Trekking in the
KARAKORAM
& HINDUKUSH

John Mock
Kimberley O'Neil

LONELY PLANET PUBLICATIONS
Melbourne • Oakland • London • Paris

KARAKORAM & HINDUKUSH

TAJIKISTAN

GHIZAR
An untouched gem: rugged and remote valleys of Hindu Raj with alpine lakes, meadows, peaks and glaciers

NAGYR & HUNZA
Karakoram's Shangri-La: ultimate mountain splendour with snow-clad Rakaposhi and magnificent tumbling glaciers

Karambar An
(4320m)

Garmush
(6243m)

Shani
(5887m)

HINDUKUSH RANGE

Yarkhun River

HINDU RAJ RANGE

Noshaq
(7492m)

Tirich Mir
(7706m)

Mastuj River

Mastuj

Chatorkhand

Ghizar River

Gupis

Gilgit River

Shandur Pass
(3800m)

Chitral

NORTHERN   AREAS

Gilgit

CHITRAL
Tirich Mir and the high Hindukush, enormous cedar trees & ancient pre-Islamic culture of Kalasha Valleys

Chitral River

Drosh

Indus River

Karakoram Hwy

Chilas

Lowari Pass
(3118m)

AFGHANISTAN

Babusar Pass

Dir

Besham

Timurgarh

Saidu Sharif

Muzaffarabad

NORTH-WEST FRONTIER PROVINCE

Mansehra

Abbottabad

Khyber Pass

Mardan

Tarbela Reservoir

Peshawar

Grand Trunk Rd

Karakoram Hwy

Murree

AZAD JAMMU & KASHMIR

Kohat

PAKISTAN

ISLAMABAD

Rawalpindi

Contents

2 Contents

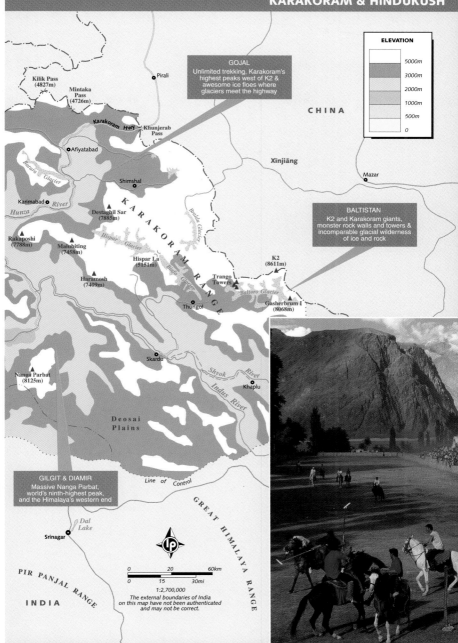

ELEVATION

5000m
3000m
2000m
1000m
500m
0

GOJAL
Unlimited trekking, Karakoram's highest peaks west of K2 & awesome ice floes where glaciers meet the highway

Kilik Pass (4827m)

Mintaka Pass (4726m)

Pirali

Karakoram Hwy

Khunjerab Pass

CHINA

Afiyatabad

Xīnjiāng

Shimshal

Mazar

Karimabad

Hunza River

Batura Glacier

KARAKORAM RANGE

Braldu Glacier

BALTISTAN
K2 and Karakoram giants, monster rock walls and towers & incomparable glacial wilderness of ice and rock

Destaghil Sar (7885m)

Hispar Glacier

Rakaposhi (7788m)

Malubiting (7458m)

Hispar La (5151m)

Biafo Glacier

K2 (8611m)

Trango Towers

Haramosh (7409m)

Baltoro Glacier

Thungol

Gasherbrum I (8068m)

Skardu

Shyok River

Khaplu

Indus River

Nanga Parbat (8125m)

Deosai Plains

GILGIT & DIAMIR
Massive Nanga Parbat, world's ninth-highest peak, and the Himalaya's western end

Line of Control

Dal Lake

Srinagar

GREAT HIMALAYA RANGE

PIR PANJAL RANGE

INDIA

0   20   60km
0   15   30mi

1:2,700,000
The external boundaries of India on this map have not been authenticated and may not be correct.

Trekking in the Karakoram & Hindukush
2nd edition – January 2002
First published – November 1996

Published by
Lonely Planet Publications Pty Ltd ABN 36 005 607 983
90 Maribyrnong St, Footscray, Victoria 3011, Australia

Lonely Planet Offices
Australia Locked Bag 1, Footscray, Victoria 3011
USA 150 Linden St, Oakland, CA 94607
UK 10a Spring Place, London NW5 3BH
France 1 rue du Dahomey, 75011 Paris

Photographs
Many of the images in this guide are available for licensing from
Lonely Planet Images.
e lpi@lonelyplanet.com.au
w www.lonelyplanetimages.com

Front cover photograph
Sun sets on Bal Chhīsh Peaks above Hispar Glacier from Dachigan
camp site, Nagyr (John Mock)

Small front cover photograph
Trekkers on the Biafo Glacier on the way to Marpogoro (John Mock)

Photographs on colour map
Left: View of Shīshpar and the Passu Glacier from the Karakoram
Highway; Right: Polo in Skardu (both photographs by John Mock)

ISBN 1 74059 086 4

Printed through Colorcraft Ltd, Hong Kong
Printed in China

The Maps

The Treks	Duration	Standard	Season
Chitral			
Gree An	5–7 hours	easy	mid-April–mid-Oct
Donson Pass & Kundyak An	2 days	easy	mid-April–mid-Oct
Kasavir	2 days	easy	April–Oct
Gokhshal An & Dooni An	3 days	moderate	July–Sept
Owir An	3 days	moderate	mid-June–mid-Sept
Roghili Gol	4 days	moderate	mid-June–Sept
Lohigal An	4 days	moderate	July–mid-Sept
Phargam An	4 days	demanding	July–mid-Sept
Zani An	5½–6 hours	easy	late April–Oct
Tirich Mir Base Camp	6 days	demanding	mid-June–mid-Sept
Shah Jinali An	4 days	moderate	mid-June–mid-Sept
Khot An	2 days	moderate	June–mid-Sept
Broghil & Karambar An	10 days	moderate	June–Sept
Kachakani An	6 days	very demanding	July–Sept
Ghizar			
Asumbar Haghost	4 days	moderate	June–Sept
Karambar An & Darkot An	11 days	demanding, technical	July–Sept
Punji Pass	4 days	demanding	July–Sept
Thui An	5 days	moderate	July–Sept
Naz Bar An	4 days	very demanding	July–mid-Sept
Zagaro An	6 days	very demanding	July–August
Chumarkhan An	2 days	easy	June–Oct
Gilgit & Diamir			
Diran Base Camp	4 days	moderate	mid-June–Sept
Rakhan Gali	4 days	demanding	mid-June–Sept
Fairy Meadow	3 days	easy	May–mid-Oct
Rupal	5 days	easy	June–Oct
Mazeno La	8 days	extreme, technical	mid-June–mid-Sept
Nagyr & Hunza			
Pakora Pass	5 days	moderate	mid-June–Sept
Daintar Pass	5 days	demanding, technical	July–Sept
Rakaposhi Base Camp	3 days	easy	June–Sept
Barpu Glacier	6 days	moderate	mid-June–Oct
Rush Phari	5 days	demanding	mid-June–Sept
Ultar	2 days	easy	May–Oct

O Open zone   **R** Restricted zone   **P** Permit (US$50)   **T** Toll Tax (Rs 100)

The Treks	Duration	Standard	Season
Gojal			
Avdegar	2 days	moderate	May–Oct
Patundas	3 days	moderate, technical	June–Sept
Batura Glacier	5 days	moderate	June–Oct
Werthum Pass	7 days	very demanding, technical	mid-June–Sept
Shimshal Village	5 days	easy	April–Oct
Lupgar Sar Base Camp	3 days	moderate	June–Sept
Shimshal Pamir	5 days	moderate	June–Sept
Boisum & Chafchingol Passes	7 days	very demanding, technical	mid-June–Sept
Qachqar-e-Dur & Shpodeen Pass	7 days	demanding	mid-June–Sept
Mai Dur Pass	8 days	extreme, technical	mid-June–Sept
Boibar	3 days	easy	mid-June–Sept
Lupgar Pir Pass	6 days	very demanding	mid-June–Sept
Chilinji An & Qalander Uween	6 days	very demanding, technical	mid-June–Sept
Kilik & Mintaka Passes	6 days	moderate	June–Sept
Baltistan			
Chogo Lungma Glacier	5 days	demanding	mid-June–Sept
Burji La	3 days	moderate	mid-June–mid-Oct
Hispar La	12 days	extreme, technical	mid-June–Sept
Baltoro Glacier	15 days	demanding	June–Sept
Gondogoro La	15 days	extreme, technical	late June–Aug
Thalle La	3 days	moderate	mid-June–Sept
Gondogoro Valley	9 days	demanding	mid-July–Sept
Masherbrum Base Camp	4 days	moderate	mid-June–Sept
K7 Base Camp	5 days	moderate	mid-June–Sept

JOHN MOCK

Tirich Mir (7706m) framed by apricot blossoms at Birmogh Lasht, Kasavir trek.

View from near Kilik Pass on the Kilik & Mintaka Passes trek.

⊙ Open zone   R Restricted zone   P Permit (US$50)   T Toll Tax (Rs 100)

The Authors

John Mock & Kimberley O'Neil

Ever since John's first Himalayan trek in 1977 and Kimberley's in 1984, each has spent much of their time in Pakistan, India and Nepal studying, working and trekking. In the Karakoram and Hindukush alone, they have crossed more than 40 passes, traversed or crossed more than 50 glaciers and visited more valleys than anyone else still active today. Married in a Tibetan *gompa* in Kathmandu in 1991, today they divide their time between northern Pakistan and their northern California home. John's PhD in South Asian language and literature from the University of California at Berkeley and Kimberley's years of experience in the adventure travel industry have enabled them to also work as consultants on ecotourism in northern Pakistan for the World Conservation Union (IUCN), on the Khunjerab National Park for the WorldWide Fund for Nature (WWF), and with *National Geographic* magazine. Avid cyclists and hikers, they have also coauthored Lonely Planet's *Hiking in the Sierra Nevada* and contributed to *Hiking in the USA*, *Pakistan*, *Rocky Mountains* and *Lonely Planet Unpacked*.

From the Authors

We dedicate this book to the memories of departed friends: beloved Shimshali raconteur Mohammad Habib and Hunza's renowned chef and hotelier Kalbi Ali.

We would like to acknowledge and thank the many people and organisations for their friendship, support and cooperation. First, we thank the government of Pakistan, Secretary of the Ministry of Tourism, the Tourism Division's Deputy Chief of Operations, PTDC Motels' Managing Director and Pakistan International Airlines. A special thanks is due to Squadron Leader Mian Waheed ud Din, former Deputy Commissioner of Gilgit.

It's not possible to name all the people with whom we've walked and the drivers who have gotten us safely to and from trailheads, but we're grateful for their help. We appreciate the true Chitrali hospitality conveyed by Maqsood ul Mulk of Hindukush Trails and his family, Haider Ali Shah of the Mountain Inn, and Babu Mohammad. In Diamir we're grateful to Rehmat Nabi and Aziz Rehman of Tato-Raikot, and Abdul Bari Rana of Astor. In Nagyr, we're indebted to Shafi Ahmed of Mountain Movers, and appreciate the hospitality at Minapin's Diran Guest House. Many old Hunza friends continue to help us in countless ways: Baig Rehmatullah Baig, Ikram Beg, Hoor Shah, Ejazullah Baig, Didar Ali, FA Khan Changazi, Wajid Ali, Noor Hayat, Amjad Ayub and Noonihal Shah. Waljis Adventure Pakistan's staff and drivers in Gilgit and Karimabad provided amazing support in countless ways. We appreciate the continuing support from Nazir Sabir and his staff at Nazir Sabir Expeditions, and the warm hospitality of the staff of Lodgings Guest House (F-7/2) in Islamabad.

In Gojal, Passu is our home and we're particularly grateful to Ali Qurban and his family, Izzatullah Beg, Ahmed Karim, Ghulam Mohammad, Qamar Jan and Safdar Hussain. A heartfelt thanks to Altaf Hussain and everyone at Passu Tourist Lodge, especially Sher Ghazi, whose culinary talents powered us between many treks. We also thank Sarfaraz Shah of Ghulkin and Ghulam Sarwar of Khaibar. From Misgar, we acknowledge the extraordinary co-operation of Shifaullah, Fida Ali, Ataullah, Karim Beg and the Misgar Board of Governors.

We owe continuing gratitude to the entire village of Shimshal. In particular, we want to thank the dream team of Farhad Khan, Fazal Ali, Laili Shah, Mirza Khan, Sarwar Ali and Yahya Beg. Rajab Shah, Mohabat Shah, Khyal Beg, Mohammad Ullah, Mohammad Shifa and Mehman Khan extended tremendous friendship and hospitality over the years. Ali Sher and Bakht Nabi also helped.

Several Pakistanis working in conservation shared their experiences: Vaqar Zakaria, Shafqat Hussain and Abdul Haleem Siddiqui. Western scholars who contributed insights are: geographers Ken Hewitt, David Butz and Ken MacDonald; botanist Einar Eberhardt; biologist Dan Blumstein; historian Haruko Tsuchiya; anthropologist Wynne Maggi; and linguist Elena Bashir. Of the many trekkers and mountaineers with whom we've communicated, we want to acknowledge Walter Keller, Amy Rice, Simon Wood, Jimmy Chin and David Hamilton.

This Book

The 1st and 2nd editions of *Trekking in the Karakoram & Hindukush* were researched and written by John Mock and Kimberley O'Neil.

From the Publisher

The 2nd edition of *Trekking in the Karakoram & Hindukush* was coordinated in Lonely Planet's Melbourne office by editor Janet Brunckhorst and designer/cartographer Helen Rowley. Janet was assisted by Andrew Bain and Helen was assisted by Jarrad Needham and Karen Fry. Karen designed new symbols and prepared the climate charts and the map legend. Chris Klep provided mapping technical assistance, and Quentin Frayne and Emma Koch edited the language chapter. Andrew Tudor, Mark Germanchis, David Burnett, Morgan Dennithorne, Nick Forward and George Dunford offered invaluable technical support. David also answered geological queries, and Miranda Wills and David Andrew lent their considerable expertise to the flora and fauna sections. Images were organised by the good people of Lonely Planet Images, illustrations were coordinated by Matt King, and Martin Harris provided new illustrations. Jamieson Gross designed the cover. Fiona Siseman and Briony Grogan offered administrative and marketing support. Sally Dillon, Glenn van der Knijff, Chris Klep and Lindsay Brown checked the book during layout.

Thanks

Thanks to the readers who wrote in with useful comments about the 1st edition of *Trekking in the Karakoram & Hindukush*:

Eddy de Wilde, Daniel Fabian, Michael Green, Marcus Hardie, Robert Klaassen, Fiona Martin, Murray Robbins, Valerie Sloan, Ann & Arthur Ward, Jack Zektzer

Foreword

ABOUT LONELY PLANET GUIDEBOOKS

The story begins with a classic travel adventure: Tony and Maureen Wheeler's 1972 journey across Europe and Asia to Australia. Useful information about the overland trail did not exist at that time, so Tony and Maureen published the first Lonely Planet guidebook to meet a growing need.

From a kitchen table, then from a tiny office in Melbourne (Australia), Lonely Planet has become the largest independent travel publisher in the world, an international company with offices in Melbourne, Oakland (USA), London (UK) and Paris (France).

Today Lonely Planet guidebooks cover the globe. There is an ever-growing list of books and there's information in a variety of forms and media. Some things haven't changed. The main aim is still to help make it possible for adventurous travellers to get out there – to explore and better understand the world.

At Lonely Planet we believe travellers can make a positive contribution to the countries they visit – if they respect their host communities and spend their money wisely. Since 1986 a percentage of the income from each book has been donated to aid projects and human rights campaigns.

Updates Lonely Planet thoroughly updates each guidebook as often as possible. This usually means there are around two years between editions, although for more unusual or more stable destinations the gap can be longer. Check the imprint page (following the colour map at the beginning of the book) for publication dates.

Between editions up-to-date information is available in two free newsletters – the paper *Planet Talk* and email *Comet* (to subscribe, contact any Lonely Planet office) – and on our Web site at Ⓦ www.lonelyplanet.com. The *Upgrades* section of the Web site covers a number of important and volatile destinations and is regularly updated by Lonely Planet authors. *Scoop* covers news and current affairs relevant to travellers. And, lastly, the *Thorn Tree* bulletin board and *Postcards* section of the site carry unverified, but fascinating, reports from travellers.

Correspondence The process of creating new editions begins with the letters, postcards and emails received from travellers. This correspondence often includes suggestions, criticisms and comments about the current editions. Interesting excerpts are immediately passed on via newsletters and the Web site, and everything goes to our authors to be verified when they're researching on the road. We're keen to get more feedback from organisations or individuals who represent communities visited by travellers.

Lonely Planet gathers information for everyone who's curious about the planet – and especially for those who explore it first-hand. Through guidebooks, phrasebooks, activity guides, maps, literature, newsletters, image library, TV series and Web site we act as an information exchange for a worldwide community of travellers.

Research Authors aim to gather sufficient practical information to enable travellers to make informed choices and to make the mechanics of a journey run smoothly. They also research historical and cultural background to help enrich the travel experience and allow travellers to understand and respond appropriately to cultural and environmental issues.

Authors don't stay in every hotel because that would mean spending a couple of months in each medium-sized city and, no, they don't eat at every restaurant because that would mean stretching belts beyond capacity. They do visit hotels and restaurants to check standards and prices, but feedback based on readers' direct experiences can be very helpful.

Many of our authors work undercover, others aren't so secretive. None of them accept freebies in exchange for positive write-ups. And none of our guidebooks contain any advertising.

Production Authors submit their manuscripts and maps to offices in Australia, USA, UK or France. Editors and cartographers – all experienced travellers themselves – then begin the process of assembling the pieces. When the book finally hits the shops, some things are already out of date, we start getting feedback from readers and the process begins again…

WARNING & REQUEST

Things change – prices go up, schedules change, good places go bad and bad places go bankrupt – nothing stays the same. So, if you find things better or worse, recently opened or long since closed, please tell us and help make the next edition even more accurate and useful. We genuinely value all the feedback we receive. A well-travelled team reads and acknowledges every letter, postcard and email and ensures that every morsel of information finds its way to the appropriate authors, editors and cartographers for verification.

Everyone who writes to us will find their name listed in the next edition of the appropriate guidebook. They will also receive the latest issue of *Planet Talk*, our quarterly printed newsletter, or *Comet*, our monthly email newsletter. Subscriptions to both newsletters are free. The very best contributions will be rewarded with a free guidebook.

We may edit, reproduce and incorporate your comments in all Lonely Planet products, such as guidebooks, Web sites and digital products, so let us know if you don't want your comments reproduced or your name acknowledged.

Send all correspondence to the Lonely Planet office closest to you:

Australia: Locked Bag 1, Footscray, Victoria 3011
USA: 150 Linden St, Oakland, CA 94607
UK: 10a Spring Place, London NW5 3BH
France: 1 rue du Dahomey, 75011 Paris

Or email us at: e talk2us@lonelyplanet.com.au

For news, views and updates see our Web site: w www.lonelyplanet.com

Introduction

At the western end of the great Asian high-mountain system, the Karakoram, Hindukush and Himalaya ranges all converge in a landscape of truly breathtaking scale. Mountains typically rise above 6000m, with more than 160 summits higher than 7000m. In the Karakoram alone, 30 peaks reach higher than 7500m.

Here is the world's greatest concentration of high peaks and glaciers, with a beauty, isolation and sheer immensity like nothing else on the planet. This wilderness of ice and rock has drawn mountaineers and trekkers since its discovery by European explorers in the mid-19th century.

The star attraction is the Baltoro Glacier, with its huge rock towers, giant peaks and the real mountain heavyweight, K2. This is heaven for mountain lovers; a place you dream of going. Yet there are other places, equally sublime, and whether you trek in the high Hindukush or the mighty Karakoram ice mountains, you experience a wilderness of heartaching beauty that encompasses the extremes of climate and terrain.

Mammoth highways of ice – the Biafo, Hispar, Chogo Lungma, Tirich and Batura glaciers – offer the longest glacier traverses outside the subpolar zones. Nanga Parbat, an 8000m colossus, has three of the most easily reached base camps of any major peak in the world.

Whenever you venture off the well-travelled trekking routes, you embark on a journey through areas visited by only handfuls of trekkers each year. There are valleys and glaciers virtually unknown, awaiting the adventurous. Beyond Shimshal village lies

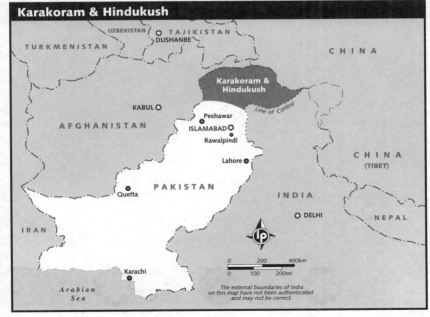

an area of thousands of square kilometres, almost completely unexplored. West of the Karambar River are mountains and valleys that don't even appear on maps.

Even on the most well-trodden routes, you can walk for days and never meet another trekker. Northern Pakistan is not the victim of tourist floods and remains an undiscovered gem. You can find plenty of day hikes and short treks where no glacier travel is involved, all of them uncrowded and inviting.

This book is a tool to give you information to get started on your own adventure. Its goal is to demystify a region that still has many unknown areas and to make them accessible to you. There are many great places waiting to be explored and enough adventures to last a lifetime.

Although most trekkers first go for the mountains, many return for the people. The diversity and uniqueness of the people who live in the Karakoram and Hindukush offer a personal counterpoint to the immensity of the terrain and climatic extremes. The religious tension and political convulsions that often wrack down-country Pakistan are conspicuously absent in the mountains. Wherever you go you meet friendly, inquisitive people who want to get to know you and the reasons why you choose to visit their valleys.

Trekking through Pakistan's northern mountains calls for a spirit of adventure and a sense of humour, and brings the rewards of perhaps the most spectacular mountain scenery in the world, the gracious warmth and hospitality of the people, and a feeling of accomplishing something remarkable.

Facts about the Karakoram & Hindukush

HISTORY

The Karakoram and Hindukush have always been rather porous barriers, offering short, seasonal routes between South Asia and Central Asia. Over the course of history, Indo-Aryans, Persians, Greeks, Scythians, Huns, Tibetans, Chinese, Mongols, Russians and Britons all traversed the mountains. Although the remarkable crossings of armies are the events history records most precisely, the travels of traders and pilgrims have been equally significant. Three of the world's great religions – Zoroastrianism, Buddhism, and Islam – flowed through the mountains with deep and profound effect. The spread of Buddhism outward from India followed one of the world's greatest trade routes, the Silk Route, through these mountains. For more than 1000 years, overland trade between the civilisations of the Mediterranean, China and India carried religion, art, technology and wealth. The empires involved vied for control of the passes, exerting considerable effort to control trade. Chinese and Tibetan armies fought over Chitral, Gilgit and Baltistan during the 7th and 8th centuries. The Silk Route experienced one last resurgence in the 13th century. Chenghiz (Genghiz) Khan ruthlessly subdued all the land between China and the Mediterranean, and under the harsh power of the Mongol dynasty, trade once again flowed freely. It was during this time that Marco Polo and his uncles passed just north of the Karakoram and Hindukush on their way to the Mongol court in China.

The small states of the Karakoram and Hindukush and their warlike chiefs, however, remained largely independent in their mountain strongholds, forming strategic alliances with their more powerful neighbours to the north and south.

By the early 19th century, the Sikh empire controlled Kashmir from the Punjab. The Sikhs also attempted to rule Gilgit and Baltistan but growing British power led to the annexation of the Sikh mountain territories in 1846. Calling them the state of Jammu and Kashmir, the British sold the territories to Gulab Singh and declared him Maharaja of Kashmir. This included all of what are now Pakistan's Northern Areas and Azad Jammu & Kashmir, plus Indian-controlled Jammu, Kashmir and Ladakh. This newly created Kashmir functioned as a dependent border state against Russian expansion from the north-west. In what became known as 'The Great Game', Britain dispatched military and diplomatic missions to the mountainous no-man's land to counter Russian influence. The mountain chiefs of Chitral and Hunza fought the British but, by the early 20th century, British power was secure in the area.

When Britain finally left India, Pakistan and India divided Kashmir. India claimed territory all the way to the Chitral border, but Muslim troops in the Northern Areas secured the territory for Pakistan. A United Nations-supervised cease-fire has been in effect since 1949, but shelling and firing is a regular occurrence along the line. In the far east, the line was never demarcated. Taking advantage of this indeterminacy, Indian troops moved onto the Siachen Glacier in 1984, seizing control of territory Pakistan claimed. The Siachen's two western tributary glaciers, the Kondus and Bilafond, are still held by Pakistani troops. The Siachen and the Baltoro Glaciers are separated by a line of high peaks, with Pakistani troops stationed on the Baltoro side and Indian forces on the Siachen. More soldiers die from altitude and avalanches than from bullets in this high-altitude war.

500 BC – Darius the Great of Persia conquers the Indus Valley

333–326 BC – Alexander the Great of Macedonia defeats the Persian army, crosses the Hindukush and reaches the Indus River

325–150 BC – Indo-Greek kingdoms established south of the Hindukush

185 BC–AD 40 – Scythians and Kushans cross the high passes from Central Asia, displacing the Indo-Greeks as rulers of the Buddhist kingdoms

100 BC–AD 900 – Silk Route, the great overland trade between the Mediterranean and Asia, flourishes under a *pax Buddhica* and Buddhism spreads from India to Tibet and China

5th century – Chinese Buddhist monk Fa-Hsien journeys through the mountains on the way to India in search of sources of Buddhism

570–632 – life of Prophet Mohammad (PBUH), founder of Islamic religion

7th century – Chinese Buddhist monk Hsuan-Tsang journeys through Gilgit and Swat on his way to India in search of sources of Buddhism

1220 – Genghiz Khan sweeps through Turkestan and conquers Peshawar and Lahore

1271–5 – Marco Polo and his uncles travel from Venice through the Pamir to China

1398 – Timur the Lame (Tamerlane), the Mongol Khan, invades India from Central Asia and conquers Delhi

1526–1739 – Moghul empire rules much of India from Delhi

1540 – Kashgar conquers Chitral and Gilgit

1586–92 – Moghul emperor Akbar the Magnificent conquers Kashmir

1612 – British East India Company founds its first trading post in India

1759 – Hunza begins tribute relations with China

1821 – British begin Great Trigonometrical Survey of India

1835–8 – explorer GT Vigne travels in Kashmir and Baltistan

1847 – Lieutenants Vans Agnew and Young reach Gilgit

1856 – triangulation and survey of Kashmir starts

1857 – Adolph Schlagintweit killed near Kashgar

1858 – height of K2 determined

1869 – Hunza begins tribute relations with Kashmir

1876 – John Biddulph becomes first British officer to reach Hunza

1887 – Francis Younghusband crosses Muztagh Pass

1889 – Gilgit Agency established; Younghusband visits Shimshal Pamir and Hunza

1891 – Hunza-Nagyr campaign; British control over Hunza established

1892 – Sir W Martin Conway's expedition to Biafo and Hispar glaciers

1893 – Durand Line established, separating Chitral and Afghanistan

1895 – Pamir Boundary Commission divides Russian and British empires in Pamir; Alfred Mummery makes first attempt on an 8000m peak, reaching 6000m on Nanga Parbat's Diamir face, then vanishes exploring Raikot Gah

1902 – Oscar Eckenstein's expedition to K2

1909 – Italian Duke of Abruzzi's K2 expedition reaches 6000m via south-east ridge and 7500m on Chogolisa

1926 – Kenneth Mason's Shaksgam exploration

1929 – Duke of Spoleto's Baltoro Glacier expedition

1932 – first German Nanga Parbat expedition

1934 – second German Nanga Parbat expedition reaches 7705m; deaths of four Germans and six porters

1936 – French expedition to Gasherbrum I

1937 – third German Nanga Parbat attempt; death of seven Germans and nine porters; Shipton-Tilman Shaksgam expedition

1938 – C Secord and M Vyvyan reconnoitre Rakaposhi

1939 – German-born Fritz Wiessner reaches 8370m on second American K2 expedition, but turns back when sherpa refuses to go higher; K2's first fatalities with deaths of Dudley Wolfe and three sherpas on descent

1947 – Pakistan and India gain independence from Britain; HW Tilman and Hans Gyr make second reconnaissance of Rakaposhi

1949 – United Nations-sponsored cease-fire in Kashmir between India and Pakistan

1953 – Austrian Herman Buhl makes miraculous solo first ascent of Nanga Parbat's Raikot face after 17-hour solo push to summit without oxygen; American K2 expedition led by Charles Houston reaches 7800m; death of Arthur Gilkey

1954 – Ardito Desio's Italian expedition makes first ascent of K2 via Abruzzi ridge

1957 – Austrian expedition summits Broad Peak without oxygen or high-altitude porters

1957 – Buhl and Kurt Diemberger summit Chogolisa; Buhl dies

1958 – Pete Schoening and Andy Kauffman make first American ascent of an 8000m peak, Gasherbrum I

1969 – princely state of Chitral merges with Pakistan

1970 – Reinhold Messner makes first ascent of Nanga Parbat's Rupal face

1974 – princely state of Hunza becomes part of Pakistan

1975 – Messner and Peter Habeler make first three-day alpine ascent of Gasherbrum I

1977 – Chris Bonington and Doug Scott climb Baintha Brak

1978 – Karakoram Highway completed to Hunza

1980 – Soviet occupation of Afghanistan starts; Galen Rowell, Ned Gillette, Kim Schmitz and Dan Asay complete first ski traverse of Siachen, Baltoro, Biafo and Hispar glaciers

1983 – Jerzy Kukuczka and Voytek Kurtyka summit Gasherbrum I, II and III on single expedition

1984 – Kukuczka and Kurtyka make first alpine traverse of Broad Peak's three summits; Indian troops occupy Siachen Glacier; Messner and Hans Kammerlander traverse Gasherbrum I and II in one week from base camp

1985 – Kurtyka and Robert Schauer make 10-day alpine ascent of Gasherbrum V's west face, still regarded as the world's greatest alpine climb

1986 – Khunjerab Pass opens to overland travel

1989 – Soviets withdraw from Afghanistan

1998 – Rajab Shah becomes first Pakistani to summit Pakistan's five 8000m peaks

History of Exploration

When British explorers began probing the region in the 19th century, they were confronted by a bewildering landscape of high mountains, deep river valleys and enormous glaciers. Driven by the need to protect the north-west flank of their Indian empire from Russian expansion, they set out from Kashmir to explore and map these great ranges.

The first to reach Skardu was GT Vigne in 1835. With a shotgun in hand and a kettle always ready to brew tea, he made four explorations into the Karakoram, giving the first description of its vastness and height.

In 1847 Lieutenants Vans Agnew and Young were the first to reach Gilgit. Thereafter, a steady stream of explorers sounded out the passes and routes through the mountains. The most notable among them included Frederic Drew, George Robertson, Francis Younghusband, Colonel Reginald CF Schomberg and Lieutenant George Cockerill.

Drew, a keen and systematic observer, explored the Ishkoman, Shimshal and Basha valleys between 1862 and 1871. He also had the unenviable task of burying in Gilgit's British Cemetery the less fortunate British explorer George Hayward, who was murdered in Darkot in 1870. Robertson made prolonged official visits to the Afghan Hindukush people between 1889 and 1891, before their conversion to Islam. In 1889 Younghusband visited the Shimshal Pass, then crossed the Mintaka Pass and entered Hunza from the north. Cockerill, in a flying survey of the borders of Chitral in 1892 and 1894, saw more of that country than anyone else of the time. Schomberg, who travelled for British intelligence in the 1930s and 1940s, is still remembered today by some village greybeards in Bagrot, Chapursan

and Shimshal. Less known are the travels of native secret agents, the 'pundits' as they were called, who went in disguise where British officers could not in the mid-19th century. Swat, Dir, Chitral, Yarkhun, Wakhan, and Yasin were all first visited by these remarkable travellers.

The first scientific explorers, interested not in potential chinks in the British empire's borders, but in a wide range of natural and anthropological phenomena, were the Schlagintweit brothers, Hermann, Adolf and Robert. Recommended to the British East India Company by Alexander von Humboldt, they travelled the Karakoram between 1855 and 1857. Among their achievements were the description of the Deosai Plains, Nanga Parbat's glaciers, and of the Chogo Lungma, Biafo, Baltoro, and Bilafond glaciers. Adolf reached Concordia and was first to explore the Muztagh Pass.

The scientist-explorers of the Survey of India continued to map the region, establishing a triangulation network from Ladakh to Hunza by 1863. In 1856 Captain TG Montgomerie recognised K2 (8611m) as the highest Karakoram peak and HH Godwin-Austen advanced knowledge of the Karakoram glaciers, travelling up the Panmah, Biafo and Baltoro glaciers in 1860 and 1861. The final step to link the British survey with that of Russia was begun in 1913, supervised by Lieutenant Colonel Kenneth Mason.

The Schlagintweits' work was surpassed only by the scientist Giotto Dainelli, who first came to the Karakoram with Filippo de Filippi's 1913–14 expedition. Much of the region's exploration was accomplished by such expeditions to high peaks and glaciers. Sir W Martin Conway's expedition to the Central Karakoram, which in 1892 first crossed the Hispar La, was one such expedition, as were Workman's seven expeditions to the Chogo Lungma, Biafo, Hispar, Aling, Masherbrum, Gondogoro, Bilafond, Siachen and Kondus glaciers between 1899 and 1912. The Vissers made four expeditions between 1922 and 1935; on one of which they made the first crossing of the Chafchingol and Mai Dur passes through the Ghuzherav Mountains. The pivotal Shipton-Tilman expeditions to Shaksgam and Shimshal in 1937 and to the Biafo and Hispar glaciers in 1939 provided the basis for today's maps of the area. The Baltoro Glacier was accurately mapped by Norman Dyhrenfurth's 1935 and 1939 expeditions and Ardito Desio's 1954 expedition, which made the first ascent of K2.

Organised trekking was an outgrowth of mountaineering expeditions to the region. The earliest trekking party was led by Major GD Langlands over Kachakani An in 1963. Most of the Karakoram was closed to foreigners between 1962 and 1974 because of internal and regional political tension, although a few people went to Swat and Chitral. Upon the reopening of the Karakoram came the first independent trekkers and organised trekking parties. Trekking has grown slowly and, compared with the Nepal Himalaya, it remains in its infancy. It's fair to say that the exploration of this part of the planet, still in many ways *terra incognita* for most of humanity, continues today.

GEOGRAPHY

The Karakoram, Hindukush and Himalaya are the western part of the great chain of high mountains that form the watershed between the plains of South Asia and the deserts of Central Asia. The Karakoram range includes the mountains north of the lower Shyok, the Indus and lower Gilgit rivers as far west as the Ishkoman and Karambar valleys. The name Karakoram means 'black rock' in Turkic, an apt description of the mountains. To the west, stretching into Afghanistan, the mountains are known as the Hindukush. According to Afghan tradition, the name Hindukush means 'Hindu killer', but more probably it's a variant of Hindu Kuh, meaning 'Hindu mountains'. The Nanga Parbat massif rises south of the Karakoram, at the western end of the Great Himalayan range.

The region's topography is a convoluted series of ridges and valleys, with 10 of the world's 25 highest peaks and the longest glaciers outside the subpolar regions. The Karakoram alone has more than 100 peaks

above 7000m. Most of the highest peaks are in the more-than-300km-long Great Karakoram range, which forms the main crest line of the entire system and is divided into sections termed *muztagh*, the Turkic word for any great ice mountain. From the Batura Muztagh running east are the Hispar Muztagh, Panmah Muztagh and Baltoro Muztagh. The shorter ranges on either side of this great icebound crest are collectively termed the Lesser Karakoram range. On the north side are the Lupgar and Ghuzherav mountains. On the south side are the Naltar, Rakaposhi-Haramosh, Spantik-Sosbun, Mango Gusor, Shimshak, Masherbrum and Saltoro mountains.

The snows and glaciers from these mountains are the source for an extensive network of rivers that cut deeply through them. All of them flow into the Indus River, which, older than the mountains themselves, is the only river to transect the Karakoram range. The Chitral and upper Ghizar rivers drain the Hindukush range and its offshoot, the Hindu Raj range. From the heavily glaciated Karakoram flow the Hunza and Shyok rivers. Nanga Parbat's glaciers flow into the Indus River, which separates this Himalayan massif from the Karakoram. Devastating events have left their mark throughout the landscape. Massive landslides and sudden surging advances of glaciers have dammed rivers, causing destructive outburst floods. Massive spring and early summer mudflows block roads and occasionally bury villages.

Around Nanga Parbat and on the southern slope of the Great Karakoram, forests are nurtured by summer monsoon rains. North of the crest the monsoon has little effect. Trees appear only along stream beds and in sheltered places, giving the landscape a stark and austere aura. Yet on this inhospitable land live hospitable people, who manage to use the rivers, the rocks and the meadows along the margins of ice and snow to maintain their cultures. Irrigation is essential for cultivation, but no more than 1% of the land is farmed. Villages are green oases that sit on alluvial fans of side streams or on terraces above the main rivers.

Major 7000m & 8000m Peaks

peak	elevation	first ascent	nationality
HINDUKUSH RANGE			
Tirich Mir	7706m	1950	Norwegian
Noshaq	7492m	1960	Japanese
Istor-o-Nal	7403m	1969	Spanish
Saraghrar	7349m	1959	Italian
Udren Zom	7108m	1964	Austrian
Nobiasum	7070m	1967	Austrian
Akher Chhīsh	7020m	1966	Austrian
GREAT KARAKORAM RANGE			
Batura Muztagh			
Batura I	7795m	1976	German
Shīshpar	7611m	1974	Polish-German
Passu Sar	7478m	nr	
Muchu Chhīsh	7453m	nr	
Ultar	7388m	1996	Japanese
Boyohagur-Duanasir	7329m	1984	Japanese
Passu Dior	7295m	1978	Japanese-Pakistani
Kampir Dior	7168m	1975	Japanese
Hachindar Chhīsh	7163m	1982	Japanese
Sangemarmar Sar	7050m	1984	Japanese
Pamiri Sar	7016m	1986	Italian
Hispar Muztagh			
Destaghil Sar	7885m	1960	Austrian
Kunyang Chhīsh	7852m	1971	Polish
Kanjut Sar	7760m	1959	Italian
Trivor	7728m	1960	British-American
Yazghil Dome South	7559m	1980	Polish
Yukshin Gardan	7530m	1984	Austrian
Pumari Chhīsh	7492m	1979	Japanese
Momhil Sar	7343m	1964	Austrian
Jutmo Sar	7330m	1980	Japanese
Yazghil Dome North	7324m	1983	Italian
Lupgar Sar	7200m	1979	Japanese
Mulungutti Sar	7025m	1985	Japanese

nr – no record

peak	elevation	first ascent	nationality
GREAT KARAKORAM RANGE *(cont)*			
Panmah Muztagh			
Baintha Brak	7285m	1977	British
Latok I	7151m	1977	Italian
Latok II	7145m	1979	Japanese
Baltoro Muztagh			
K2	8611m	1954	Italian
Gasherbrum I	8068m	1958	American
Broad Peak	8047m	1957	Austrian
Gasherbrum II	8035m	1956	Austrian
Gasherbrum III	7952m	1975	Polish
Gasherbrum IV	7925m	1958	Italian
Skyang Kangri	7544m	1976	Japanese
Sia Kangri	7422m	1934	multinational
Skilbrum	7360m	1957	Austrian
Muztagh Tower	7284m	1956	British
Baltoro Kangri	7280m	1963	Japanese
Savoia Kangri	7263m	nr	
LESSER KARAKORAM RANGE			
Rakaposhi-Haramosh Range			
Rakaposhi	7788m	1958	British-Pakistani
Malubiting	7458m	1971	German
Haramosh	7409m	1958	Austrian
Diran	7266m	1968	German-Austrian
Spantik	7027m	1955	German
Rakaposhi East	7010m	1985	Austrian
Northern Karakoram Range			
Qarūn Koh	7164m	1984	Austrian
Masherbrum Range			
Masherbrum	7821m	1960	American-Pakistani
Chogolisa	7665m	1975	Austrian
K6	7281m	1970	Austrian
HIMALAYAN RANGE			
Nanga Parbat	8125m	1953	Austrian-German
Silberzacken	7597m	nr	
Raikot	7070m	1932	German

Village life follows a pattern of subsistence agriculture combined with animal husbandry. As high as 2400m, it's possible to grow two crops per year. Winter-sown wheat is followed closely by corn, buckwheat, or millet. Above this elevation, only a single crop, almost always wheat, is grown. In the highest villages, those above 3000m, wheat ripens with difficulty. Soil fertility is maintained by the application of carefully collected animal dung and, in some areas, human waste. In parts of Baltistan, stone toilets are built in the fields, and the waste allowed to compost before spreading on the fields once a year. Trees grown for fruit and timber are carefully tended.

In Gojal, the introduction of potatoes in the early 1970s brought sweeping changes. Before, the people barely subsisted on a single wheat crop per year. Now Gojal produces bumper crops of virus-free seed potatoes to meet the insatiable down-country demand. With the money earned from potatoes, people buy all the wheat they need and still have money left over for education, travel and consumer goods. The Karakoram Highway (KKH) makes this trade possible and in autumn truck-loads of potatoes roll down-country.

Most households grow their own green vegetables, which is why they're rare in bazaars. In some areas, particularly the Yarkhun Valley, cannabis and opium are cultivated in small plots. These used to be major trade commodities, but now the demand has dwindled and the production reduced to meet the low local demand. It's not actually legal, of course.

Sheep and goats are the most numerous livestock; poor indeed is the household that doesn't have a few goats. Milk cows are also kept and bulls are essential for ploughing the small terraced plots where tractors are impractical. Bulls are still used for threshing in roadless areas, yoked together and driven over the harvested grain stalks around a central pole. This method is now being replaced by tractor-driven threshing machines in most villages. In high-altitude regions, especially among Wakhi people, yaks are the prized livestock. In Baltistan, crosses of cows and yaks, called *dzo,* are the favoured livestock.

GEOLOGY

The Karakoram and Hindukush ranges, as well as the Pamir and Himalayan ranges, are a result of the ongoing collision of the Indian land mass with that of Eurasia. More than 100 million years ago, the Indian land mass separated from the African land mass (then a primordial super continent known as Gondwanaland) and began its inexorable drift northward. Some 50 million years ago, it collided with the Eurasian continent and began the most spectacular period of mountain building in earth's history. The Indian land mass buckled and slid under Eurasia, which crumpled and heaved upward, forming the Karakoram and Hindukush. Between the two land masses, an area of what were once islands has been compressed and raised. Geologists term this area the Kohistan Arc. It includes Chilas, upper Swat, Gilgit and Skardu. Geologically, what geographers call the Karakoram and Hindukush is actually a single continuous upthrust block that runs north of the main suture line between the Indian and Eurasian land masses. The suture line roughly corresponds with the Indus River, which originates on the older upraised sea bed of the Tibetan Plateau and has carved its gigantic canyon through the rising Karakoram range. The great massif of Nanga Parbat represents the prow of the Indian continent, and is still rising by 7mm every year. Across from Nanga Parbat, separated by the Indus River, is Rakaposhi, the prow of the Eurasian landmass. Between these two lies the area where continents collide.

The inexorable force of this collision resulted in enormous pressures and temperatures deep in the earth. Rocks melted, ran together and cooled. Over millions of years crystalline pockets have risen to the surface and over the last 25 years Pakistan has become renowned as a major producer of mineral specimens and rough gems. Trekkers may meet villagers offering gem crystals mined high in the mountains. Fine aquamarine comes from Dassu in Baltistan's

Braldu Valley and Sumayar in Nagyr. Tourmaline comes from Stak Nala, garnet from Shengus along the Indus River, topaz from Dassu and Nyet in the Braldu Valley, and tanzanite from Alchuri in the Shigar Valley.

CLIMATE

Chitral and the Northern Areas, far from the moderating influence of the ocean, lie between 35 degrees and 37 degrees north latitude and 71 degrees and 77 degrees east longitude. There are four distinct seasons, typified by extreme seasonal heat and cold: a pleasant spring (March to May); a hot summer (June to mid-September); a cool autumn (mid-September to November); and a cold winter (December to February).

Rain can fall any time in the mountains, but most precipitation occurs from December to May, with the peak in March. The summer monsoon in the Bay of Bengal moves westward and usually reaches Pakistan by late June and continues through September. Being north of, and in the rain shadow of, the Himalaya, the Karakoram and Hindukush receive little monsoonal rain. Southern Chitral, Swat, Kaghan and Rupal on Nanga Parbat's southern flanks, however, get some monsoonal rain, as do all areas above 5000m. When the monsoon first breaks in down-country Pakistan, it's usually stormy in the mountains too. A curious precipitation peak in the mountains also occurs in late August.

Chitral town receives about 450mm of precipitation per year, with 270mm falling between February and April. Gilgit receives about 165mm per year with 95mm from March to May. Skardu receives about 100mm per year with most between March and May. Above 5000m annual precipitation ranges from 1000mm to 2000mm. Up to one third of the annual Karakoram snow pack comes from the monsoon.

Temperature varies with elevation, with a marked difference in daytime and night-time temperatures in all seasons. Temperatures generally fall 6.2°C for each 1000m rise in elevation. During the peak trekking season, Gilgit and Chitral are hot in the daytime – around 40°C during midsummer – but dry. Skardu, 1000m higher, is about 5°C cooler and also very dry.

The many rivers rise dramatically during summer, carrying 20 times more water than in winter. This isn't due to rainfall, but rather to melting glaciers and snow. The key factor isn't air temperature, but rather the duration of sunshine on the ice and snow. This accounts for the dramatic rise or fall in some streams and rivers on sunny or cloudy days. The silt from melting glaciers and river-bank erosion turns most rivers a grey-brown colour. Only snow-melt streams remain blue. The Chitral River catchment area is about 20% glaciated, the Hunza River 40%, the Shigar River 50%, but the Ghizar River only about 10%.

ECOLOGY & ENVIRONMENT

In the extreme environment of the Karakoram and Hindukush – arid, steep, rocky, and both blisteringly hot and cold – life clings to any toehold it can, and humans are no exception. People use every bit of land, every blade of grass, every drop of water, and every stick of wood to survive. Animal husbandry and agriculture have always been their mainstays, but pastures are far away and only a tiny fraction of land can be cultivated. The sheer effort required is overwhelming. All livestock must be herded through a series of summer pastures, carefully exploiting all available grass. Crops are possible only through intensive irrigation from canals, engineering marvels laboriously constructed across sheer cliffs and treacherous scree slopes, that carry the life-giving water from distant glacial streams.

Only the most inaccessible part of the mountains is wilderness – area unaltered by

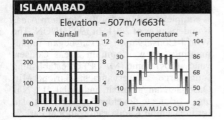

ISLAMABAD
Elevation – 507m/1663ft

human use. Trekkers see signs of human presence from the villages to the high pastures. Historically, human impact has been small, with people living in small village-states. Isolated in the mountain fastness, these marginal states had little opportunity for growth. But in the late 1960s and early 1970s these tiny states were absorbed into Pakistan and the government began building roads into the mountains. A growing population coupled with improved access placed greater pressure on natural resources. Settlements expanded, and logging, grazing and hunting all increased, resulting in deforestation, loss of habitat and sharp declines in wildlife populations.

Villagers are only now realising that forests, grasslands and wildlife are a sort of natural capital that once gone, cannot easily be replaced. The beauty and wildness of the landscape is also what attracts trekkers, and villagers now realise that the future of trekking depends on the continued wellbeing of the environment. The paradox of trekking in northern Pakistan is that visitors are attracted by the very lack of other trekkers and as Pakistan seeks more travellers it risks losing its unvisited, unspoiled landscape.

The greatest threat to the environment comes from the increased demands placed on resources and habitat by ever-increasing human use. Local people, business, government and visitors face the challenge of reconciling this conflict.

Conservation

Conservation was not a high priority for post-independence Pakistan. But, alarmed at the decline of wildlife in the 1950s and 1960s, the government asked the World Wildlife Fund (WWF) to survey wildlife status and make recommendations. As a result, between 1972 and 1979 the government established a system of protected areas that continues today, recognising just three categories: national parks, wildlife sanctuaries and game reserves. These now outdated categories and the equally outdated legislation behind them severely restrict how Pakistan manages its unique mountain habitats. Game reserves exist largely for controlled

hunting and can be on either privately owned or government-owned land, whereas national parks and wildlife sanctuaries are required to be on government-owned land. Local people, who rely on the resources within the protected areas for their own survival, see themselves as the rightful owners and stewards of the mountain forests and grasslands, and view protected areas as a threat to their way of life. The resulting disputes are still with the courts.

In addition, mountain areas have now also become the object of desire for a number of competing interests – resort hotels, polo tournaments, adventure tourism, big-game hunting and the military. Pakistan's understaffed, under-equipped and under-trained wildlife officers are unable to handle the growing complexity of management. With the government as owner, and others as users, no one has sufficient control over resources and effective management seems impossible. Whether the government can revise legislation and resolve conflicts resulting from multiple users remains to be seen.

While village conservation projects do exist throughout Chitral and the Northern Areas, these are essentially designed to translate wildlife into rupees. These projects sell trophy-hunting permits to wealthy Pakistanis and foreigners. Some of the money goes to the village to encourage conservation, but most of the money goes to other parties higher up the food chain.

The government, seeking to revitalise the conservation ethic and community spirit (*qannat* and *haqūq ul-ibād* in Arabic), set up a high-level Environmental Protection Council. The Environment & Urban Affairs Division of the government devised a National Conservation Strategy (NCS). A provincial conservation strategy for NWFP is complete, and one for the Northern Areas is underway as of 2001. In 1999, IUCN–The World Conservation Union began implementing a new Mountain Areas Conservancy Programme (MACP) by establishing four large conservancies: Tirich Mir, Qashqar, Nanga Parbat, and Gojal. IUCN is also working to develop a management plan for the Central Karakoram National Park.

The international conservation organisations largely responsible for advising the government and implementing strategy are:

Worldwide Fund for Nature (WWF, ☎ 042-5869429, 58692360, 5882069, 5839536, fax 5862358, ✉ wwf@lhr.comsats.net.pk) PO Box 5180, Lahore. Works to protect migratory birds in Chitral, and is the main adviser for Khunjerab National Park.

IUCN (☎ 051-270686/90, fax 270688, ✉ mail@isb.iucnp.org) House 26, Street 87, G-6/3, Islamabad. The world's largest alliance of conservation authorities and interest groups, and the driving force behind the NCS and provincial conservation strategies.

Small environmental groups are working to introduce the concept of the interdependence of all living beings in a web of life, but the realities of day-to-day survival often mean that villagers must put their immediate needs first and foremost. Some of the organisations working in areas that trekkers visit are:

Himalayan Wildlife Foundation (☎ 051-2276113, fax 2824484) F-7/2, Street 15, Center One, Islamabad. Works to safeguard biodiversity in Deosai National Park.

Central Asia Institute (☎ 406-585 7841, ✉ info@ikat.org) 617 South 5th Ave, Bozeman, MT 59715, USA. Runs education and public-health programs, including porter training and latrine construction.

Khunjerab Student Welfare Organisation Works to prevent hunting in the buffer zone around Khunjerab National Park.

PARKS & PROTECTED AREAS

In the West, and especially in the USA, parks are typically wilderness areas, remnants of a once vast, wild landscape. In the Karakoram and Hindukush, however, most protected areas were previously hunting reserves of local rulers that were also used by people eking out a tenuous subsistence on the steep, fragile mountain slopes. Established to protect a particular animal species, they're largely ineffective at conserving habitat. Most fail to conform with international criteria or classification standards. Boundaries are absent or poorly defined,

and aren't ecologically sound. Communities find themselves in conflict with the authoritarian and strongly protectionist management system over land tenure and resource access rights.

For example, Chitral Gol National Park, the former hunting preserve of the Mehtar of Chitral, has one of the few remaining viable populations of the endangered markhor. Chitral Gol's ownership is tied up in a three-way dispute between the Mehtar, who claims it is still his private property, the government and local people. The case has been in litigation since 1975. It would be a loss to all if this litigation resulted in an end to the protection of this special wildlife habitat.

Khunjerab National Park was established to protect Marco Polo sheep, a magnificent species once abundant around the Khunjerab Pass. But, despite the park status, hunting in the area continued indiscriminately. The government's inability to implement management practices that respect the rights of communities and involve them in decision making jeopardises the recovery of Marco Polo sheep.

The very heart of the Karakoram has been designated as the Central Karakoram National Park. But on the Baltoro Glacier, military hardware and debris from the long-simmering conflict with India continues to accumulate. A park management plan has yet to be developed and time will tell if the park can avoid repeating problems that have plagued other parks.

National Parks

National parks are administered by the government's Forestry Division. The National Council for the Conservation of Wildlife (NCCW), of the Ministry of Food, Agriculture & Cooperatives, has the major responsibility for national-park development.

Chitral Gol National Park Chitral Gol was declared a wildlife sanctuary in 1979 and a national park in 1984. This 7750-hectare area lies just west of the town of Chitral, encompassing the watershed of Chitral Gol. Park management is in town.

Khunjerab National Park The renowned wildlife biologist George Schaller recommended the establishment of Khunjerab National Park in 1975 to the prime minister, Zulfiqar Ali Bhutto, who then declared it done. This 2269 sq km area of Gojal lies on both sides of the KKH between Dih and the Pakistan-China border at the Khunjerab Pass. Most of the Shimshal Pamir and Ghuzherav are also included but, currently, only the area along the KKH is being actively managed. The Directorate of Khunjerab National Park (DKNP) is responsible for management, but operates more as a bureaucracy with administrative headquarters in Gilgit. Wildlife protection is the responsibility of villagers living near the park.

Central Karakoram National Park Established in 1993 in response to growing environmental pressure on Baltistan's once pristine Baltoro Glacier, the Central Karakoram National Park also includes the Biafo and Hispar glaciers and their tributaries. The crown jewel, of course, is K2.

Handrap-Shandur National Park The Handrap-Shandur National Park, established in 1993, includes two separate areas in Ghizar district; the 996 sq km Handrap Valley south to the Dadarelli An, and the 644 sq km Shandur Pass area. Handrap Lake and Handrap River have world-class trout and the Shandur Pass (3800m) is the site of an annual July polo tournament, which draws more than 10,000 people to the lakes and meadows. The park was established largely to rein in polo players and fans, a group not prone to be the most respectful towards the fragile mountain ecology.

Deosai National Park The 3464 sq km high-altitude Deosai plateau in Baltistan borders Indian-controlled Kashmir. Uninhabited and little-used, it's home to a significant Himalayan brown bear population, numerous marmots, and unusual snow trout in its clear streams. Deosai National Park, established in 1993, covers 1400 sq km of this unique habitat. Designated camping areas, open between June and September,

are at Ali Malik Mar, Shatung, and Chogo Chu (Bara Pani) where daily tent rentals and meals cost Rs 250–350. Himalayan Wildlife Foundation works in the park, and its nature guides take visitors from Chogo Chu on marked trails to designated bear-viewing points for Rs 500 per day.

Wildlife Sanctuaries

Wildlife sanctuaries are all remote former hunting grounds or *shikar gah* of local rulers. For each sanctuary there is at least one designated game watcher. There is no visible indication of the sanctuary status of these areas. In theory, hunting is banned. The six wildlife sanctuaries in northern Pakistan – one in Chitral district and five in the Northern Areas – cover more than 2000 sq km and most are contiguous with game reserves.

Game Reserves

Game Reserves, too, were former hunting grounds. Hunting is theoretically still permitted, but most of the game now is scarce and hard to find. There are five in Chitral district and eight in the Northern Areas (four in Ghizar, one each in Gilgit and Gojal, and two in Baltistan).

Khunjerab or Khunzherav?

The renowned Khunjerab Pass marks both the highest point on the Karakoram Highway and the Pakistan-China border. The name Khunjerab, however, is an inaccurate rendition of Khunzherav, the actual Wakhi name for the pass. Place names indicate the significance of a location for local people, so it's important to understand their real meaning. In Urdu, *jerab* means 'socks', but in Wakhi *zherav* (a stream) is distinguished from *jerab* (socks). This distinction is lost on non-Wakhi speakers, resulting in the absurdity of a valley being confused with a pair of socks. As for *khun*, in Urdu it means 'blood', but in Wakhi it means 'house'. Thus in Urdu, the common pronunciation 'Khunjerab' actually means something like 'bloody socks', a painful distortion of the original Wakhi place name Khunzherav.

FAUNA

The wildlife of the mountains is generally known, but much less is known about its distribution and status. Large mammals can be hard to see, as human pressure has confined them to remote and high places. You're more likely to see them in protected areas. The wildlife department conducts an annual valley-by-valley census in Chitral, and less regularly in the Northern Areas, maintaining records of large mammals and game birds.

Mammals

Trekkers are very likely to see pikas, voles, marmots, hares, foxes and ibexes, and in specific locations, blue sheep and bears. You're much more likely to see signs (droppings, hoof or paw prints, scrapes) of large mammals than the animals themselves.

Predators & Scavengers At the top of the food chain are the predators and scavengers. In the family Canidae are wolves, foxes and wild dogs. Wolves *(Canis lupus pallipes)*, an infrequently seen, although common, predator, are poisoned or shot on sight by herders. They're most frequent along the China border. The Tibetan red fox *(Vulpes vulpes montana)* isn't necessarily red. It can be grey, blonde or black, but its white-tipped tail is characteristic. It's frequently seen, even along the KKH. The wild dog or dhole *(Cuon alpinus)* has been reported around Shimshal Pamir.

The wolf's fawn coat may bleach
to grey in the summer months.

The family Mustelidae includes martens, weasels and otters. The stone marten *(Martes foina)*, with dense caramel fur, inhabits the artemisia steppe zone and is infrequently seen. It reportedly loves ripe apricots! The alpine weasel *(Mustela altaica)* is widespread from Chitral to Baltistan. The ermine or stoat *(Mustela erminea)* has a characteristic black-tipped tail with brown fur in summer that turns white in winter. Smaller than the marten, it's common in Gojal and Baltistan. The common otter *(Lutra lutra)*, once abundant on the Indus River and its tributaries, is now scarce because of fur hunting.

The bear family Ursidae includes the Himalayan brown bear *(Ursus arctos isabellinus)* and Himalayan black bear *(Ursus thibetanus)*. Bears can be dangerous, although it's much more common to see bear signs (greenish scat, paw prints, excavated marmot burrows) than to encounter one. Brown bears inhabit the alpine zone, especially the Deosai Plains, where the Himalayan Wildlife Foundation counted 25 bears (including cubs) in 1996.

Cats belong to the family Felidae. The medium-sized, powerfully built Himalayan lynx *(Felis lynx isabellina)* has a short tail and tufted ears. It's a solitary and resourceful hunter, and though rarely seen, widely inhabits the alpine zone from Ghizar to Baltistan. See also snow leopard under Endangered Species (p28).

Hoofed Mammals Tiny musk deer *(Moschus moschiferus)*, with their tusk-like canine teeth, inhabit eastern Indus Kohistan, Astor and the Deosai's southern edge. Relentlessly hunted for their musk gland, they're rarely seen. Two impressive mountain goats are the Himalayan ibex *(Capra ibex sibirica)* and Kashmir markhor (see Endangered Species, p29). Himalayan ibex, which live in or above the alpine zone, are common enough to support limited hunting and are often seen throughout Khunjerab National Park. Intermediate between goats and sheep, blue sheep *(Pseudois nayaur)* are found only north of the main Karakoram crest, in Ghuzherav and Shimshal Pamir, which marks the westernmost extent of their distribution. Two wild mountain sheep are urial and Marco Polo sheep (see Endangered Species, p29).

Horses and asses are represented by the Tibetan wild ass, or kiang, *(Equus hemionus kiang)*, which may visit Shimshal's remote Braldu River near the Chinese border in winter.

Royle's high mountain vole lives in burrows on alpine grasslands.

Blue sheep are prized as a trophy animal because of their magnificent horns.

Small Mammals In Kaghan, near Babusar Pass, the furry Asiatic pygmy shrew *(Sorex thibetanus)*, with red-tipped teeth, is abundant. At dusk around Gilgit or Chitral, you can see insectivorous bats (order Chiroptera). Species include horseshoe bats, whiskered bats, mouse-eared bats, long-eared bats, and Pipistrelle bats.

Hares and pikas belong to the order Lagomorpha. The Cape hare *(Lepus capensis)*, with black-edged ear tips, is common in the artemisia steppe zone, especially among tamarisks and willows near streams. Royle's pika *(Ochotona roylei)* abounds on talus slopes or among rocks, often near shrubs, from Chitral to Baltistan.

The order Rodentia includes voles, marmots, flying squirrels, mice and rats. Royle's high mountain vole *(Alticola roylei)* is abundant from tree line to snow line everywhere. Charmingly bold, with attractive raised furry ears, large eyes, and

dense velvety silver-grey fur, it frequents herders' huts in alpine pastures.

Marmots, highly social high-alpine rodents found in large colonies, are burrowing denizens of the alpine zone. Golden marmots *(Marmota caudata aurea)* abound on the Deosai Plains and in high sedge meadows close to the Chinese border. Long-tailed marmots *(M. caudata)* have black fur along their back and populate a similar niche in Kaghan, Astor and Baltistan. The Himalayan marmot *(M. himalayana)* is found in Baltistan. Marmots have a whistling alarm call that alerts you to their presence and dive into their burrows when approached. The ancient Greek historian Herodotus, who wrote of 'gold-digging ants' in the region was probably writing about marmots. Check out the Marmot Burrow at Ⓦ www.marmotburrow.ucla.edu.

Long-tailed marmots are only active for a few months each year.

Flying squirrels are rarely seen nocturnal creatures. The giant red flying squirrel *(Petaurista petaurista)* and the small Kashmir flying squirrel *(Hyloptes fimbriatus)* live in coniferous forests of Kaghan, Swat and around Nanga Parbat, although the small Kashmir flying squirrel also occurs farther north. See the woolly flying squirrel under Endangered Species (p29).

Rodents include the Chinese birch mouse *(Sicista concolor)*, a nocturnal inhabitant of the alpine, subalpine and artemisia steppe zones down to the edge of cultivated fields, which has a semi-prehensile tail; the field mouse *(Apodemus rusiges)*, found throughout Gilgit, Swat, Chitral and Ghizar; the Turkestan rat *(Rattus turkestanicus)* from Chitral to Baltistan; and the migratory hamster *(Cricetulis migratorius)* that inhabits the mountain artemisia steppe zone from Ghizar, Gilgit and Gojal to Baltistan.

Birds

Larger birds, especially raptors, are easily spotted, as are doves and waterfowl, although they're still hunted. Alpine and moraine lakes are important stopovers on the Indus flyway, one of the largest migratory bird routes in the world, with rare storks and cranes and at least 10 species of ducks and geese migrating from Siberia. About 200,000 of these wetland birds migrate through Chitral alone between September and April. Waterfowl are under severe hunting pressure and the most significant lakes, such as Karambar Lake, deserve recognition and protection.

Falcons are often trapped in northern Chitral and sold in Peshawar to falconers. Wealthy falconers from Arab states then use them to hunt Houbara bustard, a severely endangered bird of Pakistan's southern desert.

Both migratory and resident birds are observable in northern Pakistan. Grebes and waterfowl such as teals, mallards and pintails are seasonal. Among the raptors are the migratory sparrowhawk *(Accipiter* spp.) and marsh harrier *(Circus aeruginosus)*. The golden eagle *(Aquila chrysaetos)*, lammergeier or bearded vulture *(Gypaetos barbatus)*, Eurasian black vulture *(Aegypius*

♀   ♂

MARTIN HARRIS

Trekker's view of common raptors, top to bottom: sparrowhawk; marsh harrier; golden eagle; lammergeier; cinereous vulture; Himalayan vulture.

The lammergeier's wedge-shaped tail is clearly visible in flight.

monarchus) and Himalayan griffon vulture *(Gyps himalayensis)* are present year-round. Eagles prey on snowcocks, hares and marmots. Lammergeiers have a wedge-shaped tail that distinguishes them from golden eagles.

Kestrels and falcons *(Falco* spp.) can be seen year-round, as can the western tragopan *(Tragopan melanocephalus)* and Himalayan monal *(murgh zarin; Lophophorus impejanus),* both hunted for their iridescent plumage. Partridges, also common year-round residents, include chukors *(Alectoris chukar),* snow partridges *(Lerwa lerwa),* and the larger Himalayan snowcock (ram chukor, *Tetraogallus himalayensis)* are

readily seen. Herons, shorebirds, and gulls, including grey herons, black winged stilts, plovers and sandpipers, are transient visitors. Pigeons *(Columba* spp.) and doves *(Streptopelia* spp.) are permanent residents.

Nocturnal birds such as the eagle owl *(Bubo bubo)* and nightjar *(Caprimulgus europaeus)* are present, but poorly known. Cuckoos *(Cuculus* spp.), kingfishers and rollers pass through on migration. The unmistakably crested hoopoe *(Upupa epops)* is widespread. The horned lark *(Euemophilia alpestris)* is a year-round resident, while other larks *(Calandrella* spp.*)* migrate, as do swallows, swifts, and martins. Pipits *(Anthus)* and wagtails *(Motacilla)* visit year-round. Much-hunted thrushes include redstarts *(Phoenicurus* spp.), wheatears *(Oenanthe* spp.) and blue and whistling thrushes.

Others common birds are warblers, accentors, sparrows and buntings, rosefinches *(Carpodacus* spp.), mountain finches *(Leucostite* spp.) and many songbirds (dippers, wrens, tits, shrikes, orioles and starlings). Trekkers also see yellow and red-billed choughs *(Pyrrhocorax* spp.), as well as magpies *(Pica pica)* and the all-black croaking ravens *(Corvus corax),* called *shend* by Wakhi people, who consider them inauspicious.

Endangered Species

Some species, such as Himalayan brown bear and blue sheep, appear to be endangered in Pakistan, although globally they are not. Intense hunting pressure and habitat loss threatens all large or attractive species, no matter their official status. IUCN attempts to track the status of species worldwide and classifies the following species as endangered.

Snow Leopard The magnificent snow leopard *(Uncia uncia)* is an elusive, solitary inhabitant of many Karakoram valleys. Its distinctive, very long, thick tail helps it balance on cliffs in the alpine zone. Northern Pakistan may hold one of the world's largest populations of snow leopards, so look for its scat and scrapings.

Golden eagles, distinguished by their gold head and neck, are found above the tree line.

The beauty of the snow leopard's coat tempts poaching of this endangered cat.

Kashmir Markhor The mountain monarchs, Kashmir markhors *(Capra falconeri cashmiriensis)*, able to cope with wide temperature fluctuations, live on cliffs in the subalpine and artemisia steppe zones. They belong to the goat family, but are a far cry from the common domestic variety. The males weigh up to 90kg and have unique long spiralling horns and a flowing white ruff at the neck. Fortunately, Chitral has perhaps the largest population of these magnificent animals on the planet. Sightings are most easily made in Chitral Gol National Park and Tooshi Gol Game Reserve.

The striking Kashmir markhor may be seen in Chitral Gol National Park.

Marco Polo Sheep As recently as 1968, hundreds of Marco Polo sheep *(Ovis ammon polii)*, whose males have massive outward curving horns, could be seen around Khunjerab Pass. But during the construction of the KKH they were slaughtered to feed workers and soldiers and hunted by visiting bigwigs. Called *roosh* in Wakhi, they now only occasionally visit the Chinese border area in remote valleys west of Khunjerab Pass. They're active only around dawn and dusk, retreating to higher places to rest during the day.

Ladakhi Urial Urial *(Ovis vignei)*, whose males have massive, curving horns, tolerate the relatively warmer temperatures of valley floors in Baltistan, and are infrequently seen. Smaller in size than Marco Polo sheep, males have a distinctive thick chest ruff. Called *shapu* in Balti, they're most active before dawn.

Dignified male urials have a thick ruff on their neck and chest.

Woolly Flying Squirrel The cliff-dwelling woolly flying squirrel *(Eupetaurus cinereus)*, one of the world's rarer mammals, is known only in northern Pakistan. It was rediscovered in the 1990s near Gilgit and Astor and is adapted to the drier, rocky northern region with its dense silky fur and bushy tail.

Flora of the Karakoram & Hindukush

Pakistan has over 5000 species of trees, shrubs and wildflowers. This diversity is particularly notable in the mountainous north where more than 55% of the species are found. With plenty of sunlight in the mountains, moisture is the key factor for plant growth. Precipitation increases with elevation, from desert-like conditions on low valley floors to moist, dense forest on shaded higher slopes. Precipitation from the summer monsoon is also greater on the southern side of mountain ranges, notably southern Chitral, the southern Hindu Raj, south of Rakaposhi and Haramosh, and around Nanga Parbat. The northern slopes, devoid of monsoon moisture, tend to be dry, rocky and barren.

As you rise in elevation, you pass through a series of four vegetation zones, each with its characteristic plants and animals. The extensive **artemisia steppe zone** starts as low as 1500m and continues as high as 2400m on north-facing slopes and 3400m on south-facing slopes. The **dry temperate coniferous forest zone** stretches in a narrow band along the mountains' southern flanks between 1800m and 3400m. In southern Chitral, oak forest predominates below 2400m. In other areas reached by moist monsoon air, conifer forests dominate the upper level of this zone (2400m to 3400m). Where accessible by road, forests have been heavily cut. Tree line roughly corresponds with a 10° to 12°C midday summer temperature, usually around 3300m. Above the timberline is the **subalpine zone**, with scattered stands of birch, willow and juniper bent by snow and wind. Higher still and reaching to the snow line is the **alpine zone**. Where the snow line recedes, colourful flowers appear, literally carpeting these meadows for the short, intense summer.

Artemisia steppe landscape, Yarkhun Valley.

TREES

Forests are scarce, due to general lack of precipitation and to extensive felling. Oak (*Quercus ilex*) forests, prevalent in the dry temperate zone of southern Chitral, but scarce elsewhere, extend from valley floors as high as 2400m. The common white-barked birch *(Betula utilis)*, is found from 3000m to 4600m in the subalpine zone. Herders often wrap and store butter in its paper-like bark.

The prolific pine family (Pinaceae) is represented by four genera: firs (Abies), spruces (Picea), cedars (Cedrus) and pines (Pinus). Common species include: silver fir (*Abies pindrow*), found from 2100m to 3500m on northern aspects; Himalayan spruce *(Picea smithiana)*, from 2500m to 3400m on exposed slopes with firs and pines; Himalayan cedar (*Cedrus deodara*), called *deodar*, a

Oak forest at Guru village, Birir Valley.

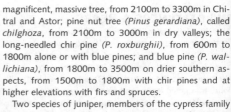

JOHN MOCK

Birch grove near Dok summer village.

magnificent, massive tree, from 2100m to 3300m in Chitral and Astor; pine nut tree *(Pinus gerardiana)*, called *chilghoza*, from 2100m to 3000m in dry valleys; the long-needled chir pine *(P. roxburghii)*, from 600m to 1800m alone or with blue pines; and blue pine *(P. wallichiana)*, from 1800m to 3500m on drier southern aspects, from 1500m to 1800m with chir pines and at higher elevations with firs and spruces.

Two species of juniper, members of the cypress family (Cupressaceae), are the slow-growing, magnificent, ancient *Juniperus excelsa* trees found from 2000m to 4000m in dry open forests; and *J. communis*, a low-growing shrub found from 2200m to 4500m, and especially above the tree line.

Two genera of the willow family (Salicaceae), willow (Salix) and poplar or aspen (Populus), are very common and easily recognisable trees. Salix species abound from 2100m to 4500m along streams and canals, especially in the subalpine zone. The long, narrow, dark green leaves have a pale undersurface. Distinctively tall, quick-growing Lombardy poplars *(Populus nigra)* are much planted near villages and provide timber for house construction.

SHRUBS

Artemisia brevifolia, a pale, greyish-green, highly aromatic shrub that gives its name to the vegetation zone, grows in dry, sandy soil. It has small yellow flower clusters. In Europe, it's better known as wormwood. Other species also flourish in this zone. Berberis species are spiny shrubs, found in dry places, with pale yellow flower clusters and edible blue-back berries. *Ephedra gerardiana*, a common and easily recognisable shrub, grows in dry, sandy places, and has smooth green branchlets with small, red berry-like fruit. *Perovskia abrotanoides*, whose many frond-like branches grow from a single base, displays profuse, tiny, pale violet flowers all along its branches in late summer. It's very common in dry sandy soil, especially around Passu, where it's called *poop-shing*. The common tamarisk *(Tamaricaria elegans)* flourishes along streams. This shrub has long, profuse, dark red-brown spreading branches and produces pinkish-white flowers between July and August. *Hippophae rhaminoides*, a prolific thorny shrub, also called buckthorn, has clusters of small orange fruit. It often lines canals and is used as quick-kindling firewood. *Rosa webbiana* has thorny canes and fragrant, delicate pink flowers that delight trekkers. Its rosehip is an edible source of vitamin C. It grows from 1400m to 4000m near water in dry, rocky areas, especially ablation valleys.

JOHN MOCK

Junipers near Batura Glacier.

WILDFLOWERS & HERBS

The abundance of wildflowers, which peak in early July, in the alpine zone is remarkable and rewards trekkers who visit these high elevations. In the artemisia steppe zone, look on sandy wasteland for *Peganum harmala* (see the boxed text 'Ritual Rue', p263), a medicinal herb with long, thin green leaves and creamy white flowers growing low to the ground, and the conspicuous *Capparis spinosa* with its round green leaves on low-growing runners and solitary, showy white flowers.

Common genera of the buttercup family (Ranunculaceae) are: monks hoods (Acontium), found in alpine meadows; blue delphiniums, common in Swat and Chitral; columbines (Aquilegia); Paraquilegias, a cushion plant of higher elevations; anemones on alpine stone outcrops; buttercups (Ranunculus), which trekkers can hardly miss; and the bright yellow, shiny flowers of globe flowers (Trollius) on rocky slopes.

Delicate herbs of the gentian family (Gentianaceae) have tubular or funnel-shaped, usually purple, flowers that flourish in salt-rich soil. *Gentianodes argentea* carpets open slopes from April to June between 1500m and 3500m. *G. marginata* blooms from June to July in the subalpine zone between 2400m and 3600m, and *G. paludosa* blooms in the alpine zone.

The geranium family (Geranicae) of familiar five-petalled flowers with colours ranging from pink and lilac

Peganum harmala

JOHN MOCK

Passion for Primrose

JOHN MOCK

Clusters of magenta flowers on tall green stems line summer snow melt rivulets in meadows above 4000m. Unequivocally identifiable by its sweet, intoxicating fragrance, the alpine primrose *(Primula macrophylla)* is revered by mountain people throughout northern Pakistan. Wakhi call it *banafsha*, the 'king of flowers'; Kho call it *milkhon*. Burusho and Shina speakers call it *sujo punar* and *suji punar*, the 'sacred flower'.

According to Hunza and Gilgit legends, it's cultivated by the mountain fairies, who hold it dear. In Gojal, it's the subject of songs and poems. The flower extract is used as a cold remedy in Ayurvedic medicine, and the flower itself is used locally as eye medicine. Herders decorate their hats with its blossoms, a symbol of all that is beautiful in their mountain home.

Buttercups and polygonums *Primula denticulata* Myosotis

At Pakora High Camp (4230m), buttercups snake towards Sentinel Peak.

Stenotus, Rost-e-Dur Valley

Aconitum

Viola

Wildflowers at Khani Basa camp site, along Hispar Glacier.

Clematis orientalis

JOHN MOCK

Papaver nudicaule

to purple abound along alpine streams, especially *Geranium wallachianum*.

The poppy family (Papaveraceae) is represented by *Papaver nudicaule*, with its yellow-orange papery petals, growing in alpine rocky places. The beautiful blue Himalayan poppy *(Meconopsis grandis)* is rare.

With their often showy flowers, the attractive herbs of the primrose family (Primulaceae) are always a delight, growing in moist alpine areas near snow melt. Cortusas, with their nodding, bell-shaped red-pink flowers, grow in Kaghan. Androsace grow in tight clusters, with *Androsace mucronifolia* found in cushions of pale pink flowers with a tiny red eye between 3300m and 4700m from Chitral to Baltistan. Alpine primroses rise in proud red to purple clusters on singular stems in moist areas. Mauve-pink dog-tooth primula *(Primula denticulata)* grows as high as 4300m, flowering from April to June. Purple-blue *P. elliptica* grows from 3300m to 4900m in Swat and throughout the Karakoram, and flowers from July to August near snowmelt. The pink-purple, deeply scented *P. macrophylla* (see the 'Passion for Primrose' boxed text) grows between 3300m and 4500m in Chitral, Swat, Deosai, Hunza and Gojal, blooming from May to July.

In addition to the easily recognisable wild rose and wild strawberry (Fragaria), the Potentilla genus is a widely represented member of the rose family (Rosacae). These perennial herbs have a woody base, numerous small, smooth, nut-like fruitlets, and five-petalled flowers ranging from white to reddish to yellow, with the yellow *Potentilla pamiro-altaica* and *P. peduncularis* common in alpine meadows.

Several species of perennial herbs in the saxifrage family (Saxifragaceae) decorate alpine meadows. Perhaps

JOHN MOCK

Pale pink *Androsace mucronifolia* has red or yellow centres.

most common is yellow *Saxifraga hirculus* in meadows and moist places from 3900m to 4500m in Hunza, Gojal and Baltistan.

Lagotis cashmeriana, a member of the snapdragon family (Scrophulariaceae), with its bluish flower spikes on short stems, is found from 3100m to 4000m in the Hunza Valley and the Deosai Plains. *Verbascum thapsus*, with its broad spikes of yellow flowers on tall stems, is found as high as 3600m in rocky places of Chitral. The lovely *Veronica lanosa* with its broad, four-petalled lavender flowers having a pink ring at the base, rises on tall stems to decorate rocky places from Chitral to Baltistan as high as 3800m. *Leptorhabdos parvifolia* is a tall plant with pale pink flowers found in clearings near juniper in Chitral, Gilgit and Baltistan. *Pedicularis* spp., or lousewort, with their multiple elongated flowers with an exaggerated lip along a single tall stalk, are found from 2600m to 4200m throughout northern Pakistan.

Yellow Potentilla and Rhodiola species.

The herbaceous succulents of the stonecrop family (Crassulaceae) have thick fleshy leaves, many stems and flat-topped flower clusters ranging from rose-pink and reddish-brown to yellow. Some high-altitude species form cushions. As the family name 'stonecrop' implies, they grow next to stones or rocks. Common species are *Sedum ewersii*, with rose-pink flowers found in crevices as high as 4500m, and *Rhodiola himalensis* and *R. quadrifida*, both having reddish flowers and growing between 3200m and 4300m from Chitral to Baltistan.

Familiar members of the very large sunflower family (Compositae) include asters and daisies. Several species of aster, with flower heads radiating white or bluish from yellow central discs, are common in high rocky places from Chitral to Baltistan. Very similar are the *Erigeron* species, with large-flowered *Erigeron mutliradiatus*, found from 2200m to 4200m in the Hunza Valley. Blue-flowered chicory *(Cichorium inthybus)* is common along roads from 1300m to 3000m. The spiny thistle herbs, pink-purple flowered *Cousinea thomsonii* and white-flowered globe thistle *(Echinops cornigerus)*, are common from 2400m to 4000m. Near the snow line look for *Saussurea obvallata*, with small purple flowers inside a yellow papery cover, and dense, woolly, dome-like *S. simpsoniana*, growing up to 5000m, tiny purple flowers emerging from the woolly dome. The familiar tufted woolly white flowers of edelweiss *(Leontopodium himalayanum)* grow in open areas of subalpine and alpine zones. In open rocky places, the many tall slender stems and small yellow flower heads of *Tanacetum gracile* are common in Gojal and Baltistan, as is the similar but feathery-leafed, aromatic *T. artemisioides*.

Pink alpine asters amongst the rocks.

POPULATION & PEOPLE

The Karakoram and Hindukush are home to a kaleidoscope of people. Cultural borrowing over millennia has led to a sharing of words and customs between many of the peoples, yet each group has retained its own unique identity. The region's population is approximately 1.5 million, with 53% male and 47% female.

Kho

Kho, whose language is Khowar, make up about 80% of Chitral's population of 350,000 and also predominate in the Northern Areas' Ghizar district and Swat's Ushu Gol. Mulkho and Turikho in Chitral are regarded as the original Kho homeland. Most Kho are Sunni Muslims, but many Kho in upper Chitral are Isma'ilis. Kho society is made up of three classes: an aristocracy, a gentry, and landless labourers. Kho are regarded as highly cultured people, and Khowar poetry and song is greatly esteemed.

Kalasha

Kalasha, whose language is Kalashamun, are the only remaining non-Muslims in northern Pakistan. About 3000 Kalasha live in three valleys in southern Chitral. Kalasha once controlled a much greater area, ruling the Chitral Valley as far north as Reshun. The entire Hindukush was once populated by people with similar beliefs, but the people in the Afghanistan Hindukush were converted to Islam in the 1890s. Kalasha are farmers and herders.

Burusho

The people who speak the Burushaski language are called Burusho. Most of the approximately 80,000 Burusho live in Nagyr and Hunza. Burusho also live in the Yasin Valley. The terms Nagyrkutz and Hunzakutz (people of Nagyr and Hunza respectively) refer not only to Burusho, but also to the non-Burushaski-speaking people living in Nagyr and Hunza. Notable among the minority groups are the Bericho, who speak Dumaki and are the musicians and blacksmiths for the Burusho. Most Burusho in Hunza and Yasin are Isma'ili Muslims, and Burusho in Nagyr and Ganesh are Shi'a Muslims.

Burusho are renowned for their agricultural skills and abilities to construct irrigation systems. Burusho men often work as guides for treks, and are friendly and open-minded. The reputed longevity and extraordinary health of Hunzakutz and Nagyrkutz portrayed in Western literature is just fiction, originating from the romantic fantasies of early-20th-century visitors who found the Shangri-la of their dreams in Hunza.

Gujars

The nomadic Gujar people are widespread throughout South Asia and have migrated into the mountains of northern Pakistan, living in southern Chitral and Ghizar. The name Gujar indicates their close link with cow *(ghu)* herding. These people have taken the opportunity to tend animals and grow crops in marginal areas, and so have found a niche among the Kho, Shins and Yeshkuns. They're exclusively Sunni Muslims and marry within their own group. In Chitral, they speak Khowar, and in Ghizar they speak Khowar and/or Shina.

Shina-speaking people

The Northern Areas' 410,000 Shina-speaking people live in the lower Ishkoman Valley, Lower Hunza, Gilgit, Astor and the Indus Valley from Haramosh to Jalkot and Palas, including Chilas, Darel and Tangir. Some Shina speakers have settled in Baltistan, where they're called Brok-pa. Although most Shina-speaking people are Sunni Muslims, those west of Gilgit are usually Isma'ili Muslims, and those in Gilgit and east of Gilgit are usually Shi'a Muslims. Shina-speaking people are not to be confused with Shins, who are a separate group of Shina-speaking people. In the Gilgit and Hunza valleys, as well as in Darel and Tangir, there are four communities: Shins, Yeshkuns, Kamins and Doms. The Yeshkun are probably the original inhabitants, but the Shins have higher status. Kamins are labourers, and Doms are blacksmiths and musicians. Some scholars believe that the Yeshkun are Burusho who long ago adopted the Shina language from conquerors who came from the south.

Wakhi

Wakhi people, or Xik as they call themselves, migrated to northern Pakistan several hundred years ago from Afghanistan's Wakhan corridor, where they've been living for over 2500 years. They view themselves as part of the larger Tajik ethnic community of the Tajikistan Pamir, Afghanistan's Wakhan, and China's Xinjiang province. Approximately 12,000 Wakhi live in Broghil, Gojal and a few villages in Ishkoman, and are Isma'ili Muslims.

Wakhi depend on livestock husbandry, including yaks, as their villages are at the upper limit of cultivation. Among Wakhi, and unlike other people in northern Pakistan, the livestock are the women's responsibility. Men generally do not go to the high pastures, but rather stay in the village to tend the crops. Wakhi men are renowned for their endurance and often work as guides and high-altitude porters.

Balti-pa

Balti-pa, whose language is Balti, are an Islamicised Tibetan people. Their land, known as Baltistan, lies along the Shyok and Indus rivers. The 365,000 Balti-pa follow Shi'a Islam, and have been Muslims for about five centuries. Their Tibetan cultural roots are evident in their language, clothing, food, yak husbandry and folklore. Balti villages are densely packed clusters of interconnected houses, surrounded by intensively cultivated and irrigated terraces. They make a striking contrast to the huge vertical mountains and arid glacial valleys of Baltistan. Balti men have long worked as porters, cooks and guides for mountaineering expeditions and trekking parties.

Myth of Dards

No people in northern Pakistan today refer to themselves as Dards, and the term is unknown in any local languages. Although rock inscriptions from the 4th or 5th century refer to a great king of the Dards, and the Kashmiri Chronicle of Kings mentions Darad

rulers of the 9th and 10th centuries, the idea that there is today an area populated by Dard people that is called Dardistan is essentially a colonialist construction. The person most responsible for this vexed term is Dr GW Leitner. Leitner was candid about his construction, writing, 'the country is known, since my visit in 1866, as Dardistan' despite the fact that 'the name Dard was not claimed by any of the race I met'. Even the linguistic classification of a Dardic language group is dubious. Georg Morgenstierne, the definitive scholar of northern Pakistani linguistics, wrote that Dardic is 'simply a convenient term to denote a bundle of aberrant Indo-Aryan hill languages'. Linguists now regard Dardic as a geographic rather than a linguistic expression. Dardistan is a problematic inheritance from colonial times that only obscures the identity of, and the relationship between, the people living in northern Pakistan.

RELIGION

Islam is the state religion and nearly all (ie, 97%) Pakistanis are Muslim. Islam became the dominant religion around the 13th century. Islam translates loosely from Arabic as 'the peace that comes from total surrender to God'. God's will is articulated in the Koran, the revelations made to the Prophet Mohammad (Peace be upon him; PBUH) by the archangel Gabriel. In addition to the creeds set out in the Koran, Muslims express their surrender in the form of daily prayers, alms-giving, fasting, proselytism and pilgrimage to Mecca. In its fullest sense, Islam is an entire way of life, with guidelines for doing nearly everything.

In AD 612 Mohammad, a wealthy Arab merchant of Mecca, began preaching Islam. In 622 Mohammad and his followers went to Medina; the Islamic calendar counts its year from this *hijrah* (flight). There he established a religiously organised society that quickly spread throughout Arabia. The new and militant faith meshed nicely with a latent Arab nationalism, and within a century the empire reached from Spain to Central Asia.

Succession disputes after Mohammad's death soon split the community. When the fourth caliph (ruler), the Prophet's son-in-law Ali, was assassinated in 661, his followers and descendants became the leaders of the Shi'a (or Shi'ite) branch. Others accepted the governor of Syria as caliph, a brother-in-law of Mohammad, and this line has become the modern-day orthodox Sunni (or Sunnite) branch. In 680, a chance for reconciliation was lost when Ali's surviving son Hussain and most of his male relatives were killed at Karbala in Iraq by Sunni partisans. Today more than 90% of Muslims worldwide are Sunni.

Among Shi'a doctrines is that of the *imam*, or infallible leader, who continues to unfold the true meaning of the Koran and provides guidance in daily affairs. Most Shi'as recognise a hereditary line of 12 imams ending in the 9th century. These Shi'as are known as Ithna Ashariyas. The Nurbakhshiyya, a Sufi sect of the Shi'a tradition, has about 70,000 followers in Baltistan, particularly along the Shyok River from Kiris to Chorbat, on the Shigar River's west bank, and in the Thalle, Hushe and Saltoro valleys.

An 8th-century split among Shi'as, as to which son of the sixth imam would succeed him, gave rise to the Isma'ili branch. For Isma'ili Shi'as, the line of imams continues to the present. The present leader is Prince Karim Aga Khan, who is revered as the 49th imam. The 11th-century Persian poet and philosopher Nasir Khusro brought Isma'ili teachings to the Hindukush.

Christians, Hindus, Parsis (Zoroastrians) and Kalasha are officially recognised minority religions with elected representatives in the National Assembly.

Islamic Holidays

Many Islamic holidays are national holidays in Pakistan; those marked with an asterisk (*) are also public holidays. The Islamic calendar is lunar, each month beginning with the new moon's first appearance. Religious officials have formal authority to declare the beginning of each lunar month, based on sightings of the moon's first crescent. Future holidays can be estimated, but are in doubt by a day or two until the start of that month. Islamic holidays normally last from sunset

until the next sunset. Sunni and Shi'a officials occasionally disagree by a day or more about when the first crescent appears, and therefore about the holiday's start. This can lead to sectarian tension, even violence, especially at Eid ul-Fitr and Eid Milad-ul-Nabi. Trekking may be affected during Ramazan, Eid ul-Fitr, Eid ul-Azha and Muharram, when guides, cooks and porters may prefer being with their families.

Ramazan (begins 6 November 2002, 27 October 2003, 15 October 2004, 4 October 2005) The month of total sunrise-to-sunset fasting (smoking is also forbidden), called *roza*. Children, pregnant women, non-Muslims, the ill and infirm, and Muslims who travel far from home are exempt from fasting though they're expected to not eat, drink or smoke in front of those who are fasting. Most food shops and restaurants are closed during daylight hours. People take meals in the evening and just before sunrise. The best places for non-Muslims to find food and drink are tourist hotels and, sometimes, Chinese restaurants. Even a nonfasting foreigner may be under stress, so pay attention to your nutrition. Carry a water bottle and snacks, but be compassionate about consuming around those who are not. When trekking, cook, eat and camp in a discreet location away from villages.

*Eid ul-Fitr** (Chhoti Eid or Small Eid; 6 December 2002, 26 November 2003, 14 November 2004, 3 November 2005) Two or three days of celebrations mark the end of Ramazan when the new moon is sighted. This is the Islamic world's most joyous holiday. Families visit, give gifts, enjoy banquets, get bonuses at work and make donations to the poor.

*Eid ul-Azha** (Bari Eid or Qurban; 23 February 2002, 12 February 2003, 2 February 2004, 21 January 2005) The feast of sacrifice, which coincides with the climax of the *hajj* 40 days after the end of Ramazan, commemorates the Prophet Abraham's promise to God to sacrifice his son. Abraham's willing submission found favour and, in place of his son, a ram was offered. Those who can afford it sacrifice a ram, billy goat or bull, sharing the meat with relatives and the poor. Businesses and shops are usually closed for several days.

*Ashura** (24–25 March 2002, 14–15 March 2003, 2–3 March 2004, 19–20 February 2005) The 9th and 10th day of the month of Muharram, is the anniversary of the martyrdom of Imam Hussain, grandson of the Prophet Mohammad. Shi'as begin 40 days of mourning the death of

Hussain, who was killed at Karbala, Iraq. On the 10th day, in trance-like processions sometimes led by a riderless white horse, men and boys pound their chests and chant the names of those killed at Karbala. Some practice *zuljinnah*, an awesome and bloody spectacle of self-flagellation with blade-tipped chains. Sunnis also mourn Hussain's death in a less dramatic way. In the Northern Areas especially, Sunni-Shi'a tension may be high at this time. Travel on the 10th day is inadvisable.

Chhelum (2 May 2002, 22 April 2003, 10 April 2004, 31 March 2005) Forty days after Ashura, with similar but smaller processions.

*****Eid Milad-ul-Nabi** (24 May 2002, 14 May 2003, 2 May 2004, 21 April 2005) Celebrates the Prophet's birthday.

SOCIETY & CONDUCT
Traditional Culture

Mountain societies cannot afford to remove half their population from the labour force, so you can expect to see women working outside the home as well as inside. Although village women are rarely veiled, approaching them risks drawing the ire of male relatives. Women trekkers, however, can freely do so and thus have an opportunity to see more of traditional life than male trekkers. Some religious groups, such as Isma'ili Muslims, place fewer restrictions on women, although the increasingly strong role model of idealised female behaviour projected by Pakistani media and down-country behaviour is influencing even these communities.

People within communities share a broad network of kinship and refer to any fellow villager as a relative, whether actually related or not. The corresponding sense of communal responsibility creates a warm and close social fabric that supports all within it. You may catch glimpses of this while trekking, as younger men help their elders, and fellow-villagers support each other, sharing loads, food and sleeping arrangements.

As schools proliferate and children spend more time in them, they have less time for tending flocks. In villages along the KKH, for example, numbers of livestock have decreased, due to a lack of available labour. Men also are often gone from the village, exploiting opportunities to earn money outside.

Portering, driving a vehicle or keeping a shop are a few examples of these ever-increasing changes.

But all people want to return to their home village for ceremonies and festivals. The social fabric may be stretched through contact with the larger world, but it's not broken. Being sensitive to the concerns and feelings of people you meet, or with whom you trek, will enrich your experience greatly.

Hospitality The tradition of hospitality is deeply cherished throughout the mountains, where people almost bend over backwards to welcome you. Learning a few Urdu language phrases of greeting and thanks will make these encounters more than a pantomime for all. In villages you will likely be offered tea, snacks or fruit. If invited into a home, emulate your hosts' actions – take off your shoes if they do, sit where they indicate and rise if they do. Bowls of food are often shared communally. Whatever you are offered, it's polite to take a bit – you don't have to eat it all!

Dos & Don'ts

Respect local values by dressing and acting conservatively.

Clothing Conservative dress is very important and trekkers should be sensitive to this issue. Dressing in a culturally appropriate fashion will increase your own comfort level. Clothing that reveals any body parts other than the face, hands and feet, or that reveals the shape of the body is deeply offensive. Tight-fitting or revealing dress offends and embarrasses residents who are usually too polite to say anything. Shorts, halter tops and lycra are particularly offensive. Wear loose, non-revealing, long-sleeved shirts and full-length pants for cultural and practical reasons. Western dress is common in cities, but you may want to wear the very comfortable *shalwar kameez* (local baggy pants and long shirt) in towns and villages.

Eating Muslims avoid handling or eating food with the left hand, and so should you. Use your right hand for eating.

Bathing Nude bathing in public is considered vulgar and shameless. On trek, wash your body in your tent, using a wash cloth and a basin of water. Washing hair, face, hands and feet outside is fine as Islam emphasises personal cleanliness.

Public Displays of Affection Holding hands, hugging and kissing are considered private acts, not to be openly displayed.

Public hand holding between men, however, is common as an expression of friendship and rarely has any sexual overtones.

Smoking Although most Pakistani men smoke, remember that many people find smoking offensive. The Aga Khan actually encourages Isma'ili Muslims not to smoke. Please respect the wishes of others and set a positive, healthy example.

Begging Don't give anything to beggars; begging is a superficial and negative interaction. If you want to make a contribution, ask a school headmaster or a representative of a village organisation how you can best make a donation.

LANGUAGE

Many languages are spoken in Pakistan, but only Urdu is readily understood throughout the country. Urdu is the single best language for a trekker to know. Almost all men know Urdu. English is taught in schools, but only used for communication by the educated elite. Still, many people have a smattering of English words or phrases. In the mountains, there are many local languages (mother tongues). The main ones are: Balti, Burushaski, Kalashamun, Khowar, Shina and Wakhi. Women mostly speak only their mother tongue, although with the spread of education more women are learning Urdu.

Balti, the language of the Balti-pa, is the spoken version of classical literary Tibetan and is closely related to Ladakhi, which is spoken in adjacent Indian territory. Burushaski, the language of the Burusho, is unrelated to any other spoken language in the world. Neighbouring Khowar and Wakhi speakers call it Werchikwor. Kalashamun, which is spoken in the three Kalasha valleys and in Jinjeret Kuh, is an Indic language, somewhat related to Khowar with which it has been in long contact. Khowar, the language of the Kho, is an archaic Indic language with significant Iranian influence. The Khowar spoken in Turikho is regarded as the purest. Shina is an Indic language, whose original speakers probably migrated from the south. Several dialects exist, notably Gilgiti, Kohistani and Astori, with Gilgiti the main one. Shina gives its name to Shinaki, the areas in Lower Nagyr and Lower Hunza where Shina speakers live. Brok-pa, the Shina-speakers in Baltistan, call their language Brokskat. Wakhi, or Xikwor as the Wakhi people who speak it call it, belongs to the Pamir group of Iranian languages, all of which belong to the greater Indo-European language family. To speak to people in their own language, see the Language chapter (p353) for useful words and phrases.

Facts for the Trekker

Trekking in the Karakoram and Hindukush encompasses much more than just walking along trails. It's more aptly characterised as cross-country trekking rather than as trail hiking. Trekking here requires a high level of fitness, self-sufficiency and competence, and frequently involves glacier travel, high pass crossings and route-finding since there are no signposts or trail markers and often not even visible trails.

Most treks start from the highest village at the head of a valley, go up through summer pastures, cross a high pass and descend to the highest village in an adjacent valley. As a trekking route wends up valley and over a pass, trails often becomes faint, hard to find, or nonexistent. Occasionally, crossing a pass may involve a scramble over loose scree and rock.

Many other treks involve glacier traverses, where prior experience with glacier travel, rope technique and crevasse rescue are essential. These basic alpine techniques are necessary on many treks, but you don't need to be a climber to trek through these mountains. Many qualified guides can safely see you across difficult sections, demonstrating and letting you practice any technique you may need. Excepting a few treks through heavily glaciated regions, you're usually on such terrain for no more than one day. For most trekkers, attempting such treks without a guide would be an ill-advised risk.

Highlights

In a region of extremes, superlatives abound. Whatever turns you on in the mountains, you can find it in the Karakoram and Hindukush. Here are some themes, with recommended treks listed for each, to help you pick a trek to satisfy your craving for adventure. And don't forget that most treks begin from villages, so the cultural side of trekking comes with each and every one.

Gentle Treks
Donson Pass & Kundyak An, Asumbar Haghost, Fairy Meadow, Rakaposhi Base Camp, Ultar, Kilik & Mintaka Passes

Treks with Views of K2
Baltoro Glacier, Gondogoro La, Rush Phari, Burji La

Treks to 8000m Peak Base Camps
Baltoro Glacier, Fairy Meadow, Rupal, Mazeno La

Treks to 7000m Peak Base Camps
Tirich Mir Base Camp, Diran Base Camp, Rakaposhi Base Camp, Lupgar Sar Base Camp, Masherbrum Base Camp

Rock & Ice – Traversing Gargantuan Glaciers
Hispar La, Baltoro Glacier, Batura Glacier, Chogo Lungma Glacier, Barpu Glacier

Trekking Beneath Monster Walls & Towers of Rock
Baltoro Glacier, K7 Base Camp

High-Altitude Trekking Challenges
Gondogoro La, Mai Dur Pass, Chilinji An & Qalander Uween, Karambar An & Darkot An

Hard & Far Away Treks
Naz Bar An, Zagaro An, Phargam An

Treks with Peak Possibilities
Fairy Meadow, Werthum Pass, Naz Bar An, Rush Phari, Shimshal Pamir, Pakora Pass, Gondogoro Valley

Authors' Favourites
Broghil & Karambar An, Thui An, Punji Pass, Lupgar Pir Pass, Baltoro Glacier, Boisum & Chafchingol Passes

Trekking is a physically and mentally exacting way of travelling. Day after day, you walk for hours, often gaining and losing hundreds of metres in elevation every day. In order not to turn trekking into a gruelling endurance contest, it's useful to cultivate an easy-going attitude. During the first few days, when you're getting used to life on trek, plan short walking days and don't push yourself too far. The scale of the terrain is enormous, and getting there first isn't the most important thing. Pace yourself and stop for rests whenever you need them. To make your trek an enjoyable experience, take time to look at the mountains and sit amid the wildflowers. If your itinerary is leisurely, you can have opportunities to explore an interesting side valley or to spend a little more time in pastures. Take time to get to know your companions, whether they are your compatriots or local residents.

Being physically and mentally prepared for an extended period of mountain travel means cultivating self-reliance. The key factors are judgment and planning. You must know how to integrate your knowledge and experience to make sound decisions and recognise the limits of your own abilities.

SUGGESTED ITINERARIES

Usually the first step in choosing which trek(s) to do is deciding whether to trek in an open zone or a restricted zone (see the discussion of zones under Trekking Permits, p70), because this will affect logistics and costs significantly. It is crucial to plan any restricted-zone trek for the start of your trip and allow time in Islamabad for permit formalities. No matter which zone you choose, allow plenty of time to get to and from trailheads.

One Week

With one week, it's best to pick one open-zone trek near the Karakoram Highway (KKH) and travel by road to avoid any potential flight delays. From Gilgit, the Fairy Meadow trek, followed by a few days sightseeing in Karimabad, is ideal. When coming from China, visit Karimabad first, followed by the Rakaposhi Base Camp trek.

Two Weeks

With two weeks, it's possible to combine two or three open-zone treks in the same region. Flying to a gateway town is recommended to maximise your trekking time. From Chitral, a traverse of five gentle passes from the Kalasha Valleys to Chitral Gol National Park combines three treks: Gree An, Donson Pass & Kundyak An and Gokhshal An & Dooni An. From Gilgit, the Rakaposhi Base Camp trek gets you to a 7000m peak base camp and the Batura Glacier trek gives a taste of huge peaks, ice floes, and a Karakoram glacier; reverse treks when coming from China.

Three Weeks

Either of two classic glacier traverses in Baltistan fit perfectly into a three-week trip: the open-zone Hispar La trek; and the restricted-zone Baltoro Glacier trek or Gondogoro La trek.

One Month

With one month, it's possible to do two or three treks in succession traversing from one region to another. Good open-zone and restricted-zone options exist. A near-loop from Gilgit combines three open-zone treks over three passes: Pakora Pass, Asumbar Haghost and Punji Pass.

An open-zone traverse from Chitral to Gilgit crosses four passes: Owir An, Thui An, Punji Pass or Asumbar Haghost, and Pakora Pass. Shimshal is the ideal place if you wanted to spend the entire time in one place; try combining the open-zone Shimshal Pamir trek, the Qachqar-e-Dur & Shpodeen Pass trek or Mai Dur Pass trek followed by the Boisum & Chafchingol Passes trek. In Baltistan, you can follow the restricted-zone Gondogoro La trek with the restricted-zone Masherbrum Base Camp trek. Alternatively, you can follow the open-zone Hispar La trek with a week in the Hunza Valley either sightseeing or going on day hikes. Arguably the most outstanding restricted-zone combination is a traverse from Chitral to Gojal via three passes on these treks: Shah Jinali An, Broghil & Karambar An and Chilinji An & Qalander Uween.

Three Months

Anything is possible in three months, which allows plenty of time to check out all the main trekking areas. Plan to spend a month in each, basing your treks from Chitral, Gilgit, and Skardu. Traverse the Kalasha Valleys, then trek from Chitral to Gojal as mentioned above. Once in Gojal, do either the Batura Glacier trek or enjoy a few day hikes or short treks listed in that chapter's Other Treks section. From Gojal, travel down the KKH to Gilgit, spending a few days in Karimabad en route. From Gilgit, travel by road to Skardu. In Baltistan, try either the Chogo Lungma Glacier trek to see traditional Balti villages or the Hispar La trek. Next, head to Hushe in eastern Baltistan. Hushe village is a base for several great treks. Remember, if you want to include any restricted-zone treks, it's crucial to do these first.

WHEN TO TREK

The trekking season is late April to late October. Late April to mid-June choose treks that avoid crossing passes, or that cross passes less than 3000m in Chitral because much snow remains on higher passes and north-facing slopes. This is a pleasant time to trek in lower valleys, where fields turn bright green with new wheat and fruit blossoms decorate the trees. Around late May or early June, enough snow has melted for villagers to move flocks to alpine pastures.

Mid-June to mid-September is the peak season and optimal time to traverse glaciers and cross passes higher than 4000m. During late spring and summer, the snow line recedes by about 10m per day, and on southern slopes it recedes to 5500m by late summer. Alpine meadows are in bloom, valleys below 2500m are intensely hot and dry, narrow canyon walls reflect the intense midday heat, and rivers are swollen from glacial melt. By mid-August, the snow pack has melted, exposing crevasses on glaciers and softening remaining snow.

The Karakoram Measures Up to the Himalaya – Way Up

Those willing to put aside negative media reports to travel to northern Pakistan are usually amazed by the hospitality and friendly interactions with the welcoming people they meet. First-time trekkers in the Karakoram usually have trekked previously in the Nepal or Indian Himalaya. So, how does the Karakoram compare to its more well-known neighbours?

The peak Karakoram trekking season is summer, whereas in the Himalaya it's spring and fall. Summer trekking has two major advantages – the weather is warm, even at higher elevations, and the days are long. On most treks, it never freezes at night, so you can forget about packing that down jacket. Sunrise is as early as 4am and daylight lasts until after 8pm. You can hike as long and far as you want, and still have plenty of daylight to settle into camp each evening and have dinner.

The Karakoram has incredible access to the highest mountains. A network of roads extends to almost every village, even in remote valleys. You can jump in a jeep and trek to an 8000m peak base camps in as little as two to seven days. Equivalent Himalayan treks can take as long as two to three weeks! If you're looking for adventure, the Karakoram's glaciers descend to 3000m and sometimes to within 15 minutes' walk from a road. You'd have to hike for days and to elevations as high as 4300m in the Himalaya to reach similar terrain.

You want to get away from crowded trails? The Karakoram exemplifies the untrammelled wilderness experience. So few trekkers visit the region that it's possible to do 'popular' treks and never see another person for as long as 10 days, let alone another foreigner. When you do run into someone else, it's a welcome chance for a visit.

Add up the incredible scenery, traditional cultures and friendly people, and you'll wonder why more people can't get beyond the media reports and trek in northern Pakistan. But you'll be glad they don't!

Mid-September to late October has cooler, yet pleasant, temperatures and crisp nights, often dipping below freezing, that suits lower-elevation treks. Snowfall begins to accumulate, closing passes higher than 4000m. Glacial melt ceases and rivers recede.

During major election campaigns, political expression sometimes takes violent forms. Be cautious while travelling through cities and towns, but once in trekking areas, you're removed from such distractions.

WHAT KIND OF TREK?

Every trek in the Karakoram and Hindukush means a camping trip, because nothing is available once you are on the trek. All trekkers must cultivate self-sufficiency, which means having all the shelter, bedding, camping and cooking equipment, food and fuel for your entire trip. Careful planning and preparation is the key to the success or failure of any trek.

Basically you can follow either of two approaches to organising your trek – either do it yourself, or hire someone to do it for you. Organising things yourself offers the greatest flexibility and is the least expensive style. However, it requires time and initiative to shop, pack and arrange transport to the trailhead, and basic language skills to communicate with everyone from shopkeepers and drivers to porters.

The vast majority of trekkers hire someone to help them. This can mean anything from hiring a porter or two to carry loads and show the way to hiring a trekking company (see Organised Treks, p44) or an adventure travel company abroad (see Trekking Holidays, p113) to take care of everything. The two key criteria in deciding whether or not to hire someone are your physical ability to deal with the terrain and your ability to communicate with local people. Anyone lacking basic route-finding, mountaineering and wilderness-survival skills or the language skills necessary to ask permission to travel in a valley and explain themselves, should either hire someone or go on an organised trek. Anyone planning a restricted-zone trek is required to book through a trekking company.

Whatever arrangements you make, no-one should trek alone. It's always a good idea to trek with a partner and, if you haven't done this kind of trekking before, go with someone who has. You can travel with friends or take a chance on finding another like-minded trekker or two to share the work and support each other on trek. No organised system exists to hook up independent trekkers, so it can be difficult to meet people. If you're looking for a trekking companion, you can hang around hotels and ask around town. Be sure prospective trekkers share the same objectives as you.

Backpacking

You may be inclined to heft everything yourself, but remember that backpacking is the most physically and mentally taxing way to trek. Backpacking suits the patient and outgoing individual with a high degree of self-reliance in adverse conditions and enough physical conditioning and endurance to carry a full load and still do all the camp chores (eg, cooking, cleaning, hauling water, and setting up and striking tents). You also need good trail sense and good maps. The length of your trek is limited by your physical ability to carry food and fuel, usually from seven to 10 days. This rules out longer open-zone routes and all restricted-zone treks. In a few areas, trekkers may be tempted to do short treks to pastures, living off the generosity of herders and sleeping in the herders' huts. You will be less of an imposition on local hospitality, and have a safer and more comfortable experience, if you're supplied and equipped to deal with the conditions you'll encounter while trekking.

Backpacking is not recommended on routes that traverse glaciers unless you have extensive experience with glacier travel. Certain areas are very tolerant of independent trekkers wandering around – valleys in northern Chitral such as Owir and Yarkhun, Ishkoman and Yasin, and all of Hunza, Gojal and Baltistan. Other areas, however, are not as tolerant and backpacking should be avoided – the Shina-speaking areas around Gilgit, Bagrot, Haramosh and Nanga Parbat.

Of course, if you can do all this, backpacking can be the most rewarding way to trek. It offers you the most flexible itinerary, the greatest freedom to go at your own pace and the most open potential for discovery and interaction with people and their culture.

Trekking with Porters

You can reduce the sheer physical effort of trekking, extend your range and still run your own show by hiring a porter to carry the bulk of your gear and food. Some porters may also cook and do camp chores. For comfort's sake, it makes sense to allow at least one porter per trekker for trips up to 10 days. You need to know porters' wages, stages, load sizes (see Guides & Porters, p46) and be able to adequately discuss all this with whoever you hire. If you don't want to prepare your own meals, or if you have a large enough trekking party to make cooking a full-time job, you may want your porter to do some cooking, or to hire a separate cook. Be sure he knows how to cook your food and operate your stove. Any porter can help you buy supplies and arrange transport.

Trekking with savvy porters can offer the best of both worlds; you carry less and enjoy the trail more, have more time to do as you like, and still keep expenses low enough not to break the bank. Moreover, trekking with a knowledgeable porter can open a world of experience not possible on your own. A porter can invite you into his home and introduce you to fellow villagers in pastoral settlements. He can also explain to his compatriots just what it is you are doing in their territory. Having spent his life walking the trails you're on, he can help you across difficult sections, he will know about every rock and tree, and all the stories and lore about the places you visit. For many trekkers, their warmest memories are of the energetic and helpful porter who made their trip possible.

ORGANISED TREKS

Trekking companies provide a range of services to match most styles and budgets. They can suggest treks that match your schedule and physical abilities. This enables you to choose your fellow trekkers and create a flexible itinerary that you can modify along the way. Some offer fixed group departures for certain treks. The trekking company provides an experienced trek crew (ie, a guide, cook, kitchen and camp helpers and porters) and food and equipment. Ask for a list of personal equipment (eg, sleeping bags, sleeping pads and tents) and camping equipment (eg, dining or mess tent, tables, chairs, toilet tent, kitchen tent and kit, stoves, dishes, utensils and washbasins) they provide. They can also book hotels and arrange transport. Trekking companies quote a fixed price inclusive of all services you request and you pay them one lump sum.

Working with a trekking company increases the likelihood of your trekking with a reliable trek crew. It's worthwhile to shop around and get quotes from three or four companies. This process is easier when you know where you want to trek and what services you want them to provide, so be specific before you start spending money.

Contact trekking companies about six months in advance, otherwise their best trek crews may not be available. When you contact trekking companies after you arrive in Pakistan, it can take as long as a week to compare companies and select one, inquire about the quality of services, decide what services you want, agree on costs and complete the trek arrangements.

Many trekking companies have a main office and smaller branch offices. An alphabetised list of reputable licensed companies by cities and towns follows; street addresses follow mailing addresses when different.

Islamabad & Rawalpindi

Adventure Tours Pakistan (☎ 051-2252759, 2260820/1, fax 2252145, e enquiry@atp.com.pk, w www.atp.com.pk) Ashraf Aman, PO Box 1780, Islamabad; G-9/1, St 53, House 551
Adventure Travel (☎ 051-2272490, ☎/fax 28 22728, fax 2821407, e adventur@isb.coms ats.net.pk, w www.adventure-touroperator.com) SN Malik, PO Box 2062, Islamabad; 15 Wali Centre, 86 South Blue Area

Alpine Trekkers & Tours (Pvt) Ltd (☎ 051-5519815, 5592126, 5593149, fax 5517330, e alpine@meganet.com.pk, W www.alpine .com.pk) PO Box 2488, Islamabad; 21 Al Amin Plaza, 1st floor, The Mall, Rawalpindi Cantt

Baltistan Tours (☎ 051-2270338, fax 227 8620, e btadvent@karakorm.sdnpk.undp.org, W www.baltistantours.com.pk) Muhammad Iqbal, PO Box 1285, Islamabad

Concordia Expeditions Pakistan (☎ 051-5510308, fax 5527505, e concordi@isb.com sats.net.pk, W www.concordia-expeditions. com) GPO Box 1800, Rawalpindi

Concordia Tours & Trekking Services (☎/fax 051-5503495, e ctt@isb.compol.com) Haji Ahmad Khan, 132 Millat Colony, Rawalpindi

Himalaya Nature Tours (☎/fax 051-2820836, e urgent@hotmail.com) F-7/1, St 45, House 5, Islamabad

Himalaya Treks & Tours (Pvt) Ltd (☎ 051-5515371, fax 5563014, e himalia@isb.com sats.net.pk, W www.himalayatrekstours.com) Muhammad Ali Changazi, PO Box 918, Rawalpindi; 112 Rahim Plaza, Murree Rd

Hushe Treks & Tours (☎ 051-2263594, fax 226 1360, e hushe@isb.comsats.net.pk, W www .hushe.com.pk) PO Box 471, Islamabad; G-9/1, St 25, House 764

Jasmine Tours (☎ 051-5586823, fax 5584566, e jtours@isb.apollo.net.pk, W www.jasminet ours.com) Asghar Ali Porik, PO Box 859, Rawalpindi; 24 Canning Rd, Saddar Bazaar

Karakorum Explorers (☎ 051-4441258, fax 444 2127, e hunza@isb.comsats.net.pk, W www .karakorumexplorers.com.pk) Mubarak Hussain, PO Box 2994, Islamabad; I-10/1, St 90, House 1295

Karakurum Treks & Tours NA (Pvt) Ltd (☎ 051-2250317, fax 2264192, e karakurm@ isb.comsats.net.pk, W www.karakurum .com.pk) Anchan Ali Mirza, PO Box 2803, Islamabad; Hotel Metropole, 21-B G-9 Markaz

Mountain Movers (☎ 051-5470519, fax 547 0518, e isb01315@paknet2.ptc.pk, W www .it-warehouse.com/mountainmovers) Musarat Wali Khan, PO Box 985 GPO, Rawalpindi

Mountain Travels Pakistan (☎ 051-5528595, 5525795, fax 5528596, e mtp@isb.comsats .net.pk, W members.home.net/mtntravelspakis tan) Ghulam Ahmad, PO Box 622, Rawalpindi; 507 Poonch House Complex, Adamjee Rd

Nazir Sabir Expeditions (☎ 051-2252580/53, 2853672, fax 2250293, e nazir@isb.comsats .net.pk, W www.nazirsabir.com) Nazir Sabir, PO Box 1442, Islamabad 44000; F-8/1, 28/B, Nazimuddin Rd

North Pakistan Treks, Tours and Expeditions (☎ 051-2281655, 2251034, fax 2260835, e north@isb.compol.com) Ishaq Ali, PO Box 463, Islamabad; G-9/1, Street 52, House 505

Pakistan Guides (☎ 051-5525633, ☎/fax 552 4808, fax 5539497, e guides@isb.paknet .com.pk) Kaiser Khan, PO Box 1692, Rawalpindi 46000; 62/2 Bank Rd, 3rd floor

Siachen Travels & Tours (☎ 051-4426340, e si chenttpak@yahoo.com) Ghulam Ali, PO Box 1213, Islamabad

Sitara Travel Consultants (Pvt) Ltd (☎ 051-2873372, 2274892, fax 2279651, e islam abad@sitara.com, W www.sitara.com) PO Box 1662, Islamabad; Waheed Plaza, 3rd floor, 52-West, Jinnah Ave, Blue Area

Trans Asian Tours (☎ 051-4414231, fax 4426614, e tat_pak@yahoo.com) Ashraf Khan, PO Box 1535, Islamabad

Vista Tours (☎ 051-2253092, fax 2253093, e vista@vista-tourism.com, W www.vista -tourism.com) Bilal Ahmad, G-8 Markaz, Flat B, First Floor, Block 20-D, Islamabad

Walji's Adventure Pakistan (☎ 051-2270757/8, 2870201/9, fax 2270753, e waljis@comsats.net.pk, W www.waljis .com) Iqbal Walji, PO Box 1088, Islamabad; Walji's Building, 10 Khayaban-e-Suhrawardy

Chitral

Hindukush Trails (☎ 0933-412800, fax 412668, e info@hindukushtrails.com, W www.hin dukushtrails.com) Mountain Inn, Chitral

Gilgit

Adventure Center Pakistan (Pvt) Ltd (☎ 0572-2409, fax 3695, e info@adventu recenterpak.com, W www.adventurecente rpak.com) Ikram Beg, PO Box 516, Gilgit; 468 Sir Aga Khan Rd, Jamat Khana Bazaar

Adventure Tours Pakistan (☎ 0572-2663), Airport Rd, Gilgit

Concordia Tours & Trekking Services (☎ 0572-3739, 3956) NLI Chowk, Gilgit

Himalaya Nature Tours Pakistan (☎ 0572-2946, ☎/fax 55359, fax 55900, e himalaya@ glt.comsats.net.pk) Asif Khan, PO Box 535, Gilgit; Chinar Bagh Link Rd

Mountain Movers (☎ 0572-2967, fax 2525) PO Box 534, Gilgit; Airport Rd

Trans Asian Tours (☎ 0572-3419) Chinar Bagh Link Rd, Gilgit

Walji's Adventure Pakistan (☎ 0572-2665, fax 4129) PO Box 515, Gilgit; Airport Rd

Hunza Proper

Concordia Expeditions Pakistan (☎ 0572-77181/2) Karimabad
Karakorum Explorers (☎ 0572-77078) Ganesh
Nazir Sabir Expeditions (☎ 0572-2661) Aliabad
Sitara Travel Consultants (☎ 0572-77194) Zero Point, Karimabad
Walji's Adventure Pakistan (☎ 0572-77203, 77087) Karimabad

Skardu

Baltistan Tours (☎ 0575-2626, fax 2108) PO Box 604, Skardu; Satellite Town
Concordia Trekking Services (☎ 0575-3440) Syed Abbas Kazmi, PO Box 626, Skardu
Concordia Tours & Trekking Services (☎ 0575-2947) Naya Bazaar, Skardu
Himalaya Treks & Tours (Pvt) Ltd (☎ 0575-2528) College Rd, Skardu
Karakorum Explorers (☎ 0575-55072) Hospital Rd, Skardu
Karakurum Treks & Tours (☎ 0575-2856) Link Rd, Satellite Town, Skardu
Mountain Travels Pakistan (☎ 0575-2750) PO Box 621, Skardu; Satellite Town
Nazir Sabir Expeditions (☎/fax 0575-2778) near K2 Motel, Skardu
Siachen Travels & Tours (☎/fax 0575-2844) PO Box 622, Skardu
Walji's Adventure Pakistan (☎ 0575-3468) Prince Market, College Rd, Skardu

GUIDES & PORTERS

When hiring a guide and/or porters, you need to understand the details outlined in the Tourism Division's *Trekking Rules and Regulations* (see Trekking Permits, p70). Guides and porters are savvy and surprisingly well-informed, so familiarise yourself with this information before hiring anyone. When a trekking company organises your trek, it employs the guide and porters. Guides and porters are always men; women don't do this type of work for social and cultural reasons. The majority of trekkers hire at least one local person to help them navigate through these rugged mountains.

Guides

Competent guides are good-natured, know the route, know where to locate water and where to camp, have basic mountaineering skills and speak some English. Guides also hire and supervise porters, buy supplies and organise transport. Guides carry only their own personal gear, expect you to equip them fully and generally don't help with cooking. Guides usually work as a team with their own cook. Guides should make your trek easier and more enjoyable – that is why you pay them. A good guide can be the key to a successful trek.

Tourism Division licenses guides, assigning a registration number that entitles them to work as mountain guides. The fact that Tourism Division has licensed a guide doesn't mean he has any specific training. Ask prospective guides if they are licensed and have completed any training courses. Often their experiences and abilities vary widely, so ask the guide about his experience and if he has done the route before. Guides may be familiar with one area, but be completely unfamiliar with another. Most guides are employed by trekking companies, some run their own trekking companies and others work as freelance guides.

Guides are less useful for small parties (eg, four trekkers or fewer) on open-zone treks, unless you hire enough porters to justify having a guide to manage them. Guides, however, are indispensable on some challenging open-zone treks for route-finding and recruiting reliable porters. Licensed mountain guides are required for restricted-zone treks. On these treks, Tourism Division requires the guide to meet you in Islamabad for your briefing at its office and remain with you until you return to Islamabad and complete your debriefing. During this time, you pay their daily wages plus expenses, including food and lodging.

Porters

A low-altitude porter works with trekking parties below 6000m and a high-altitude porter works with mountaineering expeditions above 6000m. Porters aren't licensed by the government. Most porters carry heavy loads, cook their own food, have excellent route knowledge and experience, but speak limited English. Often porters travel only in familiar areas, close to where they live. Porters are indispensable on glacier crossings, where the route can change daily, and in remote areas where finding water can be problematic. For open-zone treks that don't require a licensed guide, it makes sense to hire a porter. When trekking in a restricted zone, you have to hire porters in addition to a guide.

When you have more than 25 porters, the government requires you to hire a head porter (called a porter *sirdar*) to manage the other porters. When you have fewer than 25, you can do it yourself, have your guide do it, or have the porters select one of themselves to manage the others.

Porter Loads The government sets a load limit of 25kg below 5000m and 20kg between 5001m and 6000m per porter, not including the porter's personal gear and food. Porters prefer to tie loads onto a metal-frame carrier with shoulder straps, if they have one, and carry them on their backs. Otherwise, they use rope to fashion shoulder straps. The 1kg to 2kg carrier's weight isn't usually included in the load limit.

Buy a hand-held scale to weigh porters' loads daily. A double-spring scale (Rs 240, maximum 100kg) is more accurate than a single-spring scale (Rs 140, maximum 50kg). Porters are accustomed to using these scales and usually sort out the loads themselves. This is a very easy way to ensure fairness and resolve disputes. Scales are available in Rawalpindi, Islamabad's Aabpara market, Chitral, Gilgit, and Skardu. Trekking companies typically set their own per trekker weight limit for personal gear, which can be well below the government limits. Ask about weight limits and what the charges per kilogram are for overweight gear, if any.

It's important to make up all the loads before leaving your hotel or trek's staging place. It's impractical to make up loads at the trailhead. Usually there's too much confusion at the trailhead, resulting in light loads and an additional porter or two you don't need.

When you cross a high pass or glacier, you can keep the pace from becoming too slow

by lightening loads a few kilograms or hiring an extra porter. Porters usually reciprocate with hard work and fewer complaints. In some areas, porters may ask for wage increases or for their loads to be lightened as elevation is gained, although you may be nowhere near the 5000m or 6000m limits. In the face of a unified demand, all you can do is bargain hard and consider whatever extra you pay as *baksheesh*.

Hiring Guides & Porters
The key to hiring both guides and porters is knowing who to hire and how much to pay. It's best to hire porters from the valley or area through which you will be trekking. Upon arrival in the highest village in a valley or at the trailhead, ask if anyone is available. Avoid hiring anyone along the trail; instead, hire in the presence of others so at least one person witnesses who goes off with you. This increases the likelihood of hiring a reliable, responsible person and deters thieves and troublemakers. Some foreigners who have hired people along the trail or who have opted to trek alone have faced the extreme consequences of robbery, rape, and murder.

In late August and September, villagers are busy with the harvest. At this time, finding a few porters isn't usually a problem, but when you need a lot of porters, or when an expedition is in the area, it can be tough. Along some trekking routes that pass through different valleys, you're expected to hire new porters in each valley and release your porters if they're from a different area. At the start of your trek, before you hire any porters, verify if you need to change porters along the way.

Ask trekking companies, hotels and shopkeepers for recommendations. Ask prospective guides and porters to show you a *chit*, or letter of recommendation, from any foreigners for whom they have previously worked. These will help you to ascertain their range of skills and experience. If you're pleased with any guides or porters after your trek, take the time to write them a similar letter.

When hiring a freelance licensed guide, try to find one who is associated with (and somewhat accountable to) an established, licensed trekking company. The guide is then less likely to create problems and may have more of an incentive to do a good job.

In some villages, a porters' union exists that assigns porters based on a rotational numbering system. The names of men available for work are posted (usually in a public place) and whoever is next on the list goes with you. Avoid hiring school-age boys. This robs them of their chance at an education, which is far more valuable than any money they may earn.

Be thorough when hiring: make your requirements clear, set any limitations and agree on loads, wages, stages, food, clothing and equipment. Count and weigh your porters' loads and check your gear daily. Have each porter sign a contract (an example is in the *Trekking Rules and Regulations*). The contract may not be legally binding, but serves its purpose. If possible, also collect each porter's *shenakti* or national identity card (NIC). A photocopy may work, but the original is better. Keep these with you until your trek finishes; they're the cheapest insurance against disputes and strikes en route.

Keep a list of anyone you hire, noting their name, their father's name, village and place and date of hire. When you release someone, refer to this list to calculate wages. Pay wages when you release someone – not in advance or on a daily basis. It's helpful to count out the wages in the privacy of your tent the night before you release them and pay their wages. Carry a small note pad and make a receipt by again noting their name and their father's name, village, and the date and amount you paid them. Then fold the receipt and money in half, so the next day it's easy to pull this out discreetly and give the correct wage to each individual. Ask them to sign the receipt or give a thumb print. This can resolve disputes that may arise after the fact about payment of fair wages, but be prepared for haggling anyway.

Stages

The distance covered on most treks is divided into *parāo* or stages, loosely defined as a traditional day's walk for the people who live in an area. The government, trying to avoid abuses and unify disparate systems of payment, initially established the stage scheme for mountaineering expeditions in restricted zones. Later, porters working in open zones also began to demand wages on the stage basis, although it's rarely clear to outsiders what a stage really is. Stage lengths vary widely, often depend upon the difficulty of the terrain, and may be as short as a one-hour walk or as long as a full day. Trekkers often walk several stages in one day because the stage length varies. Walking only one stage per day is too slow a pace for most trekkers; an average of two stages per day is common. Occasionally it might be necessary to walk three or more stages in one day, particularly when crossing a high pass and descending to the first possible camp site.

This unofficial system of payment by stages is now prevalent for trekking in both open and restricted zones. The stage system is pervasive throughout the Northern Areas. Thankfully, the stage system is not as prevalent throughout Chitral where wages are typically paid on a daily basis, which is understood to be after six or seven hours of walking.

The number of stages on many treks isn't fixed and can vary according to whom you ask and can change from year to year. Recognised halting places exist on most treks and many of these comprise stages. On popular treks, such as the Baltoro Glacier, stages are fixed and non-negotiable. On some routes, however, as new place names are recognised, porters attempt to define new stages. For example, over a five-year period the number of stages on the Biafo Glacier increased by 40%, substantially increasing the cost of hiring porters. As roads are pushed farther up some valleys, the traditional trailheads change, thus altering the starting stages on some treks. Ask the village headman nearest the trailhead how many stages a trek covers. Often he can confirm what guides or porters may have said. When you bring porters to the headman, everyone can hear and agree upon what he says. Be sure everyone agrees on where the stages start and finish and on the total number of stages. Write down these details so you can refer to them when paying wages later. Think in terms of the number of stages and not of the number of days on a trek since wage negotiation is usually based on stages. The cost difference between a per-stage basis and a daily basis can be dramatic. Some 'amateur' guides are demanding per-stage wages, which is ridiculous since they carry almost no load.

Tourism Division has no authoritative list of stages for treks and the stage system is widely abused. The accepted number of stages is in the Planning section for each trek, and represents the authors' best understanding from experience and after speaking with an exhaustive number of guides, porters, village leaders and trekking companies. This may help you to avoid being ripped off or inadvertently embroiled in wage disputes or strikes.

Stage inflation is a problem in Pakistan. If a stage means a normal day's walk, why pay two or three stages for an easy day of trekking? Porters don't yet understand that stage inflation discourages trekkers, leading to a decrease in the number of trekkers and hence a decrease in potential overall earnings. Use this book as a source to counter any attempts at stage inflation.

Wages

Wages in Pakistan may seem high among developing countries, but they reasonably reflect the comparatively higher standard of living. For example, guides' and porters' wages are three to four times higher than those for trekking in the neighbouring Indian or Nepal Himalaya. When you pay your guide and porters fair wages, they, in turn, look after you. When you keep in mind that everyone's in it together, the neo-colonial hierarchy of *sahib* and servant fades and the trek is more enjoyable.

Guides Freelance licensed guides earn Rs 1000–1200 per day, not per stage, for every day they accompany you. This includes rest days on trek, and days spent at hotels or en route to and from trailheads.

Cooks A cook earns Rs 500–600 per day plus food rations. A porter who doubles as a cook earns Rs 50–100 per stage in addition to the per-stage porters' wage.

Porters Total porters' wages are divided into categories: stage; *wāpasi* (return); food rations; clothing and equipment allowance; rest days; and halts due to bad weather. The system is complex and often confusing, but it helps to try to understand it to minimise disputes and avoid porter strikes.

When expeditions and trekkers use the same routes, it generally becomes more expensive for trekkers to walk to base camp. Expeditions need to transport large loads to base camp and equip porters for conditions beyond, so stages tend to become shorter and more numerous and porters tend to expect more substantial clothing and equipment.

Stage For many years, Tourism Division set and published the maximum porters' wage per stage. This maximum wage became the going wage with few exceptions. (These wages were outlined on a sheet of paper physically separate from the *Trekking Rules and Regulations*.) In theory, these maximum wages were to be reviewed, set and published annually by Tourism Division. This didn't happen, so actual wages were often fixed locally by the Deputy Commissioner (DC) for each district and superseded the maximum wages set by the government. The government last published maximum wages in 1994 and, out of necessity, many villages have largely abandoned this system and now set their own wages annually to keep up with inflation or to react to market forces. The locally set wages tend to be a flat rate of Rs 220–300, inclusive of the stage wage and food rations. It's imperative to ask for the current wage in each valley for each trek before setting out.

That said, Tourism Division has stated that it's planning to publish new wages in 2001. If that happens and these wages are higher than the current locally set wages, wages are likely to increase. If they're lower, it may have no effect on actual wages. Since it's still technically the law, the 1994 maximum wages per stage, which correlated loosely with the regional standards of living, are: Rs 160 for Chitral, Ghizar and Gilgit (Hunza and Gojal); and Rs 120 for Diamir and Baltistan.

Wāpasi (Return) Wāpasi equals half of the wage for one stage and is paid in addition to the per stage porter's wage on all treks. When exceptions exist, it's explained in the Planning section for each trek. Wāpasi is intended to cover a porter's expenses to walk with only his personal belongings (not a load) back to the point where he was hired. For example, if a porter has to walk several stages to return to his village where he was hired, it's fair to compensate him for his time to get there and for the cost of food he eats en route.

Sometimes wāpasi is not paid. When you hire a porter for a trek that starts and finishes at the same place, don't pay wāpasi since the porter has incurred no out-of-pocket expenses nor extra time to return to where he was hired. When a trek finishes in a different place from where it starts and finishes at a roadhead where public transport is available, it doesn't make sense to pay wāpasi since the porter isn't walking back. Instead pay your porter's fare on public transport back to where he was hired plus a fair amount for his food and/or lodging en route. When you and your porters travel together to and from trailheads, you are usually expected to cover the costs of their transport and do not pay wāpasi. Some porters may demand wāpasi even when it may not seem logical to pay it. Use your best bargaining skills to negotiate an acceptable compromise before starting your trek, or look for other porters.

Food Rations Porters need to eat and they simply use the term 'rations' when they're talking about their food. It's essential to agree upon what kind of food they eat, who buys it, who carries it and who cooks it before hiring someone. Trekkers can either pay porters a per diem for rations or buy porters' rations.

The maximum porter's food ration is Rs 60 per day, which is interpreted to mean Rs 60 per stage. If you insist on paying food rations per day instead of per stage, you may inadvertently find yourself walking only one stage per day. When you pay a flat-rate wage that includes payment for rations, porters buy and bring all their own food. Their food is typically not weighed as part of the government's load limit. Hence, it can be cheaper to pay food rations rather than provide food and then hire more porters to carry the porters' food.

Alternatively, when providing rations, you're required to comply with the government's itemised list of minimum daily food rations detailed in the *Trekking Rules and Regulations*. Most porters, however, don't want to eat the food on the list, which then necessitates negotiating what food they want. Typically, porters eat bread with sweet and milky tea. Figuring out what and how much to buy and buying and packing it takes time. On the trail, you then distribute food to porters every few days. Otherwise, they may eat all the food quickly and five days into a 15-day trek you may learn that food is running out.

An unexpected food shortage can also happen when porters provide their own food. Be sure they have sufficient food for the number of days you plan to be trekking.

Porters' Feast

On a long glacier traverse or high pass crossing, there's no wood to make a fire to bake bread. All you're eating is stale bread and tea, and hunger pains knot your stomach. Who wouldn't want a special feast! Tradition dictates that trekkers buy a sheep or goat for their porters to butcher. At camp before stepping out onto that big glacier or in celebration after that high pass crossing, porters cook, eat and then distribute the leftover meat among themselves. Since you paid for it, they'll offer you your choice of meat. The cost of an animal depends on its size and who is doing the bargaining, but it's a big budget item (Rs 2000–2500) and much-appreciated morale booster that trekkers should anticipate.

Somehow, porters may expect to eat your 'extra' food, which usually doesn't exist.

Clothing & Equipment Allowance Technically, the government requires trekkers to provide porters with clothing and equipment itemised in the *Trekking Rules and Regulations*. Alternatively, you can pay each porter an allowance of Rs 200, which is usually less than buying every item on the list. It's unlikely that porters will buy new gear with Rs 200, but the money helps cover the wear and tear on their clothes and shoes. On some treks, it's not necessary to pay the allowance. Often on treks lasting less than one week you can negotiate a lower rate, say Rs 100–120. When doing multiple treks back-to-back with the same porters, a single clothing and equipment allowance covers all treks. The allowance is mentioned in the Planning section for each trek only when you're expected to pay it.

Payment of this allowance in no way minimises your responsibility to ensure that each porter is properly equipped for the specific conditions of your trek. Ask to see porters' gear before the trek to ensure it's suitable.

Rest Days Porters expect compensation either in time off or additional wages for rest days. Porters earn one day off for seven days worked, which is often interpreted as seven stages, to their advantage. It's not difficult to walk seven stages in four or five days, so don't agree to stop for a day each seven stages unless it's for rest or acclimatisation.

Porters are always paid half the wage for one stage for a rest day, whether you actually take it or not. Wāpasi is never paid for a rest day. If you take a rest day, you also pay food rations. If your porters earn a rest day, but agree not to take it, you don't pay food rations. When day hikes or side trips do not require shifting camp and your porters stay put, pay your porters for a rest day. Remember that it's cheaper to walk one stage a day for two days than to walk two stages in one day and then take a rest day!

Bad Weather If a trekking party halts due to bad weather, government regulations require you to pay your porters one full-stage wage per day. Porters, however, often accept a rest day (or half a stage) wage for such days. Full rations are expected, but wāpasi is not.

Clothing & Equipment

As their employer, you're responsible for the wellbeing of anyone you hire. Ensure they're adequately equipped because their lives can depend on it. This includes providing them with warm clothing, including hats, gloves, socks, jackets or sweaters and shoes. You will be expected to dispense medicine for headaches, clean and bandage cuts and organise any more serious medical help if the need arises.

Essential equipment when camping on snow or ice or higher than 4000m includes: windproof shelter (tarp or tent that several men can share); sleeping bag and/or heavy blankets; sleeping pad per person; and sunglasses or glacier goggles per person. Ask each crew member if they have any of these items; many have their own blankets or sleeping bag and sleeping pad. The extent to which you supply your crew with adequate shelter is a personal choice, but ask yourself if you would be warm enough sleeping in the shelter you intend to provide. Tarps need to be large enough to cover the roofless stone-walled shelters porters use along many trekking routes. The cost of providing this equipment is usually less than the cost of paying porters' wages to carry the amount of kerosene a crew would consume trying to stay warm on cold nights at higher elevations.

Additional considerations exist when you hire a guide. It is reasonable to provide a tent for the guide separate from the porters' shelter. When you expect a guide to break trail through fresh snow or over a difficult pass, provide him with gaiters, snow pants and glacier goggles (not sunglasses).

When guides or porters don't have their own equipment, you can either purchase or lend them gear. When you lend gear, distribute it only on the day(s) when it's needed and collect it immediately afterward.

Cooking Equipment You also need to supply a trek crew with cooking equipment separate from your own. Their basic kitchen includes: stove with spare parts and cleaning wires (also see Stoves, p60, and Fuel, p61); plastic container(s) with good seal to transport kerosene; funnel to pour kerosene; fuel; matches or butane lighter; large cooking pot; tea kettle; *tawa* (an iron griddle for cooking chapattis); rolling pin; large flat pan to mix and knead dough; and one plate, mug and spoon per person.

Insurance

No insurance requirements apply to open-zone treks, but on restricted-zone treks the government requires trekkers to purchase a personal accident policy for guides, cooks, and porters. The government sets a minimum per-person coverage limit of Rs 200,000 for guides and cooks and Rs 100,000 for low-altitude porters. Premiums vary with the trek length (ie, the insured period). For example, the approximate base premiums for a one- to four-week trek for Rs 200,000 coverage is Rs 248 and for Rs 100,000 coverage is Rs 105; 9% taxes are added to the base premiums. When you organise your own trek, purchase the insurance policy before submitting a permit application to Tourism Division. It's easiest to hire a trekking company to help you.

ACCOMMODATION

In Towns

Accommodation at hotels and village guest-houses ranges from a *charpoy* (a rope bed) without privacy, security or bedding to three-star hotels with private rooms with attached bathrooms. Many budget hotels lack running hot water. Chitral, Gilgit and Skardu have public bathhouses called *hammams*. These male-only establishments, usually attached to a barber shop and identifiable by the rows of towels hanging outside, offer a good place to bathe with a bucket of hot water for a few rupees. Women can ask the hotelkeeper to provide a bucket of hot water in their room.

Occasionally, villagers welcome you into their homes. Conventional camping grounds don't exist, although some hotels allow you to pitch a tent in their garden and charge a per-tent camping fee. No hostel system exists in northern Pakistan, although there are hostels in a few down-country cities.

On the Trek

No camp sites or facilities exist anywhere along trekking routes. Once on trek, you're snoozing on the ground in your tent unless you prefer sleeping under the stars. Some villages charge a per-tent camping fee.

FOOD

Local Food

Meat is the basic theme of Pakistani meals and travel is taxing on vegetarians. Meat generically is called *gosht*. Mutton is *chota gosht* and beef is *bara gosht*. Chicken is called *murgi* and is not considered gosht. Pieces of meat or chicken are typically served in a sauce, occasionally with potatoes or other vegetables. Everyone uses flat rounds of *chapattis* (bread) for grabbing, spooning or soaking up all the pieces and juices. Flat fried bread called *paratha* is commonly eaten for breakfast.

Common vegetables *(sabzi)* are spinach, potatoes, cabbage, okra and peas. The universal vegetarian dish is *dal* (lentils). Rice can be ordered steamed, or fried with vegetables or meat *(biryani)*. *Dahi* (plain yogurt) or *raita* (spicy curd with vegetables) is also served. Salad consists of sliced cucumber, tomato and onion. Seasonal fresh fruit includes mangoes, pomegranates, papayas, bananas, melons and limes brought from down country and apricots, peaches, pears, plums, apples, cherries, mulberries and grapes grown in the mountains. Walnuts and apricot kernels are common in the mountains.

Most hotels can produce a Western breakfast of fried or boiled eggs, toast and jam, sometimes porridge or cornflakes and tea or coffee.

On the Trek

Cooking Food is vital to the success of any trek. For long-distance travel in uninhabited country or at high elevations, lightweight freeze-dried food (which is not available in Pakistan) cooks fast and reduces the weight of food and fuel you carry and can, therefore, extend your trekking range. You may be used to a shot of caffeine in the morning

to get you going, but it's not really going to help you get down the trail. Mixing coffee with powdered chocolate or Ovaltine and powdered milk is a better hot energy drink. Morning oatmeal is vastly improved by

Mountain Cuisine

Wheat and dairy are staples of mountain cuisine. But how many interesting dishes can you prepare with just flour, butter, milk and cheese? When you ask at hotels in Hunza, Gojal and Ghizar, or visit homes and summer pastures, you may be invited to sample some of the following dishes and drinks.

Burusho Cuisine

baghundo – sourdough chapatti

batering-e-daudo – soup made with dried apricots (batering)

berikutz – chapattis layered with *burus* and *maska*

burus – curd cheese prepared by first making yogurt, separating the butter and then draining the whey

burus shapik – two chapattis with *burus* spread in between

chap shuro – a pot pie filled with meat (chap)

daudo – a soup, usually with dumplings or home-made noodles

dechirum – bread broken and mixed with ground walnuts and butter

deskulum tel – clarified butter

diltar – buttermilk

diram phiti – a sweet bread made from sprouted wheat flour, cooked on a griddle

dumana mamu – yogurt

giyaling – batter of flour and water cooked on a very hot griddle and served with butter

hani – apricot kernels

harisa – coarse ground wheat boiled in meat stock and butter in a large pot until thick, served with meat and melted butter

hoy garma – chapatti cooked in the same pot with leafy greens (hoy)

kamali – large thin chapatti

malida – broken bread mixed with *dumana mamu* and *maska* or apricot kernel oil (hani tel), which is eaten with a spoon from a communal bowl

maltash – aged butter with a strong flavor

maska – fresh butter

mull – fine ground wheat flour boiled in water until thick, served with melted butter or sugar

phiti – thick bread made from wheat flour, milk and sometimes an egg, baked in an oven

shiqam chai – green tea, often synonymous with *tumuru chai*

shiru – chopped onions baked into a chapatti, often served for breakfast

tili chai – walnut tea

tumuru chai – wild thyme-flower tea

Wakhi Cuisine

chelpindook – a stack of thin chapattis, each layer covered with clarified butter and melted *qurut*

daudo – a soup, usually with dumplings or home-made noodles

dogov – bread broken into a bowl of *tsimik*

garal – crepe covered with clarified butter

kemishdūn – a thick bread, made with milk, baked in a Dutch oven

khisht – roasted wheat flour, cooked in ghee, and then moulded into a thick saucer-shaped paste, which is then set aside to cool before being eaten

kista – sourdough bread baked on the stove top

mirik – cream

malida – broken chapatti mixed with melted *tsimik* with clarified butter (rugen) poured on top of it; the richest dish

pai – yogurt

qurut – a hard cheese made from buttermilk

ruxen tabaq or **ruxen pituk** – a thin white, shiny bread (nigan) placed on a large wooden plate around a bowl of milk

sharbat (**bat**) – a pudding-like dish of boiled wheat flour mixed with melted butter or animal fat on top

tsimik – *qurut* dissolved in water

urzok – fried and salted nuggets of bread

stewing dried apricots and raisins with it. Cooking a hot lunch can become a time-consuming hassle; carrying a simple meal or snacks is easier. Pasta is an easy and fast-cooking dinner. Rice won't cook higher than 4500m, and takes a long time. You need a pressure cooker to cook lentils, so they're not a viable option unless you hire a porter to carry it. See Cooking Equipment (p60) for a list of everything you need to bring to outfit a trek kitchen.

When to Eat When backpacking, you can eat whenever you like. But when trekking with porters, you need to consider their rou-tine. Porters arise at first light (about 4am), make tea and eat bread. Then they're ready to go. If you'd rather not follow this routine, let them know. Porters usually stop mid-morning for more tea and bread, when you can eat lunch. On an organised trek, the cook will usually serve lunch whenever you choose. Stops, however, are often dictated by where water is available, rather than by the clock or by your stomach. Consider car-rying some food with you on the trail to help between meals. Most trekking parties stop for the day by mid-afternoon and eat dinner whenever the food is ready, ideally before it gets dark.

Trek Food

This is a guide to trek food available in Pakistan. When backpacking or trekking with porters, you usu-ally want to plan your menus from this list. When booking an organised trek, they buy and cook all food. What and how much you eat depends on the difficulty of your trek, how much weight you want to carry, your enthusiasm for cooking and your tolerance for eating the same foods day in, day out.

Staples & Local Food
- wholemeal flour and wholemeal bread
- oatmeal, porridge and cornflakes
- rice and lentils
- tea and tea bags
- instant coffee
- milk powder (full-cream or 2% milk fat)
- sugar
- goat cheese and yogurt
- cooking oil (sunflower, corn, canola/rape seed)
- jam
- honey
- noodles, macaroni and spaghetti
- biscuits (crackers and cookies)
- dried fruits (apricots, mulberries, raisins)
- nuts (walnuts, almonds, peanuts, pistachios, cashews)
- seasonal fresh vegetables (potatoes, cabbage, carrots, okra, tomatoes, onions, garlic, ginger)
- seasonal fresh fruit
- custard, pudding, jelly (gelatin-based dessert)
- bouillon cubes (chicken or beef)
- spices
- salt
- dried onions and tomatoes
- eggs

Imported Packaged Food
- oatmeal, cream of wheat and porridge
- Parmesan cheese and soft cheese
- soy sauce
- mustard
- peanut butter
- pasta
- soup mix
- powdered drink mixes (eg, cocoa mix, drinking chocolate, Ovaltine)
- powdered fruit drinks (eg, Tang)
- sweets (candy)

Imported Tinned Food
- tuna chunks or flakes in brine or oil
- sardines, mackerel or salmon
- cheddar cheese
- tomato sauce
- tomato paste
- butter
- meat (corned beef, chicken, Spam)
- vegetables (peas, beans, baked beans)
- fruit
- fruit cocktail

Buying Food Most trekkers easily buy all the trek food they need after arriving in Pakistan. Those who import food usually bring 'goodies' or supplementary items unavailable in Pakistan. These may include energy bars, freeze-dried meals, dried soup and sauce mixes and powdered drink or electrolyte mixes. Basic staples and local food are readily available in the bazaars of Chitral, Gilgit, Skardu and even Aliabad and Karimabad. Down-country speciality stores have a wide variety of imported tinned food that can supplement grain-based meals and local food. Many of these items can be found by scouring the bazaars of Peshawar, Chitral, Gilgit and Skardu. Food left by expeditions sometimes shows up in Chitral, Gilgit and Skardu. Butter, Parmesan cheese, soy sauce and mustard are usually not found outside Islamabad and Rawalpindi. Once you set off into the mountains, you can't expect to purchase much, if anything, from villagers.

The recommended serving sizes on packaged foods aren't enough for trekking, so double or triple daily measurements when determining how much to buy. Buy extra food in case of unexpected delays; plan on one to two extra meals per week.

Check any food you buy in Pakistan for spoilage and bugs before reaching the trailhead. Look for an expiry date on tinned food. Open any packaged food and inspect any items bought in bulk. Then repack all food in resealable plastic bags; use two bags just in case one opens while it's being carried. It's a good idea to measure food into daily and/or weekly serving sizes before putting it into bags. Then pack your sorted food into larger plastic storage bags, waterproof stuff sacks or cloth bags that can easily be stitched in any bazaar. Compression stuff sacks or dry bags are very handy because they keep your food load intact, clean and dry.

When flying into Chitral, Gilgit or Skardu, remember a 20kg total weight limit per person applies. This prevents most trekkers from buying too much food in down-country cities. When you travel by road, however, it's easier, more reliable and less expensive to purchase food in Islamabad, Rawalpindi or Peshawar. A strategy to get around weight

> ## What Fuels These Authors
>
> Eating the same meals every day is a simple approach to trek food that works for us. Quick-cooking, nutritious, flavourful, easy-to-pack food keeps life on the trail uncomplicated. Our typical per person minimum daily quantities follow.
>
> **Breakfast** – a tea bag or one spoonful instant coffee, a spoonful Ovaltine and/or spoonful drinking chocolate, 230g (1 cup dry) oatmeal with currants and/or dried blueberries, 45g (1½ tbs) sugar, 115g (½ cup dry) powdered milk (for hot drinks and oatmeal)
> **Lunch** – one energy bar or 230g (1 cup) dried nuts and fruit, four pieces of cheese, eight to 12 biscuits
> **Dinner** – one soup packet, 285g (1¼ cup dry) macaroni, ½ can tinned fish or tuna, a sauce packet, five dried tomatoes, 30g (1 tbs) Parmesan cheese
>
> **John Mock & Kimberley O'Neil**

limits is to fly yourself and organise to send your gear and food by road; a trekking company may be able to help with these logistics. If you want to stock up before heading for the mountains, try shopping in Islamabad's Jinnah Market (F-7/2) or Covered Market (G-6/4), Rawalpindi's Saddar Bazaar, or Peshawar's Saddar Bazaar.

Wild Food
Living off the land may be a romantic concept, but in the Karakoram and Hindukush you're likely to go hungry. Nibbling a few stalks of rhubarb here and there isn't going to provide enough fuel to power you anywhere. Other edible foods include mushrooms (edible fungi such as morels and chanterelles), wild mustard, wild onion (allium), purslane *(Portulaca oleracea)* and watercress *(Nasturtium officinale)*.

DRINKS
Nonalcoholic Drinks
Tea is the preferred drink. *Dudh chai* (milky tea) is usually equal parts water, leaves,

Apricots

Every household strives to have one apricot tree; most have many, and Hunzakutz won't live without them. Apparently introduced from Baltistan, today a multitude of varieties – all delicious – are grown. Some are produced through grafting onto existing trees; others grow from root stock. Their pale-pink blossoms brighten the hillsides in April and May, and their autumn leaves splash crimson and gold in October. When in season – July to August – trekkers are almost guaranteed to be presented with a large plate of fresh-picked sweet golden apricots. The early-ripening, large, whitish Burum-dru are delicious, but the late-ripening, smaller, red Shikandah are the tastiest. Whatever the variety, a proper apricot binge at the finish of a trek is a traditional treat. Dried apricots make good trail snacks, and reportedly are excellent high-altitude energy food. The delicately sweet almond-flavoured kernel is equally tasty and often is reinserted between two dried halves. Apricot soup is a delicacy and stewed dried apricots are excellent.

Famous Hunza apricots being dried on woven willow racks.

sugar and milk brought to a raging boil. Chinese-style green tea is called *sabz chai*. In villages, tea is usually served salted. Bottled soft drinks are ubiquitous. Sweetened fruit juice and natural orange juice sold in hygienic Tetra packs are great thirst quenchers and are found in some towns.

Alcoholic Drinks

In Pakistan, it's illegal for Muslims to drink alcohol. Non-Muslims are allowed to purchase alcohol if they obtain a liquor permit. A liquor permit is available for a nominal fee from some five-star hotels in major down-country cities, allowing you to drink in your room. When you stay in one city for a while, you can get a liquor permit for Rs 25 per month from city Excise & Tax offices, entitling you to buy a monthly quota of alcohol. They also tell you where to buy it. Some offices may ask for a letter from the Pakistan Tourism Development Corporation. You need to bring your passport, photocopies of its front page and your Pakistani visa and entry stamp and sign a form saying you are a non-Muslim. Bringing alcohol into Pakistan without prior permission is against the law. If you choose to do so and officials find any liquor, it may be confiscated and returned to you upon departure from Pakistan. Typically, no penalties or fines apply.

Alcohol is legally produced at two places in Pakistan, the Murree Brewery in Rawalpindi and the Quetta Brewery in Quetta, which produce beer and several kinds of vodka, gin, rum and whisky. Imported alcohol is unavailable. Liquor is not available in North-west Frontier Province or the Northern Areas. In Hunza and Punial, some people still brew *mel*, a coarse grape wine, and a powerful mulberry brandy called *arak*. Some local wine may also be found in Chitral.

On the Trek

Purifying water for drinking is just one of several steps for staying hydrated on trek. The more crucial first step is obtaining what people call *saf pani*, which means 'clear' or 'clean' water. The Urdu phrase refers to water suitable for drinking, not purified water devoid of bacteria, cysts and viruses but, rather, visually clear water.

The most desirable drinking water, of course, is spring water, and locations of springs are detailed in the trek descriptions. Sometimes springs are in improbable locations just a few inches from the edge of a raging glacial river. More often than not, though, water comes from the rivers themselves. Glacial rivers carry sediment and silt, giving the water a murky, unappealing colour. You can make glacial water more appealing by letting it stand for several hours in a container until the sediment settles to the bottom. Then collect and transfer the clear water from the top into another container for purification, repeating the process as many times as necessary. When water is really muddy, first filter it through sand or fine cloth and then let it settle.

Some water sources play tricks. Some springs only flow in the afternoon, when snow above has melted and recharged the spring. At higher elevations, snow melt may yield a trickle in the afternoon that freezes overnight and stays frozen until the next afternoon. Rising waters can cover a morning riverside spring by afternoon. The basic rule of thumb at camp sites is to fill up every available vessel – bottles, pots and pans – whenever water is flowing, because there's no guarantee it'll continue.

Nothing else is available to drink once on trek, so bring tea, instant coffee, milk powder, hot chocolate and flavoured drink mixes to vary the routine of drinking purified water (see Water, p92).

CLOTHING & EQUIPMENT
Clothing
For travelling around cities and towns, light-coloured 100% cotton clothing, not synthetic blends, is best. Cotton *shalwar kameez* are ideal for the hot climate. Ready-made men's and women's versions are available, starting at Rs 350, or a tailor can make you one using 6m of cloth. When arriving in Pakistan from China, you have to bring your own or go down to Gilgit to buy one.

On trek, however, avoid cotton clothes, which are cold when wet from rain or sweat

and take a long time to dry. Avoid bulky clothing. Instead, select fabrics that compress and are easy to clean. A hat is essential because from 40% to 75% of body heat is lost through the head.

Footwear
Footwear is the most important item you bring. Your choice depends on the length of trek and whether the trek crosses snow-covered passes or traverses glaciers. Sturdy leather boots with scree collars and a stiff sole are essential for rocky terrain. Waterproof breathable boots, made from fabrics such as Gore-Tex, are preferable and essential for snow or glaciers. If you plan to use crampons, make sure your boots can accommodate them. Lightweight nonleather boots are not recommended for any trek, but might last for a few day hikes or one short trek – maybe! Break your boots in thoroughly before going trekking. Wear them on your flights, as it's very difficult to replace boots if they're lost. Bring a pair of sandals with ankle straps or training shoes to wear when fording rivers and when you reach camp.

Camping Equipment
Backpack The most comfortable type of backpack has an internal frame with a padded waistband to take weight off your shoulders and sternum straps to stabilise the

---

The Layering Principle

Maintaining a comfortable body temperature when trekking and still being warm enough at night in camp, or when resting along the trail, is vital. The best way to deal with the wide range of temperatures and weather conditions you encounter is to bring several thin insulating garments that can be layered for maximum flexibility. A wicking layer of Capilene, wool or silk next to your skin keeps you warm and dry. An insulating layer of pile, wool, down or Thinsulate adds warmth. An outer breathable, waterproof shell layer – preferably a hooded jacket and pants – protects you from wind, rain or snow.

load. One with a zippered internal compartment to store valuables is helpful. Select the lightest backpack that's large enough to meet your needs. An 80L (5000 cubic inch) backpack is typically large enough to carry a week's worth of food, clothing and equipment. When trekking with porters, bring a daypack that's smaller than 32L (2000 cubic inches) and pack the rest of your gear into a duffel bag.

Duffel Bag Duffel bags are indispensable when trekking with porters. They are also very useful for securely storing your extra

Clothing & Equipment Check List

This list is a general guide to what to bring on a trek. When backpacking or trekking with porters, you need to bring most of the equipment on this check list. When booking an organised trek through a trekking company or an adventure travel company, however, ask what equipment it provides and what you need to bring. What you bring depends on what kind of trek you do, how much weight you want to carry, the terrain, weather conditions and time of year.

CLOTHING
General Clothing
☐ shalwar kameez
☐ loose-fitting long pants
☐ long-sleeve shirt with collar
☐ underwear
☐ lightweight thermal underwear top and bottom

Outerwear
☐ waterproof hooded jacket and pants
☐ pile or fleece jacket
☐ liner gloves
☐ woollen gloves or mittens
☐ woollen or pile hat or balaclava
☐ sun hat

For Glacier Traverses & Pass Crossings Higher than 4500m
☐ gaiters
☐ waterproof mitt shells
☐ mid-weight thermal underwear top and bottom
☐ mid-weight hooded down or fibre-filled jacket
☐ fingerless gloves for cooking
☐ down booties

Footwear
☐ waterproof leather boots with spare laces
☐ boot waterproofing liquid or wax
☐ tube of silicone shoe repair

☐ sandals with ankle straps or training shoes
☐ liner socks
☐ woollen or pile socks

EQUIPMENT
Personal Items
☐ 1L water bottles (two or three)
☐ torch (flashlight) or head lamp with spare battery cells and bulbs
☐ pocket knife
☐ shatterproof sunglasses with UV and infrared radiation protection
☐ first-aid kit (see the First-Aid Kit Check List, p91)

Toiletries
☐ toothbrush and toothpaste
☐ moisturiser
☐ toilet paper
☐ butane lighter and lightweight trowel
☐ bath and laundry soap
☐ shampoo
☐ small towel

Camping Equipment
☐ backpack or daypack with waterproof cover
☐ duffel bags with locks
☐ tent with waterproof fly and ground cover
☐ sleeping bag
☐ sleeping sheet and insulating sleeping pad
☐ repair kit (needle, thread, tape, glue, cord)
☐ collapsible plastic basin

belongings at a hotel while you're trekking. For the duffel bag you take trekking, get the most durable one you can find with strong fabric and a zipper along the side. End-loading duffel bags are less practical. A combination lock, preferable to a key lock, is essential to protect its contents.

Most duffel bags aren't waterproof, so pack your gear in waterproof stuff sacks or in large sturdy plastic bags inside the duffel. Dry bags are excellent for storing sleeping bags and other gear that must stay dry. Plastic sheets to cover the outside of duffel bags on the trail during inclement weather

Clothing & Equipment Check List

Cooking Equipment
- [ ] portable stove with wind screen, spare parts and cleaning wires
- [ ] fuel
- [ ] fuel containers, funnel and fuel filter
- [ ] nesting stainless-steel cooking pots (1.5L and 2L) with lids
- [ ] gripper or hot pads
- [ ] waterproof matches or butane lighter
- [ ] eating utensils (one spoon minimum)
- [ ] plate and insulated mug with lid
- [ ] dish soap
- [ ] scourer, wash cloth and towel
- [ ] mesh storage bag

Optional Cooking Equipment
- [ ] expedition barrel
- [ ] kerosene lantern, spare mantles and padded carrying box
- [ ] candles
- [ ] pressure cooker
- [ ] ladle
- [ ] knife
- [ ] vegetable peeler
- [ ] plastic or collapsible wash basin(s)
- [ ] tea kettle and strainer
- [ ] aluminium pan
- [ ] rolling pin
- [ ] wooden board
- [ ] griddle

Mountaineering Equipment
For each trekker:
- [ ] glacier goggles
- [ ] gaiters
- [ ] crampons
- [ ] aluminium locking carabiner

- [ ] climbing harness
- [ ] mechanical ascenders or prusiks
- [ ] climbing helmet
- [ ] trekking poles or snow probe and avalanche wands

For each trekking party:
- [ ] ice axe
- [ ] climbing rope
- [ ] snow anchors
- [ ] slings and carabiners

OPTIONAL
Photography
- [ ] camera
- [ ] spare batteries
- [ ] lenses
- [ ] lens-cleaning supplies
- [ ] film

Navigation
- [ ] maps
- [ ] guidebook
- [ ] altimeter
- [ ] compass

Optional Miscellaneous Items
- [ ] bandanna
- [ ] waterproof compression stuff sacks
- [ ] umbrella
- [ ] thermometer
- [ ] binoculars
- [ ] journal and pen/pencil
- [ ] plastic bags
- [ ] solar battery recharger and rechargeable cells
- [ ] short-wave radio
- [ ] portable chair

usually tear and become useless for protecting the contents from rain or wet snow.

Despite their best efforts, porters treat duffels roughly. They get dropped, bumped against rocks and put in livestock pens and the like. It's worthwhile to invest in a bombproof duffel bag that might withstand being dropped from a helicopter or stepped on by a yak. The waterproof North Face Base Camp Duffel meets the challenge.

Tent A three-season tent is suitable for most treks. On treks where you sleep on a glacier or cross passes higher than 5000m, an all-season tent is better. Select the lightest tent that meets your needs. Remember to evaluate the weight of the tent including a waterproof fly sheet and ground cloth. A fully free-standing design, which allows you to set up and move the tent without stakes, is best for camping in rocky terrain where it's often impossible to put stakes in the ground. It's important to have a tent that stands up to high winds. It must be large enough to fit your backpack or duffel inside at night without being too cramped. A vestibule is useful for additional storage space and for maintaining privacy by keeping curious onlookers away. Waterproof all the seams of the tent and fly prior to your trek. A small combination lock on tent windows and doors helps protect your gear when going on day hikes.

Sleeping Bag The main choice in a sleeping bag is between down or synthetic insulating material. Down is warmer and lighter, but useless when wet. Synthetic material is durable, cheaper and insulates when wet, but is heavier and more bulky. A down bag with a water-resistant, breathable shell is best, but is the most expensive. Sleeping bags are rated for temperature. The choice you make depends on your personal optimal sleeping temperature. When you're backpacking, also consider weight, because bags rated for colder temperatures are usually heavier than bags rated for warmer temperatures. A bag rated to -7° C (20° F) is suitable for most treks. On treks where you sleep on a glacier or cross passes higher than 5000m, a bag rated to -18° C (0° F) is more appropriate.

Sleeping in an all-season tent and using a cotton sleeping sheet, easily made in Pakistan, make a bag feel warmer. An insulting foam mattress is indispensable. A self-inflating mattress is comfortable on rocky terrain and snow. A closed-cell foam mattress is a less expensive, but more bulky and less comfortable alternative.

Cooking Equipment
When cooking for yourself, you need all the cooking equipment on the Clothing & Equipment Check List (p58). Transporting everything in expedition barrels keeps contents clean and dry, ensures your food and gear are not damaged along the trail, deters theft and packs easily into a porter's load. Barrels are readily available in Skardu for Rs 650 (medium) or Rs 750 (large), but are less easily found in Gilgit. Check that the barrel is in good condition, its opening is wide enough for your gear to pass through easily and that it seals properly.

Stoves The choice of stove depends upon its durability, ease of use and fuel efficiency, who will be cooking and who will be carrying the stove and fuel. When cooking for yourself and carrying your own stove and fuel, bring a stove, wind screen, cleaning tools and fuel bottles from home.

Multifuel liquid stoves where the fuel container is connected to the stove by a fuel line offer the greatest flexibility. The MSR X-GK (II) stove is highly recommended because it's compact, rugged, burns almost anything and burns wells at high altitude. Other recommendations include the MSR Dragonfly, Optimus Explorer No 11, and Primus Multifuel. Cooks and porters, however, find them too delicate and complicated to use. Cartridge stoves where the burner screws onto a gas cartridge are lightweight and easy to use, but fuel problems make them less preferable. Cooks and porters, however, have no trouble cooking with them. Hanging stove systems aren't necessary on the treks in this book. On trek, it's advisable to carry your stove in the backpack you carry yourself instead of putting it into a porter's load where there's a greater chance of it being damaged.

When hiring a cook or porters, you can buy locally made kerosene stoves. These stoves have a large and heavy steel frame, variable-sized fuel tank and one or two burners. Stoves are readily available in Chitral, Gilgit and Skardu for Rs 215–360. They make awkward loads, but people know how to use and repair them and you can usually sell them back for half what you paid after the trek. Russian-made brass stoves, surplus from the Afghan war, also available in Chitral and Gilgit, cost slightly less. Although more compact, they don't burn as hot.

Fuel Kerosene is the fuel of choice, although Pakistani kerosene burns sootily. It's inexpensive and widely available in bazaars, at petrol pumps and even in small amounts in many villages. Bring a filter or strain it through a cloth, especially if resupplying in a village. White gas (white spirit/Shellite) is not available, and denatured alcohol (methylated spirits) is available only in Rawalpindi and Islamabad. Butane cartridges (eg, Gaz, EPI Gas) are sporadically available in Skardu and less reliably so in Gilgit for Rs 500 per 250cc canister. These cartridges aren't allowed in checked or carry-on baggage on any flights, so you can't bring your own supply. Because you cannot rely on buying them in Pakistan and they create disposal problems, using a butane stove is a poor choice. Some trekkers report that petrol burns hot and clean in MSR stoves, but it is explosive on ignition. Mixing petrol and kerosene is a better solution.

Bring MSR or equivalent fuel bottles if you need fuel for only a few days, as they are easier to carry and don't leak. Alternatively, bring ordinary fuel bottles to use as storage vessels and one MSR bottle to use as a pressurised vessel. Carry any pressurised fuel bottle yourself so it doesn't get damaged in a porter's load. Plastic containers to transport larger quantities of kerosene are readily available in Gilgit and Skardu bazaars. Container sizes and costs vary: Rs 50/75/100/120 per 5/10/25/30L. The screw-on lids usually leak, so carry some extra plastic to cover the opening and reduce spillage.

When you share fuel with porters, monitor its usage diligently to ensure it's not used too hastily. Fuel will be used for cooking, heating and starting fires (to burn rubbish). In colder conditions, porters can easily burn from 3L to 4L per night to keep warm. Supplying your porters with a windproof shelter and sleeping pads is less expensive than paying a porter to carry extra kerosene. Ask your crew how much kerosene they think they need, and bring more. Plan to use from 125mL to 250mL of fuel per trekker per day.

Mountaineering Equipment

Most treks that traverse glaciers or cross glaciated passes where trekkers travel in roped teams and/or fix ropes require some mountaineering equipment. Any trek that requires mountaineering equipment for safe completion of the route mentions this in the trek's Planning section.

For these treks, each trekker needs: glacier goggles; full-length gaiters; one aluminium locking carabiner; a climbing harness (seat and chest or full body harness for glacier travel) or 2.5cm tubular webbing to make a harness or swami belt (another way to tie into a rope); mechanical ascenders or prusiks (5mm to 7mm cord) for crevasse rescue; lightweight alloy 10- or 12-pointed crampons; and trekking poles and/or dedicated snow probes for using on scree slopes and for probing crevasse fields. Each trekking party needs: one ice axe with leash for self belay, self arrest and step cutting; rope for glacier travel, one 9mm dry rope (40m to 50m in length) for every three or four people (including each member of your trek crew), and one 8mm or 9mm dry rope (30m long) for emergency rescue; two snow anchors (such as a deadman or picket) for belays; slings and carabiners; and at least one pair of hinged adjustable-width crampons for crevasse rescue. Four-pointed in-step crampons are indispensable for porters' use on extreme treks.

Buying & Hiring Locally

You can't be sure of finding anything either for sale or rent, so bring essential clothing and equipment with you. A very limited selection of basic equipment, typically used expedition gear, is for sale or rent in Chitral, Gilgit, Karimabad, Passu, Skardu and Hushe. Generally available are closed-cell foam sleeping mattresses (Rs 300-600), expedition barrels, rope, carabiners, ice screws, snow anchors, crampons, ice axes, tarpaulins, porters' clothing, sunglasses (Rs 300) and basic cooking equipment (eg, aluminium cooking pots with flat lids, aluminium tea kettles, steel spoons, plates and enamelled tin mugs). Used boots can be found, but any selection is meagre. Backpacks, sleeping bags, down jackets and gaiters are much harder to find. Buying and then reselling an item, such as stoves or sleeping mattresses, after your trek usually works out cheaper than renting. Ask if any expeditions are around and also check with trekking companies.

MAPS & NAVIGATION

Maps may not be the territory, but a good two-dimensional representation of the terrain is an indispensable tool. Knowing how to read maps and being familiar with the information they provide is essential in both planning and doing a trek. Don't even try to trek on your own without a map. Maps, however, are still no substitute for local expertise.

Small-Scale Maps

The following 1:500,000 and smaller-scale maps are excellent for trek planning. Their scales, however, are too small for route finding.

US Geological Survey (USGS) In 1997,

the USGS published a seven-map series of remarkable satellite images of Pakistan. Two sheets (US$7 per map) show all of northern Pakistan between 26° and 34° standard north parallels:

1:500,000 Pakistan Satellite Image Maps
NW Frontier Pakistan Map I-2587-B
Northern Areas Pakistan Map I-2587-C

US Defense Mapping Agency (DMA)

US DMA published these two series of topographic maps for pilots:

1:1,000,000 Operational Navigation Chart (ONC)
ONC G-6 – NWFP, Ghizar, Diamir
ONC G-7 – Diamir, Hunza, Gojal, Baltistan

1:500,000 Tactical Pilotage Chart (TPC)
TPC G-6B – Northern Chitral, Ghizar
TPC G-6C – Southern Chitral, Swat
TPC G-7A – Nagyr, Hunza, Gojal
TPC G-7D – Diamir, Baltistan

The TPC series has unreliable place names and locations, but up-to-date landsat-derived topographic data. Both series show landforms, but not all the roads and villages. Maps cost US$7 each.

Large-Scale Maps

For all but a few areas, the best available maps are at a scale of 1:250,000. No maps cover all trekking areas. Specialised maps of the Baltoro and Batura Glacier are detailed in the Planning sections for treks to those areas.

Swiss Foundation for Alpine Research

The Swiss Foundation for Alpine Research's two-sheet series (US$35 per set) of orographical sketch maps give the most accurate rendering of the major mountain ranges and valleys it covers:

1:250,000 Karakoram Series
Sheet 1 – Nagyr, Hunza, Gojal (except Misgar), Baltistan north of Indus River
Sheet 2 – Eastern Baltistan

US Army Map Service (AMS) The US

AMS published two series of topographic maps: U502 India and Pakistan, and Afghanistan – NW Frontier Province. These maps are old, but still useful in areas not covered by the Swiss maps, such as Chitral, Swat, Ghizar and Diamir.

The U502 India and Pakistan series covers almost all trekking areas. Last revised in 1962, these maps (US$15 per map for colour reprints) show most villages, but not roads built since then. The series is, however, highly accurate for much topographic detail. Each map, which has 500-foot contour intervals and covers one degree of latitude and 1½ degrees of longitude, has a reliability diagram showing its degree of accuracy because some mountain areas aren't accurately mapped.

1:250,000 Series U502 India and Pakistan

NI 43-1 Churrai – Southern Chitral, Upper Ghizar, Kalam Kohistan
NI 43-2 Gilgit – Diamir
NI 43-3 Mundik – Baltistan
NI 43-4 Chulung – Eastern Baltistan
NI 43-6 Srinagar – Kaghan, Azad Jammu & Kashmir
NI 43-7 Kargil – Southern Deosai
NJ 43-13 Mastuj – Chitral, Ghizar
NJ 43-14 Baltit – Ghizar, Nagyr, Hunza, Gojal
NJ 43-15 Shimshal – Gojal

In 1942, the US AMS published the Afghanistan – NW Frontier Province series. These accurate yet out-of-print maps are only found at university libraries. Two maps cover western Chitral:

1:253,440 (ie, one inch to four miles)
Afghanistan – NW Frontier Province Series

I 42-F Chitral – Kalasha Valleys, Begusht, lower Shishi and Golen, upper Roghili (areas west of *NI 43-1 Churrai* sheet)
J 42-X Zebak – Lutkho, Tirich (areas west of *NJ 43-13 Mastuj* sheet)

Leomann Maps Leomann's 1:200,000 orographic Karakoram Trekking and Mountaineering Maps are: *Sheet 1: Gilgit, Hunza, Rakaposhi, Batura; Sheet 2: Skardu, Hispar, Biafo; Sheet 3: K2, Baltoro, Gasherbrum, Masherbrum, Saltoro;* and *Sheet 4: Siachen, Rimo, Saser.* Apparently based on the US AMS Series U502 maps with the same inaccuracies, the Leomann maps (US$15 per map) have imprecise details and vague and useless trek descriptions on the back. Though readily available, they're of little use for trekking. West Col Productions of the UK produces an identical four-map 1:200,000 Karakoram Himalaya series.

British Survey of India Published in 1930, this accurate topographic series of Chitral, which is out of print and only found at university libraries, still gives the best available detail of the region:

1:63,360 (ie, one inch to one mile)
Afghanistan – NW Frontier Province Series

38 M/9 – Chitral Gol (west of Chaghbini and Merin), Rumbur
38 M/10 – Jinjeret Kuh, Birir, Bumboret
38 M/13 – Chitral town, Jughor, Golen, Roghili
38 M/14 – Drosh, Shishi, Jughor, Roghili
42 D/4 – Upper Golen
42 D/8 – Phargam
43 A/1 – Madaglasht, upper Shishi, Dok, Lohigal

Deutscher Alpenverein (DAV) DAV publishes two 1:50,000 topographic maps (US$18 per map): *Minapin* shows Rakaposhi's north slopes; and *Nanga Parbat – Gruppe*, based on the 1934 Deutsche Himalaya Expedition and first published in 1936 and reproduced in 1980, shows the Nanga Parbat massif. These three-colour maps have 50m contour intervals and are the best and only readily available maps of these peaks. DAV also publishes the 1:100,000 *Hunza-Karakorum* map of the Hunza Valley.

Russian Military The Russian military published two series of highly detailed topographic maps labelled in Russian showing all areas of Chitral and the Northern Areas. More than 40 sheets (US$75 per map) are in the 1:100,000 series, and more than 20 sheets (US$95 per map) are in the 1:200,000 series. The relevant 1:100,000 maps with 40m contour intervals are: J-42 sheets 132 and 144; J-43 sheets 101–103, 109–116, 121–129, and 133–141; and I-43 sheets 2–10, 15–24, 28–36, and 40–46. The relevant 1:200,000 maps are: J-42 XXXVI; J-43 sheets XXV–XXVIII, XXXI–XXXV; and I-43 sheets I–VI and VIII–XII.

Buying Maps

No matter which maps you select, have them with you when you arrive in Pakistan. You cannot count on finding any maps inside Pakistan. Good sources (most with on-line stores) include:

The UK
Cordee (☎ 0116-254 3579, fax 247 1176, ⓔ info@cordee.co.uk, Ⓦ www.cordee.co.uk) 3A De Montfort St, Leicester, LE1 7HD, UK. Stocks Swiss, U502, Leomann and specialised maps of the Baltoro and Batura glaciers.

Stanfords (☎ 020-7836 1321, fax 7836 0189, e sal es@stanfords.co.uk, W www.stanfords.co.uk) 12–14 Long Acre, Covent Garden, London WC2E 9LP, UK. Stocks Swiss, U502, DAV, Leomann, TPC, ONC and Baltoro maps.

The USA
Chessler Books (☎ 303-670 0093, 800-654 8502, fax 303-670 9727, e chesslerbk@aol.com, W www.chesslerbooks.com) PO Box 4359, Evergreen, CO 80437-4359, USA. Stocks Swiss, DAV and Leomann maps, as well as specialised maps of the Baltoro and Batura glaciers.

East View Information Services (☎ 888-694 5917, e orders@eastview.com, W www.east view.com/mm/kashmir.html) 3020 Harbor Lane North, Minneapolis, MN 55447, USA. Stocks Russian maps.

Maplink (☎ 805-692 6777, fax 692 6787, e cu stserv@maplink.com, W www.maplink.com) 30 S La Patera Lane, Unit 5, Santa Barbara, CA 93117, USA. Stocks ONC and TPC maps.

Omni Resources (☎ 336-227 8300, fax 227 3748, e custserv@omnimap.com, W www.om nimap.com) PO Box 2096, 1004 S Bebane St, Burlington, NC 27216-2096, USA. Stocks Swiss, Russian, Leomann, TPC and ONC maps.

US Geological Survey Information Services (☎ 888-275 8747, fax 303-202 4693, W earth explorer.usgs.gov) PO Box 25286, Denver, CO 80225, USA. Stocks USGS maps.

US Library of Congress, Geography & Map Division, 101 Independence Ave, Washington, DC 20540, USA. Sells B&W copies of British Survey of India maps.

Germany
Aree Greul (☎ 069-666 18 17, e greulalpin@ cs.com, W www.greulmountain-books.de) Am Goldsteinpark 28, 60529 Frankfurt am Main, Germany. Stocks Swiss, DAV, U502, Leomann and specialised maps of the Baltoro and Batura glaciers.

Deutscher Alpenverein (DAV) – Service GmbH (☎ 089-82 99 94 94, fax 82 99 94 14, W www .alpenverein.de/kartografie) Post Fach 60 03 03, 81203 München, Germany. Stocks DAV maps.

GeoCenter ILH (☎ 07348-5562, fax 5563, e ge ocenterilh@t-online.de, W www.geocenter.de) T&M, Kornackerweg 11, 89179 Beimerstetten, Germany. Stocks DAV maps.

Italy
Libreria Stella Alpina (☎ 055-411688, fax 436 0877, e libreria@stella-alpina.com, W www .explorer.it/stellalpina) via F Corridoni, 14 B/r-50134 Firenze, Italy. Stocks IGM maps.

Global Positioning System (GPS)
GPS is a network of more than 20 earth-orbiting satellites that continually beam encoded signals back to earth. GPS receivers decode these signals to give users an extremely accurate reading of their location – to within 30m, anywhere on the planet, at any time of day, in almost any weather. A GPS receiver is of little use to trekkers unless used with an accurate, detailed topographical map – the GPS receiver simply gives your position, which you must then locate on the map. GPS receivers are more vulnerable to breakdowns (including dead batteries) than the humble magnetic compass or an altimeter, but do give altitude unaffected by changes in atmospheric pressure. Technically, carrying a GPS receiver in Pakistan is forbidden by law, so if you have one keep it out of sight.

Using a Compass
To be an effective navigational tool, a compass requires more detailed maps than the 1:250,000 scale maps generally available for this area. Travelling with a local person is a more effective guarantee against navigational difficulties, rather than checking the general direction you're going.

TREKS IN THIS BOOK
The six trekking chapters contain 55 detailed self-guiding trek descriptions and 77 other treks – summaries of notable routes. It's impossible to describe every possible trek and this book makes no attempt to do so. See the Table of Treks (pp4–8) for a summary of what's in the book. All treks are within the boundaries of Pakistan's North-west Frontier Province (NWFP) and Northern Areas. Most treks in NWFP are in Chitral district. Those in the Northern Areas are in all five districts: Ghizar, Gilgit, Diamir, Baltistan and Ghanche. Most trekkers will select one of the treks described in this book. Your choice will depend upon the season, length of time you want to trek and the level of difficulty.

About 70% of the treks in this book are long treks between four and 15 days, and 30% are short treks ranging from a few

The expansive alpine meadows of Shah Jinali An offer relatively easy trekking.

Porters and their donkeys climb towards Shah Jinali An.

Joshi festival, Batrik, Kalasha Valleys.

Wakhi girls at Top Khana summer village, Broghil, sporting local 'sunscreen' on their foreheads.

Form follows function: the architecture of Shekhanandeh village.

A Wakhi man sharpens his scythe, Chilma Rabot village, Broghil & Karambar An trek.

hours to three days. Generally, long treks require commitment to the route and cannot be done in segments or shortened, unless you walk really fast or abort the route and turn back. Similarly, short treks that cross a pass cannot be shortened. Short treks to viewpoints, however, can often be tackled as prodigious day hikes. Side trips accompany both long and short treks, recommending scenic view points and nearby peaks below 6000m. Of the treks in this book, 60% cross one or more passes, 20% involve glacier travel and the other 20% avoid both passes and glaciers.

The Other Treks section at the end of each trekking chapter highlights many equally outstanding routes that, due to space constraints, could not be covered in detail in this edition. Many of the these routes suggest ideas for exploration and climbing possibilities.

The book includes only open-zone and restricted-zone treks, not any closed-zone treks at the time of writing. Nor does it include treks in the notoriously dangerous valleys of Indus Kohistan. More adventurous or experienced trekkers may go to these and other valleys, but most trekkers would be ill-advised to attempt to do so. Perusing maps, reading accounts of previous explorers and travellers and talking to local people provides information about the possibilities.

Route Descriptions

Route descriptions are described in actual walking days. The trek's stages (see the Stages section, p48) are detailed in each trek's Planning section. An average trekker can comfortably complete each trek day, which starts or finishes at a place to pitch a tent where water is available or at a trailhead. When an intermediate camp site exists, it's indicated in **bold italics**. Trekkers may choose to use intermediate camp sites when going at a more leisurely pace or in case of illness. Some trek days have no alternative camp sites because of terrain constraints or lack of water, and trekkers must make it all the way.

Trek descriptions exclude segments on roads unless there's a high likelihood of

walking on the road to find transport. Most villages are now accessible via a link road. In some areas, roads seems to lengthen a bit each year. In a few years, existing trailheads may change. Eventually, all villages will be accessible by road. The majority of trailheads have no facilities. When a trek starts or finishes at or near a village with hotels it's explained in the Nearest Village or Nearest Facilities sections.

You can do many of the treks in either direction. If there's a good reason for going one way or the other, the text explains it.

Level of Difficulty

As a guide to help pick suitable treks, each trek has a relative grading based on the authors' subjective impressions of its level of difficulty in relation to all other treks in this book. The grading appears next to the heading 'Standard' in the Facts Box at the beginning of each trek:

Easy treks, suitable for most trekkers in good health, have trails below 3500m possibly with moderate elevation changes, usually for two or three days, and less than half a day nontechnical glacier travel or gentle pass crossings.

Moderate treks, suitable for reasonably fit trekkers, cover trails usually for no more than one week, with significant elevation change and usually cross a pass below 4500m, and not more than half a day of usually nontechnical glacier travel.

Demanding treks, suitable for regular trekkers who are fit and competent on difficult terrain, cover trails often for more than a week where some route-finding is necessary with significant elevation change. Any pass crossings are usually below 5000m, and nontechnical or technical glacier travel is usually for not more than one day.

Very Demanding treks, suitable for fit trekkers who are accustomed to rigorous trekking, are through rugged terrain over a longer and more committed route where route-finding is required, with glaciated or difficult pass crossings usually below 5000m, involving nontechnical or technical glacier travel for one or more days.

Extreme treks, suitable for highly fit and experienced trekkers, may involve multiple days of extended technical glacier travel and trekking on rugged terrain above 4500m, require serious commitment to the route, and cross a glaciated pass higher than 5000m.

The term 'technical' and the ice-axe symbol at left also appear next to the grading in the Fact Box for any route that involves technical trekking. Technical trekking requires the use of mountaineering equipment and basic mountaineering and glacier travel skills for safe completion of the route. Of the treks in this book, 60% range from easy to demanding and 40% are very demanding or extreme with 16% of treks being technical.

Factors considered with each trek's grading include: the number of days, the maximum elevation, the total daily elevation gain and loss, whether the trek involves glacier travel or crosses any passes, its remoteness and isolation, any technical mountaineering requirements and the necessary fitness level. A further difficulty of grading treks that traverse glaciers or cross glaciated passes is that conditions change during each season and from year to year. Adverse weather can make relatively easy treks seem difficult, and a trek done quickly can seem harder than one done slowly. Anyone trekking for the first time will probably find many easy and most moderate treks quite challenging.

Read the trek descriptions carefully before setting out. Note any significant difficulties and objective dangers, when a route crosses scree or talus slopes, glaciated passes, or traverses any glaciers or crevasse fields and if any mountaineering experience and equipment is needed. For treks over glaciated passes, note the details about the angle of snow slopes and any danger from avalanche, crevasses or cornices. This forethought will help you decide which trek to choose.

International rating systems used for climbing are somewhat useful for describing some treks because they categorise terrain according to the techniques and equipment required to tackle it. No specific standardised rating system for trekking, however, exists as it does for climbing. The Yosemite Decimal System (YDS), the rating system used in the USA and the one referred to in this book, includes these ratings:

Class 1 – Trekking with possible scrambling; hands generally not needed.
Class 2 – Off-trail scrambling through rough terrain (eg, talus); likely use of hands.
Class 3 – Simple climbing or scrambling with moderate exposure possible where beginners may want a rope; frequent use of handholds and footholds.
Class 4 – Intermediate climbing where use of rope (by beginners and average climbers) for belay is necessary because of exposure; a fall could be serious.
Class 5.0 – Climbing with rope and natural or artificial protection to protect against fall.

Whenever a trek involves difficulties greater than YDS Class 1 or its equivalent, the trek description details the nature of the difficult section and give a YDS class rating. The table opposite shows how the YDS corresponds with the French Union Internationale des Associations d'Alpinisme

Maidan

When trekking, you will no doubt hear the word *maidan* used to describe an upcoming section of trail. This Urdu word has the literal meaning of 'a level plain', but beware when you hear it used! It can be applied to any slope up to about 15 degrees in angle or a trail that gains as much as 500m in elevation. That's the bad news. The good news is that it signifies a visible footpath over a generally broad and consistent slope where the walking is relatively easy. With a little experience, you too will learn to recognise sloping alpine grassland as the easiest of all trekking terrain, a maidan.

JOHN MOCK

Maidan walking: trekker on the way to Kilik Pass, Kilik & Mintaka Passes Trek.

(UIAA), Welzenbach (German), Australian, and British rating systems, up to Class 5, where technical climbing starts.

YDS	UIAA	German	Australian	British
Class 1	I	1	1	E
Class 2	II	2	2	E
Class 3	II	3	3	MOD 1a,b,c
Class 4	III	4	4	MOD 1a,b,c
Class 5	III	5	5	DIFF

Times & Distances

Each trek description details the number of days the trek takes and gives the approximate daily trekking time. The number of days doesn't include side trips or alternative routes, the details of which are listed separately. The daily trekking times are based on actual walking times, excluding stops for resting, eating or photographing.

Most trekkers walk at a pace from 2km to 3km per hour, or 10km to 15km per day. Most trekking days involve six to eight hours of walking; some days are longer, some shorter. The trekking days are realistic for most reasonably fit trekkers going at a moderate pace. Since everyone walks at their own pace, these times may not reflect your actual trekking time.

Times are provided for a few reasons. Clear water is rarely abundant on most treks, and it's important to know how long it might take to reach the next water source. The only camp sites on glacier traverses can be several hours apart, so it helps to know approximate times to avoid having an unplanned or undesirable camp site. You infrequently meet local people on many treks and when you meet them, they may happily tell you how long it takes to reach somewhere, but their walking times are likely to be two or three times faster than yours.

Distances, when given, are in kilometres and are based on GPS data. While it's easy to judge distances from maps, it's almost impossible to determine how far you actually walk taking into account elevation gain and loss, twists and turns along trails, or zigzags through crevasse fields on glaciers. Frankly, it's unrealistic to have such detailed data for all possible trekking routes in this wild terrain.

Maps in This Book

The maps in this book, which show the general route of individual treks, are intended to be used in conjunction with the maps recommended in each trek's Planning section. At the start of each trekking chapter is a small-scale regional map with boxes showing the borders of the treks mapped in greater detail. The scale, marked beneath the north arrow, varies from map to map. A wide line of brown stipple shows the entire trek route, and a wide dashed line of brown stipple shows any alternative routes. Boxes mark the start and finish points, and symbols indicate camp sites and other features. A wide band of grey stipple shows land boundaries and borders, beyond which are notes about any adjoining or overlapping maps along with their page numbers.

Altitude Measurements

The elevations given are composites, based on the authors' averaged readings using a GPS and an altimeter. Existing published map altitudes not infrequently were estimated by early 20th-century British explorers, and therefore tend to be inaccurate. The elevations given are not absolutely precise, but represent elevations more accurate than those on existing maps. The best use of these elevations is to evaluate your rate of acclimatisation and elevation gain or loss over a stretch of trail, not to determine whether you've cracked the 5000m mark.

Place Names & Terminology

Some place names given in this book, especially for places other than cities, towns, and villages, differ from those given on maps. The Maps section for each trek details any discrepancies. Errors in place names on some maps occurred for a few reasons: some early explorers' local guides were not native speakers of the language in the area where they went; mistakes were made in transliterating place names from local languages to English; and some names were simply made up.

Glaciers & Dragons

Robert LeMoyne Barrett (Gypsy Davy), when describing the Braldu Valley and Baltoro Glacier in 1927, wrote:

> There are ice-dragons here, which maul the valleys. This valley was mauled by one old fellow, incredibly long and fat. His tail lay on the high passes, and his horrid snout vomited gravel and grey water. His many feet clawed the very mountain tops, and his wings covered the mountains. For spines he had ice pinnacles, and on his back, long ridges of moraine.

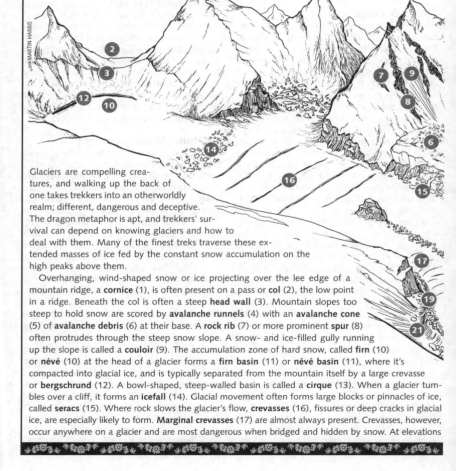

Glaciers are compelling creatures, and walking up the back of one takes trekkers into an otherworldly realm; different, dangerous and deceptive. The dragon metaphor is apt, and trekkers' survival can depend on knowing glaciers and how to deal with them. Many of the finest treks traverse these extended masses of ice fed by the constant snow accumulation on the high peaks above them.

Overhanging, wind-shaped snow or ice projecting over the lee edge of a mountain ridge, a **cornice** (1), is often present on a pass or **col** (2), the low point in a ridge. Beneath the col is often a steep **head wall** (3). Mountain slopes too steep to hold snow are scored by **avalanche runnels** (4) with an **avalanche cone** (5) of **avalanche debris** (6) at their base. A **rock rib** (7) or more prominent **spur** (8) often protrudes through the steep snow slope. A snow- and ice-filled gully running up the slope is called a **couloir** (9). The accumulation zone of hard snow, called **firn** (10) or **névé** (10) at the head of a glacier forms a **firn basin** (11) or **névé basin** (11), where it's compacted into glacial ice, and is typically separated from the mountain itself by a large crevasse or **bergschrund** (12). A bowl-shaped, steep-walled basin is called a **cirque** (13). When a glacier tumbles over a cliff, it forms an **icefall** (14). Glacial movement often forms large blocks or pinnacles of ice, called **seracs** (15). Where rock slows the glacier's flow, **crevasses** (16), fissures or deep cracks in glacial ice, are especially likely to form. **Marginal crevasses** (17) are almost always present. Crevasses, however, occur anywhere on a glacier and are most dangerous when bridged and hidden by snow. At elevations

Glaciers & Dragons

at or above 5000m, the snow pack is permanent; below, the ice often lies exposed. At elevations below 4000m, the surface of a glacier is mostly covered by ridges, mounds or irregular masses of rock debris called moraine. Moraine varies in size from gravel to boulders, and, when densely piled, makes for tedious and difficult walking. The moraine in the middle of a glacier is called **medial moraine** (18), and as one gets higher on the glacier, it usually offers the easiest walking. Moraine along the glacier's margins, called **lateral moraine** (19), is typically dense and jumbled, since a glacier's margins are more broken than its mid-sections. A boulder carried by glacial ice and deposited some distance from its place of origin is an **erratic** (20). Where glaciers recede from the valley walls on either side, they leave an **ablation valley** (21), where moraine rubble may form a **moraine lake** (22). Glaciers descend as low as 2500m where they deposit **terminal moraine** (23), and the **outwash stream** (24) issues forth from the glacier's **snout** (25) or **terminus** (25).

Particular attention has been paid to the accurate recording of both the place names and their meanings in that particular local language throughout this book. Because the many languages of northern Pakistan have sounds unknown in English or other languages, attempts to render local names in English inevitably fall short. Because place names also describe what is present in the landscape and provide information about the significance of a location for the people, it's important to include that as well (eg, *yarzeen* means 'the place where juniper grows'). Distortions through inaccurate renditions corrupt such meanings and are resented by the local populations. For example, two place names on the Baltoro Glacier are Muztagh Pass and Muztagh Tower; *muztagh* means 'ice mountain' in Turkic. On some recent Pakistani maps, Muztagh has been inaccurately replaced by Mushtaq, an Arabic word and common male name. A serious effort has been made in this book to avoid the dilution and loss of local values through such chauvinistic distortions of place names.

Because so many languages are spoken, many terms exist for features such as 'pass', 'valley' or 'stream'. For example, pass is *la* in Balti, *haghost* in Burushaski, *an* in Khowar, *gali* in Shina, and *uween* in Wakhi. Place names are given in local terminology and avoid the redundancy of adding the English term. Thus, the preferred usage is 'Burji La' rather than 'Burji La Pass'.

The term 'trail' is used to describe a visible path to follow. 'Route' is used for cross-country trekking (even though it's understood that technically a 'trail' is also a 'route'). The term 'hut' refers to the private property of herders who live in pasture settlements, while the term 'shelter' refers to a roofless enclosure made of stone walls that porters use to block the wind.

PERMITS & FEES
Trekking Permits
Regulations The Tourism Division of the Ministry of Tourism regulates trekking, which it defines as any walking below 6000m. It publishes the brochure *Trekking*

Rules and Regulations, which is available at the following offices.

Deputy Chief of Operations, Tourism Division (☎ 051-9203509, fax 9202347) Ministry of Tourism, Sports Complex, Kashmir Highway, Near Aabpara, Behind Liaqat Gymnasium, Islamabad. Open 8am to 3pm Monday to Thursday and Saturday, and 8am to noon Friday.
PTDC Tourist Information Centres In Islamabad and Rawalpindi (see Tourist Offices, p78).

The brochure *Trekking Rules and Regulations* details the permit process and fees, the duties of the licensed mountain guide and low-altitude porters, insurance requirements and equipment and rations you're required to provide them. Rules about payment of porters' wages and transport, the import and export of equipment, foreign exchange and photography are described. Guidelines are given for providing medical treatment and what to do when an accident occurs.

The appendices include a 'List of the Treks Approved by the Government'. Each approved trek on this list has a serial number, lists place names along the approved route and is classified into a zone. These treks are called 'specified treks', despite the zone in which they lie. Any trek not on this list is called an 'unspecified trek'. Unless you suspect an unspecified trek is in a restricted or closed zone, you can assume it's in an open zone and go. Tourism Division, however, considers applications for unspecified treks and notifies you if permission is granted within 15 days upon receipt of a completed application and a map detailing your proposed route. If permission is granted, a liaison officer usually accompanies the party. The list of approved treks changes – a new trek may appear, an old trek may disappear, or the zone in which a trek is classified may change – so check the status of any trek with Tourism Division before planning your trek.

Zones Tourism Division has designated three zones for trekking: open, restricted and closed. Know what type of zone you're trekking through to avoid any conflict with authorities.

Open Zones Foreigners are allowed to trek anywhere in open zones as high as 6000m without a permit or guide. Ongoing discussions may someday raise this to 6500m, but meanwhile the regulation isn't always strictly enforced.

Restricted Zones Foreigners are allowed to trek in restricted zones as high as 6000m, but are required to pay a fee and obtain a permit, hire a licensed mountain guide, insure the guide and each porter and register at check posts along these routes. The leader of the trekking party and the licensed mountain guide are required to attend mandatory briefing and debriefing meetings at Tourism Division. In order to complete the permit application you need to know the trek's serial number, start date and length, the name of your licensed mountain guide and his government registration number, and the number of porters you will engage.

You're required to obtain a personal accident insurance policy for the guide and porters (see Guides & Porters, p46). You also deposit a fee of US$50 for each non-Pakistani person per trek directly into the Tourism Division's account at the National Bank of Pakistan. Then you submit the bank receipt along with the insurance policy and six copies of your completed application form with two passport-sized photographs per person per trek to Tourism Division.

Tourism Division can help you in this process. It is, however, easiest to work with a licensed trekking company. They can provide a licensed mountain guide, collect the insurance premium and prepare the policy, collect and deposit the permit fee and submit a letter of request to Tourism Division along with the application. Permits for a specified trek in a restricted zone are, in theory, issued within 24 hours of receipt of the completed application.

The trekking party then contacts Tourism Division who sets meeting dates and times for the briefing before and the debriefing after a trek. Supposedly, meetings can be scheduled within 24 hours excluding Sundays and holidays.

Trekking in a restricted zone requires considerable planning. When organising yourself, allow four to six days in Islamabad upon arrival to complete the tedious formalities. You can reduce this time by hiring a trekking company to handle some of these arrangements in advance of your arrival. When you book through an adventure travel company abroad, it handles these formalities.

Closed Zones Foreigners are prohibited in closed zones, which, in theory, include areas within 48km of the Afghan border and within 16km of the Line of Control with Indian-controlled Kashmir. It may be possible to get a permit for a closed zone, but you could still be turned back by authorities.

Check Posts Formal check posts are rare while trekking. On open-zone treks, you're unlikely to encounter any. On restricted-zone treks, though, plain-clothed and uniformed border police, Khunjerab Security Force (KSF) police, the army at any military outpost, or forestry personnel may ask to see your permit. Carry at least six photocopies of your permit to give to such authorities. Your guide also has to meet any of these officials. Often, these guardians of the frontier are bored, and look upon your arrival as an opportunity to talk and relieve the tedium of a remote post. Accepting any invitation for tea earns goodwill not only for yourself and your trekking party, but also for any future parties. This helps to alleviate any anxiety about trekkers and encourages the policy of allowing trekkers in such areas.

National Park Entry Permits

No permits or fees are required to enter national parks, except Deosai National Park, which has a Rs 200 entry fee payable at either the Satpara or Chilam entrance stations.

RESPONSIBLE TREKKING

In many parts of the world, tourists, tour operators and host communities follow voluntary codes of conduct. In Pakistan, guidelines are not yet readily available and little is done to implement ecotrekking principles. Hence, much depends upon you as an individual adopting an activist approach. Much of the Karakoram and Hindukush is still 'clean' and unpolluted; ensure it remains that way for those who come after you.

Ask yourself what you can do to lessen the negative impact your trek might have on the environment and culture. Taking care of yourself and responsibility for your actions is a basic obligation of all trekkers. Perhaps the most important single action you can take is to reduce the size of your trekking party, which minimises your overall impact. Avoid overvisited trekking areas by selecting a lesser-known trekking destination and travelling in the off-peak season when possible.

Fires

Trees grow slowly in these arid mountains, making wood a scarce and highly valued local resource. Wood belongs to the area's inhabitants and you, as a visitor, have no right to use it. Cook on a kerosene stove and not on wood fires. When trekking with a guide, trek crew or porters, outfit everyone properly to avoid depending on fires for warmth. Also provide stoves and fuel or cooked food for everyone and consider preparing the same food for everyone simultaneously to conserve fuel. Bathe with warm water only when the water is heated without wood (eg, by solar heat or on stoves). Bring adequate warm clothes so you don't depend on campfires for warmth. Be especially careful about throwing cigarettes and matches in hot, dry places where they might cause fires.

Water

Water contamination occurs when human waste and other contaminants enter open water sources. This spreads disease and poses a health risk for residents, trekkers and wildlife. Be careful when washing, bathing and going to the toilet. Wash yourself, your dishes and your clothes in a basin and discard soapy water at least 50m from water sources. Don't put soaps, even biodegradable soaps, or toothpaste in water sources.

Toilets

Toilets don't exist on trekking routes, so during the day find a discreet location at least 50m from any open water source to relieve yourself. How to best deal with human faeces depends on where you are. Below the tree line, bury it with other organic matter where soil microbes and worms will decompose it. Above the tree line in remote, uninhabited areas, spread faeces thinly on rocks to dry it where the sun's ultraviolet (UV) rays kill bacteria and microorganisms. On a glacier, use a crevasse (straddle a small crevasse or bag faeces and toss the bag into the crevasse) where the glacier's crushing motion kills some bacteria and the waste will be dispersed and diluted over the many years it will take it to emerge into the river below.

At camp sites, create a toilet pit when none exists and ensure it's at least 50m from any open water source and half a metre deep. Ask people if they have any concerns about the spot you've selected. Make sure it's not where others may want to sleep or cook. When you hire a trekking company that carries a portable toilet tent, ensure it follows these guidelines. Burn toilet paper rather than discarding it in a toilet pit or crevasse. Sprinkle some dirt in the pit after each use; this helps faeces to decompose and reduces odours. Encourage your guide, trek crew or porters to use the same toilet site. When leaving the camp site, cover the pit with dirt at least 3cm to 4cm above ground level to allow for decomposition and settling.

Rubbish

Rubbish disposal systems don't exist along trekking routes, so be sure none in your party pollutes. Separate rubbish into organic, rubbish that can be burnt and rubbish that can't be burnt. Dispose of organic trash, such as food scraps, by feeding it to domestic animals. When no animals are around, bury it. Above 4000m, organic waste takes decades to decay, so carry it to lower elevations for disposal. Collect rubbish that can be burnt and organise a camp routine to burn it, preferably where a fire scar already exists. Candy wrappers and cigarette butts should not be discarded along the trail. Rubbish that can't be burnt, such as tins, bottles, aluminium foil and plastics should not be buried because it doesn't decompose and animals may dig it up and scatter it. Give tins and bottles to people along the trail if they want them, but don't leave them if no-one is there to take them. Aluminium foil, foil-lined packages and plastics release toxic ozone-depleting gases when burned, so carry out rubbish that can't be burnt and dispose of it in the nearest town. No formal recycling facilities exist, but bottles, aluminium and plastic are informally recycled. Please take used battery cells to your home country for recycling or disposal. When you find an existing rubbish hole at a camp site, ideally bury, burn or pack its contents out. When this isn't possible, partially cover the hole with large flat stones or wood to keep the rubbish from being scattered by weather or animals. Pick up others' rubbish when you see it along the trail.

You can minimise the rubbish you produce on trek by removing packaging from foods and repacking them into sturdy reusable containers before your trek. Don't buy or drink beverages in nonrecyclable plastic containers or tin cans. None of this is difficult or time consuming, but it makes a substantial difference.

Economic Considerations

Tourism is a major source of foreign currency for Pakistan. It provides economic incentives to promote conservation of wild lands, generates income for park management and brings needed income to rural populations. Patronise adventure travel companies abroad, trekking companies in Pakistan, airlines, and hotels that make a commitment to environmentally responsible tourism.

When people benefit from tourism, they respond positively and work to protect and manage their natural resource base. Give business to locally owned and operated trekking companies and hotels, hire porters and buy local products. When you bring freeze-dried food from home, or buy imported food in big city shops, you're not contributing to the local economy. Often when you enter a new valley you are expected to hire new porters from that valley and release any porters from a different

area. Instead of viewing this as an inconvenience, realise that the people through whose area you're walking will now benefit directly from your being there.

Purchase locally grown grains and vegetables in market towns like Chitral, Gilgit and Skardu whenever possible and plan to be self sufficient while trekking. Villagers often grow barely enough food for themselves. Where villagers have a surplus of fruits, nuts or dairy products, buying these helps put needed cash into the local economy. Inform yourself about current wages and prices for food, lodging and other services. Paying too much contributes to inflation by forcing wages and prices up, while paying too little denies a fair return.

Other Considerations

Using established camp sites and places for cooking, sleeping and relieving yourself concentrates the environmental impact and minimises overall disturbance. Select a level site at least 50m from open water sources and the trail. Avoid camping in fragile meadows. Don't clear vegetation, cut trees and limbs or brush to make camp improvements. Making trenches around tents leaves soil prone to wind and rain erosion. Before leaving a camp site, naturalise the area and replace rocks, wood, or anything else you moved. Repair anything you may have damaged, such as a stone wall or canal.

Graffiti on rocks is a permanent form of environmental pollution. Discourage your trek crew from writing their names or drawing on rocks. Don't make any unnecessary noise, and ask your trek crew to do the same. It's astounding how noisy a crowded camp site along the Baltoro Glacier can be at 4.30am!

Unauthorised hunting of, and trade in, endangered species is illegal, so don't condone or engage in it. And don't harass or feed wildlife, or eat wild game.

WOMEN TREKKERS
Attitudes to Women

Most Muslim women stay out of sight (or at least out of reach) of other men, remaining in the house, behind the veil, in special sections of buses and in the 'family' areas of restaurants. By the same token, most Muslim men also go out of their way to avoid direct contact with women outside their family. In some places (eg, the Tribal Areas of NWFP), such contact may bring a threat to their lives. That is why answers to a foreign woman's questions, for example, are often directed to her male companion. It's not a sign of contempt, but of respect. Most Muslim men's views of 'other' women come largely from the media. To make matters worse, popular films full of full-hipped women, guns and violence inflame the sexuality suppressed by traditional culture. Younger Pakistani men rarely miss the chance to point out to Western women how sexually frustrated all men are, and then ask, 'Where is your husband?'

Paradoxically, women travellers are more likely to get a look into people's private lives. Women travellers have the benefit of speaking to both men and women. Even in the most traditional areas, women may invite you into their home, feed you and show you around. Public areas (eg, at airports) often have separate waiting rooms or queues. Where they don't, women are expected to go straight to the head of the queue.

Safety Precautions

Women should not be deterred from trekking by fear of Islam or Muslim culture. By planning your trek carefully you can minimise any risk to your personal safety and increase your chances of a positive experience. Local people, however, strongly advise women never to trek or go on day hikes alone, particularly anywhere outside Hunza and Gojal. In all the authors' years of trekking here, they've never seen a female trekker backpacking on her own and rarely encountered female trekkers who are not part of an organised trek or without a male companion. The obvious alternative for women is to trek with a male partner or with a small group of male and female companions. Many women prefer to trek with a group organised by an adventure travel company, which makes planning easy and provides security and comfort on the trail.

Trying to understand how Pakistanis would think about a given situation will help you evaluate appropriate behaviour. Don't allow a man who is unknown to you to sit next to you. If travelling alone by vehicle, buy the seat next to you and refuse to allow any man to sit there. Ask him to select another seat.

Women should anticipate that most Pakistani men will make unwanted sexual overtures given the opportunity. It's definitely inappropriate for anyone to touch you for any reason. It helps to position yourself so that it would be difficult for a man to get close enough to touch you. A Western woman shaking hands with a Pakistani man is accepted. Don't let anyone into your tent for any reason. Bring a small combination lock for your tent zippers to deter any would-be Romeos. 'Holiday romances' with local men harm the image of Western women. Most men are married and either see the relationship as a ticket to the West, or as validation of the misconception that most Western women are sexually available.

When camping in, or passing through, villages on trek, it's often difficult to find a discreet place to relieve yourself. To avoid an unpleasant ambush by local men and boys, it's sometimes necessary to relieve yourself in your tent. Some trekkers merely use plastic bags. Using a collapsible plastic basin, however, is easier.

Often, a Western woman is simply ignored in social settings, even in cities. If you're outgoing and greet a local man by extending your hand, they usually respond politely and address you directly. Typically, this is not received negatively. Actual physical harassment is rare, but it does happen. If someone annoys or threatens you, don't hesitate to make a scene, particularly in public.

Local men aren't aware that they interrupt conversations between Western women and men. This usually happens when the local men want to speak with the Western men. They simply ignore the Western woman's presence. You can handle this situation first by being aware of it and then simply asking the local man not to interrupt and to wait until you are done speaking to one another.

Segregation of Women

Women and families are seated separately from men in all types of road transport. Women are usually placed in the front seats or towards the front of vehicles. If you are not assigned one of these seats, ask to move. In vans, coasters and buses, it's preferable for a woman to sit next to the window while her male travelling companion sits in the aisle seat. On passenger and cargo jeeps, women are likely to be seated up front with the driver. Women shouldn't pay extra for sitting in the front seat.

It's acceptable to ask that a woman sit in the front seat of Suzukis that run up and down the Gilgit and Skardu bazaars. When the front seat is already occupied by a man, ask him to move into the back. When a woman is travelling with a man, it's preferable that he also sit in the front seat between the woman and the driver. Some Suzuki drivers may not stop to give a woman a ride; try again – someone always does. When a woman travels alone, avoid inviting trouble and don't sit in the back of a crowded Suzuki. It's OK to ride in the back of a Suzuki when a woman has a companion, but it can become uncomfortable when it fills with other male passengers.

Women sit in a separate departure lounge at Chitral, Gilgit and Skardu airports, but not on aeroplanes.

Chitral and Skardu have *purdah* bazaars where local women don't go, although on rare occasions you may see a young girl or elderly woman. Foreign women are tolerated in the bazaar, but it's preferable to be accompanied by a man and to dress appropriately. When travelling alone, ask someone from your hotel or a jeep driver to accompany you.

What to Wear

Wear loose, long-sleeved, unrevealing shirts and full-length pants that cover your ankles, even when seated on the ground. The shalwar kameez is the dress of choice for cities, towns and villages. Get a kameez with buttons close to the neck and make sure the sleeves extend to the wrist covering the forearm completely. Most Western-style pants

still show the outline of the body and, hence, aren't the best choice. Loose skirts or dresses, unless ankle length, are a poor choice.

A shalwar kameez can also be comfortable to wear while trekking, but this largely depends on the terrain and weather. Three style features make a difference: the length of the kameez; whether the sides of the kameez are slit; and the size of the leg openings of the shalwar. Many kameez are too long (ie, well below the knees), which is impractical when you might have to jump or take big steps. You can also step on the tail of a long kameez when standing up and trip yourself. Look for a kameez with side slits, so the front and back panels move independently, increasing mobility. The size of leg openings on men's shalwar are larger than women's. Larger openings enable you to pull the shalwar up over your knees, which helps when fording rivers. The legs of some shalwar are so voluminous, however, that they're hazardous on the trail. On glacier traverses and high pass crossings, you may choose not to wear a kameez. Instead, wear a shalwar or baggy long pants, long-sleeved lightweight shirt, thermal underwear top and an oversize T-shirt over that (worn loose and not tucked in). It's not too stylish, but it's comfortable and functional. Regardless, bring a shalwar kameez on every trek to wear when travelling to and from trailheads and when walking around villages and herders' settlements.

Local women feel more comfortable if you're dressed appropriately, which is a visible sign of your interest in their culture. Chitral is particularly conservative and you may want to have a *dupatta* or scarf to cover your hair. Wearing a shalwar kameez may be overt camouflage, but remember others still see you as a conspicuous Western woman.

TREKKING WITH CHILDREN

Lonely Planet's *Travel with Children* is a valuable resource for anyone planning to trek with children. Parents should know their children's needs and abilities well. Select your trek carefully and choose easier treks, such as Fairy Meadow or Rakaposhi Base Camp and avoid treks that traverse difficult glaciers or cross high passes. That said, children under eight years of age have done extraordinary treks such as Gondogoro La, Shimshal Pamir and Dadarelli An, so anything is possible. The experience and competence of these parents is the reason their treks were successful.

Hiring a guide, cook and porters to carry gear allows parents to turn their attention to their children, and to stop and explore interesting sights along the way together. Hire a porter to carry children under eight years of age who cannot walk a full day by themselves. Older children can walk most of a day, but still may need or want to be carried part of the way. Bring your own child-carrier and a child's bicycle helmet for routes where rock-fall danger is present. Be sure to protect your children from the harsh environment. Dress them in lightweight long-sleeved shirts and pants. Apply sunscreen to all exposed skin and have your child wear a wide-brimmed hat and sunglasses. Children are always welcomed and treated with respect and their presence opens many doors.

DANGERS & ANNOYANCES

Heat, pollution, noise, impossible bureaucracy and overcrowded public transport are facts of life in Pakistan, which you'll share with Pakistanis. A smile helps, as does knowing your own limits and when to take a break. Pakistanis are amazingly hospitable, straightforward and honest, but a few pitfalls exist for the unwary. Beware of demonstrations and parades, called *jaloose*, especially religious ones. These can quickly turn violent, so avoid getting caught in any sectarian clash.

Road travel can be risky. Vehicles may not be properly maintained, drivers may be exhausted from too much driving, or have an overly macho attitude towards others on the road. Unfortunately, it's hard to recognise such conditions in advance. It's best to travel with larger, more reputable companies.

Also see the Money section (p81) and the Safety on the Trek section (p101).

Guns

In the 1990s, a combination of corrupt and incompetent police and bureaucrats, carte blanche passage for heavily armed Afghan guerrillas and a vigorous tribal arms industry allowed sectarian, political and criminal violence to flourish. Some areas of the country are now simply too dangerous to visit and few middle- or upper-class Pakistanis live without a gun at home.

Even celebrations can be dangerous. Pashtuns fire their weapons into the air on happy occasions, and the bullets have to fall somewhere. Peshawar residents instinctively move indoors when they hear a Pashtun wedding.

Drugs

Penalties for possession of drugs are stiff. Drug traffickers can receive the death penalty. Be wary of absolutely anyone who approaches you with drugs for sale. Some dealers, especially in Lahore and Peshawar, are in cahoots with the police, and will set you up in exchange for a cut of the fine or bribe. Police roadblocks along the Grand Trunk (GT) Rd make spot checks of traffic from Peshawar and the NWFP, and may search you or your bags for drugs.

OTHER ACTIVITIES
Rock Climbing

Baltistan's big walls and towers make it an international hot spot for climbers. The Baltoro Glacier and Hushe Valley are the main centres. Eastern Baltistan's Kondus and Saltoro valleys have some of the biggest unclimbed walls in the world, but their proximity to the Line of Control with India have kept them out of bounds, although a permit to this dream region was issued in 2000. Most of the rock is high-quality granite, with both free and aid routes established. Sport climbing is undeveloped. Walls along the KKH north of Hunza offer possibilities, as do boulder fields along the road west of Skardu. No climbing shops exist, other than some used-equipment stores in towns, so bring your own gear, including a helmet.

Mountaineering

The same rules and regulations apply to climbing peaks below 6000m as for trekking.

The trekking chapters feature many of these popular peaks as side trips to treks. Some hot spots and peaks are: Ghizar's Mashpa Gol and side valleys off Gazin Gol in the Hindu Raj Range; South Jalipur Peak (5206m) and Buldar (5602m) in Raikot Gah; Bort Valley in the lower Karambar Valley; Shani (5887m), Sentinel (5260m) and Snow Dome (5029m) in the Naltar Mountains; peaks above the Shireen Maidan Glacier and Werthum Peak (5844m) north of the Batura Glacier; unclimbed summits in Qachqar-e-Dur and Mungalig Sar in the Shimshal Pamir in Shimshal; and Gondogoro Peak (5650m) in Hushe. It's easy to hire a jeep to within a day's walk of many places. A few shops in Gilgit and Skardu sell used gear. See the Mountaineering chapter for peaks higher than 6000m.

Cycling
The KKH could have been invented for cyclists. It's a demanding, incredibly exhilarating and increasingly popular trip. The best riding is north of Gilgit, especially north of Hunza. For more about the KKH, see Lonely Planet's *Pakistan* and *Karakoram Highway*. The Gilgit-Skardu road along the Indus River is sealed and has small hotels in the few oasis villages along the way. The Skardu-Khaplu road is also sealed, but has almost no hotels along the way. The mostly unsealed Gilgit-Chitral road over Shandur Pass is a harder ride than the KKH where a mountain bike with good brakes, front suspension and a dust mask are essential. Accommodation and food are harder to find on this ride, so bicycles tend to be heavily loaded. Cyclists also cross the Deosai Plains between Skardu and Astor in five days via a rough unsealed road. Most cyclists will want to bring their own bike. For those who don't, Himalaya Nature Tours in Gilgit (see p45) is the only place that rents mountain bikes. The cycling season is June to September. Avoid riding in the intense midday heat.

Rafting & Kayaking
Rivers open for white-water rafting and kayaking usually lie well below 3000m. Class II to IV rivers are run commercially, although commercial rafting is still in its infancy. The best rafting season is from mid-September to late November, followed by April to mid-June. Most rivers, except the Ishkoman River, cannot be run between mid-June and early September because of high water levels. Flow volume usually peaks in mid-July, when kayaking is still possible.

Popular runs include: the Chitral, Laspur and Lutkho rivers in Chitral; the Ishkoman, Ghizar, and Gilgit rivers in Gilgit; the Kunhar River in Kaghan; the Indus River in Indus Kohistan; the upper Hunza River in Gojal; and the Braldu, upper Indus, Shigar, and Shyok rivers in Baltistan. The Ishkoman and Gilgit rivers and the upper Hunza River are possible during the summer, and combine nicely with treks in the area. Mountain Movers in Gilgit is the only company that rents kayaks.

Fishing
Since the beginning of the 20th century, many of Pakistan's mountain rivers and lakes have been stocked with trout. World-record trout have been taken out of Ghizar's Handrap River. Popular reaches are in Chitral, Swat, the Gilgit River basin (eg, Singal, Kargah and Naltar), Astor Valley, Baltistan and Kaghan. The season is 10 March to 9 October. Information and licences are available at fisheries offices in towns, and sometimes from wardens on the spot.

Ski Touring
The Deosai Plains and the Karakoram's largest glaciers, such as the Biafo, Hispar, Baltoro and Batura, attract adventurous and experienced ski mountaineers. Ski traverses are best done from mid-March to mid-May. It's recommended to tow gear on lightweight plastic sledges.

USEFUL ORGANISATIONS
No formal organisations, such as trekking clubs or associations of mountain guides, exist. The Alpine Club of Pakistan (☎ 051-5562887, fax 5581987), 509 Kashmir Rd, Rawalpindi, however, operates a mountaineering centre in Naltar, where it trains and certifies mountain guides and liaison

officers. Adventure Foundation Pakistan (☎ 0992-382190, fax 34537), 151 Workshop Rd, Habib Ullah Colony, Kakul, Abbottabad, founded by retired Brigadier Jan Nadir Khan, is a nonprofit organisation that promotes special-skills training and Outward Bound-style adventures for young Pakistanis. Although not a trekking company, it will organise small-group mountaineering, trekking and clean-up expeditions for anyone able to contact it several months in advance. It also publishes a useful *Green Trekking* brochure. Although its headquarters is in Abbottabad, direct inquiries can be made to PO Box 1807, Islamabad 44000, c/o Adventure Inn (☎/fax 051-2272538, ☎ 825805, e adventure@pimail.com.pk), Garden Ave, National Park Area, Islamabad.

TOURIST OFFICES

Pakistan Tourism Development Corporation (PTDC) is the promotional arm of the Tourism Division of the Ministry of Tourism. (The ministry has at different times also included divisions for culture, sport, youth affairs, minorities etc, and its official name changes accordingly and with regularity. Ministry of Tourism is being used for simplicity throughout this book.) PTDC runs motels, maintains tourist information centres, and books vehicles. PTDC does not maintain any official offices abroad. Its subsidiary, Pakistan Tours Ltd (PTL), books domestic flights, vehicles, hotels and tours. Its staff, although knowledgeable about general information, is much less helpful for trekking-specific queries, which are better directed to trekking companies.

Contact the PTDC Information and Reservations Line (☎ 111-555 999, e tourism@isb .comsats.net.pk), visit its Web site (W www .tourism.gov.pk) or visit these offices:

PTDC
Head Office (☎ 051-2877039/40, 2275754, fax 2274507) 4th floor, 22/A Saeed Plaza (enter unmarked stairway facing Blue Area), Jinnah Avenue, Blue Area, Islamabad 44000
Motels Booking Office (☎ 051-9208948/49, fax 9218233, e ptdcibd@apollo.net.pk) F-7 Markaz, Bhitai Rd, Block 4-B, Islamabad

Tourist Information Centre 2nd floor, Head Office
Tourist Information Centre (☎ 051-9202766, 9212760, fax 9204027) F-6 Markaz, Super Market, Islamabad
Tourist Information Centre (☎ 051-5514672, fax 5513054) Rm 7, Flashman's Hotel, The Mall, Rawalpindi

PTL
Head Office (☎ 051-5563038, 5565449, fax 551 3054, e ptl@isb.comsats.net.pk) Rm 17, Flashman's Hotel, The Mall, Rawalpindi

VISAS & DOCUMENTS
Passports

Your most important travel document is a passport. If it's about to expire, renew it before you go as this may not be easy to do abroad. Pakistan requires your passport be valid for at least six months after your visit.

Visas

A visa is a stamp in your passport issued by a foreign government that permits you to enter and/or travel in a country for a specified period of time. You can apply for a tourist visa at any Pakistani embassy or consulate. A multiple-entry tourist visa is valid for three months from the date of arrival in Pakistan and for six months from the date of issue.

Tourists entering Pakistan without a visa can get a 30-day landing permit at any immigration check post. A fee may be assessed according to nationality. This is a new policy implemented in October 2000, so getting a visa before arrival eliminates any uncertainty, particularly when entering the country by road.

Visa requirements and fees vary according to length and nationality and can change without notice, so check with any Pakistani embassy or consulate, visa service, or reputable travel agency before travelling.

Visa Extension Anyone entering Pakistan on a 30-day landing permit can get an entry visa valid for three months from the date of entry into Pakistan, issued at the Regional Passport Office (☎ 051-9261566) at Peshawar Chowk, G-8/1, Mauve Area, INT

Centre, Islamabad. The Regional Passport Office and the Deputy Commissioners (DC) in Gilgit and Skardu can issue one three-month extension to any tourist or entry visa.

An expired visa is a problem to avoid at all costs, because the Regional Passport Office in Islamabad states that it doesn't deal with expired visas. It usually means a tedious and time-consuming detour to the Ministry of Interior, R Block of the Secretariat in Islamabad. If you're somewhere else and time is running out on your visa, police may give you an authorisation letter giving a few extra days to get to the border.

Re-entry Visas When you want to depart and then return to Pakistan and don't already have a multiple-entry tourist or entry visa, you can get a re-entry visa stamped into your passport for a minimum US$10 fee, which varies according to nationality. The Regional Passport Office in Islamabad can issue not more than two re-entries, and the DC in Gilgit or Skardu can issue one.

Foreigners' Registration
The arcane and troublesome system of Foreigners' Registration was abolished in October 2000, except for Indian nationals, foreigners of Indian origin and passport holders from certain African and Middle East countries.

Onward Tickets
To get a visa, you may be asked to produce an onward/return ticket in addition to submitting the completed visa application, fee, your passport and passport-size photos. This request may be deflected by saying you're leaving Pakistan via the Khunjerab Pass to China.

Travel Insurance
It's worth taking out travel insurance to cover medical care, emergency evacuation, personal property and trip interruption. Consider insuring yourself for the worst possible scenario – an accident requiring helicopter evacuation, hospitalisation, ambulances and medi-vac and possibly a flight home. For an extended trip, travel insurance may seem very expensive, but if you cannot afford the insurance premiums, you probably cannot afford a medical emergency abroad either. Some policies pay only for a medical emergency abroad and not for nonemergency care. You may prefer a policy that pays doctors or hospitals directly rather than your paying on the spot and filing a claim later. If you file a claim later, ensure you keep all documentation. Some policies require you to call (reversing the charges) the insurance company at a centre in your home country to authorise treatment or to assess your situation. Others may require you to get a second opinion before receiving any medical care.

Personal property covers loss or theft of your belongings. Remember to report any incident to the nearest police and obtain a police report, which you may need to file a claim. If you have prepaid any travel arrangements, trip-interruption or cancellation insurance covers any unreimbursed expenses if you cannot complete your trip due to illness, an accident or the illness or death of family members.

Before you purchase travel insurance, check any existing policy you may own to see what it covers abroad. Some policies refuse to pay claims when you engage in certain 'dangerous' activities; verify that trekking is a covered activity.

Travel insurance is available from private companies; you can also ask any travel agency or adventure travel company for recommendations. The international student-travel policies handled by STA Travel and other student-travel organisations are good value. They frequently include major medical and emergency-evacuation coverage in the cost of the student-travel ID card.

Other Documents
Youth cards aren't recognised in northern Pakistan, so just ask for a discount if you want one. Record all immunisations on an International Certificates of Vaccination, available from your physician or health department, and carry this yellow booklet with you to show proof of immunisation (see Immunisations, p89, for recommended immunisations).

Copies

Copy all important documents (passport data page and visa page, credit cards, travel insurance policy, air/bus/train tickets, driving licence etc) before you leave home. Leave one copy with someone at home and keep another with you, separate from the originals.

EMBASSIES & CONSULATES
Pakistan Embassies & Consulates

A partial list of embassies abroad follows; high commissions and consulates are noted as such.

Australia & New Zealand
Embassy: (☎ 02-6290 1879) 4 Timbarra Crescent, O'Malley, ACT 2206; PO Box 684, Mawson 2607 Canberra
Consulate: (☎ 02-9299 3066) 49–51 York St, Sydney, NSW 2000
Consulate: (☎ 03-9866 1200) 492 St Kilda Rd, Melbourne, VIC 3004

Belgium
Embassy: (☎ 02-733 97 83) 25 Ave Delleur 57, Boitsfort 1170, Brussels

Canada
Embassy: (☎ 613-238 7881) 151 Slater St, Ste 608, Ottawa, Ontario K1P 5H3
Consulate: (☎ 514-845 2297) 3421 Peel St, Montreal, Quebec H3A 1W7
Consulate: (☎ 416-250 1255) 4881 Yonge St, Ste 810, Willowdale, Toronto, Ontario M2N 5X2

China
Embassy: (☎ 10-6532 2504) 1 Dong Zhi Menwai Dajie, San Li Tun, Beijing 100600

France
Embassy: (☎ 01 45 61 09 24) 18 rue Lord Byron, 75008 Paris

Germany
Embassy: (☎ 0228-9 55 30) Rheinallee 24, 53173 Bonn
Consulate: (☎ 069-42 10 12) Wachterbacher St 83, 60386 Frankfurt

India
Embassy: (☎ 011-600 603, 688 9229) 2/50-G Shantipath, Chanakyapuri-21, New Delhi

Iran
Embassy: (☎ 021-934 332) Khayaban-e Dr Fatimi, Koocha-e-Ahmed Eitmadzadeh, Block No 1, Jamshedabad, Shomali Tehran
Consulate: (☎ 051-29845) Khayaban-e-Imam Khomeini, Opposite Bagh-e-Milli, Meshed
Consulate: (☎ 0541-23389) Khayaban-e-Razmju, Moqaddam, Zahidan

Ireland
Embassy: (☎ 01-6611055) 34 Fitzwilliam Square, Dublin 2

Italy
Embassy: (☎ 06-329 4836) Via Della Camilluccia 682, 00135 Rome

Japan
Embassy: (☎ 0334-54 4864) 2-14-9 Moto Azabu, Minato-ku, Tokyo 106

Netherlands
Embassy: (☎ 070-3648948) Amaliastraat-8, 2514 JC, The Hague

Spain
Embassy: (☎ 01-345 89 86) Av Pio XII-II, 28016 Madrid

UK
Embassy: (☎ 020-7664 9200, W 212.106.96.110) 34–36 Lowndes Square, London SW1X 9JN
Consulate: (☎ 0274-721921) Fraternal House, 45 Cheapside, Bradford BD1 4HP. Vice-consulates are in Birmingham, Glasgow and Manchester

USA
Embassy: (☎ 202-939 6200, W www.pakistan-embassy.com) 2315 Massachusetts Ave NW, Washington, DC 20008
Consulate: (☎ 212-879 5800) 12 East 65th St, New York, NY 10021
Consulate: (☎ 310-441 5114) 10850 Wilshire Blvd, Suite 1100, Los Angeles, CA 90024

Embassies & Consulates in Pakistan

Most embassies, unless otherwise noted, are in the Diplomatic Enclave (G-5) at Islamabad's east end. It's possible to get foreign visas only from embassies in Islamabad, not from consulates in other cities. Some applicants may need a letter of request from their own embassy.

From Aabpara, vans to Quaid-e-Azam University pass the US, Chinese and Australian embassies. The No 3 van to Bari Imam (Nurpur Shahan) passes near the Iranian, Indian, Japanese and British embassies. For others, consult the telephone directory or PTDC Tourist Information Centres (see p78).

Australia (☎ 051-2279233/7)
Canada (☎ 051-2279100)
China (☎ 051-2824786)
France (☎ 051-2278730/2)
Germany (☎ 051-2279430)

India (☎ 051-814371/5, ext 257)
Iran (☎ 051-2276270)
Ireland (☎ 051-2277912)
Italy (☎ 051-2210791), F-6/3, 54 Khayaban-e-
  Margalla
Japan (☎ 051-2279320)
Netherlands (☎ 051-2214336)
New Zealand contact the UK embassy
Spain (☎ 051-2211088)
UK (☎ 051-822131/5)
USA (☎ 051-826161/79)

Trekkers are advised to check with their high commission or embassy's consular section in Pakistan to see what services are available for citizens visiting Pakistan. Some embassies may offer emergency medical treatment or financial assistance if you run out of money. Most embassies also assist with emergency evacuation. In the event someone at home needs to reach you in an emergency, most foreign offices maintain 24-hour operators who can contact your embassy in Pakistan.

CUSTOMS
Arrival
Pakistan prohibits the import of alcohol and firearms. No other significant import restrictions apply, and none apply to trekking gear. If you exchange other currencies for a large sum of Pakistani rupees before you enter Pakistan, keep them out of sight.

Departure
Baggage inspection is cursory for foreigners. Customs officials may ask for sales receipts and bank encashment certificates for major purchases. Put battery cells into your checked baggage, as airport security may confiscate them from carry-on baggage. Officials are sharp-eyed about pen guns and other disguised firearms. Penalties are stiff and foreigners have been busted. Drug smuggling is punishable by death.

Export Permit
An export permit is necessary to post out any purchase with a declared value of more than Rs 500 and to carry out carpets. Obtaining an export permit on your own can be tedious. PTDC, shopkeepers, or your hotel

staff may help. Bring the purchase receipt, encashment certificates for at least the value of the purchase, an explanatory letter to the Controller (Import & Export) and photocopies of these documents and the front pages of your passport to the export office.

Pakistan bans the export of antiquities. When in doubt, ask a museum curator or shopkeeper who deals in them.

MONEY
Currency
The unit of money is the rupee (Rs), divided into 100 paisa. Paper notes come in denominations of Rs 1000, Rs 500, Rs 100, Rs 50, Rs 20, Rs 10, Rs 2 and Rs 1. Rs 2, Rs 1 and half-rupee coins are used (and a few 25 paisa and 10 paisa). Very worn or tattered notes are often refused by villagers and porters.

The freely convertible rupee fluctuates on the open market, and generally depreciates against major international currencies. The rupee lost half its value during the 1990s. Since anyone can buy major foreign currencies, the black market has largely finished.

Exchange Rates
The cash exchange rates at the time of publication were:

country	unit		rupee
Australia	A$1	=	Rs 32.30
Canada	C$1	=	Rs 40.88
euro	€1	=	Rs 59.41
India	Rs 1	=	Rs 1.34
Japan	¥100	=	Rs 54.49
New Zealand	NZ$1	=	Rs 26.35
UK	UK£1	=	Rs 94.03
USA	US$1	=	Rs 64.17

Exchanging Money
US dollars, either cash or travellers cheques, are by far the easiest currency to exchange, followed by British pounds sterling. Neither Euros nor Euro cheques are accepted, even by moneychangers. Exchange rates are higher in down-country cities than in towns in NWFP or the Northern Areas. It's best to exchange the bulk of your money before heading into the mountains.

You can exchange money at domestic banks, such as United Bank Limited (UBL) and National Bank of Pakistan, in cities and at international airports. Domestic banks are also in Chitral, Gilgit, Aliabad, Karimabad, Afiyatabad and Skardu. Foreign banks, including ANZ Grindlays, Bank of America, CitiBank and American Express, are only in down-country cities. Some banks exchange other foreign currencies in cash only. Banks, however, don't give the best rates. Top-end hotels also exchange money at an even worse rate. Along the KKH, rates in Afiyatabad are generally slightly higher than Gilgit because of Chinese trade, yet still lower than those in Islamabad.

The best way to change money is with a moneychanger. Ask for an encashment certificate whenever you exchange money, which you may need to reconvert unspent rupees, purchase airline tickets or get export permits. Unspent rupees can be reconverted by moneychangers and by certain branch banks at customs, immigration posts and international airports, if the bank is open.

Cash & Travellers Cheques Cash gets a slightly higher rate than travellers cheques at banks and moneychangers. Moneychangers are not authorised to accept travellers cheques. Moneychangers give their best rate for US$100 and US$50 notes.

ATMs Automatic Teller Machines aren't prevalent in Pakistan and don't exist in the mountains. You have to go in to a bank to conduct any business.

Credit & Debit Cards American Express and Visa are the most widely accepted credit cards. Mastercard and Diners Club are only accepted in down-country cities. Credit cards aren't widely accepted anywhere in northern Pakistan.

Travel agencies usually charge a percentage fee to charge airline tickets to credit cards. Foreign banks can arrange a cash advance against a credit card. This may take a day (or more) to process and you can expect to pay a percentage commission. At American Express in Islamabad's Blue Area in Ali Plaza (☎ 051-2272425) and in Rawalpindi on Murree Rd, Saddar Bazaar (☎ 051-5582864), card holders can get rupees for no fee or travellers cheques for a 1% fee from their personal cheques.

International Transfers Banks may suggest that you arrange a telex or telegraphic transfer of funds from your home bank, which can take a week or more. It's safer and simpler to have someone post a bank draft by express registered, insured mail to you at a reliable address in Pakistan.

Moneychangers Authorised moneychangers, licensed by the State Bank of Pakistan, are in major down-country cities and in Gilgit, Karimabad, Afiyatabad and Skardu. They're quicker than banks, keep longer hours and give a better rate. Rates on the Mall in Rawalpindi are as much as Rs 0.20 higher than in Islamabad.

On the Trek

Cash is the only viable option to pay for expenses on trek. Exchange all the money you need before departing the nearest town. Carry small notes ranging from Rs 1–100 on trek. When going on a longer trek, carry 100-note bundles of Rs 5, Rs 10, Rs 20 and even Rs 100 notes to avoid overpaying because of lack of correct change. Guides and porters seldom have change for larger bank notes.

Security

Theft is almost unheard of. To people on marginal incomes, however, the money and expensive baggage of foreigners can be hard to resist. Using common sense prevents most theft. Always carry your money yourself; don't let a guide, trek crew or porter do so. This makes you responsible for your own money and keeps everyone travelling with you honest. As a general rule, keep your valuables (ie, passport and money) in the backpack you carry and in your line of sight and never flash large wads of cash. The backpack's top pocket isn't recommended; an interior zippered pocket is better. Put all money in a resealable plastic bag or other waterproof pouch. When trekking with a guide or porters, ideally put your gear in a duffel bag and lock it. Keep all your gear inside your tent at night, particularly your boots.

Costs

The costs are valid at the time of writing, but expect an annual inflation rate as high as 10%. Despite inflation, actual costs have remained about the same or even decreased during the 1990s because of the rupee's loss in value.

Cities & Towns By staying in budget hotels, eating local-style food and using public transport, you can spend less than US$15 per person per day. This includes daily per-person accommodation (double rooms) costing US$6–8, and US$4–7 each for food. When staying in mid-range hotels, budget US$20–25 per person per day.

On the Trek Per-person daily costs vary significantly with the kind of trek you choose. Backpacking costs US$10–15 when you carry your own pack or hire one porter, buy food locally, provide your own equipment and use public transport to trailheads. When you organise a special hire, guide, cook and/or porters on your own, it costs US$25–50. (See Wages under Guides & Porters, p49.) Open-zone treks cost less than restricted-zone treks (self-organised restricted-zone treks cost as much as US$50 per person per day). The cost of transport to the trailheads is listed under each trek.

Trekking companies charge US$35–100 per person per day, depending upon the services you request. Adventure travel companies charge US$100–175.

Tipping & Bargaining

Tipping (around 10%) is expected in top end hotels and restaurants in cities and towns. Airport porters charge Rs 15 per trip to carry baggage. Taxi drivers don't expect tips, but it's OK to leave them loose change. Staff in guesthouses and mid-range hotels don't ask for tips, but it's appropriate to leave Rs 10–20 per day.

When you pay guides, cooks, trek crew and/or porters fair wages, tipping isn't necessary. Tipping is a way to acknowledge and reward performance above and beyond the call of duty. You may choose to give gifts. If you choose to give cash, a tip of 10%, or roughly one day's wage per person per week, is adequate. When you book a trek with an adventure travel company, your tour leader gives you appropriate guidelines for tipping all staff when the trek finishes. The easiest way is for all trekkers to pool their tip money and have the tour leader give it out equitably to the trek crew.

Giving baksheesh, a Persian word meaning 'to bestow a blessing', has become a way of life in Pakistan and throughout South Asia. You might best think of it as another form of tipping. It greases the wheels, and if you can afford to distribute small bits of largesse as you pass through, it eases your way. It doesn't take much – Rs 5–10 for any small service rendered in the private sector. Government employees shouldn't accept it, but always enjoy a tea or a dinner invitation. Resist the temptation to see those who ask for baksheesh as beggars. It's part of the Islamic code that better-off people give part of their income to the less well off. At the finish of a trek, porters may ask for baksheesh. You can give them money but, often, what they really have their eye on is some trek gear or any items that are unavailable in Pakistan, which make truly well-appreciated baksheesh for the hard-working porter.

Hotels and restaurants have fixed rates. Hotels, however, frequently offer discounts if you ask for them. Generally, if the management knows you from a previous stay, they're more amenable to giving you a discount. In the bazaar, shopping without bargaining is like giving your money away. Bargaining is a knack most travellers develop quickly. Shops with fixed prices tell you so. Some basic necessities, including wheat flour, milk powder, sugar, tea, and kerosene, are also sold at fixed prices. Fares for bus tickets and airfares are fixed. Private vehicle hires and costs for trekking are negotiable. It's usually advantageous to negotiate in rupees instead of foreign currency.

Remember that politeness always works best, especially when negotiating over the cost of services you will receive.

Taxes

A 15% General Sales Tax (GST) is levied on consumer goods, including restaurant meals; books and clothing are excepted. A 15% Central Excise Duty (CED) is levied on airline tickets (but not road transport), major hotels and restaurants with air-conditioning. When you need a receipt, CED is assessed. See Departure Tax (p108) for the applicable international departure tax.

POST & COMMUNICATIONS
Post

Postal rates in Pakistan are only Rs 2. International rates from Pakistan are roughly the same as rates to Pakistan. International service is fast for letters and parcels from cities, but longer from remote places. To eliminate the risk of stamp theft, have letters franked in front of you. Send important letters via registered mail. Have outgoing parcels sewn into cloth bags that a tailor in the bazaar can quickly make. These need a customs declaration and postal inspection, so leave it open and finish the job yourself.

Receiving mail is fairly dependable when the address is well known. Parcels are less likely to arrive. American Express card and travellers cheque holders can have letters (but not registered letters or parcels) held for up to one month at their down-country offices. Receiving mail via poste restante in Chitral, Gilgit or Skardu is less reliable. In these towns, it's better to arrange for a trekking company or shopkeeper to receive mail for you at their postal box.

Telephone & Fax

You can place domestic and international telephone calls and send faxes from telephone exchanges, public call offices (PCOs), and hotels. Exchanges are usually open 24 hours a day. A minimum three-minute international call costs Rs 250; person-to-person calls cost about 15% more. A one-page fax costs the same as a three-minute call. Hotels usually charge higher rates.

Most large towns now have direct dialling, so you can receive international calls almost anywhere in Pakistan. When calling from abroad, the international country code for Pakistan is ☎ 92. To place an international call from Pakistan, book the call with the international operator, or dial direct from a telephone with International Direct Dialling (IDD) service. The international access code from Pakistan is ☎ 001.

Gilgit has IDD service, but Skardu is linked to the international gateway in Islamabad through a satellite relay. You can receive international calls and faxes in Skardu, but you cannot direct dial international calls. You have to book calls through the international operator in Islamabad. You can, however, direct dial to anywhere within Pakistan. From Skardu, the best way to send a fax is to prearrange with a trekking company, hotel or one of the many private business centres in Islamabad to act as a relay. You can send them a fax, and they can send it again via IDD from Islamabad.

Placing and receiving international calls and faxes in Chitral is easier because it's linked to the international gateway in Peshawar by a series of microwave relay towers, referred to locally as 'boosters'. Along the KKH north of Hunza, telephone calls are made through an operator at a switchboard, where just reaching Gilgit is difficult.

The army's Signal Battalion in Gilgit (☎ 0572-55066, 66226) and Skardu (☎ 0575-2990, 2555) rent satellite telephones; you need a refundable US$4000 deposit or equivalent. Outgoing calls are US$2.85 per minute.

Email

Travelling with a portable computer is a great way to stay in touch with life back home, but hardly practical for trekkers. Email and Internet, however, is accessible through cybercafes, which have sprung up throughout down-country Pakistan. The rates are generally Rs 40 per hour with a 30-minute minimum of Rs 20. Major Internet Service Providers, such as AOL and CompuServe, do not have dial-up nodes in Pakistan. You need to use a Web-based email account such as Yahoo or Hotmail. Set up an account before leaving home and let everyone know your travelling address. Alternatively, you can access your existing Internet email accounts if you carry three pieces of information: your incoming (POP or IMAP) mail server name; your account name; and your password. Your ISP or network supervisor can give you these. With this information, you should be able to access your Internet mail account from any net-connected machine in the world, provided it runs some kind of email software (Netscape and Internet Explorer both have mail modules). It pays to become familiar with the process for doing this before leaving home.

At the time of writing, northern Pakistan's only cybercafe is in Gilgit. Comsats Internet Services, opposite the army mess in Jutial, is open from 9am to 8pm. The rate is Rs 120 per hour with a 30-minute minimum. Cybercafes will no doubt come to Chitral and Skardu soon.

INTERNET RESOURCES

The World Wide Web is a rich resource for travellers. You can research your trip, hunt down bargain air fares, book hotels, check on weather conditions or chat with people and other travellers about the best places to visit (or avoid!).

There's no better place to start your Web explorations than the Lonely Planet Web site (**W** www.lonelyplanet.com). Here you'll find succinct summaries on travelling to most places on earth, postcards from other travellers and the Thorn Tree bulletin board, where you can ask questions before you go or dispense advice when you get back. You can also find travel news and updates to many of our most popular guidebooks, and the subWWWay section links you to the most useful travel resources elsewhere on the Web.

BOOKS

Reading about where you intend to go makes excellent preparation, and a few of the best books are listed here. Trekkers who visit libraries and book stores will find many more accounts of exploration and expeditions, too numerous to mention.

Lonely Planet

Other useful Lonely Planet titles are: *Pakistan*, *Karakoram Highway* and *Hindi & Urdu phrasebook*.

Travel & Exploration

de Filippi, Filippo, *Himalaya, Karakoram and Eastern Turkestan*. Recounts the Italian expedition of 1913–14 to the region.

Mason, Kenneth, *Abode of Snow*. Presents an authoritative history of early exploration and mountaineering.

Neate, Jill, *High Asia*. Gives a comprehensive illustrated history of the 7000m peaks.

Schomberg, Reginald. A retired British army colonel chronicles his travels around Gilgit, Yasin and Hunza in *Between the Oxus and the Indus*, his explorations of Chitral in *Kafirs and Glaciers*, and his remarkable journeys beyond Shimshal in *Unknown Karakoram*.

Shipton, Eric. The master of small expeditions treats Baltistan, Shimshal and Hunza in *Blank on the Map*.

Tilman, HW, *Two Mountains and a River*. Accounts of travels to Rakaposhi, Gilgit, Chalt, Bar and crossing the Mintaka Pass.

Vigne, Godfrey, *Travels in Kashmir, Ladak, Iskardo*. In 1835, Vigne was the first Westerner to visit these parts.

Workman, WH & Bullock, Fanny. The authors undertook six expeditions between 1899 and 1912, recount their exploration in *The Call of The Snowy Hispar* about Nagyr and the Hispar Glacier, *In the Ice World of Himalaya* about the Biafo Glacier and Snow Lake, *Ice-Bound Heights of the Mustagh* and *Two Summers in the Ice-Wilds of Eastern Karakoram* about Baltistan's glaciers, including the Kondus, Bilafond and Siachen (hardcover).

Natural History

Roberts, TJ, *The Birds of Pakistan* (Vol I & II) and *The Mammals of Pakistan*. The standard references, but not field guides. The latter serves as a reminder of how quickly large mammals disappear when modern roads and weapons appear.

Nasir, Yasin and Raif, Rubina, *Wild Flowers of Pakistan*. Describes and illustrates more than 650 flowering plants (hardcover).

General

Biddulph, John, *Tribes of the Hindoo Kush*. A reprint of a 19th-century classic by the first political agent in Gilgit.

Child, Greg, *Thin Air*. An award-winning account of Karakoram alpine-style climbs.

Jettmar, Karl, *Bolor and Dardistan*. A learned exposition of the ancient history of Gilgit, Hunza and Baltistan.

Keay, John, *The Gilgit Game: The Explorers of the Western Himalaya 1865–95*. A very readable account of the explorers and oddballs who played in the 'Great Game', the imperial rivalry between Britain and Russia across the Pamirs, Hindukush and Karakoram in the late 19th century.

Messner, Reinhold, *All 14 Eight-Thousanders*. Recounts his ascents without oxygen and many of them solo. This is probably the greatest mountaineering feat of all time.

Rashid, Ahmed, *Taliban: Miltant Islam, Oil, and Fundmentalism in Central Asia*. Required reading to understand how Afghanistan affects the entire region.

Staley, John, *Words For My Brother*. Discusses the culture, politics, religious traditions and recent history of pre-KKH Chitral, Kohistan, Gilgit and Hunza (hardcover).

Wirsing, Robert G, *India, Pakistan & The Kashmir Dispute*. The best study of the seemingly unending Kashmir imbroglio.

Buying Books

Many of the stores that sell maps also sell books (see Buying Maps, p63). Pakistan is a gold mine of inexpensive reprints of travel classics.

Book stores abound in Islamabad, Rawalpindi and Peshawar. Gilgit has a few book stores, including the Northern Areas' oldest, GM Baig Son's in Jamat Khana Bazaar. Karimabad has several book stores. In Skardu, Kazmi's store has books on Balti culture.

RADIO & TV

State-owned Pakistan Broadcasting Corporation's radio and TV programming is mostly in Urdu, with some English and regional language programming. Pakistan TV (PTV) has two channels and rebroadcasts some BBC and CNN programs. Most hotels and many restaurants in northern Pakistan have satellite-dish antennas and show CNN and BBC news, Star TV and the wildly popular Hindi videos on Zee TV. Bring a short-wave radio and listen to BBC World Service, Voice of America or your country's short-wave service to keep up on world news while trekking.

WEATHER INFORMATION

Unpredictable and changeable weather, a given in the mountains, presents a small yet inherent risk to trekkers. Before starting your trek, it's a sensible idea to determine the weather forecast. Radio Pakistan broadcasts English-language weather reports from Gilgit and Skardu each evening. Check locally for precise times. Regardless of the forecast, carry rain gear at all times and hope for the best, but be prepared for the worst.

Relying on a radio forecast is not always very practical. Not all trekkers carry a radio, battery cells can go dead, or you might miss the daily broadcast. Learning how to anticipate storms by understanding the shapes and movements of clouds that foreshadow a change in weather patterns is important general knowledge for anyone heading into the mountains. Watching the sky on trek along with carrying a pressure-sensitive altimeter or barometer may help you decide when, and if, to take a rest day, move to a higher camp site or cross a pass.

Cirrus, cirrocumulus and altostratus clouds are indicative of warm fronts, which gradually move in to replace cooler air masses. Cirrus and cirrocumulus clouds are composed of ice particles usually 8km or more above the earth. Cirrus clouds appear feathery and are often described as resembling horse tails. Cirrocumulus clouds appear as rows of small balls and wisps. Altostratus clouds are water droplets usually between 3km and 6km above the earth, which appear as a thick veil that diffuses sunlight. Warm fronts rarely produce storms, but when they do they linger longer than storms generated by cold fronts. Warm fronts start with high cirrus clouds that become low, dense stratus clouds and produce snow or rain.

Cumulus and cumulonimbus clouds are present with cold fronts when cold air masses move beneath warmer air masses causing the barometric pressure and temperature to fall and the wind direction to change. Cumulus and cumulonimbus clouds appear dense, woolly or dark and tower high into the air. They are often called thunderclouds. Cold fronts develop quickly, travelling about twice as fast as warm fronts. Keep in mind that an approaching cold front can cause the elevation reading on an altimeter to rise when you're not moving, meaning the air pressure has dropped and a storm might be on the way. *Reading Weather – Where Will You Be When the Storm Hits* by meteorologist Jim Woodmency delves deeper into the topic.

PHOTOGRAPHY
Film & Equipment
Colour print film (Rs 200–300), slide film (Rs 300–400) and print processing (Rs 300) are only available in down-country cities and some towns. Kodachrome is scarce and cannot be processed in Pakistan. B&W film is rare and of doubtful quality, and costs more to process than colour. Posting exposed film from anywhere in Pakistan is asking for trouble; better to carry it out with you.

Choice of equipment is a personal matter, but an SLR camera with a mid-range zoom (eg, 35mm to 135mm) covers a wide range of situations. A good second lens to carry might be a 24mm or 28mm for panoramas and indoor shots. A 'skylite' filter protects the lens and cuts down on high-altitude UV glare. A polarising filter darkens the sky to avoid underexposing the landscape. A soft fill-flash eliminates shadows and keeps midday photographs of people from looking like they are wearing masks.

Tourism Division regulations for mountaineering currently prohibit digital cameras.

Technical Tips
Heat, condensation, dust and sand present hazards to film and equipment. Film stays cooler through the fiercest summer day if you line a stuff sack with a patch cut from an aluminised-mylar 'survival blanket'. Camera batteries get sluggish in cold weather. Keep the camera inside your jacket and some spare batteries warm in your pocket. In very cold weather, avoid ruinous moisture on film and inside of the camera by putting them in plastic bags before going indoors or exposing

them to warmer temperatures, and leave them until they have warmed. Keep everything bagged up, and carry a squeeze-bulb for blowing dust from inside the camera. Putting a clear plastic bag over your camera protects it from dust so you can carry it over your shoulder while trekking.

For tips and techniques particular to photography on the road, read Lonely Planet's *Travel Photography* by Richard I'Anson.

Restrictions
Prohibited subjects to photograph are military installations and equipment, airports, railway stations, major bridges and women.

Photographing People
When photographing, respect people's dignity and right to privacy. Establish a friendly rapport, ask permission and get their name and address so you can mail photos back to them. Letting people know you will do so may overcome their reluctance to be photographed and make friends. Photographing women is considered improper. Avoid paying people for taking their photo. This commercialises and cheapens cross-cultural interactions, allowing your economic power to dominate and overwhelm any cultural or personal reluctance to be photographed.

Airport Security
One dose of airport X-rays for inspecting carry-on bags should not harm slow- or medium-speed films. The effects of X-rays, however, are cumulative and too many may fog your pictures. Lead 'film-safe' pouches help, but the best solution is hand inspection. Officials usually hand-inspect film if you persist. This is crucial for high speed (ISO 1000+) film. Having all your film in clear film canisters and all your canisters in one or two large clear plastic bags makes it easier. A customs regulation says you can bring in only one camera and five rolls of film, but foreigners routinely bring much more.

TIME
Pakistan has a single time zone, which is five hours ahead of Universal Time (UT). Daylight saving time is not observed.

ELECTRICITY

Electricity is 220V, 50 cycle AC. Load-shedding, a periodic cut in power, is very common in May and June down-country when the weather is hot and the reservoirs are low. Power cuts are common occurrences any time in all cities and towns.

In the mountains, rotating power outages are common in the face of high demand and low generating capacity. Most towns and villages rely on overextended small-scale hydroelectric power.

Current fluctuation is severe, and you must use a voltage stabiliser to protect all sensitive electronic equipment. Many kinds of plugs are used, mostly the round-pin variety. Electrical shops in down-country cities and in mountain towns can make an adapter (for less than Rs 50) for whatever plug you have. A high-quality and powerful solar battery recharger is useful if you prefer to carry rechargeable battery cells.

WEIGHTS & MEASURES

Pakistan uses the metric system; see this book's inside back cover for a conversion chart.

LAUNDRY

On trek and in villages, everyone does their own laundry. Laundry detergent is readily available, although none is biodegradable. In towns and cities, a *dhobi* (washer man) does laundry; ask at your hotel for details on this inexpensive service.

BUSINESS HOURS

Government offices are open 9am to 5pm Monday to Thursday and Saturday and 9am to 1pm Friday. Private businesses have similar hours, except Friday when they reopen 3pm to 5pm. Banks are open 9am to 5pm Monday to Friday and 9am to 1pm Saturday. Banks usually exchange currency, however, only 9am to 1pm Monday to Friday and 9am to noon Saturday.

Bazaars in Rawalpindi and Islamabad are open Monday to Saturday; those in NWFP are open Saturday to Thursday. Shops generally open at 9 or 10am, may close in the late afternoon, and reopen in the evening until at least 8pm. In towns and villages, expect shops to be closed on Friday as well as Sunday.

PUBLIC HOLIDAYS

Government offices, businesses and banks are closed on secular holidays except where noted. Also see Islamic Holidays (p37).

23 March Pakistan Day, celebrating the 1940 demand by the All-India Muslim League for an independent Muslim state (or, some say, the proclamation of the Pakistan republic in 1956)

1 July Bank holiday only

14 August Independence Day, the anniversary of the birth of Pakistan in 1947

9 November Iqbal Day, honouring the poet Alama Mohammed Iqbal, who, in 1930, first proposed a Muslim Pakistan

25 December Birthday of Pakistan's founder, Mohammed Ali Jinnah

31 December Bank holiday only

Health & Safety

Staying healthy on your treks and travels depends on your predeparture preparations, your daily health care while travelling and your response to any medical problem or emergency that develops. While potential problems can seem quite frightening, in reality few travellers experience anything more than an upset stomach.

PREDEPARTURE PLANNING
Health Insurance
Make sure you have adequate health insurance. See Travel Insurance (p79) for details.

Immunisations
Immunisations against several diseases are recommended. Discuss immunisations with your physician at least six weeks before travelling. Don't leave everything to the last minute. Some immunisations require more than one injection, while others shouldn't be given together.

Make sure your immunisations are recorded and carry your record as proof. Certain immunisations are sometimes needed to enter some countries. Yellow fever immunisation as an entry requirement is usually only enforced when coming from an infected area, and isn't required for travel in South Asia. No immunisations are required by law for entry into Pakistan. Consider the following immunisations for your trip.

Diphtheria & Tetanus Immunisations for diphtheria and tetanus are usually combined and are recommended for everyone. After an initial course of three injections (usually given in childhood), boosters are necessary every 10 years.

Polio Everyone should keep their polio immunisation up to date. It's normally given in childhood, and a booster every 10 years maintains immunity.

Hepatitis In northern Pakistan, hepatitis A is common. The Havrix vaccine conveys immunity to hepatitis A, possibly for more than 10 years, after an initial injection and a booster at six to 12 months. Alternatively, an injection of ready-made antibody gamma globulin, which is collected from blood donations, provides short-term protection. Have it administered one to two weeks after your last vaccination and as close as possible to departure. It's most effective in the first few weeks after administration, tapering off gradually depending upon the dosage given (eg, 2cc for three months or 5cc for six months). It's reasonably effective and, unlike the vaccine, it's immediately protective. Concerns about its long-term safety linger, however, because it's a blood product.

Hepatitis A vaccine is also available in a combined form with the hepatitis B vaccine. It requires three injections over a six-month period, the first two conveying substantial protection against hepatitis A.

Hepatitis B is endemic in northern Pakistan, and appears in 10% of the population throughout Pakistan, so immunisation is advisable. Immunisation involves three injections with a booster at 12 months. More rapid courses are available if necessary.

No vaccines exist for hepatitis C, D or E.

Typhoid Immunisation against typhoid is available either as an injection, which protects for three years, or as capsules taken orally, which protect for five years. Neither confers total immunity, but is advisable. A combined typhoid/hepatitis A vaccine was launched recently but its availability is still limited – check with your doctor to find out its status in your country.

Cholera The current injectable vaccine against cholera gives minimal protection for six months, but has many side effects and is not generally recommended for trekkers, who have a low risk of infection.

Rabies Immunisation for pre-exposure to rabies is only recommended for individuals who travel for a month or longer, especially if handling animals, caving (where bat bites could be dangerous) or travelling to remote areas, and for children (who may not report a bite). It requires three injections over 21 to 28 days. If someone who has been immunised is bitten or scratched by an animal, they require two booster injections; those not immunised require more.

Tuberculosis (TB) Although widespread, TB isn't generally a serious risk to travellers. TB is commonly spread by coughing or by consuming unpasteurised dairy products from infected animals. TB is prevalent in high-elevation villages where people live closely with livestock. Avoid staying in homes in such villages where anyone has a persistent cough. Immunisation is recommended when spending three or more months in areas where people are known to have TB. It's advisable to get a TB skin test after you return home.

Malaria Prophylaxis Vivax and falciparum are two types of malaria parasites spread by mosquitoes. Both occur in Pakistan, although they're not prevalent in northern Pakistan. Vivax is more common, but isn't severe and is never fatal. Falciparum is a serious, cerebral malaria and can be fatal when untreated. These parasites may lie dormant in the liver, so symptoms may not appear until long after you leave an infected area. Vivax parasites are sensitive to chloroquine. Falciparum parasites are resistant to many drugs. Prophylaxis doesn't prevent you from being infected, but kills the parasites during a stage in their development and significantly reduces the risk of becoming very ill or dying.

For malaria prophylaxis that protects you from both parasites choose any one of three methods: 500mg chloroquine weekly, plus 200mg daily proguanil (Paludrine); 250mg mefloquine (Lariam) weekly; or 10mg doxycycline (Vibramycin, Doryx) daily. If you buy your chloroquine tablets in Pakistan, they will probably be 250mg chloroquine phosphate tablets, containing 150mg chloroquine. With each method, begin the

week you arrive in a risk area, and continue for four weeks after you leave.

Discuss the best dosage, side effects and potential treatment with your physician. Factors to consider are the areas you will visit, the risk of exposure to malaria-carrying mosquitoes, your current medical condition and your age and pregnancy status.

First Aid

It's essential to know the appropriate responses in the event of a major accident or illness, especially when trekking in remote areas. Consider learning basic first aid on a recognised course before you go, and carrying a first-aid manual. Although detailed first-aid instruction is beyond this book's scope, some basic points and tips for prevention are listed under Traumatic Injuries (p100) and Safety on the Trek (p101).

Physical Preparations

Being both mentally and physically prepared for trail conditions best enables you to enjoy trekking. Any physically fit person who is experienced in mountain travel can undertake a trek. Several months before your trek, however, begin an aerobic conditioning program. Regular exercise (running, cycling or swimming) is essential. Hiking is the best preparation, so plan weekend or longer outings in hilly areas near your home. Typically, fit trekkers are less bothered by minor illness. The degree of physical conditioning, however, doesn't reduce the potential for altitude problems (see Altitude, p94). See also Level of Difficulty (p65) for an overview of a trek's rigours.

Other Preparations

It's a good idea to have a full check-up before you go. It's far better to have any problems recognised and treated at home than to find out about them on trek. Visit your dentist to make sure your teeth are OK. Air trapped in cavities or cracked fillings may expand at high altitude and cause tooth trauma. If you wear glasses, take a spare pair and your prescription.

If you require a particular medication, take enough to last the trip. Take part of the

Trekking First-Aid Kit Check List

The following is a list of items to consider including in your first-aid kit.

First-Aid Supplies

- [ ] sterile **adhesive bandages** (for minor cuts, abrasions and puncture wounds)
- [ ] waterproof **adhesive tape** (to secure dressings)
- [ ] topical **antibiotic ointment**
- [ ] **antiseptic swabs** or liquid
- [ ] fingertip and knuckle **bandages**
- [ ] sterile and nonsterile **bandages** (for dressing wounds)
- [ ] **ammonia inhalant** (for faintness, dizziness)
- [ ] **blister treatment** (eg, molefoam)
- [ ] knee or ankle **brace**
- [ ] waterproof **butterfly closures** (to hold wound edges together)
- [ ] **cotton swabs**
- [ ] high-compression **elastic bandage** with Velcro closure
- [ ] oval **eye pads**
- [ ] flexible rolled **gauze** (to secure dressings)
- [ ] disposable **needles** and **syringes** (in case you need injections)
- [ ] absorbent, nonstick, **nonsterile pads** (to cushion and protect larger wounds)
- [ ] **safety pins**
- [ ] bandage **scissors**
- [ ] **'space' blanket**
- [ ] absorbent, nonstick, **sterile pads** (for bleeding or draining wounds)
- [ ] eight-ply **sterile pads** (to cleanse open wounds and dress minor wounds)
- [ ] latex **surgical gloves**
- [ ] **thermometer** (note that airlines will not allow mercury thermometers)
- [ ] **triangular bandage**
- [ ] **tweezers**

Miscellaneous

- [ ] **eye drops** (for washing out dust)
- [ ] **insect repellent**
- [ ] **lip salve** with sunscreen
- [ ] **matches**
- [ ] **oral rehydration salts** (ORS)
- [ ] **skin applications** for irritations (sunburn, bites and sore muscles)
- [ ] waterproof **sunscreen**
- [ ] **vitamins**
- [ ] **water purification treatment**

Medications

The generic names are listed with common brand names in parentheses. Consult your pharmacist for locally available brands. If you're allergic to commonly prescribed antibiotics, such as penicillin or sulpha drugs, carry this information with you at all times.

Bring enough analgesic and anti-inflammatory medications to treat the minor aches and pains of anyone you may hire or villagers who will ask. Because local people may be allergic to aspirin or ibuprofen, acetaminophen (paracetamol) is the best choice. For medications to treat altitude-related illness, see the Altitude section (p94).

- [ ] **analgesics** for pain and fever – aspirin, paracetamol, acetaminophen (Tylenol, Atasol) with codeine (Beserol, Panadeine)
- [ ] **antibiotics** – ampicillin, amoxycillin (Zoxicillin), azithromycin, cephalexin (Keflex, Sporidex), ciprofloxacin, erythromycin, metronidazole (Flagyl), norfloxacin (Noroxin), tinidazole (Fasigyn), trimethoprim sulfamethoxazole (Bactrim, Septra DS)
- [ ] **antidiarrhoeal** – kaolin or sodium bismuth preparation (Pepto Bismol)
- [ ] **antifungal** – tolnaftate (Tiniderm, Tinactin, Tineafax)
- [ ] **antihelminthic** – mebendazole (Vermox, Wormin)
- [ ] **antihistamines** for allergic reactions, itchiness – diphenhydramine (Benadryl, Vistaril)
- [ ] **anti-inflammatory** – ibuprofen (Advil, Motrin, Novofen, Brufen, Nurofen), naproxen sodium (Aleve)
- [ ] **antimotility** – diphenoxylate hydrochloride (Lomotil, Phenatol), loperamide (Imodium A-D)
- [ ] **antimotion** – dimenhydrinate (Dramamine)
- [ ] **antinausea** – promethazine (Phenergan), prochlorperazine (Compazine)
- [ ] **antispasmodic/antacids** to soothe upset stomachs – Mylanta, Maalox, Gelusil
- [ ] **decongestant** – pseudoephedrine hydrochloride (Sudafed) with triploidine (Actifed), slow-release decongestant (Ornade or Histade)
- [ ] **laxative** – bisacodyl (Dulcolax)

packaging showing the generic name, rather than the brand, as this makes getting replacements easier. To avoid problems at customs, it's also a good idea to have a legible prescription or letter from your physician to prove that you legally use the medication.

Health & Safety Guides

Lonely Planet's *Healthy Travel: Asia & India* is a handy pocket-sized reference packed with useful information including pre-trip planning, emergency first aid, immunisation and disease information, and what to do if you get sick on the road. Consider bringing a more detailed health guide: *Medicine for Mountaineering* by James A Wilkerson, MD; the pocket-sized *Mountaineering Medicine* by Fred T Darvill, MD; *Hypothermia, Frostbite & Cold Injuries* by James A Wilkerson, MD; and *Mountain Sickness: Prevention, Recognition, and Treatment* by Peter H Hackett, MD.

When planning a trek that traverses glaciers, read up on techniques and safety issues before you go. *The Illustrated Guide to Glacier Travel and Crevasse Rescue* by Andy Tyson and Mike Clelland, and *Mountaineering: The Freedom of the Hills* by the Mountaineers, Seattle, Washington both contain excellent information.

Online Resources

Excellent travel health sites are on the Internet. From the Lonely Planet site (W www.lonelyplanet.com/weblinks/wlheal.htm) there are links to many sites, including the World Health Organisation (W www.who.ch) and US Centers for Disease Control and Prevention (W www.cdc.gov/travel).

STAYING HEALTHY
Hygiene

To reduce the chances of contracting an illness, wash your hands with soap frequently, particularly before handling or eating food. When on an organised trek, ensure the cook and kitchen crew also wash their hands thoroughly. Make sure dishes and utensils are washed properly with soap and not just rinsed off. Avoid drinking from cups or eating from plates that aren't thoroughly dried.

Beware of dirty towels used to dry dishes and utensils.

Brush your teeth with purified water. When trekking, change sweaty clothes, including socks, immediately when you get into camp. Wear shoes at all times and wear rubber sandals when you bathe.

Avoid insect bites by covering bare skin when insects are around, screen windows or bedding and use insect repellents.

Nutrition

If your food is poor or limited in quantity or availability, if you're travelling hard and fast and therefore missing meals, or if you simply lose your appetite, you can soon start to lose weight and place your health at risk. To trek long distances over rugged terrain, you need to eat between 3000 and 4500 calories per day. It's hard to trek when you're not eating enough. Make sure your diet is well balanced. You need extra calories, especially carbohydrates found in grains, bread and potatoes. Dairy products, eggs, beans, lentils and nuts are all good sources of protein.

Consider using vitamin supplements if your intake of vitamin-rich foods is insufficient, or when travelling for an extended period.

Food

Follow the old adage 'cook it, boil it, peel it or forget it'. Locally available dried fruit is safe to eat only when it is sulphured to kill fly larvae. Unfortunately, sulphured fruit is not as tasty as the unsulphured variety. Soaking dried fruit overnight in iodised water or boiling it are effective solutions. Milk is often unpasteurised, which transmits tuberculosis and brucellosis. Drink milk only if it's boiled and stored hygienically. Yogurt is safe to eat, if flies have not been landing on it. Take care with *lassi* (yogurt drink) as water may have been added. Busy restaurants where food is being cooked and eaten quickly are best. Avoid food that has been left to cool or has been reheated.

Water

Water is often contaminated with bacteria, cysts and viruses. When you don't know for certain that the water is uncontaminated, it's necessary to purify drinking water. When buying bottled water, choose containers with a serrated seal; not pop or screw tops or corks. Studies show that most bottled water produced in Pakistan is contaminated. Generally, the Nestlé brand is safe, as are imported brands.

Water Purification Boiling, treating chemically and filtering are three practical ways to purify water.

Boiling The best way of purifying water is to bring it to a rolling boil for at least one minute, which kills all intestinal-disease-causing organisms. At higher elevation, water boils at a lower temperature, but still adequately for disinfection. When you can't boil water, treat it chemically or filter it.

Chemical Treatment When used correctly, iodine is a very effective chemical treatment to purify water. It's available in three forms: tablets, tincture and crystals. Iodine products are lightweight and easy to use, although their effectiveness depends on concentration, exposure time, temperature, pH and turbidity of the water. After treating water with any form of iodine, let the water stand for at least 20 minutes before drinking. If the water is particularly cold, let it warm up in the sun before treating it. Otherwise, allow treated water to stand longer.

Iodine in tablet form is marketed under various brand names (eg, Potable Aqua). Tablets are easy to carry and use and dissolve quickly. If the tablets get wet, however, they become ineffective. Tincture of iodine is a liquid form typically sold in a glass bottle (eg, Lugol's solution, Povidone or Betadine). The recommended dosage is two to three drops per 1L of water.

Iodine crystals also come in glass bottles. Prepare a saturated solution by filling the bottle with water. After this solution stands for one hour, it's ready to use. Remember to protect glass bottles from breakage.

Add flavoured drinking powder, rehydration salts or herbal tea bags only after the water is completely disinfected. Vitamin C binds with any excess iodine and also improves the taste.

Chlorine tablets, sold under various brand names (Puritabs, Steritabs), don't kill all pathogens (eg, *Giardia lamblia* and amoebic cysts) and aren't recommended.

Filtration Chemicals, microorganisms and suspended solids can be strained out via filtration. The size of the pores in a water filter determines its effectiveness. All filters should remove *Giardia lamblia*, some remove smaller bacteria, but none remove viruses. To kill viruses, chemical disinfection or boiling is necessary. Only filters that combine filtration with disinfection produce water safe to drink.

Common Ailments

Blisters Prevent blisters by making sure your trekking boots are well worn in before your trip. At the very least, wear them on a few short walks before tackling longer outings. Your boots should fit comfortably with enough room to move your toes; boots that are too big or too small cause blisters. Be sure socks fit properly and no seams cross the widest part of your foot. Wet or dirty socks also cause blisters, so carry a spare pair and change them regularly. Keep your toenails clipped, but not too short. As soon as you feel a hot spot coming on, apply tape or an adhesive foam pad to act as a second skin. If a blister develops, don't pop it. Pad it, wait for it to burst and keep the new skin clean. Blisters eventually turn into calluses.

Fatigue Most injuries happen towards the end of the day when you're tired. Tiredness can be life-threatening on a narrow or exposed trail or in bad weather. Never set out on a walk that's beyond your capabilities that day. To reduce the risk, don't push yourself too hard and take regular rest breaks. Towards the end of the day, relax your pace and increase your concentration. Eat energy-giving snacks throughout the day to replenish depleted reserves.

Knee Pain Swelling of the knee from pounding descents can be incapacitating. If prone to this, take anti-inflammatory medications before you start walking. A brace may also help. Minimise the pounding by carrying less weight and taking small steps with slightly bent knees, making sure that your heels hit the ground before the rest of your foot. Trekking poles are effective in taking some of the weight off the knees.

MEDICAL PROBLEMS & TREATMENTS

Wherever possible seek qualified medical help before treating any illness or injury. Although this section gives advice and treatments, it's intended only for reference in an emergency.

Environmental Hazards

Trekkers are at more risk than most groups from environmental hazards. The risk, however, can be significantly reduced by using common sense.

Altitude Acute mountain sickness (AMS) occurs from a failure of the body to adapt to high elevations resulting in a build-up of intercellular fluid, which accumulates in the lungs (high-altitude pulmonary oedema or HAPE) and/or in the brain (high-altitude cerebral oedema or HACE). HAPE and HACE are both progressive, life-threatening conditions, which may occur simultaneously. Ignoring progressive symptoms may lead to unconsciousness and death within hours. AMS is easily preventable and should never be fatal.

Prevention & Symptoms Watch for symptoms at intermediate altitudes between 1500m and 2500m as AMS is known to

Warning

Self-diagnosis and treatment can be risky, so you should always seek medical help. An embassy, consulate or five-star hotel in down-country cities can usually recommend a local doctor or clinic. Although drug dosages appear in this section, they're for emergency use only. Correct diagnosis is vital.

occur as low as 1800m. 'High altitude' is an arbitrary descriptive term, but for medical purposes could be understood to mean elevations above 2500m. These categories help gauge the range of higher elevations where AMS generally occurs and is more severe: high altitudes between 2500m and 3500m; very high altitudes between 3500m and 5800m; and extreme altitudes above 5800m.

The key to preventing AMS is to ascend slowly so acclimatisation can take place. When trekking above 3000m, limit your daily increase in sleeping elevation to 300m. Exercise caution when flying to Chitral, Gilgit or Skardu. Do not drive to high-elevation villages or trailheads on the same day you fly into these towns. Spend at least one night in Chitral or Gilgit and two nights in Skardu. Keep your fluid intake high and avoid diuretics, such as caffeine and alcohol. Since the body takes in less oxygen while sleeping, avoid taking sedatives to help you sleep; sedatives lower your breathing rate and decrease oxygen levels in your blood.

In areas where no educational material about AMS is available, guides and porters are inadequately trained in recognition and treatment of AMS. Trekkers need to understand and recognise the symptoms of AMS, be aware of its risks and know how to respond to symptoms. Be alert for symptoms in yourself and those in your trekking party.

AMS progresses slowly but steadily over 24 to 48 hours. Early signs of AMS are headache, persistent yawning, hyperventilation, shortness of breath, loss of appetite, poor sleep and waking at night gasping for breath (ie, Cheyne-Stokes breathing). It's not uncommon to experience these symptoms when ascending. They indicate you have reached your limit of acclimatisation and that you need to stop and rest in order to acclimatise further.

When you continue to ascend, symptoms will steadily worsen. As fluid accumulates in the lungs, the person with HAPE becomes progressively more breathless, at first while walking and eventually even at rest. Breathlessness is accompanied by a cough, dry at first, and a discernible rattling or gurgling in the lungs, which progresses to production of pink, frothy sputum, then bloody sputum. Death from drowning results. As fluid collects in the brain, a person with HACE experiences headache, loss of appetite and nausea, and becomes lethargic and tired. As the severity increases, disorientation and loss of coordination develop. A trekker with HACE has difficulty lacing boots, putting on crampons or tying knots. With increasing lethargy comes a desire to lie down, followed by coma. Without immediate descent, death is inevitable.

Studies conducted by the Himalayan Rescue Association of Nepal found that 80% of fatalities from AMS occurred in groups, even though only 40% of trekkers travel in groups. The reason for this is that fixed trekking itineraries put pressure on trekkers and tour leaders to continue ascending even when AMS symptoms appear. Trekkers often hide their early symptoms and inexperienced tour leaders hesitate to split the group and trek crew. These mistakes in judgment can have fatal consequences.

Treatment AMS treatment is simple. When you experience any symptoms, especially headache and/or breathlessness, stop and rest until they go away. Symptoms may be confused with a cold or an upset stomach or being out of shape. Do not ascend when you have any symptoms. If the symptoms don't go away, or get worse, descend immediately to the last elevation where you were symptom-free, regardless of the time of day. A person suffering from AMS may not think clearly and may have to be forced to descend. Even if the diagnosis of AMS is uncertain, descend when you suspect AMS, as a prompt descent always relieves symptoms. You can always reascend later.

Prophylaxis is not recommended to prevent AMS. It's safer to rely on planned, slow ascent. Some medications, however, have proven effective to treat AMS. Acetazolamide 250mg (Diamox) can be taken before ascent to prevent or to relieve mild AMS symptoms, such as headache and nausea, and promote sleep at altitude. Recent studies indicate that 125mg is just as effective with fewer side effects. Dexamethasone

0.5mg (Decadron and Oradexon), a steroid drug thought to reduce brain swelling, is useful for HACE. Don't take it to prevent the onset of AMS. Nifedipine 10mg (Procardia and Adalat) lowers pulmonary artery pressure and is useful for HAPE. Don't take it as a prophylaxis. Treatment with nifedipine should be accompanied by immediate descent.

A portable hyperbaric chamber (eg, Gamow Bag) is an effective device to treat altitude-related illness by simulating descent. It's used when the victim is unable to walk or be moved to lower elevations. None are available in Pakistan. Suppliers in some countries offer weekly and monthly rentals.

Sun Protecting your skin and eyes from the intense solar radiation in the mountains should always be taken seriously.

Sunburn At high altitude you can get sunburnt quickly, even on hazy, cloudy or overcast days, and even when it snows. Use a high-quality sunblock or sunscreen and lip moisturiser with a Sun Protection Factor (SPF) of 30 or 50 with UV-A and UV-B protection, and reapply throughout the day. Remember to cover areas that don't normally see sun, such as under your nose and chin. Wear protective clothing for your face, ears and neck. A wide-brimmed hat, scarf, bandanna or an umbrella offer added protection. Use zinc oxide or another cream or physical barrier for your nose when travelling on snow for extended periods. If, despite these precautions, you get burnt, calamine lotion, aloe vera or other commercial sunburn-relief preparations are soothing.

Snowblindness Exposure to UV light can burn the cornea, or eye's surface, in as little as two hours. At 5000m there is 75% more UV penetration than at sea level. Any time you walk on snow or go above 3500m your eyes need protection that filters a minimum of 90% UV-A and UV-B radiation. Extend precautions on cloudy days as well.

Snowblindness usually occurs when someone walks on snow without eye protection. Buy sunglasses for anyone you hire;

don't give them money to buy glasses for themselves. If you don't have sunglasses for someone you hire, insist on wrapping a cloth around their head and face, leaving the smallest slit possible for them to see. Snowblindness is temporary, but extremely painful. If it occurs, patch both eyes and apply a cold compress and give analgesics for pain. It can take two days or longer for symptoms to subside. Ophthalmic ointment or drops may soothe the eyes and prevent possible infection.

Heat Daytime temperatures often soar, even when at altitude. Drink plenty of noncaffeinated liquids and treat heat with respect.

Dehydration A condition caused by excessive fluid loss, dehydration occurs in cold as well as hot conditions and because of diarrhoea and vomiting. The body expends fluids in saliva, urine and sweat that need to be replenished. Make sure you drink enough and don't wait until you feel thirsty to drink. Always carry water when you trek or take long road journeys. Urine is normally pale yellow and darkening urine and decreased urination are symptoms of dehydration. Drink more fluid and avoid diuretics, such as caffeine; a minimum intake of 3L per day is recommended. ORS and powdered electrolyte mixes can be added to drinking water to replace essential salts lost through diarrhoea or sweating.

Heat Exhaustion Overexposure to heat and sun, dehydration or deficiency of salts can cause heat exhaustion. Symptoms include faintness, a weak and rapid pulse, shallow breathing, cold or clammy skin and profuse perspiration. Lie a victim down in a cool, shaded area. Elevate their feet and massage their legs towards the heart. Give them a drink of cool salty water (ie, ½ teaspoon of salt in a glass of water) or a sweet drink. Allow them to rest and don't let them sit up too soon.

Heatstroke A life-threatening emergency condition, heatstroke is the onset of a high fever caused by sun exposure when the

body's heat-regulating mechanism breaks down. Symptoms are extremely high body temperature (39° to 41°C), rapid pulse, profuse sweating followed by its cessation, and then dry, red, hot skin. Severe, throbbing headaches and lack of coordination may also occur, and a victim may be confused or aggressive. Eventually, a victim convulses and becomes unconscious. Hospitalisation is essential, but meanwhile it's imperative to lower the body temperature by getting the victim out of the sun, cooling them in water, sponging briskly with a cool cloth, or wrapping in cold clothes or a wet sheet or towel and then fanning continually. Give fluids if they're conscious, but avoid caffeinated drinks.

Cold When trekking and camping at high altitudes always be prepared for cold, wet or windy conditions, even when just out for a few days.

Hypothermia When the body loses heat faster than it produces it, lowering the core body temperature, hypothermia occurs. Even when the air temperature is above freezing, the combination of wind, wet clothing, fatigue and hunger can lead to hypothermia. Dress in insulating layers and wear a hat, as much heat is lost through the head. On the trail, keep fluid intake high and carry food containing simple sugars to quickly generate heat.

Symptoms are shivering, loss of coordination (slurred speech) and disorientation or confusion. This can be accompanied by exhaustion, numb skin (particularly toes and fingers), irrational or violent behaviour, lethargy, dizzy spells, muscle cramps and violent bursts of energy. To treat the early stages of hypothermia, first get the victim out of the elements like wind, rain or snow. Then prevent heat loss by replacing any wet clothes with layers of dry, warm ones. Next have the victim drink warm liquids, avoiding alcohol, and eat high-caloric food with sugars or carbohydrates. Don't rub the victim, but place them near a fire or gently bathe with warm, not hot, water. It may be necessary to place the victim, naked, in sleeping bags and get in with them. Early recognition and treatment of mild hypothermia is the only way to prevent severe hypothermia, a critical condition.

Frostbite When extremities freeze, frostbite occurs. Signs include crystals on the skin, a whitish or waxy skin accompanied by itching, numbness and pain. Warm affected areas by immersing in warm water or covering with clothing or sleeping bags. When skin becomes flushed, stop warming, elevate, and expect pain and swelling. Exercise the area if possible, but don't break blisters or rub affected areas. Apply dressings only if the victim must be moved. When fingers or toes are affected, separate the digits with sterile pads. Seek medical attention.

Infectious Diseases

Diarrhoea When diarrhoea results from ingesting toxins produced by bacteria growing on food, it is called food poisoning. Most diarrhoea, however, results from infection caused by consuming faecally contaminated food or water. Diarrhoea leaves you miserable, interrupts travel plans and can jeopardise the success of your trek. In other mountain areas of South Asia, bacterial diarrhoea has been found to cause 85% of travellers' diarrhoea. Giardiasis, often thought to be the most common, is responsible for only 12% and amoebiasis accounts for only 1%. The good news is that almost all travellers' diarrhoea can be effectively treated with antibiotics. Fluid replacement remains the mainstay of management. Taking frequent sips of liquid is the best approach. Diphenoxylate hydrochloride or loperamide can bring symptomatic relief, although neither treats the problem. Don't take them if blood or pus is present in stool. Because they keep the pathogens from passing through your gut, use them as a last resort to keep from dehydrating or when absolutely necessary (eg, when you have to travel). Infectious diarrhoea can be treated with antibiotics. Although a stool test is necessary to identify which pathogen is causing diarrhoea, the nature of the onset of symptoms is a useful diagnostic as to the cause of diarrhoea.

Bacterial Diarrhoea Although bacterial diarrhoea is self-limiting and will usually go away within a week, there's no reason to avoid treatment. Bacterial diarrhoea is characterised by its sudden onset, and is often accompanied by vomiting, fever and blood in the stool. You will probably be able to recall what time of day the diarrhoea began, and the symptoms will be uncomfortable from the start. Treat with either 400mg norfloxacin or 500mg ciprofloxacin twice daily for three days. Alternative antibiotics haven't proven useful in other Himalayan regions where 30% to 95% of bacteria are resistant.

Giardiasis The parasite responsible for giardiasis, *Giardia lamblia,* resides in the upper intestine and moves from host to host as nonactive cysts that exit the body with faeces. The cysts survive in streams and dust. This infection is characterised by a slow onset and a grumbly, gassy gut. Symptoms occur one to two weeks after ingesting the parasite. The symptoms may disappear for a few days and then return. This often goes on for several weeks before travellers decide to seek treatment.

The best antibiotic treatment for giardiasis is 100mg quinacrine three times daily for five to seven days. This drug, however, is often hard to get. The more common treatment is 2g tinidazole for two days. In the USA, metronidazole is used in a 250mg dose three times daily for seven days. Both drugs produce mild nausea, fatigue and a metallic taste in the mouth. Neither can be taken with alcohol.

Amoebiasis Caused by a single species of amoeba, *Entamoeba histolytica,* amoebiasis symptoms usually appear gradually, often over several weeks, with infrequent cramping and vomiting. The diarrhoea may come and go every few days, even alternating with constipation. It's not a self-limiting disease; it will persist until treated and can recur and cause long-term health problems. The treatment is 2g tinidazole daily for three days followed by 500mg diloxanide furoate three times daily for 10 days to prevent reinfection from amoebic cysts. In Pakistan, a combination of diloxanide furoate and metronidazole is sold as Entamizole DS. In the USA, treatment is 750mg metronidazole three times daily for 10 days.

Worms These are parasites that enter the intestines, consume digested food and its nutrients and lay eggs that hatch and multiply. They can be present on unwashed vegetables or in undercooked meat and you can pick them up through your skin by walking barefoot. Infestations may not show up for some time, and although they are generally not serious, they can lead to severe health problems if left untreated. Symptoms include upper abdominal pain, feelings of fatigue or hunger even when eating regularly, reduced quantity of, or irregular, bowel movements and spaghetti-like strands in your faeces. A stool test is necessary to pinpoint the problem and is not a bad idea when you return home. Treatment is 100mg mebendazole twice daily for three days. Mebendazole is very safe, with few side effects.

Fungal Infections To prevent fungal infections wear loose, comfortable clothing, avoid artificial fibres, wash frequently and dry thoroughly. If you get an infection, wash and dry the infected area daily. Apply a topical antifungal powder or cream with 1% tolnaftate. Try to expose the infected area to air or sunlight as much as possible. Wash all socks and underwear in hot water and change them regularly.

Hepatitis Several different viruses cause hepatitis, a preventable viral infection that causes liver inflammation, but differ in the way they're transmitted. Symptoms are similar in all forms of the illness and include fever, chills, headache, fatigue, feelings of weakness and aches and pains, followed by loss of appetite, nausea, vomiting, abdominal pain, dark urine, light-coloured faeces, jaundiced (yellow) skin and yellowing of the whites of the eyes. The incubation period is two weeks to two months. You're contagious before the onset of symptoms and for some time afterwards. Once jaundice appears, you're no longer infectious.

People who have had hepatitis should avoid alcohol for some time afterwards, as the liver needs time to recover. Hepatitis A is transmitted by faecally contaminated food or water. Seek medical advice, but there's not much you can do apart from resting, drinking lots of fluid, eating lightly and avoiding fatty foods and alcohol. Hepatitis E is transmitted the same way as hepatitis A, and can be particularly serious in pregnant women.

Hepatitis B, which has close to 300 million chronic carriers worldwide, is spread through contact with infected blood, blood products or body fluids. For example, it can be transmitted through sexual contact, unsterilised needles, blood transfusions or contact with blood via small breaks in the skin, which can even occur while having a shave. The symptoms of hepatitis B may be more severe than hepatitis A and the disease can lead to long-term problems such as chronic liver damage, liver cancer or long-term carrier state. Hepatitis C and D are spread in the same way as hepatitis B and can also lead to long-term complications.

Anyone suspected of having hepatitis can confirm the diagnosis with a simple blood test. Tests to detect hepatitis strains, which only differentiate types A, B and E, are only available at a few medical facilities in Pakistan's major down-country cities.

HIV & AIDS Human Immunodeficiency Virus (HIV) attacks the body's cells that protect against infections. A person infected with HIV may be asymptomatic, may have symptoms, or may have Acquired Immune Deficiency Syndrome (AIDS), a fatal disease. It's impossible to know if an otherwise healthy-looking person is infected with HIV or has AIDS without doing a blood test.

Any exposure to blood, blood products or bodily fluids may put an individual at risk of transmission. HIV/AIDS can also be spread by transfusions with infected blood. Pakistan only began screening blood at some hospitals in 1994; blood is still not screened at most facilities.

HIV/AIDS can also be spread by use of dirty needles. Immunisations, acupuncture, tattooing and body piercing can potentially be as dangerous as intravenous drug use if the equipment isn't sterilised. If you need an injection, ask to see the syringe unwrapped in front of you, or better still, bring a needle and syringe pack with you.

Rabies A fatal viral infection, rabies is caused by a bite or scratch from an infected animal. Dogs are noted carriers, as are bats, monkeys, wolves, foxes and cats. It's their saliva that carries the infection. Any bite, scratch or even lick from a warm-blooded, furry animal needs to be cleaned immediately with soap and water, and then with an alcohol disinfectant and antibiotic ointment. If any possibility exists that the animal is rabid, seek medical help immediately in order to receive a series of booster injections administered over a few weeks that prevent symptoms and death. Treatment can be difficult to get and is expensive, but be conservative in your judgment.

Tetanus A potentially fatal infection also known as lockjaw, tetanus occurs when a wound becomes infected by a bacteria that lives in soil and animal faeces, so clean all cuts, punctures or animal bites.

Viral Gastroenteritis As the name suggests, viral gastroenteritis is caused by a virus. It's characterised by stomach cramps, diarrhoea and sometimes by vomiting and/or a slight fever. All you can do is rest and drink lots of fluids. It typically lasts no more than one week.

Cholera The bacteria responsible for cholera are found in faecally contaminated water. The disease is characterised by a sudden onset of acute diarrhoea with 'rice water' stools, vomiting, muscular cramps and extreme weakness. You need immediate medical help. Treat for dehydration, which can be extreme, and if there is an appreciable delay in getting to a hospital then begin taking 250mg tetracycline four times daily. Ampicillin is an alternative drug. While antibiotics might kill the bacteria, remember that it's the toxin produced by the

bacteria that causes the massive fluid loss. Fluid replacement is by far the most important aspect of treatment.

Typhoid Enteric fever, or typhoid, is a dangerous intestinal infection with *Salmonella typhi* or *S. paratyphi* bacteria that travels the faecal-oral route. In the early stages, a victim may feel like they have a bad cold or flu on the way. Early symptoms are headache, sore throat and a fever which rises a little each day until it is around 40°C or more. The victim's pulse is often slow compared with the degree of fever present and gets slower as the fever rises – unlike a normal fever where the pulse increases. There may also be vomiting, diarrhoea or constipation. Typically, in the second week, the high fever and slow pulse continue and a few pink spots may appear on the body; trembling, delirium, weakness, muscle aches, bone-rattling chills, weight loss and dehydration are other symptoms. If no further complications develop, the fever and other symptoms will slowly go away during the third week. Seek medical help before this, however, because pneumonia (acute infection of the lungs) or peritonitis (perforated bowel) are common complications, and because typhoid is very infectious. Treat the fever by keeping the victim cool and watch for dehydration. Recommended treatment is 1g ciprofloxacin for 14 days. Chloramphenicol is an alternative drug that has been the mainstay of treatment for many years. In many countries it's still the recommended antibiotic but there are fewer side effects with ampicillin. The adult dosage is 500mg four times a day.

Upper Respiratory Tract Infections Colds, sore throats, sinusitis and bronchitis commonly occur on trek. Treat a cold with decongestants and analgesics. If it progresses to sinusitis, treat with an antibiotic. Sore throats can be soothed by moistening the throat with a lozenge or hard sweets (candy). This is particularly helpful when making long ascents and crossing passes. Bronchitis is characterised by a yellow-green sputum with fever and needs to be treated with antibiotics. Be cautious at higher elevations;

bronchitis can predispose you to AMS. Accompanying cough or complaint of chest pain may be indicative of HAPE.

Insect-Borne Diseases

Malaria Primary prevention of malaria is mosquito avoidance. *Anopheles bifurcatus*, the mosquito that transmits malaria, is a nocturnal feeder that bites from dusk to dawn. Trekkers are at greater risk in Pakistan's down-country cities where malaria is more prevalent. Pakistan's malarial season is July to August and November to December. During these periods travellers are advised to: wear light-coloured long pants and long-sleeved shirts; use mosquito repellents containing the compound DEET on exposed areas of skin and on clothing; avoid highly scented perfumes or aftershave; and use a mosquito net.

Malaria symptoms include headache, fever, chills and sweating that may subside and recur. Headaches, abdominal pains and a vague feeling of ill-health may be present. Without treatment malaria can develop more serious, potentially fatal effects. Malaria is treatable and can be diagnosed by a simple blood test, so seek medical help immediately when symptoms occur.

Typhus Spread by ticks, mites and lice, typhus begins like a bad cold, followed by a fever, chills, headache, muscle pains and a body rash. There is often a large painful sore at the site of the bite and nearby lymph nodes are swollen and painful. Lice are common where people live closely with sheep and goats. Always check your body and clothing carefully for ticks after walking through a tick-infested area. Ticks are rare, but not unknown in northern Pakistan. A strong insect repellent (with DEET) can help.

Traumatic Injuries

Sprains Ankle and knee sprains are common trekking injuries. To help prevent ankle sprains, wear an all-leather boot that has adequate ankle support. If you do suffer a sprain, immobilise the joint with a firm bandage, and relieve pain and swelling by keeping the joint elevated for the first 24 hours and, where possible, by using ice or snow on the swollen joint. Take analgesic or anti-inflammatory medication to ease discomfort. If the sprain is mild, you may be able to continue your trek after a couple of days. For more severe sprains, seek medical attention as it may be necessary to have an X-ray in order to rule out the possibility of a broken bone.

Major Accidents For large wounds with gaping skin, irrigate the wound with disinfected water to wash out any debris and an iodine solution to kill any bacteria. Tape the wound shut and bandage. For serious head wounds, open fractures and penetrating wounds, no treatment you can administer while trekking is effective. Administer antibiotics (250mg penicillin or erythromycin four times a day for five days) and evacuate the victim as quickly as possible. Treat for shock and use pressure to control bleeding. For extensive trauma when bones or tendons are visible, treat the victim for shock, use pressure to control bleeding, administer antibiotics and evacuate.

Cuts & Scratches Cleanse small wounds with soap and an antiseptic solution (Povidone or iodine). Apply a topical antibiotic ointment (bacitracin, neosporin, polysporin or mycolog) to disinfect wounds and prevent infection, and bandage to keep the wound clean. Keep the wound dry, and watch for swelling or redness around the wound, indicative of infection.

Bites & Stings

Bedbugs, Lice, Fleas & Scabies These pests are a major nuisance. If encountered, shake your bedding thoroughly and expose it to sunlight. Avoid sleeping in homes or herders' huts, many of which harbour these pests. Sleep in your tent rather than accepting invitations to share others' shelter.

Bedbugs found in bedding and bed frames are relatively large and leave itchy bites. Bedbugs come out when it's dark or when body heat is present. They can be difficult to spot as they disappear quickly when exposed to light.

Lice cause itching and discomfort and can cause typhus. Lice make themselves at home in your hair (head lice), the seams of your clothing (body lice) or in your pubic hair (crabs). You can see lice and may notice a small welt after they bite. You catch lice through direct contact with infected people, animals or bedding, or by sharing combs, clothing and the like. Powder, cream, lotion or shampoo treatment of 1% lindane (Kwell, Gamene, Gammexane) will kill lice and the many eggs or nits they lay. Other effective treatments are 1% permethrin (Nix) and pyretrins with piperonyl butoxide (Rid, XXX). These are toxic, so wash your hands thoroughly after using and avoid applying to your face or any broken skin. Washing infested clothing in very hot water may help, but doesn't always get rid of lice.

Fleas are tiny jumping insects whose bites itch for some time. Look closely in the seams of your sleeping sheet and bag and try to catch any fleas. You can also use a commercial pet flea collar. Put the flea collar in your sleeping bag before you pack your sleeping bag into its stuff sack. During the day, this kills any fleas that may have jumped in. Then, at night, take the flea collar out of your sleeping bag before you go to sleep.

Scabies is caused by a tiny mite that burrows under the skin, causing intense itching. The mites are too small to see. Use the same treatment as for lice.

Women's Health

Gynaecological Concerns Women often find their menstrual cycles become irregular or even cease while they travel. This is not uncommon when travelling or engaging in strenuous activities, such as trekking. Remember that a missed period in these circumstances doesn't necessarily suggest pregnancy. You can seek advice and get a pregnancy test at family-planning clinics in some cities and towns.

Poor diet, lowered resistance due to the use of antibiotics and even taking contraceptive pills can lead to vaginal infections, particularly in hot climates. Keeping the genital area clean and wearing loose-fitting pants and cotton underwear helps prevent infections.

Pregnancy If you think you might be, or know you are, pregnant and decide to go trekking, you should plan on extra time for acclimatisation. Most authorities recommend not travelling above 3500m while pregnant. It may be prudent to limit your trek to a week or two, keeping in mind the distance you'll be from transport and medical care if complications arise. Miscarriage is not uncommon and most miscarriages occur during the first three months of pregnancy, so this is the most risky time to travel as far as your own health is concerned. Spend the last three months of pregnancy within reasonable distance of good medical care.

Pregnant women generally should avoid all unnecessary medication, but inoculations and malaria prophylaxis can be taken. Avoid inoculations with live viruses, however, such as polio and measles. During the first trimester, cholera and typhoid inoculations are contraindicated. Consult your physician.

Oral Contraceptives There is a theoretical risk that side effects, such as blood clots in the legs or lungs, may result from taking oral contraceptives while spending extended periods of time at high altitude. No conclusive examples, however, support this theory. Women already taking oral contraceptives could face other problems, such as irregular bleeding or pregnancy, if they were to stop taking the Pill while on the trail. If you take oral contraceptives, discuss these issues with your physician prior to your trek.

SAFETY ON THE TREK

Trekking in remote mountain areas has inherent risks and uncertainties. Medical facilities are limited or nonexistent. The environment is inhospitable and the weather is unpredictable. Most treks are through sparsely populated areas where trekkers risk becoming lost or injured. A twisted ankle or a fall down a hillside can be life-threatening if you're alone.

To help make your trek a safe one, plan to be self-sufficient. Obtain the best available maps, recognising that many regions are not fully or accurately mapped. Be prepared for changeable and severe weather by carrying adequate clothing and equipment. Choose a trek that is within your range of physical ability and commitment. Always seek local advice on trails, routes, equipment and climate extremes before heading out. Be aware of your trek's objective dangers and pay attention on the trail. It's a good idea to assign a rear guard to keep watch on slower trekkers.

Promote mountain safety by following a few basic rules: don't trek alone; don't hike too high too fast; be law-abiding; don't trek in restricted areas without a permit; don't go higher than the government's 6000m limit; and register your name with your embassy or consulate before starting your trek.

Dogs

In Baltistan, Chitral (including Broghil and the Kalasha Valleys) and Yasin, herders keep dogs to reduce livestock depredation. These dogs are territorial, so exercise caution when approaching or entering walled compounds. If approached by a growling dog, pick up and throw or pretend to throw a rock and it will usually go away. A trekking pole can also come in useful. Dogs aren't kept in Gilgit, Hunza and Gojal.

Objective Dangers

The verticality of the mountains, the extensive glaciation and the lack of vegetation produce objective dangers on the trail such as exposure, rock fall on unstable scree slopes, river crossings, crevasses on glaciers and avalanche. Trails can be hard to follow, so route-finding skills and local expertise are essential. Recognition of these conditions and a sensible approach to them reduce any chance of accident or injury. People euphemistically term these conditions 'adventure'. They add excitement to trekking, but to keep your adventure from turning into a nightmare, it's important to be aware of your immediate surroundings and use proper techniques to reduce your exposure to objective dangers. If you have no experience with such conditions, or you

are at all uncertain of your ability to deal with them, hire a competent guide.

Scree slopes These common slopes can be 1500m high and more than 1km wide. These can take 30 minutes to cross. Before stepping onto any scree slope, look up carefully for any rock fall. Rocks fall any time, but be especially cautious when it's windy or rainy. Winds typically come up in the afternoon, so plan to cross scree slopes in the morning, if possible. Often it's necessary to traverse a scree slope one person at a time or in very close groups, so those waiting can watch for rock fall and warn those crossing. Be aware if a scree slope is above you, even if you are not walking directly on one. If any rock is falling, stop and wait until all falling rock has stopped. Check with any local person, your guide or porters before proceeding.

Stop and look for any trail across the entire slope. The scree will be more stable where footprints are visible. Often a left-right order to footsteps exists. Take footsteps in the correct sequence; don't cross your legs or you are likely to trip yourself.

If you're inexperienced walking on scree slopes, get out on one to see what it feels like. Take one or two steps to see how far, or if, you slide down as you walk. It's similar to walking on a sand dune. Make sure you are comfortable with this feeling before setting off to cross a longer scree slope. You want to be able to stand on the scree slope and to take a step up or down and feel some sense of stability. If you're hesitant, ask someone to take your hand. If they walk in front and support you, it's quite easy to hang on and to follow in their footsteps. Once you start traversing a scree slope, keep moving steadily and as quickly as possible. Don't panic if you slip. Walking on scree is a skill that gets easier with practice.

Local people usually use a walking stick. Hold the stick with both hands in front of you, keeping the long end of the stick on the uphill side of the slope. Lean into the uphill side if you feel yourself slipping. When descending a scree slope, use the stick like a rudder. Hold the stick to one side and lean back gently onto it for support and 'ski' down in a standing glissade. This is an amazingly effective technique that enables you to descend quickly. Ascending scree is slow and tedious. When ascending or descending scree, be careful not to kick rocks loose that may fall on, or in the path of, others. If rocks are sliding and falling, increase the distance between yourself and others for safety.

Talus Piles of large boulders, called talus, are common, especially on glaciers. Talus is usually unstable and always tiring and tedious to cross. A few techniques can make it easier. Test your foothold before placing your weight on it. Give the rock a little push; if it feels solid you can step on it, and if not, try another rock. Look several steps ahead to where you want to go. Pick out your route and figure out a sequence of three or four steps, rather than stopping on every rock to figure out your next step. You can use angled rocks for intermediate steps. You may not be able to stop and stand on such rocks, but you can step on them as you move to a flatter rock, thereby keeping your forward momentum.

River Crossings Always ask for current conditions. Footbridges over rivers often wash away in high water and may not be present where they once used to be, or may be missing essential parts. Be prepared to ford a stream or river if necessary.

Footbridges Infrequent or nonexistent on most trekking routes, footbridges may be constructed of any combination of logs, planks, rocks or dirt and usually don't have any handhold. Many bridges are poorly maintained and were constructed solely for one-time use to bring skittish livestock over a river when going to or from summer pastures. Take deliberate steps and watch for loose planks or rocks or for gaping holes in the bridge material. Even a short fall into a raging river can be fatal.

Cables & Pulleys When resources are unavailable to construct a footbridge, a cable may span a river's width. A small metal or wooden basket in varying degrees of repair may be suspended from the cable. A rope hangs beneath the cable and is used to pull the basket across the river. If the setup looks dubious, back it up by securing a short piece of 2.5cm-wide tubular webbing or rope to the cable with a locking steel carabiner. Don't use an aluminium carabiner on a steel cable since the friction destroys it. Secure the other end of the webbing or rope to the passenger with a carabiner secured to either a harness or equivalent. Secure backpacks and other loads to the basket and/or cable with a carabiner or rope. The rope used to pull the basket may be frayed, too short or nonexistent. Carry extra rope or tubular webbing in case an on-the-spot repair job is needed. When no basket is present, the local style of crossing is to grab the cable with both hands, and swing one leg up over the cable. A short rope is tied around the waist and secured to a steel shackle or wire loop around the cable for safety. Then the person pulls hand over hand across the length of the cable. Don't try this; instead rig a seat with a rope or harness.

Fording Rivers More often than not, you'll be getting your feet wet. Find the widest spot to ford where water is more shallow and flows more slowly. Always choose braided sections instead of a single channel. Water that is more than knee-deep may be too dangerous to cross. The deeper the water is, the more swiftly the current flows, and the greater likelihood that rocks or boulders are being carried downstream. Even small rocks can knock you off your feet or break an ankle or leg. Before fording, listen carefully for any rocks that may be rolling down the river. Don't cross if you hear anything; wait for a safer time.

River levels rise and fall dramatically, dependent more upon the daily weather than the month or season. Water levels are lowest in the morning and on cloudy or overcast days and are highest in the afternoon and on sunny days. When water is too high in the afternoon, wait until the next morning to cross.

Don't ford a river alone; cross with one or more partners, preferably with a local person. When crossing with one other person, position the stronger person upstream. When crossing with two or more other people, position the stronger people on either side of the person(s) in the middle. Avoid holding hands since this grip isn't adequate to support someone if they lose their balance. Try interlocking one another's forearms or upper arms or slipping your whole arm through the shoulder straps of your partners' backpacks. Use a trekking pole for greater stability and to probe the water before each step to find out the water's depth. Allow someone else to carry your backpack across the river if you're hesitant.

Take your boots off first; tie the laces from each boot together and put them around your neck. Don't carry your boots in your hands. If you lose your balance while crossing, you can't afford to risk losing your boots. Sandals with ankle straps or old training shoes protect your feet from rocks. Socks can help if the water is icy or if the crossing is very wide. Wear loose-fitting pants that you can pull up over your knees. When you know a crossing will be icy, deep or wide, or that you will have multiple crossings on a given day, wear long underwear bottoms for insulation. Unfasten any waist and chest straps on your backpack in case you fall and need to swim, requiring you to quickly discard your backpack.

Ford a river on a diagonal from upstream to downstream, crossing with the current. Don't cross perpendicular to or against the current. When the water level is knee to crotch deep and you must cross, you could use a rope for a handline though this can be dangerous (eg, avoid belaying a person across a river where it is possible the belay could trap a person under water) and is not generally recommended. Secure the rope across the river on a diagonal from upstream to downstream. When the current is swift, clip onto the rope with a locking carabiner and use a trekking pole or partner(s) for balance.

Men often insist on carrying trekkers piggyback-style across raging torrents, which may seem crazy, but it's almost tradition for younger men to carry elders and guests. Feel comfortable accepting this wonderful gesture. Consider anyone who offers to be very strong and capable.

Glacier Travel Most trekking involves some walking next to glaciers. Routes that traverse glaciers or cross glaciated passes are only for those experienced and equipped for route-finding on glaciers, camping on snow and ice, travelling in roped teams through extensive crevasse fields, using an ice axe and crampons, and knowing crevasse rescue.

The ablation valleys alongside glaciers are often the easiest routes up and down the lower sections of most glaciers, and also offer grassy camp sites and clear water. When you plan to walk on a glacier, hire a local guide to show you the best route, both on the glacier and to the exit and entry routes to camp sites in ablation valleys. When you go onto the upper, snow-covered section of a glacier where there are crevasses, it's necessary to rope up. Go with at least two other people, making a roped team of three or four people for a rope length between 40m and 50m. It's preferable to travel with two rope teams for safety. Use an ice axe or trekking pole to probe the snow for hidden crevasses. When you find a crevasse, you can either do an 'end run' around it, cross it under belay if it's bridged by snow, or jump it if you're prepared to self arrest. It's best to avoid traversing these sections when snow is soft, but to avoid postholing, try to distribute your weight evenly over the snow to prevent breaking through by either creating three points with a trekking pole or sliding on your hands and knees.

Glacier camping requires carefully probing the camp site in a grid pattern for hidden crevasses, and using wands to mark in a circle the perimeter of the safe, crevasse-free zone. Crevasse rescue requires use of rope, mechanical ascenders or prusiks, crampons and ice axe; essential gear for any trekking party crossing crevasse fields.

If you don't have this technical experience or gear, you can travel safely across such terrain only in the company of a trained, experienced and properly equipped guide. Never go onto a glacier alone. An explanation of proper techniques for glacier travel and crevasse rescue is beyond this book's scope.

Ropes & Knots Learn to use and tie your own knots before you actually need to on trek. Local people very rarely know how to tie secure knots. The basic knots are: figure eight (for tying into a harness at the end of a rope); water knot, also called ringbend or tape knot (to tie a length of tubular webbing into a runner); double bowline or double figure eight (to clip onto the rope); and a double fisherman's knot (to secure two dissimilar ropes). These knots are also useful when crossing a river via a cable.

Rescue & Evacuation

When rescue and evacuation become necessary, assess your situation and don't panic. Rescue doesn't always imply someone else coming to 'rescue' you. No search and rescue organisations exist in Pakistan, so you must be resourceful and not rely on others to get you out of trouble. On long treks, especially over glaciers, you may have to rescue yourself or a fellow trekker. Carry the proper equipment and know crevasse-rescue techniques.

Evacuation can mean shortening a trek because of a minor illness or injury, or responding immediately to a serious illness or injury. For minor illness or injury, a victim may be able to walk with assistance. When a victim can't walk, perhaps they can be carried on a porter's back or on a donkey, horse or yak. Helicopter rescue and evacuation can't be guaranteed and is to be considered only for life-threatening medical emergencies such as serious trauma caused by falling, rock fall or avalanche, or frostbite, serious illness or advanced AMS.

When someone in your party is injured or falls ill and can't move, leave somebody with them while another person goes for help. If there are only two of you, leave the injured person with as much warm clothing, food and water as it's sensible to spare, plus a whistle and torch. Mark the position with something conspicuous, eg, an orange bivvy bag or a large stone cross on the ground.

If you need to call for help, use these internationally recognised emergency signals. Give six short signals, such as a whistle, a yell or the flash of a light, at 10-second intervals, followed by a minute of rest. Repeat the sequence until you get a response. If the responder knows the signals, this will be three signals at 20-second intervals, followed by a minute's pause and a repetition of the sequence.

Helicopter Rescue & Evacuation Tourism Division no longer requires permit holders to post a bond for helicopter evacuation. Askari Aviation (Pvt) Ltd (☎ 051-5505760/62, fax 5590414, mobile 0300-502701, ✉ askarin@isb.paknet.com.pk) H59, Lane 2, Chaklala-1, Rawalpindi, a Pakistan Army-operated organisation, now coordinates and operates helicopter rescue. It requires a US$6000 up front, refundable cash deposit before it will fly. If you're carrying insurance that covers helicopter rescue, a trekking company or your embassy may agree to put up the cash bond in an emergency. Arrange this before heading out on trek. Askari also requires a pre-trek briefing at its office.

In these mountains, it isn't possible to radio for a helicopter once you're out there. Helicopter evacuations usually take more than 48 hours to arrange because of the remoteness of most trekking areas, poor communication systems and variable mountain weather. Helicopter landing or take off is very difficult or impossible at elevations above 5500m. Studies in the Nepal Himalaya show that severely ill or injured trekkers are likely to die before a helicopter arrives. For those who are rescued by helicopter, however, the survival rate is almost 100%. No statistics are available for Pakistan.

Helicopter evacuation may fail to save a life because of lack of details. Assess the need for a physician to accompany the helicopter and communicate this clearly with whoever is sent to request a helicopter. Detail the number of victims, their conditions and the degree of urgency of the evacuation (eg, is the patient unconscious?). This critical information may alter a pilot's decision to fly in marginal weather. Place names are confusing, so be explicit about the location and stay put for two days once you send a message. In order for the helicopter to land, there must be a cleared space of 25m by 25m, with a flat landing pad area of 6m by 6m. Don't mark the centre of the landing spot with materials or objects that can get caught in and damage the helicopter's rotors. Secure all gear. Erect a streamer or make smoke downwind of the pad to indicate wind direction. Helicopters fly into the wind when landing. In cases of emergency, where no landing area is available, a person or harness might be lowered. Take extreme care to avoid the rotors when approaching a landed helicopter. When you see a helicopter and haven't sent for one, don't wave at it. This avoids pilots having to make unnecessary landings and minimises their risk. If a helicopter arrives on the scene, use these conventions standing face on to the chopper: arms up in the shape of a letter 'V' means 'I/We need help;' and arms in a straight diagonal line like one diagonal of the letter 'X' means 'All OK.'

Getting There & Away

Flying is the most convenient way for trekkers to get to and from Pakistan. Travelling overland, although more interesting, is neither the quickest nor most practical.

AIR
Airports & Airlines
Pakistan has four international airports of interest to trekkers: Islamabad, Karachi, Lahore and Peshawar. Pakistan International Airlines (PIA, W www.fly-pia.com) is the state-owned airline.

Islamabad, the gateway to most of northern Pakistan's trekking destinations, is the most convenient city in which to arrive on international flights. Flying into Islamabad also avoids paying excess-baggage charges on domestic flights where a 20kg total weight limit applies. Only a handful of airlines, however, have rights to land here. Airlines that operate direct flights include PIA, British Airways, Emirates Airlines, Saudi Arabian Airlines and Xinjiang Airlines.

Most airlines fly to Karachi, Pakistan's main international airport. It offers travellers the cheapest air fares and the most scheduling options with frequent daily connections to Islamabad and Peshawar. As Karachi's law-and-order situation has deteriorated in recent years, it's best to schedule an immediate domestic connection to your final destination. If scheduling forces an overnight in Karachi, stay at one of the hotels near the airport instead of going into the city.

PIA, Indian Airlines, Saudi Arabian Airlines, Kuwait Airways, Singapore Airlines and Thai Airways International are the only airlines that operate direct flights to Lahore. From Lahore, it's easy to travel by air or road to Islamabad or Peshawar.

A few airlines, including PIA, operate several flights per week to Peshawar, but only from Dubai and Abu Dhabi.

Buying Tickets
An airline ticket can gouge a great slice out of anyone's budget, but you can reduce the cost by finding widely available discounted airfares. You need to buy carefully and flexibly to avoid paying additional fares or fees. For long-term travel, many discounted fares are valid for 12 months, allowing multiple stopovers with open dates.

When looking for bargain fares, go to a travel agency rather than directly to the airline. Airlines generally only sell published fares, although many offer discounted fares to Web surfers. Many travel agencies have Web sites, making the Internet a quick and easy way to compare fares. On-line ticket sales are no substitute for a travel agent who knows all about special deals, has strategies for avoiding layovers, and offers advice on everything from which airline has the best vegetarian food to the best travel insurance to bundle with your ticket.

Most travel agencies are honest. Paying by credit card generally protects purchasers from rip-offs, as most card issuers provide

Warning

The information in this chapter is particularly vulnerable to change: prices for international travel are volatile, routes are introduced and cancelled, schedules change, special deals come and go, and rules and visa requirements are amended. Airlines and governments seem to take a perverse pleasure in making price structures and regulations as complicated as possible. You should check directly with the airline or a travel agent to make sure you understand how a fare (and ticket you may buy) works. In addition, the travel industry is highly competitive and there are many lurks and perks.

The upshot of this is that you should get opinions, quotes and advice from as many airlines and travel agents as possible before you part with your hard-earned cash. The details given in this chapter should be regarded as pointers and not a substitute for your own careful, up-to-date research.

refunds if you can prove that you did not get what you paid for. Similar protection can be obtained by buying a ticket from a bonded agency, such as one covered by the Air Transport Organiser's Licensing (ATOL) scheme in the UK. After you have made a booking or paid your deposit, call the airline and confirm that the booking was made. It is generally not advisable to send money (even cheques) through the post unless the agency is very well established. Some travellers have reported being ripped off by unscrupulous fly-by-night mail-order ticket agents.

Better known travel agencies, such as STA Travel, which has offices worldwide, Council Travel in the USA and Usit Campus (formerly Campus Travel) in the UK, are not going to disappear overnight and offer good fares to most destinations.

If you purchase a ticket and later want to make changes to your route or get a refund, you need to contact the original travel agency. Airlines only issue refunds to the purchaser of a ticket, which is usually the travel agency that bought the ticket on your behalf. Many travellers change their routes halfway through their trips, so think carefully before you buy a ticket that's not easily changed or refunded.

If you plan to buy international airline tickets in Pakistan, shop around for travel agencies. Some discount published fares, but may not do so unless you ask. As elsewhere, airlines themselves don't always sell the cheapest tickets. Typically, travel agencies in Pakistan don't offer very big discounts on international flights. When paying for tickets in rupees, travel agencies and airlines may require a bank encashment certificate (at least for the full value of the ticket) issued in the same month as the month of travel. Others accept payment by credit card (no processing fee should be charged) or in US dollars and other major currencies.

Reconfirm your outbound international flights at least 72 hours in advance or the airline will cancel your reservation. When you reconfirm, make sure that the airline puts a reconfirmation stamp directly onto the ticket coupon and/or staples a hard copy of the reconfirmed reservation to your ticket. Many flights are overbooked and therefore proof of reconfirmation may become necessary.

If you don't have an outbound reservation, book a seat before your trek. If you wait until after your trek, it may take several days to get a confirmed reservation. When you plan to fly from Chitral, Gilgit or Skardu, allow a two to three-day buffer after your trek before an international departure. Due to security procedures, the reporting time for check-in is three hours for international flights and usually two hours for domestic flights.

Student & Youth Fares Full-time students and people under 26 have access to cheaper international fares and more flexibility to change dates, flights and/or routes. You have to show a document proving your date of birth or a valid International Student Identity Card (ISIC) when buying your ticket and boarding the plane.

Departure Tax
International departure tax, usually payable at check-in, costs Rs 400 for economy class, Rs 500 for business class and Rs 600 for 1st class.

The UK
Airline ticket discounters are known here as bucket shops. Despite the name, there's nothing under-the-counter about them. Discount air travel is big business in London. Advertisements appear in the travel pages of the weekend broadsheets, such as the *Independent* on Saturday and the *Sunday Times*. Look for the widely available free magazines, such as *TNT* and *SX*, outside the main railway and underground stations.

For students or travellers under 26, STA Travel (☎ 08701-600 599, W www.sta travel.co.uk) has an office at 86 Old Brompton Rd, London SW7 3LQ, and other offices in London and Manchester. Usit Campus (☎ 0870-240 1010, W www.usi tcampus.com), 52 Grosvenor Gardens, London SW1W 0AG, has branches throughout the UK. Both of these agencies sell tickets to all travellers but cater especially to young people and students.

Other recommended travel agencies include: Trailfinders (☎ 020-7938 3939), 194 Kensington High St, London W8 7RG; Bridge the World (☎ 020-7734 7447), 4 Regent Place, London W1R 5FB; and Flight-bookers (☎ 020-7757 2000), 177–178 Tottenham Court Rd, London W1P 9LF.

PIA has daily flights to either Karachi, Lahore or Islamabad. British Airways flies thrice weekly to Islamabad. Kuwait Airways offers the cheapest fares from London to Karachi (UK£310), Lahore (UK£362) and Islamabad (UK£362). Emirates Airlines flies Manchester-Lahore (UK£494) and Manchester-Islamabad (UK£494). Swiss Air flies Manchester-Karachi (UK£458).

Continental Europe

Although London is Europe's travel-discount capital, other cities also offer good deals. Generally, there's not much variation in air fares for departures from main European cities. All major airlines usually offer some sort of deal as do travel agencies, so shop around.

Across Europe, many travel agencies have ties with STA Travel, where cheap tickets can be purchased and STA-issued tickets can be altered (usually for a US$25 fee). Outlets in major cities include: Voyages Wasteels (☎ 08 03 88 70 04 within France only, fax 01 43 25 46 25), 11 rue Dupuytren, 756006 Paris; STA Travel (☎ 030-311 0950, fax 313 0948), Goethestrasse 73, 10625 Berlin; Passaggi (☎ 06-474 0923, fax 482 7436), Stazione Termini FS, Galleria Di Tesla, Rome; and ISYTS (☎ 01-322 1267, fax 323 3767), 11 Nikis St, Upper Floor, Syntagma Square, Athens.

France has a network of student travel agencies that sell discount tickets to travellers of all ages. OTU Voyages (☎ 01 44 41 38 50, ⓦ www.otu.fr) has a central Paris office at 39 ave Georges Bernanos (5e) and another 42 offices around the country. Acceuil des Jeunes en France (☎ 01 42 77 87 80), 119 rue Saint Martin (4e), is another popular discount travel agency. Travel agencies in Paris that offer some of the best

services and deals include Nouvelles Frontières (☎ 08 03 33 33 33, ⓦ www.nouvelles-frontieres.com), 5 ave de l'Opéra (1er), and Voyageurs du Monde (☎ 01 42 86 16 00), 55 rue Sainte Anne (2e).

Belgium, Switzerland, the Netherlands and Greece are also good places for discount tickets. In Belgium, Acotra Student Travel Agency (☎ 02-512 86 07), Rue de la Madeline, Brussels, and WATS Reizen (☎ 03 226 16 26), de Keyserlei 44, Antwerp, are both well-known agencies. In Switzerland, SSR Voyages (☎ 01 297 11 11, ⓦ www.ssr.ch) specialises in student and budget fares, with a Zurich branch at Leonhardstrasse 10 and branches in most major Swiss cities.

In the Netherlands, NBBS Reizen (☎ 020-624 09 89), Rokin 66, Amsterdam, is the official student travel agency. It has several other agencies around the city. Another recommended travel agency in Amsterdam is Malibu Travel (☎ 020-626 32 30), Prinsengracht 230.

In Athens, check the many travel agencies in the backstreets between Syntagma and Omonia squares. For student and non-concessionary fares, try Magic Bus (☎ 01-323 7471, fax 322 0219).

PIA and many other carriers have several flights weekly to/from Amsterdam, Athens, Frankfurt, Istanbul, Oslo, Paris, Rome, and Zurich to the Pakistan cities of Islamabad, Lahore and Karachi. Kuwait Airways has cheap fares to Karachi and Lahore from many cities including Munich and Madrid. One-way/return airfares from most of these cities start from US$790/1467. Sample airfares are: Paris-Karachi €1600/3022 and Paris-Islamabad €1700/3090; Frankfurt-Karachi €844/1534; Frankfurt-Islamabad €863/1568; Rome-Karachi €930/1659; and Rome-Islamabad €954/1700.

The USA

Discount travel agents in the USA are known as consolidators (although you won't see a sign on the door saying Consolidator). San Francisco is the USA's ticket consolidator capital, but good deals can be found in Los Angeles, New York and other major cities. Consolidators can be found through the *Yellow Pages* or the major daily newspapers. The *New York Times, Los Angeles Times, Chicago Tribune* and *San Francisco Chronicle* all produce weekly travel sections in which you find their ads. Ticket Planet (W www.ticketplanet.com) is the USA's leading consolidator.

Council Travel (W www.counciltravel .com), the USA's largest student travel organisation, has around 60 US offices. Call its head office (☎ 800-226 8624), 205 E 42 St, New York, NY 10017 for the office nearest you. STA Travel (☎ 800-781 4040, W www.statravel.com) has offices in Boston, Chicago, Miami, New York, Philadelphia, San Francisco and other major cities.

PIA flies via Europe from New York and Washington to Islamabad, Lahore and Karachi. Airfares are US$720/1250 one-way/ return. Kuwait Airways also offers cheap fares from New York. British Airways flies into Islamabad nonstop from London; air fares from New York cost US$1043/1390 and from San Francisco US$1181/1575. Thai Airways International and Singapore Airlines have Trans-Pacific service from San Francisco and Los Angeles to Karachi and Lahore; fares cost US$1031/1375.

Canada

Canadian discount air ticket sellers are also known as consolidators and their fares tend to be about 10% higher than those sold in the USA. The *Globe & Mail, Toronto Star, Montreal Gazette* and *Vancouver Sun* carry travel agencies' ads and are a good place to look for cheap fares. Travel CUTS (☎ 866-246 9762, W www.travelcuts.com), Canada's national student travel agency, has offices in major cities.

Australia

Many travel agencies specialise in discount air tickets. Some agencies, particularly smaller ones, advertise cheap airfares in the travel sections of weekend newspapers, such as the *Age* in Melbourne and the *Sydney Morning Herald*.

STA Travel (W www.statravel.com.au) and Flight Centre (W www.flightcentre .com.au) are well-known travel agencies for

cheap fares. STA Travel (☎ 03-9349 2411) has its main office at 224 Faraday St, Carlton, Victoria 3053, and offices in all major cities and on many university campuses. Call ☎ 131 776 Australia-wide for the location of your nearest branch. Flight Centre (☎ 131 600 Australia-wide) has a central office at 82 Elizabeth St, Sydney, with dozens more offices throughout Australia.

The cheapest fares are to Karachi with Air Lanka via Colombo. Return fares start at A$1340. Singapore Airlines has flights from Sydney via Singapore, which start at A$2188 return. Other connections are possible through Bangkok and Kuala Lumpur.

New Zealand

The *New Zealand Herald* has a travel section in which travel agencies advertise fares. Flight Centre (☎ 09-309 6171) has a large central office in Auckland at National Bank Towers (corner Queen and Darby Sts) and many branches throughout the country. STA Travel (☎ 09-309 0458, W www.sta .travel.com.au) has its main office at 10 High St, Auckland, and has other offices in Auckland as well as in Hamilton, Palmerston North, Wellington, Christchurch and Dunedin.

Return fares to Karachi start at NZ$1799 via Kuala Lumpur, and NZ$2059 with Singapore Airlines via Singapore.

East & South-East Asia

Most Asian countries offer fairly competitive airfare deals, but Bangkok, Singapore and Hong Kong are the best places to shop for discount tickets.

Khao San Rd in Bangkok is the budget travellers' headquarters. Bangkok has many excellent travel agencies, but also some suspect ones; ask the advice of other travellers before handing over your cash. STA Travel (☎ 02-236 0262), 33 Surawong Rd, is a good and reliable place to start.

In Singapore, STA Travel (☎ 737 7188), in the Orchard Parade Hotel, 1 Tanglin Rd, offers competitive discount fares for Asian destinations and beyond. Singapore, like Bangkok, has hundreds of travel agencies, so you can compare fares. Several are at

Chinatown Point shopping centre on New Bridge Rd.

Hong Kong has many excellent, reliable travel agencies and some not-so-reliable ones. A good way to check on a travel agent is to look it up in the telephone book: fly-by-night operators don't usually stay around long enough to get listed. Many travellers use the Hong Kong Student Travel Bureau (☎ 2730 3269), 8th floor, Star House, Tsimshatsui. You could also try Phoenix Services (☎ 2722 7378), 7th floor, Milton Mansion, 96 Nathan Rd, Tsimshatsui.

PIA flies to Bangkok, Jakarta, Kuala Lumpur, Manila and Singapore. One-way/return Bangkok-Karachi fares cost 17,360/33,020B. Thai Airways International flies Bangkok-Karachi three times per week and Bangkok-Lahore four times per week for US$216/431. PIA and Malaysian Airlines have once-weekly Kuala Lumpur–Karachi flights. Singapore Airlines flies thrice weekly Singapore-Karachi via Lahore for US$247/392; the fares are the same with connections from Manila or Kuala Lumpur. Cathay Pacific has three weekly flights Hong Kong–Karachi via Singapore for US$247/392.

PIA has two flights per week Beijing-Islamabad for US$711/875. Tokyo-Karachi fares cost US$999/1499.

South & Central Asia
Within Pakistan PIA and three private airlines, Aero Asia, Bhoja Air and Shaheen Air International, operate several daily flights to Islamabad and Peshawar from Karachi and Lahore. It's usually cheaper to wait and purchase domestic tickets for these flights in Pakistan, but it can be difficult to get reservations on short notice.

One-way airfares from Karachi to Islamabad or Peshawar cost Rs 3740; those to Lahore cost Rs 3146. Fares from Lahore to Islamabad cost Rs 1430; those to Peshawar cost Rs 1958. Flights between Islamabad and Peshawar cost Rs 770.

India Delhi is the centre of the real wheeling and dealing, although you can buy cheap tickets in Mumbai (Bombay) and Kolkata (Calcutta). Many discount travel agencies are around Connaught Place but, as always, be careful before handing over your cash. Always double-check with the airline to make sure that the booking has been made. STIC Travels (☎ 011-332 5559), an agent for STA Travel, has an office in Delhi in Room 6 at the Hotel Imperial in Janpath.

In Mumbai, STIC Travels (☎ 022-218 1431) is at 6 Maker Arcade, Cuffe Parade. Transway International (☎ 022-262 6066), 2nd floor, Pantaky House, 8 Maruti Cross Lane, Fort, is also recommended. Most of the international airline offices in Mumbai are in or around Nariman Point.

PIA and Indian Airlines fly Delhi-Karachi twice weekly, Delhi-Lahore four times weekly and Mumbai-Karachi five times per week. Malaysian Airlines flies Delhi-Karachi and Air Lanka flies Mumbai-Karachi. Flights to/from Delhi can fill up weeks ahead, so book as far in advance as possible. Typical one-way/return air fares cost: Delhi-Lahore Indian Rs 3240/5880; Delhi-Karachi Rs 4910/8920; and Mumbai-Karachi Rs 3960/7195.

Nepal PIA has once-weekly Kathmandu-Islamabad flights for US$168/304 one-way/return and Kathmandu-Karachi flights for US$253/461.

Central Asia Xinjiang Airlines schedules twice-weekly Urumchi-Islamabad flights for US$210 one-way. PIA has once weekly Tashkent-Karachi flights for US$393/714 one-way/return.

LAND
China
The Karakoram Highway (KKH) links Kashgar in Xinjiang, China to Islamabad via the Khunjerab Pass, the only border crossing. The Khunjerab Pass is formally open from 1 May to 30 November. Snow, however, often keeps the pass closed longer in the spring or closes it earlier in the fall. Pakistan's customs and immigration check post at Afiyatabad is open from 8.30am to 11am for departing foreigners, and as late as 4pm for people arriving from China.

NATCO buses depart Afiyatabad from 8am to noon for Tashkurgan (Rs 1380, five hours, 220km), the Chinese check post from where you continue in Chinese vehicles to Kashgar. Chinese vehicles take you from Kashgar all the way to Afiyatabad. The trip takes two days in either direction with an overnight stop at Tashkurgan. Between June and September as many buses as necessary operate daily; earlier or later in the year buses may not operate daily. You can also organise special hires. By jeep, you can travel from Kashgar to Afiyatabad in one long day.

India

The only border crossing, open from 8.30am to 2.30pm daily, is east of Lahore at Wagah (on the Pakistani side) or Attari (on the Indian side). The crossing, however, remains hostage to Pakistan-India relations, so get current information before heading there. You can cross by road or rail, although it's usually much quicker and easier by road (eg, Lahore-Amritsar in 3½ hours). On each side you clear immigrations, customs and security and walk across 100m of neutral territory.

No direct bus service operates between Lahore and Amritsar, but plenty of vehicles go to and from the border on both sides. Minibus No 12 costs Rs 11 and departs the Lahore railway station every 15 minutes all day long, taking one hour to Jila Mor (*mor* means crossing). From Jila Mor, another van takes you the last 5km to the border for Rs 3. Taking a taxi from Jila Mor may save you queuing with bus or train passengers. Taxis from the Lahore railway station to the border cost Rs 450.

An air-conditioned luxury bus from Lahore to Delhi (Rs 950 including breakfast, lunch and tea, 11 hours) departs from Faletti's Hotel (☎ 042-6311961) at 6am Tuesday, Wednesday, Friday and Saturday. A simultaneous Delhi-Lahore bus departs from Dr Ambedkar Terminal, Delhi Gate, New Delhi at the same time and days.

Regular train service operates between Lahore and Amritsar (Rs 60 economy class, Rs 120 1st class). Trains depart from Lahore at 11am Monday and Thursday, reach Attari in one hour, and arrive in Amritsar at 3pm. Trains depart from Platform 1 near the main Lahore railway station in an unlabelled shed-like building called *musāfir khānā* (traveller's house) some 150m to the right of the main station's entrance, just beyond a large pipal tree. All signs in both buildings are in Urdu, not English, so allow extra time to find your way. Trains depart Amritsar at 9.30am, arriving in Lahore at 2pm. The Lahore-Delhi *Samjhota Express* train (Rs 180 economy class, Rs 600 1st class) departs Lahore at 11am Monday and Thursday. Reporting time is three hours before departure.

Iran

The only border crossing is at Taftan, also called Kuh-i-Taftan (on the Pakistani side) or Mirjavé (on the Iranian side), between Quetta and Zahedan. The border is open from 9am to 5pm daily. A weekly Quetta-Zahedan train (27 hours, Rs 600 economy class, Rs 780 sleeper) departs Quetta at midday on Saturday and Zahedan on Monday mornings. Another train departs Quetta on Tuesday and Taftan on Thursday, and takes 34 hours.

Several buses travel daily Quetta-Taftan (Rs 480, 650km), from where frequent buses go to Zahedan (two hours). Check current information before you head for the border. Expect to spend at least four hours in Taftan. Take food and water whichever way you go. Anyone driving their own vehicle through the interior of Baluchistan is advised to travel in a convoy.

Afghanistan

Two decades of civil war means it's unsafe and almost impossible for foreigners to cross legally between Pakistan and Afghanistan. Typically, only Pakistani and Afghan nationals and UN personnel are allowed to cross the border either at Torkham (on the Khyber Pass along the road between Peshawar and Kabul) or at Chaman (on the road and railway line between Quetta and Kandahar). Afghan consulates in Quetta and in Peshawar may provide updates on current regulations. Any illegal crossing is a highly dangerous prospect with millions of unexploded landmines across the country, ongoing fighting and bandits. Foreigners have been kidnapped and killed.

TREKKING HOLIDAYS

Adventure travel companies market trekking holidays where all you have to do is show up fit and ready to go. This is the most expensive kind of trek, but it maximises your holiday time since all the 'work' of organising a trek is done for you. These companies advertise popular itineraries where you join a group of like-minded trekkers. It's an ideal option for single women and for those interested in meeting people with similar interests. Most companies also customise private treks. This is convenient when you want to travel with friends but don't want to join a large group, or are interested in a route not advertised by the company. All adventure travel companies work with Pakistani trekking companies. Therefore, the quality of services provided by the trekking company is crucial to your trek's success.

Many companies also book international flights. They answer pre-trek questions and are aware of difficulties in the region in which you plan to trek. They can help select a trek that's compatible with your interests and abilities. A single tour price usually includes hotels, transport and trek services.

Group trekking itineraries, while normally planned carefully, are essentially fixed. You're committed to staying with the group and following the itinerary. Itineraries usually allow extra days for acclimatisation or inclement weather, but minimal flexibility exists in case of illness. Trekking with a group can provide a support network in case of illness or accident. Many groups have a trip physician and resources for an evacuation if required. Large trekking parties tend to insulate trekkers more from local culture.

Before making a booking, ask how long the company has been in business and operated treks in the region. Ask about the tour leader's qualifications, degree of familiarity with the country, local languages and culture, and whether they have previously done the trek. Request references of previous clients who have done the same trek, or trekked in the region, or travelled with that company or tour leader. Avoid any company that's reluctant or unwilling to give references. A list of reputable companies follows.

The UK

Exodus Expeditions (☎ 020-8675 5550, 8673 0859, fax 8673 0779, ℮ info@exodus.co.uk, ⓦ www.exodus.co.uk) 9 Weir Rd, London SW12 0LT

Himalayan Kingdoms Ltd (☎ 01453-844 400, fax 844 422, ℮ info@himalayankingdoms .com, ⓦ www.himalayankingdoms.com) 18 Market St, Wotton-under-Edge, Gloucestershire GL12 7AE

KE Adventure Travel, Inc (☎ 017687-73966, fax 74693, ℮ keadventure@enterprise.net, ⓦ www .keadventure.com) 32 Lake Rd, Keswick, Cumbria CA12 5DQ

Continental Europe

Allibert (☎ 08 25 09 01 90, fax 04 76 45 27 28, ℮ info@allibert-voyages.com, ⓦ www.allib ert-voyages.com) route de Grenoble, 38530 Chapareillan, France

Beek Trekking Pakistan (☎ 0864-0 81 45, ℮ beek-trekking-pakistan@t-online.de, ⓦ www.beek-pakistan.de) Brem 3, 83246 Oberwössen-Chiemgau, Germany

DAV Summit Club GmbH (☎ 089-6 42 400, fax 6 42 40 100, ℮ info@dav-summit-club.de, ⓦ www.dav-summit-club.de) Am Perlacher Forst 186, 81545 München, Germany

Hauser Exkursionen International GmbH (☎ 089-2 35 00 60, fax 2 91 37 14, ℮ hauser@ hauser-exkursionen.de, ⓦ www.hauser-exkur sionen.de) Marienstrasse 17, 80331 München, Germany

ITMC – Germany (☎ 6201-3 37 15, fax 3 37 16, ℮ infos@itmc-germany.com, ⓦ www .itmc-germany.com) Heddesheimer Strasse 9, 69469 Weinheim-Ofling, Germany

Pineapple Tours Reisen GmbH (☎ 01-403 98 83 0, fax 403 98 83 3, ℮ office@pineapple.at, ⓦ www.pineapple.at) Währinger Strasse 135, 1180 Vienna, Austria

Seven C's (☎ 033-14 70 77, fax 14 70 30, ℮ ad min@sevenc.dk, ⓦ www.albatros-travel.dk/ov erseas) Bredgade 58, 1260 Copenhagen K, Denmark

Terres d'Aventure (☎ 08 25 84 78 00, fax 01 43 25 69 37, ⓔ terdav@terdav.com, ⓦ www.terdav.com) 6 rue Saint Victor, 75005 Paris, France

Trekking Y Aventura (☎ 91-522 86 81, fax 523 16 64, ⓔ mad@trekkingviajes.com, ⓦ www.trekkingviajes.com) Calle Pez 12, 28004 Madrid, Spain; (☎ 93-454 37 02, fax 323 52 88) Calle Gran Vía 523, 08011 Barcelona, Spain

Trekking Tours R Hoffmann (☎ 040-819 62 129, fax 819 62 135, ⓔ hoffmann@tth.de, ⓦ www.trh-reisen.de) Nagelshof 24, 22559 Hamburg, Germany

Viaggi Nel Mondo (☎ 06-588 0661, fax 580 9540, ⓔ info@viaggiavventurenelmondo.it ⓦ www.viaggiavventurenelmondo.it) Circonvallazione Gianicolense 41, 00152 Roma, Italy

Viajes Sanga (☎ 91-445 59 60, fax 445 60 54, ⓔ sanga@vsanga.com, ⓦ www.vsanga.com) Calle Donoso Cortés 36, 28015 Madrid, Spain

Zig Zag (☎ 01 42 85 13 93, 01 42 85 13 18, fax 01 45 26 32 85, ⓔ thierry@zig-zag.tm.fr, ⓦ www.zig-zag.tm.fr) 54 rue de Dunkerque, 75009 Paris, France

The USA

Concordia Expeditions (☎ 719-539 6687, fax 702-975 7075, ⓔ info@concordiaexpeditions.com, ⓦ www.concordiaexpeditions.com) PO Box 4159, Buena Vista, CO 81211

Explore South Asia Tours Inc (☎ 203-961 8194, 800-221 6941, fax 203-348 6489, ⓔ explorasia@aol.com) Abdul Aslam, 6 Pond Rd, Stamford, CT 06901

KE Adventure Travel, Inc (☎ 970-384 0001, 800-497 9675, fax 970-384 0004, ⓔ info@keadventure.com, ⓦ www.keadventure.com) 1131 Grand Ave, Glenwood Springs, CO, 81601

Peter Owens' Asian Treks (☎ 510-222 5307, 800-223 1813, fax 510-223 5309, ⓔ govindsh@himtreks.com, ⓔ petertrek@worldnet.att.net, ⓦ www.instantweb.com/p/peterowens) c/o Govind Shahi, Himalayan Treasures & Travel, 3596 Ponderosa Trail, Pinole, CA 94564

Snow Lion Expeditions (☎ 801-355 6555, 800-525 8735, fax 801-355 6566, ⓔ info@snowlion.com, ⓦ www.snowlion.com) Oquirrh Place, 350 S 400 East, Suite G2, Salt Lake City, UT 84111

Australia & New Zealand

World Expeditions (☎ 1300-720 000 Australiawide, ⓦ www.worldexpeditions.com.au)

Sydney: (☎ 02-9264 3366, fax 9261 1974, ⓔ enquiries@worldexpeditions.com.au), 3rd floor, 441 Kent St, Sydney, NSW 2000, Australia

Melbourne: (☎ 03-9670 8400, fax 9670 7474, ⓔ travel@worldexpeditions.com.au), 1st floor, 393 Little Bourke St, Melbourne, Victoria 3000, Australia

Brisbane: (☎ 07-3216 0823, fax 3216 0827, ⓔ adventure@worldexpeditions.com.au), Shop 2, 36 Agnes St, Fortitude Valley, Queensland 4006, Australia

Perth: (☎ 08-9221 8240, fax 9221-8238, ⓔ holiday@worldexpeditions.com.au), Suite 2, 544 Hay St, Perth, Western Australia 6000, Australia

Auckland: (☎ 09-522 9161, 0800-350 354, fax 09-522 9162, ⓔ enquiries@worldexpeditions.co.nz), 21 Remuera Rd, Newmarket, Auckland, New Zealand

Asia

Alpine Tour Service Co Ltd (☎ 0335-06 8411, fax 0335-06 8417), 5-F Shimbashi Towa Bldg, 2-13-8 Shimbashi, Minato-Ku, Tokyo 105, Japan

Country Holidays Travel Pte Ltd (☎ 334 6120, fax 337 4166, ⓔ enquiries@countryholidays.com.sg, ⓦ www.countryholidays.com.sg), 111 North Bridge Rd, #02-02 Peninsula Plaza, Singapore 179098

Himalaya Treks & Tours (Pvt) Ltd (☎ 075-491 3060, fax 491 4200), Sayed Sajaad Hussain Shahji, Kyoto Shi Kita, Ku Shichiku, Kamitake Dono Cho, 42-2, Japan T603

Independent Tours Centre (ITC) (☎ 0334-31 7497, fax 0334-38 1280), Tsukasa Bldg, 3-23-7, Nishi-Shimbashi, Minatoku, Tokyo 105, Japan

Saiyu Travel Co Ltd (☎ 03-3237 1391), Shinekai Bldg 5F, 2-2 Kanda Jimbocho, Chiyoda-Ku, Tokyo, Japan and (☎ 06-367 1391, fax 367 1966, ⓔ saiyu@gol.com), Kitagawa Bldg 5F, 6-4 Kamiyamacho, Kita-ku, Osaka, Japan

Getting Around

The easiest way to reach trekking destinations in northern Pakistan is to fly from Islamabad or Peshawar. The heavily booked flights are subject to delays and cancellations year-round, and many people choose to travel by road. All transport in Northwest Frontier Province's (NWFP) Chitral district and the Northern Areas is by road. Note that domestic transport up to Islamabad and Peshawar falls within the scope of the Getting There & Away chapter.

AIR
Domestic Air Service
PIA is the only airline operating flights to northern Pakistan's three airports: Chitral, Gilgit and Skardu. The Peshawar-Chitral (Rs 2825, 45 minutes) and Islamabad-Gilgit (Rs 2825, 1¼ hours) flights are on ageing, prop-driven Fokker F27 Friendships, which seat a maximum of 44 passengers. Flights from Islamabad to Skardu (Rs 2825, 1½ hours) are on a Boeing 737, and business-class fares are also available on this sector. The government subsidises the cost of these flights for its nationals and charges significantly higher fares for foreigners. Taxes from 10% to 15% are added to the one-way base airfares for foreigners listed above.

Northern Areas Flights PIA refers to all flights to Chitral, Gilgit and Skardu as 'Northern Areas Routes' or 'Northern Areas Ticketing' (even though technically Chitral is in NWFP).

Reservations Flights are always heavily booked, so at least one week's advance booking is necessary. It is advisable to work with a trekking company with a Rawalpindi or Islamabad office (see Organised Treks, p44) to book flights in advance of your arrival in Pakistan.

Bookings for Northern Areas flights are handled differently from bookings for other domestic down-country flights, because these flights operate subject to weather conditions year-round. During monsoon (July to September), perhaps only 30% of flights to Chitral and Gilgit and 50% to Skardu operate as scheduled. Delays of up to one week are not uncommon. Northern Areas fares are not discounted and flights can only be booked and tickets purchased at certain PIA offices in Pakistan.

Flights to Chitral are only handled at the PIA office in Peshawar (☎ 0521-273081, ext 230) in Saddar Bazaar. Go to the 'Northern Area Ticketing' office, which has a separate entrance on the left side of the building towards the rear. Flights to Gilgit and Skardu are handled only at the PIA office in Rawalpindi (☎ 051-5568071/8 reservations and ☎ 114 or 5567011 flight inquiry) on The Mall. Go to the Northern Areas section, which has a separate entrance on the right side of the building towards the rear.

You can buy an 'open' ticket for any Northern Areas flight anytime. Then, when you make a reservation, it's either confirmed or put on a waiting list. PIA gives priority to higher-fare-paying foreigners, so your chances of getting a confirmed reservation are much better than Pakistani nationals. Having a confirmed reservation is necessary, but it doesn't guarantee you will actually fly on a given day. Two factors affect this: backlog; and the weather. Backlog refers to passengers whose flights were cancelled in the day(s) preceding your flight and who are still waiting to fly. These passengers are given priority to fly on the next flights that operate. Regardless of whether you have a confirmed reservation, you have to wait for any backlog to clear. Unless you want to wait, it can be quicker to travel by road. If, however, there's no backlog and inclement weather cancels your flight, you know you will go on the next flight that operates.

Reconfirmation The day before your flight, go to the PIA office to drop off your ticket (usually before 12.30pm). Then, later that same afternoon (typically after 1pm or

2pm), you pick up your ticket. If your ticket is confirmed, PIA puts the next day's flight information in your ticket. If you aren't confirmed, your ticket is returned to you unchanged.

Flight Operation Call PIA Flight Inquiry before reporting to the airport. The final determination to operate any flight isn't made until shortly before the scheduled departure time. Reporting time for check-in is one hour before the scheduled flight time, but can be delayed and may not begin until PIA feels there is a good chance the flight can operate. Particularly in hot weather, Fokker F27s cannot get enough lift when they are filled to capacity. Hence, PIA may not fill every seat with passengers when a flight has a lot of cargo or may fill every seat with passengers and off-load cargo. A strict 20kg weight limit for baggage applies.

Cancellation Flights can be cancelled at any stage of the process. This can be before you report to the airport, after you have checked in and gone through security, even after you have boarded the aircraft. The most extreme case is after the flight has taken off. You can be 30 minutes into an hour-long flight, sipping milky tea, when the pilot announces that the aircraft is turning back! If your flight is cancelled and there are later flights scheduled that same day, you're given priority for the next flight. If there are no later flights scheduled that day, go back to the PIA office to reconfirm your seat for the next day. You can either try again for a flight the next day or ask for a refund and travel by road.

Helicopter Charters Advanced approval of each helicopter flight route is mandatory and takes about three weeks. A passenger manifest and photocopies of passports are also required at the time of booking. For security reasons, an army officer is on board each charter flight.

Askari Aviation (Pvt) Ltd (☎ 051-550 5760/62, mobile 0300-502701, fax 5590414, e askarin@isb.paknet.com.pk), H59, Lane 2, Chaklala-1, Rawalpindi, an army-run organisation, charters two types of helicopters:

the Allouette 3 at US$1085 per hour with a maximum of four passengers; and the MI-17 at US$1665 per hour with a maximum of 20 passengers. A 25% refundable deposit is required to make a booking. Charter costs are based on round-trip flying time from Islamabad. Approximate one-way flight times are: Islamabad-Gilgit, two hours; Islamabad-Skardu, three hours; Islamabad-Peshawar one hour; and Islamabad-Chitral 1¾ hours.

PIA charters 20-seat Russian-made MI-8 MTV helicopters with a 4000m ceiling. It costs US$2000 per hour, with a three-hour minimum charge. A US$1000 overnight fee applies with a six-hour minimum charge for any flights requiring an overnight stay. Contact PIA's Manager of Helicopter Services in Islamabad (☎ 051-815041, ext 225) or the PIA information officer (☎ 051-815041, ext 227/8).

Domestic Departure Tax
Departure tax for domestic flights, payable at check-in, is Rs 20.

ROAD
Travelling by road is gruelling – vehicles aren't usually comfortable, they're crowded, and many journeys seem to take forever. You may be crowded onto a bench seat with other people, or travel with livestock or vermin. The windows may be stuck, closed or missing, and the vehicle full of cigarette smoke. The suspension may make a bumpy road seem worse. Only a few main roads are sealed; the rest are unsealed. Vehicles travelling on sealed roads probably average no more than 30km/h, and vehicles travelling on unsealed roads only go about 15km/h. The mechanical condition of the vehicle may not be good, but more crucial to your safety is the driver. Private transport-company drivers may be driving with inadequate rest. Every year drivers fall asleep and plunge off the road at night. It's best to avoid overnight road travel. Travelling by road is, however, affordable, readily available between most towns, and the scenery is spectacular.

In NWFP, private transport companies operate vehicles between Peshawar, Dir and

Chitral. The government-run Northern Areas Transportation Company (NATCO) and several private transport companies operate buses between Rawalpindi, Gilgit, Skardu and Afiyatabad (Sost) in the Northern Areas. NATCO also operates services from Gilgit to Chatorkhand, Gupis and Yasin. Buses usually run on fixed schedules and are the cheapest transport, but they're also the slowest. Other vehicles usually depart only when full of passengers.

For treks that start or finish close to main roads, you can usually rely on scheduled transport, which is cheap and generally dependable. For more remote trailheads, you can take a jeep or hire your own vehicle. The type of transport you take depends on the trailhead for your trek and your budget.

Minibus, Van & Wagon

Twenty-one-seat Toyota Coasters run regional and long-distance routes. They're faster, more comfortable and slightly more expensive than buses, and usually operate from different stands. They usually have air-conditioning, although drivers rarely use it. 15-seat Toyota Hiace vans and old 15-seat Ford wagons are common on regional routes.

Pick-up Trucks

The most common short-haul transport is the converted Suzuki light-duty pick-up truck, which seats eight to 10 passengers on two rows of benches. Avoid Suzukis on longer trips since they are slow and don't have much power. Datsun and Toyota pick-up trucks are also common. Some 4WD pick-ups go to remote villages.

Jeeps

Jeeps are the most commonly used transport in northern Pakistan where unsealed mountain roads to remote villages, often referred to as 'jeep roads' in this book, permit nothing else. Jeeps have removable canvas rooftops and plastic sides that roll up and down. Jeeps are differentiated as either VIP, cargo or passenger. VIP jeeps cater to the tourist trade and are typically in superb condition. The driver of a VIP jeep typically allows a maximum of four passengers plus

baggage. In Hunza and Gojal, many jeeps for hire are VIP jeeps. Cargo and passenger jeeps are more common in Chitral, Ghizar, Diamir and Baltistan. These jeeps serve as the local form of public transport for remote villages and trailheads, operating on loose schedules and departing when full of passengers. Passenger jeeps may load as many as 20 people, all standing, into the vehicle. Cargo jeeps tend to be loaded well beyond capacity. Seating on top of the cargo, or perhaps standing, is first-come, first-served. Jeeps departing villages are usually loaded with passengers, and those returning from towns to villages are loaded with cargo. Be prepared for a dusty, rough ride and don't plan to reach a destination at any particular time. Throughout this book, 'jeep' refers to cargo or passenger jeeps.

4WD

Enclosed 4WD vehicles, which include Toyota Land Cruisers and Mitsubishi Pajeros, are much less common than jeeps. More importantly, 4WD vehicles are only available for special hires at a cost about three times higher than jeeps. An air-conditioned vehicle costs as much as Rs 3000 per day.

Road Distances in Northern Pakistan

Signs, maps, officials and drivers all give varying distances. The road distances in the table below (in kilometres) are probably accurate to within 5%. Distances for Rawalpindi are approximately the same as for Islamabad.

	Chitral	Gilgit	Islamabad	Khunjerab Pass	Peshawar	Saidu Sharif	Skardu
Chitral	---						
Gilgit	620	---					
Islamabad	382	564	---				
Khunjerab Pass	885	265	829	---			
Peshawar	304	565	167	830	---		
Saidu Sharif	216	406	243	671	159	---	
Skardu	790	170	734	435	735	576	---

Driving & Rental

Few foreign drivers bring their vehicles into Pakistan (and even fewer who do go trekking). Self-drive car rental is available only in major down-country cities. You can bring in your own vehicle, duty-free, for up to three months. You need a *carnet de passage en douane* (effectively a passport for the vehicle and temporary waiver of import duty), plus registration papers, liability insurance and an international driver's permit. Contact your local automobile association for details about all documentation. On entry, you sign a form saying you promise not to sell the vehicle in Pakistan. Traffic drives on the left.

When you hire a vehicle exclusively for your use, it's known as a 'special hire' or 'booking'. Renting your own vehicle, which comes with a driver, is easy to organise and is a common way to get to and from remote trailheads. This is the most expensive transport, but allows you to choose your departure time, determine rest stops and overnight stays, and is the only way to reach some trailheads. It's also possible to prearrange to be picked up at your trek's finish when there's no public transport. When you require a drop-off in a remote area, prepare to pay for the return journey as well, as the vehicle may have to return empty. If people are waiting for a ride at the trailhead when you're dropped off, be sure to negotiate with them directly. After all, you paid for it.

Internal Customs Checks

At police check posts along some roads in NWFP, the Northern Areas and on the KKH, foreigners are required to write their name, nationality and passport details on a register. It's appropriate that a woman ask the police to bring the register to the vehicle, so she doesn't have to get out. Sometimes these registers have been successfully used to trace a missing foreigner. Foreigners may be searched or questioned any time when in budget hotels, on public transport or on known routes favoured by smugglers.

It's cheaper to organise a special hire directly with the vehicle's owner than through a travel agency, trekking company or hotel. In some towns, such as Skardu, it's best to negotiate directly with jeep contractors who control most special hires. Payment is by day or by distance, or a combination of both. The longer you want it, the more leverage you have in negotiating a price. Typical rates for special jeep hires are Rs 300 per day or Rs 8 per kilometre on sealed roads and Rs 10 per kilometre on unsealed roads, plus Rs 300 per overnight on multi-day hires. Common destinations typically have a fixed price.

Some towns have special stands with for-hire Suzukis or jeeps, and you can often hire one right off the street. A special hire can be good value when sharing costs with others. Before you reach an agreement make sure the driver knows the road you intend to travel and the location of your final destination, and inspect the vehicle (ie, its tyres, including the spare, brakes, jack, tyre repair kit, tools and pump).

Reliable 24-hour rent-a-car services based in Islamabad's Blue Area that offer Coasters, vans, Land Cruisers, and cars are: Quik Tours (☎ 051-2274791/2, 2206993/4, fax 828115, e quiktour@isb.comsats.net .pk); Khurram (☎ 051-820427); Voyager Pvt Ltd (☎ 051-818855, 2276073, 2278030, fax 817812), 2–37 Fazal-e-Haq Rd in Sethi Plaza; and Riaz Travels (☎ 051-812782, 2218723, 2218967, fax 2218976), 87 Al Abbas Centre, Flat 7. Avis Rent-a-Car has offices in Islamabad (☎ 051-2270751), Karachi, Lahore and Gilgit.

Bicycle

Few roads are sealed, and the surface is typically rough with plenty of holes. The Karakoram Hwy (KKH) is in the best condition, but cyclists will find sections of road damaged by landslides, which means riding over gravel and rocks or carrying your bike across impassable sections. Unsealed roads are rough, challenging, mountain-bike rides. Beware of deep sand alongside large rivers. Cyclists report that unfriendly, rock-throwing children are a danger on the KKH south of Chilas.

Himalaya Nature Tours (see p45) in Gilgit is the only company that rents mountain bikes. It has some parts and can make basic repairs. Elsewhere, you have to be self-reliant. No permit is necessary to take a bicycle into or out of Pakistan.

Hitching

Hitching isn't entirely safe and isn't recommended. Travellers who hitch should understand that they're taking a potentially serious risk. Hitching is safer when travelling in pairs and letting someone know where you're planning to go. Hitching is possible for men, but it's highly risky for unaccompanied women.

Hitching strikes Pakistanis as odd. Bus fares are so cheap, no-one understands why you might want to bump along in a truck cab when you could be travelling more quickly and comfortably on a bus. You can signal drivers by holding your hand in front of you parallel to the ground and making a downward patting motion. If drivers have space they usually stop, but may ask for a fare. Some drivers have been known to offer lifts and then, on arrival, demand payment. Along the KKH between Gilgit and Afiyatabad, drivers usually pick up hitchers. Hitching on the KKH in Indus Kohistan is inadvisable.

LOCAL TRANSPORT

Fixed-fare Suzukis ply the bazaars in Gilgit and Skardu. They often don't have a conductor, so stomp on the floor or tap on the cab window to signal when you want out. There are also a few taxis in Gilgit and Skardu. The meter is usually turned off or broken, even in down-country cities, so settle on the fare before you get in.

Chitral

Tucked into Pakistan's north-west corner, Chitral is remote, isolated and completely surrounded by mountains. The Kafiristan range to the west and the Hindukush range to the north separate it from Afghanistan. To the east and south, the Shandur and Hindu Raj ranges separate Chitral from the rest of Pakistan. Chitral's wild alpine country, narrow forested valleys, ancient cultures and hospitable inhabitants impart a unique and charming character. Above its cultivated valleys tower snowcapped peaks, and from vantage points throughout Chitral, Tirich Mir (7706m), the Hindukush's highest peak, is visible. The Hindukush has 38 summits above 7000m, including Noshaq (7492m), Istor-o-Nal (7403m) and Saraghrar (7349m). Draped on the flanks of the peaks, a multitude of large glaciers disgorge torrents that all flow eventually into the Chitral River. From its densely forested southern valleys to its arid and open northern highlands, Chitral, perhaps because of its isolation, remains a trekker's delight.

HISTORY

Chitral has been populated for more than 3000 years. Under the Persian empire in the 5th and 4th centuries BC, the Zoroastrian religion was widespread. Later, under the Kushan empire, Buddhism took root and spread. Chitral's location south of the passes linking China to the West made it an important state along the Silk Route. By the 6th century, China's Han dynasty had extended its control to Chitral. In the 8th century, the Tibetans displaced the Chinese, but in the 9th century, Arab armies defeated Chitral's Buddhist ruler. In the 11th century, the Kalasha moved into southern Chitral, ruling up to the present-day town of Reshun. Upper Chitral was ruled by Kho kings whose power extended to Gilgit. The Chaghatai Khan rulers of Kashgar extended their supremacy over Chitral and Yasin in the 16th century, and Islam began to take hold. In the 17th century, Chitral was invaded from neighbouring

Badakshan. The Kalasha were defeated and the so-called Rais dynasty established itself in Chitral and Yasin. Islam spread under this dynasty, which continued until the 18th century when it was displaced by the Katur dynasty, which claimed descent from the Mongol emperor Timur.

Two Katur brothers, Muhtaram Shah and Kushwaqt, divided the state, with southern

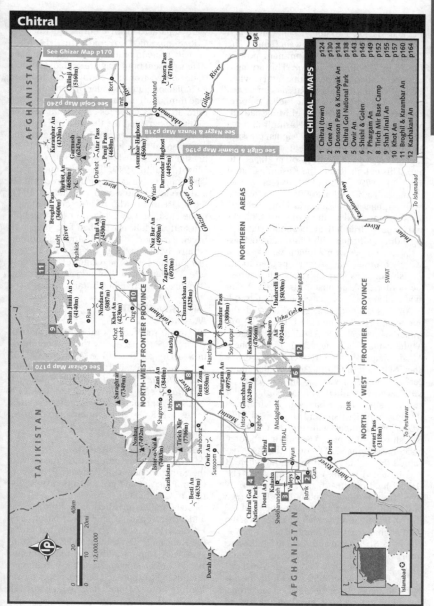

Chitral

See Ghizar Map p170

AFGHANISTAN

See Gojal Map p240

Chilinji An (5166m)

Kumbar An (4320m)
Garmush (6243m)
Atar Pass
Darkot Pass (4688m)

Broghil Pass (3800m)
Darkot An (4650m)
Punji Pass (4600m)

Lasht
Yishkist

River

Thui An (4500m)
Darkot

Asumbar Haghost (4560m)

Darmodar Haghost (4495m)

Yasin

Gupis

River Ghizar

See Nagyr & Hunza Map p218

Gilgit

Imit

River

Chatorkhand

Ishkoman

Pakora Pass (4710m)

Bort

See Gilgit & Diamir Map p196

NORTHERN
AREAS

To Islamabad

Karakoram Hwy

TAJIKISTAN

Saraghrar (7349m)

Naz Bar An (4980m)

Zagaro An (4920m)

Shah Jinali An (4140m)

Nizhdaru An (5087m)

Khot An (4230m)

Dizg

10

Khot
Lasht

Chumarkhan An (4328m)

Mastuj

Yarkhun

Shandur Pass (3800m)

Sor Laspur

Dadarelli An (5030m)

Machiangos

NORTH-WEST FRONTIER PROVINCE

See Ghizar Map p170

9

11

Rua

Noshaq (7492m)
Istor-o-Nal (7403m)

Zani An (3840m)

Shagrom

Uthool

River

8

Bumi Zom (6550m)

Harchin

Kachakani An (4766m)

Bashkaro An (4924m)

Ushu Gol

12

SWAT

Indus River

To Islamabad

Gazikistan

Besti An (4633m)

Tirich Mir (7706m)

Shahbronz

Pharghan An (4975m)
Ghuchhar Sar (6249m)

Istor

Izghor

Madaglasht

NORTH - WEST

DIR

Lowari Pass (3118m)

To Peshawar

Owir An (4760m)

Sussoom

5

Shagrom

Chitral

1

CHITRAL

Ayun

FRONTIER PROVINCE

Chitral Gol National Park

Dooni An

Shekhanandeh

Kalasha

4

3

Valleys

2

Batrik

Guru

Drosh

Chitral River

AFGHANISTAN

Dorah An

40km
20ml

1:2,000,000

0   10   20
0   20   40km

Islamabad

Chitral, Mulkho and Turikho going to the former and Mastuj, Yarkhun, Yasin, Ghizar and Ishkoman going to the Kushwaqt family. The Katur ruler became the dominant power, known by the title of *mehtar*. This arrangement continued into the 19th century, when the British, anxious about Russian advances towards the borders of their Indian empire, learned that Mehtar Aman ul Mulk had approached the Maharaja of Kashmir about a possible treaty to counteract Afghan pressure on Chitral. They advised the maharaja to accept and suggested the basis of an alliance to him. This culminated in the Kashmir-Chitral treaty of 1879. Aman ul Mulk received an annual subsidy of Rs 8000 and protection from Afghan aggression. Kashmir received his allegiance and a tribute of horses, hawks and hounds. Britain then set about establishing a direct alliance with Chitral and demarcating the border with Afghanistan. Aman ul Mulk's brother, Sher Afzal, opposed to the British and Kashmir alliances, fled across the border to Afghanistan. In 1892, Aman died and a bloody succession fight ensued.

Aman's second son, Afzal, seized the throne and Nizam, the eldest, fled to Gilgit. Aman's brother Sher Afzal returned from Afghanistan and murdered his nephew Afzal. Nizam returned from Gilgit and drove Sher Afzal out of Chitral, but was then murdered by his own younger brother Amir ul Mulk, who was allied with the Afghan ruler of Dir state, Umra Khan. Umra Khan was strongly anti-British, and the exiled Sher Afzal joined forces with him to throw the British out of Chitral. A small British force under the command of George Robertson occupied the mehtar's fort in Chitral where it was besieged by the Chitral partisans. The British held out for 46 days until relief arrived from Peshawar and Gilgit. The Siege of Chitral, as it became known, captured the British imagination as a heroic exploit on the wild Afghan frontier. George Robertson was knighted, Sher Afzal and Amir ul Mulk were imprisoned and eventually died in South India, and Umra Khan fled to Afghanistan.

The British placed Shuja ul Mulk, the 14-year-old son of Aman ul Mulk, on the throne, but only gave him Chitral, Mulkho and Turikho to rule. Mastuj, Yasin and Ghizar were separated from Chitral and ruled by British-appointed governors. In 1914, Mastuj was reincorporated into Chitral and the state's present borders were settled. Chitral's trade shifted from a Central Asian focus to an Indian orientation under British influence. One third of all exports were opium, and one third of all tax revenues came from hashish. Shuja was granted the title of His Highness in 1919 with a personal salute of 11 guns and a substantial subsidy. Shuja ruled until 1936, his son Nasir until 1943, and Nasir's brother Muzaffar until 1949. These mehtars abolished oppressive taxes, opened free schools and brought Chitral into Pakistan in 1947. Saifur Rehman, Muzaffar's son, died in a plane crash on Lowari Pass in 1954 and his son Saif ul Mulk Nasir, then five years old, became mehtar. In 1969, Chitral was administratively merged with the rest of Pakistan, bringing an end to the centuries of princely rule. The large family of princes remains influential and active in Chitral's affairs.

INFORMATION
Maps

No single map covers all or even most of Chitral, so it's necessary to use a combination of maps: the US AMS Series U502 India and Pakistan 1:250,000 topographic maps *Churrai (NI 43-1)*, *Mastuj (NJ 43-13)* and *Baltit (NJ 43-14)*; and the 1942 US AMS Afghanistan – NW Frontier Province series 1:253,400 topographic maps *Chitral (I-42F)* and *Zebak (J-42X)*.

Permits & Regulations

All foreigners are required to register with the Superintendent of Police (SP) when in Chitral district and get a Temporary Registration Certificate.

Local police jurisdictions in border areas and other sensitive spots (eg, North-west Frontier Province's (NWFP) tribal areas, the Kalasha Valleys, Swat and Kalam Kohistan) may impose additional requirements. Border police stop and arrest any foreigners attempting to approach and cross any passes leading into Afghanistan, which are all strictly off limits.

CHITRAL

Once the capital of a princely state, Chitral (1518m) is now the administrative seat for NWFP's Chitral district. Along the Chitral River, it has long been a trade centre. Although trade with Afghanistan has largely halted, the occasional mule-load of lapis lazuli from the Badakshan mines still makes its way through Chitral to Peshawar markets. Afghans, including refugees and Taliban partisans of Afghanistan's ongoing civil war, are now a fixture of the bazaar. Tirich Mir's snowy summit provides a dramatic backdrop to the town and surrounding wooded hills.

Information Sources

The PTDC Information Centre (☎ 0933-412683) is at the PTDC Chitral Motel (p125).

Supplies & Equipment

It's difficult, if not impossible, to buy enough food here to outfit a trek, so bring it with you. Little is available in villages. Shops in Shahi Bazaar and Naya Bazaar sell stoves, shoes, barrels, fuel containers and cooking equipment. Also check with Hindukush Trails at the Mountain Inn.

Places to Stay & Eat

Most hotels need advance notice to prepare food. Near PIA Chowk and Ataliq Bridge,

---

Warning

When travelling through tribal areas (eg, Malakand and Khyber Agency), Pakistani law has little force and government authorities are almost powerless to help you. Since the early 1990s, fundamentalist Islamic groups have forcibly brought their demand for total enforcement of Shariat Law (Koranic laws and courts) to Malakand, Swat and Dir. When you travel through these areas act and look like a sympathetic traveller in the Islamic world. Men may be expected to have a full beard, but no moustache. Women are advised to wear a burqa in public. It's easier to wander into trouble in Indus Kohistan. Trekkers are advised to stay out of Darel, Tangir and Kandia valleys, where they may be unwelcome intruders.

Afghans run *teashops* and *tandoor ovens* that offer fresh hot bread at meal times. In late summer, nearly invisible sandflies are a nuisance; cover your arms and ankles when sitting outside in the evening. Mid-range and top-end hotels have hot running water in attached bathrooms.

Budget In Ataliq Bazaar, *Garden Hotel* has a Rs 25 camping fee for sites on a lawn near the river and Rs 30 charpoys in uninviting rooms, but it's inappropriate for Western women.

Few budget hotels cater to foreigners, although all welcome them. All have charpoys; some have beds. Most rooms have an attached bathroom with toilet and tap with cold water, and buckets of hot water available on request. Across from Allied Bank, *Al-Farooq Hotel* (☎ 0933-412726, 412509, Naya Bazaar) has singles/doubles/triples with attached bathrooms and morning hot running water for Rs 100/200/300. Popular and friendly, it has nice views from terraces on each floor. Behind it is *Lasani Restaurant*. Near Ataliq Bridge, *Fairland Hotel & Restaurant* has a dorm that costs Rs 30 and rooms for Rs 100/150/200. *Hotel Savanna* (☎ 0933-412294), off Jami' Masjid Rd, has reasonably clean singles without bathroom (Rs 50). Singles/doubles with attached bathroom and hot water are Rs 75/100, all built around a central car park. *Chitral City Tower* (☎ 0933-412912, Jami' Masjid Rd), has good rooftop views. Rooms cost Rs 100/200/300, or Rs 200/300/400 with a view. *Hotel Tourist Lodge* (☎ 0933-412452, Jami' Masjid Rd), offers shabby rooms for Rs 150/200/300.

The following all-male establishments are inappropriate for Western women. On the 2nd floor next to Hotel Savanna, *Mastuj Hotel* is managed by Wazir Khan from Gazin. Singles/doubles cost Rs 100/150. *Chitral Luxuary Hotel*, behind Al-Farooq Hotel, has uninviting Rs 35 charpoys and rooms for Rs 70. *YZ Hotel* (☎ 0933-412690), above PIA Chowk, faces a small garden. Rooms cost Rs 80/100. *Damdam Hotel*, behind Hotel Savanna, is friendly, but rock bottom; charpoys cost Rs 20. *Pakistan Hotel &*

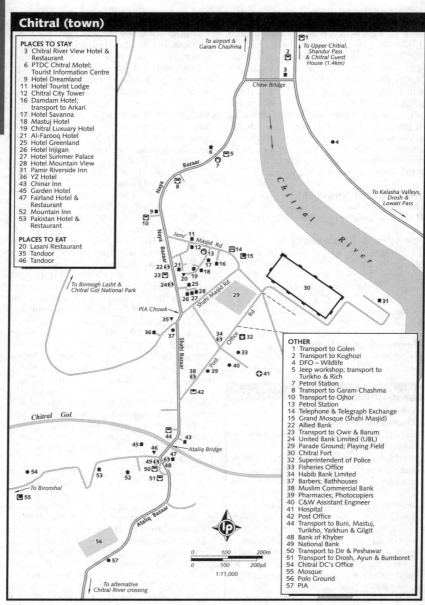

Chitral (town)

PLACES TO STAY
3 Chitral River View Hotel & Restaurant
6 PTDC Chitral Motel; Tourist Information Centre
9 Hotel Dreamland
11 Hotel Tourist Lodge
12 Chitral City Tower
16 Damdam Hotel; transport to Arkari
17 Hotel Savanna
18 Mastuj Hotel
19 Chitral Luxuary Hotel
21 Al-Farooq Hotel
25 Hotel Greenland
26 Hotel Injigan
27 Hotel Summer Palace
28 Hotel Mountain View
31 Pamir Riverside Inn
36 YZ Hotel
43 Chinar Inn
45 Garden Hotel
47 Fairland Hotel & Restaurant
52 Mountain Inn
53 Pakistan Hotel & Restaurant

PLACES TO EAT
20 Lasani Restaurant
35 Tandoor
46 Tandoor

OTHER
1 Transport to Golen
2 Transport to Koghozi
4 DFO – Wildlife
5 Jeep workshop; transport to Turikho & Rich
7 Petrol Station
8 Transport to Garam Chashma
10 Transport to Ojhor
13 Petrol Station
14 Telephone & Telegraph Exchange
15 Grand Mosque (Shahi Masjid)
22 Allied Bank
23 Transport to Owir & Barum
24 United Bank Limited (UBL)
29 Parade Ground; Playing Field
30 Chitral Fort
32 Superintendent of Police
33 Fisheries Office
34 Habib Bank Limited
37 Barbers; Bathhouses
38 Muslim Commercial Bank
39 Pharmacies; Photocopiers
40 C&W Assistant Engineer
41 Hospital
42 Post Office
44 Transport to Buni, Mastuj, Turikho, Yarkhun & Gilgit
48 Bank of Khyber
49 National Bank
50 Transport to Dir & Peshawar
51 Transport to Drosh, Ayun & Bumboret
54 Chitral DC's Office
55 Mosque
56 Polo Ground
57 PIA

To airport & Garam Chashma

To Upper Chitral, Shandur Pass & Chitral Guest House (1.4km)

Chew Bridge

Chitral River

To Kalasha Valleys, Drosh & Lowari Pass

Bazaar

Naya Bazaar

Jami' Masjid Rd

To Birmogh Lasht & Chitral Gol National Park

PIA Chowk

Shahi Masjid Rd

Shahi Bazaar

Office Rd

Post Office Rd

Chitral Gol

To Bironshal

Ataliq Bridge

Ataliq Bazaar

To alternative Chitral River crossing

0   100   200m
0   100   200yd
1:11,000

Restaurant (Ataliq Bazaar) has rooms with two or three charpoys for Rs 80. *Hotel Mountain View* (☎ 0933-412559), *Hotel Summer Palace* and *Hotel Injigan* are all in a row in an alley off Naya Bazaar across from United Bank Limited. These grimy three-storey buildings lack charm, but offer rooftop views. Doubles cost Rs 100. *Hotel Greenland*, nearby in the same alley, is comparable. *Chitral River View Hotel & Restaurant* (☎ 0933-413416), east of Chew Bridge on the river's left bank, is a Pathan-run dive with Rs 20 charpoys.

Mid-Range Near Ataliq Bridge *Chinar Inn* (☎ 0933-412582, *Shahi Bazaar*) has doubles that cost Rs 250; ones with carpeting cost Rs 300. The place has well-kept rooms, a small garden and a peaceful atmosphere off the road. *Hotel Dreamland* (☎ 0933-412614, 412806, fax 412770, Airport Rd) in Naya Bazaar has rooms around a cool, shady courtyard with rooftop views. Singles/doubles cost Rs 250/350, and carpeted rooms cost Rs 350/550.

Top End A favourite for old Chitral hands, *Mountain Inn* (☎ 0933-412581, 412800, 412781, fax 412668, e mountain@inn.isb .sdnpk.org, Ataliq Bazaar) has friendly, helpful staff. The relaxing, sheltered garden is tended by its gracious owner, Haider Ali Shah. Singles/doubles/suites cost Rs 600/800/900. Deluxe rooms cost Rs 1000/1200/1500. *Pamir Riverside Inn* (☎ 0933-412525, fax 413365) is the former guest quarters of the Mehtar of Chitral in a peaceful, cooler location along the river beyond the fort. A handball/squash court is available. Single/double cottages with TV cost Rs 800/1000; deluxe ones cost Rs 1500/2000. *PTDC Chitral Motel* (☎ 0933-412683, Naya Bazaar), costs Rs 1250/1500. *Chitral Guest House* (☎ 0933-413077, 412461), Danin Shandoor Rd 1.5km north of Chew Bridge on its east side, is set around a garden and costs Rs 1200/1500. *Hindu Kush Heights*, in Dalamutz 10 minutes' drive north of the airport, is Chitral's most luxurious property, built with traditional architecture on a panoramic ridge. Rooms cost Rs 2300/2800.

Getting There & Away

Chitral can be reached by air or road, although its only road links with the rest of Pakistan are two unsealed roads, one from Peshawar and one from Gilgit.

Air PIA schedules three daily Peshawar-Chitral flights (Rs 2825). The first two daily flights originate in Peshawar and, hence, are more reliable than the third flight, whose aircraft comes from Islamabad. The PIA office (☎ 0933-412863, 412963) is in Ataliq Bazaar.

Road The road between Peshawar and Chitral crosses the Lowari Pass (3118m), which is usually open 15 May to 15 November. Snow may keep the pass closed longer in the spring or close it earlier in the fall. The road is subject to blockage by avalanche until June.

Peshawar Peshawar-bound vehicles depart from Chitral's Ataliq Bazaar (Rs 250–260, 10 hours). It's fastest in jeeps and small vehicles. Wagons and Coasters go to Peshawar's Qissa Khawani Bazaar and GTS bus stand or Haji Camp on GT Rd. If your destination is Swat, get off in Dir and transfer onto a Swat-bound bus. Transport between Chitral and Dir costs Rs 150 for Coasters and Rs 180 for jeeps. Chitral-Dir special hires cost Rs 1600. In sometimes xenophobic Dir, *Al Mansur Hotel*, owned by Rauf, is the only reliable place for meals, rooms and organising transport.

Peshawar-Chitral wagons cost Rs 250 and depart from Peshawar's Spogmey Hotel at 8pm, Chitrali Bazaar at 8pm, and the Sultan Hotel in Qissa Khawani Bazaar at 8pm. Peshawar-Chitral Coasters (Rs 260) depart Haji Camp at 8pm.

Gilgit No public transport operates between Gilgit and Chitral across the Shandur Pass (3800m), which is usually open 1 June to 15 November. Access to the pass can be blocked by avalanches on either side for longer periods of time.

continued on p136

KALASHA VALLEYS

Kalasha are the only non-Muslim people left in the Hindukush. About 3000 Kalasha still practice their pre-Islamic religion. 'Kalash', which has negative connotations, is the Chitrali word for the Kalasha. Birir, Bumboret and Rumbur are the common Khowar names for three valleys inhabited by the Kalasha. In Kalashamun, the language of the Kalasha, Birir is called Biriyoo, Rumbur is called Roghmo, and Bumboret is more accurately pronounced as Bomboret. These valleys lie south and west of Chitral town, and west of the Chitral River.

Kalasha are subsistence farmers who herd goats in pastures. Their fields, while irrigated, are not terraced. Villages are just above fields, at the base of rocky hills. The flat-roofed houses are tightly clustered. Carved wooden figures of Kalasha men, standing or mounted on horse, are called *gandao*, and honour ancestors. These are now scarce, most having been removed by collectors and museums.

Below: Kalasha boys in school uniform, Bumboret, Kalasha Valleys.

Since the construction of roads into the Kalasha Valleys in the 1970s, tourists have flocked to see the last survivors of an ancient culture. Unfortunately, some tourists, particularly Pakistani men, leer and gawk at the unveiled Kalasha women. Tourism is often promoted with little regard for the sensibilities of the Kalasha people, and much of the income generated from tourism never reaches them. In addition, Muslim and Christian missionaries are working to convert young Kalasha. The Kalasha want roads, bridges and hospitals, but they don't want interference in their culture or religion. They want to be asked before development projects are brought to the valleys, and for those projects to work through Kalasha village organisations.

When visiting, be sensitive to their condition and try to ensure that at least some financial benefit goes to Kalasha. Some English-speaking Kalasha men are happy to tell you more about their culture. Trekking from valley to valley offers the opportunity to travel with the Kalasha, and to get to know, respect and appreciate them and their land.

RICHARD I'ANSON

Religion

Kalasha religion may represent a branch of the Vedic religion that entered the Indian subcontinent through the Hindukush more than 3000 years ago, and until the late 19th century was widespread throughout the region. Kalasha believe in one god, the creator *dezau*. Their other *dewa* (gods) function like messengers between Dezau and the Kalasha.

The two principles of their religion are the 'pure' (*onjesta*) and 'impure' *(pragata)*. Altars for the gods, the mountains, and their goats are examples of the pure, whereas the valley floor and the *bashali*, or women's birthing and menstrual house, are examples of the impure. For Kalasha, these two realms meet at the *jestak han*, the house of jestak, the female deity of hearth and home in a Kalasha village. The skylight opening in the ceiling of the jestak han is the place where a mythological iron pillar connects heaven and the underworld. Its doorway is flanked by wooden carved ram heads. The doorway is always on the impure downhill, valley side. The purest part of the jestak han is opposite the doorway, inside, below the mountain above. Here are found the statues of gods and sacred juniper branches.

Below: Kalasha men have adopted the Chitrali woollen cap and shalwar kameez.

JOHN MOCK

Dress

Colourful traditional dress, both men's and women's, is the most conspicuous aspect of Kalasha culture. The ceremonial big headdress worn by women is a *kupas*. Made of wool, it's decorated with cowrie shells and other ornaments that hang down the back and provide protection from fierce summer sun. The minor headdress worn regularly by women is a *shushut*. It's a woollen ring decorated with cowries that goes around the head, with a woven or fringed tail that hangs down the back. The shushut is worn daily, under the kupas. Women wear black woollen or cotton dresses called *pirhan*, decorated with embroidery. All women braid their hair in five plaits; two on each side and one in front. Around their waist is a *pati*, a woollen-fringed and decorated belt. Kalasha men have adopted Chitrali-style *shalwar-kameez* and woollen cap, in which they wear a feather. Traditionally, men wore a woven woollen jacket and white woollen trousers called *boodt*. In winter, men wrap colourful leggings, called *kutawati*, around the lower part of their trousers. Women honour men by presenting them with embroidered or woven sashes called *shuman*.

Festivals

Kalasha celebrate their festivals with reunions, feasts, ceremonies, singing and dancing. Ask locally for exact dates. Their main festivals are:

Chilimjust or **Joshi** (mid-May) Dedicated to spring and to future harvests. Festivities are held in each of the three valleys on consecutive days.

Utchal (mid-August) Celebrates the wheat and barley harvests. It includes evening dancing every few days in successive villages in Bumboret and Rumbur.

Phool (late September) Celebrated only in Birir to mark the walnut and grape harvest and the end of wine making. Its origins concern the return of herders from the pastures.

Chaumos (mid-December) A solstice festival with feasting and evening dancing, closed to Muslims. Foreigners are expected to participate and possibly offer a goat for sacrifice.

PLANNING
Books

Kalash Solstice by Jean-Yves & Vivianne Lièvre Loude is a passionate and detailed study of the Kalasha's religious traditions (hardcover). *Beyond the Northwest Frontier: Hindukush & Karakoram* by Maureen Lines has a special focus on Kalasha and current environmental issues.

Permits & Regulations

A Tourism Division permit and a licensed mountain guide aren't necessary, although the Kalasha Valleys are in a restricted zone. Tourism Division's zone classification is superseded by three Chitral district requirements for foreigners: registering with SP in Chitral; requesting permission from the DC in Chitral for visits longer than seven days, although staying an extra day or two seems to go unnoticed; and paying a toll tax to the border police.

The border police maintain two check posts for the three valleys. Border police are stationed in Guru in Birir (and usually find foreigners) and at the check post at the confluence of Bumboret Gol and Rumbur Gol. Carry your Temporary Registration Certificate since the police ask for its serial number. Then fill out a toll-tax form and pay a one-time toll tax of Rs 100, which is valid for all valleys. Keep your receipt when you plan to visit more than one valley.

JOHN MOCK

Left & Right: Kalasha women during the Joshi festival in Birir Valley.

Warning

Extra concern for safety is warranted because many 'outsiders' come and go through all the Kalasha Valleys, and unregulated passes into Afghanistan lie at these valleys' heads. Never hire anyone along the trail. Instead, hire someone in a village in the presence of others, so at least one responsible person witnesses who goes off with you. This ensures you're hiring a reliable person rather than troublemakers or thieves. When trekking between valleys, hire a person from the valley in which you start. When you reach the next valley, they can introduce you to a responsible person there whom they know, such as a relative, friend or hotel owner. They can also suggest secure camp sites, preferably inside a compound.

Guides & Porters

Kalasha prefer that trekkers hire a local guide or porter(s). It's useful to have someone show you the trails, which are steep and not always obvious. Ask for recommendations at a hotel or school. Wages are a flat rate of Rs 200 per day.

You may see sign boards in some hotels from the Kalash Environmental Protection Society (KEPS). KEPS has issued permits to eight Kalasha guides who are identifiable by their blue uniforms. For your security, KEPS encourages everyone to take a guide. KEPS guides earn a nominal salary and ask for no pay for their service. A gratuity, however, is appreciated. Ask at the Mountain Inn in Chitral, Jinnah Kalash Hotel & Restaurant in Anish or at Kalash Guest House in Guru.

Gree An

Duration	5–7 hours
Distance	6.9km
Standard	easy
Season	mid-April–mid-October
Start	Guru
Finish	Gumbak
Zone & Permit	restricted, no permit, Rs 100 toll tax
Public Transport	finish only

Summary A superb day-long trek over a forested ridge between Birir and Bumboret offers a glimpse of Kalasha hill country and sweeping views of Hindukush peaks.

JOHN MOCK

A pass (3060m) over the scenic ridge between Guru in Birir and Gumbak in Bumboret is called Gree An by Birir villagers and Gumbak An by Bumboret villagers. The trail, steep on both sides of the pass, is 2km longer on the Birir side, and entails 132m ascent and 930m descent. Gree An, one of two passes linking Birir and Bumboret, is west of Gorimun Zom (3157m). Maskor Pass (2745m), which lies to its east, is a slightly longer route between Nojhbiu, east of Guru, in Birir and Brun in Bumboret.

PLANNING
Maps
The US AMS 1:253,440 topographic map *Chitral (I-42F)* covers the Kalasha Valleys, but its scale is not useful for trekking. It does not name any of the villages in Bumboret, and it only shows the route over Maskor Pass not Gree An. The British Survey of India 1:63,360 topographic map *38 M/10* shows more detail, and labels Gree An as Ghumbak Gri.

NEAREST VILLAGE
Guru
Birir's hotels are in Guru (1740m). *Paradise Hotel* has rooms for Rs 100–150. *Mehran Hotel*, just up the road from the school, costs Rs 100–150. Rooms are upstairs; each hotel has a shop with expensive basic supplies downstairs. *Kalash Guest House*, a traditional Kalasha house, offers rooms and meals for Rs 300 per person. Book the *C&W Resthouse* (Rs 400), in a walled compound, with the Assistant Engineer in Chitral or Drosh.

Catch any vehicle heading south from Chitral to Drosh (Rs 35), departing from Chitral's Ataliq Bazaar, and get off near Ghariet Gol at Gasheriat where a bridge to Birir crosses the Chitral River. Then try to catch a jeep going upvalley or walk two to three hours to Guru. Ayun-Birir special hires cost Rs 300–350, and Chitral-Birir cost Rs 600.

GETTING TO/FROM THE TREK
For details of transport to the start of the trek, see Guru above and, from the finish of the trek, see Bumboret (p133).

THE TREK
Walk upvalley along the Birir Gol 20 minutes to Bishala and cross the river. A *bashali* is on the true left bank just below the footbridge. Continue up the true left bank 10 minutes to **Gaskuru**. Turn north up a side valley, and go through the village 15 minutes to where the trail splits. Two trails lead from this point towards the pass. Straight ahead up a rocky slope with a few trees is a much steeper, but shorter, herders' trail. Instead take the trail to the right, entering a narrow black-walled gorge (*tang* in Persian) with high rock walls that provide morning shade. Most of the way to the pass is dry, so get water from the canal before heading up the canyon. Follow the relentlessly steep, rocky trail 1½ to 2¼ hours. Gradually the canyon opens up as the trail passes scattered oaks, hollies, pines, cedars and occasional junipers. Water may be found halfway up, but isn't reliable. The steepness lessens as you reach an open grazing area with a lot of deadwood.

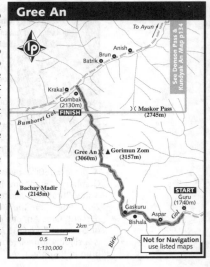

Gree An

To Ayun
Anish
Brun
Batrik
Krakal
Gumbak (2130m)
FINISH
Bumboret Gol
Maskor Pass (2745m)
Gree An (3060m)
Gorimun Zom (3157m)
Bachay Madir (2145m)
START
Guru (1740m)
Gaskuru
Aspar
Bishala
Birir

See Donson Pass & Kundyak An Map p134

0 1 2km
0 0.5 1mi
1:130,000

Not for Navigation use listed maps

The steeper herders' trail meets the trail up the gorge here. (If descending to Birir from the pass, the herders' trail is clearly visible traversing the hillside. The trail down into the gorge is less distinct, but bears east or left). The pass is first visible from the head of this grazing area. Turn north-east (right) and continue to the pass in 45 minutes to one hour up switchbacks of loose, steep rock through chilghoza pines. **Gree An** (3060m) has superb views north to Tirich Mir and Noshaq; Istor-o-Nal hides behind Tirich Mir.

The descent is to Gumbak, a Muslim village in Bumboret. Descend through forest along the true right side of a gully (snow-filled early in the season and dry later on). Where the first side stream joins from the east, the trail crosses and then shortly recrosses the gully. A second side stream farther down offers water. Reach **Gumbak** (2130m) in 1½ to two hours. The pass is easily visible from Bumboret. It lies at the east of the forested low point on the ridge, where the trees meet the rock of Gorimun Zom. The darker peak west of the pass is called both Bachay Madir and Onjesta Zom.

JOHN MOCK

Donson Pass & Kundyak An

Duration	2 days
Distance	10.2km
Standard	easy
Season	mid-April–mid-October
Start	Batrik
Finish	Rumbur Gol
Nearest Facilities	Bumboret, Rumbur
Zone & Permits	restricted, no permit, Rs 100 toll tax
Public Transport	yes

Summary Giant ridge-top cedars, the relatively intact forests of Acholgah, and stunning Hindukush vistas feature in this traverse of passes and valleys.

A scenic, forested route connects Bumboret to the upper Rumbur Gol via the Donson Pass (2970m), the intervening Acholgah Gol, and Kundyak An (2855m). The villages in Acholgah are inhabited year-round by Kalasha men from Anish and Batrik villages who tend their livestock. A few Kalasha women come in July and August to tend the fields. This trek is best done south to north with Bumboret villagers who know the way. Rumbur villagers rarely travel this route and may not know the way.

PLANNING
Maps

The US AMS 1:253,440 topographic map *Chitral (I-42F)* covers the Kalasha Valleys, but its scale isn't useful for trekking. It shows only the western alternative crossing of Kundyak An. It shows the higher trail into the upper Rumbur Gol that leads to Shekhanandeh (labelled as Bashgaliandeh), and doesn't show the riverside trail. It doesn't label any settlements in Acholgah or along Rumbur Gol.

Above right: Kalasha woman at Joshi festival.

The British Survey of India 1:63,360 topographic maps *38 M/10* and *38 M/9* show more detail. A trail is shown incorrectly along the true right bank of the stream coming from the Kundyak An. Ravelik is not labelled, and Balanguru is positioned incorrectly and mislabelled Kalashan Deh.

NEAREST VILLAGES

In peak season and during festivals, rates may be higher than those listed. At other times, most hotels are willing to negotiate.

Bumboret

Accommodation is in the villages of Anish, Brun, Batrik and Krakal. Shops with basic supplies are in each village. With nearly two dozen hotels, Bumboret has been overbuilt and many rooms are vacant except during festivals. Generally, hotels that advertise a dorm or double rooms cater to foreigners, whereas hotels that advertise quadruple rooms cater to domestic tourism where a bunch of guys share a room.

Anish Off the road and quiet, *Jinnah Kalash Hotel & Restaurant* has a Rs 100 camping fee for sites on flat grassy areas in front of the hotel. Singles/doubles upstairs cost Rs 150/250 and Rs 100/150 downstairs with shared bathrooms.

Zahid Kalash Guest House has doubles for Rs 400. *Benazir Hotel & Restaurant*, on the road, has a walled compound with a garden. Doubles cost Rs 600 or Rs 200 with shared bathrooms. *Hotel Alexander Post* is set back from the road. Doubles cost Rs 700. If you're looking for comfort, *PTDC Motel Kalash (☎ 0933-412683, fax 412722)* is Bumboret's best accommodation. Rooms cost Rs 1250/1500.

Batrik The friendly *Peace Hotel* costs Rs 100/200. *Green Hotel and Restaurant* has a Rs 25 dorm and doubles with shared bathroom for Rs 200. *Kalash Continental*, an inviting place set in a large compound with a lawn back from the road, has doubles for Rs 500.

Brun Up a short steep road with good views overlooking the valley, *Kalash View Hotel* is a traditional Kalasha house in the centre of the village with rooms for Rs 100. Nearby *Kalash Guest House* offers rooms for Rs 100. *Ishpata Inn and Restaurant* is set back from the road with a pleasantly designed garden. The dorm costs Rs 50 and singles/doubles cost Rs 100/200. *Foreigner's Tourist Inn* lacks an English sign, but it's the walled compound below the mosque. Doubles/triples cost Rs 600/700.

Krakal Inside its compound, *Alexandra Hotel and Camps* charges a Rs 100 camping fee. *Abdul Kalash Hotel* has a Rs 50 camping fee for sites on a large grassy lawn. *Shishoyak Hotel & Village Restaurant*, Bumboret's best place to camp, asks for a Rs 60 camping fee for sites in its large compound and grassy lawn. Doubles at this hotel cost Rs 150.

Getting There & Away Chitral-Bumboret jeeps (Rs 30, 1½ to two hours) depart regularly from Chitral's Ataliq Bazaar. Alternatively, take any Chitral-Ayun vehicle (Rs 7) and look for a ride from there. Jeeps Ayun-Bumboret cost Rs 20 and special hires cost Rs 300–350.

Rumbur

Accommodation is in the villages of Balanguru (1860m) and Grom, which are on opposites sides of the river. *Saifullah Guest House*, run by Saifullah Jan and Washlim Gul in their Kalasha home in Balanguru, has a relaxing rooftop terrace shaded by walnut trees. Rooms with a shared bathroom cost Rs 250 per person, including tea and meals. Their newer, popular compound close to the river costs Rs 300 without meals.

Kalash Guest House, newly built with a large compound near the river in Grom, has doubles for Rs 200. *Exlant Hotel & Restaurant* in Grom has an inviting shaded garden across the road from its older, plain singles/doubles with charpoys and a shared bathroom for Rs 50/ 90. *Kalash Guest House*, a concrete two-storey building (with different owners from the hotel of the same name), is several minutes' walk outside Grom and above the road. It costs Rs 100 per person and offers free camping behind the hotel when you eat meals there. *Kalash Home Guest House*, a popular place five minutes' walk outside Grom, has rooms with a shared bathroom attached to a traditional Kalasha house. It costs Rs 150–200 per person, including meals, which are cooked in the family's kitchen.

Getting There & Away Transport to and from Rumbur can be sporadic. Chitral-Rumbur jeeps (Rs 30) depart from Chitral's Ataliq Bazaar. Alternatively, take any Chitral-Ayun vehicle (Rs 7) and walk or look for a ride from there, or take a Chitral-Bumboret jeep and get off at the check post, 8km before Grom. Either walk from there or look for a jeep. Ayun-Rumbur jeeps cost Rs 20 and special hires cost Rs 300–350.

GETTING TO/FROM THE TREK
To the Start

For information on transport to the trailhead, see Bumboret (p132).

Right: Kalasha girls dressed for the Joshi festival.

RICHARD I'ANSON

From the Finish

Unless you flag down a vehicle, walk on the road along the Rumbur Gol's true left bank for 3.5km, or one hour, to Balanguru and Grom, passing the footbridge to Sajigor 15 minutes before reaching Balanguru.

THE TREK
Day 1: Batrik to Gomenah

3½–4½ hours, 5.7km, 930m ascent, 990m descent

Ascend the gully behind Batrik (2040m) on a steep, but solid and well-defined trail. Pass through forest of cedars and occasional chilghoza pines, where aggressive logging and milling is evident. Alternatively, you can walk from **Krakal** on the more gentle and wide donkey trail that traverses east and north to join the path up from Batrik in two hours at 2700m.

Proceed up gentle switchbacks on the wide trail 45 minutes to one hour to **Donson Pass** (2970m), 2.5km from Batrik. Donson Pass is crowned by massive, stunning cedars, at least 1000 years old. A rocky pyramid called Gorasin lies to the east, with a forested ridge to the west. Goats and cows graze on the grassy slopes to the north. Acholgah Gol is visible below while the Rumbur Valley is hidden behind the Kundyak An ridge. Tirich Mir and Noshaq are prominent to the north.

Descend north through flower-filled meadows and then steeply down a spur for 30 minutes, following a trail. The trunks of some cedars in this forest are 3m in diameter. Just west of the spur is a small gully. Cross the gully to its true left side. In five to 10 minutes pass through forest to a wooden shelter called Owzurie (2460m). Continue down 45 minutes, crossing a side stream and traversing high above the Donson Gol on a good trail. Pass below Gogalog, a herders' hut above the trail, to an obvious view point and westward bend in the trail (2220m).

Below, Donson Gol meets the **Acholgah Gol** near a hot spring. Ghariet Peak dominates the view downvalley to the east. Looking south up the Donson Gol, the entire valley is forested and the route back to the pass is visible with Gorasin rising east of the pass. Continuing north, just around the bend of the trail, are two enormous cedars. From here, either drop down to the fields below or continue 15 minutes on the trail to the settlement of Shigala. *Camp* anywhere in the three settlements of Passuwala, Shigala or across the river in **Gomenah** (1980m), 3.5km below the pass. Several log and stone footbridges cross the Acholgah Gol.

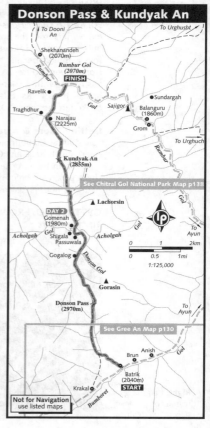

Donson Pass & Kundyak An

To Dooni An
To Urghusht
Shekhanandeh (2070m)
Rumbur Gol (2070m)
FINISH
Rumbur Gol
Ravelik
Sundargah
Gol
Sajigor
Balanguru (1860m)
Traghdhur
Narajau (2225m)
Grom
To Urghuch
Rumbur
Kundyak An (2855m)
See Chitral Gol National Park Map p138
Lachorsin
Gol
DAY 2
Gomenah (1980m)
To Ayun
Acholgah Gol
Shigala
Acholgah
Passuwala
0   1   2km
Gogalog
Donson Gol
0   0.5   1mi
1:125,000
Gorasin
Donson Pass (2970m)
To Ayun
See Gree An Map p130
Anish
Gol
Brun
Batrik (2040m)
START
Krakal
Not for Navigation use listed maps
Bumboret

A road connects the Acholgah Gol to lower Rumbur Gol 3km above the border police check post. The road is open only in low water and is usually impassable from May to July. To the east of Gomenah rises Lachorsin peak. In Kalashamun, it's called *pushak* (snow leopard hill) because of the snow leopard that is known to come down and raid the villages' livestock. A mineral-water spring is two hours' walk west up the Acholgah Gol.

Day 2: Gomenah to Rumbur Gol
4–5 hours, 4.5km, 875m ascent, 785m descent

Once across the Acholgah Gol, walk north 30 minutes up the road to its end, passing through an impressive cedar forest (2460m). Ascend either the slope to the west or the barren hillside, both of which cross the Kundyak An a short distance apart. Climb up the barren hillside, also called Kundyak, 15 to 30 minutes on goat paths to a small wooden shelter (2670m). Notches cut into trees are to encourage bees to build hives so Kalasha can collect honey.

Continue up a 10m-wide logging scar one to 1½ hours. Eventually this strip narrows and becomes a gully with deadwood lying around. The trail then disappears and the heavily forested route to the pass heads up and to the right of the gully. In May and June, the forest floor offers *qutsi,* or morel mushrooms, and later, wild strawberries. **Kundyak An** (2855m) is forested and is not visible from below. Views to the north from the pass are obscured by trees. The sweeping views south towards the Donson Pass, however, are excellent. This 1.25km ascent is through an old-growth forest with trees ranging from 300 to 1000 years old.

No obvious trail exists north of the Kundyak An until you reach the first settlements below in 1¼ to 1½ hours. A local companion who knows the way down is essential, as the overgrown trail appears and disappears. The route stays to the right, bearing north-north-east, and traverses high for an hour before descending steeply to a Kalasha house and barley field at **Narajau** (2225m), 2km below the pass. Traghdhur, a Muslim and Gujar settlement, is across the valley. Ravelik, a Kalasha village, lies high above the confluence of this side stream and Rumbur Gol. The fields of Shekhanandeh are to the distant north.

It's a short descent to the footbridge over the side stream below Narajau. Cross to the true left bank on the first of eight footbridges (the number of footbridges changes depending on the water level). Steep cliffs flank the true right bank and the stream enters a gorge. After 30 minutes and several river crossings reach the **Rumbur Gol** (2070m). From the confluence are views west up the Gangalwat Gol towards the Afghan border. Cross the Rumbur Gol on a sturdy plank footbridge to the road along its true left bank.

Sajigor

In the midst of an oak grove, the Kalasha shrine of Sajigor lies beneath a giant oak tree. Elaborately carved wooden pillars stand behind the altar and the Sajigor tree. Only males can visit this sacred place where men gather for festival rituals and young virgin boys offer goats as sacrifice.

CHITRAL

continued from p125

It's possible, however, to piece together several forms of transport. A daily NATCO bus (Rs 81) operates between Gilgit and Gupis. Beyond Gupis, jeeps go as far as Teru and Barsat. It's usually difficult to catch a ride over the Shandur Pass between Gupis and Mastuj. Daily Mastuj-Chitral jeeps cost Rs 80. Only jeeps can travel the road between Mastuj and Buni. The 75km between Buni and Chitral is sealed and has regular van and Coaster service (Rs 35).

In light of these logistics, some trekkers opt for special hires that cost Rs 8000–9000. Under the best circumstances, the trip from Gilgit to Chitral takes two long days with an overnight stop. The driving times on the largely unsealed road are: Gilgit-Gupis, six hours; Gupis-Phundar, 3½ hours; Phundar-Mastuj, five hours; and Mastuj-Chitral, four hours. The best camp sites are in Phundar and 4km beyond Mastuj in Shachar.

Getting Around
Outside the gate of the airport, jeeps and Suzukis to town cost Rs 5 per person plus Rs 5 per bag. Special hires to or from the airport cost Rs 40. The bazaar is small and everyone walks.

Chitral Gol National Park

The beautiful, easily accessible, but rarely visited Chitral Gol National Park is Chitral's best-kept secret. It provides sanctuary to several hundred magnificent markhor, and at least one mating pair of snow leopards that move between Kasavir, Dooni Gol and Gokhshal as the snow level changes. World-renowned wildlife biologist George Schaller spotted his first snow leopard here. Other mammals are black bears, wolves, ibex, marmots and weasels, and birds include falcons, hawks, eagles, lammergeiers, monals, snowcocks and many smaller species that thrive in the park's lovely old-growth cedar and pine forests.

Hunting is prohibited, although the long and sinuously twisted horns of the male markhor once made Chitral Gol the mehtar's royal hunting reserve. The national park conducts an annual wildlife census, regulates livestock grazing, the chopping of fuel wood and timber and the gathering of qutsi in May and June and chilghoza pine nuts in September and October.

Chitral Gol National Park is to the immediate west of Chitral town. Chitral Gol flows under the bridge between Ataliq and Shahi bazaars. The park is ideal for spring trekking, but passes only open in July.

PLANNING
Guides & Porters
The District Forestry Officer (DFO) – Wildlife is in charge of the park, as well as all wildlife sanctuaries and game reserves in Chitral. The office is across the Chitral River from town (☎ 0933-412101). The office can organise for a game watcher to work as a guide, but most don't speak English. Since game watchers are salaried employees, a daily wage isn't expected. It's appropriate, however, to compensate them for extra work. Game watchers must buy and carry all their own food from Chitral town, so you should bring extra food (eg, rice, dal, flour, bread, eggs, tea, sugar or milk powder) for them.

ACCESS FACILITIES
Chaghbini
The DFO operates two-room rest houses called *Inspection & Watchers' Houses* at Merin, Gokhshal and Chaghbini. The one at Merin is sometimes referred to as the *Merin Special Hut*. Rooms have a single bed with attached toilets. At Chaghbini, carry water from a spring 30 minutes away or melt snow. When starting a trek at Chaghbini (2925m), bring full water bottles from Chitral. Contact the DFO to book a room; no rate is set. Camping is free. Bring your own food; the game watchers are happy to cook it for you.

Getting There & Away Only special hires go Chitral-Chaghbini (Rs 750, one hour, 17km). From Chitral, jeeps follow a sealed road west from PIA Chowk, then take the first unsealed road up to the left (the sealed road continues to the governor's cottage). The unsealed road forks to the left to the microwave relay tower (locally called the 'booster') and to the right into Chitral Gol National Park (a park sign is posted there). Birmogh Lasht (2580m), the abandoned summer residence of the Mehtar of Chitral, is 2km before Chaghbini.

Alternatively, walk to or from Chaghbini or the booster, which usually adds one day to the trek. Follow the more direct, but steeper, route up the ridge to avoid the lengthy switchbacks on the road. Walking uphill to Chaghbini takes 3½ to five hours and downhill two to 3½ hours. Walking to the booster takes two hours uphill or one to 1½ hours downhill. Either way, it's hot and dry.

Kasavir

Duration	2 days
Distance	7km
Standard	easy
Season	April–October
Start/Finish	Chaghbini
Zone & Permit	open, no permit
Public Transport	no

Summary Easily accessible Kasavir, the location of the mehtar's former hunting lodge in the heart of Chitral Gol, has fine markhor watching and, at the right time of year, snow leopards can be seen.

The beautiful trek to Kasavir takes you into the park's central sanctuary. An overnight trip to Kasavir is worthwhile to watch the markhor at dusk and dawn. In Kalashamun, *kasavir* means 'a sanctuary for hunting'. In spring and early summer, markhor are readily visible on the cliffs above Kasavir. In winter and early spring, snow leopards have been photographed here.

PLANNING
Maps
The US AMS 1:253,440 topographic map *Chitral (I-42F)* covers the park, but its scale isn't useful for trekking. It labels Ishperudeh Zom (4156m) as Sowarmapur Tak.

The British Survey of India 1:63,360 topographic maps *38 M/9* and *38 M/13* show more detail. They don't show the booster, the road beyond Birmogh Lasht, or the game-watchers' route to Kasavir.

Stages
It's two stages total round trip from Chaghbini: (1) Kasavir; and (2) Chaghbini.

GETTING TO/FROM THE TREK
For information on transport to/from the trek, see Chaghbini (p136).

At the end of the trek, unless you prearrange a special hire, walk down to Chitral town from Chaghbini. At Birmogh Lasht (2580m), 30 to 45 minutes below Chaghbini, you may get lucky and find a jeep that has brought tourists up and is willing to take you down if there's room.

THE TREK (see map p138)
Day 1: Chaghbini to Kasavir
3½–4 hours, 3.5km, 880m descent

Chaghbini means 'place where there is always shade' for the space beneath a huge cedar tree (whose top was lopped off by a lightning strike) below the Inspection & Watchers' House. The views from Birmogh Lasht and Chaghbini are spectacular, an almost 360-degree panorama. Tirich Mir is to the north, Buni Zom to the north-east and the sheer rock summit of Ghariet to the south-east.

Traverse west from the rest house (2925m) along a level trail on the ridge's south-facing side through conifer forest. Where the trail makes an obvious bend north, choose between two routes to Kasavir. Both routes are shaded by cedar and chilghoza pine forests with scattered oaks, hollies and junipers. A steep route drops dramatically down a lateral ridge to Kasavir in two hours, but you need a game watcher to show the way. Or, you can follow the longer, but more gradual, trail down the Ishperudeh Nala. *Ishperudeh* means 'white place' for the light-coloured cliffs above. From the bend, continue to traverse

CHITRAL

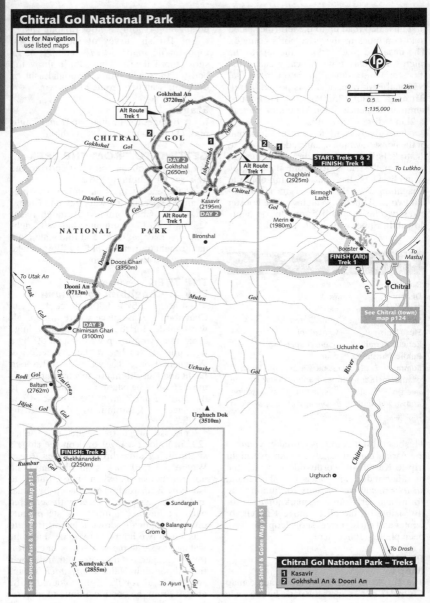

Chitral Gol National Park

Not for Navigation
use listed maps

Gokhshal An
(3720m)

Alt Route
Trek 1

CHITRAL GOL

2

1

Gokhshal Gol

Isperuakh Nala

To Lutkho

2 1

START: Treks 1 & 2
FINISH: Trek 1

Chaghbini
(2925m)

Birmogh
Lasht

DAY 2
Gokhshal
(2650m)

Alt Route
Trek 1

Dúndini Goi

Kushunisuk

Chitral Gol

Kasavir
(2195m)
DAY 2

Merin
(1980m)

Alt Route
Trek 1

NATIONAL PARK

Dooni Gol

Bironshal

To Mastuj

FINISH (Alt):
Trek 1

Chitral

2

Dooni Ghari
(3350m)

See Chitral (town)
map p124

To Utak An

Utak Gol

Dooni An
(3713m)

Mulen Gol

DAY 3
Chimirsan Ghari
(3100m)

Chimirsan Gol

Uchusht

Uchusht Gol

River

Rodi Gol

Baltum
(2762m)

Jájok Gol

Chitral

Urghuch Dok
(3510m)

See Donson Pass & Kundyak An Map p134

FINISH: Trek 2
Shekhánandeh
(2250m)

Rumbur Gol

See Shishi & Golen Map p145

Urghuch

Sundargah

Balanguru

Grom

Rumbur Gol

Kundyak An
(2855m)

To Ayun

To Drosh

0   1   2km
0   0.5   1mi
1:135,000

Chitral Gol National Park – Treks
1 Kasavir
2 Gokhshal An & Dooni An

north, passing a spring in 15 minutes and meeting the Ishperudeh Nala in another 15 minutes. Cross the river and descend along its banks.

If you come down the game watchers' route, you pass through abandoned apple and walnut orchards and cross two canals above the Chitral Gol's left bank as you near Kasavir. Cross the Ishperudeh Nala and head upstream a short distance to find a suitable place to ford the Chitral Gol. **Kasavir** (2195m), the location of the now-dilapidated hunting bungalow of the ex-Mehtar of Chitral, Saif ul Mulk Nasir, on the river's opposite side.

A few minutes' climb above Kasavir is **Mroi Lodini** (the markhor viewing place), a distinctive rock outcrop visible from Chaghbini. Climb onto Mroi Lodini and look west across the river to the grassy plateau and the rocky cliffs above. At dusk, markhor can usually be spotted. *Mroi* refers to markhor in general whereas the term *shahrah* refers to adult males and *majher* to females and young.

Day 2: Kasavir to Chaghbini
5–6 hours, 3.5km, 880m ascent
The climb from Kasavir is steep and hot, so start early to minimise the time climbing in direct sunlight. The trail up the Ishperudeh Nala is more gradual, easier to follow, and the best choice.

Alternative Finish: Kasavir to Booster
3½ hours, 7km, 215m descent, 220m ascent
An alternative route follows the Chitral Gol downstream to Merin (1980m) in two hours and continues to the booster in another 1½ hours. In June and July, however, high water makes this route impossible (see Merin under Other Treks, p165).

Alternative Route: Kasavir to Chaghbini
It is possible to make a circuit by returning to Chaghbini via Gokhshal. It is, however, much easier to visit Gokhshal first, and then Kasavir in a counterclockwise loop.

Alternative Day 2: Kasavir to Gokhshal
2–3 hours, 3.3km, 800m ascent, 345m descent
Cross the river to the grassy Kasavir Lasht (plain) and ascend a trail, climbing above the gorge to reach Kushunisuk. Then continue on an exposed and narrow trail along the ridge overlooking the gorge 15 minutes and descend north-west 30 to 45 minutes to *Gokhshal* (2650m).

Alternative Day 3: Gokhshal to Chaghbini
5½–6½ hours, 5.8km, 1070m ascent, 795m descent
See Day 1 of the Gokhshal An & Dooni An trek (p140) for a description.

Gokhshal An & Dooni An

Duration	3 days
Distance	24.8km
Standard	moderate
Season	July–September
Start	Chaghbini
Finish	Shekhanandeh
Zone & Permit	open and restricted, no permit, Rs 100 toll tax
Public Transport	finish only

Summary A classic traverse of Chitral Gol National Park into the Kalasha Valleys rewards with excellent views of Tirich Mir and the likelihood of spotting markhor.

Two passes, Gokhshal An and Dooni An (also called Chimirsan An by people in Rumbur), combine for an exciting trek from Chitral Gol National Park into Rumbur, the northernmost Kalasha Valley. The often faint, rugged trails offer mountain views and enhance the wildlife-watching opportunities.

PLANNING
Maps
The US AMS 1:253,440 topographic map *Chitral (I-42F)* covers the park, but its scale isn't useful for trekking. It doesn't show the route across Gokhshal An.

The British Survey of India 1:63,360 topographic maps *38 M/9*, *38 M/13* and *38 M/10* show more detail, but don't show the trail between Gokhshal and Dooni Gol. They indicate a route up Chitral Gol from Kasavir via Krui Dheri to Dooni Gol, which has been destroyed by landslides. The maps name the pass between Gokhshal and Awireth Gol to the north as Gokhshal An, but game watchers call that pass Chikan and the pass over the Ishperudeh ridge Gokhshal An.

Stages

Due to its popularity, the stage system is in effect on this trek. It's four stages total from Chaghbini: (1) Gokhshal (or Kasavir); (2) Dooni Ghari; (3) Chimirsan Ghari; and (4) Shekhanandeh.

GETTING TO/FROM THE TREK
To the Start

For information on transport to the start of the trek, see Chaghbini (p136).

From the Finish

Shekhanandeh-Grom jeeps cost Rs 20. Special hires cost Rs 600. Alternatively, it takes one to 1½ hours to walk on the road to Balanguru and Grom. For transport information from Grom, see Rumbur (p133).

THE TREK (see map p138)
Day 1: Chaghbini to Gokhshal

5–6½ hours, 5.8km, 795m ascent, 1070m descent

From Chaghbini (2925m), follow the trail along the ridge's south-facing side through open forest at the head of the Ishperudeh stream, passing a spring. (Avoid the ridge-top trail, which leads to a Class 3 traverse across a rock face before joining the easier trail described here.) Then angle up a grassy slope towards the rocky Ishperudeh ridge. The pass, the lowest point, is a small notch to the south (left) of a larger, but higher saddle. Follow a livestock trail (used by cows) up, passing the junction with the Class 3 route from the right two hours from Chaghbini. Reach **Gokhshal An** (3720m) in another 45 minutes to one hour, with sweeping views from Lowari Pass to Buni Zom.

Carefully descend over steep, loose gravel switchbacks to reach the gentler vegetated slopes 30 minutes below. After 10 to 15 minutes, pass a tiny spring then cross two small clear streams and follow the trail above the second stream's true right bank. Fifteen minutes farther, cross another small stream and follow down its true right bank rather than going ahead into cedar forest. Reach the valley floor in 30 minutes, and follow the trail down the Gokhshal stream's true left bank to reach the tin-roofed game-watchers' house at *Gokhshal* (2650m) in another 30 minutes. Nearby are walnut trees and a spring near willows. The house sits in an amazing amphitheatre-like rocky gorge with a pine-forested boulder area nearby. Unfortunately, cows graze nearby, so all grass is gone and dung piles lie under the trees.

Day 2: Gokhshal to Chimirsan Ghari

7–8 hours, 11km, 1340m ascent, 890m descent

Cross the stream, heading west-south-west and ascend the easternmost (first) of three forested spurs from the prominent ridge separating the Gokhshal Gol and Dūndini Gol. A former bridle trail, now faint, works south-east, contouring up one hour to the ridge top (3049m) due south of Gokhshal visible below. Descend 10 minutes, then leave the trail and follow a very faint game-watchers' route to the west and south (right).

The main trail into Dooni Gol was wiped out by a slide. Contour 45 minutes to Dūndini Gol (2772m), locally called Chhato Ush (water from the lake), and a good water and rest spot. Cross a log footbridge and climb steeply 20 minutes to a forested ridge. Contour south-south-west along the Dooni Gol's true left (west) bank and meet the stream in 30 minutes. Cross it via a snow bridge, which is present even late in the season, and climb a grassy hill along its true right (east) bank 30 minutes to *Dooni Ghari* (3350m). A small spring amid willows here makes it a possible camp site for trekkers coming in the opposite direction.

Follow the remains of the old trail steeply up switchbacks well above the Dooni Gol's true right (east) bank, passing some stone shelters adjacent to boulders. A few small cairns occasionally mark the faint trail. Pass 100m beneath a prominent isolated stand of five or six large cedars. Ascend a gully south of these trees a short distance and emerge onto a grassy ridge with scrub juniper. Tirich Mir comes prominently into view. Follow livestock trails, switchbacking up the grassy, flower-covered slopes another hour to **Dooni An** (3713m), the southern boundary of the Chitral Gol watershed. Tirich Mir is impressive and Buni Zom is visible in the distance. To the west above the many feeder streams of the Dooni Gol is the summer habitat of markhor herds.

From Dooni An, descend and contour the east (left) side of the bowl below the pass. Aim for the level plain's north end where herders' huts are visible below on the Chimirsan Gol's true right (west) side. Follow the middle spur that leads to this point. Cross the stream and reach the level area one to 1½ hours from the pass. Just 15 minutes ahead, behind the low spur at the plain's south end, are the huts (*ghari* in Khowar) of **Chimirsan Ghari** (3100m) along both sides of the Utak Gol, the stream coming from Utak An (see Utak An under Other Treks, p165). Rumbur and Uchusht people, both Kalasha and Muslim, herd goats here. *Camp* on the slightly sloping grassy area with abundant clear water.

Day 3: Chimirsan Ghari to Shekhanandeh
4–4½ hours, 8km, 850m descent
Descend 30 minutes on old lateral moraine and cross Utak Gol. A steady descent through 500-year-old cedar forests and across small side streams leads in 1½ to two hours to the start of a canal near Baltum hut (2762m) on the Rodi Gol's south bank. Continue down another hour, contouring through forest above Chimirsan Gol's true right (west) bank to Nuristani-style homes above the Jājok Gol's north bank. Descend through cornfields along the spur separating Jājok Gol and Chimirsan Gol and cross Jājok Gol. The trail stays well above Chimirsan Gol's true right bank one hour, and then descends

the ridge separating the Chimirsan Gol and Rumbur Gol to reach the roadhead at **Shekhanandeh** (2250m). This village, where Kati-speaking people of the Bashgali tribe live, used to be called Bashgaliandeh. *Shekh* is a term used for converts to Islam.

Lutkho

Lutkho *tehsil* covers the western portion of Chitral north of Chitral town and south of Tirich Mir. It's an area drained by the Lutkho River, which flows from the Afghan border, and its main tributary, the Arkari River. The area is known for the hot springs of Garam Chashma, with a town of the same name at the end of the sealed road. Ojhor and Arkari, the valleys that drain the south and western flanks of Tirich Mir (7706m) and Gul Lasht Zom (6657m), offer the best trekking.

Owir An

Duration	3 days
Distance	15.7km
Standard	moderate
Season	mid-June–mid-September
Start	Shahguch
Finish	Mujhen
Zone & Permit	open, no permit
Public Transport	yes

Summary This popular and easily accessible trek crosses a ridge-top pass along the southern flanks of mighty Tirich Mir, visiting friendly villages along the way.

Crossing the Owir An (4337m) is a short and popular trek that offers wonderful close-up views of the southern flanks of the Tirich Mir massif. The description that follows is from Ojhor, south-west of Tirich Mir, to Owir, south-east of Tirich Mir, but it can be done in the reverse direction.

PLANNING
Maps & Books
The topographic US AMS 1:250,000 map *Mastuj (NJ 43-13)* and 1:253,400 map

Zebak (J-42X) cover the trek. They don't label Lasht in Ojhor, or Mujhen along the Owir Gol's true right bank across from Shungush. Riri is labelled as Reri.

Tirich Mir: The Norwegian Himalaya Expedition by Aarne Naess et al is the story of the first ascent of Tirich Mir (hardcover).

Guides & Porters

The trail over the pass isn't hard to find, so a guide is optional. Ojhor porters, who work between Kiyar or Lasht and the first village in Owir, ask for a flat rate of Rs 250 per day, including payment for food rations. When going up the North Barum Glacier to Tirich Mir Base Camp, hire Owir porters from Shahbronz, who ask for Rs 230.

GETTING TO/FROM THE TREK
To the Start

Jeeps depart from Chitral's Ojhor *sarai* (stopping place) behind Hotel Dreamland to Sussoom (Rs 35) and Kiyar (Rs 40, two hours, 30km). Special hires cost Rs 800. The first 20km (45 minutes) is along the sealed road to Garam Chashma and the bridge at Shoghor. The last 10km (1¼ hours) is a steep ride up a narrow jeep road.

From the Finish

Mujhen-Chitral or Shahbronz-Chitral jeeps cost Rs 100. Special hires cost Rs 1500. If no jeeps are in Mujhen, walk 4.8km on a trail across barren land to Riri and look for one there. Riri-Chitral jeeps cost Rs 80. You

Tirich Mir as seen from Kiyar village.

JOHN MOCK

can also keep walking on the road 3.2km beyond Riri to Parpish and the bridge over the Mastuj River to the Chitral-Gilgit road. Parpish-Chitral jeeps cost Rs 35–40. A seat in a Buni-Chitral van costs Rs 20–25.

When doing this trek in the reverse direction, jeeps to Riri, Mujhen and Shahbronz depart from Chitral's Owir sarai next to the Allied Bank, across the street from the Al-Farooq Hotel, in Naya Bazaar. The proprietor of a teashop in the corner of the sarai can help you get on a jeep. Jeeps to Mujhen and Shahbronz use a newer bridge 3km north of the Parpish Bridge.

THE TREK
Day 1: Shahguch to Kiyar High Camp

2–2½ hours, 4km, 330m ascent

Ojhor Gol separates Sussoom (2896m) and Kiyar villages. Along its true right bank is Lasht. Shahguch, a large, well-watered grassy area, lies between the two villages just upstream from the bridge. Camp in *Shahguch* (3000m) before ascending farther. From Shahguch, follow the road 15 minutes to Kiyar. From Kiyar's polo field, head left and follow a trail up through fields. Keep the obvious dry rocky spur with a small cairn on it to your left and head for the highest trees and fields. On your right, but farther away, are three vertical rock outcrops, and a waterfall upvalley from them. Reach the highest fields and houses and continue on a trail to the saddle crossing the dry rocky spur on your left, one hour from Kiyar.

This vantage point has a superb view of Tirich Mir and upper Ojhor Gol. From the saddle, contour gently up the Ojhor Gol's east side 45 minutes to one hour, crossing several small clear streams, to *Kiyar High Camp* (3500m), a sheltered level grassy area with room for many tents.

Day 2: Kiyar High Camp to Owir High Camp

4–4½ hours, 4.7km, 837m ascent, 150m descent

The trail reaches a ridge in 15 minutes and turns east to head up the south side of the valley leading towards the pass. Contour around 30 minutes to the snow pack at the confluence of two small streams. The ascent to the Owir An is up the north (left) side of the rocky bluffs above. From the snowfield, ascend to the gully with a small stream, left of the rocky outcrop, in 30 minutes. From here, it's a steep one- to 1½-hour climb to the pass itself. A small black outcrop lies just left of **Owir An** (4337m). In heavy snow years, or early in the season, a snowfield lies on both sides of the pass. From the pass, the Buni Zom massif dominates the view with the Shandur range stretching to the distant horizon. The fields of Shungush are visible below.

Descend along the small stream, crossing another small side stream from the left. The trail descends a ridge, well above the main stream's true left side. One hour from the pass, reach a level area with some grass and a few tent sites where two streams meet. This is where the alternative trail to the **Barum Glacier** starts (see the Alternative Finish, p144).

If trekking in the reverse direction, ascending to the pass from Owir High Camp, follow the ridge trail up steeply. The pass isn't visible until you reach the ridge top, above the true left bank of the stream below. As the trail and the stream near each other, a small hill is visible ahead with a prominent squared-off rock outcrop to its south (left). The Owir An lies just to the north of this hill.

To continue towards Mujhen, follow the trail that crosses to the main stream's true right bank, and continues across rolling hills and grassland 45 minutes to another stream and a large grassy area. Large *Owir High Camp* (4187m) is near a small pool at the base of a rock outcrop.

Day 3: Owir High Camp to Mujhen
2–2½ hours, 7km, 1260m descent

Cross to the stream's east side and follow an abandoned canal. The trail contours around

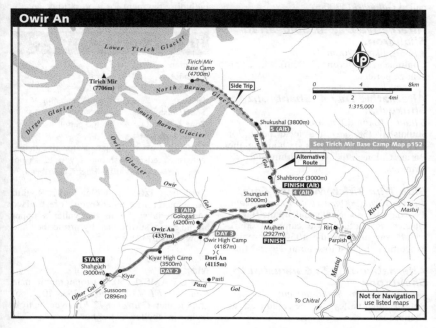

several ridges and as you leave camp you can see the square-topped outcrop and small hill that mark Owir An. The view up to Tirich Mir is impressive. Contour to a ridge overlooking fields and houses, then descend to the upper settlement, one hour from the high camp. Follow the large trail through the village one hour to **Mujhen** (2927m).

Alternative Finish: Kiyar High Camp to Shahbronz

This route takes you to Shukushal, and gives you the option to continue to Tirich Mir Base Camp.

Alternative Day 2: Kiyar High Camp to Gologari

4 hours, 4.7km, 837m ascent, 137m descent

From the level grassy area with a few tent sites one hour below (east of) the pass, follow a trail along the main stream's true left bank 30 minutes ahead to the grassy area called *Gologari* (4200m).

Alternative Day 3: Gologari to Shahbronz

4 hours, 9km, 1200m descent

Continue to **Shahbronz** (3000m), where you change porters.

Alternative Day 4: Shahbronz to Shukushal

6 hours, 10km, 800m ascent

Shukushal (3800m), the local name for *Tirich Mir Base Camp*, is six hours up the Barum Gol, near the North Barum Glacier's terminus.

Side Trip: Tirich Mir Base Camp

4 days, 30km, 900m ascent, 900m descent

Two days beyond Shukushal, up the Barum Glacier, is another base camp (4700m), which was used by the 1950 Norwegian expedition, the first to summit Tirich Mir.

Alternative Day 5: Shukushal to Shahbronz

4–5 hours, 10km, 800m descent

Return downvalley to the roadhead at **Shahbronz**.

Shishi & Golen

Shishi and Golen, two large valleys east of the Chitral River, form the principal watersheds for the chain of peaks including Buni Zom (6550m) and Ghuchhar Sar (6249m). The long Shishi Gol flows into the Chitral River 40km south of Chitral, just north of Drosh. The highest village in Shishi Gol, Madaglasht, is a community of Persian-speaking Isma'ilis who migrated in the 19th century from northern Afghanistan to make guns for the Mehtar of Chitral. Golen Gol refers broadly to the main Golen Gol and its side valleys: Roghili, Dok, Lohigal and Sachiokuh. *Golen* means 'many valleys' in Khowar. The entire area has exceptional biodiversity and a largely intact habitat.

PLANNING
Guides & Porters

Porters ask for a flat rate of Rs 250 per day, including payment for food rations.

Roghili Gol

Duration	4 days
Distance	27.8km
Standard	moderate
Season	mid-June–September
Start/Finish	Izghor
Zone & Permit	open, no permit
Public Transport	yes

Summary Trekking along clear streams through extensive cedar forest brings you to alpine meadows and lakes at the Roghili Gol's head.

South from Izghor in Golen Gol is Roghili Gol named for its cedar *(rogh)* forests. Two turquoise lakes lie in the valley's upper alpine basin, surrounded by prime ibex and snow leopard habitat.

PLANNING
Maps

The US AMS 1:250,000 topographic map *Churrai (NI 43-1)* and 1:253,440 topographic map *Chitral (I 42-F)* cover the trek. Izghor is labelled as Uzghor.

The British Survey of India 1:63,360 topographic maps *38 M/13* and *38 M/14* show more detail. Local people call the lower lake Tsak Chhat (*tsak* means 'little'; *chhat*, a 'lake') and the upper one Lut Chhat (big lake). They also sometimes refer to them as Muli Chhat (lower lake) and Turi Chhat (upper lake). The British *38 M/13* and *38 M/14* sheets are a little confusing as they label Tsak Chhat as More Chhat, and Lut Chhat as Tore Chhat.

GETTING TO/FROM THE TREK

Chitral-Izghor jeeps cost Rs 35 (1½ hours). Jeeps usually depart Chitral in the late morning for Golen and depart Golen in the early morning for Chitral. The staging area is a small teashop, the Kohinoor Hotel, across Chew Bridge, just north of Chitral town on the road's east side. Hakim Khan, who also runs the adjacent store, can help you find the right jeep. Chitral-Izghor special hires cost Rs 500–600.

Alternatively, get off any Chitral-Buni van at Golen Gol (Rs 7, 18km), north of Koghozi. From here, it's three to four hours' walk to Izghor following the jeep road and traversing steep cliffs high above the river. Pass through Golen (1890m), the valley's first village, where the houses are built of the ever-present speckled granite. Beyond Golen, fragrant yellow-blossomed laburnums *(beshoo)* blanket the valley walls early in the season.

THE TREK (see map below)
Day 1: Izghor to Lochuk
2 hours, 5.2km, 415m ascent

An enormous spring pours forth at the base of the cliff just north of Izghor (2225m), the valley's second village. Near where the road crosses the stream coming from the spring is an open, grassy *camp site*. When you reach Izghor from Chitral in the morning, walk to Lochuk in the pleasant late-afternoon shade. Follow the Roghili stream's true left bank

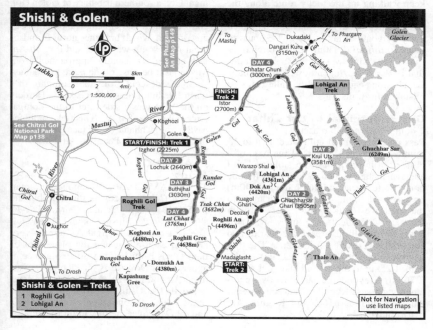

up a good, but steep, trail through a rich cedar forest. The clear stream, enormous in early summer, subsides by July. In 1¾ hours reach huts at Molassi amid a mixed pine and cedar forest. Cross an alluvial fan and a log footbridge over a stream, and in 15 minutes reach the pleasant, flat, grassy forested area and huts of **Lochuk** (2640m). The views downvalley and north-west to Tirich Mir are good. Uncontrolled cutting of trees in these magnificent, but finite, forests for timber, fuel wood and clearing of fields is evident. Izghor villagers now realise that if it continues at its present rate, no forest will be left for their children.

Day 2: Lochuk to Buthijhal
1½ hours, 2.5km, 390m ascent

Continue up the trail through pine forest, passing occasional huts. In 15 minutes, the forest ends. Kundar Gol, the side stream to the east, is home to ibex herds. Overgrazing by livestock is apparent. As the trail fades, keep walking up the rocky route along the true left bank of the Roghili Gol. Willows line the stream, but many have been nibbled away by goats. It takes one to 1½ hours to reach **Buthijhal** (3030m). Large birch trees *(buthi)* are visible west of the stream. Buthijhal is also a grazing area with a few huts. Canals along each side of the valley may be mistaken for trails.

Day 3: Buthijhal to Lut Chhat
3 hours, 6.2km, 735m ascent

Pass one more small cultivated area in 15 minutes, with its few huts at the base of a cliff, right in the path of possible rock fall and avalanche. Ascend rocky rubble for one hour to a few scattered birch trees (3240m) on a rise. Continue upvalley as it turns to the south-west and narrows. Pass through the narrow defile *(tang)* and 1½ to two hours from Buthijhal reach the first of two aqua lakes, Tsak Chhat (3682m). The trail continues up the stream's true left (west) bank 1.25km to the second lake, **Lut Chhat** (3765m). Beyond the lake are two challenging passes: Roghili Gree and Roghili An (see Jughor, p166, and Roghili An, p167, under Other Treks).

Day 4: Lut Chhat to Izghor
4–6 hours, 13.9km, 1540m descent

Easily return from the lakes to **Izghor**.

Lohigal An	
Duration	4 days
Distance	47.5km
Standard	moderate
Season	July–mid-September
Start	Madaglasht
Finish	Istor
Zone & Permit	open, no permit
Public Transport	yes
Summary Forested slopes, meadows, springs, wildflowers, friendly herders, big snowy peaks and a gentle pass make this one of Chitral's most enjoyable treks.	

Lohigal An is a nonglaciated pass at the Shishi Gol's head that leads north-east to Lohigal Gol, a southern tributary of Golen Gol. It's also the easternmost of three passes that connect Shishi and Golen. The other passes are Dok An, which branches north from Lohigal An's south-west side, and Roghili An. Lohigal An is usually approached from Madaglasht because of the more gradual ascent; the descent from the Lohigal An's north side into Lohigal Gol is steep. Herders on the Madaglasht side refer to the Lohigal An as Ghuchhar Sar An. This trek combines easily, from Chhatar Ghuni (see Day 3), with the more strenuous Phargam An trek.

PLANNING
Maps

The US AMS 1:250,000 topographic map *Churrai (NI 43-1)* covers the trek, but the 1:253,440 topographic map *Chitral (I 42-F)* shows the lower Shishi Gol and Golen Gol. The Dok An and Lohigal An appear very close to each other, and the placement of their labels is misleading. At first glance, it appears that Dok An is mislabelled as Lohigal An and Lohigal An as Dok An. Istor is labelled as Ustur. The British Survey of India 1:63,360 topographic maps *43 A/1* and *42 D/4* cover the trek in more detail.

GETTING TO/FROM THE TREK
To the Start
Chitral-Drosh vans (Rs 35) depart regularly from Chitral's Ataliq Bazaar. Drosh-Madaglasht special hires cost Rs 1000 and Chitral-Madaglasht costs Rs 2000.

From the Finish
Jeeps only go as far as Istor, above Izghor, although the road continues to Chhatar Ghuni and Dukadaki. Istor-Chitral jeeps cost Rs 40 (two hours), departing in the early morning. Special hires cost Rs 600–700. You can also walk on the road between Istor and the Chitral-Gilgit road in four to five hours and look for a ride there.

THE TREK (see map p145)
Day 1: Madaglasht to Ghuchharsar Ghari
4–6 hours, 14km, 905m ascent
Follow Shishi Gol's true right (north) bank north-east. Pass through fields and pastures two to three hours (10km) to Deozari. After 500m, another trail branches east up the Andowir Glacier's outwash stream. Some maps show a route to the Andowir An at the glacier's head that leads to Dir's upper Panjkora Valley just south of Thalo An. The route, however, is over crevassed glaciers, rarely used, and neither feasible nor advisable for trekkers. The trail to the Lohigal An continues another hour, or 1.5km, from this junction through trees to Ruagol Ghari. From this Gujar settlement, follow the trail up, steeply at times, one to two hours to the huts at *Ghuchharsar Ghari* (3505m). Several good camp sites are nearby.

Day 2: Ghuchharsar Ghari to Krui Uts
4½–6 hours, 11km, 856m ascent, 780m descent
Follow the stream's true right (north) bank. In one hour, the route to the Dok An branches north, climbing quickly to that pass. The trail continues north-east one hour to Lohigal An (4361m) with a good view of Ghuchhar Sar (6249m). In Khowar, *ghuchhar* means 'waterfall'; *sar*, 'head'. Descend into the upper Lohigal Gol through flower-filled

meadows for 6.5km, or two to three hours, to huts at *Krui Uts* (red spring, 3581m).

Day 3: Krui Uts to Chhatar Ghuni
4–5 hours, 13.5km, 581m descent
Head north, following the Lohigal Gol's true left (west) bank a short way, then cross to the opposite bank. Continue downvalley through several summer settlements to the confluence of the Lohigal Gol and Golen Gol at *Chhatar Ghuni* (3000m). Camp anywhere in this valley with springs and meadows.

Day 4: Chhatar Ghuni to Istor
3–4 hours, 9km, 300m descent
Descend Golen Gol to Istor (2700m).

Phargam An

Duration	4 days
Distance	52.5km
Standard	demanding
Season	July–mid-September
Start	Istor
Finish	Harchin
Zone & Permit	open, no permit
Public Transport	yes
Summary	Traversing wild Hindukush country, this rugged trek follows an old route over a high pass, skirting the south and east shoulders of Buni Zom.

Phargam An (4975m) links the infrequently visited Golen Gol with the Laspur Valley at the western base of Shandur Pass. This route was used regularly in summer before construction of the Chitral-Gilgit road. It passes between Buni Zom and Ghuchhar Sar, offering glimpses of these peaks. Crossing the steep Phargam An involves several hours of Class 2 scrambling up huge talus on an obscure route where route-finding skills are useful.

PLANNING
Maps
The US AMS 1:250,000 topographic maps *Churrai (NI 43-1)* and *Mastuj (NJ 43-13)*

cover the trek. The British Survey of India 1:63,360 topographic maps *43 A/1*, *42 D/4* and *42 D/8* cover the trek in more detail.

Guides & Porters

A guide or knowledgeable porter is essential for this tricky route. One trekker, a 'jungly' veteran of long solo journeys, spent several days looking for the pass before finally making it over. The trek involves two nights at high camps above the tree line on either side of the pass, so equip anyone going with you adequately.

When doing this trek after the Lohigal An trek, detour down Golen Gol to Istor since Madaglasht men don't know Phargam An and you can't count on hiring someone at Chakoli Bokht, the highest summer hut used by Golen people. Other summer settlements in Golen Gol are used by Gujars, who aren't familiar with Phargam An.

GETTING TO/FROM THE TREK
To the Start

Chitral-Istor jeeps cost Rs 40 (two hours), departing in the late morning. The staging area is a small teashop, the Kohinoor Hotel, across Chew Bridge, just north of Chitral town on the road's east side. Hakim Khan, who also runs the adjacent store, can help you find the right jeep.

Jeeps only go as far as Istor, a steep 8km above Izghor, but the road continues beyond Istor to Chhatar Ghuni and Dukadaki. Chitral–Chhatar Ghuni special hires cost Rs 1000 and Chitral-Dukadaki costs Rs 1200–1500, shortening the trek by one to 1½ days.

From the Finish

Harchin-Mastuj jeeps cost Rs 25 for the 20km ride. It's easy to catch a Mastuj-Chitral jeep (Rs 80), but it may require spending the night in Mastuj. Prearranged special hires can meet you at Phargam village.

THE TREK
Day 1: Istor to Chhatar Ghuni

5½ hours, 7.5km, 300m ascent
Istor (2700m), Golen Gol's highest village, means 'horse' in Khowar. Across the river from Istor is a spring and a grassy, shaded

camp site. The trail up Golen Gol narrows and continues 5km to Romen, a level place with huts, fields and clear springs. Another 2.5km on is a broad, grassy plain with clear streams, a few huts and some fields. This is called ***Chhatar Ghuni*** (3000m) on maps, but Jungal locally. Lohigal Gol branches south from Jungal to the Lohigal An.

Day 2: Chhatar Ghuni to Jeshtanan Camp

5 hours, 16km, 1050m ascent
An easy 5km beyond Chhatar Ghuni, come to the Gujar huts of Dangari Kuru (3150m). From here, a side valley, Sachiokuh Gol, leads south over a pass and then east via the Bashqar Gol to Sor Laspur. The U502 *Churrai (NI 43-1)* map inaccurately depicts this unnamed pass. The pass is higher (5070m) and completely glaciated. It involves a steep glaciated ascent and descent with serious crevasses, and isn't feasible for trekkers.

One kilometre beyond Dangari Kuru are the Gujar huts of Dukadaki. The U502 *Mastuj (NJ 43-13)* map shows a route north from Dukadaki over a 4633m pass to Reshun along the Mastuj River. Neither villagers in Golen, nor those in Reshun, are familiar with this steep route, which seems to be no longer used. Some 5km beyond Dukadaki, in a stony barren area, are the huts of Chakoli Bokht (3600m), where the Golen Gol villagers tend their sheep and goats. Springs flow from the base of the cliff here, and a bit of grass is surrounded by talus-covered hills.

Beyond the last grass at Chakoli Bokht, cross the talus fields and two side streams from the north, and head for the cliffs at the base of the Golen Glacier. Reach the three small stone shelters against the cliff known as ***Jeshtanan Camp*** (4050m), 6km from Chakoli Bokht. There is good, clear water near to this picturesque, although sometimes windy, camp. Local people tell that at this place *jeshtan* spirits are sometimes seen. They are small beings, the size of children, and wear only a small, pointed hat the colour of juniper wood. The name is cognate with the Kalashamun term *jestak* and derives from Sanskrit *jyeshtah*, which means eldest or first.

Day 3: Jeshtanan Camp to Phargam High Camp

8–10 hours, 9km, 925m ascent, 1075m descent

Ascend the lateral moraine along the true right (north) bank of the Golen Glacier's outwash stream. Some sparse grass grows on the moraine, but it's mostly talus and the route is steep. Reach the top of the ascent 1½ to two hours from camp. Where the route levels off with a black moraine ahead and a grassy hillock on the right, turn left 40 degrees and head up an unlikely seeming talus slope. Ascend huge Class 2 granite blocks one to 1½ hours to a lovely grassy area where wildflowers bloom in profusion and snowcocks abound. From here, ascend more gradual talus towards the pass. You may find the remains of an old trail, built for a past Mehtar of Chitral to ride his horse over. On the final steep climb to the pass, the old trail is obliterated until close to the top, where water and the trail are again encountered. It takes from 4½ to six hours to reach **Phargam An** (4975m). On a cairn at the top is a metal plaque commemorating an Austrian mountaineering casualty, Georg Kronberger, who 'sleeps forever in the glacier'.

Expect to find a fair amount of snow on the pass through mid-August, and a small cornice on its north side. The descent is across talus, where the old trail is occasionally encountered, until you reach grassy, flower-strewn ibex habitat. No doubt snow leopards are also about, although rarely seen. You can *camp* here (and still reach Harchin in a long day by starting early the next morning).

Just beyond this spot is a rocky hill. Leave it on your left and head right and down a scree slope. Below you can see the old trail and clear streams. Flowers and low willows abound, and the stream is cool and clear on a hot day, inviting you to wash the dust out of your hair under a waterfall. Descend into the upper Phargam Gol with its steep, jagged cliffs. On your left to the north, a spectacular waterfall booms off the Khora Bort Glacier from Buni Zom. On summer days, the river from this huge waterfall can be crossed only in the morning. In the afternoon, large boulders roll down the river bed, and it's impossible to ford. Camp before the river at *Phargam High Camp* (3900m) in a grassy area among clear streams three to four hours from the pass. Enjoy the sunset

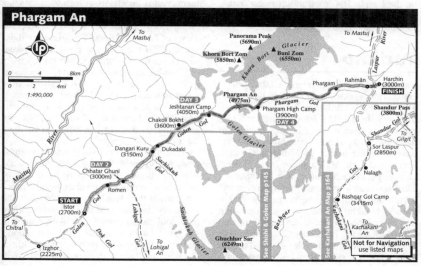

CHITRAL

on the cliffs and mountains of this lovely upper valley.

Climbers attempting Buni Zom, first climbed in 1957 by a New Zealand expedition, make their base camp here. A steep narrow gully near Gulabmali with loose rocks leads to the Khora Bort Glacier and Khora Bort Zom (5850m), as well as the route to Buni Zom. Wearing a climbing helmet is prudent. Beyond the gully, steep moraine leads to a snowy basin where you can camp. Above the basin, the route splits and is confusing, so a local guide is necessary. Less ambitious climbers can get excellent views from nearby Panorama Peak (5690m).

Day 4: Phargam High Camp to Harchin

6–8 hours, 20km, 900m descent

In the morning, the river is no longer muddy brown, but a cool, milky white, and is easily forded. Descending, cross another glacial side stream and pick up the trail downvalley, passing awesome hanging glaciers on either side of Phargam Gol. Above Phargam village is a small spring, and an unsealed road leading from Phargam to Rahmān. Jeeps are infrequent, so walk on the road to Rahmān on the Laspur River's true left (west) bank, and cross the bridge to reach **Harchin** (3000m) on the Gilgit-Chitral road.

Turikho

The high Hindukush forms a labyrinth of peaks, ridges, glaciers and valleys that march along Chitral's north-west border. Through it all flows the Turikho River, which receives the waters from the everlasting snows and glaciers. Turikho and its tributary valleys are known by the names of Mulkho, Turikho, Tirich and Rich. *Muli* and *turi* mean 'lower' and 'upper' in Khowar; hence Mulkho and Turikho mean lower and upper Kho country; Tirich and Rich may be originally Wakhi names. Mulkho's green villages are south and east of the long ridge running north-east from Tirich Mir. Turikho's villages lie north of Mulkho along both sides of the Turikho River. Tirich, a side valley leading west into

the heart of the Hindukush, is the route to several base camps. The upland Rich Gol is the northernmost section, including the entire area above the Uzhnu Valley to Pakistan's northern border with Afghanistan.

Zani An

Duration	5½–6 hours
Distance	12.2km
Standard	easy
Season	late April–October
Start	Uthool
Finish	Shagrom
Zone & Permit	restricted, no permit
Public Transport	yes

Summary Crossing the Zani An on the ridge above Mulkho offers spectacular sweeping views and the best and quickest approach to the Tirich Valley.

Zani An (3840m) is a pass that links Uthool in Mulkho to Shagrom in the Tirich Valley. Tirich villagers use the pass, the quickest and shortest route to their valley. Tirich villagers call the pass Zani An, although Uthool villagers call it Tirich An. A jeep road makes a pleasant, wide trail that eases the 1200m climb from Uthool to the pass, where the views of Istor-o-Nal and Saraghrar are magnificent. To the east, the Buni Zom massif soars over the Turikho and Mastuj rivers.

Crossing the Zani An to get to Tirich significantly reduces transport cost and time spent in a jeep and is the best way to start the Tirich Mir Base Camp trek. Large parties can send the bulk of their supplies by road and walk over the Zani An to meet their crew in Shagrom.

Although this is a short and easy pass crossing, proper acclimatisation is necessary. Uthool villagers have plenty of stories of trekkers who quickly develop altitude problems when they reach Uthool (2640m) and begin walking the same day. Spend one night in Uthool (larger parties may like camping in the large meadow across from the school) and cross the pass the next morning. Uthool is a scenic village with sweeping views over

Mulkho and Buni. Friendly villagers may show you to a lovely camp site in the village amid an open grassy area beneath walnut trees with a gushing spring nearby.

PLANNING
Maps
The US AMS 1:250,000 topographic map *Mastuj (NJ 43-13)* covers the trek. The road beyond Uthool isn't shown. It spells Uthool as Uthul, Warijun as Warinjun and Shagrom as Shagram. (Three villages have similar names, which are often confused and are misprinted on maps. Shagrom is Tirich Valley's highest village, Shagram is Turikho's main village and Shogram is along the Mastuj River's true right bank opposite Reshun.)

Guides & Porters
The route is fairly obvious, so a guide isn't necessary. Porters usually spend the night in Shagrom and recross the pass the next day, so their wages (Rs 375–475) include payment for wāpasi and food rations. Let your needs be known when you arrive in Uthool, where the helpful school teacher speaks some English.

GETTING TO/FROM THE TREK
To the Start
A link road before Warijun, Mulkho's main village, leads to Uthool; don't take the road just beyond Warijun that leads to Zani village. From Uthool, the road continues a few kilometres to Zani An. It was built to get an air compressor to a canal construction site. The canal, under construction since 1992, is to bring water to Mulkho from a ridge-top lake. The road isn't well maintained beyond Uthool, so you can only rely on taking a jeep as far as Uthool. Drivers may take you further if conditions permit and you pay extra.

Chitral-Mulkho jeeps cost Rs 50. Any Tirich-bound jeep can drop you in Warijun. From there, you can wait for a local jeep to Uthool, organise a Warijun-Uthool special hire, or walk several hours to Uthool, some 675m above Warijun. Chitral-Uthool jeeps cost Rs 60 (five hours), but are infrequent since there are only a few in the village. Special hires cost Rs 1200.

From the Finish
Shagrom-Chitral jeeps cost Rs 120 (nine hours), departing Shagrom at 4am. Jeeps don't go on Friday and depart only every three or four days. Alternatively, walk along the road downvalley to Zindrauli, cross the bridge to Warkup, and wait for a jeep coming from Turikho to Chitral. Special hires cost Rs 2500–3000.

THE TREK (see map p152)
Follow the road from Uthool (2640m) to the pass. The trail climbs quickly, ascending 300m in the first hour. Water is available at the last green area near a few willow trees two hours above the village. Later in the season, when snow in the gullies above has melted, water is unavailable higher. Continue another hour to **Zani An** (3840m), 7.7km from Uthool. Snow typically remains, especially on its north side, until June.

Several large cairns mark the good trail as you descend into the narrow Tirich Valley. Shagrom is visible upvalley, 4.5km and 1080m below the pass. Descend through fields and past houses to a footbridge over Tirich Gol two to 2½ hours from the pass. Cross the footbridge and head downstream along the road five to 10 minutes and *camp* under poplar trees along the river or walk upstream 30 minutes to **Shagrom** (2760m).

Tirich Mir Base Camp

Duration	6 days
Distance	58km
Standard	demanding
Season	mid-June–mid-September
Start/Finish	Shagrom
Zone & Permit	restricted, US$50 permit
Public Transport	yes

Summary Tirich Mir, the Hindukush's highest peak, rises above a vast wilderness of glaciers and 20 other impressive 7000m summits, making this a trek into the very centre of the high Hindukush.

Tirich Valley, a long, western branch of the Turikho Valley, leads towards the base of the

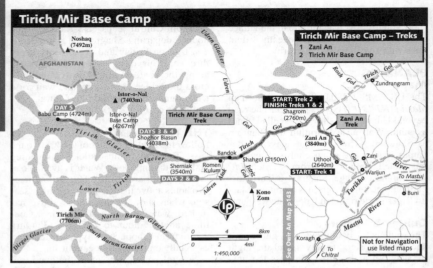

Tirich Mir Base Camp

Tirich Mir Base Camp – Treks
1   Zani An
2   Tirich Mir Base Camp

highest Hindukush peaks; Noshaq, Istor-o-Nal and Tirich Mir. The popular trek to Tirich Mir Base Camp traverses the Lower Tirich Glacier, so experience with glacier travel is helpful. The base camp is known locally as Babu Camp, named after Babu Mohammad, a veteran guide who, when not on trek, can be found at Chitral's Mountain Inn. Reminiscent of the Baltoro Glacier trek, but much shorter and less demanding, this trek delights fans of big mountains and mighty glaciers.

PLANNING
What to Bring
Mountaineering equipment necessary to travel in roped teams is optional, but may be helpful for a short icy section (see Mountaineering Equipment, p61).

Maps
The US AMS 1:250,000 topographic map *Mastuj (NJ 43-13)* and 1:253,440 topographic map *Zebak (J-42X)* cover the trek. Udren Gol is labelled as Atrak Gol, but villagers say that the map mistakenly names this major side valley. Sherniak is labelled Shekhniyak, and the trail and camp sites beyond Bandok are not shown.

Permits & Regulations
This trek is in a restricted zone where a permit and licensed guide are required (see Trekking Permits, p70).

Guides & Porters
Porters ask for a flat Rs 250 per stage, including payment for food rations. They also ask for the clothing and equipment allowance. Small parties or those with loads less than 25kg may be able to negotiate a compromise. No huts exist on this route and deforestation is evident at Sherniak, the last available wood source, so provide porters with shelter, stoves and fuel.

Stages
Because numerous mountaineering expeditions visit the Tirich Valley, the stage system applies. Fortunately, the stages correspond to reasonable walking days. It's eight stages total round trip from Shagrom: (1) Sherniak; (2) Shoghor Biasun; (3) Istor-o-Nal; and (4) Babu Camp; and four stages (5–8) to return via the same route. The start of the first stage is referred to as Shagrom, but it means the large, shaded area along the river 30 minutes below the village where large parties camp.

GETTING TO/FROM THE TREK

Chitral-Shagrom jeeps cost Rs 150 and special hires cost Rs 3000–3500. Jeeps to Tirich and Turikho have no fixed sarai in Chitral, so ask at the Mastuj sarai just north of Ataliq Bridge or at the jeep workshop behind the petrol pump across from the PTDC Chitral Motel.

Jeeps coming from Chitral take 14 hours, but jeeps down do it in nine hours (usually departing Shagrom at 4am). Jeeps don't go on Friday and depart only every three or four days. You can also take any jeep going to Turikho and get off at Warkup, cross the bridge to Zindrauli and wait for a jeep going up Tirich Valley, or walk. It's quicker, less expensive and more fun to walk over Zani An to Shagrom.

THE TREK
Day 1: Shagrom to Sherniak

3½–5 hours, 12.5km, 780m ascent

Follow the trail out of Shagrom (2760m) through willow groves. Beyond them lie several ponds, built by Shagrom villagers to attract migratory ducks, which visit in spring and fall, when Shagrom men sneak up behind the rock walls of the ponds, poke shotguns through small holes in the walls and fire away. Hunting is great sport in Tirich.

Beyond these ponds cross a wooden footbridge to the Tirich Gol's true right bank, one hour from the village. After another 15 minutes on a level trail through dry, rocky terrain is the confluence (2880m) of the Tirich Gol and **Udren Gol**, which leads to the north-east sides of Istor-o-Nal and Noshaq (see Udren under Other Treks, p167). Gradually ascend the main valley for 30 minutes to some springs. Water also flows here from cultivated moraine terraces above. Cross a gully, usually choked with snow until July, and after 30 minutes come to the fields and summer huts of **Shahgol** (3150m). Kono Zom is the prominent rocky peak ahead.

Follow the good trail for 15 minutes, ascending slightly to more huts at **Bandok**. Beyond Bandok, a narrow valley called Adren Atak heads south (left). Reportedly, a difficult pass at its head leads to Owir. Cross the Adren Atak stream to the highest huts of Romen Kulum in 15 minutes. When Tirich Gol is swollen by glacial melt, the trail climbs the scree slope 50m above the true right bank and contours high to reach Sherniak in one hour. Before July, follow the river, crossing and recrossing it over snow bridges to reach the birch and willow grove at **Sherniak** (3540m).

Days 2–3: Sherniak to Shoghor Biasun

5–6 hours, 6.5km, 498m ascent

A small trail goes through willow stands, under a rock perched over two large boulders, and climbs the Lower Tirich Glacier's terminal moraine one hour from Sherniak. From here, follow the true right bank of the main outwash stream. Head towards the glacier's north side near its snout. Beyond the snout, ascend onto the moraine and move up the glacier, working towards its north margin. A large channel can be difficult to cross in midsummer. The ice slope on its up-glacier side is steep and slippery, and the use of a rope here may be warranted for safety. Ascend the ice slope and reach more level moraine. The route continues up the glacier's north margin, past a prominent lateral moraine from a northern side stream. In the glacier's centre, across from this side stream, are white seracs. Stay close to the north margin. **Shoghor Biasun** (4038m) is just beyond and west of the large mound of moraine. Leave the glacier and descend into camp. Shoghor Biasun (sandy base) has the best views of Tirich Mir and Lower Tirich Glacier. The peak is obscured by the time you reach Babu Camp. Spend Day 3 here for acclimatisation.

Day 4: Shoghor Biasun to Babu Camp

5–7 hours, 10km, 686m ascent

The route to Babu Camp stays in an ablation valley and doesn't go out on the Upper Tirich Glacier. Follow the crest of an old lateral moraine to **Istor-o-Nal Base Camp** (4267m), a good lunch spot. Continue another two to three hours to **Babu Camp** (4724m). You may want to spend an extra day or two to explore the area.

Days 5–6: Babu Camp to Shagrom

2 days, 29km, 1964m descent
Retrace your steps downvalley to Shagrom, camping at **Sherniak** on Day 5.

Shah Jinali An

Duration	4 days
Distance	39km
Standard	moderate
Season	mid-June–mid-September
Start	Rua
Finish	Yashkist
Zone & Permit	restricted, no permit
Public Transport	yes

Summary Broad, rolling alpine meadows and sparkling streams offer open strolling through the pass called the king's polo ground, or Shah Jinali An.

Shah Jinali An (4140m) is a pass linking the Rich Gol's north end to Yashkist in the upper Yarkhun Valley. This popular and relatively easy pass parallels the Afghan border less than 8km from the Wakhan Corridor.

This trek is often combined with at least one other trek. It can precede the Broghil & Karambar An trek (see p158) and the Chilinji An & Qalander Uween trek (see p285) to make an incredible west-east trek over three passes along Pakistan's northern border. The Shah Jinali An trek can also follow an east to west crossing of the Thui An (see p183).

PLANNING
Maps

The US AMS 1:250,000 topographic map *Mastuj (NJ 43-13)* covers the trek. Shah Jinali, west of Dershal, is known locally as Jinali Ghari.

Guides & Porters

Porters ask for a flat rate of Rs 250 per stage including payment for food rations.

Stages

Porters from Phargam or Rua ask for 3½ stages from Rua: (1) Dershal; (2) Shah Ghari; (3) Siru Gol and (3½) Yashkist or Shusht.

When walking east to west, Yarkhun porters have advantageously created two stages out of one between Lasht and Siru Gol: Lasht to Shusht or Yashkist; and Shusht or Yashkist to Siru Gol.

GETTING TO/FROM THE TREK
To the Start

Chitral-Rua jeeps cost Rs 150–180 (eight hours) and special hires cost Rs 3000–5000. Jeeps to Rich Gol have no fixed sarai in Chitral, so ask at the Mastuj jeep sarai just north of Ataliq Bridge or at the jeep workshop behind the petrol pump across from the PTDC Chitral Motel.

From the Finish

Walk 15 minutes upvalley to the new bridge below Shusht that crosses to the Yarkhun's true left bank and meets the main road. Look for a ride here. Lasht-Mastuj jeeps cost Rs 160. Special hires cost Rs 3000. If the road is blocked below Yashkist, walk downvalley as needed. It takes eight hours to walk to Sholkuch. Sholkuch-Mastuj jeeps cost Rs 80 and special hires cost Rs 1500.

When walking down the Yarkhun Valley, it's half a stage from Yashkist to Dobargar and one stage from Dobargar to Sholkuch.

THE TREK
Day 1: Rua to Dershal

6–7 hours, 16km, 480m ascent
From Rua (2820m), the Rich Gol's highest village, walk one hour along the river's true right (west) bank, then cross a footbridge to its true left (east) bank. Continue one hour to **Moghlang** (2926m), a possible camp site just north of a side stream, the Hazgo Gol. A cairn on a large boulder with adjacent livestock pens marks the spot. Thirty minutes beyond Moghlang, the trail turns east into the Shah Jinali Gol.

Head up the Shah Jinali Gol's true left (south) bank, crossing a small side stream. After 30 minutes, cross the river over a natural bridge of boulders to the true right (north) bank. The narrow trail climbs loose scree 45 minutes to level terraces above, where the gorge opens into a limestone and marble valley. The trail rolls through scattered birch and juniper, and crosses several clear side streams.

After another two to 2½ hours, reach a footbridge leading to **Dershal** (3300m), along the true left bank. Dershal has shaded camp sites along a sometimes silty stream named for the nearby piles of boulders (*der* in Khowar). If the footbridge is washed out, you can camp along the true right bank.

Day 2: Dershal to Shah Ghari
2–2½ hours, 6.2km, 390m ascent
Follow the trail along the true left bank, crossing many birch-lined tributaries along the way. Above the confluence of the clear stream coming from the Shah Jinali An and the larger outwash stream from the Shah Jinali and Ochilli glaciers, cross the stream that runs down from the pass. **Shah Ghari** (3690m), an old Gujar camp with some stone shelters and a livestock pen, is on the true right bank of the stream coming from the pass. If you are previously acclimatised, it is possible to continue on to the Ishperu Dok High Camp.

If the footbridge to Dershal is washed out and you camp along the true right (north) bank, continue along the true right bank and cross a snow bridge over the outwash stream from the Shah Jinali and Ochilli glaciers just above where the stream coming from the Shah Jinali An joins it to reach Shah Ghari.

Day 3: Shah Ghari to Ishperu Dok High Camp
4–5 hours, 7.1km, 450m ascent, 150m descent
Ascend along the true right bank one to 1½ hours to the start of the pass area. The entire area, over 3km long, offers fine **camp sites** with sweeping views. The actual **Shah Jinali An** (4140m), marked by a cairn, is three hours from Shah Ghari. Just west of the pass is the level Shah Jinali, which means 'king's polo field' in Khowar.

Descend the gentle trail, bearing left from the pass, contouring around into the Ishperu Dok Gol. Reach the **Ishperu Dok High Camp** (3990m), a grassy camp site along the stream's true right bank, one hour below the pass. At the Ishperu Dok Gol's head stands the prominent white mountain that gives its name to the valley.

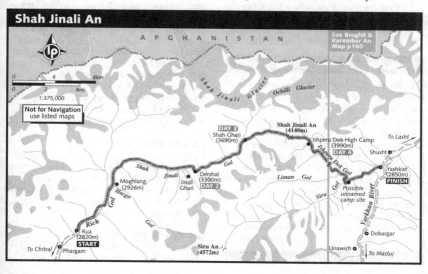

Shah Jinali An

CHITRAL

Day 4: Ishperu Dok High Camp to Yashkist

4 hours, 9.7km, 1140m descent

Cross the clear stream here, or 15 minutes below the camp site via a small footbridge, to the herders' huts of Ishperu Dok on the true left bank, where people from Shusht, Yakhdan and Yashkist bring their livestock. Another 15 minutes farther the trail enters a canyon and descends steeply 45 minutes to a footbridge. Cross it to the true right bank and descend 10 minutes to another footbridge and cross it to the true left bank. Pass the confluence with the glacial Liman Gol after 10 minutes. Then five minutes farther, cross a third footbridge (before which are several springs) back to the true right bank.

Continue down the gorge 30 minutes to the confluence with the often brown **Siru Gol**. Head 150m up the Siru Gol's true left bank and cross a footbridge to its true right bank. About 250m downstream is a possible *camp site* (3120m), which marks the end of a stage, with a small trickle of water, some porters' shelters and a flat area for tents. (When doing the trek from east to west, camp here rather than trying to reach Ishperu Dok High Camp from Lasht.)

Follow the trail high above the river for 20 minutes, then descend 10 minutes to a well-built footbridge to the true left bank. The trail climbs 30 minutes out of the river

Pass Bagging in the Hindukush

Sometimes the best treks are spontaneous. Bill Tilman, who with Eric Shipton set the standard for small, lightweight trekking expeditions in the early 20th century, wrote, 'an expedition that cannot organise itself on the back of an old envelope is bound to suffer from the effects of too much organisation'. In Chitral, with time on my hands, I planned a whirlwind solo trek, bought supplies and set out all in one morning. Seventeen days later, I returned to Chitral after crossing these seven passes: Owir An; Khot An; Thui An; Naz Bar An; Zagaro An; Gokhshal An; and Dooni An.

John Mock

valley to cross the shoulder of a ridge, then descends for 10 minutes to the outskirts of Yashkist. Continue to descend through **Yashkist** (2850m) on a road 30 minutes to the Yarkhun Valley's floor, which can be very hot on midsummer afternoons. *Camp* on an old polo field, amid shrub, near a shallow pool.

Khot An

Duration	2 days
Distance	16.2km
Standard	moderate
Season	June–mid-September
Start	Khot Lasht
Finish	Dizg
Zone & Permit	restricted, no permit
Public Transport	yes

Summary Khot An is a gentle and panoramic pass that traverses the Hindu Raj Range through upland yak pastures and provides a short and direct route between Turikho and Yarkhun.

Khot An (4230m) is a grassy pass between Turikho's Khot (Cloud) Valley and Dizg in the Yarkhun Valley. It's an ancient route, as shown by a three-tiered Buddhist stupa carved on a large boulder along the road from Turikho to Khot. The pass is regularly used by villagers of upper Khot to visit their relatives in Dizg. They make the trip in one day, but trekkers can enjoy the pretty yak pastures when taking two days. The trail is quite gentle on the Khot side, but the 8km descent to Dizg is tedious. Hence, the trek description is from west to east.

PLANNING
Maps

The US AMS 1:250,000 topographic map *Mastuj (NJ 43-13)* covers the trek. It doesn't give proper names for Ewatch and Purkhot. Shahglasht is labelled Shah Lasht and other herders' huts aren't shown.

Guides & Porters

Porters, who are easiest to hire in Khot Lasht, ask for a lump sum of Rs 500.

GETTING TO/FROM THE TREK
To the Start
Chitral-Khot Lasht jeeps cost Rs 150 (six hours). Special hires cost Rs 3000, and may go to Shahglasht for more money. Jeeps to Turikho have no fixed departure place in Chitral, so ask at the Mastuj jeep sarai just north of Ataliq Bridge or at the jeep workshop behind the petrol pump across from the PTDC Chitral Motel.

From the Finish
Dizg-Mastuj jeeps cost Rs 35 and special hires cost Rs 750. Dizg-Chitral jeeps cost Rs 120 and special hires cost Rs 3000.

THE TREK
Day 1: Khot Lasht to Shahglasht
3½–4 hours, 4.7km, 732m ascent

First, spend a night at Khot Lasht (3048m) for acclimatisation. The road continues beyond Khot Lasht to Shahglasht. Follow the road one to 1½ hours to the bridge over the Khot Gol above Ewatch (3180m). Forty-five minutes farther, and across the river, is Purkhot, the valley's highest year-round village. The highest houses, used in summer only, are another 30 minutes farther. Continue climbing another 45 minutes through rolling hills, then enter the level Shahglasht area, reaching a solar-powered weather station in another 15 minutes. Here, several streams join to form Khot Gol. Above and south-east of the weather station are the Pushet huts. Across the river to the north-west are the Jinali Shah huts, and upstream from them are the Tarwatin huts. The stream

coming from the east is Warmin Gol, and from the north is Jacha Gol. A trail leads up it to the Ghochhar Gol and Ghochhar An, a high pass leading to Bang Gol (see Hindu Raj Crest under Other Treks, p168). Across from Tarwatin on the Jacha Gol's true left bank are the Jharogh huts. Camp in the meadows at *Shahglasht* (3780m) and visit the herders' huts, where porters appreciate being able to stay.

Day 2: Shahglasht to Dizg
5–7 hours, 11.5km, 450m ascent, 1730m descent

Follow the trail up the Warmin Gol's true left bank passing between two large rocky hills. As the stream bears to the north (left), continue straight, reaching a level grassy area called *Graz*, 1¼ hours from Shahglasht. This is a good alternative high camp to Shahglasht when your porters are equipped to sleep at 3900m.

Beyond Graz 30 minutes is another grassy area called *Trushko Chhat* (3950m). This is the last reliable water until over the Khot An, and the last possible camp site. Bear south-south-east, passing below the base of the large rock face. Reach a knoll in 15 minutes and turn south-east towards the Khot An, which is first visible from the small knoll. Reach **Khot An** (4230m) 30 minutes from the knoll. Yaks graze on the pass in summer. Ahead and east are the peaks above Thui. Behind to the west are the high Hindukush peaks, including infrequently seen Akher Chhīsh (7019m) at the Uzhnu Gol's head. Descend south-south-east

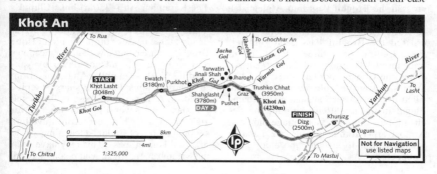

CHITRAL

across scree 30 minutes to a small, cold spring. This is the only water until Dizg! Contour around the valley's south slopes, with fine views of the Shandur range and Yarkhun Valley below. After one to 1½ hours, reach a ridge directly above Yarkhun, and turn north-east heading down the ridge top. After passing a solitary juniper, zigzag down the ridge's east face one hour on a steep, loose gravel trail. Then descend a steep gully between fantastic eroded loess towers on loose gravel another hour to the valley floor. Follow a trail across the alluvial fan 30 minutes to the jeep road into **Dizg** (2500m), and another 15 minutes to the shops. Shopkeepers of this pleasant well-watered Isma'ili village can offer trekkers grassy areas to *camp*.

Upper Yarkhun

Two passes link the upper Yarkhun Valley to Ghizar. The glaciated Darkot An leads south to the Yasin Valley, and the grassy Karambar An leads east to the Karambar Valley, which joins the Ishkoman Valley below Imit. The western approach from Yarkhun to both passes goes through Broghil, an area populated by Wakhi. Wakhi living in Broghil have large herds of yaks, sheep and goats and also horses and camels. These border areas have only opened to foreigners since the end of the Russian occupation of Afghanistan in 1989.

An important Central Asian trade route passed through the Yarkhun Valley and crossed the Broghil Pass into Afghanistan and on to Kashgar and Yarkand. As recently as 1930, more than 1000 horse loads crossed the Broghil Pass each summer. From Central Asia, three quarters of all trade through Chitral was hashish *(charas)*. When the Chinese border closed in 1950, increased cannabis cultivation in Yarkhun filled the gap. After Pakistan made charas illegal in the late 1970s, production declined, but continues as a cottage industry. Almost all Yarkhun people are Isma'ili Muslims, friendly people who enjoy song and poetry.

ACCESS TOWN
Mastuj

In the bazaar, *Nasir Hotel & Restaurant* has Rs 30 charpoys. East of the bazaar are a few hotels catering to tourists. *Tourist Guest House* costs Rs 300-500. *Tourist Paradise* (☎ 48), run by Asif Khan, is quaint, with a nice garden and enclosed compound. The dorm costs Rs 50 and rooms cost Rs 150–200. *Tourist Garden* (☎ 66), run by Ghulam Nabi, is down a small lane and has no sign. Its peaceful compound has a well-tended garden. The dorm (Rs 60) and rooms (Rs 200) are clean. A PTDC motel was under construction at the time of research.

Chitral-Mastuj jeeps, which depart from the sarai north of Ataliq Bridge, cost Rs 80; special hires cost Rs 2000. No public transport goes between Mastuj and Shandur Pass.

Broghil & Karambar An

Duration	10 days
Distance	125.7km
Standard	moderate
Season	June–September
Start	Lasht
Finish	Bort
Zone & Permit	restricted, US$50 permit
Public Transport	yes

Summary An historic caravan route through Broghil's lake- and peak-dotted landscape crosses a gentle lake-crowned pass, traversing from the Hindu Raj Range to the Karakoram.

The Karambar An (4320m) links Chitral's Yarkhun Valley with Ghizar's Karambar Valley. The trek up the Yarkhun River headwaters passes through picturesque Broghil, an area dotted with green meadows and small lakes, and populated by yak-herding Wakhi. Karambar An is, apart from the Deosai Plains, Pakistan's largest alpine meadow. At the crest of these well-watered grasslands are several pristine lakes. Over 1000 years ago, Chinese pilgrims travelling south in search of Buddhist teachings wrote of a 'wild onion' pass. This may have been the Karambar An, where wild onions abound.

The trek is often preceded by the Shah Jinali An trek (p154) and followed by the Chilinji An & Qalander Uween trek (p285), making a spectacular traverse of Pakistan's northernmost borders over three passes.

PLANNING
Maps
The highly reliable US AMS 1:250,000 topographic map *Mastuj (NJ 43-13)* shows the Yarkhun Valley and Broghil Pass. The *Baltit (NJ 43-14)* sheet is the only readily available map showing Broghil and the Karambar An. It doesn't show the Karambar lakes and slightly alters place names. It labels Shuwor Sheer as Shuwar Shur, Qul Quldi as Qiu Quldi, Boree Mergich as Margach, and Rabot as Ribat. It doesn't show Top Khāna. It calls the river flowing west from the Karambar An the Ribat Bar. Local people call it Karambar Chhat (valley of Karambar Lake).

Permits & Regulations
This trek is in a restricted zone where a permit and licensed guide are required (see Trekking Permits, p70). Police in Lasht and Imit, and the Chitral Scouts in Ishkarwaz may ask to see your permit.

Guides & Porters
Chitrali porters ask for Rs 230 per day, including payment for food rations. The constantly changing Chattiboi and Karambar glaciers are tricky and require route-finding, so hire a nearby herder to show the way.

Stages
The stage system isn't instituted on this trek, but it's begun to take hold. Between Lasht and Karambar Lake, each day is roughly equivalent to a stage. In Karambar, Chitralis ask for three stages between Sokhter Rabot and Bort.

GETTING TO/FROM THE TREK
To the Start
The road goes as far as Lutgaz, just beyond Lasht but, in summer, high water may block the road near Sholkuch. When it's blocked, walk along the road. It takes two days (and two stages) to walk between Sholkuch and Lasht, so allow time for this possibility. Chitral-Mastuj jeeps cost Rs 80 and Mastuj-Lasht jeeps cost Rs 160. Mastuj-Lasht special hires cost Rs 3000 and Chitral-Lasht costs Rs 7000. In Lasht, the Shushar Gol occasionally blocks the road, leaving 45 minutes' walk to Lutgaz on Lasht's north end.

From the Finish
The road goes as far as Bort, but in summer, high water may block the road at Bilhanz. When it's blocked, walk along the road, fording side streams as needed. It takes four hours to walk between Bort and Bilhanz. One stage is fixed between Bort and Bad Swat. You may have to pay for an additional partial stage between Bad Swat and Bilhanz.

Jeeps to Gilgit cost Rs 120 from Bort, Rs 115 from Bilhanz and Rs 110 from Imit. Special hires cost Rs 3000 from Bort, Rs 2750 from Bilhanz, and Rs 2500 from Imit. Alternatively, you can walk or take a jeep to Chatorkhand and get on a NATCO bus (Rs 75) to Gilgit.

THE TREK
Day 1: Lasht to Kishmanja
5½–6½ hours, 16km, 252m ascent
Delightful *Lutgaz* (3048m, 'big grass' in Khowar), with its abundant springs and splendid view of the Shotor (camel) Glacier across the wide Yarkhun River, is the trek's staging ground. Follow a good trail along the Yarkhun's true right bank 50 minutes to the outskirts of Zirch village. Across the valley, large glaciers descend from snowy peaks. Cross a large alluvial fan and ford the Kan Khun Gol's several shallow channels after another 45 minutes. The trail bends east as it ascends, reaching the small settlement along the Bazhdung Gol in 30 minutes. The trail climbs 15 minutes to a saddle, then descends for 15 minutes to the small settlement and clear springs of Romenu. The high-water trail, usually used during July and August, climbs the hillside above the river. The low-water trail stays in the river bed beyond Romenu, around the base of a rock ridge, then along the base of scree slopes.

Reach an alluvial fan, one hour from Romenu, called Ishkore Kunj. Continue 30 minutes across this area, then 15 minutes through a large stand of trees. Beyond, skirt a scree slope at the river's edge and reach the Wakhi settlement of **Kishmanja** (3300m) in 30 minutes. Kishmanja, with its spring, is run by Momin, who collects a Rs 30 camping fee.

Day 2: Kishmanja to Ishkarwaz
4½–5½ hours, 12.9km, 210m ascent

Cross the stream at Kishmanja's east end via a footbridge and traverse a large scree slope above the river. At the base of the scree, 45 minutes from Kishmanja, are some springs and willow trees and a great view across the valley of Koyo Zom (6872m), which Broghil villagers call Ghaliyat. It was first climbed in 1968 by an Austrian expedition. Continue for another hour to a juniper-dotted plain. After 10 minutes the trail turns sharply left and climbs 10 minutes to **Vidinkot**, with a

clear stream and several houses. A footbridge over the Yarkhun River leads to the village of Garam Chashma, called Pechugh in Khowar, and a **hot spring**.

From Vidinkot, stay on the trail along the Yarkhun's true right (north) bank with great views of the enormous Chattiboi Glacier (not to be confused with a glacier of the same name in the Karambar Valley) for 30 minutes and cross the footbridge to its true left (south) side. Here you're directly opposite the Chattiboi Glacier's snout, which protrudes into the Yarkhun River calving off in massive chunks.

The trail divides 10 minutes beyond the footbridge. The right fork leads in one hour to Chikar and the trail south-east to Darkot An (see the Karambar An & Darkot An trek, p174). Take the left fork, following the Yarkhun River 15 minutes to a house and fields, with a small trickle of water. Another hour leads to the Chitral Scouts post at *Ishkarwaz*. Camp in the grassy area (3510m)

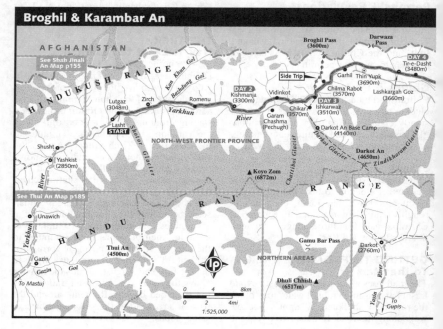

Broghil & Karambar An

AFGHANISTAN

HINDUKUSH RANGE

See Shah Jinali
An Map p155

Kan Khun Gol

Bazhdung Gol

Broghil Pass
(3600m)

Darwaza
Pass

DAY 4
Tir-e-Dasht
(3480m)

Garhil Thin Yupk
(3690m)

Side Trip

Lutgaz
(3048m)

Zirch   Romenu

DAY 2
Kishmanja
(3300m)

Vidinkot

Yarkhun

Chilma Rabot
(3570m)

Lashkargah Goz
(3660m)

Lasht
START

River

Garam
Chashma
(Pechugh)

DAY 3
Chikar Ishkarwaz
(3570m) (3510m)

Shusht

NORTH-WEST FRONTIER PROVINCE

Chattiboi Glacier

Darkot An Base Camp
(4140m)

Darkot Glacier

Yashkist
(2850m)

Koyo Zom
(6872m)

Darkot An
(4650m)

Zindikharam Glacier

RANGE

See Thui An Map p185

River

Unawich

HINDU

RAJ

Yarkhun

Thui An
(4500m)

Gamu Bar Pass

Darkot
(2760m)

Gazin

Gazin Gol

NORTHERN AREAS

To Mastuj

Dhuli Chhish ▲
(6517m)

0   4   8km

0   2   4mi

1:525,000

River

Yasin

To
Gupis

with a small spring above the river, just east of the footbridge spanning the gorge. From the ridge above Ishkarwaz are views of the Broghil Pass to the north, and the Darkot Glacier and Chattiboi icefall to the south.

Side Trip: Broghil Pass
3–5 hours, 13km, 90m ascent, 90m descent
Ask at the Chitral Scouts post in Ishkarwaz for permission to visit the Broghil Pass (3600m) for a day. You can rent horses in Chilma Rabot or Garhil.

Day 3: Ishkarwaz to Tir-e-Dasht
6–7 hours, 17.9km, 180m ascent, 210m descent
Cross the footbridge and climb gently 30 to 45 minutes to Chilma Rabot (3570m), a south-facing village, spread out amid open, terraced fields with the Broghil stream passing through the middle of the village.

Continue through grasslands above the true right bank, as the river runs through a

gorge with two watchtowers perched high above the opposite bank, one hour to picturesque **Garhil** (sheep pen by the rock), a settlement with a spring by big rocks north of the trail. From Garhil, the Darwaza Pass leads north into Afghanistan's Wakhan Corridor and is closed to foreigners, although Wakhi riders regularly cross the pass during summer.

Continue along the level trail one hour, skirting peat bogs. A newer trail carved from the river terrace parallels the river and leads in another hour to Thin Yupk (3690m, 'hot water' in Wakhi), where a hot spring flows into a small warm lake. (In low water, you can proceed from Garhil up the main river valley to Thin Yupk, but in high water avoid this route because of the seven or eight difficult fords.) From Thin Yupk, the trail goes over a low hill 30 minutes to a grassy swale with a clear stream. Continue 15 minutes past two picturesque ponds, then 15 minutes more onto the plain below

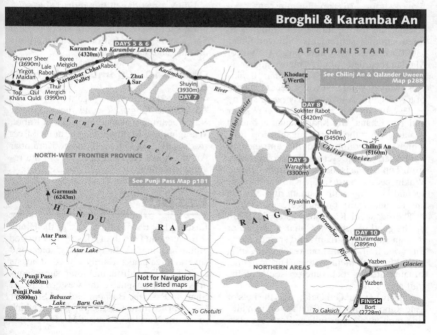

Broghil & Karambar An

Lashkargah Goz (3660m), where 22 Wakhi households are spread out along the hillside. *Lashkar* means 'army', *gah*, a 'place' and *goz*, 'grass', and the plain is a perfect place for an army to camp and graze its horses. This is the winter home of Broghil's nambardar Umar Rafi, son of the late Mirza Rafi. The Wakhi in Broghil are sadly much habituated to opium. On their plentiful grasslands, they produce surplus livestock. With the money they earn from selling it, some buy opium to while away the cold winter months.

Continue along the base of hills on the valley's north side to a mill house along a stream. Head up a short narrow defile along a clear stream, passing a large spring. The defile opens onto a large peat bog and the grassy camp site of *Tir-e-Dasht* (3480m), 1½ hours beyond Lashkargah Goz.

Days 4–5: Tir-e-Dasht to Karambar Lake

5½–6½ hours, 16.9km, 840m ascent, 60m descent

Ascend the rolling hills for 45 minutes to three summer settlements: Shuwor Sheer (3690m), the first and largest; Yirgot Maidan (bearded vulture's plain), higher on the eastern hillside; and Top Khāna, 10 minutes' walk beyond Shuwor Sheer at the base of a rocky hill. A level, grassy *camp site* by a clear stream lies between Shuwor Sheer and Top Khāna. **Top Khāna** (cannon house) is named for the crumbling hill-top fort, which once commanded the entrance to **Karambar Chhat**. Across the broad valley from Top Khāna is the **Zindikharam Glacier**. Wakhi people here speak Khowar as their second language with a smattering of Urdu and Persian. Dairy products are abundant.

The beautiful Karambar lakes lie 10km up the gentle Karambar Chhat. Clear water is abundant from streams and springs along this good trail. In one hour reach Qul Quldi, a Wakhi settlement with a Turkic name, situated atop a rock outcrop south of the trail above the river.

Shortly beyond Qul Quldi, pass the huts of Lale Rabot, which perch on the northern hillside high above the trail, and cross a clear

stream just beyond. The huts at Thur Mergich (3990m), a large summer settlement, are almost hidden from view south of (below) the trail along a clear stream one hour from Qul Quldi. Boree Mergich lies beyond another stream one hour from Thur Mergich. Rabot's two crumbling huts lie beyond another stream one hour from Boree Mergich.

This entire valley is considered *mergich* by the Wakhi, a term that means 'a pure, clean place where female fairy spirits *(pari)* dwell'. Thirty minutes beyond Rabot, a large cairn marks the **Karambar An** (4320m). The western, smaller lake lies 15 minutes farther on and is connected to the much larger lake by a stream that flows through another small lake. Follow the stream another 15 minutes to a large boulder with a cairn overlooking the largest lake. Several stone porters' shelters cluster around the boulder's base. Several excellent *camp sites* lie near the west end of the enormous blue **Karambar Lake** (4260m).

Enjoy a rest day at this remarkable spot. It takes 1¼ hours to walk along the lake's north shore. Above its south shore is Zhui Sar, a snowy peak with a glacier that falls into the lake itself.

Days 6–10: Karambar Lake to Bort

4 days, 62km, 1532m descent

To head to Gilgit, descend the Karambar Valley, camping at Shuyinj, Sokhter Rabot, Waraghut and Maturamdan en route to Bort (for details, see Days 1–6 of the Karambar An & Darkot An trek, pp175–7, in the reverse direction).

Laspur

Laspur, the area of Chitral east of the Hindu Raj Range and south of Mastuj, has rugged alpine terrain with many lakes, glaciers and several huge peaks. Rarely visited, it boasts considerable wildlife, including snow leopards. At Sor Laspur, at the western base of Shandur Pass, the Bashqar Gol and Shandur Gol join to form the Laspur River, which meets the Yarkhun River at Mastuj.

Kachakani An

Duration	6 days
Distance	57.5km
Standard	very demanding
Season	July–September
Start	Machiangaas
Finish	Sor Laspur
Nearest Town	Kalam
Zone & Permit	open, no permit
Public Transport	yes

Summary This trek through forested glades and flower-filled meadows along sparkling trout streams leads over the high Kachakani An from intimidating Swat into more peaceful Chitral.

The scenic Kachakani An trek crosses a glacier and a pass (4766m) between Swat's Ushu Gol and Chitral's Bashqar Gol. Upper Ushu Gol has lush pastures, forested hill sides and turquoise lakes.

PLANNING
Maps
The US AMS 1:250,000 topographic maps *Churrai (NI 43-1)* and *Mastuj (NJ 43-13)* cover the trek.

Guides & Porters
A reliable, responsible guide is indispensable. Hire a guide associated with a trekking company or the government. Porters from Laspur may be more reliable than those from Swat. Porters ask for a flat rate of Rs 250 per day, including payment for food rations.

NEAREST TOWN
Kalam
Many inexpensive hotels and eateries line the road. *PTDC Motel (☎ 0936-830014)* has singles/doubles for Rs 1200/1400; deluxe rooms cost Rs 1400/1800. Basic supplies are available in the bazaar.

Access to Kalam Kohistan is from Saidu Sharif or Mingora in the Swat Valley. PTDC operates a luxury bus from Rawalpindi to Saidu Sharif (Rs 350) that departs at 9am. From Mingora's general bus stand, regular transport runs all day to Kalam. The trip Mingora-Kalam costs Rs 50 (2½ hours).

GETTING TO/FROM THE TREK
To the Start
The road is sealed as far up Ushu Gol as Matiltan, 16km beyond Kalam, but jeeps go beyond to Mahodand Lake. Minibuses are generally available between Kalam and Matiltan. Kalam-Mahodand Lake special hires cost Rs 1000 (two to three hours). Alternatively, you can walk on the road from Matiltan to Machiangaas (six to seven hours, 13km).

From the Finish
Sor Laspur is on the Chitral-Gilgit road, but no regular transport goes to Chitral or over the Shandur Pass to Gilgit. Occasional Sor Laspur-Mastuj jeeps cost Rs 35. Mastuj-Chitral jeeps cost Rs 80. Sor Laspur-Chitral special hires cost Rs 3000, and Sor Laspur-Gilgit costs Rs 8000–9000.

THE TREK
Day 1: Machiangaas to Diwangar
4–5 hours, 9.5km, 160m ascent

Machiangaas (2890m) meadows lie just south of the cedar and pine-fringed **Mahodand Lake**, famous for its trout. Swat's highest peak, snowy Falak Sar (5918m) soars above. Follow the wide trail through alpine forest along the Ushu Gol to the summer settlement of **Diwangar** (3050m). The Dadarelli An route (see Ghizar's Other Treks, p194) heads north from here.

Day 2: Diwangar to Shonz
4–5 hours, 10km, 150m ascent

The broad trail rises through pine forest. Cross to the Ushu Gol's true right bank and continue to *Shonz* (3200m), a Gujar summer camp at the foot of Bashkaro An (see Ghizar's Other Treks, p194).

Warning

The area has a heavily armed populace, which necessitates trekking with an armed escort. Reports of robbery (or worse) of unescorted trekkers are not uncommon. Register with the police on arrival in Kalam. Beware of thievery and post guards at night.

Day 3: Shonz to Bokhtshal

4–5 hours, 8km, 675m ascent

The trail follows the stream, rising steadily through willow and birch groves, past a series of small falls and blue-green lakes to **Bokhtshal** (3875m), a summer pasture. Alpine scenery of birch trees, wildflowers and a sparkling stream makes this a pleasant camp site at the base of Kachakani An.

Day 4: Bokhtshal to Khunza Uts

8–9 hours, 11km, 891m ascent, 1016m descent

Start early and follow an ever-steepening trail. The view opens as you climb, with side glaciers and peaks coming into view. Climb over snow slopes, which are difficult when soft, to the **Kachakani An** (4766m).

Descend steeply on snow-covered glacier, then move onto moraine along its true right margin. Beware of rock fall, especially late in the season. Pass the Kachakani Glacier's snout and continue downstream to the

grassy camp site of **Khunza Uts** (3750m, 'Queen's Spring'), with a clear stream and fine mountain views.

Day 5: Khunza Uts to Bashqar Gol Camp

4 hours, 9km, 335m descent

Follow the Kachakani Gol downstream to its confluence with the Bashqar Gol and **Bashqar Gol Camp** (3415m).

Day 6: Bashqar Gol Camp to Sor Laspur

4–5 hours, 10km, 565m descent

Follow the Bashqar Gol's true right bank downstream. Pass through the hamlet of **Nalagh** to reach **Sor Laspur** (2850m).

Other Treks

The following treks are all in an open zone, except where noted.

KALASHA VALLEYS

See Permits & Regulations in the Kalasha Valleys section (p128) for a discussion about zones.

Urghuch

An easy one-day trek goes from Rumbur Valley to Urghuch village in the Chitral Valley 6.5km south of Chitral town (see map, p138). From Rumbur, head east up the side valley south of Balanguru. Follow the true right bank for half a kilometre, then cross to the true left bank. Three quarters of a kilometre beyond the crossing, as the trail enters the higher forest, turn south, then contour east and cross the ridge south of Sunwat (3066m). The route heads north-east and half a kilometre below the ridge lies an abandoned rest house of the Mehtar of Chitral. From here, the trail descends north 1.5km to a spring (2272m) and the Urghuch Valley. Follow it 2.5km east to Urghuch village. Find a jeep in Urghuch, walk to Chitral or Ayun, or cross the footbridge over the Chitral River and wait along the Chitral-Drosh road for a ride.

Uchusht

Another route from Rumbur Valley towards Chitral goes to Uchusht, just 1.5km south of Chitral town, in two easy days (see map, p138). Take a local guide from Balanguru as the trail is seldom-used and can be tricky. From Balanguru, walk west along the road upvalley for 30 minutes. Head

Kachakani An

To Mastuj · To Barsat · *Shandur Gol* · *Shandur Lake* · Not for Navigation use listed maps

Shandur Pass (3800m)

FINISH · Sor Laspur (2850m)

Bashqar Gol

Nalagh

NORTHERN

DAY 6 · Bashqar Gol Camp (3415m)

Kachakani Gol

See Phargam An Map p149

AREAS

DAY 5 · Khunza Uts (3750m)

Kachakani An (4766m)

Kachakani Glacier

Bashkaro An (4924m)

DAY 4 · Bokhtshal (3875m)

DAY 3 · Shonz (3200m)

NORTH · WEST

Dadarelli An (5030m)

FRONTIER PROVINCE

Diwangar (3050m)

DAY 2

Ushu Gol

Mahodand Lake

START · Machiangaas (2890m) · To Matiltan & Kalam

0 · 4 · 8km
0 · 2 · 4mi
1:575,000

Khokush Gol

north-east up the true left (east) bank of the second side valley above Balanguru; the first side valley leads to Sundargah. Some 1.5km up the side valley, cross a side stream to reach the herders' hut at Palario. Then work steeply east 2km to the forested ridge top separating Rumbur from Urghuch. Turn north and contour the upper Urghuch Gol. You can camp in this upper basin where water is available. Water isn't found on the ridge top – only views. Ascend to the ridge between Urghuch Gol and Uchusht Gol, 750m south and east of the high point **Urghuch Dok** (3510m). Follow the ridge east into forest (3025m) then descend north-east past herders' huts. Follow the small stream's true left bank, then the spur north of this stream down to Uchusht village.

Bohok Pass

An enjoyable, moderate three-day loop from Rumbur follows the **Gangalwat Gol** west past Shekhanandeh. The trail along the river's true left bank passes through several small settlements to the confluence with the Shekhan Bohok Gol (3518m), 12km from Shekhanandeh. Head south up the Shekhan Bohok Gol, where the **Bohok Pass** (4725m) leads into the Kalasha Bohok Gol, which is the valley north of Acholgah. Descend the Kalasha Bohok Gol past Narajau and the junction with the trail coming from Kundyak An (see Day 2 of the Donson Pass & Kundyak An trek, p135) to the road along Rumbur Gol.

Utak An

Utak An (4647m) is one of several passes with permanent snowfields linking Begusht Gol, the large valley south of Garam Chashma, with the upper Rumbur Gol. The moderate trek starts 4km up the Begusht Gol at Turi Beshgar village, where the Mohur Gol flows in from the south and east. Head 7km up Mohur Gol to Putrik village, where two streams join. The route to the Utak An follows the stream that leads east. Across the **Utak An**, on its east side, is Dundeeni Chhat. This lake, in the upper Chitral Gol watershed, is the summer grazing area for Chitral Gol's markhor. The route continues south-east along the Utak Gol to Chimirsan Ghari and Shekhanandeh (see Day 2 of the Gokhshal An & Dooni An trek, p140).

Jinjeret

Jinjeret Kuh, a western tributary of the Chitral River south of Drosh, is inhabited by converted Kalasha, who became Muslims in the 20th century. They still speak Kalashamun, and live in Kalasha-style homes. Several interesting old Kalasha-style forts, or *kot* in Urdu, stand near the valley's highest

village. These forts aren't found elsewhere and are the subject of current research. Jinjeret Kuh is scenic, and the friendly people welcome foreigners. Kalash Historic Adventure Tours organises tours of a restored watchtower; go to Hindu Kush Heights hotel in Chitral to make a booking.

A visit to Jinjeret makes an easy day trip from Drosh or an overnight trip from Chitral. Chitral-Drosh vans cost Rs 35; special hires cost Rs 600. From Drosh, special hires 7km to Dashmanandeh cost Rs 700, or to the road's end, 5km farther, Rs 1200. Alternatively, take a vehicle to the mouth of Jinjeret Kuh, then walk three hours upvalley.

CHITRAL GOL NATIONAL PARK
Merin

The Merin bungalows sit above the Chitral Gol's south bank (see map, p138). Female and young markhor live year-round on the cliffs across the river from Merin. Although Merin is best visited from April to October, in December male markhor come to the booster and mate with the females. The aggressive displays and competition between males are an unforgettable sight. You can visit Merin on a day hike from Chitral or camp in Merin and make this an easy two-day trip. From the booster (2200m), descend 45 minutes to a footbridge over Chitral Gol and then ascend 15 minutes to *Merin* (1980m), 2.4km from the booster. The climb up the northern hillside back to the booster takes 1½ hours. Mohammad Deen, the former mehtar's huntsman, lives in Merin and can show you where the markhor are. Bring binoculars. Figs, apples, pears, apricots and grapes grow near the crumbling mehtar's bungalow, and a now-dilapidated former British officers' bungalow with fine woodwork. The British *38 M/13* sheet shows the road and trail to Merin, but not the booster, which is very near where the trail meets the road.

You can visit Kasavir (see p139) on an easy 9.2km day hike from Merin. The trail is passable only when the water in Chitral Gol is low, usually between August and October. Follow the stream upstream three hours, fording the river up to 10 times. It takes two hours to retrace your steps to Merin.

Bironshal

The mehtar's bungalow in Bironshal (3068m) sits in mixed forest and grassland. It's no longer used, in ruins and the trail is not in good repair. Bironshal is best visited from April to October. The easy 10km route to Bironshal begins from the sealed road past the DC's office in Chitral town (see map, p124). It takes six to eight hours to ascend 1600m to Bironshal. This is too far for a day hike, so plan on two days. Return via the same route in four to six hours. If you have a local guide, you could return to Chitral town via Merin and the booster.

No trail exists beyond Bironshal except a seldom-used, difficult game-watchers' route to Kasavir. Herders take goats from Merin to Bironshal over a faint track. Reaching Dooni Gol from Bironshal is very difficult. The cross-country route with Class 2 and Class 3 sections is in bad shape and not recommended.

ARKARI

Arkari is a seldom-visited area surrounded by the Hindukush peaks that form the Afghan border on its west side and the massif of Gul Lasht Zom (6657m) and Tirich Mir on its east side. Flowing through the area is the Arkari River, a northern tributary of the Lutkho River. Treks in Arkari are challenging routes for adventurous trekkers and offer good wildlife-watching opportunities. A local guide is essential. Jeeps to Owirdeh (Rs 60, four hours), at the road's end in the Arkari Valley, depart from the Damdam Hotel at 10am. Special hires cost Rs 1000–1200. This area is in a restricted zone, and the DC in Chitral authorises visits.

Besti An & Lutkho An

Agram Gol and Besti Gol are western tributaries of the Arkari River. Besti An links these valleys, which form a wildlife sanctuary bordering Afghanistan. Because of the steepness of the north side of Besti An, it's easier to start from Owirdeh in the Agram Gol and head in a counterclockwise direction to form a three-day near-loop. The demanding trek is possible July to mid-September. Exercise caution in Agram Gol, because Agram An is an uncontrolled pass leading to Afghanistan.

The first day, the trail leads up the true right (south) bank 5km, then crosses a footbridge with Gul Lasht Zom prominent to the north-east. Reach Agramdeh village in a grassy area 4km above the footbridge. After a farther 3km, the valley widens and offers views of crags above glaciers, with scree slopes descending to the valley floor. Cross the Dajal Gol coming from the north, and 6.5km from Agramdeh reach the junction (3220m) of the trail coming from the Agram An. Cross to the main river's true right (south) bank and, beyond a grove of willows, reach *Nawasin Ghari* (3447m) after another 8km, eight to nine hours from Owirdeh.

The second day, continue up Agram Gol's true right bank as it curves south. The routes to Besti An and Lutkho (Sad Qalachi) An divide 8km from Nawasin Ghari. The more difficult Lutkho An, with a steep, long ascent from Agram Gol, crosses to the Siruik Valley, with a difficult descent involving Class 3 rock. Sad Qalachi means 'seven lengths of outstretched arms' as the final 15m to

20m on its south-west side requires traversing a narrow ledge along a 75m cliff and may require fixing ropes for safety.

To continue to Besti An, take the east (left) fork of the stream, alongside a glacier, and ascend 600m to **Besti An** (4633m). Descend 1200m to **Khoin** village in the upper Besti Gol in 2.5km, six to seven hours from Nawasin Ghari.

The last day, follow the trail down the Besti Gol 6.5km to Besti village, then 9.5km more to the confluence with the Arkari Gol and the roadhead, five to six hours from Khoin. Jeeps (Rs 70) occasionally come up Besti Gol as far as Besti village.

Maps depicting these two passes are confusing: one pass heads south and west from Agram Gol into the Siruik Valley and on to Lutkho; and the other heads south and east into the Besti Gol. The *Zebak (J 42-X)* sheet names the first pass Sad Qalachi An. The British Survey of India 1930 edition Afghanistan and NW – Frontier Province 1:63,360 *37 P/SE* sheet and the editors of the Himalayan Journal, however, call this pass Lutkho An. The second pass, which leads to Besti Gol, is named on the *Zebak (J 42-X)* sheet as Lutkho An. The British *37 P/SE* sheet, as well as the editors of the Himalayan Journal, call this pass Sad Qalachi! The authors prefer to call the pass leading to the Siruik Valley and upper Lutkho the Lutkho An and the pass leading to Besti Gol the Besti An, a name given by Cockerill, who travelled here in 1894.

Gazikistan

Gazikistan (grassy place) is a pleasant camp site between the Lower and Upper Gazikistan glaciers, which descend from Gul Lasht Zom. It makes a good base camp for climbs on the surrounding peaks. The road up the Arkari Valley goes to Owirdeh, at the Agram Gol's mouth. From Owirdeh to Gazikistan is a two-day trek. Camp at Yun, a summer village 6.5km from Owirdeh, or at Kurobakh, 14.5km from Owirdeh, at the Nuqsan Valley's mouth. Gazikistan lies 6.5km beyond Kurobakh.

SHISHI & GOLEN

The steep, rocky passes at the head of Jughor Gol and Roghili Gol are not snow-free until July. They're best crossed before late September. The routes over all of these passes are infrequently used (see map, p145). When exploring them, hire a local herder who knows the way since map references are poor and routes aren't obvious.

Jughor

Jughor village, at the Jughor Gol's mouth, is south of, and across the river from, Chitral town. Plan to visit Jughor the day before you start in order to organise any trek. Four demanding passes are towards the valley's head: two head south to Shishi Gol; and two head east, one to Koghozi Gol and the other to Roghili Gol.

From Jughor, walk upvalley to a hut at Chhato Shal (3048m), where the trail crosses to the true left bank. Go 750m farther to a junction (3161m) of two trails. One trail leads south up the Kapashung Gol to the passes to Shishi Gol and the other leads east up the Bungolbahan Gol to the other two passes.

The Kapashung Gol route splits farther upvalley. Here, the route to the south-east crosses the **Domukh An** (4380m) to Kalas in Shishi Gol. The route to the south follows the Kapashung Gol's true right bank for 3km, along the highest branch, to **Kapashung Gree** (4318m), which also leads into Shishi Gol.

The route east up Bungolbahan Gol stays on the true left (south) bank and offers two options. First, from the 3161m trail junction, you can proceed 3km upvalley and cross the river. A very steep 500m climb north brings you to the difficult **Koghozi An** (4480m) from where a steep descent into the Koghozi Valley leads to Koghozi village on the Chitral-Gilgit road. This is a difficult Class 3 cross-country route.

Second, you can ascend half a kilometre farther north-east along the Bungolbahan Gol's true left bank to **Roghili Gree** (4638m). It's then a steep 850m scree descent into the basin of the upper Roghili Gol. The basin is labelled Angarbah on the *Chitral (I-42F)* sheet, but local people don't recognise this name. Follow the south bank of a stream heading north-east 8km farther to Lut Chhat (3764m), a lake. From a trail junction 500m above the lake, you can head north down Roghili Gol by crossing the stream feeding the lake and contouring along its north bank (see the Roghili Gol trek, p144). Alternatively, you can cross the Roghili An.

Roghili An

From Lut Chhat in the upper Roghili Gol (see the Roghili Gol trek, p144) a route crosses the Roghili An (4496m) to Madaglasht in Shishi Gol. Continue along the north and west shores of Lut Chhat. Go beyond the lake for 500m and cross the stream to its south bank. Here two routes divide: one to the Roghili An and the other to the more difficult Roghili Gree (see Jughor, above). The demanding route to **Roghili An** (4496m) turns south-east and crosses a steep ridge to Madaglasht in Shishi Gol.

Dok An

Dok An (4420m) links Istor, Golen Gol's highest village, with the upper Shishi Gol. It takes one day to walk to the upper Dok Gol with its streams, flowery meadows and sheer cliffs typical of Golen.

Istor villagers graze flocks in the pastures at the summer settlement of Warazo Shal. From here, it's a one-day trek over the moderate **Dok An**, which is usually open mid-June to September, to Shishi Gol. Once over Dok An, you can turn northeast into upper Shishi Gol, cross the Lohigal An, descend into Lohigal Gol and loop back to Istor.

TURIKHO

The following are specified and unspecified treks that fall within a restricted zone, but no permit is required. The DC in Chitral authorises visits.

Rosh

The moderate four-day trek up the idyllic and infrequently visited Rosh Gol begins in Zundrangram, Tirich Valley's main village. Saraghrar, one of nine 7000m peaks in the area, towers above the valley's head. The first day, cross the Tirich Gol and walk 13km up the Rosh Gol to Duru (3600m), labelled Bachorgaz on the U502 *Mastuj (NJ 43-13)* sheet, a lovely camp site with flowers and springs amid birches and willows. Continue the second day up the river's true left bank 2.5km to the Rosh Gol Glacier's snout, and then on the true left side of the lateral moraine 5km to the lush ablation valley of Kotgaz (4300m). Beyond Kotgaz, enjoy a day hike on the moraine-covered glacier for superb views. The fourth day return to Zundrangram.

Udren

Udren Gol and the Udren Glacier flow from a ring of 7000m peaks, including Udren Zom (7108m), Noshaq and Istor-o-Nal. A moderate four-day trek visits the glacier's head (see map, p152). From Shagrom, follow the Tirich Gol 1¼ hours, then cross a footbridge and follow the Udren Gol's true right bank north past Shang-o-Lasht to a camp site 8km from the confluence. The second day, continue 3km to the glacier's snout and walk 2km along its true right side. Head onto the moraine-covered glacier and traverse it diagonally 5km to its true left margin for views of Istor-o-Nal up the South Udren Glacier. Continue on moraine 6km to the confluence with the smaller North Udren Glacier and camp in the ablation valley (4300m). Retrace steps downvalley to Shagrom in two days.

Saraghrar Base Camp

The Saraghrar massif rises at the Ziwor Gol's head. A demanding five-day trek leads to the base camp of the successful 1959 Italian expedition. From Zang Lasht in Turikho, walk across the bridge over the Turikho River to Burzum village (2400m) at the Ziwor Gol's narrow mouth. Follow the trail north and west up its true left bank, past the hot springs of Ziwor Uts, 11.5km to Golung Shal (2800m). On Day 2 continue 12km to the once-cultivated Gram Shal (3400m), crossing the river just before it. Ziwor Gol was once inhabited, but abandoned when the glacier at its head advanced. It has since receded, but the valley hasn't been re-settled. On Day3, head up the true right bank 3.5km to the Ushko Glacier's snout (Hurusko Kuh Glacier on the U502 *Mastuj (NJ 43-13)* sheet), with the Nirogh Glacier's snout (Nuroregh Glacier on maps) just to the south. Cross the Ushko Glacier just above its snout to its true right side. Leave the glacier and continue south along the Nirogh Glacier's true left (west) margin as it heads south and bends west. Cross the Sorlawi Glacier coming from the north-west to reach **Saraghrar Base Camp** (4200m), at the base of the spur separating the Roma and Surwai Glaciers above the Nirogh Glacier. Here you're surrounded by 6000m and 7000m peaks and get the best view of Saraghrar. Return downvalley to Zang Lasht in two days.

Chikor Pass

Chikor Pass (4430m), which is usually open mid-July to mid-September, links Uzhnu and Ziwor, two uninhabited valleys branching west from Turikho Valley. A moderate five- to seven-day near-loop starts at Uzhnu village along the jeep road in Turikho. Head north and west up the Uzhnu Valley, then turn south-west into Chikor Gol. Climb to the **Chikor Pass** and descend south-west to Gram Shal in the Ziwor Gol. Go east down Ziwor Gol returning to Zang Lasht in Turikho. This is an unspecified route in a restricted zone.

Nizhdaru An

Nizhdaru An (5087m), an infrequently crossed pass, links Sor Rich in Rich Gol to Bang in the Yarkhun Valley. This demanding 25km technical trek takes two to three days and is best done in July or August. From Sor Rich (2785m) walk up the Chakosh Gol's true left (south) bank 5km to Ghari Chhan. Continue another 8km and camp below a small glacier descending from the pass. The next day, ascend the glacier steeply to the **Nizhdaru An**, which may require fixing rope or cutting steps; bring an ice axe and crampons. Descend steeply over scree on the west side to the meadows of Garagar (4023m). Camp here or continue to Bang in a long day. Bang-Mastuj jeeps cost Rs 50. Special hires cost Rs 1000.

Hindu Raj Crest

A demanding and exciting five-day cross-country trek traverses the crest of the Hindu Raj Range, crossing three seldom-visited passes. Anyone attempting this route needs to be an experienced

trekker, accomplished at route-finding, completely self-reliant and able to communicate with herders in pastures in each separate valley. Khot herders know the Ghochhar An route, Bang herders the Bang Gol Muli An, and Paur herders the Siru An. The passes are typically snow-free between July and late September, but plan to do the trek before early September when herders depart the pastures.

Walk from Khot Lasht to Shahglasht in 3½ to four hours on Day 1 (see map, p157). It's seven to nine hours on Day 2 to reach Garagar. From Shahglasht, leave the trail to Khot An and continue to the Jharogh huts, along the Jacha Gol's true left bank. Cross to its true right bank and continue up-stream. The Jacha Gol (not marked on maps) and the Ghochhar Gol meet just beyond. Continue along the Ghochhar Gol's true right (west) bank 1.5km to the confluence with the Mazan Gol. Follow the Ghochhar Gol, and after passing beneath several small permanent snowfields, cross the stream to its true left bank and ascend to the **Ghochhar An** (4724m), involving a steep scree ascent, and descend over a small glacier. Continue to Garagar, a herders' settlement in upper Bang Gol.

On Day 3, head north-east, cross **Bang Gol Muli An** (4763m) and descend, traversing a small glacier, to the upper Paul Gol herders' settlement at Pimin Sor in five to eight hours. On Day 4, head north, then north-east to cross **Siru An** (4572m). Camp in the upper Siru Gol beyond the Siru Glacier, five to seven hours from Pimin Sor. On Day 5, continue down the herders' trail along the Siru Gol's true right bank to the confluence with the Ishperu Dok Gol. Cross a footbridge to the Ishperu Dok Gol's true left bank and follow the trail to Yashkist at the confluence with the Yarkhun River.

BASHQAR

Glacial lakes dot the upper Bashqar Gol, above which towers Ghuchhar Sar (6249m). Beyond the first lake, the valley divides: Thalo Gol heads south-west and Manali Gol heads south-south-east. These upper valleys offer interesting, demanding, trekking and climbing possibilities, and are best visited by starting/finishing in Sor Laspur. It's ill-advised to attempt the difficult passes at the head of these valleys, which lead to lawless areas where people are armed, may not welcome trekkers and should be considered dangerous.

It's tedious going up the long, rocky Thalo Gol, which has numerous hanging glaciers. The moraine of the Thalo Glacier descends to the valley floor and another glacial lake lies beyond the Thalo Glacier. Thalo An leads to Dir's Panjkora Valley. The way up the shorter Manali Gol leads over the large Manali Glacier, and on to an upper cirque. Manali An leads into Swat's upper Gabral Valley.

Ghizar

Ghizar, the Northern Areas' westernmost district, is also its least visited. Trekkers who venture here, however, discover isolated valleys, traditional Kho and Burusho villages, friendly people and glorious passes through the Western Karakoram and Hindu Raj ranges. With peaks all lower than 7000m and less heavily glaciated than the extremes of the high Karakoram or Hindukush, it's a trekkers' and mountaineers' paradise. Ghizar offers both the easiest and hardest nonglaciated passes in all northern Pakistan. Combining four or five passes can give weeks of unlimited open-zone trekking and delight beneath innumerable unclimbed 5000m peaks.

Ghizar's valleys and mountains lie west of Gilgit, along the courses of the upper Ghizar and Gilgit rivers. Two major northern tributary valleys, Ishkoman and Yasin, provide access into the heart of this area's mountain domain. The Ghizar River itself descends from the Shandur Pass (3800m) on the Northern Areas' border with North-west Frontier Province (NWFP), and its numerous southern tributaries flow from the rugged mountains along Kalam Kohistan's northern boundary. The Ghizar River joins the Yasin River near Gupis, the district's administrative centre, to form the Gilgit River.

HISTORY

Burusho appear to have once occupied all the northern valleys of present-day Ghizar. Today, they remain only in Yasin Valley, although Burushaski place names abound in Bahushtaro Gol and Ishkoman. Chinese travellers of the 5th to 8th centuries, who passed through Yasin and Ishkoman on their way to visit the renowned Buddhist monasteries in Darel and Swat, knew the region as Bru-zha, suggesting a Burusho identity for the population. Migrations of Shina speakers from the south and Khowar speakers from the west probably displaced the Burusho. The Kushwaqt family, a branch of Chitral's Katur dynasty, won control of

A trekker crosses a glacier on the trek to Punji Pass.

JOHN MOCK

upper Chitral and Ghizar, ruling from Yasin. Ghizar's lower region, known as Punial, became a bone of contention between Gilgit and Chitral, and by the 19th century, Punial had become a separate state with its own raja. During this time refugees from blood feuds in Indus Kohistan migrated north into Punial and Ghizar. Although about half of Punial's and Ghizar's present population are descendants of these refugees, almost all people in the region speak

Khowar, with Shina also widely spoken. After the settlement of Chitral's borders in 1918, Ghizar became part of the Gilgit administration. Ghizar, which long had its own identity, was made a separate district in 1974 by Zulfiqar Ali Bhutto, however, General Zia merged it with Gilgit district in 1985. In 1989 Ghizar once again became its own district.

INFORMATION
Maps
The US AMS Series U502 India and Pakistan 1:250,000 topographic maps *Baltit (NJ 43-14)*, *Mastuj (NJ 43-13)* and *Churrai (NI 43-1)* cover Ghizar.

Place Names
Note the following about Khowar place names. In Khowar, the letter 'o' at the end of a word, a common grammatical ending, means something similar to 'of' in English. For example, Bahushtaro Gol means 'the valley of the Bahushtar'. The valley itself is actually named Bahushtar. Zagaro An means 'the pass of Zagar', but the pass itself is named Zagar. Others include Ano, Bashkaro, Dedero and Kano.

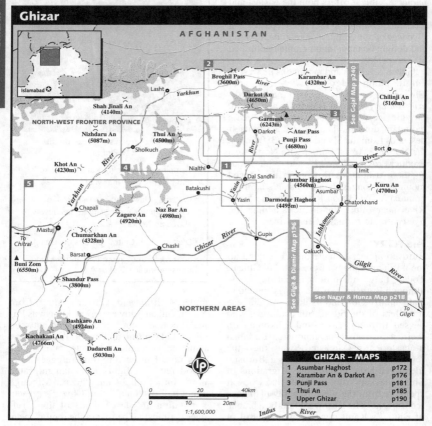

GHIZAR – MAPS	
1 Asumbar Haghost	p172
2 Karambar An & Darkot An	p176
3 Punji Pass	p181
4 Thui An	p185
5 Upper Ghizar	p190

Ishkoman

The well-cultivated Ishkoman Valley's name comes from the Burushaski word for green, *shiqam*. The Karambar, in contrast, is a glacier-scoured steep-walled valley, with jagged snowy spires and almost no inhabitants. Most Ishkoman villagers are Isma'ili Muslims, whose native language is Shina. Many so-called Gujars, who are actually migrants from Indus Kohistan, have moved into Ishkoman. The uppermost villages of Imit, Bilhanz and Bort are predominantly Wakhi. Khowar is also widely spoken in Ishkoman, which was once part of greater Chitral. Not so long ago, the Ishkoman Valley had its own raja, who ruled from Chatorkhand, the main village. His descendants still live there. Pir Sayed Karam Ali Shah, currently an elected Northern Areas Council member, and a venerated spiritual leader of Isma'ili Muslims in northern Pakistan, also lives in Chatorkhand. Trekking in Ishkoman is typically less rigorous than other areas with almost no glacier crossings. Friendly villagers and a softer, yet dramatic, landscape make it popular with those wanting to go just a bit off the beaten track.

ACCESS VILLAGE
Gakuch

Gakuch, Ghizar district's administrative centre, is in Punial on the Gilgit-Chitral road, 80km west of Gilgit, along the Gilgit River's south bank near the confluence with the Ishkoman River.

Stores sell staple food (such as salt, sugar, tea, milk powder, flour, cooking oil and lentils) and supplies such as soap, matches and kerosene, but no equipment. You can't rely on finding all your food for a trek, so it's best to bring everything from Gilgit.

Several small hotels (all with signs in Urdu) offer meals and Rs 20 charpoys. *NAPWD Rest House* has rooms that cost Rs 175–375.

NATCO buses depart from Gilgit's Punial Rd. Take the 8am Gilgit-Taus bus, the 9am Gilgit-Gupis bus, or the 11am Gilgit-Chatorkhand bus (Rs 58) and get off in Gakuch. NATCO also operates a daily Sherqila-Gakuch bus (Rs 20, two hours) that departs at 6am. Gilgit-Gakuch special hires cost Rs 1600. No regular transport operates between Chitral and Gakuch.

Asumbar Haghost

Duration	4 days
Distance	44.7km
Standard	moderate
Season	June–September
Start	Asumbar
Finish	Dal Sandhi
Zone & Permit	open, no permit
Public Transport	yes
Summary	This culturally and linguistically diverse trek through alpine meadows crosses a gentle pass with sweeping vistas.

Asumbar Haghost, a nonglaciated east-west pass, links Asumbar village in Ishkoman with Dal Sandhi in Yasin. The pass is occasionally called the Ishkoman Pass (not to be confused with the Punji Pass, which is also sometimes called Ishkoman Pass). Asumbar Haghost is one of the easiest passes to cross anywhere in the Karakoram and Hindukush. The trek is also one of the most linguistically diverse. Along the trail, Shina, Khowar, Wakhi and Burushaski are spoken, not to mention Urdu.

This trek is usually combined with at least one other trek. The Pakora Pass (p220) often precedes it, and the Punji Pass or Thui An treks (see p180 and p183 respectively) often follow it, depending on whether you're heading back to Gilgit or towards Chitral.

PLANNING
Maps

The US AMS topographic maps *Baltit (NJ 43-14)* and *Mastuj (NJ 43-13)* cover the trek. No settlements east of the pass are labelled.

Guides & Porters

The route is fairly obvious so a local guide isn't necessary. Porters use donkeys to carry their loads. The rate is Rs 500 per donkey for 50kg. The rate for a fully-loaded donkey equals the wages for two 25kg porter loads. If you have less than 50kg, try negotiating a lower rate.

When you combine this trek with the Punji Pass trek, hire porters for both passes from either Pakora or Asumbar. That way, the porters end up in the Ishkoman Valley just one stage away from their homes, minimising wāpasi.

Stages
Stages are not universally fixed, but four stages seems appropriate. Trekkers who pay three stages may have problems because the distance is difficult for trekkers, porters and donkeys to cover comfortably in three days (ie, three stages).

GETTING TO/FROM THE TREK
To the Start
Gilgit-Asumbar jeeps cost Rs 60 and depart from Wad-din Transport Service (☎ 0572-3645, 2287, 55035) on Gilgit's Punial Rd. Alternatively, you can try to find a jeep from Gakuch or Chatorkhand to Asumbar. A daily NATCO bus from Gilgit to Chatorkhand (Rs 75, 5½ hours), a half-day walk from the trailhead, departs from Gilgit's Punial Rd at 11am. Gilgit-Asumbar special hires cost Rs 2200.

When you precede this trek with the Pakora Pass trek, you can walk 3.4km between Pakora and Asumbar on the road in one hour. From Pakora, head north to the bridge over the Ishkoman River and cross to its true right bank. The trailhead is at the bridge over the Asumbar Nala along its true right bank.

From the Finish
Dal Sandhi–Gilgit jeeps cost Rs 120. Special hires cost Rs 2650. Alternatively, walk 4km south to Taus and take the daily NATCO bus (Rs 105) to Gilgit.

When following this trek with the Punji Pass trek, you need to get from Dal Sandhi to Darkot. Jeeps come infrequently to Dal Sandhi, so to find one walk 4km south to Taus or 7km north to Barkulti (two hours). Barkulti-Darkot jeeps cost Rs 30 and take two hours. Special hires cost Rs 600 Barkulti-Darkot, Rs 650 Dal Sandhi-Darkot, and Rs 700 Yasin-Darkot. If you can't find a vehicle, plan two days to walk 25km between Dal Sandhi and Darkot.

THE TREK
Day 1: Asumbar to Lower Charinj
4–6 hours, 8.4km, 270m ascent
The lower Asumbar Valley can be very hot and dry in summer; carry water and enjoy the shady places along the river. From Asumbar village (2910m), climb steadily up the Asumbar Nala's true right (south) bank passing fields and in one hour reach the first of four footbridges. Cross to the true left bank and in 15 minutes cross the second footbridge, an enormous boulder, back to the true right bank. Climb steeply 45 minutes passing corn fields to a silty stream from the south. A Gujar's house with a large willow sits across the stream. Continue 15 minutes and cross the third footbridge to the true left bank. Springs along the trail here provide the only clear water until Charinj.

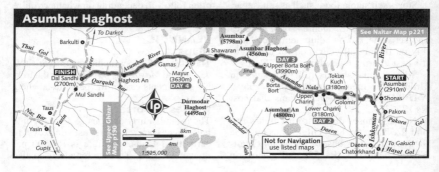

Ahead is a dark rock pile, 100m high, known as **Shah Dheri** (black rocks). Continue along the now-forested stream around Shah Dheri in 30 minutes. Back downvalley are good views of Pakora Gol. Reach the fourth footbridge in another 15 minutes and get the first views upvalley towards the pass. *Golomir*, 15 minutes farther, is an open and grassy, but rocky and shadeless, field. In 30 minutes pass above *Tokun Kuch*, an inviting forest with flat, grassy areas along both banks of the river. Tokun Kuch means the place where grass grew up to the bottom of the horse's saddle blanket *(tokun)*. The only water, however, is silty river water. Continue high above the true right bank 15 minutes to a beautiful chir pine forest called Charinj. This is a great camp site with lots of level, grassy fields, and a series of clear streams running through the forest. Gujars have conical huts here, but in midsummer, they're usually vacant. This area is also called *Lower Charinj* (3180m) and Zokhinewar by the Wakhi speakers who live farther upvalley.

Day 2: Lower Charinj to Upper Borta Bort

3¾–4 hours, 8km, 810m ascent

Continue through the dense stand of trees 15 minutes to the first of five side streams that flow in from the south. Ford this large stream and climb 30 minutes past a few huts high above the river to Upper Charinj. Continue past junipers and tall birches and pass above the tree line to reach Wakhikandeh, a year-round Wakhi settlement with three households. Just past the houses, cross a footbridge over the second side stream. This large side valley leads south across a 4500m ridge where two routes diverge: one route crosses the Asumbar An (4800m) to Darmodar Gah; and the other descends the Daeen Gol to Daeen village in the Ishkoman Valley, across the river from Chatorkhand. Although it's longer for them, Daeen villagers prefer walking along the road to Asumbar village and then up the Asumbar Valley to Charinj rather than crossing this steep pass.

A few Gujar huts are across this large side stream. Reach a third stream and more

Gujar settlements in 30 minutes. The trail begins a steady climb, contouring up the rocky hillside past scrub junipers, to emerge after one hour in a pasture. This is **Borta Bort**, an area which gets its name from the huge boulder visible upvalley. The pass is visible far ahead.

Four houses, also called Borta Bort, lie 15 minutes ahead, and are inhabited by one Isma'ili household from Shonas and three Gujar households from Asumbar. Women here wear tall pillbox-style hats.

Continue, passing several large scree slopes and more huts on the river's opposite side, and in 30 minutes come to a large alluvial fan and the fourth stream. A possible camp lies across this side stream, but a better camp site is 30 minutes ahead. Cross over a grassy knoll, with huts below its west side (beware of dogs), and cross a silty glacial side stream via a footbridge. Climb through flower-filled meadows along clear, spring-fed streams. Camp below the large boulders at *Upper Borta Bort* (3990m) and enjoy spectacular views to the east. The Hayal Pass, Shani (5887m), Twin peaks (5798m and 5700m) and distant Rakaposhi (7788m) are visible.

Day 3: Upper Borta Bort to Mayur

5½ hours, 10.6km, 570m ascent, 930m descent

The trail continues through the boulder field 45 minutes to a broad grassland called *Jinali* (polo ground in Khowar), a possible, although less desirable, high camp. Porters prefer staying in huts near Borta Bort. Ahead are two low points (passes) on either side of a hill. The route goes over the northern low point. The southern one is steep on the west side, passes close to an icefall, and cannot be crossed by donkeys. Cross Jinali, fording a silty side stream, and follow the river's north (right) fork past springs 45 minutes to the base of the hill leading to the pass.

Ascend over grass one hour to the gentle flower-carpeted **Asumbar Haghost** (4560m). Rakaposhi and Diran (7257m) peaks to the east and the peaks of the high Hindukush to the west are visible.

Snowy patches lie just below and west of the pass. Descend for one hour, following a clear willow-lined stream to meadows. Continue north (right) on a trail, skirting willows. Cross the clear side stream from Asumbar peak to the north, above its confluence with the milky main stream, and continue past small springs to the huts of **Ji Shawaran** (polo ground in Shina), two hours below the pass, which is visible from this spot.

Cross a footbridge to the river's true left (south) bank, and head downvalley. Cross a low rise with two cairns on it to a large unnamed pond, visible from the pass, 45 minutes from Ji Shawaran. The slightly green water is deep enough for a swim and this is a possible camp site. A better camp site is 45 minutes farther, through extensive junipers, at *Mayur* (3630m). Springs abound below the huts along the clear river from the south. This river is the route over Darmodar Haghost (see Other Treks, p193).

Day 4: Mayur to Dal Sandhi
5½–6 hours, 17.7km, 930m descent
The main trail follows the Asumbar River's true left bank, although another trail goes along its true right bank through three areas cultivated by Burusho from Sandhi. In one hour, reach Gamas, a huge cultivated area bisected by a large side stream, high above the main river's south bank. Below Gamas, cross a footbridge to the true right bank where the trail stays to Dal Sandhi. After 30 minutes reach the start of **Haghost An**. When villagers irrigated this land and brought it under cultivation, they changed its name from Chucho Ano Tok (in Khowar, *chucho* means 'dry place'; *ano*, the 'top of') to Haghost An. Burusho, however, refer to it as Bay Haghost.

At Haghost An's west end, descend steeply to tall willows along the river, then continue more gradually downvalley on a good trail. Pass Bericho Batan, where low-status Bericho people used to live, and ford a clear side stream. Descend the broad valley to **Dal Sandhi** (2700m), 2½ hours from Haghost An. You can *camp* in a lovely village orchard.

Karambar An & Darkot An

Duration	11 days
Distance	123.5km
Standard	demanding, technical
Season	July–September
Start	Bort
Finish	Darkot
Zone & Permit	restricted, US$50 permit
Public Transport	yes

Summary This trek ascends the glacially carved Karambar Valley across a meadow- and lake-filled pass to Pamir grasslands, then crosses a historic glaciated pass into the incredibly scenic Darkot Valley, which features springs and tumbling icefalls.

The glaciated Darkot An (4650m) at the Yasin Valley's head is more easily crossed from north to south, even though access to its north side takes several days. The most desirable route for this trek from Ishkoman to Yasin is via the Karambar Valley, the dividing line between the Hindu Raj and Karakoram ranges. The rugged Karambar Valley leads to some of northern Pakistan's most scenic places and largest alpine meadows used by Gujars in Karambar and by Wakhi in Broghil. The valley was apparently an ancient Buddhist pilgrimage route from Afghanistan's Wakhan Corridor to Gilgit via the Khodarg Werth Pass.

An alternative, more challenging start to the trek is possible from Chapursan, by preceding this trek with the Chilinji An and Qalander Uween trek (p285) joining this trek at Chilinj (see Day 3, p176).

PLANNING
What to Bring
Mountaineering equipment necessary to travel in roped teams is required; crampons are optional (see Mountaineering Equipment, p61).

Maps
The US AMS topographic maps *Baltit (NJ 43-14)* and *Mastuj (NJ 43-13)* cover the trek. The map marks incorrect trails across

the Chattiboi Glacier and along the river's true right bank between Chattiboi Glacier and Shuyinj. The Karambar lakes are not shown. Bort is labelled Bhurt, Maturamdan as Mahtram Dan, and Piyakhin as Pekhin.

Permits & Regulations
This trek is in a restricted zone where a permit and licensed guide are required (see Trekking Permits, p70). Police in Imit and Lasht, and the Chitral Scouts in Ishkarwaz may ask to see your permit.

Guides & Porters
The tricky Karambar and Chattiboi glaciers and glaciated Darkot An require route-finding. Since few porters from Imit, Bad Swat, Bilhanz or Bort know the Chattiboi Glacier, find a herder from Sokhter Rabot. This route changes from year to year, and porters who crossed the Chattiboi in previous years may still have difficulty. Hire someone from Chikar to show the route across Darkot An. Ishkoman porters ask Rs 280–300 per stage including payment for food rations. Chitrali porters in Broghil may ask for as little as Rs 230 per stage.

Stages
The stage system is not instituted on this trek, but it's begun to take hold. In Karambar, these stages are fixed and, unfortunately, short: Bort to Yazben, and Yazben to Maturamdan. Most porters consider it three stages between Chikar and Darkot village.

GETTING TO/FROM THE TREK
To the Start
The jeep road goes as far as Bort, but in summer, high water often blocks the road at Bilhanz. When it's blocked, walk along the road, fording side streams as needed. Some river crossings, such as Bad Swat River, can be difficult. It takes four hours to walk between Bilhanz and Bort. One stage is fixed between Bad Swat and Bort. You may have to pay for an additional partial stage between Bilhanz and Bad Swat.

Jeeps, which depart from Wad-din Transport Service on Gilgit's Punial Rd, cost Rs 120 to Bort, Rs 115 to Bilhanz and Rs 110 to Imit. Special hires cost Rs 3000 to Bort, Rs 2750 to Bilhanz and Rs 2500 to Imit. From Imit, you can also organise special hires as close to Bort as road conditions permit. Alternatively, you can take a daily NATCO Gilgit-Gakuch (Rs 58) or Gilgit-Chatorkhand (Rs 75) bus, which depart from Gilgit's Punial Rd, and look for a jeep there.

The trip takes five hours to Imit via the Khanchey (Chinese) Bridge over the Gilgit River, which is beyond Singal and before Gakuch, or 5½ hours via Gakuch and over the old bridges over Gilgit and Ishkoman rivers.

From the Finish
Darkot-Gilgit jeeps cost Rs 150–175 and take nine hours. Darkot-Gilgit special hires cost Rs 2500–3000. Special hires Darkot-Yasin cost Rs 700 and Darkot-Gupis cost Rs 1000–1500. Jeeps are infrequent, so you may have to wait a day or two. Darkot villagers can help you find a ride. Alternatively, you can walk along the road in two or three days to Taus or Yasin for transport. Yasin-Gilgit jeeps cost Rs 120 and special hires cost Rs 2000. A daily NATCO Taus-Gilgit bus costs Rs 105.

THE TREK
Day 1: Bort to Maturamdan
4–5 hours, 13km, 167m ascent
Above Bort (2728m), the trail stays along the Karambar River's true left bank to Yazben. Cross the **Karambar Glacier**, descending from the east and pushing its way into the valley, which can present a serious obstacle. In 1876 it stopped British officer John Biddulph who described it as 'an impassable wall of ice protruding from a side valley.' In 1916, Dr Tom Longstaff, Assistant Commandant of the Gilgit Scouts, found the glacier abutted against the rocks on the west bank, forcing the river to flow under it. In 1948, in contrast, the explorer HW Tilman found the glacier stopped well short of the river. A route leads up the Karambar Glacier's north side to Kampir Dior Base Camp (4198m). Continue upriver to **Maturamdan** (2895m), the valley's highest year-round village.

Day 2: Maturamdan to Waraghut
5–6 hours, 12km, 405m ascent

The trail crosses a footbridge to the Karambar River's true right (west) side at Piyakhin. Continue up the river's west side to **Waraghut** (3300m). An alternative and more difficult trail stays along the river's true left bank traversing the Chilinj Glacier above a small moraine lake that has formed near its west end en route to the cable crossing of the Karambar River at Chilinj (see Day 3).

Day 3: Waraghut to Sokhter Rabot
4–5 hours, 10km, 120m ascent

Continue upvalley three to four hours to the cable crossing that leads to the river's true left bank and the Gujar settlement of **Chilinj** (3450m). At Chilinj, the trail from the Chilinji An and Qalander Uween (see p285) meets the Karambar Valley. The valley here is grassy and forested with steep cliffs above the river.

Stay along the river's true right (west) bank 45 minutes beyond the cable crossing, then ascend briefly and ford the stream from a large unnamed glacier. After 15 minutes across moraine rubble, the trail descends to a broad alluvial plain and Sokhter Rabot (*rabot* means a 'dwelling place'), occupied by Uzbeks who fled Uzbekistan in the 1930s.

This plain was formed when the glacier advanced and dammed the Karambar River. Across the valley is a reddish scree slope below the mouth of a valley at the head of which Wakhi herders say is a pass to the Agh Glacier in Chapursan above Biatar. Fifteen minutes farther up the trail is a clear stream. After another 30 minutes are more huts, also called **Sokhter Rabot** (3420m), with willows and a meadow for camping.

Day 4: Sokhter Rabot to Shuyinj
5–6 hours, 14.6km, 510m ascent

Continue up the grassy plain. A route from the Wakhan over the Khodarg Werth or

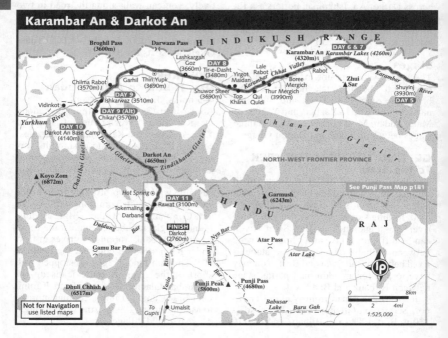

Khora Bort Pass (Wakhi and Khowar respectively for 'millstone') enters from the north. This was the route crossed by Qirghiz nomads fleeing the Russian invasion of the Wakhan in the early 1980s.

Reach the lateral moraine of the **Chattiboi Glacier** (3510m) in 1¼ hours. For the next 4km, the Karambar River runs underneath the glacier, which fills the entire valley and provides the only route upvalley. Follow the black medial moraine up the glacier's middle until it's easy to move towards the right onto white ice. Follow the ice parallel to the black medial moraine until even with the main icefall to the south (left). As crevasses become more frequent, work towards the north (right) and the polished granite cliffs until just next to them. Parallel these cliffs 10 to 15 minutes, then leave the ice and climb up the Karambar River's true left (north) bank to a trail marked by cairns. (An old trail, which is more difficult and less preferable, exits the glacier to the river's

true right (south) bank and continues upriver to a cable crossing below Shuyinj.)

A few huts are nestled against the grassy hillside above the trail. Continue upvalley one hour to the base of a hill, passing many clear streams. Ascend 15 minutes to a large cairn. Continue 30 minutes to the two huts of *Shuyinj* (3930m). A more desirable camp site is 20 minutes farther. Cross the stone footbridge over the distinctive Shuyinj (*shu* means 'black'; *yinj*, a 'narrow gorge where water comes down') stream, and ascend a short distance to a large meadow near two other huts, a rushing stream and marmot burrows.

Days 5–6: Shuyinj to Karambar Lake

4 hours, 12.4km, 330m ascent
Above Shuyinj, the Karambar River is clear. Continue through grasslands 1¼ hours to the base of a large old terminal moraine that runs north-south. A few huts are visible at its base, across the river to the south. Keep to the river's true left bank and wind around the hill and up 30 minutes onto immense grasslands. Clear streams abound and wild onions grow in profusion along their banks. Ram chukor and golden marmots are on every south-facing hillside leading you into the beautiful, gently rolling pass.

One hour farther lies the opaque turquoise water of **Karambar Lake** (4260m), a stopover for migratory water fowl. It takes 1¼ hours to walk along its north shore, and 15 minutes farther is a large boulder with a cairn at its west end. Here are several stone shelters for porters and excellent *camp sites*. Rising above the lake's south shore is Zhui Sar (peak above the lake), a snowy peak (*sar*) whose glacier tumbles dramatically into the lake (*zhui*) itself. Enjoy a rest day at this remarkable spot. The **Karambar An** (4320m) itself is 1.2km west of the camp sites.

Days 7–8: Karambar Lake to Ishkarwaz

2 days, 34.7km, 60m ascent, 810m descent
See Days 3–4 of the Broghil & Karambar An trek (pp161–2), in reverse, for details. Camp at Tir-e-Dasht on Day 7.

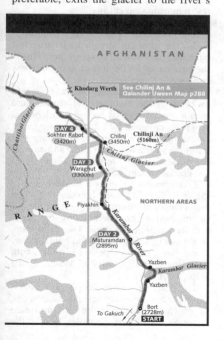

Alternative Camp Site

Chikar On Day 8 continue over a ridge 45 minutes, 2.8km, beyond Ishkarwaz (3510m) to the large meadow at *Chikar* (3570m; *chikar* means 'willow' in Khowar and in Wakhi) where the camping fee is Rs 30. Several small stores sell basic supplies such as rice, flour, salt, milk powder, tea, sugar and kerosene. Chikar men bring these goods over Darkot An from Darkot village where shops are regularly supplied from Gilgit.

The 25km route between Chikar and Darkot can be crossed in two days, and involves an 1080m ascent and 1890m descent. Camp either at the base camp or on the pass.

Day 9: Ishkarwaz to Darkot An Base Camp

3¼–3¾ hours, 7.9km, 630m ascent

Snow on the Darkot An softens by mid-morning, which makes the going tedious. It's a good idea to cross the pass before 9am. To do this, either camp farther upvalley beside the glacier, or depart Ishkarwaz or Chikar before dawn.

Thirty minutes beyond Chikar is an excellent spring at the edge of the fields. The first possible camp site is 1½ hours farther where a side valley opens into the main ablation valley along the Darkot Glacier's east margin. Water is well above camp, flowing over scree. A better camp site is 30 minutes farther up the trail, at the upper limit of scrub willow, 6km from Chikar. In a small ablation valley at the mouth of a side valley is *Darkot An Base Camp* (4140m), with space for three or four tents. Clear water flows from the side valley over rocks above the camp site. Directly across the glacier is a distinctive black rock outcrop separating two major icefalls coming down from a prominent snowy peak.

Day 10: Darkot An Base Camp to Rawat

5½–6 hours, 11.6km, 510m ascent, 1550m descent

The 6.5km ascent to the pass takes 2½ to three hours. Continue up the lateral moraine, cross a ravine to a few tent platforms on the moraine (a more exposed and less desirable camp site) and in 30 to 45 minutes, reach a

cairn. Descend onto the glacier itself and walk 45 minutes up the left side of the smooth, white Darkot Glacier. Aim for a rock outcrop at the glacier's eastern head. Travel in roped teams and ascend a steep 30-degree section just west of this rock outcrop 45 minutes. Traverse right and up, passing below and to the right of a broken section to reach the level upper pass area. Avoid the glacier's heavily crevassed middle and west margin, even though it's a lower angle. Cross the top of the crevassed, but broad and level, **Darkot An** (4650m) in 30 minutes. The **Zindikharam Glacier** branches north-east from the pass. A well-known PTDC poster shows a yak caravan crossing the pass.

The 5.1km, 1500m descent begins on the west side of the pass, and contours back east passing below a crevasse-filled bowl. Then head to the Zindikharam Glacier's west margin and descend quickly to the end of the ice, 45 minutes from the top of the pass. The slope steepens here and may be icy, requiring step cutting.

Descend over rock to the level area below the glacier's snout in 15 minutes. Cross the outwash stream to its true left bank and pass a small stone shelter. This is the *base camp* for anyone crossing the pass from south to north.

The trail becomes clear and traverses left, away from the main glacial stream, and over a small ridge that ends in a dark brown pinnacle, crowned by a large square cairn. In 30 minutes reach a possible *camp site* with room for a few tents and a stone circle for porters. Water, however, comes from the glacial stream.

Five minutes below is a boulder next to the trail. Carved on the boulder is a stupa and Tibetan inscription dating from the 8th or 9th century commemorating the meritorious donation of a stupa. The inscription, translated by AH Francke and published by Aurel Stein, names a person Lirnidor, with the clan or family name of Me-or, as the stupa's donor.

The trail descends steeply 1½ hours. Continue east, crossing several streams, one of which tumbles over the cliff in a nice waterfall. Below, on the valley floor at the base of the cliff, is the trail to a hot spring. The trail from the pass, however, doesn't go by the hot spring. The trail to the **hot spring** branches north off the main trail just outside of Rawat. This spring is said to be good for aching joints and bones and to cure infertility. Descend to *Rawat* (3100m), a lovely summer herders' settlement.

Six or seven large streams come down all around this secluded valley and three or four glaciers perch above. To the west, the rough broken tongue of a small glacier hangs down the cliff, almost licking the valley floor. This well-watered lush bowl has a sanctuary-like quality to it. The people are Burusho, and speak the Yasin dialect of Burushaski. The women wear tall stitched hats, three times the height of Hunza women's hats. Unlike other Burusho settlements, here the women tend the herds, a division of labour usually found among Wakhi.

Day 11: Rawat to Darkot
2–2½ hours, 7.3km, 100m ascent, 440m descent

Continue 15 minutes to a footbridge (2970m) and cross to the main river's true right bank. Pass by the permanent settlements of Haribaris and Tokemaling west of the trail. Climb a short, but steep, 100m to the top of **Darband**, named for the terminal moraine that almost blocks the river like a closed

Darkot or Zindikharam?

A Chinese army led by a Korean general crossed the Darkot An in AD 747 and conquered Gilgit, which was then ruled by Tibetans and called Bru-zha. The archaeological explorer Aurel Stein believed the Chinese army crossed the Zindikharam Glacier rather than the Darkot Glacier. But Stein himself in 1913 found the Zindikharam Glacier closed by enormous bergschrunds and opted for the Darkot Glacier. Broghil residents living north of the Darkot An report that it's feasible to cross the heavily crevassed Zindikharam Glacier in two or three days, but they prefer the easier and more direct route across the Darkot Glacier.

(band) door *(dar)*. Two trails cross Darband; a shorter, but steeper footpath and a more gradual livestock path. Descend steeply 15 minutes and cross the river again via a sturdy wooden footbridge, obscured from view as you descend from Darband. West of Darband is the Duldung Bar, at the head of which is a steep scree ascent to the Gamu Bar Pass, the Das Bar and Nialthi.

Follow a jeep road 45 minutes to Darkot's west end from where it takes 30 minutes more to walk on the road west to east along the village's north side. **Darkot** (2760m) is green and lush with some 300 households. The imposing mountain to the west called Dhuli Chhīsh (6517m) is usually shrouded in clouds. Beneath Dhuli Chhīsh (frowning mountain) is a rock called Lamokor and Gasun village, along the river's true right bank. Expect to pay a Rs 20 camping fee.

Yasin

Yasin Valley forms a multibranched cul-de-sac along the south and east sides of the Hindu Raj Range, offering plenty of scope for trekking. Its attractive villages with carefully cultivated fields and orchards are home to easy-going Burushaski-speaking Isma'ili Muslims. Remote Yasin is not frequently visited by foreigners, but its many excellent treks spark an increasing interest in this splendid area. Large bazaars in Yasin and Taus sell staples, but with much less variety than Gilgit.

ACCESS TOWN
Gupis
Gupis, a regional market town, is along the Gilgit-Chitral road, 30km west of Gakuch.

Stores sell basic food (such as salt, sugar, tea, milk powder, flour, cooking oil and lentils) and supplies such as soap, matches and kerosene, but no equipment. You can't rely on finding all your food for a trek, so bring everything from Gilgit.

NAPWD Resthouse is in a large walled compound along the road with a popular camp site. The camping fee is Rs 100 and rooms cost Rs 175–275. *Snow Leopard Inn* is where NATCO buses stop, so food is available. Charpoys cost Rs 30 (elsewhere they cost Rs 20); rooms cost Rs 150. *PTDC Motel*, 8km west of Gupis, has singles/ doubles for Rs 1250/1500.

A daily NATCO Gilgit-Gupis bus (Rs 81, six hours) departs from Gilgit's Punial Rd at 9am. No regular transport operates between Gupis and Chitral.

Punji Pass

Duration	4 days
Distance	40.3km
Standard	demanding
Season	July–September
Start	Darkot
Finish	Ghotulti
Zone & Permit	open, no permit
Public Transport	yes

Summary This traverse of the Hindu Raj Range, through unspoiled traditional valleys with spring-fed meadows and superb alpine vistas, crosses a straightforward pass with opportunities for climbs and first ascents.

Punji Pass (4680m) links Darkot at the Yasin Valley's head to Ghotulti in Ishkoman. The pass is named after a distinctive cairn (*punji* in Burushaski) 2.25km west of, and 350m below, the pass, marking the highest possible camp site on the west side of the pass. The pass is also called Ishkoman Haghost by Darkot villagers. It's also occasionally called the Ishkoman Pass (as is the Asumbar Haghost to the south). This trek is often preceded by the Asumbar Haghost trek (p171).

PLANNING
Maps
The US AMS topographic maps *Baltit (NJ 43-14)* and *Mastuj (NJ 43-13)* cover the trek. The map calls the pass Ishkuman Aghost. What appears as a second pass is confusingly marked Panji Pass. The Ishkoman Haghost and Punji Pass are the same; there is only one pass. Gamelti is incorrectly shown on the river's south side, but

it's on the north side east of Gartens and west of Alam Bar. Nyu Bar is labelled as Neo Bar and Hanisar Bar as Anesar Bar.

Guides & Porters
Porters occasionally use donkeys to carry loads. Porters, however, must unload the donkeys to cross the pass itself, which takes time. Darkot porters seem happy to work for a flat rate of Rs 200 per day, including payment for food rations. The stage system isn't fully instituted on this trek, although some parties pay by stages. Look for porters at Darkot's *New Tourist Camping Garden* run by Muhammad Murad. If you can't find any, walk up to Gartens and the surrounding villages and ask there.

GETTING TO/FROM THE TREK
Gilgit-Darkot jeeps (Rs 150–170, nine hours) depart from a shop run by Bahadur off Gilgit's Shaheed-e-Millat Rd. Gilgit-Darkot special hires cost Rs 2500–3000. Alternatively, take the 8am daily NATCO Gilgit-Taus bus (Rs 105, eight hours), from where you can walk along the road in two days to Darkot or look for transport. It may be easier to find Gilgit-Taus jeeps (Rs 120).

From the finish of the trek, Ghotulti-Gilgit jeeps cost Rs 110 and are infrequent. Jeeps start from Ghotulti and go through Ishkoman village, so it's better to wait for one in Ghotulti rather than walk down to Ishkoman and risk them being full by the time they gets there. Special hires cost Rs 3350. Alternatively, walk a full day downvalley to Chatorkhand and get on the daily NATCO bus (Rs 75) to Gilgit.

THE TREK
Day 1: Darkot to Boimoshani
5–6 hours, 9.6km, 1200m ascent
If you're not previously acclimatised, cover the 1200m elevation gain from Darkot to Boimoshani in two days. Ascend from Darkot to Sawarey or Mardain (camp sites for large trekking parties are limited) the first day, and then to Boimoshani the next day.

Climb the obvious trail that snakes its dusty way up the hillside east from Darkot (2760m). In 1½ hours reach Gartens

(2880m) and then **Gamelti** (3139m). Cross Alam Bar and walk along the willow-lined path through **Sawarey** and in 15 minutes reach the sturdy footbridge over the Gasho Gol. Reportedly a difficult, seldom-used two-day route goes up Gasho Gol and over a 5700m pass via the Chiantar Glacier to Shuwor Sheer in Broghil.

Continue through a cultivated area called **Mardain** 45 minutes. Pass the last trees and reach the confluence of the Nyu Bar (*nyu* means 'big') from the north-east and Hanisar Bar from the south. Local people refer to Nyu Bar as Tshili Harang, which is the name of the main summer settlement up-river. Beyond Tshili Harang lies Atar Pass (see Other Treks, p193). Pyramid-shaped Garmush (6243m) rises above the head of the Nyu Bar; the snowy peak with the distinctive glacier west of Garmush is unnamed. Farther west is the wide, flat, snowy pass between the Gasho Gol and Broghil.

Cross a footbridge (3270m) to the Nyu Bar's true left bank just above its confluence with the Hanisar Bar. A short way ahead the trail divides. The left branch follows the Nyu Bar's true left bank to Mamutshil. Take the right branch up the steep spur between

the two rivers 150m to the fields and huts of **Gawat Kutu**. Like their northern Wakhi neighbours, Burusho women here tend the livestock. They wear tall pillbox hats, with their hair in multiple braids on the sides of their head. Relatives and friends are greeted in traditional fashion by kissing the top of one another's hands. From Gawat Kutu (3450m), traverse high above the Hanisar Bar on a level trail to the small settlement of Hanisar Bar. Hapey, a large cultivated area with several huts, lies across a footbridge above the true left bank.

Beyond, both sides of the valley are barren scree slopes. The narrow, rocky trail stays on the true right bank and ascends gradually for one hour. Around a bend to the south-east, grass appears and the pass is visible. Continue along the river bank 30 minutes to **Boimoshani** (3960m), a small camp site amid willows near a spring. The name Boimoshani means Boi's vegetable garden. Larger trekking parties camp in the grassy areas along the river. Porters need shelter as there are no huts and nights get cold. Across the river are two reddish mineral springs whose waters reportedly cure upset stomachs and headaches. Access to

GHIZAR

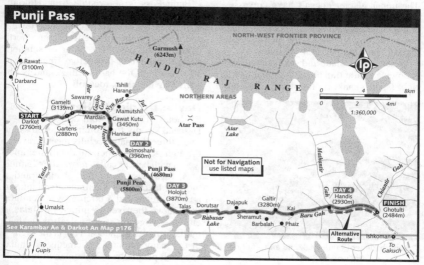

the other side of the river is usually via snow bridges.

Day 2: Boimoshani to Holojut

5 hours, 8.9km, 720m ascent, 810m descent

Follow the trail gradually up through thyme and wildflowers 45 minutes to a deep ravine. Cross the stream in the ravine, which is usually icy in the morning, and climb 15 minutes to the highest possible camp site (4250m) where a 1m-high cairn, or punji stands. Cows share the grassy well-watered slopes with marmots. Porters need adequate gear to camp here. The views downvalley are superb, especially the peaks and dramatic icefalls south of Darkot An above Rawat. South of Punji Pass rises the distinctive snowy pyramid of Punji Peak (5800m).

Continue up a faint trail, then work south (right) over moraine rubble towards the small glacial cirque flowing from the pass, reaching its margin (4410m) in one hour. Cross onto the glacier's south (right) side on the 20- to 30-degree slope, rather than lower down to the left, where it's at a 40-degree angle. The glacier's north (far left) side is exposed to rock fall from the cliffs above. Contour towards the two cairns visible on the pass. The upper glacier doesn't have crevasses, so using a rope is optional, as is wearing crampons. Reach **Punji Pass** (4680m), which has sweeping views of the peaks above Darkot and Thui An, in 45 minutes.

Descend over shale and small snowfields, following a faint trail along the stream's true right (south) bank. As the stream descends,

follow the trail south-south-east along the rocky ridge above the stream 45 minutes. At the end of the ridge, turn sharply back west (right) to avoid a deep ravine ahead. Descend steep switchbacks and a short scree slope on a trail to a flower-filled bowl below. Cross the meadow in 15 minutes to its west end and a clear stream, which tumbles down into a waterfall below the trail. Cross the stream and descend 125m on switchbacks along its true right bank to a smaller meadow. Recross the stream and pass left of many boulders, one of which is topped by a cairn.

Descend towards the alluvial plain below, traversing grassy slopes along the north (left) side of the valley 15 minutes to a cascading waterfall, which is the stream originating at the pass. Cross the stream and descend 15 minutes across scree to the valley floor. Walk along the river bed 15 minutes to **Holojut** (3870m). 'Holo' is the name of a renowned *wazir* from Nagyr and *jut* is a Burushaski word meaning 'grassy land', indicating this was a meadow he once frequented. Surrounded by peaks and hanging glaciers, this grassy expanse is a superb camp site with a large bubbling spring of deliciously cold water.

Punji Pass is not visible from Holojut. The eastern approach to the pass, however, is marked by two prominent rock towers and a large light-coloured cliff just north (right) of the pass. The taller or southern (left) tower has a distinctive finger on it. The pass is at the base of these and is obscured by the black rock rib.

Day 3: Holojut to Handis

5½ hours, 17.7km, 940m descent

Descend steeply for 15 minutes. Across the river, three dramatic icefalls meet. Traverse through scrub junipers and tall-stemmed weeds with berries called *laka*. After 15 minutes, turn east, with the glaciers and a moraine lake below. Continue 30 minutes to a clear stream and a birch grove. Continue well above the river 15 minutes to **Talas**, a cluster of wigwam-style conical-roofed huts built of juniper branches. This is the highest of the many summer settlements of Shina-speaking people from Ishkoman village.

JOHN MOCK

Superb view of Punji Peak and an icefall on the way to Punji Pass.

Continue 15 minutes through birch to the river, here called the Baru Gah, where the trail divides. A footbridge leads to the true right bank and on to *Babusar* (3480m), a settlement below a clear pond fed by a spring. Alternatively, stay on the true left side of the Baru Gah, bypass Babusar and cross another footbridge at Dorutsar, 15 minutes downstream.

Babusar sits along a side stream. Young girls here may coyly extract a bridge toll to cross the footbridge. The level grassy area along the pond makes a comfortable camp site, but leaves a long walk to Ghotulti the next day. The main trail stays on the Baru Gah's true right bank two hours to Galtir, passing through pleasant juniper and birch groves. A footbridge to Dajapuk is 30 minutes below the Dorutsar footbridge. The wigwams made from birch bark *(japuk)* here perch on a steep, dry hillside *(daj)* with no room for camp sites. Springs are on either side of the footbridge on the true right bank.

Cross several side streams, then on through a chir pine forest as the trail climbs gently and traverses high above the river. Pass the huts of Sheramut below. Then pass below four 1m-high cairns and through a mature juniper forest with a small spring. Above and out of view is the settlement of Barbalah. Descend to the river. *Galtir* (3280m) is a summer settlement with huts on both sides of the river. Cross a footbridge to the true left bank. No water is available between Galtir and Handis, so fill bottles at a clear side stream on the north bank, with a camp site nearby.

The trail climbs and stays high above the true left bank through juniper and artemisia-covered hillsides to Kai. Across the Baru Gah is the once-cultivated settlement of Phaiz. From Kai, continue high above the true left bank 45 minutes, then pass through boulders and juniper from where Handis, the first cultivated land in the valley, is 15 minutes ahead. Trails are along both sides of the Baru Gah between Handis and Ghotulti. If continuing to Ghotulti the same day, cross a footbridge over the Baru Gah above Handis and follow the trail along its true right bank two hours to Ghotulti to meet the

road just south of the bridge. Otherwise cross the footbridge over the **Mathantir Gah**, which flows from Atar Lake. Walk through *Handis* (2930m) 15 minutes to good camp sites in flat, grassy, shaded areas near a large, clear stream.

Day 4: Handis to Ghotulti
2½ hours, 4.1km, 446m descent

Continue above the true left bank, passing through cultivated fields, then high above the river 1¼ hours. The river becomes a gorge below. Just above the Chiantir Gah and Ghotulti, a large circle of stones enclosed by a square stone wall is a **shrine** to a saint who once visited the area. The saint's legend is remarkably similar to that of Baba Ghundi, whose shrine is in Gojal's Chapursan Valley. Descend steeply 30 minutes to **Ghotulti** (2484m). *Camp* in the enclosed orchard of Maiun Jan, son of Hussain Ali. The Chiantir Gah, which leads northeast towards the Chiantar Glacier, joins the Baru Gah below the village to become the Ishkoman River. In Burushaski, *chian* means 'near'; *tir*, a 'valley'. A bridge crosses the Baru Gah just below Ghotulti.

Thui An

Duration	5 days
Distance	47km
Standard	moderate
Season	July–September
Start	Nialthi
Finish	Sholkuch
Zone & Permit	open, no permit
Public Transport	yes

Summary An outstanding and popular traverse over a relatively easy pass, surrounded by tumbling glaciers and jagged 6000m peaks, this trek passes through traditional villages and links Yasin and Chitral.

Thui An (4500m) crosses the Shandur Range, a branch of the Hindu Raj Range, between the Yasin and Yarkhun valleys. The trek offers dramatic close-up views of 6000m peaks, lovely alpine meadows and the opportunity to meet the Burushaski-speaking people of the beautiful Thui Valley, as well as the Khowar speakers of the Gazin Gol. Thui Gol branches west off the Yasin Valley above Taus.

The Thui An is a deservedly popular trek, and is the most frequently trekked route between Ghizar and Chitral. The trek can be done in either direction; this description is from east to west. It's often combined with other open-zone treks. It can be preceded by the Asumbar Haghost trek (p171) and followed by the Shah Jinali An trek (p154). Done in the reverse direction (west to east), it can be combined with the Zagaro An trek (p189) to make a near loop.

PLANNING
Maps
The US AMS 1:250,000 topographic map *Mastuj (NJ 43-13)* covers the trek. It doesn't label Galpigol or Gashuchi. It shows a route along the Haghost Bar Glacier's north margin, but the route actually goes up the middle. It shows the Gazin and Thui glaciers as joined, but they're separated by a large alluvial fan.

Guides & Porters
A local guide is necessary to show the way over the Haghost Bar Glacier. Hire someone in Nialthi, or in Gazin or Nichagh when doing the trek in the reverse direction. Yasin porters seem happy to work for a flat rate of Rs 200 per stage, including payment for food rations. Porters need stoves and fuel because wood is very scarce at Gashuchi and unavailable at Galpigol.

Stages
It's 5½ stages total from Nialthi: (1) Lasht; (2) Shotaling; (3) Gashuchi; (4) Galpigol; (5) Nichagh; and (5½) half a stage to Sholkuch.

GETTING TO/FROM THE TREK
To the Start
Gilgit-Nialthi jeeps (Rs 150–170) depart from a shop run by Bahadur off Gilgit's Shaheed-e-Millat Rd. It may be easier to find Gilgit-Taus jeeps (Rs 120). Alternatively, take the 8am daily NATCO bus from Gilgit to Taus (Rs 105, eight hours), from where you can either walk along the road or look for transport. Yasin-Nialthi jeeps cost Rs 40–50 and Gilgit-Nialthi special hires cost Rs 2500–3000.

When coming from the Asumbar Haghost trek, walk 4km south to Taus or walk 7km north to Barkulti and cross to the road along the Yasin River's true left bank. Continue walking to Nialthi or look for transport.

From the Finish
Sholkuch-Mastuj jeeps cost Rs 100, and special hires cost Rs 1200. Since jeeps from Sholkuch are infrequent, you may have to settle for one from Paur, one hour's walk and half a stage below Sholkuch. If you're lucky enough to find one, Gazin Gol–Mastuj jeeps cost Rs 120 and special hires cost Rs 2000. Mastuj-Chitral jeeps cost Rs 40 and special hires cost Rs 2000.

When heading upvalley from Sholkuch, cross the bridge over the Gazin River and follow the road up the Yarkhun River's true left (east) bank and look for a ride.

THE TREK
Day 1: Nialthi to Shotaling
5½–6½ hours, 17.2km, 395m ascent
At Ali Murad Shah's store in Nialthi (2790m), the government road ends and the narrower community-constructed road continues. Spend a night in Nialthi; Mohammad Ali Shah, Ali Murad's father, makes his orchard available to trekkers.

Descend to the footbridge over Thui Gol and climb 20 minutes to Das village along the true left (north) bank. Continue up the good trail one to 1½ hours to Mushk, with its poplars and clear stream. It's another one to 1½ hours to Lasht, a summer village. Just 15 minutes farther, around the alluvial fan and across a clear stream, is **Balegarch**, a nice lunch spot.

Continue 1½ hours up the wide valley, with granite cliffs on either side over which flow waterfalls, through birch and willow stands to the well-made huts at Ramanch. Fifteen minutes farther cross the footbridge over the Kerun Bar (3078m) and reach *Shotaling* (3185m) in another hour. Here are the last birch trees *(taling)* along small grassy plots watered by a small, but very clear spring.

Day 2: Shotaling to Gashuchi
4–5 hours, 6.3km, 985m ascent

This is the trek's most strenuous day. Follow the river's true left (east) bank a short distance to where ice from the Haghost Bar Glacier bridges the river. Cross this permanent ice bridge and climb steeply, but briefly, up the moraine-covered ice to the more level glacier. (Alternatively, continue upvalley and ford the Barum Bar. In summer, this river has too much water and isn't possible to ford.) Once on the glacier, follow the fairly even, stable seam between the broken north margin and the heavily crevassed ice along its south margin, which flows from a massive icefall down a high snowy peak. Continue up the brown medial moraine, finding occasional cairns, keeping in the level, crevasse-free midsection. As you climb towards the confluence of the Qalander Gum Glacier, leave the medial moraine to the north and work onto the smooth central ice, lightly covered with small rocks. Follow this up and around to a knoll of brown moraine opposite the Qalander Gum Glacier. From here, the grassy Gashuchi area and the pass are visible ahead.

Leave the brown moraine and cross the smooth ice towards the grassy area. Follow the edge of the icy glacier and the brown moraine on the north margin, detouring around a few small crevasses, until opposite the grassy hill. Cross the moraine in 15 minutes. Climb a trail up the verdant hillside, past a large cairn on a rock, and contour through profuse wild onions, willows and flowers, over many small streams, to reach Gashuchi in another hour. *Gashuchi* (4170m) is on a level alluvial plain, near a large boulder on the hillside with a rock shelter next to it. Gashuchi means 'wild onion' in Burushaski; it's Khowar name is Kachili. Stroll these alpine meadows where ibex are occasionally spotted, surrounded by dramatic, snowy peaks in a splendid alpine amphitheatre.

Day 3: Gashuchi to Galpigol
3–4 hours, 4.8km, 330m ascent, 390m descent

Crossing the Thui An isn't difficult. The trail is clear and not overly steep. Walk

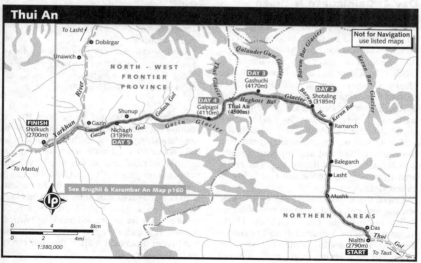

around to the west slopes of the grassy hill, then cross the stream via a solid snowfield to the grassy area on its west bank. Walk up to a small cairn that marks the point where the trail leaves the grass and begins to traverse west-south-west over scree to the pass. It takes from 1½ to two hours of steady walking to reach **Thui An** (4500m).

Descend a trail, keeping to the north (right) to avoid rockfall danger along the south side of the gully that runs west from the pass. Reach a solid snowfield at the base of the pass in 30 minutes. Cross the snowfield to rocks on its opposite side. Turn south and descend a trail over the rocky moraine towards the level alluvial area ahead. Don't go too far west; be sure to keep to the true left (east) side of the Thui Glacier's outwash stream. Continue south, towards the Gazin Glacier's northern lateral moraine (4200m). Once you reach it, bear west along the trail that parallels this moraine 20 minutes to *Galpigol* (4110m), the small grassy level area between the moraine and the outwash stream. Just over the first moraine is an enormous boulder with porters' shelters all around it.

Day 4: Galpigol to Nichagh
4–5 hours, 10.5km, 971m descent
Follow the trail along the edge of the Gazin Glacier's lateral moraine, next to the Thui Glacier's outwash stream. After 15 minutes, this stream turns and flows into the Gazin Glacier, blocking the path. Descend to the Gazin Glacier and detour 30 minutes around this obstacle, then climb back to the northern lateral moraine. Continue down a trail on moraine another 30 minutes to a small ablation valley. Follow the ablation valley 45 minutes over a small stream to a large alluvial fan and another clear stream, which makes a good lunch spot. The entire area from here to the Golash Gol below is called **Golash**.

Leave the wide alluvial fan of the side stream, and enter the more narrow ablation valley north of the Gazin Glacier. Thirty minutes from the stream, the trail begins to descend. The Yarkhun Valley is visible far below. In 30 minutes more, reach a small

hut at the ablation valley's end with a small trickle of water. Contour the hillside, descending to the alluvial plain of Golash, which is dotted with birches, willows and a few junipers.

Reach the clear Golash Gol (3450m) after 30 minutes, and cross it over a small footbridge. The first summer huts are 15 to 20 minutes farther. Thirty minutes below them are the few houses of Shunup, where the trail crosses a footbridge to the Gazin Gol's true left (south) bank. Continue down the trail 30 minutes to **Nichagh** (3139m) where the traditional *camp site* is in an orchard.

Day 5: Nichagh to Sholkuch
2½–3 hours, 8.2km, 439m descent
Walk 1½ to two hours downvalley to the Yarkhun River and follow the road for one hour to **Sholkuch** (2700m).

Naz Bar An

Duration	4 days
Distance	53.6km
Standard	very demanding
Season	July–mid-September
Start	Batakushi
Finish	Chashi
Zone & Permit	open, no permit
Public Transport	finish only

Summary This challenging route takes adventurous trekkers through wild and ruggedly scenic alpine country via a high pass with plenty of opportunity for exploration and peak bagging.

Naz Bar An (4980m) links Naz Bar, a south-west tributary of the Yasin Valley, to the Bahushtaro Gol, a northern tributary of the Ghizar River. This steep route is infrequently trekked and is not used by local people. The pass isn't glaciated, but has a brief Class 2 section at its top and a permanent cornice on its east side. It also receives strong winds. This trek is not for novice trekkers, nor for organised trekking parties. Rather, it's a challenging alternative route west from the Yasin Valley through rarely visited country.

Mountaineers heading for the 5000m peaks around Mashpar Gol and Kano Gol in upper Bahushtaro Gol may choose the Naz Bar An approach for acclimatisation. Naz Bar An is often crossed in conjunction with Zagaro An (p189), northern Pakistan's two most difficult nonglaciated passes.

PLANNING
Maps
The US AMS 1:250,000 topographic map *Mastuj (NJ 43-13)* covers the trek. It indicates the general route, but without sufficient detail to help with route-finding. The pass appears fairly level, but the map's scale causes this deceptive aberration.

Guides & Porters
Guidance from Batakushi herders, who know the not-straightforward route over the Naz Bar An, is essential. Yasin porters seem happy to work for a flat rate of Rs 200 per stage, including payment for food rations.

Stages
It's four stages total from Batakushi: (1) Naz Bar High Camp; (2) Ano Gol Huts; (3) Dedero Shal; and (4) Chashi.

GETTING TO/FROM THE TREK
To the Start
A daily NATCO Gilgit-Taus bus (Rs 105, eight hours) departs from Gilgit's Punial Rd at 8am. Get off the bus at Yasin village, from where most jeeps to Naz Bar depart. Jeeps only go up Naz Bar as far as Baltaring (2682m), where the last stores are and the electric line ends, although the jeep road goes as far as Batakushi. It takes 2½ to three hours to walk 8.5km from Baltaring to Batakushi. (If you walk from Yasin village, it takes a full day to reach Batakushi.) If you aren't previously acclimatised, avoid driving directly to Batakushi, but start walking from a lower elevation. When combining this trek with the Thui An trek, Nialthi-Baltaring special hires cost Rs 1000.

From the Finish
Jeeps sporadically pass through Chashi, on the Gilgit-Chitral road east of Phundar, en route to Gupis and very occasionally to Gilgit. Chashi-Gupis jeeps cost Rs 60. Chashi-Gupis special hires cost Rs 1500–2000 and Chashi-Gilgit special hires cost Rs 5300 (nine hours).

THE TREK (see map p190)
Day 1: Batakushi to Naz Bar High Camp
5–6 hours, 12.7km, 1050m ascent

Naz Bar An is visible from Batakushi. It's the lowest snowy saddle between the peaks to the west. From Batakushi (3400m), follow a trail up the Naz Bar's true left (north) bank. Many sheep and goats graze the grassy slopes above the wide valley. One hour beyond Batakushi, the Kha Bar enters from the south. *Shuqan* (3505m), the highest Burushaski-speaking summer settlement, is 45 minutes farther. This level grassy area with springs and willows makes a good camp site, from where the huts in upper Ano Gol could be reached in one long day.

Continue for 30 minutes to the alluvial plain (3690m) where the Yaltar Bar and Naz Bar meet. Cross the Yaltar Bar and head west. Across the alluvial plain is a small grassy area where the valley and trail turn south. The trail ascends a talus slope, climbing above the Khamit Bar's true left (west) bank, as the stream is now called. Forty-five minutes from the Yaltar Bar crossing, reach the confluence of the Khamit Bar (3810m) with a stream coming from the west. Turn west and head up the stream's true left (north) bank. Ahead is a rocky bluff. Two streams descend either side of this bluff and join to form this western tributary of Khamit Bar. Take the north (right) fork past the rocky bluff. As the stream rises to the level of the top of the rocky bluff, cross it and climb the grassy slope to the bluff's top. Continue angling south-west up a trail along the red streak that leads to the top of a grassy north-south ridge well above the small rocky bluff. It takes one hour to make this climb, or 1½ hours from the confluence with the Khamit Bar. From the top of this alpine ridge, the mountains above the pass are visible, but the pass itself is not.

Head west, contouring down to meet the stream below. Herders use these extensive alpine grasslands where you can camp along the stream. Forty-five minutes from the ridge top is a large boulder with a cairn on top and a stone shelter next to it, which is the *Naz Bar High Camp* (4450m), the highest possible camp site.

Day 2: Naz Bar High Camp to Ano Gol Huts

5–6 hours, 6.5km, 530m ascent, 1250m descent

Head along the stream's true left (east) bank. Where two streams join to form this stream, take the right fork, heading around the base of and behind the last grassy hill, where horses and cows graze in summer. This hill rises into a ridge. Curve around and behind (west of) this ridge, entering a valley with a black moraine in its centre. To the south and west is a small glacier and snowfield. Ahead is the steep scree ascent topped by a snowy cornice that is the Naz Bar An. It's the southernmost scree chute, reddish in colour, on the pass ridge. Continue along the black moraine towards the pass. From the high camp, it takes 1½ to two hours to reach the end of this moraine and the base of the pass.

Cross the top of the snowfield, working as high up the snow as possible. Then ascend the 45- to 50-degree scree slope to the pass in 45 minutes to one hour. At the top, scramble over a Class 2 rock outcrop on the north edge of the pass to get around the cornice lying on the pass itself. On top of **Naz Bar An** (4980m) is a small cairn, not visible from below. Late in the season, when more snow has melted, rock-fall danger is lower. The views all around are stunning.

Descend straight down reddish scree on the west side, moving onto the easier snow-field to the left as the angle eases. Reach the level area at the base of the pass in 20 minutes, and follow a faint trail. After 10 minutes, descend to white granite talus amid sparse grass and flowers. As the valley turns south-south-west, follow a trail, with occasional cairns, 30 minutes to the junction with a black moraine-filled valley coming from the east.

Turn west (right) and continue along a rocky moraine downvalley another hour. Keep to the grassier south-east side to avoid a steep descent over scree. At the base of this grassy hill, amid scrub willow by a stream side, is a cairn-topped boulder with an adjacent small rock shelter. This is the first possible *camp site*, two to 2½ hours below the pass. Ten minutes farther downstream is another more open area. Another 30 minutes down a grassy hillside, the stream called Naz Bar by herders opens into a large alluvial river bed and joins the larger stream coming from Kano Gol. The confluence of these two streams marks the start of the Ano Gol. In Khowar, Ano Gol simply means the valley *(gol)* coming from a pass *(an)*. Herders say it's possible to reach Pingal village over a high pass at the Kano Gol's head, where several 5000m peaks have attracted mountaineers in recent years. Cross the Naz Bar and follow a now-clear trail along the Ano Gol's true right (north) bank. Ten minutes beyond this crossing is a good level camp site near the *Ano Gol Huts* (3730m), the first herders' settlement.

Day 3: Ano Gol Huts to Dedero Shal

3½–4 hours, 12.4km, 430m descent

It's one hour down the Ano Gol to the confluence with the War Bar, which enters from the south. Cross the Ano Gol over a footbridge to the thriving summer huts on the true left bank of both the War Bar and Ano Gol. The trail downvalley stays high above Ano Gol. A trail on the true right (north) bank is a longer way down, but it's the trail to take when heading up the **Mashpar Gol** for climbing. Thirty minutes down the true left bank you're high above the confluence of the Ano Gol and Mashpar Gol (3566m). Turn left and continue high above the true left bank of the Bahushtaro Gol (formed at the confluence of the above two). In 30 minutes, you're opposite **Haringol Shal** settlement (3420m) and the grassy plain called Rushkot. Parties going up the Bahushtaro Gol's true right (west) side camp in Rushkot.

Another hour down the trail, cross a footbridge over the Bahushtaro Gol and continue down the level alluvial river bed. In 30 minutes reach the huts of Deder, also called *Dedero Shal* (3300m), at the clear Zagaro Gol's mouth.

Day 4: Dedero Shal to Chashi

6–8 hours, 22km, 679m descent

Descend the largely uninhabited Bahushtaro Gol to Chashi. The herders in the Bahushtaro Gol are friendly and hospitable Khowar-speaking Isma'ili Muslims from Chashi.

Upper Ghizar

Along the clear blue upper Ghizar River runs the unsealed Gilgit-Chitral road. But to the north and south, side valleys beckon trekkers with passes to Chitral and Kalam Kohistan, ranging from gentle strolls to adventurous out-there challenges.

ACCESS TOWN

See Gupis (p179).

Zagaro An	
Duration	6 days
Distance	57.6km
Standard	very demanding
Season	July–August
Start	Batakushi
Finish	Chapali
Zone & Permit	open, no permit
Public Transport	finish only

Summary Northern Pakistan's most challenging nonglaciated pass traverses unvisited valleys between Ghizar and Chitral, offering opportunity for exploration and alpine climbs.

Zagaro An (4920m), a difficult Class 2 pass that marks the Northern Areas' border with NWFP, connects the Bahushtaro Gol with Chitral's Yarkhun Valley. This trek is usually done from east to west preceded by the equally difficult Naz Bar An, by which it takes three days to reach Dedero Shal (3300m) in the Bahushtaro Gol. The pass has a small permanent cornice on its west side, although it's unglaciated. Adventurous trekkers who relish a challenging, little-used route through high and hard country may wish to attempt it. The pass isn't used by local people and is only infrequently crossed by trekkers. It isn't recommended for novices or organised trekking parties.

PLANNING
Maps

The US AMS 1:250,000 topographic map *Mastuj (NJ 43-13)* covers the trek. The map's scale is of little use for route-finding, particularly west of the pass.

Guides & Porters

A local guide is essential. Naz Bar men don't know the route, so even if you have a Naz Bar porter, hire a herder to show the way. You may need to send a message to Haringol Shal (or Donjo Shal) to find someone, as Dedero Shal is inhabited by a single small family. Expect to pay Rs 300–400 to hire someone to go to the top of the pass.

Stages

It's 5½ stages total from Batakushi: (1) Naz Bar High Camp; (2) Ano Gol Huts; (3) Dedero Shal; (3½) Zagar Shota, half a stage; (4½) Jambor Shal; and (5½) to Chapali.

GETTING TO/FROM THE TREK

For details on transport to the start of the walk, see the Naz Bar An trek (p187). For details on transport from the finish, see the Chumarkhan An trek (p192).

THE TREK (see map p190)
Days 1–3: Batakushi to Dedero Shal

3 days, 31.6km, 1580m ascent, 1680m descent

See Days 1–3 of the Naz Bar An trek (p187).

Day 4: Dedero Shal to Zagar Shota

1½–2 hours, 3.1km, 500m ascent

Climb the steep hill behind the huts at Dedero Shal on a trail. Contour high above the Zagaro Gol's true right (south) bank, continuously working up the slopes on live-stock trails. Reach a hut by the stream after 45 minutes, and continue upvalley. The valley opens and 1½ to two hours from Dedero Shal, reach **Zagar Shota** (3800m), a small hut and a livestock pen by the stream. This short day is necessary in order to reach the first possible camp site on Day 5.

Day 5: Zagar Shota to Jambor Shal
7–9 hours, 12.2km, 1120m ascent, 1140m descent

Leave the stream after 15 minutes and climb steeply to the shoulder of the grassy ridge ahead. Go around the shoulder of the ridge, to the right of a rock outcrop, following a faint trail. Behind the ridge is a valley with grassy slopes, one hour from Zagar Shota. Continue upvalley to a small bowl, marked by a cairn, where wild onions abound. Turn right, up grassy slopes, and 45 minutes after rounding the ridge see the

Zagaro An, the obvious low point with a scree slope beneath it. Continue up a series of hillocks with grass, herbs and flowers amid rocks, switchbacking steadily. In 30 minutes, reach the highest vegetation at the base of an old terminal moraine (4410m). Work right around the moraine's northern base, on easy scree below talus slopes for another 20 minutes. Follow the moraine's base as it turns back west and south. Reach a small snowfield and head along its west edge 20 minutes to a scree slope coming from the base of a yellowish rock outcrop. Traverse right across the scree to reach the rock rib on the south (left) side of another scree slope coming from the pass itself.

Ascend this Class 2 rock rib to avoid rock-fall danger on either side. When the rock rib becomes too steep to continue, exit right and climb the 45- to 50-degree scree slope coming from the pass. Keep close to the rock rib, the occasional protrusions of which provide solid footing. This is Class 2

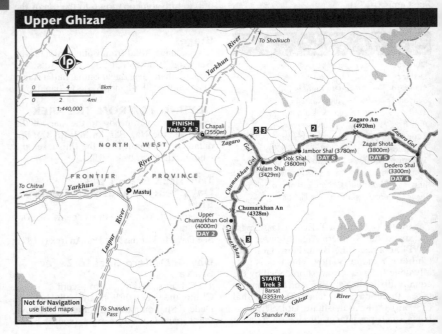

scree, and a trekking pole is essential for balance. Near the top, the angle lessens and the scree becomes more stable. It takes 1½ to two hours to ascend the pass. From the top of **Zagaro An** (4920m), Tirich Mir dominates the view west. There is no cairn.

Descend left down scree one hour to a level basin and the first water, looking straight at Buni Zom's dramatic summit. Looking back, the pass is the low point with the jagged snowy cornice in it, between two dry hills; the one to the north rounded and the one to the south more rocky. Continuing down the stream 30 minutes, the valley opens into a large bowl with some grass and flowers. An emergency high camp is possible.

Keep to the south (left) of the stream, and cross pleasant, rolling hills of ungrazed grass and flowers for 30 minutes. As they end, traverse left over and around the west edge of an awkward slate talus slope 30 minutes. Then descend a short scree slope

20 minutes to the level grassy area along the stream and to the north (right) of the enormous moraine that fills the entire valley. Follow the stream all the way past the moraine to the alluvial fan below. If the stream has too much water to make this possible, continue on the moraine's talus, working down its tedious slope to the alluvial fan below, and then cross the stream from the pass. On this more level area (4110m) find a trail along the main stream's true right bank, which flows on the valley's south (left) side. One hour downvalley, reach a grassy area to camp. Across the stream, on its true left (south) bank is the well-built hut, livestock pen and small spring at *Jambor Shal* (3780m).

Day 6: Jambor Shal to Chapali
4–5 hours, 10.7km, 1230m descent
Cross the footbridge and follow the livestock trail above the Zagaro Gol's true left bank. Reach Dok Shal (3600m), with many

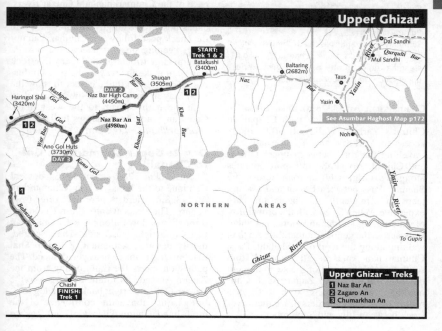

abandoned huts and a clear stream, in 45 minutes. Alternatively, stay on the Zagaro Gol's true right bank and continue past abandoned huts and once-irrigated fields to cross a footbridge at a level area before Dok Shal. A lone herders' hut is in use at Dok Shal, perched on a small spur. Continue 30 minutes on the main trail to more abandoned settlements at Kulam Shal (3429m). Meet the main trail from Chumarkhan An after another 30 minutes. Continue 2½ hours down a good trail to Chapali (2550m); see Day 2 of the Chumarkhan An trek (below) for details.

Chumarkhan An

Duration	2 days
Distance	29km
Standard	easy
Season	June–October
Start	Barsat
Finish	Chapali
Zone & Permit	open, no permit
Public Transport	yes

Summary This gentle pass leads through meadows and meanders along streams; it's an outstanding quick route between picturesque upper Ghizar and colourful Yarkhun.

Chumarkhan An (4328m) links Barsat in the upper Ghizar Valley with Chapali in Chitral's Yarkhun Valley. It offers quick access to Yarkhun and an alternative to travelling the road between upper Ghizar and Chitral. No public transport operates along the Gilgit-Chitral road across the Shandur Pass between Barsat and Mastuj, jeeps go infrequently and special hires are expensive. When faced with the probability of walking, it's shorter and more pleasant to walk across the gentle Chumarkhan An than walking along the road over Shandur Pass. Chumarkhan An is usually crossed from south to north because of the steep descent on its north side into Zagaro Gol. Chumarkhan, which means 'iron fort', is a rolling plain where herders graze their livestock between July and September.

PLANNING
Maps
The US AMS 1:250,000 topographic map *Mastuj (NJ 43-13)* covers the trek.

GETTING TO/FROM THE TREK
Jeeps go infrequently from Gupis to Barsat, which is beyond Teru where the Chumarkhan Gol joins the Ghizar River. Special hires cost Rs 6000.

Chapali-Mastuj jeeps depart in the morning and cost Rs 15. Special hires cost Rs 400. At other times of day, flag down any vehicle heading south. Jeeps also go regularly Mastuj-Chitral (Rs 40). To go upvalley, flag down any vehicle heading north.

THE TREK (see map p190)
Day 1: Barsat to Upper Chumarkhan Gol
3–4 hours, 11km, 647m ascent
Barsat (3353m) lies along the upper Ghizar's north bank. Nearby, at the confluence of the Chumarkhan and Ghizar rivers, are the tents of the Chumarkhan police check post on the Gilgit-Chitral road. From the check post, follow the Chumarkhan upriver, keeping on its true left (east) side. Several large tributaries and many livestock trails can make the way to the pass confusing. It's easiest to find a herder to show the way. Stay in the middle of the broad valley with the main stream to the west (left). Camp anywhere in meadows in the *Upper Chumarkhan Gol* (4000m).

Day 2: Upper Chumarkhan Gol to Chapali
5 hours, 18km, 328m ascent, 1778m descent
Continue to the broad, rolling **Chumarkhan An** (4328m). Herders here may offer fresh yogurt. The descent into Chitral is steep, through meadows along the Chumarkhan Gol's true right (east) side. The scattered, mostly deserted settlement of **Kulam Shal** (3429m) lies to the right as you descend. The path soon meets the trail coming from the Zagaro An and in 15 minutes crosses to the Zagaro Gol's true right bank over a log footbridge, just above the confluence of the birch-lined Chumarkhan Gol and Zagaro

Scree slopes run down to plentiful camp sites on the shores of vast Karambar Lake.

Porters lend a helping hand up a steep section on Chattiboi Glacier, Karambar An trek.

Dhuli Chhīsh, in the Hindu Raj Range, rises above well-watered Darkot Valley.

Mint flowers abound in upper Karambar Valley.

Gol. Follow the large, well-used trail one hour to the first houses. The trail widens here to jeep width. Continue another hour to the footbridge at the start of **Chapali** (2550m) and its jeep road. Follow the road 30 minutes past the water supply house through the village to the Yarkhun Valley jeep road. At this intersection is a sign reading 'Water Supply Scheme Chapari' and a store on the opposite side of the road. The shopkeeper lets trekkers *camp* in the field behind the store.

Other Treks

The following treks are all in an open zone.

KURU AN

Kuru An (4700m), a pass used by ibex hunters, crosses the ridge between the Baj Gaz Gol and Pakora Gol, eastern tributaries of the Ishkoman River. From Mujaowir village (spelled Munjawar on maps) adjacent to Imit in the Ishkoman Valley, follow a trail south-east up the Baj Gaz (where there's a lot of grass) to the pasture at Khushrui Zherav (beautiful valley in Wakhi). Local people also refer to the valley as Bazi Gah. The glaciated upper valley offers climbing possibilities, but the heavily corniced and technically difficult Baj Gaz Pass (shown on all maps) at the valley's head is never crossed. The pass was reportedly crossed by an unknown Englishman in about 1925.

From Khushrui Zherav, the route over Kuru An (marked on some, but not named on any maps) turns south-west, climbs to the ridge, and descends the Kuru An Gol, reaching Pakora Gol at the small settlement of Kuru. Cross the footbridge to the Pakora Gol's true left bank and follow the main trail downvalley. See Day 5 of the Pakora Pass trek (p223) for a description between Kuru and Pakora. Allow three or four days for this demanding near-loop trek.

ATAR PASS

Atar, a less well-known but very scenic pass between the Yasin and Ishkoman valleys, is usually open July to September (see map, p181). Atar is also the name of a large lake, which flows into the Mathantir Gah (in Burushaski, *mathan* means 'far'; *tir*, a 'valley'). Schomberg explored this route in 1933 and village elders in Ghotulti still remember him. The route shown on the U502 *Baltit* (NJ 43-14) map is based on Schomberg's notes. Atar is a longer, but seemingly easier route between Darkot and Ghotulti than the Punji Pass. A local guide is essential. Some villagers from

Darkot and Ghotulti know the route. It may be preferable to trek east to west since many Ghotulti villagers go up to Atar Lake and few people from Darkot cross the Atar Pass to the lake. Plan on three to five days for this demanding trek.

From Darkot, head east past Mardain. Cross to the Nyu Bar's true left bank and follow it to Mamutshil with its few trees, huts and livestock pens. Tshili Harang is the main summer settlement and Chordes is a pasture high above the Nyu Bar's true right bank. Recross the Nyu Bar to Tshili Harang and continue up the valley's east arm, here called the Jut Bar.

The Jut Bar divides, with the Bhorik Bar continuing south. The route to the pass turns east and heads up Atar Bar. Schomberg found a small glacier beneath the pass, which became steep near the top. The glacier isn't difficult, but could be avoided by keeping to the north side. Schomberg was met by Ishkoman men on top of the pass and so had to change porters there. He describes the view towards Ishkoman as 'an immense amphitheatre surrounded by a circle of snowy peaks and hanging glaciers'. The descent is steep to Atar Lake, a greenish lake 4km long. The path skirts its south shore with a camp site at its east end. Follow the Mathantir Gah to Handis and the confluence of the Baru Gah. From Handis trails on both sides of the Baru Gah lead to the roadhead at Ghotulti.

DARMODAR HAGHOST

A four-day moderate trek across the Darmodar Haghost (4495m) links Jundoli village, along the Gilgit River 10km upstream from its confluence with the Ishkoman River, with Dal Sandhi in Yasin. From Jundoli, head north up the Darmodar Gah, cross the pass on the second day, and on the third day reach Mayur, joining the trail from the Asumbar Haghost. Continue to Dal Sandhi (see Day 4 of the Asumbar Haghost trek, p174).

Two variations of this trek exist. An alternative and longer trek starts from Maiun in the Ishkoman Valley. It heads north-west up the Shahchoi Gah and across the Shahchoi An (4500m) to meet the Darmodar Gah below the Darmodar Haghost. An alternative three-day route starts at Jundoli, but crosses another pass, about the same elevation as Darmodar Haghost, and heads west into Qurqulti Bar meeting the Yasin Valley above Sandhi village. This route is used by Gujars from Ghizar, who ride horses to medicinal springs above Barkulti in Yasin.

KALAM KOHISTAN

Two passes, the Dadarelli An and Bashkaro An, link the upper Ghizar Valley with the Ushu Gol in Kalam Kohistan to the south. A reliable local guide and an armed escort are recommended, especially in Swat's Ushu Gol where people are heavily armed and may be hostile. A challenging loop trek can be made by combining a trek over either of these passes with the Kachakani An trek (p163). Both routes cross small glaciers, so bring a rope and ice axe for safety.

Dadarelli An

Infrequently crossed Dadarelli An (5030m) is at the head of the scenic Handrap Valley, a southern tributary of the Ghizar River. Handrap is renowned for its trout fishing, and the world-record brown trout was taken out of Handrap Lake. Although Handrap villagers speak Khowar, most are immigrants from the Darel Valley in Indus Kohistan. This demanding five-day trek is best done July to September.

From the Gilgit-Chitral road before Teru, 4½ hours' drive from Gilgit, cross a bridge over the Ghizar River to Handrap village, on the Handrap River's west bank. Follow the trail 13km to the south shore of the tree-lined Handrap Lake in four to five hours on Day 1. On Day 2 continue five to six hours, 14km, up the pleasant valley to where the valley divides (3593m), and take the main (south) fork. The other fork, which heads southeast, leads across high passes to the Kandia Valley in Indus Kohistan. Camp a few kilometres past the fork. On Day 3 push four hours up the open, barren valley, passing several lakes, and set a base camp near the highest lake. It takes seven to eight hours to cross the pass on Day 4, and because of rock-fall danger on the south side of the pass, start early. The final ascent to the pass is over a small glacier, and the descent is on steep scree with a detour around a large snowfield. Several hours from the pass, reach meadows and camp. On Day 5 descend the herders' trail along the Dadarelli stream, past summer huts to Diwangar at the confluence of the Dadarelli Valley and Ushu Gol. Continue down Ushu Gol to Machiangaas, making this a five- to six-hour day. Prearrange transport to meet you in Machiangaas or walk the next day five to six hours to Matiltan where there's transport to Kalam.

Bashkaro An

Bashkaro An (4924m) is a demanding and rarely crossed pass. West of Barsat, the Gilgit-Chitral road goes south, past peat bogs. Leave the road where it turns west to the Shandur Pass and the Khokush Gol meets the Ghizar River. The trek starts here and heads south up the Khokush Gol, which has many large lakes and good fishing. Continue upvalley, along the lakes' west shores and camp beyond the highest lake. The ascent to the Bashkaro An appears to be several kilometres over a glacier. Herders in the Khokush Gol may be able to guide you to the pass. South of the pass, descend into the Ushu Gol at Shonz and continue to Machiangaas.

Gilgit & Diamir

Gilgit and Diamir, two Northern Areas districts, are also ancient names whose history is lost in legend. Gilgit centres on Rakaposhi (7788m) whose snowy flanks and summit always charm visitors with their beauty. Diamir centres on Nanga Parbat (8125m), the ninth-highest peak in the world and the Himalaya's west end. Like the prows of two huge ships, these peaks lie on separate continental plates that here collide.

HISTORY

Most of what is known about the prehistory and early history of the Gilgit and Chilas region comes from carvings and inscriptions on polished boulders along the Indus and Gilgit rivers. The earliest petroglyphs were probably made by late–Stone Age hunters, who incised totemistic ibex and markhor figures as part of hunting rituals. Rock carvings and inscriptions indicate an extensive network of travel and communication through the region. Between Gandhara, Kashmir and Central Asia, merchants and monks travelled the Silk Route through the mountains. From the 5th through the 8th centuries, Buddhism flourished along these routes, and Gilgit and Chilas were important monastic as well as trading centres. Shatial, across from the mouth of the important Darel Valley, and Thalpan, on the Indus River's north bank across from the route to Babusar Pass, were also significant. Naupur, at the Kargah Valley's mouth near Gilgit, has a standing Buddha figure carved on the hillside. The location of these sites, at the entrances to important side valleys or where a route crossed the Indus River, shows that travel wasn't along the Indus River's deep gorges, but rather over passes joining smaller side valleys.

No doubt the wealth from Silk Route trade helped support the region's cultural and artistic achievements. Gilgit's kings belonged to the Patola Shahi dynasty, and the region was known to the Chinese as 'Little Balur'. In the 8th century, Tibetan armies conquered the Gilgit region, and the Gilgit

king married a Tibetan princess. Although the courts were cosmopolitan and learned, the mountain people retained their shamanistic beliefs coupled with a strong belief in magically endowed female spirit beings. It no doubt made for a strange mix. Gilgit became known as a centre of Bon-po practice, and in Udaiyana (Swat), the dynamic mix of Shaivism and Buddhism produced a

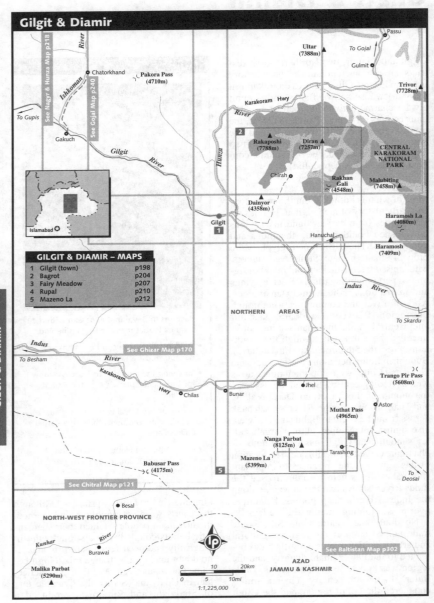

Gilgit & Diamir

GILGIT & DIAMIR – MAPS

1	Gilgit (town)	p198
2	Bagrot	p204
3	Fairy Meadow	p207
4	Rupal	p210
5	Mazeno La	p212

See Nagyr & Hunza Map p218
See Gojal Map p240
See Ghizar Map p170
See Chitral Map p121
See Baltistan Map p302

Passu
To Gojal
Gulmit
Ultar
(7388m)
Trivor
(7728m)
Chatorkhand
Pakora Pass
(4710m)
Karakoram Hwy
Ishkoman
Hunza River
Gakuch
To Gupis
Gilgit River
Rakaposhi
(7788m)
Diran
(7257m)
CENTRAL KARAKORAM NATIONAL PARK
Chirah
Rakhan Gali
(4548m)
Malubiting
(7458m)
Dainyor
(4358m)
Gilgit
Hanuchal
Haramosh La
(4080m)
Haramosh
(7409m)
Islamabad
Indus River
To Skardu
NORTHERN AREAS
Indus River
Karakoram Hwy
To Besham
Chilas
Bunar
Jhel
Trango Pir Pass
(5608m)
Astor
Muthat Pass
(4965m)
Nanga Parbat
(8125m)
Tarashing
Mazeno La
(5399m)
Babusar Pass
(4175m)
Besal
NORTH-WEST FRONTIER PROVINCE
To Deosai
Kunhar River
Burawai
Malika Parbat
(5290m)
AZAD JAMMU & KASHMIR

0   10   20km
0   5   10mi
1:1,225,000

GILGIT & DIAMIR

powerful Tantric blend that was brought to Tibet by Padmasambhava (Guru Rimpoche). Legend says Gilgit's last Buddhist king Shri Badat was a cannibal, but this is apparently just a local version of a widespread cannibal king legend that probably came to Gilgit as an exemplary Buddhist *jataka* tale.

As Arab armies pushed east along the Silk Route in the 9th century, China and Tibet lost influence in Gilgit. With no external power to unify the area, small independent kingdoms arose. These independent, unruly wine drinkers of Gilgit and Chilas continually harassed the neighbouring Kashmiri kings from the 9th to the 13th century. The coming of the Mongols brought a new power to Central Asia. Gilgit came under the influence of the mighty Mongol and Turkic rulers from the north. Gilgit legends recall one, Taj Moghul, who played a role in mid-17th-century struggles for control of Gilgit between the Chitral and Yasin rulers and the Raja of Skardu. In 1841, again pressed by the Chitrali rulers of Yasin, the Raja of Gilgit called for help from the Sikh armies holding Kashmir. The arrival of Dogra troops set off a 35-year struggle with Kashmir. Time and time again the Sikh armies captured Gilgit, only to be driven off by tribesmen. The massacre of General Bhup Singh's entire Sikh regiment in 1852 by rolling rocks down on it is known to every Gilgit schoolchild.

Britain, nervous about Russian designs on the area, sought through Kashmir to control the independent states, and sent a political agent to Gilgit in 1877. Chilas rebelled in 1892 and Chitral in 1895, but finally the British held the frontier. In 1935, Britain actually leased back the entire Gilgit Agency from Kashmir and raised a local militia, the Gilgit Scouts.

In anticipation of independence from Britain, set for 14 August 1947, Kashmir sent General Ghansara Singh to Gilgit as its new governor. On 1 August, the British political agent handed over the entire Gilgit Agency to him. Two British officers, one at Chilas and one at Gilgit, however, stayed on to command the Gilgit Scouts. As independence came and went, Kashmir's Maharaja Hari Singh hesitated to join India or Pakistan. Finally on 26 October, he acceded to India. The Gilgit people had little love for Kashmir after more than 100 years of Kashmiri rule, and they had even less desire to become part of India. On the news of Kashmir joining India, Gilgit rose to claim its independence. The Gilgit Scouts, led by Mohammad Babar Khan, arrested Ghansara Singh and the following day, 2 November, Gilgit *wazirat* joined Pakistan. Remarkably, members of the ruling families and the two British officers kept bloodshed to a minimum. The move to join Pakistan closed the old Kashmir-Gilgit route via the Astor Valley, and the Babusar Pass became the route to down-country Pakistan. The much-disliked Kashmiri shopkeepers and officials left Gilgit, and their positions were filled by local men. Gilgit now celebrates 1 November as the Northern Areas' Independence Day, *Jashan-i-Gilgit,* with music, dancing and a week-long polo tournament.

INFORMATION
Maps
The Swiss Foundation for Alpine Research 1:250,000 orographical map *Karakoram (Sheet 1)* covers Bagrot and Haramosh. The Deutscher Alpenverein (DAV) 1:50,000 topographic map *Nanga Parbat Gruppe* and US AMS Series U502 India and Pakistan 1:250,000 topographic map *Gilgit (NI 43-2)* cover Diamir.

Books
Nanga Parbat Pilgrimage by Hermann Buhl is an account of the 1953 solo first ascent of Nanga Parbat (hardcover). *Nanga Parbat – The Killer Mountain* is by Karl M Herrligkoffer, who devoted much of his life to this mountain.

GILGIT
Gilgit (1494m), Pakistan's mountain 'capital', is a booming administrative and market centre at the intersection of northern Pakistan's main north-south and east-west roads. Gilgit is spread along the Gilgit River's true right bank above the confluence with the Hunza River, 10km west of the Karakoram

GILGIT & DIAMIR

Gilgit (town)

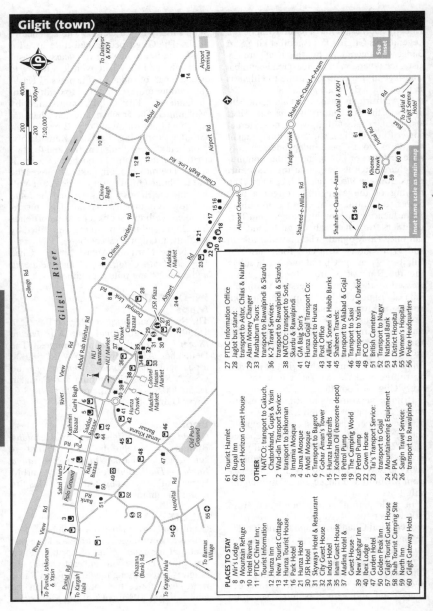

PLACES TO STAY
8 Mir's Lodge
9 Mountain Refuge
10 Hotel Riveria
11 PTDC Chinar Inn;
   Tourist Information
12 Hunza Inn
13 New Tourist Cottage
14 Hunza Tourist House
16 Park Hotel
21 Hunza Hotel
30 JSR Hotel
31 Skyways Hotel & Restaurant
32 City Guest House
34 Indus Hotel
35 Inam Guest House
37 Madina Hotel &
   Guest House
39 New Kashgar Inn
40 Ibex Lodge
47 Garden Hotel
50 Golden Peak Inn
57 Gilgit Tourist Guest House
58 Shah Tourist Camping Site
59 North Inn
60 Gilgit Gateway Hotel

61 Tourist Hamlet
62 Rupal Inn
63 Lost Horizon Guest House

OTHER
1 NATCO: transport to Gakuch,
   Chatorkhand, Gupis & Yasin
2 Wad-din Transport Service:
   transport to Ishkoman
3 Imamia Mosque
4 Jama Mosque
5 Moti Mosque
6 Transport to Bagrot
7 Gohar Aman's Tower
15 Hunza Handicrafts
17 Kohistan Oil (kerosene depot)
18 Petrol Pump
19 The Camping World
20 Petrol Pump
22 Gown House
23 Tai's Transport Service:
   transport to Gojal
24 Mountaineering Equipment
25 PIA
26 Sargin Travel Service:
   transport to Rawalpindi

27 PTDC Information Office
28 Jaglot bus stand:
   transport to Astor, Chilas & Naltar
29 Alam Money Changer
33 Mashabrum Tours:
   transport to Rawalpindi & Skardu
36 K-2 Travel Services:
   transport to Rawalpindi & Skardu
38 NATCO: transport to Sost,
   Skardu & Rawalpindi
41 GM Baig Son's
42 Hunza Gojal Transport Co:
   transport to Hunza
43 Post Office
44 Allied, Soneri & Habib Banks
45 Shaheen Travels:
   transport to Aliabad & Gojal
46 Transport to Sassi
48 Transport to Yasin & Darkot
49 PCO
51 British Cemetery
52 Transport to Nagyr
53 National Bank
54 District Hospital
55 Women's Hospital
56 Police Headquarters

Highway (KKH). Gilgit is completely enclosed by soaring rocks walls, with only the rivers providing a way in or out. Too hot in summer (often more than 40°C), it's a place to get supplies, organise transport and check email, rather than hang out. The airport is east of the bazaar and Jutial, primarily a military cantonment, is east of the airport. Another road leads into Gilgit from Dainyor along the KKH via bridges over the Gilgit and Hunza Rivers, creating a route 10km shorter to and from Nagyr and Hunza.

Gilgit's colourful, dusty bazaars are filled with myriad goods and memorable faces. The original bazaars were near the old Gilgit fort and original Gilgit River bridge. After independence, the Hindu Kashmiri cloth merchants of Kashmiri Bazaar were replaced by Pathans. Sabzi Bazaar, along the road to the bridge, specialises in food and vegetables and is run largely by Kashgaris. Khazana Bazaar is run by Nagyrkutz, and Jamat Khana Bazaar by Hunzakutz. Raja Bazaar is mostly Pathan traders, and Punial Rd Bazaar is traders from Ghizar District. After the opening of the KKH, Gilgit's bazaar grew (and is still growing) along Airport Rd, where traders of every ethnolinguistic group have shops selling almost

anything. Local people patronise shops run by those from their home valley or village.

Information Sources

The PTDC Information Centre (c/o Sargin Travel Service ☎ 0572-3939) is at 19 JSR Plaza, near the PIA office, and at the PTDC Chinar Inn.

Supplies & Equipment

The bazaar has enough food available to outfit a trek, although you may have to visit lots of shops to find what you're looking for. Ali Ahmed at Mountaineering Equipment (☎ 0572-3842), Airport Rd, sells used boots, ice axes, climbing hardware, ropes, sleeping bags and pads, jackets and occasionally EPI gas cylinders. Madina Adventure Supplies inside the Madina Hotel & Guest House sells sleeping bags, stoves (including MSR), crampons, some climbing gear and more. Gown House, Airport Rd, sells used boots, jackets, sleeping bags, ropes and climbing hardware. Hunza Handicrafts, next to the Park Hotel, has a similar assortment. The Camping World, in Super Market on Airport Rd, sells lightweight Pakistan-manufactured nylon tents (Rs 3000–3500).

Places to Stay & Eat

Camping For camping, *Mountain Refuge*, *Golden Peak Inn* and *Shah Tourist Camping Site* each charge Rs 50. See Hotels – Budget for contact details.

Hotels – Budget Numerous hotels cater to foreigners. *Madina Hotel & Guest House* (☎ 0572-2457, 3536, NLI Chowk) has a dorm that costs Rs 80, and singles/doubles for Rs 150/250. The staff is very helpful at this popular place, which serves Western food. Away from the bazaar, *Mountain Refuge (no phone, Chinar Garden Rd)*, at the end of Domyal Link Rd, is by far one of Gilgit's more peaceful corners. A Hunza man nicknamed 'German' and his friendly staff serve Western food. The dorm costs Rs 50. Singles cost Rs 100, and doubles cost Rs 150–200. *New Tourist Cottage (☎ 0572-4255, ✉ newtouristcottage@hotmail.com, Chinar Bagh Link Rd)* costs Rs 70 for the

Warning

Although most villages want tourism, persistent reports of robbery, harassment and even rape occur. Many incidents occur at gunpoint. Past incidents in Haramosh, Rupal Gah and Raikot Gah show that intolerance persists throughout this area. No one should trek alone, and female trekkers should always be accompanied by a responsible male whom they know. All trekkers should also travel with a trustworthy local guide. An armed escort may be prudent in some areas, so check the current situation before starting out.

The Northern Areas is one of the safer parts of Pakistan, but sectarian and political (factional) conflicts occasionally arise. Tense times are the holy days at the end of Ramazan, the Prophet's birthday, the month of Muharram, and during political elections.

dorm. Singles/doubles cost Rs 150/200. Run by a Japanese woman and a local man, it serves Japanese and Pakistani food. *Lost Horizon Guest House* (☎ 0572-55516, fax 2779, ⓔ *bari@glt.comsats.net.pk*), near Khomer Chowk, has rooms for Rs 100/150 with cold running water and Rs 150/200 with hot. The spacious compound is inviting and the kitchen serves Western and vegetarian food. Owner Abdul Bari Rana is helpful with trekking arrangements. *Hunza Inn* (☎ 0572-3814, Babar Rd), near Chinar Bagh, is an old favourite with a quiet, shady garden. Rooms cost Rs 100/200, deluxe cost Rs 400/500. Manager Abdullah Beg gives a discount to anyone with a Lonely Planet guidebook. *Golden Peak Inn* (☎ 0572-3890, Bank Rd), across from the British Cemetery in the old Gilgit fort, has a small garden and serves Western food. The dorm costs Rs 50. Rooms cost Rs 150/200. A double in the old fort costs Rs 250. *Shah Tourist Camping Site* (☎ 0572-55545, 55470, fax 55900, Shahrah-e-Quaid-e-Azam) is run by North Inn. The dorm costs Rs 80, and singles cost Rs 100. *Gilgit Tourist Guest House* (Shahrah-e-Quaid-e-Azam), has singles/doubles/triples with cold running water for Rs 50/100/150.

Many more hotels cater mostly to domestic tourists, and the occasional foreigner seeking local flavour. With the possible exception of the first two, none of these all-male establishments are appropriate for Western women. *Ibex Lodge* (☎ 0572-2334, 4212, NLI Rd), charges Rs 100/250/300 for clean singles/doubles/triples with a military atmosphere. Not as rough as the following hotels, it offers better value. *Garden Hotel* (☎ 0572-2444, 2898, Hospital Rd) has a small garden. The dorm costs Rs 50. Doubles with shared/attached bathroom cost Rs 100/150 and deluxe rooms with TV cost Rs 350. A newer concrete block structure in a central location, *Inam Guest House* (☎ 0572-3026, Cinema Bazaar), costs Rs 100/300. *City Guest House* (☎ 0572-3026, Cinema Bazaar) has comparable rooms with TV for Rs 150/350. *Hunza Hotel* (☎ 0572-2948, Airport Rd) has drab carpeted rooms for Rs 150/250. *JSR Hotel* (☎ 0572-2308, Cinema Bazaar) has grotty singles/doubles/triples

for Rs 100/200/250 without bathroom and Rs 150/250/300 with bathroom. *Skyways Hotel & Restaurant* (☎ 0572-3026, Cinema Bazaar) has comparable rooms with cold running water for Rs 150. *New Kashgar Inn* (☎ 0572-2648, Cinema Bazaar) costs Rs 100/150/200 for dismal rooms with cold running water. The restaurant serves Pakistani and Kashgari food. The *Indus Hotel* (☎ 0572-2632, Cinema Bazaar) costs Rs 60/80 for dismal, grotty rooms without bathroom. Its large restaurant serves Pakistani and Kashgari food.

Hotels – Mid-Range All mid-range hotels have attached bathrooms with hot running water. At *North Inn* (☎ 0572-55545, 55470, fax 55900, ⓔ *northinn@glt.comsats.net.pk*, Shahrah-e-Quaid-e-Azam), singles/doubles cost Rs 150/250; those on the small garden cost Rs 200/350. It's friendly and serves good Pakistani and Western food. *Hunza Tourist House* (☎ 0572-2338, Babar Rd), near the airport, costs Rs 660/880. It has an inviting garden, and serves Pakistani and Western food. The *Park Hotel* (☎ 0572-2379, 2479, 3379, fax 3796, Airport Rd) has singles/doubles/suites for Rs 275/450/750; deluxe versions cost Rs 425/650/950. All rooms have TV. This large, bustling hotel has a very popular restaurant serving Pakistani food. *Mir's Lodge* (☎ 0572-2875, Domyal Link Rd) costs Rs 500/650 for well-appointed rooms. Suites cost Rs 775/900. The restaurant serves good Pakistani food. *Gilgit Gateway Hotel* (☎ 0572-55014, 55467, 55813, Riaz Rd), at Khomer Chowk, has comfortable rooms with TV that cost Rs 400/600. The restaurant serves good Chinese, Pakistani and Western food. *Tourist Hamlet* (☎ 0572-55537/8), near Khomer Chowk, costs Rs 250/350. Larger rooms with TV cost Rs 350/550.

Hotels – Top End All hotels have in-room TV and serve a full range of food. *Gilgit Serena Hotel* (☎ 0572-55894, fax 55900, ⓔ *serena-sales@cyber.net.pk*), in Jutial, is Gilgit's best hotel. Rooms cost Rs 1700/2150. Its all-you-can-eat buffet meals are worthwhile. The *PTDC Chinar Inn* (☎ 0572-2562, 4262, *fax 2650, Babar Rd)*, near Chinar Bagh, has spacious rooms and the large garden is quiet and shady. Rooms cost Rs 950/1250; deluxe rooms cost Rs 1250/1500. *Hotel Riveria (☎ 0572-4184, fax 051-513129, River View Rd)* has a large pleasant garden and big rooms with double beds. Singles/doubles cost Rs 1200/1600. *Rupal Inn (☎ 0572-55161, 55846, 55471, ⓔ rupalinn@glt.coms ats.net.pk)*, near Khomer Chowk, has ostentatious decor. Rooms cost Rs 1410/1790; deluxe rooms cost Rs 2500/3000.

Getting There & Away

Air PIA schedules one to three Islamabad-Gilgit flights daily (Rs 2825) depending on the day of the week. The PIA office is on Airport Rd (☎ 0572-3389/90, airport traffic control ☎ 3947). Only the small Fokker F27 aircraft can land on Gilgit's short runway.

When flight delays happen, an alternative strategy for reaching Gilgit and avoiding the long journey up the KKH is to get a confirmed seat and fly to Skardu on a Boeing 737, which seats as many as 120 passengers. These flights have a higher ceiling and operate a greater percentage of the time. From Skardu, inexpensive public transport goes regularly to Gilgit.

Road Travel on the KKH is anything but predictable. Landslides, mudslides, rock fall and even avalanches can sever it for hours, days or weeks at a time. Vehicles travelling between Mansehra and Shatial after dark are commonly collected by police into escorted convoys to protect from nighttime robbery in Hazara and Indus Kohistan.

Rawalpindi The Gilgit-Rawalpindi trip can take as little as 12 hours, but buses often take up to 17 hours. Vans or Coasters cost Rs 400: Hameed Travels Service (☎ 0572-3181) departs from Gilgit's Skyways Hotel at 3pm; Sargin Travel Service (☎ 0572-2964, 2959) departs from Gilgit's JSR Plaza at 3 and 5pm; and K-2 Travel Services (☎ 0572-2370) departs Gilgit's NLI Chowk at 4pm. Mashabrum Tours (☎ 0572-2784, 3094) has regular buses (Rs 400) that depart from Gilgit's Cinema Bazaar near the Indus

Hotel at noon and 2, 6 and 9pm and an air-conditioned bus (Rs 450) that departs at 4.30pm. NATCO (☎ 0572-3381) has Coasters and deluxe buses (Rs 410) that depart from Gilgit's Cinema Bazaar at 9am, noon and 5 and 7pm, and air-conditioned buses (Rs 460) that depart at 3 and 9pm. Special hires cost Rs 6500–9000.

The Rawalpindi-Gilgit trip takes between 16 and 20 hours. Vans or Coasters cost Rs 400: Hameed Travels Service (☎ 051-5542970) departs from Mashriq Hotel on City-Saddar Rd, south of Fowara Chowk, at 3pm; Sargin Travel Service (☎ 051-5531776) departs from Modern Hotel opposite the Novelty Cinema in Kashmiri bazaar (southwest of Fowara Chowk) at 4 and 5pm; and K-2 Travel Services (☎ 051-4474112) departs from Anarkali Hotel in Pir Wadhai at 4pm. Mashabrum Tours (☎ 051-5477095) has regular buses (Rs 400) that depart from Pir Wadhai at noon and 2, 6 and 9pm and an air-conditioned bus (Rs 450) at 4.30pm; their 'office' (#7) is a person sitting in a chair at the yard's east end. NATCO (☎ 051-4445580) has Coasters and deluxe buses (Rs 410) that depart from Pir Wadhai at 9 and 11am and 1 and 5pm, and air-conditioned buses (Rs 460) at 3.30 and 8pm. You can buy tickets from the window at the bus stand. A 50% student discount is available on all but the deluxe service (with a maximum of four discount tickets per departure). NATCO and Mashabrum Tours buses normally cannot be booked in advance.

At the time of research, Rawalpindi was planning to establish a single new arrival/departure yard for vans and Coasters in order to minimise pollution and congestion. The transport companies' offices, however, will not move. Contact them for an update. All bus operations at Pir Wadhai will remain the same.

Afiyatabad (Sost) NATCO's deluxe bus (Rs 115, 6 hours) departs from Gilgit's Cinema Bazaar at 7am. Private transport companies operate vans and Gilgit-Afiyatabad wagons that make fewer stops and are quicker by about an hour. Shaheen Travels (☎ 0572-2330) departs Gilgit's Jamat Khana

Bazaar every two hours between 6.30am and 5pm for Rs 120. Tai's Transport Service (☎ 0572-55774) departs Gilgit's Airport Rd every two hours between 7am and 2pm for Rs 135.

From Afiyatabad, NATCO's deluxe bus departs along the roadside near NATCO's Afiyatabad office (in the customs building, the red one with a white stripe). Shaheen Travels and Tai's Transport Service vehicles depart irregularly and only when full of passengers. The first vehicles of the day depart Afiyatabad between 4.30 and 5am, and continue departing until 5 or 6pm.

Skardu The trip between Gilgit and Skardu takes six to seven hours. The Gilgit-Skardu road leaves the KKH at Alam Bridge over the Gilgit River north of its confluence with the Indus River, and follows the Indus River to Skardu.

Mashabrum Tours (☎ 0572-2784, 3095) departs Gilgit's Cinema Bazaar at 8, 10am and noon; buses cost Rs 120, and Coasters or wagons cost Rs 140. K-2 Travel Services (☎ 0572-2370) has wagons (Rs 140) that depart Gilgit's NLI Chowk at 9, 11am and 1pm. The NATCO bus (Rs 125) departs Gilgit's Cinema Bazaar at 6.30am.

The daily NATCO bus departs for Gilgit near Skardu's Chashma Bazaar at 5.30am. Mashabrum Tours has a bus that departs near Yadgar Chowk at 5am, a Coaster at 10am, and wagons at 8am and noon. K-2 Travel Services' wagons depart near the aqueduct at 9 and 11am and 1pm. Special hires Skardu-Gilgit cost Rs 3500.

Chitral No public transport exists between Chitral and Gilgit, but see Chitral (p123) for a discussion of the best strategies.

Getting Around
Suzukis to/from Airport Chowk, a few minutes' walk to the terminal, cost Rs 3. Special hires cost Rs 50 between the bazaar and airport.

Suzuki central is by the post office. Most Suzukis go through the bazaar to Jutial. Some turn at Chinar Bagh Link Rd and cross the Gilgit and Hunza rivers to Dainyor. Most

can be flagged down anywhere, although they don't run regularly after dark. Ask the driver if it's Jutial or Dainyor bound. Suzukis cost Rs 3 to the intersection of Chinar Bagh Link and Babar Roads. Anywhere beyond is Rs 7. Suzukis also run west from Punial Rd.

Travel Plus (☎ 0572-2613), A-1 Madina Super Market, offers 24-hour taxi service.

Bagrot

Most visitors only see the Bagrot Valley's broad alluvial fan across the Gilgit River, 15km downstream from Gilgit. Its narrow, lower reaches are desolate, but above Sinakkar it's a cultivated and settled valley where pre-Islamic traditions are still remembered. From Bagrot, the stunning south faces of Rakaposhi (7788m) and Diran (7257m) peaks, as well as the lovely twin summits of Bilchar Dobani (6134m) are visible. Phuparash (6785m), Malubiting (7458m), Laila (6986m) and Haramosh (7409m) peaks tower over the Haramosh Valley, which lies east of Bagrot and branches north from the Indus River. Treks in these valleys, seldom on trekkers' itineraries, are readily accessible by road with mostly easy trails and superb views.

Diran Base Camp

Duration	4 days
Distance	34km
Standard	moderate
Season	mid-June–September
Start/Finish	Chirah
Zone & Permit	open, no permit
Public Transport	yes

Summary A short and easily accessible trek goes to the seldom-seen incredible south wall of the Rakaposhi-Diran ridge and Diran Base Camp.

Rakaposhi and Diran, two towering Karakoram peaks, rise directly above Hinarche Harai, the local name for Diran Base Camp. A 16km-long ice ridge connects the peaks, and the Bagrot and Upper Hinarche glaciers roll down their flanks. The spectacular base camp is an easy two-day walk up the Hinarche Glacier from the head of the Bagrot Valley, just a short jeep ride from Gilgit.

Two routes lead to Hinarche Harai from the Bagrot Valley. The trail described here follows the Hinarche Glacier's east margin from Chirah and crosses the Upper Hinarche Glacier to base camp. The alternative route begins in Bulche, follows the Hinarche Glacier's west margin to Yurbun, a seasonal village in a grassy ablation valley, then crosses the Bagrot Glacier. Because this route is longer, more heavily crevassed and requires roping up, it's less frequently used. The six-hours to Yurbun, however, are pleasant walking through forest and cultivated areas.

PLANNING
Maps
The Swiss Foundation for Alpine Research 1:250,000 orographical map *Karakoram (Sheet 1)* covers the trek, but omits place names along the Hinarche Glacier. Hinarche Harai is mistakenly shown as being in the middle of the Upper Hinarche Glacier.

Guides & Porters
Porters ask for Rs 160 per stage plus payment for food rations. Porters don't ask for the clothing and equipment allowance. Hire someone to show the way safely across the glacier. Men in Datuchi and Chirah have worked as scholars' assistants and happily share their knowledge of local lore.

GETTING TO/FROM THE TREK
Gilgit-Chirah jeeps (Rs 30) depart from Gilgit's Garhi Bagh (between NLI Chowk and the GPO) around midday, returning early the next morning. Special hires cost Rs 600/900 one way/round trip. Don't take the bus to Jalalabad, which has no connections to Bagrot. It takes 1¼ hours to Sinakkar, 1½ hours to Datuchi and two hours to Chirah.

THE TREK (see map p204)
Day 1: Chirah to Biyabari
2 hours, 7km, 200m ascent
Chirah's welcoming *Bagrote Sarai* (☎ 37 Oshikandas), which has grassy camp sites

and prepares food, is the staging place. From Chirah (2700m), follow the trail along the Bagrot River's true left bank, past the confluence with the Hinarche Glacier's outwash stream. Cross a footbridge to the true right (north) bank of the Burche Glacier's outwash stream. Follow the Hinarche Glacier's east margin to *Biyabari* (2900m), a grassy area with chir pine trees just below Diran village.

Day 2: Biyabari to Hinarche Harai
10–12 hours, 10km, 1100m ascent
Several significant slides along the Hinarche Glacier's east margin make this a long day. At the end of the long ablation valley, cross the Upper Hinarche Glacier in one to two hours to *Hinarche Harai* (Diran Base Camp, 4000m), which is a summer herders' settlement.

Days 3–4: Hinarche Harai to Chirah
2 days, 17km, 1300m descent
Retrace your steps to Chirah, camping at Biyabari on Day 3.

Rakhan Gali

Duration	4 days
Distance	46km
Standard	demanding
Season	mid-June–September
Start	Chirah
Finish	Hanuchal
Zone & Permit	open, no permit
Public Transport	yes

Summary This dramatic close-up traverse along the south flanks of Diran and Phuparash crosses a rugged pass.

Rakhan Gali (4548m) is a pass connecting the Bagrot and Haramosh valleys that skirts the southern ramparts of the Rakaposhi-Haramosh Range. The remarkably scenic route is seldom used because people prefer to travel by vehicle along the roads between villages in these valleys.

PLANNING
Maps
The Swiss Foundation for Alpine Research 1:250,000 orographical map *Karakoram (Sheet 1)* covers the trek.

Guides & Porters
Porters ask for Rs 160 per stage, plus the payment for food rations. Porters do not ask for the clothing and equipment allowance. Porters from Bagrot only carry loads between Chirah and Rakhan Gali, which is the boundary of Bagrot's territory, and Haramosh porters carry between Rakhan Gali and the Gilgit-Skardu road. Large parties need to change porters, which can be prearranged by sending a message to Khaltaro, but smaller parties may be able to avoid it.

GETTING TO/FROM THE TREK
To the Start
See the Diran Base Camp trek (p203).

From the Finish
Sassi-Gilgit wagons cost Rs 40; vehicles travelling along the Gilgit-Skardu road are fairly frequent.

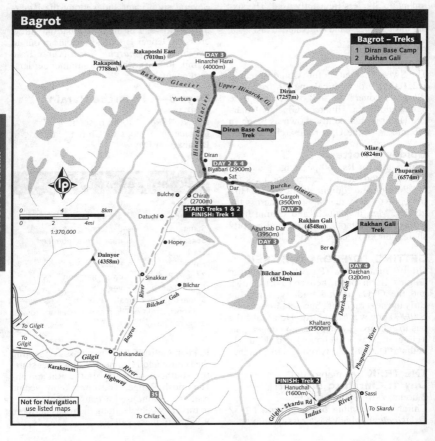

THE TREK (see map opposite)
Day 1: Chirah to Gargoh
4–5 hours, 12km, 800m ascent

From Chirah (2700m), a trail climbs the east side of the valley above the Hinarche Glacier, then drops to the Burche Glacier's silty outwash stream. Cross the footbridge and ascend through Sat village, whose fields and forests hug the Burche Valley's north side. Continue to Dar, a summer settlement two to three hours from Chirah, and descend to the glacier. The trail moves onto the glacier and in 1.5km it divides. One branch heads east to Rakhan Gali and the other heads north off the glacier. The north branch follows a clear stream through a pretty valley busy with logging activity. Beyond this valley are pastures and glaciers at the base of Miar peaks (6824m). From these pastures, it's also possible to day hike or camp on the ridge rising to the north. Continue south along the east branch of the trail two hours over moraine to *Gargoh* (3500m). These herders' huts are along the Burche Glacier's south margin, in a level area with trees and plentiful water.

Day 2: Gargoh to Agurtsab Dar
2–3 hours, 5km, 450m ascent

Continue south and east up the Gargoh Valley two to three hours to *Agurtsab Dar* (3950m), a good high camp with a clear stream. This pasture has no herders' huts.

Day 3: Agurtsab Dar to Darchan
5–6 hours, 14km, 598m ascent, 1348m descent

Agurtsab Dar to the top of Rakhan Gali takes three hours, following the stream to the pass. The grass ends 1½ hours above Agurtsab Dar after which the route ascends over tedious scree and rock. Expect to find snow in the saddle. From **Rakhan Gali** (4548m), descend very steeply two to three hours through the pastures of *Ber* (3400m) and one to 1½ hours farther down this sylvan valley to the summer settlement of *Darchan* (3200m).

Day 4: Darchan to Hanuchal
6–7 hours, 15km, 1600m descent

Continue down the Darchan Gah on a trail to Khaltaro (2500m), the main village, three hours from Ber. The main trail continues three to four hours to *Hanuchal* (1600m) on the Gilgit-Skardu road, just west of Sassi.

Diamir

Nanga Parbat (8125m), the world's ninth-highest peak and the second-highest of Pakistan's five 8000m peaks, is the westernmost peak of the Great Himalayan range. Actually a 20km-long series of peaks and ridges, Nanga Parbat forms a huge massif. Its solitary white appearance, visible from the south for at least 100km, prompted its name, which means 'naked mountain' in Urdu. It's also known as the 'Killer Mountain' because of the difficulties mountaineers have in reaching its summit.

The valleys of Raikot, Astor, Rupal and Diamir provide access to Nanga Parbat's north, east, south and west faces respectively. The peak's base camps are Raikot, Rupal and Diamir: access to Rupal is via the Astor Valley, and access to Raikot and Diamir (via Bunar Gah) are from the KKH along the Indus River. These Himalayan valleys receive more rainfall and have more forests than their Karakoram neighbours.

Most people living around Nanga Parbat are Sunni Muslims, with some Shi'a Muslims living along the Astor Valley's upper tributaries. Shina is the main language spoken.

Diamir

Nanga Parbat is known as Diamir in Shina, an archaic Indic language. The name derives from an ancient Indic word *devameru*, which means the 'sacred mountain of the gods'. In Indian cosmology, Devameru, or Mt Meru, is the mythical mountain at the centre of the world; the axis of the cosmos and the home of the gods. A journey to this mountain is a journey to the centre of the universe. Ancient Sanskrit texts describe it as a gleaming mountain, soaring to unimaginable heights, and place it north of India, near Central Asia. Perhaps there is some reality to this myth, after all.

Fairy Meadow

Duration	3 days
Distance	21km
Standard	easy
Season	May–mid-October
Start/Finish	Jhel
Nearest Facilities	Fairy Meadow
Zone & Permit	open, no permit
Public Transport	no

Summary Fairy Meadow offers easy access to an 8000m peak base camp and one of the world's finest mountain panoramas with several excellent short side trips and climbs.

The lofty summits of the Nanga Parbat massif form a glacial amphitheatre at the head of Raikot Gah. Four major icefalls converge to form the 13km-long S-shaped Raikot Glacier, beneath Nanga Parbat's north (Raikot) face. Beside the glacier are pine and fir forests, sparkling streams and open grasslands that have enchanted visitors and prompted the name Fairy Meadow. The glacier's outwash stream carves a dramatic gorge that drops 2000m to the Indus River. The 7000m descent from the summit to the Indus forms one of the world's deepest gorges. A trip to Fairy Meadow, with day hikes or side trips, has a bit of everything Himalayan trekking can offer – a hair-raising jeep ride to get there, hot and dusty trails, lush meadows, amazing glaciers and an 8000m summit. It's the area's best short trek.

PLANNING
Maps
The Deutscher Alpenverein (DAV) 1:50,000 topographic map *Nanga Parbat Gruppe* covers the trek. Fairy Meadow is labelled Märchen Wiese, Beyal (which is just north of the 3710m point) is not labelled, Nanga Parbat Base Camp is labelled Hauptlager (high camp), and Camp 1 is labelled Lager 1. It labels the peak and glacier Rakhiot, which local people call Raikot.

Guides & Porters
Porters, who transport loads on donkeys, ask for a flat rate of Rs 200 per stage including payment for food rations. Regardless of whether porters walk or ride in a jeep between Raikot Bridge and Jhel or you hire porters at the road's end in Jhel, pay all porters for one stage between Raikot Bridge and Jhel in both directions in addition to all other stages you walk. This hardly seems fair, but it's the fixed position of the

Peak Possibilities

Buldar Peak
Accessible from Nanga Parbat Base Camp (Side Trip) The snowy dome of Buldar Peak (5602m), which has a large bergschrund on its west face, lies directly east of the Raikot Glacier. The three-day climb involves 1635m ascent and 1635m descent. The first day cross the Raikot Glacier from Nanga Parbat Base Camp and ascend through forest to set a high camp (4500m). The second day, the rocky ascent continues north-east to Buldar Cleft (5150m), marked Buldar Scharte on the DAV map. The technical route continues north following the snow-covered ridge to Buldar's summit. Return to high camp, and the next day to base camp. Buldar Peak is infrequently climbed, but is certainly doable by any fit person with basic mountaineering skills, and in the company of a local person who knows the route.

South Jalipur Peak
Accessible from Beyal (Day 2) South Jalipur Peak (5206m), which is west of the Raikot Glacier and south of the Khusto (Jalipur) Pass (4837m), is the peak most frequently attempted by trekkers visiting Raikot Gah. The nontechnical ascent begins from Beyal and takes two days, with 1706m ascent and 1706m descent. The first day, follow the Jalipur stream west up the rocky side valley that leads to Khusto Pass and place a high camp west of (below) the pass, three hours from Beyal. From the high camp, it takes three to four hours to reach the summit the next day, following a ridge route that crosses some glacier. Return to high camp and descend to Beyal the same day.

porters' union who view it as compensation for road maintenance.

Stages

It's six stages total round trip from Raikot Bridge: (1) Jhel; (2) Fairy Meadow; (3) Beyal; and (4–6) three stages to return via the same route.

GETTING TO/FROM THE TREK

Raikot Bridge, which spans the Indus River along the KKH 78km, or 1½ hours, south of Gilgit and 55km, or one hour, east of Chilas, Diamir's administrative centre, is the jumping off point. To reach Raikot Bridge, take a Gilgit-Chilas van (Rs 80) that departs from the Jaglot bus stand on Domyal Link Rd every few hours. Gilgit–Raikot Bridge special hires cost Rs 1200/2000 one way/round trip. Vans or buses to Rawalpindi drop passengers at Raikot Bridge for Rs 60.

From Raikot Bridge, walk or organise a special hire to Jhel (Rs 1000/1600 one way/round trip, 1½ hours, 15km) where the road ended as of 2001. Rates are fixed and non-negotiable. A local jeep drivers' union assigns drivers based on a rotational system, so everyone gets a turn. Some people choose to walk rather than make the heart-stopping jeep ride along a dramatic cliff with awesome drop offs. The tiresome 1320m climb from Raikot Bridge (1280m) to Jhel (2600m) takes four hours. It's usually extremely hot and dry, so start before dawn when possible.

Don't organise Gilgit-Jhel special hires, which costs Rs 2400 one way, unless the driver is from Raikot. 'Outside' jeeps aren't allowed on the road between Raikot Bridge and Jhel unless you pay an additional Rs 1000 to the union. The reason for this is the road is privately owned and maintained by Chilasis, and it's also safer to have an experienced Raikot driver.

THE TREK
Day 1: Jhel to Fairy Meadow
2–2½ hours, 5.5km, 640m ascent

At Jhel (2666m) just above Tato village, a few wooden huts sell cold drinks and snacks. Rose shrubs, chilghozas, chir pines and junipers flourish in the narrow valley.

The well-established trail rises steadily along what is the future road to Fairy Meadow. Halfway, a stream meanders through pleasant forest, offering welcome shade, and the trail becomes more level. The gentle walk continues up the Raikot Gah to **Fairy Meadow** (3306m), which overlooks the Raikot Glacier to the south-east. Herders' settlements around Fairy Meadow are worth wandering through for a glimpse of village life. In May and June, they harvest the morel mushrooms *(kuchuli)* that grow here and sell for as much as Rs 15,000 per kilogram. The herders keep dogs, so exercise caution in their territory.

Camp at either of two designated grassy camping grounds, each fenced to keep livestock out. ***Raikot Sarai*** is in a picturesque setting overlooking the glacier. Tent rentals cost Rs 350 for one person and Rs 400 for two, and small huts cost Rs 1200. The camping fee is Rs 80. The compound has toilet facilities, a kitchen and dining hall. Breakfast

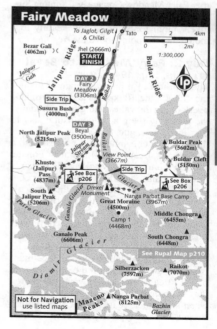

Fairy Meadow

GILGIT & DIAMIR

is Rs 160, lunch Rs 235 and dinner Rs 255. They also organise treks beyond Fairy Meadow; contact Rehmat Nabi at Fairy Meadows Tours (☎ 0572-4126, ⓔ fmtours@ glt.comsats.net.pk) on Gilgit's Chinar Bagh Link Rd. For reservations, contact the office (☎ 051-276113, fax 824484, ⓔ raikots arai@yahoo.co.uk), F-7/2, Street 15, Centre-One, Islamabad, visit Fairy Meadows Tours in Gilgit, or write to Raikot Sarai, PO Gonar Farm, Raikot Valley, District Diamir, Northern Areas.

Green Land Camping Side, adjacent to Raikot Sarai, offers welcome shade, but without glacier views. The camping fee is Rs 80 and the hut costs Rs 400.

Side Trip: Susuru Bush
3–4 hours, 4km, 694m ascent, 694m descent
Susuru Bush (4000m), which is named for the flowers *(susur)* that grow here, is the rocky ridge *(bush)* to the west. From the former Fairy Meadow Cottage & Camping Site, a trail leads through a marshy meadow and lovely birch forest. It climbs steadily to a mountain viewpoint above the tree line.

Day 2: Fairy Meadow to Beyal
1½ hours, 5km, 194m ascent
The trail to Beyal hugs the edge of the terrace above the Raikot Glacier's terminus, overlooking the valley and glacier. Initially, the trail may seem a bit confusing; stay to the left at a vague fork. The trail passes through lush chir pine and fir forest with a birch-lined stream for 30 minutes. For the next 30 minutes, it stays along the stream's true left bank, parallel to the glacier, but gradually moves away from the terrace's edge. Cross to the stream's true right bank, now lined by juniper and a few chir. The valley opens up as you reach the wildflower-filled meadows of **Beyal** (3500m) with great views downvalley of the Indus Valley and Rakaposhi. Beyal, which means 'cave-like', is named for the rocks on the opposite side of the stream. Herders stay in sod-roofed huts. Late in the season, Beyal becomes dry when snow melt ceases to feed the Jalipur stream. Beyal is typically less crowded than

Fairy Meadow, so it's worth moving your camp to this welcoming spot.

Camping is available at two fenced camping grounds, *Jalipur Inn*, with its year-round spring nearby, and *Parbat Camp* higher upvalley. The rates are the same at both places. The camping fee is Rs 70, or it costs Rs 400 to rent one of their tents. The huts cost Rs 600. Breakfast costs Rs 130, lunch Rs 220 and dinner Rs 230.

It is possible to climb South Jalipur Peak from Beyal (see the boxed text Peak Possibilities, p206).

Side Trip: Nanga Parbat Base Camp
6–7 hours, 8km, 467m ascent, 467m descent
Nanga Parbat Base Camp is between the Ganalo and Raikot glaciers, just south of their confluence. Fit hikers can visit the base camp on a day hike, but those wanting to savour its beauty or planning to go farther need at least two days.

From Beyal, an easy trail continues south 30 minutes through scattered junipers and birches to an obvious huge boulder, topped by a cow's skull balancing on a pole, at the lateral moraine's edge. People aptly call this place **View Point** (3667m). The breathtaking close-up views to the south-east include the four major icefalls coming from the Chongra peaks (ranging from 6448m to 6830m), Raikot (7070m) and Nanga Parbat's north face that converge to form the incredibly serac-covered Raikot Glacier. To the north are impressive views over the Indus Valley, and far to the north-east is the 7000m Rakaposhi-Haramosh Range.

From the boulder, the trail stays to the right. Don't take the lower still visible to its left, which has been abandoned because of surges by the Ganalo Glacier. Passing through stands of birch and pockets of the fragrant *sojo punar*, a primrose revered by local people, the trail climbs 125m in 45 minutes to the top of a moraine. The whole massif forms a sweeping glacial amphitheatre. If you only go this far, you won't be disappointed.

The trail continues 30 minutes through rolling upland to a cairn at the moraine's edge, descends to cross an outwash stream, and reaches the Ganalo Glacier. A cairn-marked route across the rubble-covered Ganalo Glacier leads from here in one hour to *Nanga Parbat Base Camp* (3967m), three to four hours from Beyal. A large spring flows from under a boulder here. Nearby is the **Drexel Monument** to German climbers killed on Nanga Parbat.

From base camp, more adventurous trekkers can continue two hours to *Camp 1* (4468m) for more big vistas, ascending steeply 500m over the **Great Moraine** (4500m), which is usually snow-free in July and August. At Camp 1 you're right under Silberzacken (7597m), Raikot and the Chongra peaks. It is also possible to ascend Buldar Peak from Base Camp (see the boxed text Peak Possibilities, p206).

The stages are: Beyal to Nanga Parbat Base Camp; Nanga Parbat Base Camp to Camp 1; and two stages to return via same route. When porters go above base camp, they carry only 15kg and get a wage increase to Rs 250 per stage.

Day 3: Beyal to Jhel
2–2½ hours, 10.5km, 834m descent
Retrace steps to Fairy Meadow in one hour, and Jhel in another one to 1½ hours.

Rupal

Duration	5 days
Distance	37km
Standard	easy
Season	June–October
Start/Finish	Tarashing
Zone & Permit	open, no permit
Public Transport	yes

Summary A quick, easy approach through lovely meadows leads to the base camp of Nanga Parbat's enormous Rupal Face.

Nanga Parbat's awesome south, or Rupal, face rises 4572m from the floor of the Rupal Gah, creating the greatest vertical rise from base camp to summit of any peak. The easy trails and two short nontechnical glacier crossings bring you directly beneath it for breathtaking close-up views. The Rupal Gah, although popular, is less frequently visited than Fairy Meadow.

PLANNING
Maps
The Deutscher Alpenverein (DAV) 1:50,000 topographic map *Nanga Parbat Gruppe* covers the trek.

Guides & Porters
It's prudent to hire a reputable, licensed guide who is accustomed to dealing with Rupal porters and villagers. Porters come from Tarashing and Chorit, which have decided that an equal number of porters for any party are to be from each village. This holds true even if you have just two porters, and also applies when releasing any porters. Porters, who transport loads on donkeys, ask for a flat rate of Rs 200 per stage, including payment for food rations, and expect large parties to buy a goat at Shaigiri.

Stages
It's six stages total round trip from Tarashing: (1) Herrligkoffer Base Camp; (2) Latobah; (3) Shaigiri; and (4–6) three stages to return via the same route.

NEAREST VILLAGE
Tarashing
Nanga Parbat Tourist Cottage, owned by Mohammad Ashraf, has a large garden. The camping fee is Rs 70, and rooms cost Rs 250/400. *Hotel Nanga Parbat* has a Rs 50 camping fee and rooms cost Rs 100/200.

Unless you organise a Gilgit-Tarashing special hire (Rs 2500/4000 one way/return), it's necessary to change transport in Astor, or walk from Astor. The narrow jeep road to Astor leaves the KKH at Jaglot, 60km south of Gilgit and 30km north of Raikot Bridge, crossing a bridge over the Indus River and heading 40km south-east up the Astor Valley skirting Nanga Parbat's northeast flank. Gilgit-Astor jeeps (Rs 100, three to four hours) go all day from Gilgit's Jaglot bus stand on Domyal Link Rd. Gilgit-Astor special hires cost Rs 1200–1500 one way. Astor-Tarashing jeeps cost Rs 50 (two hours) and special hires cost Rs 1000.

GETTING TO/FROM THE TREK
For information on transport to/from the trailhead, see Tarashing (p209).

THE TREK
Day 1: Tarashing to Herrligkoffer Base Camp
5 hours, 10km, 639m ascent

From Tarashing (2911m), climb the Tarashing (Chhungphar on some maps) Glacier's lateral moraine, near the village's north edge, and cross the glacier on a trail. Continue up the gentle valley through Rupal village.

Rising gradually through Rupal's lush fields, the trail follows the valley's north side to **Herrligkoffer Base Camp** (3550m), a beautiful, although much-used, meadow along the Bazhin Glacier's east margin. A large spring bubbles up here and a huge boulder marks the kitchen site. The camp site is named after Dr Karl M Herrligkoffer, the leader of eight German expeditions to Nanga Parbat, including the first successful expedition in 1953.

A side trip of several hours up this ablation valley leads to a point on the moraine directly above the Bazhin Glacier and across from the icefall coming from the summit.

Day 2: Herrligkoffer Base Camp to Latobah
2 hours, 3km, 20m descent

Cross the Bazhin Glacier over a trail in 1½ hours to reach **Latobah** (3530m), the broad, level meadows frequented by Rupal herders. Latobah is also known as Tupp Meadows.

Day 3: Latobah to Shaigiri
4 hours, 5.5km, 125m ascent

The trail stays to the north of the Rupal Gah, skirting the terminal moraine and a silty moraine lake. Continue through a series of alluvial fans and skirt the Shaigiri Glacier's terminal moraine. Just beyond is **Shaigiri** (3655m), a summer settlement marked by an erratic, a white boulder (*shaigiri* in Shina) and more awesome views of the south face.

Days 4–5: Shaigiri to Tarashing
2 days, 18.5km, 744m descent

Retrace steps to Tarashing, camping at base camp on Day 4.

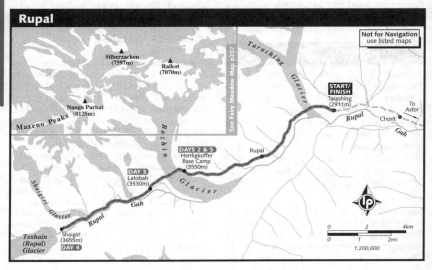

Mazeno La

Duration	8 days
Distance	74.5km
Standard	extreme, technical
Season	mid-June–mid-September
Start	Tarashing
Finish	Bunar
Zone & Permit	open, no permit
Public Transport	yes

Summary This glaciated pass brings trekkers close to the Mazeno Peaks in a traverse of the southern flanks of the Nanga Parbat massif.

Mazeno La (5399m) is a technical glaciated pass over Nanga Parbat's Mazeno ridge, with its challenging unclimbed summits of Mazeno Peak (7100m) and four subsidiary 7000m peaks. The trek skirts the southern half of the Nanga Parbat massif from the Rupal Gah to Diamir Gah. From Zangot in Diamir Gah, the standard route descends the Bunar Valleys to the KKH. An alternative, more strenuous, six-day route continues north-east from Zangot, crossing two more passes en route to Fairy Meadow. Experienced guides say most trekkers don't succeed in crossing the pass. Only fit and experienced trekkers with basic mountaineering skills should attempt this route.

PLANNING
What to Bring
Mountaineering equipment necessary to travel in roped teams and fix rope is required, depending on snow conditions (see Mountaineering Equipment, p61); wearing a climbing helmet is prudent. Heavy early-season snow pack favours the time between early August and the third week of September when less snow is present and more rock is exposed. The descent from the pass can be tricky at this time, though may require as little as 10m fixed rope. Descent is easier earlier in the season when more snow is present, but requires as much as 300m fixed rope.

Maps
The US AMS 1:250,000 topographic map *Gilgit (NI 43-2)* covers the entire trek,

whereas the Deutscher Alpenverein (DAV) 1:50,000 topographic map *Nanga Parbat Gruppe* covers the route except Diamir and Bunar. The U502 map labels Karu Sagar as Kachal Gali and Kutagali as Kachal. Khusto Pass between North Jalipur and South Jalipur Peaks isn't named on maps, but the DAV map marks it as 4837m.

Guides & Porters
Hiring an experienced Shina-speaking guide from Chilas who knows the route and can manage the complex porter logistics is strongly recommended. It's necessary to change porters as you pass through different valleys. The first group of porters, usually hired in Tarashing, go only to the top of the Mazeno La literally. Here these porters are replaced by ones from Bunar. To coordinate this change of porters, make arrangements with the shopkeeper in Bunar before your trek, telling him how many porters you need on what date. He then organises porters to meet you either on top of the Mazeno La or the Bunar porters may walk without loads up the Rupal Gah. Bunar porters then either take you to the KKH or to Shaichī depending upon your route. Bunar porters may extort camping fees in Diamir Gah. When continuing to Shaichī, Gunar porters replace the Bunar porters. Small parties, however, can usually get by without changing porters. Regardless, be prepared to change porters and be prepared for the financial consequences. Each group of porters gets wāpasi, making this an expensive route! Porters ask for a flat rate of Rs 200 per stage, including payment for food rations.

Stages
It's 11 stages total from Tarashing: (1) Herrligkoffer Base Camp; (2) Latobah; (3) Shaigiri; (4) Mazeno Base Camp; (5) Mazeno High Camp; (6) Mazeno La; (7) Upper Loibah Meadow; (8) Loibah Meadow; (9) Zangot; (10) Halalay Bridge; and (11) Bunar.

The alternative route to Fairy Meadow from Tarashing totals 18 stages: (1–9) nine stages between Tarashing and Zangot; (10) Kutagali; (11) Karu Sagar Pass; (12) Shaichī;

(13) Gutum Sagar; (14) Jalipur High Camp;
(15) Beyal; (16) Fairy Meadow; (17) Jhel;
and (18) Raikot Bridge.

GETTING TO/FROM THE TREK
To the Start
For information on transport to the trailhead, see the Rupal trek (p209).

From the Finish
From Bunar, transport is readily available
east to Chilas or up the KKH to Gilgit. Pre-
arranging Halaley-Bunar special hires,
which cost Rs 1600, shortens the trek by
one day.

THE TREK
Days 1–2: Tarashing to Shaigiri
2 days, 18.5km, 744m ascent
From Tarashing (2911m), camp at either
Herrligkoffer Base Camp or Latobah en
route to Shaigiri (3655m). (See Days 1–2 of
the Rupal trek, p210).

Day 3: Shaigiri to Mazeno Base Camp
3–5 hours, 6.5km, 395m ascent
The trail follows the Toshain (Rupal) Glacier's north margin and crosses several
streams before it reaches *Mazeno Base
Camp* (4050m), which is below the Mazeno
Glacier's terminus.

Day 4: Mazeno Base Camp to Mazeno High Camp
4–6 hours, 5.5km, 650m ascent
The route turns sharply north and then climbs
steeply to *Mazeno High Camp* (4700m),
which lies along the glacier's east margin.

Day 5: Mazeno High Camp to Upper Loibah Meadow
6–8 hours, 12km, 699m ascent, 1199m
descent
Ascend along the glacier's north-east margin, crossing it higher up, and reach
Mazeno La (5399m) in three hours. The

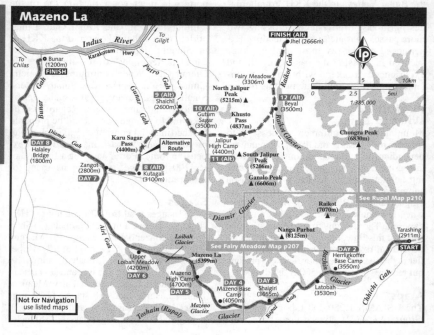

descent on the north side of the pass is very steep, has rock-fall danger, and is technical for 300m to the upper Loibah Glacier. Continue down the glacier to *Upper Loibah Meadow* (4200m).

Day 6: Upper Loibah Meadow to Zangot

5–6 hours, 10km, 1400m descent
Descend the valley passing through Loibah Meadow to *Zangot* (2800m).

Day 7: Zangot to Halaley Bridge

3–4 hours, 10km, 1000m descent
Descend north-west down the Diamir Gah to its confluence with the Bunar Gah and camp near *Halaley Bridge* (1800m). This area was first explored by British climbers AF Mummery, G Hastings and J Norman Collie, in 1895.

Day 8: Halaley Bridge to Bunar

3–4 hours, 12km, 600m descent
Descend the Bunar Gah to **Bunar** (1200m) on the KKH.

Alternative Finish: Zangot to Jhel

You can continue via two passes to Fairy Meadow in six additional days. Those interested in a complete circumambulation of Nanga Parbat can then continue from Fairy Meadow to Astor via the Muthat Pass (see Other Treks, p214, for details of this route).

Alternative Day 7: Zangot to Kutagali

3–4 hours, 4km, 300m ascent
Climb along the stream to the summer settlement at *Kutagali* (3100m). From Kutagali, a side trip several hours upvalley to the Diamir Glacier offers closer views of Nanga Parbat's west face.

Alternative Day 8: Kutagali to Shaichi

5–6 hours, 10km, 1300m ascent, 1800m descent
Climb steadily to the **Karu Sagar Pass** (4400m) and descend just as steeply to *Shaichi* (*shaich* means 'field' in Shina) in Patro Gah (2600m).

Alternative Day 9: Shaichi to Gutum Sagar

5–6 hours, 5km, 900m ascent
Head up Patro Gah through forest, crossing side streams for a few hours to the Gunar villagers' pastures. Ganalo (6606m) dominates the view. Continue upvalley to *Gutum Sagar* (3500m).

Alternative Day 10: Gutum Sagar to Jalipur High Camp

4–6 hours, 5.5km, 900m ascent
Ascend along a stream through the meadows of the bowl below the Jalipur peaks to *Jalipur High Camp* (4400m). It's possible to climb the nontechnical South Jalipur Peak (5206m) in one day from this high camp (see the climb's description in the Fairy Meadow trek, p206).

Alternative Day 11: Jalipur High Camp to Beyal

4–5 hours, 6km, 437m ascent, 1237m descent
Climb steeply east towards the east-west **Khusto Pass** (4837m), between North Jalipur Peak (5215m) and South Jalipur Peak. Ascend on a steep talus slope one to two hours and emerge near a snowfield. The descent from the pass is also steep and on loose talus one hour. Continue to meadows leading past willows and forest into Raikot Gah and *Beyal* (3500m), reaching Beyal two hours from the pass.

Alternative Day 12: Beyal to Jhel

2–2½ hours, 10.5km, 834m descent
On the final day, enjoy the easy walk down to Fairy Meadow and on to Jhel (see the Fairy Meadow trek, p206).

Other Treks

The following treks are all in an open zone.

BAGROT
Sinakkar to Dainyor

An easy three-day trek links Sinakkar village in the Bagrot Valley with Dainyor on the KKH east of Gilgit. The route is usually snow-free mid-June to mid-September, though it's best to go when herders are in the pastures late June to late August. Hire Sinakkar villagers who work as local guides/porters since the route isn't shown on maps. On Day 1, go from Sinakkar to Walo, the pasture for Sinakkar herders, in four to five hours. On Day 2 cross the 4000m ridge with views of Nanga Parbat and descend to Munugah, the pasture for Dainyor villagers, in five or six hours. On Day 3, descend to Dainyor in four or five hours. Suzukis (Rs 10) go regularly from Dainyor to Gilgit.

Hopey to Bilchar

An easy day trek begins in Bagrot Valley's Hopey village and heads south-east over a 3100m ridge to Bilchar village (2300m) in Bilchar Gah. Trekkers meet herders and have fine views of Bilchar Dobani (6134m). It takes three to four hours to reach Taisot and another hour to descend to Bilchar.

HARAMOSH
Kutwal Lake

Kutwal Lake (3260m), at the head of Haramosh Valley, nestles along the Mani Glacier's north margin, surrounded by meadows and pine and birch forest, with views of Mani (6685m), Haramosh, and Malubiting's south face. The easy six-day trek to Kutwal Lake is best done between mid-June and September. It's often done after crossing Rakhan Gali (see the Rakhan Gali trek, p203).

On Day 1, follow the jeep road, which turns north off the Gilgit-Skardu road by the bridge over the Phuparash River, north from Sassi 2km along the Phuparash River, to **Dassu** (marked as Dache on maps) on the bluffs above the river's east side. On Day 2, the trail stays along the true left bank, first climbing steeply and then continuing to Iskere (2500m). Dassu villagers graze livestock and cut timber here May to December. One kilometre above **Iskere** is a good camp site near the Mani Glacier's snout with views up the Baska Glacier of Malubiting and Laila. On Day 3, cross the river on a footbridge to Gure, a south-facing pasture, and continue east crossing the Baska Glacier's outwash stream to the summer village at **Kutwal**. Day 4 takes you along the Mani Glacier's north margin to **Kutwal Lake**. Beyond Kutwal Lake, a route continues to Haramosh La (see p346). Retrace your steps, reaching Sassi on Day 6.

Sassi is on the Gilgit-Skardu road 1½ hours from Gilgit. Daily Gilgit-Skardu NATCO and Masha-brum Tours buses pass through. Most vehicles get fuel at Sassi's petrol pump. A restaurant is nearby. A daily wagon (Rs 40) goes to Sassi in mid-afternoon from Shaheed-e-Millat Rd near Gilgit's Jamat Khana Bazaar, and returns from Sassi around 7am the next day.

It's eight stages total round trip from Sassi: (1) Dassu; (2) Iskere; (3) Kutwal; (4) Kutwal Lake; and (5–8) four stages to return via the same route.

Haramosh Base Camp

The easy approach to Haramosh Base Camp starts from Sassi village, crosses the Chonga ridge (3300m), then descends to Ishkapal village (2740m). From Ishkapal, it's a short walk up the Ishkapal Glacier's south margin to Bariyabu (3600m), beneath Haramosh's south-west face.

Phuparash Glacier

Attractive Phuparash (6574m) is visible from this trek's start. From Sassi, head upvalley to Dassu. Beyond Dassu cross the river and follow the Phu-parash River's true left (east) bank to Phuparash pastures. The easy trek is usually done in two days. Miar, the Phuparash peaks, and Malubiting (7458m) form a very imposing, steep corniced wall above the glacier.

DIAMIR
Rama Lake

Rama Lake (3482m) lies along the Sachen Glacier's south margin above Rama 6km west of Astor village (2345m) in Astor Valley. An easy two- or three-day visit to the lake (Sango Sar See on the DAV map) and the surrounding area takes you through flower-filled meadows and pine, fir, cedar and juniper forests with views of the Chongra peaks.

Gilgit-Astor jeeps (Rs 100) go all day from Gilgit's Domyal Link Rd. Gilgit-Astor special hires cost Rs 1200–1500. A jeep road goes from Astor to Rama, 1200m above Astor, so unless you want to walk, organise a special hire (Rs 600).

Muthat Pass

After successfully crossing the Mazeno La from the Rupal Gah and continuing to Fairy Meadow in Raikot Gah (see the Mazeno La trek, p211), a cir-cumambulation of Nanga Parbat is possible by continuing clockwise from Fairy Meadow over the Astor Valley over the Muthat Pass. Meat contractors supplying goats to the army reportedly use this very demanding route.

From Fairy Meadow, descend towards Tato (2475m) to cross the footbridge over Raikot Gah. Ascend north-east over a ridge (3362m) and descend to a stream, then cross the Buldar River to reach Muthat village (3000m). Follow the Buldar Glacier's south-east margin to 4000m. Then ascend a more difficult route along an ablation valley to **Muthat Pass** (4965m). (The DAV map shows a glacier west of the pass that is no longer present on this route.) Descend steeply to the Lotang Glacier, following its north margin to a point where you can cross to its south side. The route over the ridge separating the Lotang and Sachen glaciers isn't obvious. Descend to Rama and Astor villages in the Astor Valley. An experienced local guide who knows the route is helpful.

Bezar Gali

Bezar Gali (4062m) is an infrequently used pass linking Raikot Gah and Jalipur Gah. From Fairy Meadow, a moderate three-day trek over the pass leads to Gunar on the KKH, 30km from Chilas. Head north-west and cross Bezar Gali, descending to camp the first night at Bezar in the Jalipur Gah and the next day at Khusto.

KAGHAN

The 160km-long Kaghan Valley, south of Diamir in North-west Frontier Province's (NWFP) Hazara District, is renowned for its vast meadows, pine forests and sparkling alpine lakes nestled among western Himalayan 4000m to 5000m peaks. Formed by the Kunhar River, perhaps Pakistan's finest trout stream, the valley takes its name from Kaghan village. The local language is Hindko, similar to Punjabi, with Pushtu and Urdu also widely spoken. The upland meadows attract Gujars, nomadic herders who bring their flocks each spring in a colourful migration. Naran is the staging point for trips upvalley, a one-day drive from Islamabad via Mansehra.

Lake Saiful Mulk

Most visitors to Kaghan between mid-June and September make the day trip from Naran to Lake Saiful Mulk (3200m). The turquoise lake lies amid flower-filled meadows, surrounded by glacier-clad peaks. Above its far shore rises Malika Parbat (5290m), Queen of the Mountains, Kaghan's highest peak. Legend has it that fairies would gather at the lake to dance on moonlit nights. A young prince caught a glimpse of them and fell in love with the fairy princess. The illicit love between the fairy and the mortal human ended tragically, and the lake is named for the prince, Saif ul Mulk. This fairy realm has lately become spoiled by human visitors, who thoughtlessly leave trash. A small rest house and several tea stalls mark the spot.

From Naran, follow the 10km-long road through forest three hours to the lake. Walk an hour around the lake to a camp site in the meadows below the Saiful Mulk Glacier. It's possible to cross the ridge (4191m) at the valley's south-west end and descend steeply into the upper Manūr Valley, which joins the Kaghan Valley at Mahandri, 37km south of Naran.

Babusar Pass

Babusar Pass (4175m), at the Kaghan Valley's head, is really an alpine plateau marking NWFP's border with the Northern Areas. An infrequently used jeep road, once the only road linking Gilgit with down-country Pakistan, runs the Kaghan Valley's length and crosses the pass to meet the Indus River at Chilas to the north. Every year a few trekkers opt to walk along the road between mid-June and September as an alternative to travelling the KKH. The 130km walk between Naran to Chilas takes from four to six days. It's possible to jump on any vehicle (Rs 50) the last 39km between Babusar village and Chilas. At the time of writing, a project to improve the road across Babusar was underway.

Eastern Kaghan

A five-day trek between Burawai and Lulusar Lake crosses four easy passes as it dips into Azad Jammu & Kashmir, visiting the high lakes south of Babusar Pass and east of the road. A local guide from Naran is essential. Start from Burawai, 26km north-east of Naran. Follow the good trail south-east up the Jora Valley, passing the stone huts of Jora, and camp in the meadows six to eight hours from Burawai. On Day 2, cross **Ratti Gali** (4115m), a pass leading south-east into the upper Dhorian Valley and marking the NWFP and Azad Jammu & Kashmir border. Follow the stream down from the pass. At its confluence with another stream, turn north and follow the stream 5km to the gentle **Nuri Nar Gali** (4115m). Cross north into the upper Nuri Valley and camp in meadows along the stream four to five hours from Jora. On Day 3, follow the stream down to the main valley, which flows east towards the Neelum River. A trail leads north-west over a pass to Jalkhand River and back to the Kunhar River. Instead, follow the north-east fork as it bends around to the east past a small lake and then north over **Saral Gali** (4191m) into the upper Saral Valley and camp near Saral Lake, five to six hours from the upper Nuri Valley. On Day 4, walk a short way downstream, then turn west and follow a stream up 2km to a fork in the trail. The west fork leads shortly to Saral-di-Gali (4488m), a pass to Jalkhand Valley and back to the road. Follow the north fork and cross **Jor-di-Gali** (4450m), re-entering NWFP, and descend to Dudibach Lake (3962m), four to five hours from Saral Lake. On Day 5, walk six to seven hours west down Purbi Valley to the road at Besal, followed by an easy 2km walk on the road to Lulusar Lake.

Alternatively, from Dudibach Lake, head 4km west down the Purbi Valley, then north across a ridge into the Kabalbashi Valley. Camp in the upper valley and the next day continue downvalley to Gittidas. Gittidas, although south of Babusar Pass, is a Chilasi summer settlement where it's best to avoid camping.

Nagyr & Hunza

Above the carefully tended fields of Nagyr and Hunza soar Rakaposhi (7788m), known locally as Dumani (cloud-covered peak), Diran (7266m), and Ultar (7388m) in what renowned mountaineer Eric Shipton called 'the ultimate manifestation of mountain grandeur'. Beneath the snow-covered peaks, the Hunza River, the only one to cut through the Karakoram range, flows through the Hunza Valley to meet the Gilgit River east of Gilgit. Hunza is commonly and inaccurately used to refer to the entire valley, including Gojal, although Hunza and Nagyr were once independent states and still maintain separate identities. Changing rapidly due to the on-going impact of the Karakoram Highway (KKH), Nagyr and Hunza remain incomparable and are northern Pakistan's main tourist destination. The KKH provides easy access to the area's several good short treks. The valley's friendly people and breathtaking landscape continue to impress visitors.

HISTORY

The history of Hunza and Nagyr is largely the history of the rulers, the descendants of Girkis and Moglot. The story begins in Gilgit, which then ruled Hunza and Nagyr. The Ra, or king of Gilgit, gave Hunza to his son Girkis and Nagyr to his son Moglot. The rival brothers fought each other, and Moglot killed Girkis, leaving only Girkis' daughter as heir to the Hunza throne. Alarmed, the Wazir (Prime Minister) of Hunza went in search of a suitable prince. When asked where the young lad he brought back had come from, the wazir replied, 'from *ayesh* (the sky)', and therefore the Hunza dynasty became known as 'Ayesho', or 'skyborn'. The Nagyr dynasty continued through the sons of Moglot, and the descendants of both dynasties have houses in the former capitals, Baltit and Nagyr, today. The hereditary rulers of Hunza and Nagyr were called *Tham*, or *Mir*. Through their close affinity with the fairies, whose realm was the sky and the mountains, Thams controlled the

Highlights

Trekker in Ultar Meadow, across from Ultar Glacier.

- Letting your gaze sweep along the ice wall connecting Diran and Rakaposhi above the Minapin Glacier

- Standing on Rush Peak looking at Baintha Brak towering above the Hispar Glacier with K2 in the distance

- Spending a moonlit night at Ultar Meadow listening to avalanches crash down from the frozen flanks of Ultar

weather and ensured agricultural fertility. Humans contacted the fairies, who lived in the pure realm above, through shamans. The shamanic traditions still linger today, as do traces of Hinduism and Buddhism.

For most of their history, the tiny kingdoms of Hunza and Nagyr confronted each other across the Hunza River, carrying on the sibling rivalry of Girkis and Moglot through raids and intrigue. In its early days Hunza had only three villages: Altit, Baltit and Ganesh. The Altit fort is at least 800 years old. Although Hunza and Nagyr were always linked with Gilgit, by the mid-18th century Hunza had forged ties with China, which had annexed Turkestan (now Xinjiang). In 1790, Silum III became Tham in Hunza, and Hunza changed irrevocably.

Silum had spent his youth near the Afghan Pamir, where Isma'ili Islam was prevalent. Under his rule, Altit and Baltit adopted Isma'ili Islam. Ganesh, however, like neighbouring Nagyr, retained Shi'a Islam. Silum also brought new canal building techniques, and by constructing new canals established the villages of Haiderabad and Aliabad. Hunza expanded in size and strength, and Silum pushed north into Gojal, driving out the Qirghiz nomads and securing the routes to Turkestan. Hunza gained access to the rich trade route between Kashmir and Yarkand, and began raiding caravans. The loot from these raids enriched the Tham, who continued to placate the Chinese governor with annual gifts of gold dust.

As the British empire expanded northwest in the 19th century, independent Hunza became a thorn in its side. A free-booting state that intrigued with Russia and China and plundered the caravan trade grew intolerable. Hunza, however, was ready to play off one side against the other. Hunza asked China for guns and bullets to fight Kashmir, yet sent a present of gold dust to Kashmir as a sign of loyalty. Britain moved forward in 1877 to control Gilgit and the north-west frontier, yet Hunza continued to send gifts of gold to China and hold talks with Russian emissaries. Finally, in 1891, British and Kashmiri troops forcibly brought Hunza and Nagyr into the colonial fold. The Mir of Nagyr kept his throne, but his son was jailed. The Mir of Hunza fled to Xinjiang, and his stepbrother was installed on the throne.

As part of the colonial empire, Hunza and Nagyr became less involved in Central Asia and more involved with Gilgit and Kashmir. When the British empire ended, Hunza and Nagyr aided in the revolt against the Maharaja of Kashmir and joined Pakistan. The first motor road reached Hunza in 1957, and in 1963, with the Pakistan-China border settlement, Hunza and China gave up all mutual claims on each other's territory. Pakistan fully incorporated Nagyr state into the nation in 1972, and Hunza state in 1974, bringing 1000 years of Mir rule to a close. In 1978, the KKH was completed to Hunza, and with the opening of the Khunjerab Pass in 1986, the valley once again became a vital conduit between Central and South Asia.

INFORMATION
Maps
The Swiss Foundation for Alpine Research 1:250,000 orographical map *Karakoram (Sheet 1)* covers Nagyr and Hunza.

GATEWAYS
Aliabad is important as a transport centre and shopping place, but Karimabad, where many hotels have views overlooking the Hunza Valley, is a better place to stay. Both towns sell a good variety of trek food and equipment, almost as much as in Gilgit.

Aliabad
Places to Stay & Eat Run by the very friendly Ghazi Johar, *Rakaposhi Camping Site* (☎ 45-069) is 50m off the KKH's south side opposite the Village Guest House. This huge walled compound, with excellent Rakaposhi views, has good spring water, grass and shade. The camping fee is Rs 100, or Rs 150 to rent a tent. This is an ideal spot for large trekking parties, especially since there's no place to camp in Karimabad.

The *Village Guest House* (☎ 45-016), run by Ali Ahmad Shah, is towards the bazaar's west end. Singles/doubles/triples cost Rs 200/300/400.

Getting There & Away Hunza Gojal Transport Co Pvt Ltd vans (Rs 60) depart from an alley in Gilgit's Jamat Khana Bazaar throughout the day as vehicles fill with passengers; buy tickets in the adjacent booking office.

The southbound NATCO bus from Afiyatabad to Gilgit passes through Aliabad about 8am. The Aliabad-Gilgit fare is Rs 60 (2½ hours). Shaheen Travels (Rs 50) and Tai's Transport Service (Rs 65) vehicles pass through sporadically.

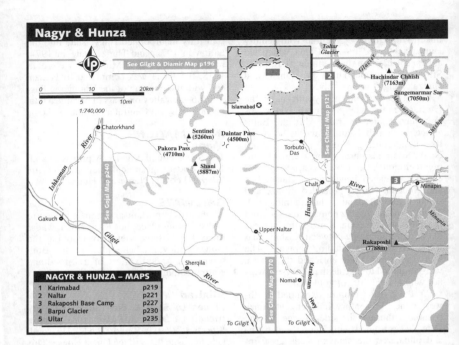

Nagyr & Hunza

See Gilgit & Diamir Map p196

1:740,000

The northbound NATCO bus from Gilgit to Afiyatabad passes through Aliabad at about 9.30am. The fare costs Rs 55 Aliabad-Afiyatabad (two hours). Shaheen Travels and Tai's Transport Service vehicles cost Rs 65.

Karimabad

Supplies & Equipment Karim's Offer (☎ 0572-77201, e karimoffer@hotmail .com), near the kerosene depot, has a good selection of backpacks and gear, including climbing hardware.

Places to Stay & Eat Head from Zero Point a minute down the original jeep road. A cluster of simple little buildings on both sides of the road is the former Hunza Inn, which was run by three brothers. Each brother now operates his own hotel: Haider Beg runs *Haider Inn*; Lal Hussain runs *Old Hunza Inn* (☎ 0572-77186); and Juwar Beg runs *Tourist Cottage*. The brothers are all friendly, serve inexpensive vegetarian and

nonvegetarian meals, and the rooms have nice views overlooking the Hunza Valley. A bed costs Rs 50. What more could you want!

Costing slightly more, *Mountain Refuge & Honeywell Restaurant* (☎ 0572-47088) is a popular local hangout. *Ultar Restaurant*, with its outdoor tables and sweeping views over Ultar Nala, is a good place for a snack.

For mid-range accommodation, *Karim Hotel & Restaurant* (☎ 0572-77091), up the road towards Baltit, has doubles with no hot running water for Rs 200. Doubles/triples with hot running water cost Rs 250/350. Its six-bed traditional house costs Rs 450, although it's not a dorm. An old favourite, *Hill Top Hotel* (☎ 0572-77129/45), costs Rs 400/450. *Tourist Park Hotel* (☎ 0572-77087), next door to Hill Top Hotel, costs Rs 400/450. *World Roof Hotel* (☎ 0572-77153) costs Rs 400/700.

At the top end, *Mountain View Hotel* (☎ 0572-77132) costs Rs 650/750; suites on

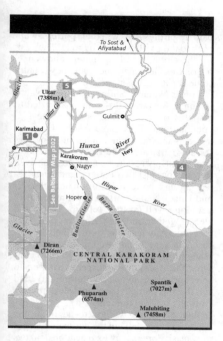

No public transport goes north on the KKH directly from Karimabad. It's best to go to Aliabad.

Naltar

The Naltar Mountains, north-west of Gilgit, have dozens of 5000m summits. Although not high by Karakoram standards, many are impressive. Naltar receives more rainfall than other areas in the Hunza Valley, and its alpine forests are a refreshing respite in the otherwise arid Karakoram. Naltar was a

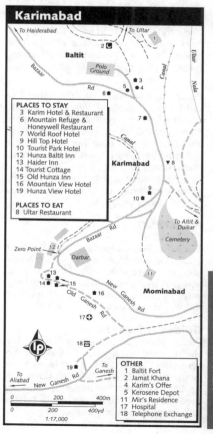

the top floor cost Rs 1000. *Hunza Baltit Inn* (☎ *0572-77012*), run by Serena Hotels, starts at Rs 1100. *Hunza View Hotel* (☎ *0572-77141/6, fax 3695*), near the telephone exchange, costs Rs 1400/1650.

Getting There & Away Hunza Gojal Transport Co Pvt Ltd vans (Rs 70, three hours) depart from an alley in Gilgit's Jamat Khana Bazaar throughout the day when vehicles are full of passengers; buy tickets in the booking office. Some vans only go as far as Aliabad or Ganesh from where you can walk steeply up to Karimabad (2286m), or organise a special hire Ganesh-Karimabad (Rs 140) or Aliabad-Karimabad (Rs 400). Other people are usually around to share the cost of this special hire. Alternatively, Gilgit-Karimabad special hires cost Rs 1500.

Vehicles (Rs 70) to Gilgit honk their horns up and down Karimabad's bazaar road between 5 and 6am in search of passengers.

NAGYR & HUNZA

British hill station and has some military facilities, including a Pakistan Air Force winter survival school.

Pakora Pass

Duration	5 days
Distance	46.9km
Standard	moderate
Season	mid-June–September
Start	Upper Naltar
Finish	Pakora
Nearest Town	Gilgit
Zone & Permit	open, no permit
Public Transport	yes

Summary A fine introduction to Karakoram trekking, this route has alpine meadows, a small glacier, a not-too-high pass, incredible scenery and it's easily accessible from Gilgit.

Pakora Pass (4710m) links the Naltar Gah and Pakora Gol. Shani and Sentinel peaks attract climbers. Naltar villagers speak Shina, and Pakora villagers speak Khowar. The trek is usually done from east to west, and combines easily with the Asumbar Haghost and then either the Punji Pass or Thui An, making superb two-week combinations over three spectacular passes (also see the Ghizar chapter).

PLANNING
Maps
The Swiss Foundation for Alpine Research 1:250,000 orographical map *Karakoram (Sheet 1)* covers the trek. Beshgiri is labelled as Bichgari. It doesn't show the trail going to Naltar lakes. In Pakora Gol, Krui Bokht, Uts and Kuru aren't labelled.

Guides & Porters
Porters cluster around Upper Naltar's few cheap hotels, but there's little reason to stay here other than for one or two hours to organise porters. Porters ask for a flat rate of Rs 250 per stage, including payment for food rations. Porters also expect large trekking parties to buy a sheep or goat, but smaller parties are usually excused or, at most, have to buy a chicken. Wāpasi is also paid regardless of whether porters walk back to their village or go by road. They ask for the clothing and equipment allowance, but on treks less than one week they usually settle for Rs 120 per person.

Lower Naltar is Shi'a, and Upper Naltar is Sunni. Sectarian differences have led to disputes over portering between the two communities. They have resolved this by agreeing that an equal number of all porters for any party are to be from Lower Naltar and from Upper Naltar. This holds true even if you have just two porters, and when releasing any porters. Unfortunately, Lower and Upper Naltar porters don't necessarily get along well on trek, refusing to eat and sleep together and bickering over the correct trail. Any tensions would likely be diffused in larger parties, but ask carefully when hiring just a few porters. Try to convince the assembly of prospective porters to select people from just one community, and for the next small party to select porters from the other community.

Porters may be willing to negotiate the wage per stage, but not the number of stages or wāpasi. Porters may load gear on donkeys to Lower Shani and carry it beyond there. A donkey might carry two loads, but wages are still paid per porter per stage and not per donkey. Horses are also available for hire. Bring a tarp for porters for the night at Pakora High Camp where there are no huts.

Stages
It's six stages total from Upper Naltar: (1) Naltar Lake; (2) Lower Shani; (3) Upper Shani; (4) Pakora Pass; (5) Lal Patthar; and (6) Pakora.

NEAREST TOWN
See Gilgit (p197).

GETTING TO/FROM THE TREK
To the Start
Several daily jeeps depart from the Jaglot bus stand on Gilgit's Domyal Link Rd to Lower Naltar (Rs 35) and Upper Naltar (Rs 65, two hours). Special hires cost Rs 1400. The road to Naltar follows the Hunza River's

true right bank 25km north-east of Gilgit to Nomal, where it narrows and turns north-west up the Naltar Valley 16km to Upper Naltar.

The jeep road continues beyond Upper Naltar to Naltar Lake. Most special hires only go as far as Upper Naltar. If you can convince a driver to go all the way to the lake, it costs up to an additional Rs 1400. Alternatively, it takes five to six hours to walk on the road between Nomal and Upper Naltar. A plan to build a bridge over the Hunza River at Nomal, linking these villages to the KKH, is under consideration.

From the Finish
Pakora-Gilgit jeeps (Rs 100, five to six hours) depart early in the morning. Pakora-Gilgit special hires, which to organise may require walking 9km on the road to Chatorkhand, cost Rs 2000. Alternatively, take the daily NATCO Chatorkhand-Gilgit bus (Rs 75) that also departs early morning.

THE TREK (see map below)
Day 1: Upper Naltar to Naltar Lake
3–3½ hours, 11.2km, 450m ascent

From Upper Naltar (2820m), also called Dumian, walk on the road up the Naltar Gah's true left (east) side. In 1¾ hours, ford a side stream at the start of **Beshgiri**, the Shina name for the distinctive red lichen-covered *(besh)* boulders *(giri)* east of the trail. Across the valley from Beshgiri, a two-day route heads south-west over a glaciated pass beneath Khaltar Peak (5591m) and descends the Bichhar Gah to Sherqila in Punial.

Beyond Beshgiri, pass through lush forest of cedar, chir pine and birch. Ford another side stream in 45 minutes, marking the start of **Bangla**, an area named after a 'bungalow' that used to be nearby. Cross a footbridge to the Naltar Gah's true right (west) bank. Continue 45 minutes to the first lake, **Naltar Lake** (3270m), at the road's end, and the *Lake View Hotel*, which

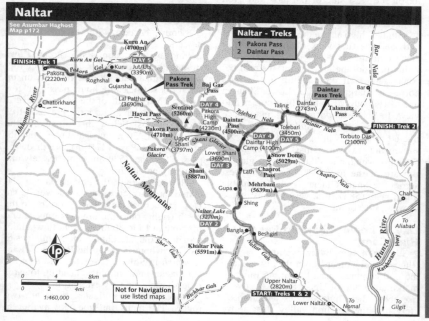

consists of a hut for food preparation and a large canvas tent with blankets for sleeping.

Day 2: Naltar Lake to Lower Shani

3½ hours, 9.5km, 420m ascent

Skirt the lake and in 15 minutes cross a footbridge to the Naltar Gah's true left (east) bank. Over a low rise, two more lakes up the western side valley come into view, and the river ahead braids out. Cross the broad area called **Shing** in 45 minutes, walking along the river bed and fording a huge side stream that tumbles from the east. Where the river narrows, the Gujar settlement of **Gupa** sits along the river's true right (west) side. Footbridges above and below Gupa give access to the settlement, but the main trail stays on the true left (east) side.

After one hour, ford a major side stream from the east, which leads to the glaciated Chaprot Pass between Snow Dome (5029m) and Mehrbani (5639m). The hanging glacier on the west side of the pass and even larger one on its east side prevent anyone from crossing this pass. Beyond the stream 15 minutes, high above the river, are huts at **Lath** and the first view of the Shani Glacier's terminus.

Junipers dot the hillside and the trail becomes faint as it skirts the Shani Glacier's north-east margin, reaching Lower Shani in one to 1½ hours as Pakora Pass comes into view. In Shina, *shani* means 'a pure place where fairies dwell', and fairies are attracted by flowers in meadows like this. A stream and grassy area marks *Lower Shani* (3690m), with herders' huts near the glacier. Beware of the herders' dogs. South-west across the Shani Glacier is the formidable Shani peak (5887m), a very serious mixed snow and ice climb.

Day 3: Lower Shani to Pakora High Camp

2–3 hours, 4.4km, 540m ascent

Rhubarb and junipers cover the hillside, and the trail continues past huts in 45 minutes, marking the start of Upper Shani. Go over a rise above these huts and descend immediately into the ablation valley. Just above

where the river goes under the glacier, cross a footbridge. Do not continue traversing above the true left bank, because the river is too wide and deep to ford higher up. Walk 15 minutes along the river bed's true right side, with the pink and orange rock of the Shani Glacier's lateral moraine to your left, to the upper end of the flat alluvial ablation valley. This is *Upper Shani* (3797m), which is well-situated in the shelter of the lateral moraine one to 1½ hours from Lower Shani. If you aren't yet acclimatised, camp here. To continue to Pakora High Camp, cross the small side stream and ascend the steep, grassy, flower-carpeted slope where horses and yaks graze. Continue through rockier terrain to where the slope levels out. Follow the true right bank of the large clear stream a short way to *Pakora High Camp* (4230m), marked by a few dilapidated stone shelters, one to 1½ hours from Upper Shani. You can also camp just before the stone shelters on either side of the stream in this very pretty area.

Day 4: Pakora High Camp to Jut/Uts

6–8 hours, 12.1km, 480m ascent, 1320m descent

Behind the high camp a side stream flows from the west, south of a large rock outcrop. An indistinct trail follows this stream up steep, loose rock one hour, passing a few cairns. The east side of the pass has several small snowfields and a large crevasse-free snowfield just below the top. Cross the snowfields in 30 minutes and reach the obvious **Pakora Pass** (4710m). North of the pass is Sentinel (5260m), a moderately difficult alpine climb.

The west side of the Pakora Pass is glaciated, but any crevasses are lower down. Descend across snowfields, working to the north (right) onto the obvious grey lateral moraine in 15 to 30 minutes. Follow a faint trail down the lateral moraine 30 minutes to its end, where it abuts the Pakora Glacier (*gomukh* in Shina). Cross the width of the icy glacier in 30 minutes, heading towards reddish rocks on its west margin.

Once across the glacier, there are two routes. The main trail goes downvalley to

Pakora. The other route crosses the seldom-used, glaciated **Hayal Pass** to Chatorkhand. From the Pakora Glacier's west margin 3km west of, and 450m below, Pakora Pass at 4230m, head west (left) ascending the rock along the Hayal Glacier's north margin. The route is incorrectly drawn on the Swiss map as splitting off at Pakora Pass itself.

To continue to Pakora, walk down the lateral moraine high above the Pakora Glacier's south-west margin, which fills the upper valley. Continue two hours on a faint trail to **Lal Patthar** (3690m), named in Urdu for the huge reddish boulder amid a few junipers. It's called Krui Bokht in Khowar. The boulder provides shelter for porters and a few possible tent sites are nearby, but the sloping hillside and distant water make this an undesirable camp.

Beyond Lal Patthar, cross a side stream in a steep ravine. Continue downvalley one hour through beautiful, dense forest of birch, pine and juniper on a pine-needle-blanketed trail and cross a footbridge (3750m) to the Pakora Gol's true right bank. The footbridge cannot be seen easily from the trail. Where the trail is level with the river continue along the river bed and walk a few minutes to the footbridge. (Don't ascend the obvious trail that climbs some 50m.) Once across the river, the narrow trail follows the river and then climbs onto a forested plateau to the Gujar huts at *Jut/Uts* (3390m) where horses, cows, sheep and goats graze, 1½ hours from Lal Patthar. *Jut* means 'grassy place' in Burushaski, and *uts* means 'spring' in Khowar.

Day 5: Jut/Uts to Pakora
3½–5 hours, 9.7km, 1170m descent
The descent from Jut to Pakora gets progressively steeper as the canyon narrows. The Pakora Gol can be hot and dry on sunny days, so start early and carry water.

From the pasture's far end, descend and cross the river on a good footbridge. The trail is in poor condition and stays on the true left (south) bank, low along the river bed one hour, passing beneath the Gujar settlements of Gujarshal and Roghshal high above. Kuru, a settlement above the confluence of the Kuru An Gol and Pakora Gol, is visible across the river. A route leads up this side stream to the Kuru An (see Ghizar's Other Treks, p193).

The trail downvalley stays on the Pakora Gol's true left side, contouring an artemisia-covered hillside on a wide donkey trail. It stays high above the raging river, often on exposed galleries. The river falls into a deep gorge with waterfalls tumbling down both sides. Reach a side stream and a large, solitary willow in 1½ hours. Cross a plank footbridge to the true right bank in 30 minutes to reach the first cultivated fields of Pakora. In 15 minutes reach the jeep road and centre of **Pakora** (2220m).

Lower Nagyr

Nagyr, with a population of 52,000 people, consists of two geographically separate administrative zones. Lower Nagyr or Nagyr 2 encompasses areas on the Hunza River's north side, including the Chaprot and Bar valleys. Attractive and prosperous Chalt, at the confluence of these valleys, is Lower Nagyr's central village where the ex-Mir of Nagyr maintains a house.

Daintar Pass

Duration	5 days
Distance	43.4km
Standard	demanding, technical
Season	July–September
Start	Upper Naltar
Finish	Torbuto Das
Nearest Town	Gilgit
Zone & Permit	open, no permit
Public Transport	yes

Summary This semi-loop alpine trek crosses a pass and explores interesting side valleys north of the lower Hunza River.

Daintar Pass (4500m) links the upper Naltar Valley with the Daintar Nala in Lower Nagyr. George Cockerill first crossed it in 1893 and described the south side as 'almost vertical'. While the pass is steep on both sides, it is easier to cross from south to north. Trevor Braham, who spent from the 1940s to the 1970s in the Himalaya, describes the northern descent as '230m of shattered rock at a 50-degree angle, ending in a wide crevasse'.

PLANNING
What to Bring

Mountaineering equipment necessary to fix ropes for safety on the descent from the pass is recommended (see Mountaineering Equipment, p61); wearing a climbing helmet is prudent.

Maps

The Swiss Foundation for Alpine Research 1:250,000 orographical map *Karakoram (Sheet 1)* covers the trek.

Guides & Porters

See Guides & Porters for the Pakora Pass trek (p220) for details. Naltar porters have the right to work only up to Daintar Pass, and Daintar porters work from the pass down to Torbuto Das. You need to pre-arrange to change porters at the pass on a specified date. These logistics and the necessity of paying wāpasi to two groups of porters adds to the trek's complexity and expense. Small trekking parties may be able to avoid changing porters.

Stages

It's six stages total from Upper Naltar: (1) Naltar Lake; (2) Daintar High Camp; (3) Khaniwal; (4) Tolebari; (5) Taling; and (6) Torbuto Das.

NEAREST TOWN

See Gilgit (p197).

GETTING TO/FROM THE TREK
To the Start

See the Pakora Pass trek (p220) for details.

From the Finish

Torbuto Das–Gilgit jeeps (Rs 30) depart in the morning. Otherwise, walk to Chalt and look for a ride. Two bridges over the Hunza River link Chalt to the KKH; a new one

below town and another above it 1km west of a petrol station. Vehicles going down or up the KKH can give you a ride.

THE TREK (see map p221)
Days 1–2: Upper Naltar to Lower Shani

2 days, 20.7km, 870m ascent
See Days 1–2 of the Pakora Pass trek (p221–2) for details. The Daintar Pass is visible from Shing. Even though you can reach the high camp from Naltar Lake on Day 2, it's better for acclimatisation to camp at *Lower Shani* (3690m). For further acclimatisation, spend another day here and explore the beautiful upper Naltar Valley.

Day 3: Lower Shani to Daintar High Camp

1–2 hours, 2km, 410m ascent
Daintar Pass is north of Lower Shani. The trail stays east (right) of the stream coming down from the ridge. *Daintar High Camp* (4100m) is in a level area below an obvious snowfield.

Day 4: Daintar High Camp to Tolebari

5–5½ hours, 6.7km, 400m ascent, 1050m descent
The ascent to the pass follows the crest of a spur from the main ridge. Near the top the angle is quite steep and a rope may be needed. It appears to be Class 2. The cornice on top can be large. A cairn marks *Daintar Pass* (4500m). The approach to beautiful Snow Dome (5029m) is along the ridge east-south-east from the pass. A steep scree gully is the standard descent from the pass. Beware of rock-fall and crevasses on the glacier below. Descend to *Tolebari* (3450m) huts and pastures, three to 3½ hours from the pass.

Day 5: Tolebari to Torbuto Das

4–5 hours, 14km, 1350m descent
Descend the Tolebari Nala to the herders' huts of Taling and Daintar (2743m) in two hours. Continue along the road down Daintar Nala through a gorge to *Torbuto Das* (2100m), at the confluence of the Daintar

Wild iris

Buddhist rock carvings, Chilas

Columbines

The Bazhin Glacier flows down from Nanga Parbat's Rupal face.

Golden Peak (Spantik) rises above the green fields and poplars of Nagyr.

Polan La & Malubiting above the icy highway of upper Sumayar Glacier, seen from Rush Phari.

Nala and Bar Nala, in two to three hours. Halfway downvalley, pass a rough trail leading north-east across the Talamutz Pass to Bar village (see Baltar & Toltar Glaciers under Other Treks, p236). Alternatively, across the river from the Daintar huts, a rugged trail leads south-east over the ridge (3657m) to Chalt on the Chaprot Nala's west bank. *Chalt Tourist Inn* has a nice camp site (Rs 50) and rooms (Rs 250–400).

Upper Nagyr

Many treks in Upper Nagyr are quite easy on good trails and offer unsurpassed views of Nagyr's well-known mountains such as Rakaposhi, Diran and Spantik (7027m). Upper Nagyr or Nagyr 1 includes the villages along the Hunza River's south bank between Nilt and the Hispar River, Nagyr Proper, Hoper and Hispar village. Nagyr Proper refers to Nagyr village, which was the capital of the former state, where the ex-Mir of Nagyr, Shaukat Ali Khan, still lives.

Rakaposhi Base Camp

Duration	3 days
Distance	17.6km
Standard	easy
Season	June–September
Start/Finish	Minapin
Zone & Permit	open, no permit
Public Transport	yes

Summary One of the shortest and easiest treks leading to a 7000m Karakoram peak base camp with sweeping views from Rakaposhi to Diran.

The Minapin Glacier sweeps down from the 16km-long fluted snowy ridge that connects Rakaposhi and Diran. Minapin village in Upper Nagyr sits along the Minapin River's true right (east) bank above the confluence of the Minapin and Hunza rivers. The excellent short trek from Minapin village to Rakaposhi Base Camp, known locally as Tagaphari, is an ideal introduction to Karakoram trekking. Easily accessible from

the KKH, the trek follows a good trail, offers sweeping vistas of Rakaposhi and Diran and is the standard route to the base camps of both peaks. Trekkers in top physical condition visit Tagaphari on a day hike from Minapin village, but most trekkers find that dividing the 1250m ascent into two days lets them enjoy the trek's many pleasures.

PLANNING
Maps
The Deutscher Alpenverein (DAV) 1:50,000 topographic map *Minapin (Rakaposhi Range)* covers the trek.

Guides & Porters
Minapin has a porters' union, which the village headman oversees. Porters, who transport loads on donkeys, ask for a flat rate of Rs 250 per stage, including payment for food rations. Porters ask for the clothing and equipment allowance only when crossing the Minapin Glacier.

Stages
It's four stages total round trip from Minapin: (1) Hapakun; (2) Tagaphari; and (3–4) two stages to return via the same route.

NEAREST VILLAGE
Minapin
Minapin is a very hospitable, yet traditional and conservative, village. Villagers ask that visitors dress in shalwar kameez and act respectfully. Women should be escorted in the village and on trek. The Burushaski name Minapin derives from compacted *(pin)* mud (resembling *mina*, the dry meal of pressed nuts, such as walnut, or apricots after their oil is extracted) that the glacier once deposited in the village.

Places to Stay & Eat Minapin's ground zero is *Diran Guest House* (e diran_gh@hotmail.com). The gracious hosts, well-prepared food and peaceful grassy compound with orchard-shaded gardens distinguish this as one of the Northern Areas' most tranquil places to stay. The dorm costs Rs 70, and singles/doubles cost Rs 400/600, all with hot running water. The camping fee is Rs 100. If you need a place to really rest and hang out for a few days between treks, this is it. It also rents tents, sleeping bags and kitchen equipment, and sells limited tinned food, but it's advisable to bring all trek food and supplies from Gilgit or Karimabad.

Getting There & Away Public vans to Pisan and Minapin depart Gilgit's Khazana (Bank) Rd near Golden Peak Inn, usually between 1 and 2pm. They're unmarked and can be hard to find. The three-hour ride costs Rs 50, plus Rs 10 per backpack or duffel bag. The 4km-long road to Minapin leaves the KKH at Pisan, just east of Ghulmet. From Pisan, it takes 45 minutes to walk to Minapin. The same public vans depart Pisan and Minapin daily for Gilgit at 6.15am.

When the Minapin vans are full, try Pisan and Miachar vans. The Pisan vans depart Gilgit before the Minapin vans, usually between noon and 1pm. The Miachar vans depart Gilgit about an hour after the Minapin vans. Gilgit-bound Miachar vans pass the Diran Guest House about 7am, but are usually already full.

No direct transport links Minapin with Karimabad, so just get to the KKH and jump on any passing vehicle. Karimabad-Minapin special hires cost Rs 1000.

GETTING TO/FROM THE TREK
See Getting There & Away, above.

THE TREK
Day 1: Minapin to Hapakun
3–4 hours, 5.8km, 792m ascent
From Diran Guest House (2012m), follow the road two minutes east. Then turn south (right) onto a dirt lane and follow it five minutes to the canal along the village's south end. Turn west (right) and follow the path along the canal 15 minutes towards the Minapin River. Walnut trees shade the path and provide a home for nesting orioles (*maiun*). The trail turns south into the canyon and crosses a footbridge (2103m) over the rushing torrent to the river's true left bank after 10 minutes.

The trail rises 183m on switchbacks for 30 minutes, then eases off and enters an open, aromatic juniper forest. Continue along the broad, shaded trail, rising gradually in one to 1½ hours to the huts at **Bang-i-das**, along a clear stream that tumbles over a cascade at the head of this pleasant side valley. The trail follows the stream 30 minutes to the base of the waterfall, where it forks. The right fork, which crosses the stream over a footbridge, leads to Gutumerung (see Alternative Day 3, p228). Follow the smaller left fork and climb 90m in 15 minutes to the grassy, tiered meadow of *Hapakun* (2804m) bordered by stands of mature fir trees. The Burushaski name Hapakun is given to a place (*kun*) within a day's walk of a main village, which is defined as 'close enough to carry a child' (*hapa*).

Camping is free in the open meadow, with northern views of Hachindar and Maiun peaks above the Hunza River. Diran and Rakaposhi remain hidden from view. Ibex inhabit the steep cliffs to the east high above the Minapin Glacier. A small, sometimes silty stream flows near the herders' huts at Hapakun, but a clear spring lies behind and five minutes below the huts. It costs Rs 40–50 to camp on private land near the spring.

Day 2: Hapakun to Tagaphari
2–3 hours, 3km, 457m ascent
Crossing the canal between the two huts, the trail (the one perpendicular to the canal, not parallel to it) heads south, rising across rock-strewn open ground beyond Hapakun's largest hut – for a minute or two – and then climbs immediately west up dusty switchbacks through fir forest for 15 minutes. The trail eases off and contours the rocky slope for 30 minutes to a verdant bowl where wildflowers and colourful songbirds thrive. Sweeping gently through the meadow, the trail enters scattered juniper stands and climbs switchbacks to the windy ridge top, where Diran, Rakaposhi and their interconnecting ice wall finally come into full view.

The trail thins and traverses a rocky cliff above the spectacularly broken Minapin Glacier 15 minutes to *Tagaphari* (3261m). Once a muddy (*taga*) lake (*phari*), as its Burushaski name indicates, it's now a level pasture where cows and oxen graze. A herders' hut is next to the rocky hillside, with plenty of good grassy camp sites along the meandering stream. A small seasonal spring lies at the base of the rocky slope towards the head of this small valley. The lateral moraine above the valley is a fun place to watch avalanches crashing down from the ridge between Rakaposhi and Diran, and to catch the sunset on Diran. Rakaposhi itself is mostly hidden from view behind the obvious snow dome of Rakaposhi East (7010m).

Side Trip: Askoreshung
3 hours, 5.8km, 1319m ascent, 1319m descent

Askoreshung (*askor* means a 'flower'; *shung*, a 'narrow path') is a view point (3780m) atop the second ridge west of Tagaphari from where the Batura, Shīshpar and Ultar peaks above Hunza are visible. From Tagaphari, ascend steeply west to the first ridge (3650m), descend and cross the intervening Gutumerung stream, reaching the second ridge in two hours. Return to Tagaphari in one hour.

Side Trip: Diran Base Camp
7–8 hours, 12km, 389m ascent, 389m descent

Diran Base Camp is locally known as Kacheli, a Burushaski word meaning 'the best grazing grass'. Minapin and Miachar villagers share these birch-dotted pastures. The area, along the Minapin Glacier's north-east margin, is similar to Tagaphari with good camp sites and a small spring nearby. Visiting Kacheli as a day hike from Tagaphari is a more strenuous, but less expensive, option than camping at Kacheli and paying porters for the two additional stages (one there, one back).

From Tagaphari, follow the crest of the lateral moraine south 20 to 30 minutes to the small cairn (3510m) marking the route onto the glacier. It takes three hours to cross

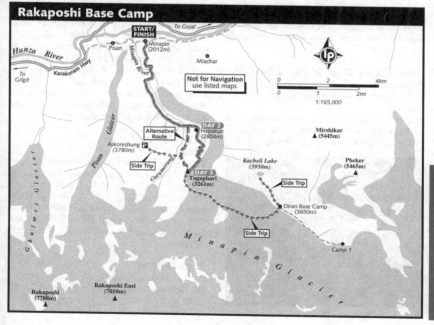

Rakaposhi Base Camp

the broad Minapin Glacier and reach ***Diran Base Camp*** (3650m). The unmarked route north-east across the glacier's alternating bands of rock and ice near many seracs is difficult to follow and changeable, so take a local guide or porter who knows the way. Carry a rope for safety. Watch for marginal crevasses when exiting the glacier.

From Diran Base Camp, trekking south-east up the ablation valley towards the rocky bend (4040m) in the glacier brings you to the point where the route to Camp 1 moves onto the glacier, close beneath Diran. Enjoy the view, but don't continue onto the heavily crevassed glacier. Experienced climbers can attempt Pheker (5465m) from base camp.

Side Trip: Kacheli Lake
3 hours, 8km, 300m ascent, 300m descent
It takes two hours to climb steeply to the small Kacheli Lake above Diran Base Camp, and half that to return.

Day 3: Tagaphari to Minapin
3–3½ hours, 8.8km, 1249m descent
Retrace your steps downvalley to Minapin via Hapakun.

Alternative Day 3: Tagaphari to Minapin
4–4½ hours, 8.4km, 389m ascent, 1638m descent
Ascend the ridge (3650m) immediately west of Tagaphari for sweeping views, and descend steeply to Gutumerung, a pasture *(rung)*

View from Tagaphari (Rakaposhi Base Camp).

in this deep *(gutum)* valley where sheep and goats graze. Follow the trail steeply downstream (north) until it passes the waterfall at the head of the Bang-i-das Valley and joins the trail between Hapakun and Minapin.

Barpu Glacier

Duration	6 days
Distance	41.9km
Standard	moderate
Season	mid-June–October
Start/Finish	Hoper
Zone & Permits	open, no permit
Public Transport	no

Summary Trails along the tree-lined upper glacier lead directly to the vertical granite north face of Spantik, or Golden Peak.

The Sumayar Bar and Miar glaciers, which flow from Malubiting (7458m) and the Miar and Phuparash peaks respectively, join to form the 33km-long Barpu Glacier. The Barpu Glacier's outwash stream flows north-west into the advancing Bualtar Glacier opposite Hoper. Trails in the ablation valleys along both sides of the Barpu Glacier offer easy, scenic walks through flower-filled meadows. This trek, however, entails five glacier crossings – twice across the Bualtar, and once each across the Barpu, Sumayar Bar and Miar glaciers.

PLANNING
Maps
The Swiss Foundation for Alpine Research 1:250,000 orographical map *Karakoram (Sheet 1)* covers the trek. The Bualtar and Barpu glaciers don't join one another as the map depicts. Bericho Kor is misplaced; it's due west of Rush Phari (Rash Lake on the map) along the Barpu Glacier's south-east margin.

Regulations
Per a 1994 ruling, the ex-Mir of Nagyr retains the right to collect a camping fee of Rs 50 from anyone camping between Tagaphari and Shuja Basa. His watchman *(chowkidar)*

JOHN MOCK

NAGYR & HUNZA

Mr Haider, wanders the valley with a type-written explanation letter in English and collects the fee.

Guides & Porters

A guide or knowledgeable porter is essential for all glacier crossings, especially the constantly shifting Bualtar Glacier, where the route changes daily. In 1999, Hoper began a porters' union to equitably assign work on a rotational basis to the people from the five villages of Hoper. This system has effectively eliminated porter disputes that plagued this area for years. The one hitch is that any trekking party hiring five or more porters must also hire a porter sirdar, who is a village representative responsible for selecting porters from his village. Porters ask for a flat rate of Rs 220 per stage, including payment for food rations. In addition, they ask for Rs 100 for shoes and for a goat from large trekking parties. A representative from the porters' union finds you at either the Hoper Hilton Inn or Hoper Inn.

Stages

This trek has suffered from stage inflation since 1986 (Lower Shishkin and Miar are relatively new stages), and today many stages are only one to 1½ hours long. It totals nine stages round trip from Hoper: (1) Lower Shishkin; (2) Barpugram; (3) Phahi Phari; (4) Girgindil; (5) Sumayar Bar; (6) Miar; (7) Hamdar; (8) Upper Shishkin; and (9) Hoper.

NEAREST VILLAGE
Hoper

Hoper refers to the five villages (Hakalshal, Ratal, Buroshal, Holshal and Gashoshal) that lie along the Bualtar Glacier's south-west margin. Hoper is also called *tsindigram*, which means 'five hamlets' in Burushaski.

Places to Stay & Eat Managed by Amir Hamza, *Hoper Hilton Inn* has singles/doubles for Rs 200/300. The camping fee is Rs 20, or it costs Rs 100/200 to sleep in one of the inn's canvas tents. *Hoper Inn* costs Rs 200. Its camp site is a little nicer and the camping fee is Rs 50. Both inns serve meals.

Getting There & Away A daily wagon (Rs 50, 4½ hours) to Hoper departs from Gilgit's Khazana (Bank) Rd near Golden Peak Inn about 8am. A daily wagon departs Hoper for Gilgit about 6am. Special hires from Ganesh or Karimabad to and from Hoper cost Rs 1100 (1½ hours).

GETTING TO/FROM THE TREK

The trailhead is at the road's end in Hoper.

THE TREK
Day 1: Hoper to Bericho Kor

4–5 hours, 10.8km, 510m ascent

Once leaving Hoper, no reliable water is available until Bericho Kor. Carry water and start early to avoid midday heat. From Hoper (2790m), descend steeply to the Bualtar Glacier's edge. The crossing is relatively short, but the constantly moving **Bualtar Glacier** is icy and broken, and has no fixed route. It can take anywhere from 30 minutes to three hours to cross.

At Lower Shishkin on the glacier's opposite side, the trail divides. The higher trail heads south-east to Upper Shishkin along the Barpu Glacier's south-west margin. Take the lower trail east to an obvious notch and the first views of the **Barpu Glacier**. The Barpu is more stable than the Bualtar, but just as bleak. Cross it on a consolidated trail in 45 minutes to the ablation valley on its south-east margin with views of Diran to the west, Spantik to the south, and Ultar Peak and Bubulimating to the north. Tagaphari is a dry, barren place in the long ablation valley. Before the Barpu Glacier retreated more than 20 years ago, Tagaphari was well watered and green. Reach **Barpugram**, the first huts, 30 minutes from the start of the ablation valley. Barpugram's water source is snow melt, unreliable after May. Two trails lead up the hillside behind Barpugram: the north-east one goes to Fetingsh in the Hispar Valley; and the south-east one leads to Gutens, an alternative route to Rush Phari (see the Rush Phari trek, p231).

The ablation valley narrows and larger junipers and wild roses appear. One hour from Barpugram, reach the huts and pastures of **Mulharai** where tamarisks offer shade. Just beyond is the grassy camp site of **Bericho Kor** (3300m) where a porters' shelter hugs a boulder, 5.5km from Tagaphari. *Bericho* are musicians, and *kor* means 'cave'. A trickle of water runs through the camp site, but its larger source is a few minutes above camp.

Day 2: Bericho Kor to Phahi Phari

1½–2 hours, 4.1km, 150m ascent

An easy trail follows the ablation valley to **Phahi Phari** (3450m), passing Dachigan one hour from Bericho Kor. A large boulder with ibex carvings at **Dachigan** marks

the spot where local people once brought ibex for the Mir of Nagyr to easily hunt.

An alternative route crosses the broken Barpu Glacier from Dachigan to Miar in two to three hours to return along the glacier's south-west side.

Day 3: Phahi Phari to Girgindil

3–4 hours, 7km, 550m ascent

Continue up the now-forested ablation valley with flower-filled meadows. In one hour, pass through Chukutans with its several huts. **Girgindil** (4000m) with its hut and beautiful meadows is two hours farther.

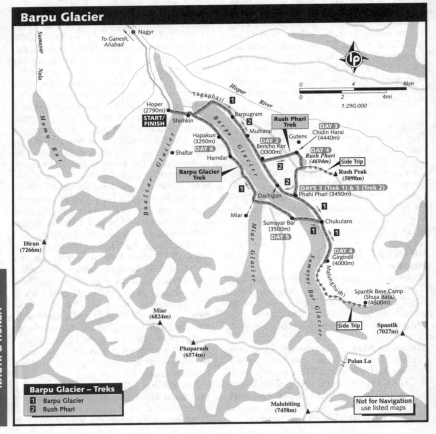

Barpu Glacier

Barpu Glacier – Treks
1 Barpu Glacier
2 Rush Phari

Not for Navigation
use listed maps

From the ridge above Girgindil are great views of Spantik.

Side Trip: Spantik Base Camp

3 days, 16km, 800m ascent, 800m descent

The Burusho of Nagyr and Hunza call the peak whose vertical granite north face soars above the Barpu Glacier's head Ganesh Chhīsh, which means Golden Peak. It's more commonly known by its Balti name Spantik and is usually climbed from the Chogo Lungma Glacier (p308). The base camp (4800m), known locally as Shuja Basa, is a two-day walk from Girgindil. The entire area between Girgindil and Shuja Basa is called Malunghushi.

The faint trail from Girgindil skirts the Sumayar Bar Glacier to the huts at Makhphona Phari in two hours, then continues for three to four hours to *Yakhzena*, at times climbing the hillside to avoid bad sections. Trekkers usually camp here. Yakhzena, with its huge boulders, means 'a place where leopards store their kill'. The next day continue along the glacier, then ascend through meadows over a ridge to *Shuja Basa* (4800m). Retrace your steps to Girgindil in one day.

The route is best done July to September. It's six stages total round trip from Girgindil: (1) Makhphona Phari; (2) Yakhzena; (3) Shuja Basa; and (4–6) three stages to return via the same route.

Day 4: Girgindil to Sumayar Bar

4–5 hours, 6km, 500m descent

Retrace your steps downvalley to Chukutans and cross the Sumayar Bar Glacier in one hour to the huts at *Sumayar Bar* (3500m), nestled near the confluence of the Sumayar Bar and Miar Glaciers below a forested ridge.

Day 5: Sumayar Bar to Hapakun

3½–4½ hours, 8km, 250m descent

Cross the wide Miar Glacier to Miar settlement at the confluence of Miar and Barpu glaciers. Follow the trail along the Barpu Glacier's south-west margin from Miar to Hamdar, reaching Hamdar in 1½ hours. Continue one hour to *Hapakun* (3250m).

Day 6: Hapakun to Hoper

3–4 hours, 6km, 460m descent

The trail passes through Upper Shishkin before dropping to Lower Shishkin at the Bualtar Glacier's edge. Cross the tricky Bualtar Glacier and return to Hoper (2790m).

Rush Phari

Duration	5 days
Distance	36.3km
Standard	demanding
Season	mid-June–September
Start/Finish	Hoper
Zone & Permit	open, no permit
Public Transport	no

Summary Incredible views of distant K2, Baintha Brak, the Hispar La and close ups of the Hispar Muztagh's giants make this a truly unforgettable trek.

Rush Phari (4694m) is a turquoise lake on a ridge between the Hispar Valley and Barpu Glacier with incredible mountain panoramas. In a 360-degree sweep, almost all the giant peaks of Hunza are visible and, remarkably, a distant K2 (8611m), Broad Peak (8047m) and Gasherbrum IV (7925m) can also be seen. The strenuous two-day 1500m climb to the lake is done in conjunction with the Barpu Glacier trek. Because of the rapid elevation gain and the high altitude at Rush Phari, do this trek only when previously acclimatised. No options for alternative camp sites exist due to lack of water, so if you experience symptoms of altitude sickness, descend to Phahi Phari or Bericho Kor immediately.

PLANNING
Maps

Refer to the Maps section for the Barpu Glacier trek (p228). Trails from Bericho Kor to the ridge and from Rush Phari to Phahi Phari aren't shown on the Swiss map. Chidin Harai and Huru aren't labelled.

Guides & Porters

See Guides & Porters under the Barpu Glacier trek (p229). Porters need bedding and

NAGYR & HUNZA

shelter for the night at Rush Phari, which can be windy and cold. The descent from Rush Phari to Phahi Phari isn't obvious, so take someone who knows the route. When you go via Gutens, hire someone to carry water.

Stages

The trek described here totals eight stages round trip from Hoper: (1) Lower Shishkin; (2) Barpugram; (2½) Bericho Kor, half a stage; (2½–4) Rush Phari, 1½ stages; (5) Phahi Phari; (6) Barpugram, with Bericho Kor being half a stage; (7) Lower Shishkin; and (8) Hoper.

Two alternative, though less desirable, trails lead to Rush Phari. One leaves the Barpu Glacier at Barpugram (see the Barpu Glacier trek, p228), climbing the hillside to Gutens, a summer settlement. From Gutens, the trail follows the ridge and joins the trail from Bericho Kor below Chidin Harai. By June, water in Gutens dries up, making these alternative trails dry and undesirable. From Barpugram, it's two stages one way to Rush Phari: (1) Gutens; and (2) Rush Phari. The second trail climbs steeply from Huru in the Hispar Valley to Gutens. From Huru, it's also two stages one way to Rush Phari: (1) Gutens; and (2) Rush Phari.

NEAREST VILLAGE

See Hoper (p229).

GETTING TO/FROM THE TREK

The trailhead is at the road's end in Hoper.

THE TREK (see map p230)
Day 1: Hoper to Bericho Kor

4–5 hours, 10.8km, 510m ascent
See Day 1 of the Barpu Glacier trek (p229).

Day 2: Bericho Kor to Chidin Harai

4½–5½ hours, 4.1km, 1140m ascent
The climb is relentlessly steep, hot and dry, with no water until Chidin Harai, so carry as much water as you can from Bericho Kor. Start early to reach the ridge top before the sun hits it. Head east from Bericho Kor (3300m) behind two large boulders. The trail rises steadily, north (left) of the scree

gully descending from the ridge. Climb 2½ to four hours through artemisia, thyme and scattered junipers to the ridge top, marked by a cairn (4020m). The trail from Gutens joins this trail at the cairn. The icy Miar Glacier below snowy Phuparash and Diran dominates the westward views.

Continue east-south-east up the grassy ridge one to 1½ hours to Chidin Harai. A faint trail follows a rocky canal, which may be dry. *Chidin Harai* (4440m) has a goat pen, a few herders' huts and grassy areas for camping. Year-round water flows five minutes above the huts. *Chidin* means a 'rounded cast-iron cooking pot', named for the shape of this *harai* (pasture). Chidin Harai enjoys late afternoon light and is a perfect spot to enjoy sunset and sunrise on the imposing Hispar Muztagh to the north-east. This wall of peaks includes: Lupgar Sar (7200m); Momhil Sar (7343m); Trivor (7728m); Mulungutti Sar (7025m); and Destaghil Sar (7885m).

Day 3: Chidin Harai to Rush Phari

1½ hours, 2.1km, 254m ascent
Head up the left side of the rocky slope above the water source. Towards the top of the slope, before it makes an obvious bend to the left, cross right to avoid talus and reach a Barpu Glacier overlook one hour above Chidin Harai. Turn south-east and cross the talus. Keep to the right of the stream and to the left of the unnamed rocky peak. Cross a low rise and reach **Rush Phari** (4694m) in 30 minutes. Although stone shelters are on the west shore, the less windy *camp sites* are along the south-west lakeshore. Enjoy the views of the Miar Glacier, Spantik, Diran and Phuparash. Two unclimbed 6000m to 6200m peaks to the south are visible behind the rocky Rush Peak.

Side Trip: Rush Peak

4 hours, 404m ascent, 404m descent
Nowhere else in the Karakoram can you get such magnificent mountain views on such a short trek, sweeping from the nearby 7500m peaks of the Hispar Muztagh to the 8000m giants of the Baltoro Muztagh, than from Rush Peak.

From Rush Phari's south shore, walk up the flower-covered slope for one hour to a hilltop (4938m) with a cairn and several tent platforms, but no water. From here, the distant pyramid of K2 is visible to the east. The best views, however, are from the summit of **Rush Peak** (5098m). From the cairn, follow the northern ridge, then ascend easy Class 2 talus to the rocky summit, also marked by a cairn. From here, K2 is dramatically larger, Broad Peak and Gasherbrum IV are visible, and Baintha Brak looms above the Hispar La.

Day 4: Rush Phari to Phahi Phari
2–3 hours, 4.4km, 1244m descent
The descent to Phahi Phari is relentlessly steep. From the stone shelters and cairns along the lake, an obvious gully descends towards the Barpu Glacier. The route stays right of the gully, traversing talus then descending juniper and grassy slopes and more steeply over artemisia steppes. Views of the Sumayar Bar and Miar glaciers, and the Malubiting and Phuparash peaks are awesome. *Phahi Phari* (3450m) has reliable water and shade.

Day 5: Phahi Phari to Hoper
5–6 hours, 14.9km, 660m descent
See Days 1–2 of the Barpu Glacier trek (pp229–30), in reverse, for details.

Hunza

Hunza's 48,000 inhabitants live in villages on the Hunza River's north bank between Maiun and Atabad. Hunza is further distinguished into two areas: Lower Hunza, the villages below Murtazabad; and Central Hunza or Hunza Proper, Murtazabad and the villages above it. The prominent rock spire of Bubulimating (6000m) and snowy summit of Ultar (7388m) tower dramatically above Hunza. Baltit, with its fort, was the capital of Hunza state. Ghazanfar Ali Khan, the ex-Mir of Hunza, resides in a modern palace in Karimabad. Karimabad, named for His Highness Prince Karim Aga Khan, is the centre of Hunza tourism.

Bubulimo Ting

Atop the soaring spire above Hunza, Lingpi Kisar left his wife Bubuli Gas with a rooster and a bag of millet. The great hero of Tibetan epics had visited Hunza and married the princess, but after accomplishing his great deeds, he departed, saying he would return when the rooster finished eating the last of the grain. So atop Bubulimo Ting (Bubuli's Peak), the 'Lady Finger', sits his wife. Climbers have since reached the top, but Kisar must have returned first, for they found neither the princess, nor the rooster and bag of grain.

Bubulimating (left) & Hunza Peak (6270m), above Hunza.

Ultar

Duration	2 days
Distance	6.2km
Standard	easy
Season	May–October
Start/Finish	Baltit
Nearest Village	Karimabad
Zone & Permit	open, no permit
Public Transport	yes

Summary This steep, but short, trek leads to a stunning glacial amphitheatre beneath the snowy summit of 7388m Ultar.

The lofty summit of Ultar (7388m), towering dramatically above Hunza, is believed to be where a fairy queen once lived in a crystal palace. It's from this sacred mountain that Hunza's irrigation water flows. Baltit Fort guards the entrance to the steep, narrow Ultar

NAGYR & HUNZA

Nala, which opens in its upper reaches into a pasture surrounded by a cascade of glaciers and granite. The walk to the meadow and back can be done as a strenuous day hike, but spending a night is an unforgettable experience. On moonlit nights, Ultar is sublime. Frequent avalanches off the icefall punctuate the stillness and echo off the peaks and cliffs surrounding the meadow.

PLANNING
Maps
The Deutschen Alpenverein (DAV) 1:100,000 topographic map *Hunza–Karakorum* depicts the area.

Guides & Porters
A local guide costs Rs 300–350 per day, but isn't absolutely necessary. Ask for a reliable guide at your hotel, because lots of unreliable ones are out there. Trekkers have been lost and injured, however, and one solo trekker in 1994 has never been seen again.

NEAREST VILLAGE
See Karimabad (p218).

GETTING TO/FROM THE TREK
Walk through Baltit towards the fort, under the house spanning the path, to the trailhead at a signed junction. It takes 15 minutes to walk here from most Karimabad hotels.

THE TREK
Day 1: Baltit to Ultar Meadow
2–3 hours, 3.1km, 770m ascent
At a signed junction (2500m), footpaths lead right to Baltit Fort, left to Diramishal, and straight (north) to Ultar Meadow. Go straight (north), following the canal into the mouth of the canyon. A spring is just past the canal's headworks, 15 minutes from Baltit.

Climb steadily for one hour on a well-used, but sometimes difficult and indistinct, trail up the steep rubble along Ultar Nala's true right bank. Rock-fall hazard is high along this section after prolonged rain, high winds or a thaw.

The trail then crosses the Dilbar canal, leaving the river's edge. Cairns mark the way over moraine rubble, staying high above

Baltit Fort, ancient guardian of Hunza.

the river and rising to the base of cliffs. Pass an overflow canal, which is usually dry in the morning and flows in the afternoon. Pass the highest canal, which flows to the Victoria Monument, 15 to 30 minutes from the Dilbar canal. Here are the first views of the black rubble of the Ultar Glacier's terminus. Follow the canal up a few minutes to the first level grassy area with a spring called **Quru Phari** (3000m). A friendly entrepreneur sells drinks and snacks, prepares hot meals and even offers free camping.

Continue up the more gradual trail one hour to *Ultar Meadow* (3270m), with good views south to Diran. Below the herders' huts at Ultar, a rock wall usually keeps livestock out of an established camping area run by Hunza clans. A stream trickles through the compound. The camping fee inside the compound is Rs 70. Camping is free elsewhere, but there are no level spots outside. Also in the compound is a kitchen hut that prepares meals and sells drinks and snacks. Sod tables and chairs invite one to hang out. It costs Rs 80 per person to sleep in one of their tents nearby. Morning sun comes late, and swirling winds off the glacier can make it quite cool.

Alternative Day 1: Baltit to Ultar Meadow
2–3 hours, 3.1km, 770m ascent
An alternative way into Ultar Nala is through Diramishal village, home to the Diramiting clan, and along the Dilbar canal. Part of this trail crosses private land and the Dilbar canal, constructed in 1998 and opened in June 2000, is technically closed

to foot traffic. Local people are concerned both about the safety of people walking along Dilbar, and also about the canal's structural integrity. Nobody wants the canal to break under the weight of excessive traffic. Ask for permission before wandering on your own. That said, it's the most direct and commonly used way to Ultar.

At the signed junction in Baltit, turn left following the arrow to Diramishal. Go up stone steps and in one minute, turn right past the house next to the house with a hanging sign in front that reads 'Hunza Fabrics Enterprise'. The narrow footpaths through Diramishal are confusing, and it's easy to get lost. Have someone show you the way. It takes about 15 minutes to wind your way up through the tightly clustered old houses. Respect the privacy of Diramishal residents whose houses and windows you walk right by. Continue climbing another 15 to 30 minutes through fields and orchards towards a rock face, topped by the Queen Victoria Monument, to reach a spectacular view point and the Dilbar canal. If you get lost, ask for the way towards Malikamo Shikari, the monument's local name.

Head right, walking carefully along the reasonably wide, but exposed path along the canal and into Ultar Nala. Reach the junction with the main trail in Ultar Nala in 30 minutes. About 50m before the canal headworks, climb (left) onto the rocky moraine towards the base of the cliff and away from the river. See Day 1 (p234) for the description from the Dilbar canal to Ultar Meadow.

Side Trip: Hon Pass
4½–6 hours, 5km, 995m ascent, 995m descent

Hon Pass (4257m), on a steep ridge above Ultar, has magnificent views of the Hunza Valley and the west end of the Hispar, Spantik-Sosbun and Rakaposhi-Haramosh ranges. The summits of Trivor, Spantik, Malubiting, Phuparash, Diran and Rakaposhi tower above the equally impressive Barpu, Minapin and Pisan glaciers. For an 'aerial' view of treks in Nagyr that you may have done or are thinking about doing, this is the place to go.

The popular day hike to Hon Pass is steep and strenuous, but well worth the effort. Plan on three to four hours from Ultar Meadow to the pass and 1½ to two hours to return. Those in really good shape can do the entire trip as a day hike from Baltit in eight hours. Carry water from Ultar because there's no reliable source above.

Looking from Ultar Meadow, Hon Pass is the obvious grassy notch on the ridge south-west of the meadow. Although many people go to Hon, there's no single established trail except for the final 20 minutes. From Ultar Meadow, head slightly northwest, and pass the grave of Japanese climber Tsuneo Hasegawa, who died in a 1991 avalanche on Ultar II. Head up along the stream paralleling the base of the cliff. Stay towards the right, and don't stray too far towards the inviting grass to the left. The relentlessly steep route rewards with increasingly spectacular views. To the south, the Barpu Glacier and peaks above it come into view first as the perspective on Ultar and its icefall becomes more dramatic. Eventually, cross to the left (south) side of the rocky rib dotted with grassy patches to reach a solitary cairn (4115m).

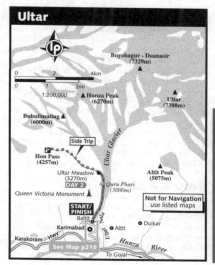

Avoid ascending the gully above the cairn. Follow the visible trail from the cairn south-south-east five minutes towards a distinctive rock outcrop. At the outcrop, the trail makes a sharp right turn and traverses the steep exposed slope 15 minutes to **Hon Pass**. Cows and sheep graze on both sides of the pass. Nobody actually crosses Hon Pass, so retrace your steps to Ultar Meadow.

Day 2: Ultar Meadow to Baltit
1½–2 hours, 3.1km, 770m descent
Be careful not to follow a canal by mistake as you descend the trail along Ultar Nala.

Other Treks

The following treks are all in an open zone.

NAGYR
Chaprot
Chaprot Valley in Lower Nagyr runs west from Chalt village above the confluence of the Chaprot and Hunza Rivers. Described as 'more beautiful than any other valley in the Gilgit Agency' by Schomberg in the 1930s, Chaprot has beautiful views of Rakaposhi and easy one- to two-day walks from mid-June to October. Horses are available for hire.

Chaprot village (2134m) is one hour's walk on the road up the valley's north side from Chalt (1981m). A one-day walk leads north-west from Chaprot, up and over the ridge (3657m) to Daintar village (2743m) in the Daintar Nala. The Ghashumaling Valley (Rashumaling on the Swiss map) branches slightly south from Chaprot village. With gentle trails through mulberry, peach, apple and walnut orchards, it's a popular day trekand picnic area. Follow the trail past Chaprot's high school to Rahbat village and continue upvalley through a canyon. The Kacheli Glacier lies at this side valley's head. Three to four hours up the Chaprot Valley from Chaprot village is Burishki (2591m), a summer settlement. A few jeeps ply between Gilgit and Chaprot.

Baltar & Toltar Glaciers
Bar Valley (*bar* means 'valley' in Burushaski) receives the water of two huge glaciers descending from the peaks at the Batura Glacier's head: Baltar from the 7500m peaks of the Batura Wall to the north-east; and Toltar from Kampir Dior (7168m) to the north-west. Two nontechnical treks through summer pastures along both glaciers

are possible mid-June to October. July and August are the most pleasant months for visiting the pastures. March to May, however, is reportedly the best time for watching the valley's sizeable ibex population. A few jeeps from Gilgit go beyond Torbuto Das to Bar village (2200m), 22km from Chalt across the KKH, but plan on starting from Torbuto Das.

The DAV 1:100,000 *Hunza–Karakorum* map is most accurate. Most place names and locations along the Baltar and Toltar Glaciers are inaccurately shown on the DAV and Swiss maps. The DAV and Swiss maps name the Baltar Glacier's large northern branch as the Toltar Glacier, but the glacier it labels as Kukuar is locally called Toltar. Baltar pastures are shown on the west side of the Baltar Glacier's northern arm, but Baltar is actually on the east side where the Swiss map has an unnamed black square. Kukuay pastures along the Toltar Glacier's west side, and Saio-daru-kush, on the hillside above the confluence of the eastern and northern arms of Toltar Glacier, aren't shown.

Baltar Glacier
It's a moderate three-day round-trip to Baltar. On Day 1, cross the river at Bar village and follow the trail along its true left bank to the pasture at **Shuwe**. On Day 2, continue up the true left bank of Baltar Glacier's outwash stream as it bends east. Cross the moraine-covered Baltar Glacier to the large south- and west-facing pastures of **Baltar**, on the Baltar Glacier's north side and east of its large northern arm. Retrace steps downvalley on Day 3. It's four stages total starting from Torbuto Das: (1) Shuwe; (2) Baltar; and (3–4) two stages to return via the same route.

Toltar Glacier
It's a demanding eight-day trek up Toltar. On Day 1, follow the road to Bar village (2200m) and continue up the river's west bank to **Bitale Tok**. If you start from Bar, you can reach Toltar the same day. On Day 2, cross the Toltar Glacier's outwash stream to **Toltar**, the main summer settlement (2900m). Above Toltar are the yak pastures of Fagurgutum (3400m), a good day hike. On Day 3, continue along the Toltar Glacier's east side, passing through Kukuay summer settlement to **Baru-daru-kush** pastures. On Day 4, beyond Baru-daru-kush, cross the Toltar Glacier to the north side and **Dudio-daru-kush**. On Day 5, continue along the main glacier's north margin, and make the difficult crossing of the north Toltar Glacier to the **Saio-daru-kush** pastures (over 4000m). The peak above (6771m) has the same name as the pastures, but is called Seiri Porkush on the Swiss map.

Retrace steps downvalley in three days, returning to Torbuto Das on Day 8. It's 10 stages total starting from Torbuto Das: (1) Bitale Tok; (2) Kukuay; (3) Baru-daru-kush; (4) Dudio-daru-kush; (5) Saio-daru-kush; and (6–10) five stages to return via the same route.

Bualtar Glacier

Two easy options exist to explore the Bualtar Glacier above Hoper. First is a 12-hour day hike to the pastures along the glacier's south-west margin. Two trails, a higher and a lower one, head to the pastures. From the ridge above the pastures are good mountain views. Second is a two-day route to Shaltar, the pastures on the Bualtar Glacier's south side. From Hoper, cross the Bualtar Glacier to Lower Shishkin and head up its south-east margin to the pastures and camp. Return the next day via the same route. The mountain views from Shaltar are limited to Diran.

Mamu Bar

High above the Sumayar Nala and Silkiang Glacier, also known as the Mamu Bar, are the mines of Chuman Bakhūr. Since 1989, the discovery of large aquamarine crystals up to 15cm across and 30cm long at this site has made Pakistan a world-famous source for these gem specimens. The easy two-day trek to these mines combines gorgeous views with a visit to a Karakoram growth industry. The large new mosque at Askordas, built with revenue from the mines, gives an idea of the wealth of the deposits.

To reach the trailhead, leave the KKH at Murtazabad and cross the bridge over the Hunza River. Head upvalley on the Minapin-Sumayar road along the river's true left bank to Sumayar village. Karimabad-Sumayar special hires cost Rs 1100. The road ends above Sumayar beyond the hydro-electric plant. Fida Hussain of Sumayar has set up tents here for visitors to stay. Climb steeply up the hillside, and enter the Mamu Bar area, the Mir of Nagyr's former hunting grounds. A large 3m by 20m flat rock one hour above the tents is where the queen of Nagyr would sit to watch her husband hunt. Cross the river twice over footbridges, with a clear spring below the second footbridge. Ascend moraine on the valley's east side, and climb 600m to a spring at the herders' huts at Madur Kushi and camp, 3½ to four hours from Sumayar.

The next day continue steeply up 750m in two hours. Then level off and traverse to the crystal mines at Chuman Bakhūr in another hour. The views of Diran above and the Silkiang Glacier below are breathtaking. From Chuman Bakhūr, either return to Sumayar in a single day, or, for an adventurous trek, cross the ridge east (behind) the mines and continue across three high ridges to Hoper. The arduous route takes several days. Few people know the route via Bartar and Supaltar pastures to Hoper, so be sure to go with someone who does.

HUNZA PROPER
Altit Peak

Above Duikar, a summer village 300m above Altit, are summer pastures and dry, rocky peaks, including little-known Altit Peak (5075m, see map p235). Duikar has spectacular views of the Hunza Valley. A road turns off Altit Link Rd west of Altit's polo ground. From Karimabad or Altit, the ride to Duikar takes one hour; walking takes five to six hours. Special hires cost Rs 800. For a magical experience, visit Duikar on a moon-lit night. It's easy to spend four or five days for the moderate trek in this area, popular in winter with hunters. Take someone who knows the way around these peaks.

Shīshpar & Muchutshil Glaciers

Hassanabad Nala drains two glaciers descending from the 7500m Batura Wall's south side: Shīshpar (also called Hassanabad) from the north-east; and Muchutshil from the north-west. Two moderate treks to summer pastures along both glaciers are possible between late May and early October. The trailheads are at the KKH where it bridges the Hassanabad Nala just above Murtazabad and 5km below Aliabad. The routes over these glaciers change from year to year, so a local guide is necessary.

Shīshpar Glacier

A four-day trek along the Shīshpar Glacier offers excellent views of seldom-seen sides of Bubulimating, Ultar and Shīshpar. On Day 1, follow the Hassanabad Nala's true left (east) bank towards the glacier's snout on the track behind the highway maintenance station. Climb the terminal moraine and continue on the glacier 1.5km to a steep gully off the glacier to the right. At the top of this gully, and in front of the ridge rising to the east is a waterless camp site called **Bras I**, three to four hours from the KKH. A short distance along the trail to the north-east, a spur drops to a glacial pool. On Day 2, head up the Shīshpar Glacier and pass Bras II, a possible camp site. Continue on moraine to **Khaltar Harai** (also called Dudara Harai), a pasture 7km, or four to five hours, from Bras I, with fine views of the glacier and Ultar and Passu peaks. Retrace steps downvalley, reaching the KKH on Day 4.

Muchutshil Glacier

The six-day trek along the Muchutshil Glacier has good views of Muchu Chhīsh (7453m) and Hachindar Chhīsh (7163m), and leads to **Sangemarmar Sar Base Camp**. On Day 1, follow the Hassanabad Nala's true right (west) bank towards the glacier's snout, following the canal that feeds Hunza's hydroelectric plant. Camp in a sandy spot below the **glacier's snout** with a spring near the river, two to three hours from the KKH. On Day 2, climb high above the Muchutshil Glacier before dropping onto the debris-covered glacier and crossing to its north-east margin. Scramble up scree to a path on a narrow plateau, which widens as you head north-west through the pastures of Tochi and Bakor. Continue to **Gaymaling** (3600m), another pasture that is now unused, five to seven hours from the previous camp site. From Gaymaling, explore the lower reaches of Sangemarmar Sar (7050m) to the north-east and visit its base camp. Head north on Day 3, climbing through scrub forest to an immense meadow with huts and a mill, four to five hours from Gaymaling. With clear, flowing water and great vistas to the east and north, this tranquil spot offers a wonderful camping respite. Retrace steps downvalley, reaching the KKH on Day 6.

The peak that the Swiss map labels Sangemar Mar (*sangemarmar* means 'marble' in Urdu) is more correctly called Sangemarmar Sar. The Muchutshil Glacier is labelled as Muchuhar, and Gaymaling is labelled as Gychalin.

Ahmedabad Glacier

Ahmedabad Glacier is east of, and parallel to, the Ultar Glacier. Few foreigners visit the village and the summer pastures above. From Altit, follow the narrow road above the Hunza River's true right bank through Faizabad to Ahmedabad. From Ahmedabad, ascend to the pastures and descend to Sarat village on the link road. Herders can show the way. Plan on five or six days for this moderate trek. It totals five stages starting from Ahmedabad: (1) Gurpi; (2) Teish; (3) Godian; (4) Baldiat; and (5) Sarat. Karimabad-Ahmedabad special hires cost Rs 450.

Gojal

Gojal, the area along the upper Hunza River between Hunza Proper and the Khunjerab Pass, lies in the heart of the Karakoram where glaciers course right to the Karakoram Highway's (KKH) edge. Outside Baltistan, Gojal is the Karakoram's most extensively glaciated region. Most treks in Gojal go to alpine pastures along or above these glaciers. Gojal boasts Destaghil Sar (7885m), the highest peak in the Karakoram west of K2, numerous other 7000m peaks and vast stretches of territory ripe for trekking. It's some of the Karakoram's most dramatic scenery, and certainly the most accessible.

Gojal, with a population of 14,700, is home to Wakhi people. Gojal's green and pleasant villages offer stunning views of towering peaks and spires. Burusho neighbours in Hunza refer to Wakhi as Guits and to Gojal as Herbar (in Burushaski, *her* means 'to weep'; *bar*, 'a valley') because of its difficult access from Hunza prior to the KKH's construction.

HISTORY

Hunza history indicates that Hunza annexed Wakhi areas in Wakhan, Taghdumbash Pamir and Raskam around AD 1700. Gojal's earliest Wakhi settlements of Avgarch and Shimshal are 250 to 400 years old. Chapursan, Wakhi history tells us, was populated even earlier, but no descendants of those early settlers survived. Chapursan's current settlement dates from the 19th century. The original ancestor of the Avgarch Wakhi, Baba Sufi, is said to have migrated with his son Quba from Afghanistan's Badakshan Province. They first settled at Sost, but soon moved to Avgarch, because Sost was too vulnerable to attack from Qirghiz nomads. Shimshalis claim descent from Mamu Sing, whose son, Sher, is said to have gained rights to the Shimshal Pamir by winning a polo contest against the Qirghiz.

The Mir of Hunza ruled the Wakhi villages of Gojal until 1974 and taxed the

A blue sheep skull greets trekkers in Qachqar-e-Dur Valley.

JOHN MOCK

Highlights

- Marvelling at the enormous ice floes tumbling into the Batura Glacier from Yashpirt

- Visiting Shimshal where Gojal's most adventurous trekking is limited only by imagination – a dozen high passes and wildlife watching await

- Visiting Chapursan's legendary Baba Ghundi Ziarat in a sacred landscape surrounded by exotic rock formations and exhilarating passes

- Standing on Kilik and Mintaka passes, along ancient caravan routes

people, required them to tend livestock, cultivate land and carry loads, in return for which he protected them from Qirghiz raiders. The Mir occasionally banished Hunza men to remote Shimshal. The Mir also had Shimshalis raid caravans travelling

GOJAL

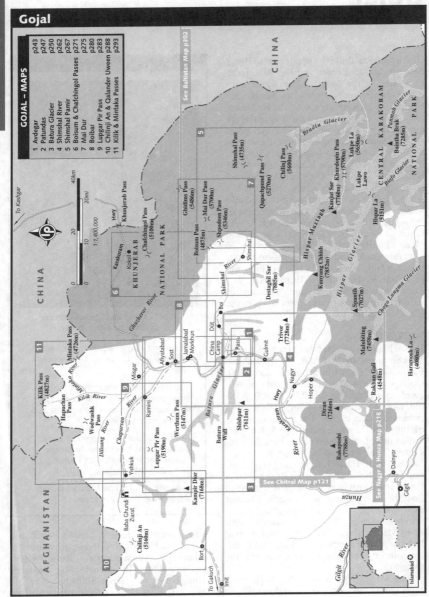

Gojal

GOJAL – MAPS

1	Avdegar	p243
2	Patundas	p247
3	Batura Glacier	p250
4	Shimshal River	p262
5	Shimshal Pamir	p267
6	Boisum & Chafchingol Passes	p271
7	Mai Dur	p275
8	Boibar	p280
9	Lupgar Pir Pass	p283
10	Chilinji An & Qalander Uween Passes	p288
11	Kilik & Mintaka Passes	p293

between Kashmir in India and Yarkand in China. The Shimshali raiders travelled over the Shimshal Pass, down the Braldu River, crossed the Muztagh River, and travelled up the Raskam River, a journey of more than one week, to raid the caravans. These raids brought Hunza to the attention of the British in the 19th century. Britain subjugated Hunza in 1891, ending the raids. Hunza's official claim to Raskam was abandoned in 1937 and the border with China was settled in 1963.

INFORMATION
Maps
The Swiss Foundation for Alpine Research 1:250,000 orographical map *Karakoram (Sheet 1)* covers Gojal except Misgar, which is mostly covered on the US AMS Series U502 India and Pakistan 1:250,000 topographic map *Baltit (NJ 43-14)*.

GATEWAYS
Afiyatabad & Sost
The Pakistan-China border check post, commonly referred to as Sost, physically moved in the early 1990s a few kilometres north of Sost village to a newly built eyesore called Afiyatabad. The customs, immigration and health check posts, and booking offices for transport are here.

The PTDC Information Centre (☎ Sost exchange 40), open May to October, is near the check post.

Despite the proliferation of shops along the KKH, it's difficult, if not impossible, to buy enough food here to outfit a trek. Less is available and it's more expensive than Hunza or Gilgit. You have to go elsewhere if you need gear.

Places to Stay & Eat Unappealing hotels, most of which are overpriced, have popped up everywhere in Afiyatabad. Cheap places line the KKH and are usually full of Pakistani men going to Kashgar for trade. Far from clean, but the best of the budget places is the Passu-run *Asia Star Hotel & Restaurant* (☎ 0572-1135). The dorm costs Rs 100, singles/doubles cost Rs 350–400, and triples cost Rs 650. *Sky Bridge Inn* (☎ 0572-77239,

ext 25) has rooms without hot running water for Rs 250; those with hot running water cost Rs 500. Singles/doubles cost Rs 1000/1200 at the *PTDC Motel*. *Hotel Riveria* (☎ 0572-77239, ext 16, 44) costs Rs 1200/1600.

Not much is left along the roadside in Sost, but staying here is more pleasant, if less convenient. *Mountain Refuge Hotel* (☎ 046-218), adjacent to the post office, has a dorm that costs Rs 50, or Rs 60 with a foam mattress. Its singles/doubles with no hot running water cost Rs 150/200. Those with hot running water cost Rs 300/400. *Khunjarab View Hotel* (☎ 046-212), farther south, costs Rs 500/600.

Getting There & Away NATCO's deluxe bus (Rs 115, six hours) departs along the roadside near the Afiyatabad office (in the red customs building with white stripe next to the money changer) at 4.30am for Gilgit. Private transport companies operate vans and wagons that make fewer stops and are quicker by about an hour. Vehicles depart irregularly and only when full of passengers. The first vehicles of the day depart Afiyatabad between 4.30 and 5am, and continue departing until 5 or 6pm. Shaheen Travels costs Rs 120 and Tai's Transport Service costs Rs 135.

From Gilgit, NATCO's deluxe bus departs from Cinema Bazaar at 7am. Shaheen Travels departs Jamat Khana Bazaar every two hours between 6.30am and 5pm. Tai's Transport Service departs from Airport Rd every two hours between 7am and 2pm.

Gulmit
Gulmit (2408m) is Gojal's main village with a post office, library and cultural museum. Accommodation is comparatively expensive, so many budget-conscious trekkers head to Passu or Borit Lake.

Places to Stay & Eat On the KKH, across from Silk Route Lodge, *Gulmit Tourist Inn* (☎ 0572-77238), owned by Abdul Bari, has a dorm in an adjacent Wakhi-style house that costs Rs 70-80. Singles cost Rs 380-760 and doubles cost Rs 500-950. *Village*

Guest House (☎ *046-12*), run by Shah Khan, is near the polo ground with a few rooms with a shared bathroom that cost Rs 200. Singles/doubles with attached bathrooms cost Rs 400/500. *Village Guest House* (☎ *046-009*), run by Ghulam Uddin, is just south of the polo ground and charges Rs 200/300. Known for its good food, *Hunza Marco Polo Inn* (☎ *0572-46107*, ℮ *marco poloinn@a1.com.pk*), starts at Rs 900/1000. *Silk Route Lodge* (☎ *046-118*, ☎/fax *0572-55359*) costs Rs 900/1200.

Getting There & Away The southbound NATCO bus from Afiyatabad to Gilgit passes through Gulmit at about 6am. The Gulmit-Gilgit fare is Rs 90 (four hours). Shaheen Travels (Rs 80) and Tai's Transport Service (Rs 90) vehicles pass through sporadically.

The northbound NATCO bus from Gilgit to Afiyatabad passes through Gulmit at about 11am. The Gulmit-Afiyatabad fare is Rs 25 (two hours). Vehicles run by Shaheen Travels and Tai's Transport Service also cover this route (Rs 35).

Passu

Peaceful Passu, which sits between the Passu and Batura glaciers along the Hunza River's true right (west) bank, is the centre of Gojal trekking. A newer settlement, Janabad, north of Passu, is quickly becoming a popular place to stay and has more hotels under construction.

PLANNING
Guides & Porters
Passu has a rotational system for assigning guides and porters, and a list of village men is kept at the Passu General Store. Porters ask for a flat rate of Rs 290 per stage, including payment for food rations and the clothing and equipment allowance.

ACCESS VILLAGES
Passu & Janabad
Supplies & Equipment Despite its deserved reputation, it's tough to outfit a trek

from here. Only a minimal amount of trek food and equipment is available.

Places to Stay & Eat With the only telephone in town, *Passu Inn* (☎ *046-101*), owned by Ghulam Muhammed, is adjacent to Passu's bus stop and shops. The dorm costs Rs 70. Singles/doubles with no hot running water cost Rs 150/300; those with hot running water cost Rs 300/450. *Batura Inn*, half a kilometre north of the bus stop, began in 1974 as a canteen for Chinese officers overseeing the KKH's construction. Owner Izzatullah Baig is a cheerful host and good cook. Camping is free, and the dorm costs Rs 60–80. Rooms have attached bathrooms, but none have hot running water. Hot water comes in buckets upon request. Singles cost Rs 100–150, and doubles cost Rs 150–200.

Passu Peak Inn, half a kilometre north of Batura Inn in Janabad, is run by the intensely friendly Akber Shah. The dorm costs Rs 50, and singles/doubles without hot running water cost Rs 100/150. It's small, but it's the cleanest place around. *Passu Tourist Lodge*, 1km north of Passu Peak Inn, or 2km (30 minutes) north of the bus stop, is a cluster of four-room cottages around a central dining hall. The cook, Sher Ghazi, may be northern Pakistan's best, which is reason enough to stay here. The dorm costs Rs 100, and singles/doubles with hot running water cost Rs 500/700. It's possible to make reservations through Walji's Adventure Pakistan offices in Gilgit (☎ *0572-2665*) and Karimabad (☎ *0572-77087*), and via telephone with Imam Shah in Gilgit (☎ *0572-2149*).

Getting There & Away The southbound NATCO bus from Afiyatabad to Gilgit passes through Passu about 5.30am. The Passu-Gilgit fare is Rs 95 (4½ hours). Shaheen Travels (Rs 90) and Tai's Transport Service (Rs 110) vehicles pass through sporadically.

The northbound NATCO bus from Gilgit to Afiyatabad passes through Passu about 11.30am. The Passu-Afiyatabad fare is Rs 20 (1½ hours). Shaheen Travels and Tai's Transport Service vehicles cost Rs 30.

Avdegar

Duration	2 days
Distance	13.4km
Standard	moderate
Season	May–October
Start/Finish	Passu
Zone & Permit	open, no permit
Public Transport	yes

Summary Being at lofty Avdegar gives the feeling of looking down at immense glaciers and peaks from a helicopter, with the area's amazing aerial-like views of the KKH and Passu far below.

Avdegar, Passu's winter yak pasture, is east of and high above, the Hunza River. Avdegar's fantastic, almost aerial views west to the Ghulkin, Passu and Batura glaciers and the peaks above them are the attraction. The trek to Avdegar is best undertaken as an overnight trip, but can be done as a very strenuous eight- to 10-hour day trek. Fitness and previous acclimatisation are necessary for this relentlessly steep route that rapidly gains elevation.

PLANNING
Maps
No maps exist that cover this trek, but the Swiss Foundation for Alpine Research 1:250,000 orographical map *Karakoram (Sheet 1)* shows the general area. It locates Yashbandan village incorrectly; it's on the Hunza River's true right (west) bank. Hussaini is labelled as Sesoni, the village's old name. Kharamabad and Avdegar aren't marked and the Avdegar Glacier is labelled as Abdigar Dur Glacier.

Guides & Porters
Hiring a porter to carry your gear makes this a more pleasant trek and removes any uncertainties about finding water or locating the route.

Stages
It's four stages total round trip from Passu: (1) Kharamabad; (2) Avdegar; and (3–4) two stages to return via the same route.

GETTING TO/FROM THE TREK
See Passu (p242).

THE TREK
Day 1: Passu to Avdegar
5–7 hours, 6.7km, 1340m ascent

From Passu (2400m), walk south along the KKH 10 minutes past the Shisper View Hotel to the first hairpin bend. On the east (river) side of the KKH is the unsealed road to the small village of Yashbandan (the place for keeping horses), where the Mir of Hunza used to keep horses. The trailhead is 20m farther south.

Follow the trail that descends east from the KKH into a small valley, skirting the stone walls around Yashbandan's fields, and continue up the other side of the valley. Looking back and to the right, is 'Welcome to Passu' in white letters on the hillside above the KKH. The well-used trail dips through rocky gullies as it heads south and east towards the Hunza River. In the second small gully, a boulder just east of the trail has ibex graffiti. The high-water trail, used from June to August, stays on the hillside above the river. In April, May, September and October, the low-water trail descends to cross the gravelly flood plain in a more direct line to the footbridge. The high-water trail takes 30 minutes from the KKH to the footbridge, while the low water trail takes 20 minutes.

Villagers call the **footbridge** *dūt*. It takes 10 minutes and more than 400 careful steps on narrow boards spaced 75cm apart to cross this suspension footbridge. This

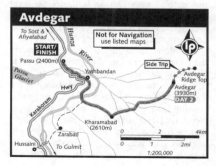

GOJAL

JOHN MOCK

Footbridge over Hunza River below Passu, leading to Kharambad & Avdegar.

would be difficult, and may not be possible, for anyone who experiences vertigo. In high winds, the footbridge tilts radically and is impossible to cross. Winds can arise anytime and are especially common in the afternoon and in spring.

Across the footbridge where the trail emerges onto the plain, it forks; the left-hand trail goes north-east to Kharamabad, and the right-hand trail goes south-east to Zarabad (see Two Bridges under Other Treks, p296). To go to Avdegar, bear north-east and follow the path 2km and one hour to pleasant **Kharamabad** (2610m), where Passu villagers produce several fodder crops during summer and pasture sheep and goats during winter.

Go along the paths between houses on the west (lower) edge of the cultivated area. From the farthest small stone house, continue over the open barren area, heading for the vegetation that lines an abandoned canal coming from the base of the Avdegar slope. No actual trail exists, but the open land makes for easy walking. If you stray too high in Kharamabad, you have to bushwhack through thorny scrub. Follow the

abandoned canal to its end in the stream bed at the base of the slope (2670m), 1.5km and one to 1½ hours from Kharamabad.

The old trail to Avdegar started from the upper end of the stream bed, where a small waterfall has worn a groove in the rock face and a willow tree stands. This trail was wiped out by rock fall in 1997, and now is a 20m-high Class 3 rock chute. Villagers use (and trekkers should too) a trail that starts several hundred metres farther west of (down from) the stream bed. The stream has year-round water, although you may have to walk up beyond the start of the correct trail to find water. Water above is scarce.

This trail begins opposite the end of the abandoned canal. Ascend the dry, rocky, steep slope for one hour, climbing 300m to 400m over 1km as the trail works gradually east, to rejoin the abandoned trail at the top of the steepest section, just below the start of scattered juniper trees (3360m). Continue up steeply through scattered junipers, as the view of the peaks above Gulmit and Ghulkin grows more impressive.

Reach the more level pasture of *Avdegar* (3930m), marked by two cairns, in another 1½ hours, or three to five hours from Kharamabad. A small three-sided stone shelter lies a short way to the south, and level areas offer camp sites. Water comes from the stream in the gully to the south, which is hard to reach. In autumn, it can be dry.

The view is spectacular, with Shīshpar dominating the horizon, and stretches from Ultar's north side to Shīshpar and Passu peaks at the Passu Glacier's head, the tops of the Batura peaks behind Passu Sar, and the peaks at the Batura Glacier's head in the distance, including Pamiri Sar (7016m). Morning sun lights the glaciers and the peaks of the Batura Muztagh nicely.

Side Trip: Avdegar Ridge Top
4–6 hours, 170m ascent, 170m descent
Even more perspective can be gained by ascending to the notch in the ridge above Avdegar, where a rock finger points up. The name Avdegar derives from this prominent rock (in Wakhi, *videk* means 'the way'; *gar*, 'stone'). From the first large grassy area,

head north (left) and cross the first large scree slope into a grassy area. Then cross a smaller scree slope and ascend the grassy area beyond, switchbacking up the rock above the highest extent of grass. Passu yaks do this, which seems unlikely, but is true. The elevations on the ridge rise to 4100m. The views, however, from the pastures below are superb and most trekkers don't attempt the more rigorous climb to the ridge top. To visit the ridge top, it's another two stages: one up, one down.

Day 2: Avdegar to Passu
5–7 hours, 6.7km, 1340m descent
Return to Passu via the same route.

Patundas

Duration	3 days
Distance	21.8km
Standard	moderate, technical
Season	June–September
Start/Finish	Passu
Zone & Permit	open, no permit
Public Transport	yes

Summary The alpine ridge between the Passu and Batura glaciers called Patundas has sweeping mountain views in all directions, but there's a tricky glacier crossing en route.

Patundas, on the ridge between the Passu and Batura glaciers, is a summer pasture used by Ghulkin villagers with a cluster of huts and livestock pens. The views from Patundas are spectacular in all directions. The rapid elevation gain of 1700m makes previous acclimatisation necessary.

PLANNING
What to Bring
Mountaineering equipment necessary to travel in roped teams and cut steps in ice for safety is recommended; crampons are helpful (see Mountaineering Equipment, p61).

Maps
The area is depicted by the Deutschen Alpenverein (DAV) 1:100,000 topographic map *Hunza–Karakorum*. If you're using the Swiss Foundation for Alpine Research 1:250,000 orographical map *Karakoram (Sheet 1)*, however, note that Luzhdur is labelled as Lazhdar and Mulungeen as Mulung Hil. The trail marked on the Passu Glacier's north side between Passu and Luzhdur no longer exists, due to glacial changes. The route shown along the glacier's north margin between Yunz and Patundas is exposed, tricky and not recommended.

Guides & Porters
A guide who knows the current route across the glacier is necessary. Patundas is the property of Ghulkin villagers, who have exclusive portering rights. When staying in Passu, organise a guide or porters by sending a message a day in advance to Ghulkin with any Ghulkin driver, or ask the owner

Warning
The Passu Glacier, known for its scenic beauty, is also known as a dangerous glacier where every year trekkers die needlessly. Its continually changing icy surface creates a maze of unforgiving crevasses and slippery seracs. Trekkers who try to manoeuvre across the glacier on their own get lost and become injured or die after falling into crevasses. Such tragedies also bring trouble to the village. Authorities in Gilgit hold villagers responsible for the trekkers' sad fate, and pressure them to stop trekkers from going onto the glacier without a local companion. Villagers, faced with imposing this requirement on budget-conscious trekkers, find themselves in an awkward situation. Trekkers should keep their own safety as well as the villagers' situation in mind, and agree to hire a local person. Trying to hire someone solely for a glacier crossing isn't likely to save money, because the rate is likely to be the same as for the entire trek. This is your cheapest insurance policy. It benefits both you and the village, and promotes safe, responsible trekking. For trekkers who refuse to hire anyone and get into trouble, self-rescue is the only option. Nobody will come looking for you.

of the Al-Rahim Hotel along the KKH, just north of Gulmit, to have a guide and/or porters meet you at your hotel. You can also organise this from Borit Lake.

Stages

It's six stages total round trip from Passu or Borit Lake: (1) Passu Ghar; (2) Luzhdur; (3) Patundas; and (4–6) three stages to return via the same route.

GETTING TO/FROM THE TREK

See Passu (p242). Borit Lake (see Alternative Start B, p247) is 1km west of the KKH above Hussaini. Most people walk up the steep road. A jeep ride takes 10 minutes, and costs Rs 100. Alternatively, it's two hours' walk north from Ghulkin village across the Ghulkin Glacier.

THE TREK
Day 1: Passu to Passu Ghar

3–4 hours, 6.6km, 810m ascent

From Passu (2400m), walk along the KKH five minutes south of the Shisper View Hotel. The trail leaves the road 50m beyond where the canal on the KKH's south side goes underground and the vegetation ends, before the first hairpin curve in the road.

Leave the KKH and go up 5m to a good trail heading west. Ascend gradually along a spur, then follow telephone lines, zigzagging 20 to 30 minutes to a saddle. Hussaini and the KKH to the south are visible. The rock above the saddle has many pockets, which provide nesting sites for crows. Just to the west of the saddle is a boulder with ibex graffiti low on its west side. The trail to Passu Ghar turns west and curves behind (south-west) a ridge above the Passu Glacier. The trail joins an abandoned canal that curves back to the valley's edge. Ascend briefly to a **slate platform** (2730m) at the base of Borit Sar 45 minutes to one hour from the saddle. The slate platform overlooks Passu Lake at the Passu Glacier's snout and the trails north to Yunz Valley and south to Borit Lake.

Continue 30 minutes along the abandoned canal that traverses the cliff face above the Passu Glacier to a level ablation valley. From the ablation valley's west end, ascend steadily, climbing 240m in 30 minutes to a well-deserved rest point at the lateral moraine's edge, overlooking the incredibly broken white seracs of the Passu Glacier to the north. Descend slightly to meet another abandoned canal through an ablation valley. Thirty years ago, the Passu Glacier extended farther downvalley and had a higher level. Then, streams flowed in these now-dry ablation valleys, which enabled people to irrigate the now-arid land between Passu, Hussaini and Borit Lake.

At the ablation valley's west end is a level area with room for several tents. At the base of the slope is a small water source that is often cloudy with glacial silt. A better camp site with five or six small, level tent sites amid junipers is above on the east-facing hillside. Where junipers first appear along the abandoned canal, take a well-worn path up five to 10 minutes to a clear, small, year-round stream. A good pit toilet, with a high stone wall for privacy, is on the stream's opposite (east) side. This camp site, and the larger one below, are called *Passu Ghar* (3210m).

It's feasible to visit Passu Ghar on a day trek from Passu village, but better views are obtained on the Borit Sar and Two Bridges day treks (see Other Treks, p296).

Alternative Start A: Passu to Passu Ghar

3–4 hours, 6km, 810m ascent

Villagers use an alternative, steeper, cross-country route between Passu village and the slate platform at the base of Borit Sar (see Day 1). Consider this route only when accompanied by someone from Passu who knows the way. From Passu, leave the KKH at the south side of the bridge over the Passu Glacier's outwash stream. Turn west (right) up its true right bank towards a small hotel (perpetually under construction) overlooking the river and KKH. Continue through scrub and thorny brush, cross a low stone wall and continue through open waste land, heading towards the largest medial moraine. Ascend this moraine heap and follow along the crest until it's possible to traverse to the ablation valley between the moraine ridge and the cliffs to the south. Walk up the ablation valley to its end and climb easy Class 2 shale to the abandoned canal just west of the slate platform. Going quickly, it takes one hour to reach this point. Continue to Passu Ghar as described in Day 1.

Alternative Start B: Borit Lake to Passu Ghar
3–4 hours, 6km, 600m ascent
From picturesque Borit Lake (2610m; in Burushaski, *bor* means 'salty earth'), a wetlands stopping station for migratory waterfowl, a trail ascends north towards the ridge above the Passu Glacier and joins the abandoned canal (see Day 1) before the slate platform at the base of Borit Sar. It takes one hour from Borit Lake to this point. Continue to Passu Ghar as described in Day 1.

Borith Lake Hotel & Restaurant, run by the cheerful Tawakal Khan, overlooks Borith Lake's south-east shore. The dorms costs

Rs 60, and doubles/triples cost Rs 160/200. The electricity is dubious, so despite the geysers in the rooms there is no guarantee of hot running water. The camping fee for a site on a grassy area in the peaceful flower garden is Rs 30–40.

Day 2: Passu Ghar to Patundas
3–6 hours, 4.3km, 890m ascent
Ascend through junipers 15 minutes to the four huts and livestock pen, and continue five minutes to the top of the lateral moraine of the heavily broken Passu Glacier. The route across the Passu Glacier changes from year to year as the glacier shifts. Its substantial marginal crevasses are difficult and dangerous, and its seracs are beautiful, but deadly. Fix a rope along narrow ice ramps above these crevasses. Cut steps on the steep, slippery ice, or wear crampons. This dangerous section eases after the first 100m. Go directly out to the glacier's centre, then turn west and head up the middle. When

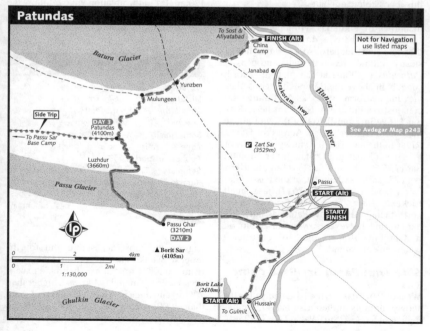

opposite the light-coloured cliffs on the glacier's north margin, turn north and head for the cliffs. It takes from one to 2½ hours to cross the glacier, moving steadily.

Luzhdur (3660m), with its five huts and livestock pen, is in the ablation valley at the base of the light-coloured cliffs on the glacier's north side, five minutes up from the ice's edge. Luzhdur has water early in the season, but by late August, carry water from the glacier. Beyond Luzhdur, water is scarce, so carry all the water you need.

Zigzag steeply up a clear trail. Pause at the several rest benches to admire the view. Reach the first ridge 250m above Luzhdur, overlooking the Passu Glacier, in 30 to 45 minutes. Continue up switchbacks another 150m amid large, ancient juniper trees, with several more rest benches along the trail. After 30 to 45 minutes reach the tumbledown walls of an old hut called **Luzhdur Sar**, where the angle lessens. From April to early June, water from snow melt makes this a possible camp site.

Work westward through the rolling alpine meadows of Patundas. Himalayan snowcocks abound here as do the more elusive ibex and snow leopard. After 30 minutes of steady walking, reach the huts and pens at *Patundas* (4100m) at the plateau's north edge, high above the Batura Glacier. A slate viewing platform overlooks the Batura Glacier just behind the huts. From here, Kuk Sar I (6943m) and II (6925m) tower above the Batura Glacier's head. Across the Hunza River to the east rise the snowy summits of the Hispar Muztagh; Destaghil Sar, Momhil Sar (7343m), Kanjut Sar (7760m), and Trivor (7728m). To the west, at the Passu Glacier's head, is Shīshpar (7611m). A small trickle of water comes out of the rock on the north-facing cliff below Patundas huts. It's hard to find, however, so you can't count on it. Ghulkin villagers plan to construct a water tank at Patundas.

Side Trip: Passu Sar Base Camp
2 days

West of Patundas are the base camps for the snowy summits of the Passu massif, including Passu Sar (7478m), Passu Dior (7295m),

Shīshpar and Ghenta. From Patundas, it's enjoyable to stroll through the alpine meadows along the ridge on a day trek with no fixed destination or to spend a night at base camp. To reach Passu Sar Base Camp, follow the ridge line until it becomes necessary to angle south-west (left) and down towards the upper Passu Glacier. Camp here and get water from the nearby glacier.

Day 3: Patundas to Passu
3–5 hours, 10.9km, 1700m descent
Return to Passu via the same route with the descent to **Luzhdur** taking half the time of the ascent.

Alternative Finish: Patundas to China Camp
4–5 hours, 8.7km, 1670m descent
An alternative return route descends from Patundas to **Mulungeen** on the Batura Glacier's south margin. Start just west (left) of the view point, and descend precipitously 1200m. From the ablation valley, follow the main trail back to China Camp (see Alternative Day 6 of the Batura Glacier trek, p254).

Batura Glacier

Duration	5 days
Distance	64.6km
Standard	moderate
Season	June–October
Start/Finish	China Camp
Zone & Permit	open, no permit
Public Transport	yes

Summary The classic trek along a giant Karakoram glacier passes beneath the peaks of the imposing Batura Wall and Batura Ice Floes with some of the Karakoram's best mountain scenery.

Batura, the most accessible and fourth-longest Karakoram glacier, stretches west from the KKH for 56km. The trek's exceptional scenery includes 14 peaks higher than 7000m and huge ice floes plummeting more than 4000m from the Batura Wall to the glacier. Most of the trek is through ablation valleys and along streams. With almost no steep segments, it affords gradual acclimatisation and presents no major difficulties. Even the trek's two glacier crossings are relatively easy. Trekkers also get a glimpse into the unique way of life of Passu villagers, who tend livestock in the summer pastures along the glacier's north margin.

The alternative route along the glacier's south margin and glacier crossing (see Alternative Days 4–5) presents a more shaded and cooler alternative to trekking along its sunny north margin on hot July and August days. Trekkers with less time or those disinclined to undertake any glacier crossings can simply trek along the south margin to Maidūn and return by the same route. This makes a pleasant three- to four-day trek, but doesn't give any views of the Batura Wall or ice floes.

PLANNING
What to Bring
Wakhi people are generous and traditionally share food with visitors, but it's unrealistic to expect food from people in pasture settlements. The herders' huts are private property and aren't available for trekkers' use. Respect the people and their property; bring your own food and shelter.

Maps
The Swiss Foundation for Alpine Research 1:250,000 orographical map *Karakoram (Sheet 1)* and Deutschen Alpenverein (DAV) 1:100,000 topographic map *Hunza–Karakorum* cover the trek. Other maps feature the Batura Glacier and surrounding peaks. In 1978, the Institute of Glaciology, Cryopedology & Desert Research, Academia Sinica, Lanchow, China published a 1:60,000 topographic *The Map of the Batura Glacier* (US$27), but it can be hard to find. Jerzy Wala published two orographical sketch maps (US$14) with text in English and Polish: the 1:100,000 *Batura Wall* in 1984; and the 1:125,000 *Batura Mustagh* in 1988.

Uzhokpirt, which isn't marked on the Swiss map, is beneath the peak labelled Shanoz (3922m). The Werthum stream,

which is labelled Wartom Nala, isn't depicted accurately. The map shows it flowing directly into (ie, perpendicular to) the Batura Glacier at Shilmin, but it turns south-east from the side valley and parallels the glacier for 7.5km before flowing into it between Kukhil and Fatima'il Sheet. The Yukshgoz Glacier is labelled as Yoksugoz Ice Flow, and Shireen Maidan Glacier is labelled as Shelin Maidan. The DAV map does not show Werthum Nala, labels Uzhokpirt as Verzokpirt, and indicates a lake east of Yashpirt that doesn't exist.

Guides & Porters
Trekkers often get lost trying to cross the glacier, so hiring someone is recommended. Additionally, government authorities insist that all trekkers going onto the glacier be accompanied by someone from Passu. Typically, porters are hired for the duration of a trek and aren't released along the way. Porters may expect large trekking parties to buy a goat or sheep.

Stages
It's nine stages total round trip from Passu: (1) Yunzben; (2) Uzhokpirt; (3) Yashpirt; (4) Kukhil; (4½) Guchesham; and (4½–9) 4½ stages to return via the same route. The traditional first stage began, literally, in Passu village. (This was before the KKH was built.) Today, it's understood to mean starting from China Camp or Janabad to Yunzben. Unfortunately, this makes for a short stage, much to porters' advantage. When you camp at Lupdur, it's half a stage beyond Guchesham; it's one stage between Kukhil and Lupdur. Despite the fact that most trekkers only camp at Guchesham, porters often ask for five stages one way from Passu instead of 4½ stages, much to their advantage. Additionally, porters may ask for an extra stage when crossing the glacier anywhere other than between Yunzben and Uzhokpirt. Negotiate the exact stages before starting.

GETTING TO/FROM THE TREK
From Passu (2400m) a tractor or jeep to China Camp (2430m), named for the Chinese road labourers who stayed here while

building the KKH, costs Rs 100. It's 15 minutes' drive north on the KKH to China Camp, a green area on the KKH's west side south of the bridge over the Batura Glacier's outwash stream.

Starting from the Janabad trailhead (2430m) is 1.3km longer than from the China Camp trailhead, but you can easily walk there from all hotels and don't have to pay for transport.

THE TREK

The trek description below crosses the glacier between Yunzben and Uzhokpirt. Two longer and more difficult glacier crossings are between Piyakh Sheet and Maidūn (see Alternative Day 5), and between Kush Bel and Kirgus Washk.

Day 1: China Camp to Uzhokpirt
5–6 hours, 11.5 km, 645m ascent

Follow the canal upstream 10 minutes to its head along the true right bank of the Batura Glacier's outwash stream. The trail ascends along the lateral moraine, passing a cairn that marks the junction with the trail from Janabad, and in 45 minutes to one hour reaches a high point. Continue through a

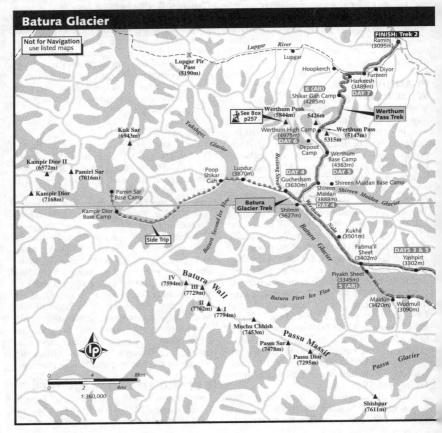

Batura Glacier

Not for Navigation
use listed maps

FINISH: Trek 2
Raminj (3095m)

Lupgar River

Lupgar Pir Pass (5190m)

Lupgar

Hoopkerch

Diyor
Furzeen
Harkeesh (3489m)
DAY 7

6 (Alt)
Shikar Gah Camp (4285m)
Werthum Peak (5844m)

See Box p257

5426m

Werthum Pass Trek

Kuk Sar (6943m)

Werthum High Camp (4975m)
DAY 6

Werthum Pass (5147m)

5315m

Yakshgoz Glacier

Deposit Camp

Werthum Base Camp (4363m)
DAY 5

Kampir Dior II (6572m)

Pamiri Sar (7016m)

Poop Shikar Gah

Lupdur (3870m)

Guchesham (3630m)
DAY 4

Shireen Maidan Base Camp

Kampir Dior (7168m)

Pamiri Sar Base Camp

Shireen Maidan (3888m)
DAY 4

Shireen Maidan Glacier

Bosidong Stream

Kampir Dior Base Camp

Batura Second Ice Floe

Batura Glacier Trek

Shilmin (3627m)

Werthum Nala

Batura Glacier

Side Trip

Kukhil (3501m)

Fatima'il Sheet (3402m)

DAYS 3 & 5

Yashpirt (3302m)

Piyakh Sheet (3345m)
5 (Alt)

Batura Wall
IV (7594m)
III (7729m)

II (7762m)   I (7794m)

Batura First Ice Floe

Maidūn (3420m)

Wudmull (3090m)

Muchu Chhish (7453m)

Passu Massif

Passu Sar (7478m)

Passu Dior (7295m)

Passu Glacier

0   4   8km
0   2   4mi
1:360,000

Shishpar (7611m)

dusty ablation valley 20 minutes, then pass through a wooden doorway past scattered rose bushes to reach *Yunzben* (2880m, at the base of Yunz Valley) in 10 minutes. The hut here is called Summer House in memory of the late Summer Beg, the father of Passu guides Sanjar Beg and Safdar Hussain. Yunzben is a large level camp site in a starkly dry and dusty area. Water comes from moraine pools.

The shortest and most frequently used route across the Batura Glacier, preferred by Passu people both going to and coming from the pastures, begins a few minutes beyond

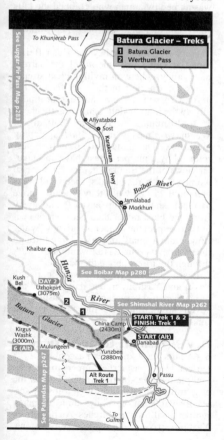

Yunzben. Bits of dung and small cairns faintly mark the convoluted 2km route across the glacier (much of it talus), which takes one to 1½ hours. Aim for the yellow rock face on the glacier's far side with a prominent white streak on its east (right) edge separating it from a black rock face.

Near the glacier's north margin, beneath the yellow rock face, turn north-west and continue up the unshaded narrow lateral moraine 1½ to two hours to another wooden doorway across the trail. As the first juniper appears, continue 30 to 45 minutes to a sizable silty lake. Follow the trail along its north shore and a few minutes beyond its west shore to *Uzhokpirt* (3075m), named for a triangular-shaped millstone *(uzhok)* once used here. The hut here was built in memory of Ali Dad, son of Passu guide Hunar Beg, who died in 1999. Mature willows and junipers offer ample shade, welcoming trekkers to pitch their tents and relax. A stream provides water, but by August it's dry and water comes from the lake.

Alternative Start: Janabad to Uzhokpirt
5–6 hours, 13.1km, 645m ascent
The Janabad trailhead is on the KKH's west side, where an old rectangular sign (between a large hotel under construction at the time of research and Passu Tourist Lodge) reads 'AKRSP Passu Orchard – Funded by SWAP'. Trekkers staying at the Passu Tourist Lodge can shorten this day's trek by 1.3km (making it 11.8km) by simply walking out the back of the property, up the hill and 10 minutes across the upper Janabad plateau to join this alternative trail at the base of the scree slope.

From the sign at the KKH, take the obvious trail past some ruined buildings 15 minutes to the base of a scree slope. Above the slope in white-painted rocks are the words 'Long Live Pakistan'. Ascend a stable trail 15 minutes to the top of the scree slope. The trail crosses a large, level, boulder-dotted plateau between Janabad and the Batura Glacier. Continue 20 minutes past numerous small livestock shelters adjacent to boulders. Head up past a rocky outcrop, then contour

GOJAL

10 minutes across a slope to a cairn-marked junction. Take the left fork up to the top of the lateral moraine, also marked by a cairn, offering the first views of the Batura Glacier. Descend a few minutes to meet the main trail between China Camp and Yunzben. Turn left and continue an hour to Yunzben.

Küch: The Annual Livestock Migration

All Wakhi villages depend upon livestock. To maintain their sheep, goats and yaks, villagers move their herds to distant upland pastures as the summer progresses and return to their villages in late autumn. The migratory unit of livestock tended by village women and children is referred to as the *küch*. Küch is a Persian word meaning 'migration,' and *küchi* are people who do this work. Although most villages have only a single küch, Shimshal village (see p260) has several that got to different pastures.

Women milk the livestock morning and evening in large stone-walled pens near their huts. During the day, when young women and children take the livestock out to graze, the older women are busy in their huts turning milk into yogurt, butter and cheese, much of which is stored to eat during winter. This division of labour contrasts with that of Hunza where tending livestock and making butter is men's work. Although all Wakhi visit the summer pastures, men recognise it as the women's zone. These flower-filled grasslands with sparkling streams beneath snowy mountains are more than just a pleasant place for the Wakhi. They're places of renewal and contentment, perhaps the main source of their well-being.

The return of the küch to the village in mid-October is a time of reunion and celebration in all Wakhi villages. After the return of the küch to the village, livestock are then tended by *shpūn*, a small group of men who take the livestock to low-elevation winter pastures. In mid-May, the shpūn turn the livestock back over to the community and the annual cycle begins again.

See Day 1 (p250) for the description between Yunzben and Uzhokpirt.

Day 2: Uzhokpirt to Yashpirt
2–3 hours, 5.1km, 227m ascent
The easy trail between Uzhokpirt and Yashpirt meanders through pretty ablation valleys, amid substantial willows, wild roses, tamarisks and junipers. The first impressive views of the upper Batura Glacier and Batura First Ice Floe are 45 minutes beyond Uzhokpirt at **Kush Bel**. (Kush Bel is also an alternative place to cross the glacier to Kirgus Washk on its south margin.) The place was named by a man who grabbed the tails of two oxen (*bel* in Urdu) in order to ford a water channel that was once here (and is now dry).

Forty-five minutes beyond Kush Bel is **Yinj Gar Dur Gush** (mouth of the narrow rock valley) where an inviting clear stream flows from a cleft in the rock face to the north. Cross the stream and contour gradually up the juniper-dotted hill directly ahead 15 to 30 minutes to *Yashpirt* (3302m). In Wakhi, *yash* means 'horse'; *pirt*, a 'sloping meadow'. The huts and pastures, surrounded by a juniper forest, have spectacular views of the Batura First Ice Floe. Passu women tend herds of yaks, sheep and goats here until 25 July when they typically move to Guchesham. Camp east of, and away from, the huts, rather than between or near huts, to respect the residents' privacy. Water flows from a small stream trickling through the pasture; its source is a few minutes' walk through the forest above the pasture.

Passu people typically walk between Passu and Yashpirt in one day. Fit and acclimatised trekkers can reach Yashpirt in seven hours, but it's too far for most trekkers to tackle in a day.

Day 3: Yashpirt to Guchesham
5–6 hours, 15.7 km, 328m ascent
Descend west past large junipers to the alluvial plain in the ablation valley. Follow the easy trail north-west, through a lovely series of small ablation valleys, amid abundant junipers, willows and birches. An hour from Yashpirt, pass an old distinctive millstone,

which was used until the late 1970s when barley was cultivated at Yashpirt and the primary summer pasture was Fatima'il Sheet. Occasional willows line the trail along a meandering stream. In 15 minutes, reach **Piyakh Sheet** (3345m) where a strange stand of *turugokh*, a kind of poplar, grows. The terrain opens onto a broad alluvial fan called **Fatima'il Sheet** (3402m). A side stream, Fatima'il stream, flows across the fan as the trail continues north-west with the Batura First Ice Floe in full view. The picturesque, yet largely unused Fatima'il huts are at the plain's west end, nestled against an Eolian fluted cliff, 30 minutes from Piyakh Sheet.

Continue up the ablation valley, passing through a wooden doorway, and reach the confluence of the good-sized Werthum Nala and the Batura Glacier 30 minutes from the Fatima'il huts. Werthum Nala, the stream draining the Werthum Valley, parallels the Batura Glacier for 7.5km before disappearing dramatically under the Batura Glacier here. Ford the stream just above the confluence and continue along its true right (south) bank one hour to **Kukhil** (springside sheep pen) where a wooden footbridge leads to the hillside huts and livestock pens. Camp sites at Kukhil (3501m) are small and dusty. The best camp site is a gravelly spot along the stream's true right (south) bank 100m below Kukhil.

From Kukhil, go along the true right (south) bank 1½ to two hours to another large alluvial fan called **Shilmin** (3627m), named after an abundant purple flower (*shilm*). It's possible to camp in a level and slightly rocky area below (south of) the trail and above seasonal pools adequate for bathing. Werthum Nala leaves the Batura Glacier at Shilmin, making a 90-degree bend north-east. Cross the alluvial fan and descend to a ford of the Bostong stream. Climb onto a level terrace and, 30 minutes from Shilmin, reach **Guchesham** (*gul* means 'flower' in Persian; *chesham*, an 'eye' in Wakhi), with its 10 huts and livestock pen. A camp site is directly across the Bostong stream from Guchesham (3630m) on a flat plain at the base of a white scree slope, from where a spring emerges. The views of the Batura Wall from the moraine south of Guchesham are spectacular. In the distance to the east is Destaghil Sar.

Side Trip: Lupdur
6 hours, 5km, 240m ascent
The day trek to Lupdur (big meadow) offers great views of the Batura Second Ice Floe, the upper Batura Glacier and Kampir Dior (7168m). From Guchesham, stay along the Bostong stream's true right (south) bank and go upvalley 30 minutes towards the obvious trail up the grassy slope. The trail eases after the first steep 100m. Follow the trail for one hour to **Lupdur** (3870m). Ibex and Himalayan snowcocks frequent these slopes. The views from here are worth the whole trek. Lupdur is bisected by a large ravine with a small pool at its bottom. Cross this ravine, continue through more pastures for better views of the Batura Second Ice Floe, and a view up the Yukshgoz (ibex grass) Glacier.

Side Trip: Kampir Dior & Pamiri Sar Base Camps
2–3 days
From Lupdur, cross to the Yukshgoz Glacier's west side to another meadow called **Poop Shikar Gah** (grandfather's hunting grounds). A guide is necessary to show the route across the glacier. Another day beyond are Kampir Dior and Pamiri Sar Base Camps. Alternatively, it's possible to climb the peak above Poop Shikar Gah, marked as peak 5735m on the Swiss map, which is the

The Upper Batura Glacier, as seen from Lupdur pastures.

culmination of a long ridge running east from Kuk Sar.

Days 4–5: Guchesham to China Camp

2 days, 32.3km, 1200m descent

Retrace steps to China Camp, camping at Yashpirt or Uzhokpirt on Day 4.

Alternative Route: Guchesham to China Camp

Rather than returning on the same trail along the glacier's north margin, it's possible to cross the Batura Glacier higher up and return along its south margin.

Alternative Day 4: Guchesham to Piyakh Sheet

4–5 hours, 12.4km, 285m descent

Retrace your steps to **Piyakh Sheet**. Camp here and get water from the Fatima'il stream or, if it's too silty, from the glacier. It's necessary to spend the night at Piyakh Sheet from where the glacier crossing begins, because it's too far to trek from Guchesham to Piyakh Sheet and cross the glacier in one day.

Alternative Day 5: Piyakh Sheet to Kirgus Washk

4–5 hours, 8km, 75m ascent, 420m descent

Turn south and cross moraine rubble five minutes, then descend the lateral moraine to reach the Batura Glacier in a few minutes. Crossing the glacier here isn't easy. Toil up and down on steep moraine 45 minutes to one hour. Then reach white ice and go up and down and around crevasses 30 to 45 minutes, after which again come heaps of moraine that take another 30 to 45 minutes to navigate. Most of the rock is very loose and unstable. No trail exists, so a local guide is essential. After two to three hours on the glacier, emerge on its south margin at the five huts at **Maidūn** (3420m), the highest pasture used by Hussaini villagers. Rising south of Maidūn in is the prominent peak marked 6090m on the Swiss map.

Follow a trail down the ablation valley 10 minutes to a small stream on an alluvial fan.

Twenty minutes beyond this, reach the two huts and livestock pen of **Wudmull** (3090m). Below Wudmull, leave the ablation valley and walk on a juniper-forested terrace well above the ablation valley. The trail grows faint as it crosses a rocky fan, which it ascends to avoid cliffs. Thirty to 45 minutes from Wudmull, a deep, narrow ravine slices through this terrace, just beyond the end of the nice juniper forest. Cross the ravine, which can be difficult in the summer when it holds a rushing stream, and descend five minutes to cross a small flat area at the base of a juniper-forested cliff. Descend gradually to a large alluvial fan covered by some snow pack, and cross it in 15 minutes. On its east side is a small stream beyond which is **Kirgus Washk** (in Wakhi, *kirgus* is a 'Himalayan griffon'; *washk*, a 'broken stone wall'), with two huts and a livestock pen. Just before Kirgus Washk, near a small hillside and close to the stream, is a good flat, grassy *camp site* (3000m).

Alternative Day 6: Kirgus Washk to China Camp

5–7 hours, 13km, 570m descent

The trail goes along the top of the southern and lower of two parallel moraines. Some 30 minutes below Kirgus Washk are two small blue lakes, suitable for a dip. Skirt the hillside beyond these lakes, staying high above the ablation valley, passing through nice stands of juniper and wild rose. Below Kirgus Washk 1½ hours is a very large, light-coloured boulder with a cairn on top and a livestock pen underneath. This area, with its mixed grass and scree slopes, is called Landgarben (the base of the big rock). Thirty minutes below the boulder is a dry lake bed, and 15 minutes beyond that are the four huts and livestock pen at **Mulungeen**, where a steep trail from Patundas meets this trail. Just below Mulungeen are two helipads, built by the Pakistan Army. The trail bends slightly north-east as it descends the ablation valley, reaching **Yunzben** 45 minutes to one hour from Mulungeen. See Day 1 (p250) for the description between Yunzben and China Camp or Alternative Start (p251) for the description between Yunzben and Janabad.

Werthum Pass

Duration	7 days
Distance	52.4km
Standard	very demanding, technical
Season	mid-June–September
Start	China Camp
Finish	Raminj
Zone & Permit	open, no permit
Public Transport	yes

Summary Werthum Pass offers a rugged mountaineers' route between the Batura Glacier and Chapursan's Lupgar Valley through un-visited areas with scope for climbing and watch-ing wildlife.

Werthum ('millstone' in Wakhi) is an in-frequently crossed nonglaciated pass (5147m) linking the Batura Glacier to Cha-pursan's Lupgar Valley to its north. The pass offers an alternative exit from the upper Batura Glacier, especially attractive for those climbing in the Werthum Valley. This rugged side valley north of the Batura Glacier has some easy nontechnical snowy peaks, and several technical peaks ranging from 5400m to 5900m at the valley's head and along the Shireen Maidan (sweet field) Glacier. The views from the pass include the six Batura peaks and Shīshpar. Crossing Werthum Pass isn't technically difficult, but requires basic mountaineering skills.

PLANNING
What to Bring

A rope, ice axe and mountaineering equip-ment necessary to cut steps in the ice cornice on the north side of the pass are required (see Mountaineering Equipment, p61). Crampons aren't necessary when crossing from south to north, but are when crossing from north to south. When trekking with porters bring a tarp or tent for their use be-cause no huts exist for the two nights be-tween Kukhil and Harkeesh.

Maps

Refer to Maps under the Batura Glacier trek (p249). The Swiss map incorrectly marks the trail between Shireen Maidan and Werthum

Base Camp (unmarked), and misrepresents the confluence of the streams that form Werthum Nala. The actual trail is on the opposite side of the river from where the trail is drawn on the map; the map has it backwards. Unsuspecting trekkers have dangled on nasty scree slopes and cliffs try-ing to follow the trail depicted on the map. Werthum Pass isn't marked and the glacier on its north side is much smaller than the map shows. Harkeesh isn't marked either. It's on the south side of the Lupgar River along the first side stream west (left) of the place name Purzin.

Guides & Porters

Hiring a local guide and porters is unavoid-able. Only four Passu men – Qamar Jan, Sanjar Beg, Ali Aman and Safdar Hussain – know the route over the Werthum Pass, although more will learn the route after the authors' crossing and opening of this route in July 2000.

When crossing from north to south, hire men from Raminj or Khaibar. Ghulam Sar-war from Khaibar and several men from Raminj also know the route. It may, how-ever, be difficult to find any porters willing to do it, because of the steepness and diffi-culty from this direction.

Stages

Passu porters ask for 11 stages total be-tween Passu and Raminj, although it's only 10 stages. Passu to Guchesham or Shilmin is 4½ stages total, but porters usually charge five stages for this distance (see the Batura Glacier trek, p248, for more details). They also ask for one stage between Shilmin or Guchesham and Shireen Maidan, which should be half a stage, thereby effectively inserting an additional stage, much to their benefit. The five stages beyond Shireen Maidan are: (1) Werthum Base Camp; (2) Werthum High Camp; (3) Shikar Gah; (4) Harkeesh; and (5) Raminj.

GETTING TO/FROM THE TREK
To the Start

See the Batura Glacier trek (p248) for a de-scription of how to reach China Camp.

GOJAL

From the Finish
See the Lupgar Pir Pass trek (p281) for a description of where to go from Raminj.

THE TREK (see map p250)
Days 1–2: China Camp to Yashpirt
2 days, 16.6km, 872m ascent
See Days 1–2 of the Batura Glacier trek (p250) for the description between China Camp and Yashpirt.

Day 3: Yashpirt to Shireen Maidan
6 hours, 16.9km, 586m ascent
See Day 3 of the Batura Glacier trek (p252) for a description of the 4½-hour walk between Yashpirt and Shilmin. From Shilmin, the trail up the Werthum Valley leaves the Batura Glacier's north margin bending 90 degrees and follows the Werthum Nala's true right (west) bank north-east. Massive scree slopes on both the valley's east and west walls guard its entrance. Stay close to the hillside (on the left) 15 minutes to the place where dwarf willows (chikor) grow. Begin a steady climb over scree on a faint trail. Early in the season, when snow is melting, be cautious for extreme rock-fall danger. After 30 minutes, the trail reaches the top of the scree and continues level for 15 minutes to Furzeen. The predominant birches (furz) and scrub junipers shade this attractive grove where a seasonal stream trickles. Ibex frequent the opposite rocky slopes as they migrate between the Batura Glacier and Khaibar Nala via the Shireen Maidan Glacier. The trail descends steeply a short distance to the river, and follows the river bed to the confluence of the Werthum Nala and the Shireen Maidan Glacier's outwash stream. Cross the Werthum Nala via two enormous adjacent boulders that bridge the torrent 300m upstream from the confluence, or ford the river when water is low. Along the true left bank at the confluence is a level camp site, sheltered from the wind, with six stone circles. A spring trickles near the river's edge. Shireen Maidan (3888m) is a preferable camp site to Shilmin, well worth the additional 1½ hours' walk. The

peaks above the glacier offer climbing possibilities (see the boxed text 'Peak Possibilities', p257).

Day 4: Shireen Maidan to Werthum Base Camp
3 hours, 3.8km, 475m ascent
Recross the river to the Werthum Nala's true right (west) bank and immediately ascend the steep scree slope on a yak trail to the grassy slopes above. Traversing high above the river gorge, the trail crosses three small ravines, the last two of which offer clear water. Before the second stream, 1½ hours from Shireen Maidan, a difficult section of trail rounds a yellowish rock face called Dzug Band (literally, 'difficult yak trail' in Wakhi). A few minutes farther ahead, a house-sized overhanging boulder offers shelter and marks the beginning of the huge area known as Werthum, which extends all thye way to the valley's head. Fifteen minutes past the third stream the going gets a little easier, and a cauliflower-like edible plant (yamush) and purple flower (bozlunj), whose dried petals can be used to make a tea that assists with acclimatisation, pop up between the shale, ephedra and patches of grass.

The trail descends to the river where it disappears among rocks and boulders along the river's true right bank. Stay close to the water's edge, hopping rocks and scampering across boulders 15 to 30 minutes. This section could be difficult in the afternoon when water levels are typically higher. The route then fords the Werthum Nala to its true left bank shortly beyond the confluence with a side stream. This is the outwash stream coming from the unnamed glacier to the east. Once across the river, a trail ascends the steep rhubarb-dotted scree slope five minutes to a cairn at the top.

A lone stone circle, which is used as a porters' shelter, marks **Werthum Base Camp** (4363m) in the middle of an exposed, broad grassy plateau above the confluence of the two unnamed streams that join to form Werthum Nala. The stream from the northwest issues from the glacier lying at the base of Werthum Peak, whose summit dominates the valley's head. The other is the outwash stream from the sizable unnamed glacier that descends from several 5000m peaks east of Werthum Base Camp. Water is accessible in a small ravine east of the stone shelter.

This is a relatively short day, but the 475m elevation gain is an argument for stopping. When previously acclimatised, it's possible to move up to Werthum High Camp. Otherwise, enjoy an afternoon spent strolling in the meadows. It is possible to climb Werthum Peak or one of the other peaks in the area (see the boxed text 'Peak Possibilities').

Day 5: Werthum Base Camp to Werthum High Camp

3–4 hours, 3.4km, 612m ascent

From Werthum Base Camp, it's advisable to set a high camp below the pass. Follow a faint yak trail for 1½ hours, staying very high above the true left bank of the Werthum Nala's north-west branch. The route traverses north-north-east over stable slate and talus heading towards the rounded peak (5426m on the Swiss map) whose dry slopes are capped by snow. Werthum Pass lies on the ridge that runs south-east between this peak and peak 5315m. The route to the pass is via the side valley immediately

Peak Possibilities

Werthum Valley is a climbing destination with many peaks accessible to trekkers with mountaineering experience. Here are a few options.

Peaks above Shireen Maidan Glacier
Accessible from Shireen Maidan (Day 3) A dozen jagged 5000m and 6000m summits encircle the Shireen Maidan Glacier, beckoning climbers to this picturesque side valley. Most climbs are along the glacier's north side and are mostly mixed ice and rock. These technical routes are more difficult than those accessed from Werthum Base Camp (Day 4). Beneath the Shireen Maidan Glacier's terminal moraine, 10 minutes east of the confluence camp site on Day 3, is an extremely clear and deep blue-green lake. The grassy area nearby is the base camp.

Werthum Peak
Accessible from Werthum Base Camp (Day 4) Werthum Peak (peak 5844m on the Swiss map), the valley's only named peak, is a technical peak north-west of Werthum Base Camp. The three-day climb involves an ascent/descent of 1481m each way. On the first day, move from Werthum Base Camp upvalley to the high camp called Deposit Camp, where porters 'deposit' climbers' loads. The route to Deposit Camp stays low along the true left bank of the Werthum Nala's north-west branch, and crosses

the stream descending from Werthum Pass. Continue past the confluence of outwash streams from two glaciers, the southernmost of which ends in an icefall from peak 5539m. Cross the northern glacier's outwash stream and move onto the black rocky moraine between the two glaciers. Deposit Camp is at the west edge of the northern glacier. On the second day, summit and return to Deposit Camp. Climb steeply to the ridge, staying far to the left (south), and then head right (north) to make the long traverse of the corniced north-south ridge to the summit. A rope, ice axe and crampons are essential, and anchors may be necessary depending on snow conditions. Return to Werthum Base Camp on the third day. It's a fairly serious route, not recommended for novices.

Unnamed Peaks around Werthum Base Camp
Accessible from Werthum Base Camp (Day 4) North and north-east of Werthum Base Camp are several unnamed, rounded snow-covered summits. These non-technical 'walk-ups' range from 5300m to 5500m, easily engaging most trekkers for a day or two. A rope and ice axe are necessary, but crampons are optional.

in front of peak 5426m. The last reliable clear water flows in the second side stream before the highest grassy patch where yaks sometimes graze.

Cross a dry gully 30 minutes beyond the grass, then head north another 30 minutes up a relentlessly steep rock- and scree-covered hillside. The angle steepens to 25 degrees towards the ridge top, which separates the main Werthum Valley from the barren, snow-filled upper basin beneath the pass. A stream flows through this upper basin and down a steep ravine to meet the Werthum Nala's north-west branch far below. Traverse scree 45 minutes to one hour to **Werthum High Camp** (4975m) on a level rocky terrace high above the true left bank of the stream descending from the pass. Water trickles from afternoon snow melt.

It's possible to break up the knee-pounding 1658m descent from Werthum Pass to Harkeesh by forgoing a high camp on the south side and crossing Werthum Pass in one long day. This also avoids sleeping at high altitude. The 6.9km between Werthum Base Camp and Shikar Gah Camp can be covered in 6½–8½ hours, with a 784m ascent and 862m descent. The following day, the 1190m descent to Raminj takes 5–5½ hours (8.2km; see Days 6–7 for a description).

Day 6: Werthum High Camp to Harkeesh
6–7 hours, 6.1km, 172m ascent, 1658m descent

Continue up the snow and scree slope to reach **Werthum Pass** (5147m) 45 minutes from the high camp. The pass has 20- to 25-degree slopes on both sides and a permanent 3m to 4m vertical cornice on its north side. Use a rope belay while breaking through the cornice and cutting steps in the ice to reach the talus below the pass. The pass is more difficult before mid-July when there's more snow and a larger cornice.

Descend the talus and scree slope, then cross a tiny bergschrund onto a small unnamed glacier. Cross the glacier in 15 minutes to moraine and a stream. Cross to its true left bank, and follow the stream down 30 minutes to a level area (4694m). It is

possible to make a high camp here when trekking from north to south.

Cross to the stream's true right bank where the valley begins to drop steeply. Reach the confluence with another stream coming from the south-west in 15 minutes. The route stays along the main stream's true right bank as the valley turns northward and narrows. When trekking from north to south, take caution to stay to the east (left), and follow the true right bank of the easternmost (left) stream.

The stream plunges steeply between two enormous reddish rock walls into the canyon-like area called **Shikar Gah** (4285m) 30 minutes below the confluence. (Some people also call this area Bayeen Shikar Gah, a hunting place named after Bayeen, a man from Chapursan.) The level stream bed here has some grass, flowers and rhubarb amid the curious conglomerate boulders that dot the valley floor. Fifteen minutes farther, at this area's north end, is an overhanging boulder with a level rocky area nearby that offers a reasonable lunch spot and possible camp site. Ibex droppings indicate these wild mountain goats roam the cliffs above.

Begin the steep descent of the boulder-choked gorge immediately below Shikar Gah on the stream's true right bank. The only way down the gorge is literally right at the water's edge. In very high water, the difficult route might be impassable. For the next 1½ to two hours it hugs the banks. You clamber over boulder after boulder and cross the torrent as needed. Steep scree slopes on both sides of the valley make this the only route.

Eventually you reach the highest pastures along the stream's true right bank, and pick up a faint, but obvious, livestock trail. The going becomes easier, and in 15 minutes the trail descends to cross a convenient boulder to the stream's true left bank. Pungent junipers dot the slope. From a ridge five minutes beyond the natural bridge, Harkeesh ('place of cultivation' in Burushaski), a level grassy area, is visible below. Descend the steep slope on a poor trail past junipers, wild roses and abundant birches 30 minutes to a log footbridge. Pause to marvel at the colourful sculpted rock cleft from which the stream emerges. Follow the path along a canal 15 minutes to *Harkeesh* (3489m). Water from the canal flows to Harkeesh in the afternoon, but can be dry by morning.

Day 7: Harkeesh to Raminj

2½–3 hours, 5.6km, 394m descent
See Day 6 of the Lupgar Pir Pass trek (p285) for a description between Harkeesh and Raminj (3095m).

Shimshal

Shimshal, Gojal's oldest Wakhi-speaking village, maintains many traditional customs. Shimshal's 1300 residents have Gojal's largest livestock herds and grazing rights to nearly 5000 sq km of territory, including the only part of Pakistan in Central Asia. The rolling grasslands of the Shimshal Pamir, on the watershed divide between South Asia and Central Asia, are their primary summer pastures. Ghuzherav and Lupgar are their main pastures.

Shimshal was closed to outsiders until 1986. Since then, increasing numbers of foreigners make the trek each year. Beyond the village lies Gojal's best trekking. When

JOHN MOCK

Author Kimberley O'Neil near Shimshal village.

Peak Prowess

Twenty men from Shimshal have summitted one or more of Pakistan's 8000m peaks, a feat unrivalled by any other village. In 1998, Rajab Shah at age 49 became the first Pakistani to summit all five of Pakistan's 8000m peaks, climbing Nanga Parbat in 1989, Gasherbrum I in 1990 and 1992, Broad Peak in 1994, K2 in 1995 and Gasherbrum II in 1998. Rajab's climbing partner Mehrban Shah summitted K2, Gasherbrums I and II, and Broad Peak. Mohammad Ullah climbed Nanga Parbat twice and Gasherbrum I once, Qudrat Ali reached the summits of Broad Peak, Gasherbrum II and Nanga Parbat, and Qurban Mohammad summited Gasherbrum II and Broad Peak. Fifteen other men have summitted one 8000m peak. In 2000 alone, eight Shimshalis reached an 8000m summit, and midway through the 2001 season, seven Shimshalis had stood on an 8000m peak! This is only the beginning of a legacy of remarkable climbing success for the young generation of Shimshali climbers.

you go to Shimshal and beyond, you travel with Shimshalis. These amazing men carry heavy loads all day long over trails that leave most trekkers exhausted. They're also the choice as high-altitude porters on most mountaineering expeditions.

Shimshal's vast area is home to snow leopards, brown bears and sizable herds of blue sheep and ibex. Although these mammals usually stay at inaccessible heights, Shimshal offers some of northern Pakistan's best wildlife-watching opportunities. Shimshal has banned hunting, although displays of ibex horns along trails testify to its previous popularity.

PLANNING
Guides & Porters

Shimshalis eager to work often wait in Passu and Gulmit. Passu porters have rights to work only as far as Shugardan, so it's essential to hire Shimshalis. For all Shimshal treks, porters ask for a flat rate of Rs 280 per stage, including payment for food rations.

They don't ask for the clothing and equipment allowance. It's not necessary to pay for rest days in Shimshal village when porters are at their own homes.

Beyond Shimshal village, yaks sometimes carry loads. These shaggy beasts can also be ridden. A yak carries two porters' loads. You pay a standard porter's wage for each yak. The yak's owner also comes along, and receives a standard porter's wage, even though the yak carries the load. This strategy saves money only if one person handles two or more yaks at a time.

NEAREST VILLAGES
See Passu & Janabad (p242).

Shimshal Village

Duration	5 days
Distance	62.8km
Standard	easy
Season	April–October
Start/Finish	Boi
Zone & Permit	open, no permit
Public Transport	no

Summary Walk through a spectacular river gorge, past impossibly huge scree slopes and the mighty Mulungutti Glacier flowing from Destaghil Sar, to reach Gojal's most remote and traditional Wakhi village.

Shimshal is the only village in Gojal not yet linked to the KKH by road. In 1985, Shimshalis began building their own road through the polished limestone gorge of the Shimshal River. Their effort garnered government support to build bridges and blast difficult sections through the gorge. As of summer 2000, the road reached Boi, 4km beyond Dūt – a little more than halfway between Passu and Shimshal. By 2001, the road should be open another 4.9km beyond Boi to Uween-e-Ben, leaving just 26.5km to reach Shimshal village. This last stretch could optimistically be done by 2002. Trekking to Shimshal village gets shorter and easier every year. But the trail and ever-lengthening road cross massive scree slopes

and raging torrents, and are prone to dangerous rock fall. Trekkers always need to be prepared to walk in and out of the village. Rainfall and strong late afternoon katabatic winds frequently start rock slides. Watch carefully for falling rock, and wait until it subsides before attempting to cross a slide.

Shimshal incorporates three separate settlements; Aminabad, Centre Shimshal, and Khizarabad. Occasionally Aminabad and Khizarabad are referred to by their former names, Shulalaksh and Chukurth Dasht respectively. The Adver stream, which separates Aminabad to the west from Centre Shimshal to the east, rushes down from snowy, unclimbed Adver Sar (6400m, marked on the Swiss map as Shimshal White Horn). Chukurth Dasht is the plateau above and east of Centre Shimshal. Chukurth-e-Dur is the glacially fed stream flowing into Chukurth Dasht, named for a triangular *(chuk)* millstone *(werth)*. Centre Shimshal has a Jamat Khana, an Aga Khan Diamond Jubilee Middle School for girls, a government boy's school and cultural museum. The dispenser for the Aga Khan Health Services, Farman Ullah, appreciates any donations of medicine or medical supplies, which are always scarce.

PLANNING
Maps
The Swiss Foundation for Alpine Research 1:250,000 orographical map *Karakoram (Sheet 1)* covers the trek. It doesn't show Jurjur, the road, jeep bridges or footbridges. Kuk and the trails leading to and from Kuk, bypassing the Mulungutti Glacier, aren't shown either.

Guides & Porters
It's fun to travel with a Shimshali who can provide essential help through the rugged terrain and welcome you to the village.

Stages
Traditionally, it's five stages one way to Shimshal village from Passu: (1) Jurjur; (2) Dūt; (3) Ziarat; (4) Kuk (or Mulungutti); and (5) Shimshal village. Pay only for stages over which loads are carried. As of 2000, the

road ends at Boi, between Dūt and Ziarat. Shimshalis don't accept payment for partial stages so, until the road is completed to Ziarat, you pay for a full stage even though you only walk a portion of a stage. This totals three stages one way, or six stages round trip, between Boi and Shimshal village.

GETTING TO/FROM THE TREK

The signed, unsealed Shimshal Link Rd turns off the KKH just south of the bridge over the Batura Glacier's outwash stream. From the suspension bridge over the Hunza River, the road contours low along the Shimshal River's true right bank beneath Tupopdan's spires and into the gorge where clear water is scarce. After 5km, it passes **Jurjur**, a deep cleft in the rock wall, and home to road workers, where a spring flows down the rock face just west of the actual cave-like camp.

Two kilometres beyond Jurjur the road passes Nagarmushk, an area with willows, roses, tamarisks and a clear stream, about 750m beyond which the road bridges a glacial stream. Ahead, the road crosses and re-crosses the Shimshal River to avoid Shugardan (*shu* means 'black'; *gardan*, the 'raised or high place'), one of the valley's many enormous scree slopes. A third bridge crosses to the river's true left bank just before **Dūt**. Beyond Dūt, the road rises between dark boulders over barren ground and descends to a bridge over the Momhil River at **Dikut**, and ends, at the time of research, at the base of cliffs called **Boi** high above the Shimshal River's true left bank. Passu-Boi special vehicles cost Rs 1000 and take 1½ hours. When leaving the village, send a message ahead to arrange a vehicle to meet you at the roadhead.

Walking on the road takes 2½ to three hours between Passu and Jurjur, another two hours to Dūt, and one to 1½ hours more to Boi. When walking from Passu, follow the KKH north 2km to Janabad and turn east (right) and follow the unsealed road across this cultivated plateau, then descend to and cross the suspension bridge over the Hunza River to join the link road. This is much shorter than walking on the KKH to the link road's start. It's 19km between this bridge and Boi.

THE TREK (see map p262)
Day 1: Boi to Kuk
5½–7 hours, 18.6km, 180m ascent, 190m descent

From Boi (2850m), the trail climbs galleries constructed across the cliff face and crosses several scree slopes, where it's only a faint line across the ever-shifting scree. This is how all trails throughout Hunza used to be. Reach **Uween-e-Sar**, marked by cairns, in 30 minutes.

From Uween-e-Sar, the trail levels out high above the river and crosses several scree slopes for one hour. Ascend a short series of steep, loose switchbacks to **Kampir Uween** (the highest place the old woman, or *kampir*, reached). Ahead lies an enormous and dangerous scree slope. Stop and look carefully for any rock fall before venturing onto the scree. Once on it, keep moving steadily. Descend in 45 minutes to **Uween-e-Ben** (2720m, 'the base of the high place'), the sandy wastes along the Shimshal River. At the river's edge, an intermittent spring flows from beneath rocks.

About 250m ahead, the trail crosses, and then in 2km recrosses, the river over footbridges to avoid the 1000m-high and 2km-long **Shams** slides on the river's true left bank. These constantly active scree slopes rain rock on the old left bank trail. Even before the footbridges were constructed in 1993, the previously existing cable crossings were preferable to the dangers of Shams.

Just beyond the second footbridge on the river's true left bank, the two huts at *Ziarat* (2760m) sit on a small terrace above the river bed. The huts are stocked with utensils and blankets, but beware sleeping inside, due to omnipresent bed bugs. If you or your porters use these communal huts, leave a donation in the wooden box inside for continued maintenance. You will also receive the blessing of the saint, Shams-e-Tabriz, whose grave site lies across the river, high on a narrow terrace, and is marked by a tiny white flag. Ziarat means 'saint's tomb'. The huts are technically the *langar*, or kitchen, for the actual shrine. The area for prayer lies behind the huts and is marked by numerous coloured flags. A few tents can be pitched near the huts, but larger parties camp below. A small spring, marked by cairns, is near the river's edge. A more reliable source of clear water is along the trail a few minutes' walk east of Ziarat. Many trekkers stay here, but it's worth camping at Kuk for the impressive perspective on the Mulungutti Glacier's terminus and the sunset and sunrise views of Destaghil Sar.

From Ziarat, the trail follows the river's edge beneath 10m-high cliffs. Fifteen minutes from Ziarat, a stream from a side glacier may present a broad, brown, knee-deep obstacle. Beyond this stream 50 minutes is a willow grove at the base of a talus slope. A stream here, although clear in the morning, is usually muddy in the afternoon. The area is called **Shikar Zhui**, or hunters' lake, but the lake where they once hunted ducks is now dry. Continue beyond this pleasant

shady spot 30 to 45 minutes to **Perk Zhirek**, a larger glacial tributary that usually must be forded. Its name means the place where a vole *(perk)* got stuck *(zhirek)*.

Follow the river bed one hour beneath riverine terraces carved by glacial outburst floods to the faint junction of the trail to Mulungutti (in Wakhi, *mulung* means 'middle'; *di*, a 'village'). The old route across the 22km-long Mulungutti Glacier has been largely abandoned in favour of a trail to Kuk that opened in 1994. The old trail forks right at the trail junction and ascends the loose, steep sandy slope to the western ablation valley of the Mulungutti Glacier where a small, clear stream flows near a hut. Beyond the hut, the old route descends onto the immense Mulungutti Glacier. The route across this glacier has no cairns and is tricky, so local assistance is recommended.

The substantially easier trail to Kuk forks left at the junction and continues along the Shimshal River's true left bank 15 minutes,

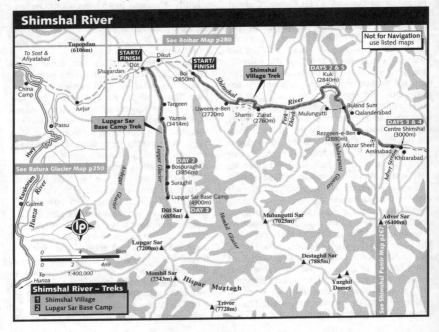

then crosses a footbridge to its true right bank. Cross a black rock outcrop, following cairns and in 30 minutes reach **Kuk** (2840m), a delightful oasis with a warm spring *(kuk)* amid tamarisks, roses, willows and some junipers just east of Kuk's two huts. Kuk is directly across the river from the advancing Mulungutti Glacier's terminus with dramatic views of the 7000m peaks at the glacier's head, including Destaghil Sar's unclimbed north face.

Day 2: Kuk to Shimshal Village

3½–4 hours, 12.8km, 160m ascent

The trail heads east and fords a side stream, sizable in full melt, and in 30 minutes passes a lone hut. Fifteen minutes beyond the hut, cross a footbridge to the Shimshal River's true left bank. Follow the trail along the river as it climbs steadily one hour to **Buland Sum** (the place high above) and the junction of the trail from the Class 1 powdery chute in the terrace wall called Kuth Dur and the Mulungutti Glacier. Qalanderabad, formerly called Tang-e-Gush Dasht, is a pocket of cultivated land across the river.

Descend to the river bed and the first cultivated area, **Rezgeen-e-Ben** (2880m) in 30 to 45 minutes. Rezgeen-e-Ben gets its name from *rezg*, a white clay used to plaster the fireplaces in Shimshali homes. It's a level, but long, 7.5km or 1½ to two hours' walk on a wide trail to the broad cultivated area of Shimshal. Forty-five minutes from Rezgeen-e-Ben is a small cold spring (which may be dry early in the season) just below the trail and east of **Mazar Sheet** (plain of tombs). Two tombs marked by white flags give this plain its name. Beyond the spring, the herb *spandr* is abundant. Forty-five minutes from the spring, ford the Adver stream. On rare occasions when the water is too high to ford, climb to Aminabad on the terraces above and cross the Adver stream via a footbridge and then descend to **Centre Shimshal** (3000m).

Day 3: Shimshal Village

A few families make their orchards and spare rooms available for trekkers and may offer to cook Shimshal-style meals in their homes. Clear water flows seasonally at springs below the cluster of original houses in Centre Shimshal, along the river's edge towards Centre Shimshal's east end, and west of Michael Bridge, a 15-minute walk east of the village. When staying for a few days, it's helpful to bring a 10L or 20L plastic container to haul water. Bathe and do laundry along the stream west of Michael Bridge. All treks beyond Shimshal village gain elevation quickly, and hence trekkers should spend at least one day in the village for acclimatisation.

Side Trip: Gar-e-Sar

6–8 hours, 16.3km, 500m ascent, 500m descent

Gar-e-Sar is a view point with superb vistas of the Yazghil Glacier, Adver Sar and hard-to-see 7000m peaks of the Hispar Muztagh. Although strenuous, it's by far the best day trek from Shimshal village with views superior to those seen from Yazben (see Yazghil Sar Base Camp under Other Treks, p297). See Day 1 of the Shimshal Pamir trek (p266) for a description.

Days 4–5: Shimshal Village to Boi

2 days, 31.4km, 190m ascent, 340m descent

Retrace your steps to Boi, camping at Kuk or Ziarat en route.

Ritual Rue

Peganum harmala (wild rue) is an aromatic, perennial herb. Known as *spandr* in Wakhi, its five-petalled white flowers bloom in late June. The seeds inside its berries are harvested from late September to early October. Once dried, Wakhi villagers burn the seeds as a purifying incense on ceremonial occasions. Burning spandr is a widespread Iranian folk custom that may go back to the ritual consumption of a hallucinogenic blend of rue and ephedra in the ancient Zoroastrian Haoma divination ceremony.

Lupgar Sar Base Camp

Duration	3 days
Distance	29km
Standard	moderate
Season	June–September
Start/Finish	Dūt
Zone & Permit	open, no permit
Public Transport	no

Summary Shimshal's oldest summer pastures with awesome views of 7000m peaks and large glaciers are just a short walk from the roadhead.

Lupgar (big rock) is an alpine pasture high on a sunny ridge above the Lupgar Glacier. The glacier descends from Lupgar Sar (7200m), and its subsequent surging dark stream joins the Shimshal River at Dūt. This wonderful valley is rarely visited by trekkers, but occasional mountaineers come to attempt Lupgar Sar.

Six Shimshali families tend livestock in Lupgar. They stay at Bospuraghil 1 June to 1 August, when they move to Suraghil where they stay until early October before returning to Shimshal village. This is the quickest trek into the world of Shimshal's alpine pastures, and offers big mountain views just one day from the KKH. The trail is steep, though, and not for the faint of heart.

PLANNING
Maps

The Swiss Foundation for Alpine Research 1:250,000 orographical map *Karakoram (Sheet 1)* covers the trek.

Stages

It's six stages total round trip from Dūt: (1) Targeen; (2) Bospuraghil; (3) Suraghil; and (4–6) three stages to return via the same route.

GETTING TO/FROM THE TREK

Passu-Dūt special hires cost Rs 700 (one hour). Beyond Dūt (2600m), the road winds 1km, or a few minutes' drive, to a level area between the Lupgar and Momhil Rivers. The trailhead is visible along the road before the bridge over the Momhil River. Clear

water can usually be found at Dūt in a small pool in the sand along the Lupgar River's true right bank below the easternmost hut.

THE TREK (see map p262)
Day 1: Dūt to Bospuraghil

4–5 hours, 9km, 1250m ascent

Ascend on a narrow, faint trail into the Lupgar Valley, along the Lupgar River's true right bank. The trail ascends to pass above a large erosion scar, then becomes extremely faint as it climbs a low-angle Class 1 slab to cross a prominent rock rib. Beyond the rib, reach a cairn. Snowy Dūt Sar is prominent up the Lupgar Valley. The meadows of Lupgar come into view as the river bends west (right). Traverse steadily upward as Lupgar Sar comes into view. Cross a broad black scree slope. Continue upward and clamber over and around another Class 2 rock rib, with significant exposure, on a faint, hard-to-follow, thin trail. Then ascend to pass above another large erosion gully, and emerge onto gentler artemisia slopes. Contour, then descend steeply almost to the riverside. Ascend, following the river's true right bank to a big boulder (3292m). Continue along and enter *Targeen*, an open area close to the river, with much tamarisk, a few tent platforms and stone-walled shelters. Continue along the river 15 minutes to the several stone-walled shelters (3414m) of **Yazmis** (glacier's snout), just below the Lupgar Glacier's black snout. Clear water is in large pools, emerging from the scree hillside. There is a good view of Qarūn Koh to the north.

Continue upvalley and soon pass the glacier's snout and follow the eastern ablation valley over moraine rubble on a faint trail. The hillside and the lateral moraine are close at times in this narrow ablation valley. Reach a cairn in 30 to 45 minutes. At the cairn, turn 90 degrees east and ascend the steep gully 15 minutes to the gentle artemisia-covered slopes above. Some juniper trees are scattered on the hillsides. Lupgar Sar's triple summit fills the view southward, with Dūt Sar to the east. Turn south and head through artemisia and grass, paralleling the glacier, to reach the huts at *Bospuraghil* (3856m; golden eagle pasture).

Bospuraghil has excellent views of Lupgar Sar and Qarūn Koh. Water is brought from the glacier.

Day 2: Bospuraghil to Lupgar Sar Base Camp

2½–3 hours, 5.5km, 1044m ascent
Continue up the herders' trail 1½ to two hours to **Suraghil** (cold pasture), Lupgar's highest settlement on the grassy ridge above Bospuraghil. One to 1½ hours beyond Suraghil is **Lupgar Sar Base Camp** (4900m). From the ridge crest you get spectacular views of Lupgar Sar, Mulungutti Sar and Destaghil Sar.

Day 3: Lupgar Sar Base Camp to Dūt

6–7 hours, 14.5km, 2320m descent
Retrace your steps downvalley to Dūt.

Shimshal Pamir

Duration	5 days
Distance	83.2km
Standard	moderate
Season	June–September
Start/Finish	Shimshal village
Zone & Permit	open, no permit
Public Transport	no

Summary Trekking to Shimshal's broad Pamir highlands takes you to the Shimshalis' favourite place, where lakes sparkle on the Central Asian watershed and herders call melodiously across the hills.

Almost 1000 yaks and several thousand sheep and goats graze in the Shimshal Pamir, an extensive alpine grassland above 4500m. In late May, women and children leave Shimshal village for Shuizherav. In June, they move to Shuwerth, the main summer settlement just beyond the Shimshal Pass. In early September, they move back to Shuizherav, and in early October, they return to Shimshal village.

Two trails from Shimshal village join at Purien-e-Ben. One, known locally as *tang* (gorge), goes by the Pamir-e-Tang River.

The other, known locally as *uween* (pass), crosses two arduous passes (Uween-e-Sar and Shachmirk, both above 4500m). The uween trail was the standard way until 1997 when an all-important footbridge across the Pamir-e-Tang River was built and the tang trail was widened. Both routes have serious exposure. Shimshalis continue to improve the tang trail and hope one day to be able to take yaks along it rather than the uween trail.

For an authentic Pamir experience, try going via the tang trail and returning via the uween trail (see Alternative Route A, p268). Another highly recommended alternative is to combine this trek with the Qachqar-e-Dur & Shpodeen Pass trek (p274) returning to Shimshal village via Shpodeen Pass. It's also possible to combine this trek with the Boisum & Chafchingol Passes trek (p270), joining it at Shpodeen.

PLANNING
Maps

The Swiss Foundation for Alpine Research 1:250,000 orographical map *Karakoram (Sheet 1)* covers the trek. It doesn't label Zardgarben, Shachmirk and Uween-e-Sar Passes, nor any place names along either route to Shuizherav. Shuwerth is labelled as Shuwari.

Guides & Porters

Local assistance is indispensable crossing exposed trail along the Pamir-e-Tang River, massive scree slopes on the uween trail, as well as the difficult trails into and out of Purien-e-Ben. Porters may ask for higher per-stage wages or for reduced weight of loads when going via the uween trail.

Stages

Traditionally, it's six stages one way (12 stages round trip) between Shimshal village and Shuwerth via the uween trail, and five stages one way (10 stages round trip) via the tang trail. The stages via the uween trail from Shimshal village are: (1) Zardgarben; (2) Yarzeen; (3) Purien-e-Ben; (4) Arbab Purien; (5) Shuizherav; (6) Shuwerth; and (7–12) six stages to return via the same route. The stages via the tang trail from

Shimshal village are: (1–2) Purien-e-Ben (two stages, not three); (3) Arbab Purien; (4) Shuizherav; (5) Shuwerth; and (6–10) five stages to return via the same route. The tang trail has always been one stage shorter in each direction than the uween trail.

Now that the tang trail is the standard way, villagers, in theory, earn one less stage in each direction. Not happy with this perceived loss of revenue, some Shimshalis say the de facto stages of the tang trail starting from Shimshal village changed from five stages one way to these six stages one way (or from 10 to 12 stages round trip): (1) Gar-e-Sar; (2) Past Furzeen; (3) Wuch Furzeen; (4) Arbab Purien; (5) Shuizherav; and (6) Shuwerth. However, the improved tang trail is significantly easier and shorter than the uween trail, and stage inflation of 20% hardly seems justified. Shimshalis actually have an opportunity to earn more money now that the easier trail enables more trekkers to make it to the Pamir. The village still needs to address and resolve this issue, so discuss this with whoever you hire before starting out.

THE TREK
Day 1: Shimshal Village to Wuch Furzeen
7–9 hours, 15.1km, 685m ascent, 320m descent

Follow the Shimshal River east (upstream) from Shimshal village (3000m) and fill water bottles at the spring before Michael Bridge, which is the only water for hours along this trail. Cross Michael Bridge, built in 1984 with money donated by Canadian Dr Michael Pflug, to the river's true right bank. Avoid the trail to Zardgarben, which climbs beyond the footbridge. Instead, veer right following the wide river bed 1½ hours, or 5km, to the confluence of the Shimshal and Pamir-e-Tang Rivers.

Ford the Pamir-e-Tang River to its true left bank, marvelling at the immense gorge. When the water is too high, cross via a footbridge some minutes upriver. Ascend the steep spur between the two rivers for 2km, or 1½ hours. On the ascent, Shachmirk Pass is visible to the north-east. After the initial

climb from the river, round a bend and enter a basin. The climb continues steadily through artemisia steppes, passing lots of igneous rock. Just above the basin, the trail splits; take the right fork to Gar-e-Sar. The left fork is a deceptively well-established trail that leads to Nogordum Uween (Bear Pass), a juniper stand in the canyon below Yarzeen. Several cairns mark **Gar-e-Sar** (3502m), which means 'top of the rock'. Here you have superb vistas of the Yazghil Glacier, Adver Sar and these hard-to-see 7000m peaks of the Hispar Muztagh: Kunyang Chhīsh, Pumori Chhīsh and Yukshin Gardan.

From Gar-e-Sar, follow level galleries passing eroded cliffs on the canyon's opposite side. Reach Shanj in 15 minutes, a scree-filled gully where an unreliable trickle of water flows below the trail in an awkward spot. *Shanj* are the boards uses to frame the place in a Wakhi home where you leave your shoes, which someone apparently got from this now-barren place. The trail and galleries deteriorate, although Shimshalis have worked to improve a dangerous Class 2 section here called Dhurik Purien. Traverse 450m above the river on exposed trail 1½ to two hours, then descend a steep 130m scree slope to **Past Furzeen** (3517m, 'lower birch grove'). A clear side stream provides the first reliable water since Shanj, but there are no level tent sites.

From Past Furzeen, the trail climbs along the clear stream, soon leaving it to ascend the tricky section of trail known as Guldin Purien. The route climbs steadily and traverses high before descending a scree gully to *Wuch Furzeen* (3365m, 'upper birch grove'). Above the Pamir-e-Tang River is a hut named Charra Khun. Just west of the hut is a small spring, which, if dry, necessitates an awkward trip down to the river for silty water.

Day 2: Wuch Furzeen to Shuizherav
6–8 hours, 18.5km, 985m ascent

Descend to the Pamir-e-Tang River in 15 minutes and cross the footbridge to its true right bank. Continue along the river for 30 minutes, climbing a short scree slope to a flat area with stone rounds 60m above the river. Follow the trail, built by Khyal Beg, climbing 150m along galleries and descend into **Purien-e-Ben** (3596m) in another 45 minutes.

Cross the Pamir Mai Dur River over a footbridge. Climb 320m on the steep 30-degree trail up the canyon wall out of Purien-e-Ben, through the doorway *(darwaza)*, and up the juniper staircase *(purien)* one hour to the level plain above, called **Purien-e-Sar** (3916m). Mungalig Sar is the prominent peak to the east, and Adver Sar the one to the west. The striking Chat Pirt massif, which rises south of the Pamir-e-Tang River, supports a blue sheep population on its grassy lower slopes, which can be reached only via faint, difficult hunters' paths.

From Purien-e-Sar, the walk to Shuizherav becomes much easier. The trail traverses dry artemisia-covered hillside high above the river (called Shuizherav above

Purien-e-Ben), crossing several tributary streams in their narrow gorges. Traverse gently to a rocky rise and reach the first side stream, Kushk Yarzeen (dry juniper) in 1¼ hours. **Arbab Purien** (3931m), the nicest of these side valleys and a good spot for lunch, is 30 minutes farther where a clear spring flows near the small hut next to the rushing stream beneath distinctive red rocks. Just beyond Arbab Purien is the grave of Ghulam Nasir, a young man who died in the Pamir in 1995 of appendicitis. In one hour, pass above Miter Kishk (where a man named Miter tried to cultivate) and descend towards the river. Follow the rocky trail along the river for 45 minutes to the confluence of the Gunj-e-Dur (in Wakhi, *gunj* means 'a distant treasure/store house'; *dur*, 'a valley where sheep are kept') and Shuizherav rivers. Cross a sturdy wooden footbridge to the Gunj-e-Dur River's true left bank. Pass the few huts at Qerqazi Kishk (where a man named Qerqazi tried to cultivate) and follow the

Shimshal Pamir

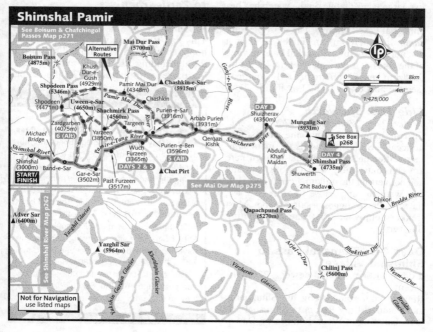

Not for Navigation
use listed maps

Shuizherav's true right bank two to 2½ hours to the large summer settlement of *Shuizherav* (in Wakhi, *shui* means a 'place with a lot of rock where it's hard to walk'; *zherav*, a 'glacial river'), with many huts on both sides of the river. Below Shuizherav (4350m), along the true right bank, is a grassy area for camping amid quiet mountain splendour.

Day 3: Shuizherav to Shimshal Pass
3 hours, 8km, 385m ascent
Cross the wooden footbridge to the Shuizherav's true left bank and ascend a side stream's true right bank. The easy climb to **Abdullah Khan Maidan** (4600m) takes one hour. These pastures are the precincts of women and children who have a rule; one cannot enter the pastures in a sad mood. Everyone must be happy and it's best to enter the pastures singing!

Stroll two hours through flowery fields amid herds of yaks and sheep, skirting the two large lakes that lie on the watershed between South Asia and Central Asia to the **Shimshal Pass** (4735m). The most pleasant *camp sites* (4700m) are in the level area just north of (below) Shimshal Pass, in view of the lakes. It is possible to climb Mungalig Sar from here if you are properly equipped (see the boxed text 'Peak Possibilities').

Side Trip: Shuwerth
1 hour, 2km, 170m ascent, 170m descent
Fifteen minutes beyond the almost unnoticeable Shimshal Pass is the main summer settlement of Shuwerth. Women here are constantly busy with milking, herding and converting the milk to *qurut* (cheese). If you want to camp close to Shuwerth, ask the villagers to suggest a suitable spot. Most trekkers enjoy at least one day visiting Shuwerth.

Days 4–5: Shimshal Pass to Shimshal Village
2 days, 41.6km, 2055m descent, 320m ascent
Retrace your route along the Shuizherav and Pamir-e-Tang Rivers to Shimshal village, camping at Wuch Furzeen on Day 4.

Alternative Route A: Shimshal Pass to Shimshal Village
The more difficult uween trail offers a challenging alternative to retracing your steps along the tang route.

Alternative Day 4: Shimshal Pass to Purien-e-Ben
6–9 hours, 16.7km, 1104m descent
Leave the Shimshal Pamir by following the trail back to *Purien-e-Ben* (3596m), where the uween trail leaves the tang trail. This camp site is in a narrow box canyon amid fantastic eroded loess towers. Water is very silty in the afternoon, but generally settles quickly. A hard-to-reach hot spring is above Purien-e-Ben. Crossing the two passes on the uween trail the next day is somewhat easier if you can go 2.5km beyond Purien-e-Ben and camp in Targeen (see Alternative Day 5).

Alternative Day 5: Purien-e-Ben to Zardgarben
8–10 hours, 15.6km, 1764m ascent, 1285m descent
This day illustrates why the term 'hardihood' aptly describes Shimshalis. Crossing the demanding Shachmirk and Uween-e-Sar passes with more than 3000m of total

---

Peak Possibilities

Mungalig Sar
Accessible from Shimshal Pass (Day 3) For those equipped and motivated, an ascent of the 5931m (elevation as per the Russian map J-43-128) snowy peak **Mungalig Sar** (the peak above where yaks graze on a grassy place), first climbed by Nazir Sabir in 1988, is possible from the lakes north of Shimshal Pass. Mungalig Sar (peak 6050 on the Swiss map) is also known as Mingli Sar. Climbing Mungalig Sar requires travelling in roped teams. It's a one-day climb, with 1480m ascent and 1480m descent.

Two other 5000m peaks, Kuz Sar (shady side peak) and Lup Zhui Sar (big lake peak), are also single-day climbs done from the Pamir.

elevation gain and loss is one of the toughest nonglacier days anywhere in the Karakoram. Starting early is essential.

The trail starts with a 240m scree ascent out of Purien-e-Ben, followed by a more gentle traverse one to 1½ hours to the stream at *Targeen* (3795m). With rockfall danger, no fuel for porters, and only room for two tents along the stream's true left bank or room for three or four tents a few minutes above on the true right bank, it's not an inviting camp site. A difficult-to-access hot spring is below Targeen.

It takes two to 2½ hours to ascend 765m over scree to reach **Shachmirk Pass** (4560m). Its name means the place where the dog (*shach*) died (*mirk*). Hopefully, you're not feeling like that dog, and can enjoy the fine views of Destaghil Sar, Adver Sar, the snowy Yazghil Glacier, Kunyang Chhīsh (7852m), Pumori Chhīsh, Yukshin Gardan (7530m), and east to Chat Pirt and Mungalig Sar.

The 1½ to two hours' and 710m steady descent to Yarzeen begins immediately. The trail is clearly visible, steep and, in a few places, loose. The rushing stream at *Yarzeen* (3850m; 'the place of juniper') makes a great, and the only, lunch spot. Years of cook fires, however, have eliminated almost all the juniper that once grew here. Yarzeen is a possible camp site, but has room for only one small tent and no more than four people, including porters. Larger trekking parties must continue over the second pass the same day.

JOHN MOCK

Descending Shachmirk Pass, with the Yazghil Glacier in the distance.

The 810m scree ascent to **Uween-e-Sar** (4650m) begins immediately from Yarzeen. It's even more arduous than the ascent to Shachmirk, and takes 2½ to three hours. The first 30 minutes or so on a faint path is extremely steep, loose and exposed, so take care not to knock rocks onto anyone below. Views from the pass extend from Destaghil Sar, Kanjut Sar and Yukshin Gardan to Chat Pirt.

The one to 1½ hour 575m descent to *Zardgarben* (4075m), visible west of the pass, is on a comparatively good trail. Head for the welcoming grassy expanse below.

Alternative Day 6: Zardgarben to Shimshal Village

2½–3 hours, 6.9km, 1075m descent
See Day 7 of the Qachqar-e-Dur & Shpodeen Pass trek (p276) for a description between Zardgarben and Shimshal village.

Alternative Route B: Shimshal Pass to Shimshal Village

Returning to Shimshal via Pamir Mai Dur and Shpodeen Pass makes an unforgettable finale to the Shimshal Pamir trek.

Alternative Day 4: Shimshal Pass to Arbab Purien

5–6 hours, 19.3km, 804m descent
Retrace your steps downvalley to *Arbab Purien* (3931m).

Alternative Day 5: Arbab Purien to Pamir Mai Dur

4 hours, 8km, 639m ascent, 222m descent
Follow the stream north-west from Arbab Purien, cross the approximately 4570m ridge, and descend to meet the Pamir Mai Dur, north of Purien-e-Sar, in 1½ hours. The trail stays high above the Pamir Mai Dur River's true left bank as it gently goes north-west upvalley. In one hour, pass **Chashkin**, a small maidan with a spring. In another 1½ hours, reach the confluence of the Pamir Mai Dur and Qachqar-e-Dur rivers. Ford the Qachqar-e-Dur River and camp along its true right bank north of the huts at *Pamir Mai Dur* (4348m). It's one stage between Arbab Purien and Pamir Mai Dur.

Alternative Days 6–8: Pamir Mai Dur to Shimshal Village

See Days 5–6 of the Qachqar-e-Dur & Shpodeen Pass trek (p276) for a description across the pass.

Boisum & Chafchingol Passes

Duration	7 days
Distance	59.6km
Standard	very demanding, technical
Season	mid-June–September
Start	Shimshal village
Finish	Koksil
Zone & Permit	open, no permit
Public Transport	no

Summary This classic traverse showcases the alpine splendour of the Ghuzherav Mountains as it follows cascading streams through meadows and crosses two dramatic passes.

Boisum and Chafchingol, two high passes in the remote Ghuzherav Mountains, link Shimshal village with Koksil on the KKH 17km west of Khunjerab Pass. Traversing the South and North Ghuzherav mountains makes for a spectacularly beautiful and challenging trek. Boisum Pass is not glaciated, but the higher Chafchingol is. The approach to Chafchingol involves fording a deep, swift torrent several times and ascending Class 2 scree and loose rock. The descent is over a crevassed glacier.

PLANNING
What to Bring

Crossing the Ghuzherav and Chafchingol rivers may require fixing ropes across the rivers for safety. Descending the Chafchingol Glacier requires bringing the mountaineering equipment necessary to fix at least 150m of rope and possibly travel in roped teams (see Mountaineering Equipment, p61).

Maps

The Swiss Foundation for Alpine Research 1:250,000 orographical map *Karakoram*

(Sheet 1) covers the trek. It labels Shpodeen as Shekhdalga, Mandikshlakh as Mandi Kushlag, and Avduzhi as Hapdija. It omits all other place names. North of Boisum Pass, the trail is incorrectly marked on the river's true right (east) side; it's on the true left (west) side to Mandikshlakh.

Several maps give the elevation of Boisum Pass above 5000m, and as high as 5090m. The authors have crossed Boisum Pass four times and have never gotten elevation readings as high as 5000m. As a base of reference, the pass elevation is probably closer to 4900m. This is supported by the Russian maps, which give it as 4930m. The Swiss map and other maps show extensive glaciation on the north-east side of Boisum Pass. In reality, the entire trail is either not on glacier or on very stable moraine. It's all rock. At no time is the trail on snow or ice, nor are there any crevasses or particular difficulties.

Permits & Regulations

This trek is usually done from south to north, but if you want start from Koksil, you may need special permission from Gilgit's DC, IG or AIG. The Khunjerab Security Force (KSF) at Koksil has the discretion to allow trekkers to enter the Koksil Valley from the KKH.

Guides & Porters

A local guide and/or porters are indispensable for the river crossings and Chafchingol Pass. Porters carry a maximum of 25kg, including their own gear and food, even though government regulations don't require you to reduce load weight. Negotiate a fair agreement about wages and weights of loads before starting. Bring tarps for shelter at Jafervask and Chafchingol where there are no huts.

Stages

Unfortunately, this trek suffered from 25% stage inflation in the 1990s. The multiple times this book's authors did this trek, it was only nine stages between Shimshal village and Koksil. Shimshalis now ask for the following 12 stages from Shimshal village:

GOJAL

(1) Zardgarben; (2) Jafervask; (3) Boisum Pass; (4) Perchodwashk; (5) Mandikshlakh; (6) Avduzhi; (7) War-e-Ben; (8) Targeen; (9) Chafchingol Base Camp; (10) Chafchingol Pass; (11) Koksil Valley; and (12) Koksil.

The three additional stages arise from these discrepancies: Jafervask to Avduzhi used to be two stages and now it's four; and Chafchingol Base Camp to Koksil Valley used to be one stage and now it's two. Reportedly, some Shimshalis have asked for as many as 15 stages, which unjustifiably asks for paying double stages over a pass.

GETTING TO/FROM THE TREK
To the Start
See the Shimshal Village trek (p261).

From the Finish
Unless you prearrange a special vehicle to meet you, catch whatever ride you can down to Afiyatabad. Daily Chinese buses are usually full and won't pick up trekkers. Vehicles returning empty from Tashkurgan may stop. Local jeeps and tractors occasionally pass and may stop. No set fares exist, so be patient and negotiate.

THE TREK
Day 1: Shimshal Village to Zardgarben
4–5 hours, 6.9km, 1075m ascent
Head east from Shimshal, cross Michael Bridge, and continue through the cultivated area of Band-e-Sar. Turn north into the steep, narrow canyon formed by the Zardgarben River, 1½ hours from Shimshal village. The trail begins along the river's true right bank, crosses it four times, and in 1½ hours reaches **Shaushau** (3360m) with a spring below the trail. *Shau* is a woody shrub with yellow flowers used to make weaving spindles. Tung-e-Ben, a sheltered flat place, is five minutes beyond.

Cross the river a final time to its true left bank and ascend a 250m steep scree slope 45 minutes to a wooden portal (3600m) called **Tung-e-Sar** (the top of the difficult dry area). Beware of rock fall on this tricky scree slope. A clear stream lies 15 minutes beyond. Continue 30 minutes to the broad,

level plain of *Zardgarben* (4075m). The yellow cliffs above Zardgarben are the source of its name, which means at the base of *(ben)* the yellow *(zart)* rock *(gar)*. This dramatic camp site has a herders' hut. The entire enormous valley is an old lake bed formed by a huge rock slide that dammed the valley. The cliffs frame views south to Shimshal and Adver Sar.

Day 2: Zardgarben to Jafervask
4 hours, 8.4km, 527m ascent
Head north from Zardgarben, fording the stream that descends from Uween-e-Sar.

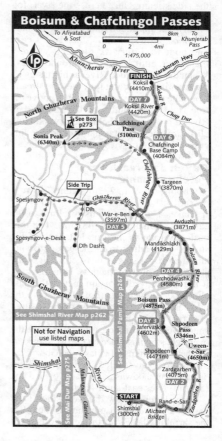

Stroll across the maidan and, towards its far end, descend to and ford the Zardgarben River to its true right bank. Immediately the trail climbs to traverse black moraine from a side glacier.

Once across the moraine, the route diverges. When the water in the Zardgarben River is very low, you can immediately descend to the river, ford it and avoid crossing the side stream coming from the west. When it's low, descend to the level plain formed by the side stream before descending to the river. Then follow the true right bank and ford the Zardgarben River above the side stream. Once across the river, follow its true left bank to the lone hut (4471m) at **Shpodeen** (place where rhubarb or *shpod* grows). Follow the river's edge one hour to *Jafervask* (4602m, where a man, Jafer, built a stone wall around fields). When the Zardgarben River is high, stay on the true right bank and ford the side stream. Continue on the river terrace high above the true right bank, and ford the Zardgarben River a few minutes below Jafervask. High cliffs provide a spectacular backdrop to this grassy flower-strewn spot, home to ibex.

Day 3: Jafervask to Perchodwashk
3–4 hours, 10.2km, 273m ascent, 295m descent
It's takes 1½ to two hours to climb to the east-west **Boisum Pass** (4875m). The trail basically follows the true left bank of the stream descending from the pass, crossing and then recrossing it just before the final steep, rocky push to the pass. In high water, it requires a ford. Boisum means the pass above *(sum)* the caves *(boi)*. It refers to the overhanging clefts at the base of the fissured cliff (on your right as you ascend) on the south-west side of the pass, which were the overnight stopping place on the two-day journey between Shimshal village and Ghuzherav long before any shelters existed at Shpodeen or Perchodwashk. Attractive Pir Peak (5915m) rises east-south-east of the pass.

Immediately below the west side of the pass is a tarn called Lup Zhui. Either skirt the shrinking lake's north-west shore or cut

across the dry section of the lake bed in 15 minutes. Cross the low rise beyond the lake to Shipkadurikh, an outwash plain, another 15 minutes farther. Beyond this is another rise that descends steeply on moraine to a vast, level outwash plain. Cairns mark the indistinct route, which takes 30 minutes to follow to the shore of the smaller Dzak Zhui. Past this lake, the trail moves onto moraine rubble and descends reasonably gently one hour to Perchodwashk beneath gigantic black terminal moraine that fills the valley. Built against an erratic is the hut (4580m) at *Perchodwashk* (meaning 'where the young girl got tired') above the confluence of two streams, which are usually silty, amid pleasant meadows.

Day 4: Perchodwashk to War-e-Ben
4½–5 hours, 14.1km, 983m descent
Between Perchodwashk and Mandikshlakh, three tongues of rocky rubble from side glaciers push into the Boisum Valley from the west. Between these obstacles are two grassy plateaus with clear streams and dilapidated structures called Qul Beg Maidan and Reza Maidan. From Perchodwashk, ford the side stream and stay close to the river's true left bank, skirting the first side glacier. Stroll across flower-carpeted rolling hills marked by cairns and in 1km pass two possible camp sites, *Shogshogeen*, named for yellow buttercups that yaks like to eat, and nearby *Pamireen*.

Beyond Pamireen, traverse Qul Beg Maidan and cross the second side moraine. The trail crosses the two-level terraces of *Reza Maidan*, dotted by ochre lichen-covered boulders, and the last side moraine. Here is the first dramatic glimpse of the rocky Ghuzherav. An imposing vertical precipice soars high above the Boisum River's true right bank. **Mandikshlakh** (4129m), an unattractive cluster of huts and livestock pens on a dusty, stark terrace, is two hours below Perchodwashk at the Boisum Valley's mouth.

Leaving the Boisum Valley, the route turns west into the Ghuzherav. When the water level in the Ghuzherav is low, the trail stays along the river's true left bank to Avduzhi. When it's high, you must ford the broad river twice – across and then back to the true left bank – to bypass a section under water. One hour west of Mandikshlakh is **Avduzhi** (3871m) with its huts and a clear stream. Beyond Avduzhi, along an easy trail, lies *War-e-Ben* (3597m), Ghuzherav's primary summer settlement. Because yaks can't cross Chafchingol Pass, they don't go beyond War-e-Ben.

Side Trip: Dīh Dasht & Spesyngov-e-Desht
2–4 days
From War-e-Ben, you can continue northwest down Ghuzherav through junipers to the summer settlements of Dīh and Spesyngov. From Dīh, a side valley rises south to the pastures of Dīh Dasht where ibex and blue sheep are reportedly plentiful. From Spesyngov, another side valley leads south to Spesyngove-Desht beneath Qarūn Koh's snowy summit (7164m). Beyond Spesyngov, a low-water route, passable between November and May, follows the Ghuzherav to its confluence with the Khunzherav. Another route to Sost over high, extreme passes is definitely inadvisable for trekkers. It's two days and four stages one way between War-e-Ben and Spesyngove-Desht, and half that to Dīh Dasht.

Day 5: War-e-Ben to Chafchingol Base Camp
4–5 hours, 10km, 487m ascent
Cross the Ghuzherav by an existing steel cable when the water is high or by wading when it's low, and enter the Chafchingol gorge. The country here is high desert with crumbly, desert-varnished granite and junipers. When water in the Chafchingol River is high, typically three and possibly as many as five difficult fords of the river are necessary. It may require fixing rope for safety.

Once through the gorge, the trail thins, rising above the river and crossing scree slopes to descend to **Targeen** (where tamarisk grows), where a small cramped hut sits by the stream (3870m), two to three hours from War-e-Ben. Beyond Targeen is the confluence of a stream from the west and

another from the glaciers at the Chafchingol's head. Ford the western stream and continue to *Chafchingol Base Camp* (4084m), a site with some low stone wall shelters, two hours from Targeen. Clear water is near the river. It is possible to climb Sonia Peak from Chafchingol Base Camp (see the boxed text 'Peak Possibilities').

Day 6: Chafchingol Base Camp to Koksil River
6–7 hours, 6km, 1016m ascent, 680m descent
It's a long, arduous day, so start early. The ascent over scree to the permanently snowcovered **Chafchingol Pass** (5100m) takes four hours. It's steep Class 2 near the top with loose rock. The pass, marked by a large cairn, is glaciated on its north side. The descent is steep. Early in the season, snow covers a large bergschrund at the glacier's west margin and the route goes down the snow and requires fixing a rope for safety and probing for crevasses. Late in the season when the bergschrund is open, the route descends the rock cliff on the glacier's west side. The rock route may require a short rappel (abseil) or fixing as much as 50m of rope for safety.

Once off the glacier, cross to the Chafchingol stream's true left bank. A small

Peak Possibilities
Sonia Peak
Accessible from Chafchingol Base Camp (Day 5) West of the Base Camp, towards the Chafchingol Valley's head, rises Sonia Peak (peak 6340m on Swiss map), first climbed by Shimshali Rahmat Ullah Baig. The three-day technical climb of 2256m ascent and 2256m descent is gaining popularity. The first day, follow the river's true right bank three to four hours from Chafchingol Base Camp to Sonia Base Camp, the high camp. The second day is a long ascent on glacier to the snowy pyramid's summit, returning to Sonia Base Camp. The third day, return to Chafchingol Base Camp.

rocky area provides a spot to make tea or camp if it becomes too long a day. From this spot, follow the Chafchingol stream down to its confluence with the Chap Dur and Koksil rivers (4420m) and *camp* along the Koksil River.

Day 7: Koksil River to Koksil
2–3 hours, 4km, 10m descent
From the confluence, it takes two to three hours to reach the KKH, the KSF check post and herders' huts at *Koksil* (4410m).

Qachqar-e-Dur & Shpodeen Pass

Duration	7 days
Distance	55.5km
Standard	demanding
Season	mid-June–September
Start/Finish	Shimshal village
Zone & Permit	open, no permit
Public Transport	no

Summary Unvisited and incredibly scenic, this loop trek crosses a spectacular snow-covered pass and offers perhaps the Karakoram's best blue sheep watching.

All treks beyond Shimshal village are strenuous, but the trek to Qachqar-e-Dur and across Shpodeen Pass is comparatively easy and offers the best views of the Hispar Muztagh. Whether making a fantastic loop by crossing Shpodeen Pass or just backtracking, the trek goes through the South Ghuzherav Mountains, including the seldom-visited Pamir Mai Dur (sheep valley) and stunning Zardgarben valleys. Abundant blue sheep populations in Pamir Mai Dur and upper Qachqar-e-Dur almost guarantee sightings of this mountain monarch.

PLANNING
Maps
The Swiss Foundation for Alpine Research 1:250,000 orographical map *Karakoram (Sheet 1)* covers the trek. Pamir Mai Dur (the east-west valley descending east from Shpodeen Pass) and Qachqar-e-Dur (the

north-south valley descending south from Mai Dur Pass) aren't named on any maps. On the Swiss map, the Pamir Mai Dur huts aren't marked. A trail between Pamir Mai Dur and Bipardah Pert is incorrectly marked on the Qachqar-e-Dur's true left bank; it's on its true right bank. The route over Shpodeen Pass isn't marked, but the pass is marked by an 'X' and is labelled Shipedin Pir. Shpodeen is labelled as Shekhdalga.

Guides & Porters
No shelter is available at Bipardah Pert, Farhad Base Camp or Khush Dur-e-Gush, so provide a tent or tarp for porters.

Stages
The loop trek totals nine stages. It's traditionally two stages between Shimshal and Purien-e-Ben via the tang trail (see Guides & Porters under the Shimshal Pamir trek, p265). From Purien-e-Ben, the rest of the trek covers seven additional stages: (1) Pamir Mai Dur; (2) Bipardah Pert or Farhad Base Camp; (3) back to Pamir Mai Dur; (4) Khush Dur-e-Gush; (5) Shpodeen; (6) Zardgarben; and (7) Shimshal village.

GETTING TO/FROM THE TREK
To the Start/Finish
See the Shimshal Village trek (p261).

THE TREK (see map opposite)
Day 1: Shimshal to Wuch Furzeen
7–9 hours, 15.1km, 685m ascent, 320m descent
See Day 1 of the Shimshal Pamir trek (p266).

Day 2: Wuch Furzeen to Pamir Mai Dur
6 hours, 11.5km, 983m ascent
See Day 2 of the Shimshal Pamir trek (p266) for a description between Wuch Furzeen and Purien-e-Sar. At Purien-e-Sar, the trail to Pamir Mai Dur turns north, and leaves the trail to the Shimshal Pamir, which continues east.

From Purien-e-Sar (3916m), the trail goes north-west through barren country and over talus, staying high above the Pamir Mai Dur

River's true left bank all the way to the Pamir Mai Dur huts, four hours away. In 2½ hours, pass **Chashkin**, a small maidan with a spring. Chashkin is the base for climbing the inviting, prominent snowy peak called Chashkin-e-Sar (5915m, not marked on the Swiss map) rising to the north-east. In another 1½ hours, reach the confluence of the Pamir Mai Dur and Qachqar-e-Dur rivers. The huts at *Pamir Mai Dur* (4348m) are on the river's opposite (north-west) side. Ford the Qachqar-e-Dur River to its true right bank and camp north of the huts on a level terrace. A spring is upstream along the river bank.

Day 3: Pamir Mai Dur to Bipardah Pert
2½–3 hours, 3.3km, 378m ascent
Head north over scree high above the Qachqar-e-Dur's true right bank. After one hour reach a small grassy area, where small purple primulas bloom and blue sheep horns sit atop a rock. Yukshin Gardan

comes into view to the south. Continue another hour over scree, traverse a gully with a spring, and then descend talus to the river. Cross to its true left bank, often via a snow bridge, just below the confluence of several glacial streams. The black rubble of the Mai Dur Glacier's snout lies ahead, and the valley opens into an extensive alpine bowl. Cross granite moraine coming from the large glacier issuing from the cirque below Chashkin-e-Sar's north face. Continue north to a small clear stream at the base of a large grassy hill called **Bipardah Pert** (4726m; the 'unveiled hill').

Side Trip: Farhad Base Camp
2½–3 hours, 2.6km, 266m ascent, 266m descent
Wander up the hill 30 minutes to its top for excellent views of the Hispar Muztagh, where Kanjut Sar and Jutmo Sar now join Yukshin Gardan. Blue sheep droppings dot the flower-covered slope as you traverse the

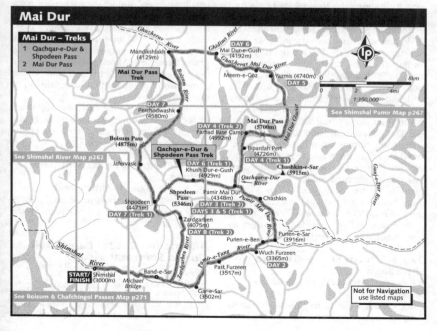

Mai Dur

crest of the hill for another 30 minutes. Cross onto the Mai Dur Glacier's black moraine, and continue another 30 minutes across the glacial rubble, past a white rock deposit, to the stone shelters and tent platforms near moraine pools at *Farhad Base Camp* (4992m). Here you're in the centre of a stunning glacial amphitheatre ringed by unclimbed snowy 5000m summits. To the south, Destaghil Sar and the other highest peaks west of K2 march along the skyline. Return to Bipardah Pert in one to 1½ hours.

Day 4: Bipardah Pert to Pamir Mai Dur
2–2½ hours, 3.3km, 378m descent
Retrace your steps back to the *Pamir Mai Dur* huts.

Day 5: Pamir Mai Dur to Khush Dur-e-Gush
3–4 hours, 6.3km, 581m ascent
Climb the hill behind the huts and continue west well above the Pamir Mai Dur's true left bank. Reach a mixed rocky and grassy area with a spring called **Rana Kuk** after one to 1½ hours. Cross a side stream in 45 minutes, then traverse the black moraine rubble coming from the north. Occasional cairns mark the 30-minute route over the shale-like rock. Staying along the true left bank, pass well above the confluence of a tributary joining from the south. The trail grows faint as you enter into a gorge. Cross to the Pamir Mai Dur's true right bank after crossing a side stream coming from the north and before the confluence of two streams. The valley divides here and the route to Shpodeen Pass, which remains hidden from view, is upvalley to the south-west (left). Ascend along the true right bank of the left branch to grassy *Khush Dur-e-Gush* (4929m, 'mouth of the happy valley'), reaching it within an hour of entering the gorge.

Day 6: Khush Dur-e-Gush to Shpodeen
5–6 hours, 3km, 417m ascent, 875m descent
Work up the slope to bypass to the south (left) of spectacular cascades and a gorge.

Shpodeen Pass becomes visible ahead. Above the cascades, cross the braided stream and continue up to where the stream emerges from a snowfield. Ascend the snowfield to reach **Shpodeen Pass** (5346m), two to 2½ hours from Khush Dur-e-Gush. From the pass, Adver Sar, Destaghil Sar, Momhil Sar and Lupgar Sar are visible. Shpodeen Pass can be snow covered and corniced early in the season, but there's no glacier on either side.

Steeply below and 2km to the west is Shpodeen in the Zardgarben Valley. The west side of the pass is dry, but the route can be icy early in the season. The descent is over extremely steep scree ranging between 25 and 35 degrees for two hours until the angle lessens as you reach the valley floor. The Class 2 route down a limestone and shale gully (slightly to the left) is preferable to avoid a Class 3 limestone rock face (a little to the right). Jenny Visser-Hooft, who crossed the pass in 1925, described the descent thus: '...on all sides the rocks rose in superb structures with beautifully sculptured, bold outline and dolomite colours'. Continue another 30 minutes, following the stream, and then another hour to the flat, grassy expanse of *Shpodeen* (4471m) above the Zardgarben River's true left bank. Water comes from an intermittent clear stream or tiny springs along the river's edge.

Looking back to the east, the Shpodeen Pass cairn is distinguishable, but barely visible on the ridge. The route lies between the golden spur and black side spur.

Day 7: Shpodeen to Shimshal Village
4–5 hours, 13km, 1471m descent
See Days 1–2 of the Boisum & Chafchingol Passes trek (p271) for a description in the reverse direction.

Alternative Route: Pamir Mai Dur to Shimshal Village
2 days, 26.6km, 1668m descent, 320m ascent
For those not wanting to cross Shpodeen Pass, it's one day shorter to retrace your steps. Return to Purien-e-Sar and head

down the Pamir-e-Tang River to Shimshal village, camping at Wuch Furzeen on Day 5.

Mai Dur Pass

Duration	8 days
Distance	80.4km
Standard	extreme, technical
Season	mid-June–September
Start/Finish	Shimshal village
Zone & Permit	open, no permit
Public Transport	no

Summary The rediscovered classic high-altitude route across Mai Dur Pass has one of the best pass views anywhere in the Karakoram, and visits virtually unknown territory.

The glaciated Mai Dur Pass (5700m), first crossed in 1925 by Dutch geographer Philips C Visser and his American wife Jenny Visser-Hooft, who were seeking the source of the Hunza River, had been neglected until this book's authors' crossing in June 2000. This exciting loop trek through the South Ghuzherav Mountains has excellent scenery with fantastic high mountain views and a good chance of watching wildlife. Crossing the pass, although technical, is relatively straightforward. It's easier when less snow is present. The trek offers a challenging and longer alternative start to the Boisum & Chafchingol Passes trek (p270) and finish to the Shimshal Pamir trek (p265).

PLANNING
What to Bring
Mountaineering equipment necessary to travel in roped teams and rappel (abseil) up to 75m is required; crampons are advisable for everyone, including porters (see Mountaineering Equipment, p61).

Maps
Refer to the Maps section for the Qachqar-e-Dur & Shpodeen Pass trek (p274). Additionally, the Swiss map shows an inaccurate route on the Mai Dur Glacier. The route is mostly on moraine along the glacier's west margin. The glaciation north-east of the

pass appears to be depicted somewhat wrongly; the actual side glaciers seem to be much larger than what's drawn.

Guides & Porters
It's imperative to go with at least one person who has previously crossed the pass: Farhad Khan, Fazal Ali, Mirza Khan or Sarwar Ali. Undoubtedly, more local men will learn this route.

Stages
The trek totals 13 stages. It's three stages between Shimshal village and Pamir Mai Dur via the tang trail (see Stages under the Qachqar-e-Dur & Shpodeen Pass trek, p274). It's five stages one way from Pamir Mai Dur to Mandikshlakh: (1) Farhad Base Camp; (2) Mai Dur Pass; (3) the Mai Dur Glacier's moraine; (4) Yazmis; and (5) Mandikshlakh. It's five more stages one way between Mandikshlakh and Shimshal village (see Stages under the Boisum & Chafchingol Passes trek, p270).

GETTING TO/FROM THE TREK
To the Start/Finish
See the Shimshal Village trek (p261).

THE TREK (see map p275)
Days 1–3: Shimshal Village to Farhad Base Camp
3 days, 31.2km, 2312m ascent, 320m descent
See Days 1–3 and the Side Trip described in the Qachqar-e-Dur & Shpodeen Pass trek (p274) for details of these days.

Day 4: Farhad Base Camp to Yazmis
6½–8 hours, 8.1km, 708m ascent, 960m descent
Farhad Base Camp (4992m), named after Farhad Khan, who in 1998 was the first to cross the pass since 1925, is rocky and cold. Get an early start when the snow is still firm. Try to depart base camp by 4am to be on top of the pass by 7am, finish the rappel by 8am, and exit the glacial basin below by 9am. A late start guarantees a tedious slog across sun-softened east-facing slopes.

GOJAL

Follow black medial moraine north-east, then move right onto glacial ice and continue up the snow-covered glacier. Travel in roped teams where necessary. About 1½ hours from base camp, the glacier turns east towards the pass, which is the obvious notch in the ridge line and the only place to cross. The 10- to 15-degree snow slope steepens to 30 degrees on the final 100m to the pass. Reach the top three to 3½ hours from base camp. **Mai Dur Pass** (5700m) is corniced on its east (Ghuzherav) side with a 10m vertical head wall and a 45-degree slope below, and requires lowering loads and making a 75m rappel. Some early-season avalanche danger may be present. Late in the season, the descent can be substantially snow-free.

Descend and cross the crevassed glacier basin below to the Mai Dur Glacier's north margin in 1½ to two hours. Once off the glacier, descend loose talus and scree along its true left margin. The glacier turns northward and is joined by another sizable glacier coming from the south-east. One hour farther is a level area (4850m) near the glacier that could be a camp site in a pinch. After another hour, reach *Yazmis* (glacier's mouth) directly beneath the imposing Mai Dur Glacier's snout. Chilling winds blow through the camp site (4740m), but there's ample clear water.

Day 5: Yazmis to Mai Dur-e-Gush
3½ hours, 8.1km, 548m descent
Follow along the Ghuzherav Mai Dur River's true left bank as it bends north-north-west, and in one hour reach **Meem-e-Goz** (Memsahib's grass), named for Jenny Visser-Hooft. Flower-carpeted and un-grazed by domestic livestock, these well-watered meadows support a good blue sheep population, and invite those with time to stop. A good flat, sandy spot by a clear stream lies 30 minutes farther.

From Meem-e-Goz's far end, climb flower-dotted moraine, then descend to another grassy area near the river in 45 minutes. Continue downvalley, at times traversing high on scree and moraine from side glaciers, and at times close to the river. Cross a glacial tongue, finally reaching a grassy boulder-dotted plateau one hour from the previous grassy area. This area marks the start of Mai Dur-e-Gush and the upper extent of livestock grazing. Descend 15 minutes to a ford of the river, and walk across the flood plain another 15 minutes to the hut (4192m) at *Mai Dur-e-Gush* (mouth of the Mai Dur) at the confluence of Ghuzherav Mai Dur and Ghidims rivers and the beginning of the Ghuzherav River. Camp anywhere in the vast open plain. Clear water is scarce, but look at the river's edge several minutes' walk away.

Day 6: Mai Dur-e-Gush to Perchodwashk
3½ hours, 10km, 388m ascent
Ford the Ghuzherav Mai Dur River above its confluence with the Ghidims River, then follow the Ghuzherav River's true left bank over stony and sandy ground to the confluence of the Boisum and Ghuzherav rivers. Head a short distance up the Boisum River's true right bank to a log footbridge and cross to Mandikshlakh (4129m), one hour from Mai Dur-e-Gush. Walk 2½ hours south up the Boisum Valley to *Perchodwashk* (4580m); see Day 4 of the Boisum & Chafchingol Passes trek (p272) for a description in the reverse direction.

Days 7–8: Perchodwashk to Shimshal Village
2 days, 23km, 295m ascent, 1875m descent
See Days 1–3 of the Boisum & Chafchingol Passes trek (p271) for a description in the reverse direction. On Day 7, it takes about two hours to reach **Boisum Pass** (4875m), 1½ hours to descend to Shpodeen, and another 1½ hours to *Zardgarben* (4075m). On Day 8, it takes 2½ to three hours from Zardgarben to Shimshal village.

Upper Gojal

At Gojal's north end, near the Chinese border, three valleys reach into the high mountains on either side of the upper Hunza River. South of Sost, the Boibar Valley leads from Morkhun towards mighty Qarūn Koh. North of Sost, the long Chapursan Valley leads west, paralleling Pakistan's border with China and Afghanistan, to Baba Ghundi Ziarat and several exciting high passes. Catastrophic outburst floods long ago devastated much of Chapursan, leaving the upper section a wasteland of huge boulders amid which the inhabitants grow wheat and potatoes. Chapursan's dramatic landscape of small fields amid red and yellow cliffs topped by snowy peaks is strikingly beautiful. Still farther north and west from Sost, the Kilik Valley leads to two passes on the Chinese border that were once part of the ancient Silk Route.

These high-altitude valleys were first settled by Wakhi immigrants from Wakhan. Bedevilled by the frequent raids of nomadic Qirghiz horsemen, the Wakhi settlers retreated to the comparative safety of the Boibar Valley. Only after the Mir of Hunza took firm control of the region around the mid-18th century were Wakhi people able to resettle Chapursan. Most Wakhi settlers migrated from lower in Gojal, but at least one village, Shutmerg, was settled more recently by migrants from the Wakhan, and Raminj was settled by Burusho from Hunza. Misgar was also resettled by Burusho from Hunza.

ACCESS VILLAGES
See Afiyatabad & Sost (p241).

Boibar

Duration	3 days
Distance	27.4km
Standard	easy
Season	mid-June–September
Start/Finish	Jamalabad
Zone & Permit	open, no permit
Public Transport	yes

Summary The beautiful and rarely visited Boibar Valley is the route to Jurjur Khun-e-Sar, Tupopdan, Parigar Sar and Qarūn Koh base camps, with Qarūn Pass offering exceptional views of the Hispar Muztagh.

Boibar is an east-west valley whose river descends from Qarūn Koh (7164m) to the Hunza River at Morkhun 10km south of Sost. Boibar is historically significant as the original Wakhi settlement in Gojal and the old route to Shimshal, and has spectacular old-growth juniper trees. Avgarch and Boibar are also names of places in the Wakhan Corridor, suggesting the original inhabitants may have come from Wakhan. Morkhun (2743m) receives more rain than other Gojal villages, as its name suggests (*mor* means 'rain'; *khun*, 'house'). At the time of research, villagers were constructing a road to Avgarch with eventual plans to extend it to the Boibar huts.

PLANNING
Maps
The Swiss Foundation for Alpine Research 1:250,000 orographical map *Karakoram (Sheet 1)* covers the trek. It labels Jamalabad as Jukulgar, Parigar Sar as Pregar, and the Boibar River as Murkhun. The glacier at the valley's head labelled Murkhun is locally called Qarūn Koh. Maidūn isn't named, but it's marked by a triangle.

Guides & Porters
Porters ask for a flat rate of Rs 240 per stage, including payment for food rations and the clothing and equipment allowance. Hire a local person to show the way, learn about the area, and support the village's economy.

GETTING TO/FROM THE TREK
Morkhun is halfway between Afiyatabad and Passu, so jump on any vehicle heading south from Afiyatabad or north from Passu. The short ride costs Rs 10 on NATCO buses and Rs 20 on vans or wagons. From Morkhun, north of the bridge and south of the Pakistan Army camp, follow the Jamalabad Link Rd half a kilometre to its end. Jamalabad (2789m), named for the late Mir of Hunza, Mohammad Jamal Khan, lies above the Boibar River's true right (north) bank.

THE TREK
Day 1: Jamalabad to Boibar
3½–4½ hours, 7.7km, 716m ascent
Follow the trail east along the canal. A shrine to **Shah Shams**, marked by white

flags, sits on the river's south side. Reach the first footbridge in 30 minutes and cross to the true left bank. Watch for rock fall between Jamalabad and Avgarch and avoid this section of trail in rain or high winds. Continue along the river's edge 30 minutes passing scattered rose bushes and the herb *spandr* to a clear side stream, which flows from **Sangar**, a scenic grassy ridge descending from Jurjur-Khun-e-Sar (6055m) to the south. (It takes five hours to reach Sangar from Morkhun, making it an eight- to nine-hour round trip.)

Just beyond the stream pass **Bandiletk**. Here red markings on the rock are said to have been made by a *bilas* (evil spirit) who licked the rock after having eaten people. Villagers say it's dangerous to travel here after dark. The area on both sides of the river, with its scattered artemisias, ephedras, and roses, is also known as **Lalazar** (beautiful place in Persian).

Continue 15 minutes to the second footbridge surrounded by tamarisks and a thorny shrub *xakh* and cross to the river's true right bank. The trail forks immediately. Both trails lead to Avgarch, but people describe the right fork as dangerous. Take the left fork

and follow the trail along the true right bank downstream, backtracking for a few minutes to the base of **Yasin Band**. Ascend a short 35-degree scree slope, and then a steep, narrow chimney with steps made out of juniper branches, to the terrace above. From this plateau are beautiful views south to Jurjur-Khun-e-Sar and east to Parigar Sar (6200m), a prominent rocky peak *(sar)* known as the rock *(gar)* where fairies *(pari)* dwell.

Continue 30 minutes along a canal at the base of a rocky rhubarb-dotted slope and through level fields and wildflowers to **Avgarch** (3200m). This large cultivated area was the first settlement of the Wakhi people living in the five villages between Sost and Morkhun who refer to themselves as Avgarchi. It has a mosque with unique wood carvings and two forts. One sits atop the central building, a reminder of the constant battles with Qirghiz people who also used the upper Hunza Valley until the 19th century. A lone giant juniper called **Baltar Yarz** is nearby. Legend says a boy, Baltar, would have died, but he sacrificed a cow near the juniper tree *(yarz)* and lived.

From Avgarch, continue up, then cross the river via a footbridge heading south-east

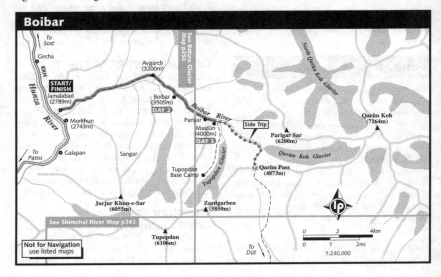

Boibar

To Sost

Gircha

KKH

Hunza River

START/ FINISH
Jamalabad (2789m)

Morkhun (2743m)

To Passu

Galapan

Avgarch (3200m)

See Batura Glacier Map p250

Boibar (3505m)
DAY 2

Sangar

Pariyar
Maidūn (4000m)
DAY 3

Boibar River

Tupopdan Base Camp

Jurjur Khun-e-Sar (6055m)

Zardgarben (5850m)

See Shimshal River Map p262

Tupopdan (6106m)

North Qarun Koh Glacier

Side Trip

Parigar Sar (6200m)

Qarūn Koh Glacier

Qarun Pass (4873m)

Qarūn Koh (7164m)

To Dūt

LP

0   2   4km
0   1   2mi
1:230,000

Not for Navigation use listed maps

to reach **Boibar** (3505m), a barren summer settlement 1½ hours from Avgarch. Boibar huts sit in a southern side valley, which has a small glacier. Above is the dramatic north face of Tupopdan (6106m), whose name means 'the sun-drenched mountain'.

Day 2: Boibar to Maidūn
2 hours, 6km, 495m ascent

Continue one hour to a cold spring called Xunza Kuk (Queen's spring), then 30 minutes to **Pariyar** (the place loved by fairies). These overgrazed pastures are at the upper limit of juniper. Many junipers have been cut, but some of those remaining are older than 1000 years. **Maidūn** (4000m), 30 minutes farther, has good water and makes a fine base camp for exploring the upper Boibar Valley. The route to Tupopdan Base Camp, used by the 1987 British expedition who were the first to summit Tupopdan, heads south up the Tupopdan Glacier from Maidūn.

Side Trip: Qarūn Pass
4–5 hours, 11km, 873m ascent, 873m descent

The original, but now abandoned, route to Shimshal village followed the Boibar Valley, crossed Qarūn Pass, and descended 2100m of treacherous scree to reach the Shimshal River at Dūt. A day trek to the top of the pass offers great views and a glimpse of how difficult access to Shimshal used to be. Legend has it that Mamu Singh, Shimshal's founder, saw the meadows along the Lupgar Glacier from the pass and so decided to take his livestock there. Shimshalis say the pass is like the legendary miser, Qarūn, because no water is available on the arduous ascent from Dūt to the pass, hence the name Qarūn Pass.

From Maidūn, ascend 1½ hours past yellow rock outcrops to the pasture of Zardgarben (the base of the yellow rock) from where the pass cairn is visible. Continue, passing right of the Qarūn Koh Glacier's black moraine to the base of the pass (4500m). From this point, the routes to Qarūn Koh and Parigar Sar base camps head across the glacier east and north-east

respectively. The route to the pass turns south, ascends a scree gully, and traverses to **Qarūn Pass** (4873m) in one hour. Lupgar Sar, Trivor and Destaghil Sar rise in front. Return from the pass to Maidūn.

Day 3: Maidūn to Jamalabad
4–5 hours, 13.7km, 1211m descent

Retrace steps downvalley to Jamalabad.

Lupgar Pir Pass

Duration	6 days
Distance	37.7km
Standard	very demanding
Season	mid-June–September
Start	Yishkuk
Finish	Raminj
Zone & Permit	open, no permit
Public Transport	yes
Summary	From the ochre landscape of Chapursan to the steep-walled, juniper-dotted canyons of Lupgar, this high pass crossing unfolds through unvisited alpine spectacle.

Little has been written about the beautiful route across the nonglaciated Lupgar Pir Pass (5190m). Following a route parallel to and south of Chapursan Valley, this trek links Yishkuk in upper Chapursan Valley with Raminj in the picturesque and rugged Lupgar Valley. People don't traditionally use the pass, but graze their livestock in the valleys on both sides of it. Renowned mountaineer Nazir Sabir, who is from Raminj, concurred that this book's authors' crossing in 1994 was probably the first since Schomberg's initial crossing in 1934. Since the 1994 'reopening' of the route, its popularity has been growing every year.

The trek can be done in either direction, but the description below is from west to east starting in Yishkuk, which allows for more gradual acclimatisation. This direction entails less ascending, since Yishkuk is 300m higher than Raminj, and the west side of the pass is shorter with less scree than the east side. The route involves two nontechnical glacier traverses.

PLANNING
Maps
The Swiss Foundation for Alpine Research 1:250,000 orographical map *Karakoram (Sheet 1)* covers the trek. The glaciers to the south-west and south-east of the pass are larger and in different positions from those drawn on the map. Many place names are inaccurate. Wyeen (on the west side of the pass), labelled as Wain, is between two spurs of the ridge descending from Peak 6006. People refer to the glacier south-east of Kit-ke-zherav (labelled as Kuk-ki-jerav) as the Wyeen Glacier, not the Kit-ke-zherav Glacier. The trail east of the summer settlement of Lupgar is inaccurately drawn. It runs along the river's true left bank until recrossing just above the place mislabelled Hapgurchi. Places names east of here to Raminj are inaccurate; Hoopkerch, Harkeesh, and Furzeen aren't shown.

Guides & Porters
Route-finding beyond (east of) Kit-ke-zherav (across the Wyeen Glacier and finding the pass itself) is tricky, so hire someone who knows the way. Most herders from Zood Khun only know the route as far as Banafshayeen where they take livestock. Herders from Raminj and Khaibar take livestock as far as Wyeen on the east side of the pass.

Porters ask for a flat rate of Rs 270 per stage, including payment for food rations. They also ask for the clothing and equipment allowance. Only pay for stages over which porters carry loads; don't pay when they ride in a vehicle. When you agree to pay for porters' transportation to and from their village, you aren't obliged to pay wāpasi.

Stages
The route totals eight stages. Prior to 1994, only these three stages were fixed west of the pass starting from Zood Khun: (1) Yishkuk (walking on the road); (2) Kit-ke-zherav (with Raud being half a stage); and (3) Wyeen (west of pass). The remaining five stages from Wyeen (west of pass) are understood to be: (4) Haji Beg Camp; (5) Wyeen (east of pass); (6) Lupgar; (7) Harkeesh; and (8) Raminj.

GETTING TO/FROM THE TREK
To the Start
Chapursan is beyond the Afiyatabad check post, so immigration officials may ask to see your passport. Vehicles depart Afiyatabad for Zood Khun (Rs 40–50, three hours) every afternoon shortly after the NATCO bus from Gilgit arrives. Special hires cost Rs 800–1000. Spend a night in Zood Khun to acclimatise. Beyond Zood Khun, either organise a special hire or walk 5.9km west-south-west along the road to Yishkuk in two hours.

From the Finish
The canal path enters the village and becomes the Raminj Link Rd. Walk 15 minutes through the village down to the Chapursan Link Rd. Raminj-Afiyatabad vehicles (Rs 30, 1¼ hours) are sporadic. Special hires cost Rs 500.

When combining multiple treks in Chapursan, you typically travel along the road between villages. Vehicles going upvalley and downvalley pick up passengers for fixed rates (eg, Raminj–Zood Khun is Rs 30 per person, plus Rs 10 per bag). Raminj–Zood Khun special hires cost 500.

THE TREK
Day 1: Yishkuk to Raud
30 minutes–1 hour, 1.4km, 150m ascent
Yishkuk (3450m) is a well-watered meadow with some willows. A good spring flows along the road just as you reach Yishkuk where *zolg (Berberis)*, with its edible blue berries, and wild rose bushes abound. Leave the road before it begins to climb towards the wooden bridge over the Yishkuk torrent. Walk south upvalley, over moraine rubble, with the Wyeen Glacier's outwash stream below to the west. Sparse junipers grow along the trail. The trail bends south-east and after 30 to 45 minutes reaches a level area, mostly sandy, next to a large, very cold, clear stream. The stream comes from a spring at the base of a south-facing scree slope. This spot, *Raud* (3600m), makes a wonderful camp site. To the west, across the 20km-long Yishkuk Glacier is the unusual red rock called Sekr, at the base of which is

a summer settlement. This is a very short walk, but most trekkers need to acclimatise before ascending farther.

Day 2: Raud to Wyeen
4½–5½ hours, 7.2km, 500m ascent

Cross the clear stream and walk five minutes along its true left bank to cross the two-part wooden footbridge over the large glacial torrent. Ascend 30 minutes above the river's true left bank amid junipers, on a small, clear herders' trail to the huts and livestock pen at **Kit-ke-zherav** (3690m). Reach the small Kit-ke-zherav stream from the south in five minutes. Cross it and continue up the narrow, rocky ablation valley 45 minutes to a side stream called **Shot Dur** (3780m; 'avalanche valley'). This is the last water until on the glacier. Continue up the valley, eventually climbing out of it to contour the green hillside, and reach a black talus slope in 45 minutes. Cross the greasy black talus called **Charva Shui** (3990m) in 15 minutes. Return to the ablation valley, ascending steadily 30 minutes until the valley curves south.

Across the Wyeen Glacier to the east is a side valley marked by red rock. Wyeen camp, south of it, is the grassy area visible

between two small ridges. Cross the glacier in two hours. The rock on the glacier is mostly stable and the crossing is easy. Stay to the north (left) of two enormous white and tan rubble mounds in the middle of the glacier. At **Wyeen** (4100m) only one or two tents can be pitched next to the huts and a couple more on rooftops. Larger trekking parties may prefer to camp by the glacial stream, which comes from Banafshayeen. Clear water is just above the livestock pen.

Day 3: Wyeen to Haji Beg Camp
4–5 hours, 5.4km, 630m ascent

Cross immediately to the Banafshayeen stream's true left bank. Go up Wyeen Glacier's lateral moraine on loose boulders one hour. Leave the moraine and walk along the stream's edge. Cross to its true right bank just below the mouth of the Banafshayeen Valley (4200m). A possible camp site for large trekking parties is across the silty stream in an open area next to a small moraine lake. Ascend east up the grassy slope 30 minutes to the level Banafshayeen Valley (4410m). The view of Kuk Sar (6943m) and its unclimbed 3000m vertical face is extraordinary. Banafshayeen, which

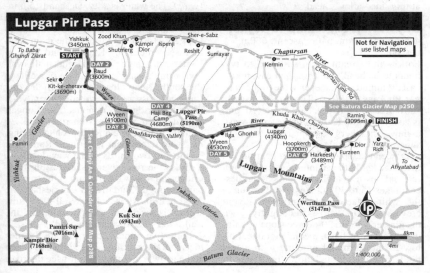

Lupgar Pir Pass

means 'the place where *banafsha (Primula macrophylla)* grows', is the highest pasture used by Wyeen herders.

From this point, no trails or cairns exist. Continue steadily up the stream's true right bank. One hour above the Banafshayeen pasture is the terminus of an unnamed glacier (4650m) that fills the valley. This glacier isn't shown on the Swiss map; it shows two small glaciers higher in the valley. These glaciers have merged and descend to below where the confluence of their outwash streams is shown on the map. Skirt the glacier on the slope high above its north margin. Walk on black lateral moraine 45 minutes to a small side valley, where a clear stream comes down. Continue another hour high above the glacier to a second side valley with a larger, clear stream tumbling down. Ascend along this stream five to 10 minutes to a large flat area where the remains of a square enclosure next to a large, prominent boulder indicates that others have been this way. This is *Haji Beg Camp* (4680m), named in 1994 by the authors after their travelling companion who embodies the spirit of these mountains. The views are remarkable and the pass is visible at this side valley's head.

Day 4: Haji Beg Camp to Wyeen
4–5 hours, 4.1km, 510m ascent, 660m descent

Follow the stream north-east one to two hours to its head (5100m), then east-north-east 30 minutes up steeper scree to the **Lupgar Pir Pass** (5190m). The pass is usually snow-free by mid-July. Pamiri Sar (7016m) is visible beyond Kuk Sar to the south-west, a view Schomberg described as 'a series of superb peaks and glaciers'.

Descend steep, loose scree, bearing left to a scree knoll, then continue over the knoll left and down to a glacier. This 300m descent takes 15 to 30 minutes. Head out on to the white glacier, zigzagging to avoid crevasses. Work across and slightly down the glacier's 15- to 20-degree slope 30 minutes to a narrow black medial moraine. Follow it onto terminal moraine with a few pools. About 500m below the glacier's

snout, more pools are visible. Rather than descending towards the mouth, stay high and traverse right on scree, well above the river 30 minutes to a clear stream and another 15 minutes to a grassy yak pasture called **Wyeen** (4530m).

The upper Lupgar Valley features striking red, yellow and brown rock formations. Climbers may be interested in the snowy 6000m peaks at the valley's head, which appear to be straightforward ascents.

Day 5: Wyeen to Hoopkerch
5–6 hours, 12.3km, 830m descent

Descend to the main river bed and pick up a faint trail. In 15 minutes, reach the large outwash stream from the big glacier to the south. Ford its several knee-deep channels. Across the stream, continue one hour to **Ilga** (4380m), a pasture with some unused huts. The water from a hanging glacier is especially silty in the afternoon. On the valley's north side are spectacular snowcapped spires with scree cascading from their base to the river. On its south side are fantastic red crags.

Descend 20 minutes to **Ghorhil**, a natural livestock pen *(hil)* amid the boulder field *(ghor)*. The water is silty. Descend 15 minutes through sharp boulders to a river from the south. Cross the river and continue to **Lupgar** (4140m, 'big rock'), the main summer settlement for Khaibar and Raminj herders who share pastoral rights in this valley. A tiny spring is at the base of a cliff to the south. Keep close to the cliffs leaving Lupgar. Cross a southern side stream via a stone footbridge, 15 minutes from Lupgar, then descend along its true right bank 30 minutes to the Lupgar River. A huge spring, the last reliable clear water until Raminj, is on the left, two-thirds of the way down.

Cross the river over an interesting footbridge and follow the trail along the true left bank through Khuda Khair Charjeshan, the 'God help us slides'. Rock fall along this section is deadly in wind or rain, and the trail is very narrow and exposed.

Forty-five minutes later, the trail comes to a natural footbridge. The gorge is so deep and narrow here that you can't see the river below. Cross to the true right bank and continue on a thin loose trail with tricky footing. Continue downvalley, crossing two side streams. The water in one is reddish, and the other is whitish. Descend one hour to a sandy area along the river, passing through a birch grove, then ascend and enter a juniper forest. Ahead and below 15 minutes is **Hoopkerch** (3700m, 'seven hunters' huts'), where a glacial side stream comes in from the south. A small spring is below the livestock pen.

Day 6: Hoopkerch to Raminj
3½–4 hours, 7.3km, 30m ascent, 605m descent

Cross the footbridge over the muddy stream and continue through beautiful ancient juniper forest one hour to **Harkeesh** (3489m, the 'place cultivated with a plough'). Harkeesh is the valley's only Burushaski place name, named by Burusho from Raminj who tried to farm here. The Wakhi name for Harkeesh is Kishtazod. The well-built hut and livestock pen are surrounded by a broad, open grassy area that makes a perfect camp site. The canyon walls rise to cliffs crowned by monumental, multicoloured rocky peaks, spires and towers. The route from the Werthum Pass comes out here (see p259). Water from the side stream can be silty.

From Harkeesh, descend steeply 10 minutes and cross a side stream via a footbridge. Birches, roses, tamarisks and junipers flourish in this area called Furzeen (Purzin on the Swiss map). Five minutes farther, cross a sturdy footbridge to the Lupgar River's true left bank. The trail from here to Raminj is considerably better, although it's still exposed in places. For the next 1¼ to 1½ hours to the Raminj canal's headworks, the trail traverses high above the river gorge occasionally dropping closer to the river. Midway, pass a footbridge to the Lupgar River's true right bank above the confluence of the Lupgar and Dior rivers leading to the Dior hut.

Follow the path along the willow-lined canal one hour to Raminj, passing several gushing springs en route. The canal, begun during the reign of Mir Muhammad Jamal Khan and completed in 1978, is a marvel of construction. Several tunnels, built through the cliff, carry the canal under scree slopes that the trail crosses. **Raminj** (3095m), which lies above the confluence of the Lupgar and Chapursan rivers, is a beautiful, well-tended east- and south-facing village.

Chilinji An & Qalander Uween

Duration	6 days
Distance	57km
Standard	very demanding, technical
Season	mid-June–September
Start	Baba Ghundi Ziarat
Finish	Bort
Zone & Permit	restricted, US$50 permit
Public Transport	finish only

Summary Cross a challenging glaciated pass along Pakistan's northernmost border between the dramatic and sacred landscape of Chapursan and the rock walls and spires of the Karambar Valley.

Chilinji An somewhat confusedly refers to two distinct passes linking Chapursan with the Karambar Valley to its west: the true Chilinji An (5160m); and the Chilinji An North, known as Qalander Uween (5220m) to people from Chapursan. (*Qalander* means 'an ascetic wanderer' in Urdu, and *uween*, a 'pass' in Wakhi.) The east sides of these passes are glaciated, whereas the west sides are steep, generally dry, scree.

Trekkers going from east to west typically cross the true Chilinji An, the pass crossed by early 20th-century explorers such as British archaeologist Aurel Stein, HW Tilman and Wilfred Thesiger. Trekkers going from west to east usually cross the Qalander Uween, although many of them mistakenly think it's the true Chilinji An. (That said, it's possible for strong parties to cross the true Chilinji An from west to east, although no high camp is set.) The descriptions for both routes follow. Only previously acclimatised trekkers should attempt crossing from east to west.

The Chilinji An frequently precedes the Karambar An & Darkot An trek (p174) by crossing to the Karambar River's true right bank at Chilinj on Day 5 and heading up the Karambar Valley. The Qalander Uween is often combined with the Broghil & Karambar An trek (p158).

PLANNING
What to Bring
Mountaineering equipment necessary for travelling in roped teams is required (see Mountaineering Equipment, p61, for a discussion of appropriate gear).

Maps
The Swiss Foundation for Alpine Research 1:250,000 orographical map *Karakoram (Sheet 1)* covers the trek. The map shows the Chilinji An, but its actual coordinates are 36° 47' 47.7" N and 74° 03' 51.8" E. It gives inaccurate place names and locations. In particular, Biatar, an important camp, is along the true right bank of the river flowing east from the passes. The glacier on the east side of the Chilinji An, above Biatar, isn't labelled. In the trek description, it's referred to as the Biatar Glacier, because the glacier on the west side of the pass is the actual Chilinji Glacier. No maps depict the Qalander Uween, whose coordinates are 36° 48' 08.8" N and 74° 03' 41.1" E, nor the route over it.

Permits & Regulations
This trek is in a restricted zone where a permit and licensed guide are required (see Trekking Permits, p70, for futher information). Bring multiple photocopies of your permit, which you may be asked to give to the army at Baba Ghundi Ziarat and the police in Imit.

Baba Ghundi

Baba Ghundi Ziarat, Hunza's most important shrine (*ziarat* or *astan*), draws pilgrims from as far as Baltistan. The current shrine, built in 1924 by Hunza's Mir Ghazin Khan, houses the tomb of the saint and his wife, along with the saint's sword. Baba Ghundi came to Chapursan from Ghund, a valley in what is today's Tajikistan. He performed numerous miracles throughout Chapursan, each commemorated by a small shrine. The shrine of Panja Shah, just before Yarz Rich, has many coloured flags. Inside is a rock with three long scrape marks, as though made by claws. The saint is said to have made these marks, and ghee is poured on them as an oblation. Kermin has a shrine, as does Reshit, where a rock bears the imprint of the saint's fist and horse whip. Baba Ghundi's main miracle is a tale of sin and retribution, very similar to other legends in Pakistan and Kashmir. When Baba Ghundi first came to Chapursan, it was a fertile, wealthy valley where the people lived in sin. He went from house to house, asking alms, but only one old woman offered him food. Angry at the villagers, but pleased with the old woman's devotion, Baba Ghundi told her to leave her house and climb the hill. As she did, she saw Baba Ghundi riding at the head of a great flood that wiped out the valley and its people in punishment for their sinful ways. Evidently, a great outburst flood from the Yishkuk Glacier actually did cover most of the valley with boulders and mud as far down as Kampir Dior village, where the remains of the old woman's house are visible today.

Baba Ghundi is also remembered as a dragon slayer. West of Zood Khun is Ravai Zhui, a lake in which lived a dragon that terrorised the villagers. The saint killed the dragon and 'dragon's bones' are still found today in the dry lake bed. Today, Baba Ghundi's main blessing is to bestow children on childless couples. The time for pilgrimage to his shrine is late September and early October, when religious songs are sung throughout the night. Goats are offered with prayers, and the meat is distributed, imbued with the *barakat*, or spiritual power, of the saint. Throughout the year, pilgrims arrive on Thursday to offer prayers on Friday. Close to the main shrine, near the river, is a spring decorated with ibex horns; its mineral water, called *ab-e-shafa*, bestows health on those who drink it.

Guides & Porters

Chapursan porters ask for a flat rate of Rs 270 per stage, including payment for food rations. They also ask for the clothing and equipment allowance. Hire someone from Chapursan who knows the route if your guide doesn't know it. When you trek from east to west, you use Chapursan porters. Having Wakhi porters opens doors for you in areas where their relatives live. When trekking from west to east, you most likely use Chitrali porters who are allowed to carry loads to Baba Ghundi Ziarat, from where they walk back to Chitral.

Some trekking companies have set a precedent to pay 'drop' fees to porters who travel by vehicle from their village to Baba Ghundi Ziarat. Since the porters carry no load and you already pay for their transportation, it makes no sense to pay an additional 'drop' fee.

Stages

It totals eight stages from Baba Ghundi Ziarat: (1) Yarz Yarz; (2) Biatar; (3) Chilinji An Base Camp; (4) Chilinji An; (5) Jungle Camp; (6) Maturamdan; (7) Yazben; and (8) Bort.

When travelling with Chitrali porters over Qalander Uween, the stages between Jungle Camp and Baba Ghundi Ziarat are: (1) Qalander Uween High Camp; (2) Biatar; and (3) Baba Ghundi Ziarat.

GETTING TO/FROM THE TREK
To the Start

Chapursan is beyond the Afiyatabad check post, so immigration officials ask to see your passport. The 70km drive between Afiyatabad and Baba Ghundi Ziarat takes four hours; three hours to Zood Khun, and another hour to Baba Ghundi Ziarat. Usually several jeeps, vans or pick-up trucks depart Afiyatabad every afternoon, shortly after the daily NATCO bus from Gilgit arrives. Most vehicles (Rs 60) go only as far as Zood Khun. Afiyatabad–Baba Ghundi Ziarat special hires cost Rs 2000; it costs Rs 1000 Afiyatabad–Zood Khun, plus Rs 1000 Zood Khun–Baba Ghundi Ziarat. Alternatively, it's two stages to walk the 10km along the road between Zood Khun and Baba Ghundi Ziarat. When you take porters in a vehicle, pay them only for stages over which they carry a load.

The grassy expanse at Baba Ghundi Ziarat offers ample room to camp. Spend one or two nights here to acclimatise and visit with Wakhi and Qirghiz from Afghanistan's Wakhan Corridor who come to Baba Ghundi Ziarat to trade livestock for supplies such as flour, tea and salt. Springs are across the footbridge on the river's true left bank.

From the Finish

The road goes as far as Bort, but in summer, high water may block the road at Bilhanz. When it's blocked, walk along the road, fording side streams as needed. It takes four hours to walk between Bort and Bilhanz. One stage is fixed between Bort and Bad Swat. You may have to pay for an additional partial stage between Bad Swat and Bilhanz.

Jeeps to Gilgit cost Rs 120 from Bort, Rs 115 from Bilhanz and Rs 110 from Imit. Special hires cost Rs 3000 from Bort, Rs 2750 from Bilhanz and Rs 2500 from Imit. Alternatively, you can take a jeep to Chatorkhand or Gakuch and get on a NATCO bus to Gilgit there.

THE TREK: CHILINJI AN
Day 1: Baba Ghundi Ziarat to Yarz Yarz

2 hours, 5.4km, 140m ascent

From Baba Ghundi Ziarat (3660m), cross the footbridge and walk one hour on a good

Qirghiz traders from Wakhan loading a yak at Baba Ghundi Ziarat, Chapursan Valley.

JOHN MOCK

trail to the footbridge over Sekr Zherav (red stream). Across the Chapursan River to the south are the huts at Shpod Kut (rhubarb on the roof), labelled Shikarkuk on the Swiss map. Continue another hour to *Yarz Yarz* (3800m). This once-fine juniper *(yarz)* stand has been decimated for firewood and timber. Huts are on either side of a small clear stream with room for a few tents.

Day 2: Yarz Yarz to Biatar
3 hours, 7km, 220m ascent

Twenty minutes along the alluvial fan, reach the base of a reddish cliff called Besk

Rui. A small camp site here is called *Beske-Ben*. A larger camp site called *Targeen* is below, along a clear stream lined with tamarisks *(targ)* just before the Kuz Glacier's terminus. The trail works up the cliffs 45 minutes, easing off near the top (3900m), then contours 15 minutes to Jamal Ilga (3810m), a livestock pen and several huts below the trail to the south. From here, another trail leads north to Zhui Werth (millstone by the lake) and Irshad Uween, a pass on the Afghan border.

Thirty minutes beyond Jamal Ilga, a stream bars the trail where a footbridge

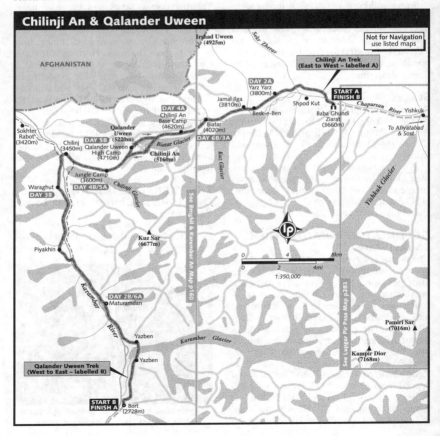

Chilinji An & Qalander Uween

Not for Navigation use listed maps

No matter how you get there, the view sure is worth it! Clockwise from bottom left: porters crossing the Shimshal River; flooded road approaching the Shimshal Village trailhead; yak transport on the Shimshal Pamir trek; cable crossing of the Ghuzherav River at War-e-Ben; Mai Dur-e-Gush camp site.

Above Passu village, Tupopdan, 'the sun-drenched mountain', lives up to its name.

Biatar camp site, Upper Chapursan Valley.

Wakhi woman cooking bread, Shimshal.

washed away. Descend onto the Kuz (shady) Glacier and cross the lateral moraine to avoid fording the deep, swift stream that disappears under the glacier. The trail continues along this stream's true right bank another hour to the huts and livestock pen at **Biatar** (4020m) with large, clear springs and grassy camp sites amid boulders.

Day 3: Biatar to Chilinji An Base Camp

3½–4 hours, 4.6km, 600m ascent

Ascend the rocky pasture directly above Biatar 45 minutes to the base of a large cliff on the valley's east side. The Biatar Glacier, which descends from Chilinji An, fills the valley. Follow a faint trail 30 minutes to the top of the Biatar Glacier's lateral moraine (4260m). Cross the glacier over terminal moraine, fording a glacial stream flowing over ice. Reach the ablation valley on the glacier's west margin, where yaks graze, in 45 minutes. Late in the season, water is scarce. Ascend the ever-narrowing ablation valley 1¾ hours, climbing steadily to reach **Chilinji An Base Camp** (4620m), with four tent platforms and five rock circles. Water comes from a nearby snow bank. This camp site has some rock-fall danger.

Day 4: Chilinji An Base Camp to Jungle Camp

5–6 hours, 7km, 540m ascent, 1560m descent

Walk up the crest of the moraine to a large cairn, which marks the high camp for trekkers coming from west to east. Follow the lateral moraine one hour along the glacier's north margin. As the moraine diminishes and bends right, cross on to the level snow-covered glacier. The pass is directly ahead. Head towards the yellowish crag that marks the north side of the pass. Some medial moraine descends from this crag. Follow this moraine a short way, until one hour after coming onto the glacier you encounter black moraine and the slope steepens to 30 degrees. From this point, travel in roped teams. Head up the middle of the glacier towards the pass, zigzagging to avoid numerous crevasses. Reach the tall cairn marking **Chilinji An** (5160m) in one hour.

Put away your rope and head down scree, traversing north (right) to a small ridge. Follow the crest of this ridge 10 to 15 minutes until you can descend right on scree to the valley below. A few small tent platforms (4560m) on rock are near a clear stream. The 600m scree descent takes 45 minutes.

Follow the stream over very steep, loose scree. Be careful of rock fall. It takes one hour to descend almost 1000m of scree to the gentler slopes and forest below. Head for the lateral moraine of the Chilinji Glacier 15 minutes ahead through dense willow and birch. In this lovely ablation valley, stop near the obvious bend in the clear stream. This forested site is called **Jungle Camp** (3600m).

Days 5–6: Jungle Camp to Bort

2 days, 33km, 872m descent

Follow the stream through the forested ablation valley, crossing it several times. Tall junipers grow farther down this enchanting sheltered valley, and a waterfall cascades from cliffs above. After one to 1½ hours, you reach the Gujar settlement of **Chilinj** (3450m) along the Karambar River's true left bank.

Head down the Karambar Valley camping at **Maturamdan** on Day 5 en route to Bort (see Days 1–3 of the Karambar An & Darkot An trek, p177, for details in the reverse direction).

THE TREK: QALANDER UWEEN
Days 1–3: Bort to Jungle Camp

3 days, 33km, 872m ascent

See Days 1–3 of the Karambar An & Darkot An trek (p177) for details, but on Day 3 leave the Karambar Valley above Waraghut by crossing the cable to the river's true left bank at Chilinj and continue 3km to **Jungle Camp** (3600m).

Day 4: Jungle Camp to Qalander Uween High Camp

3–4 hours, 3.4km, 1110m ascent

The trail heads up the vegetated slope dotted with blue salvias and other wildflowers. Continue past the highest willows and after 30 to 45 minutes head right into a steep, narrow canyon. Follow the stream bed, using the boulders as irregular stairs, one hour to the top of the ravine, where the angle eases (4560m). A clear stream flows across black scree on the right, and the trail from the true Chilinji An is visible on the scree above. Continue upvalley, working left onto light-coloured moraine, another two to 2½ hours to the valley's head. A cairn, tent platforms and stone porters' shelters mark the *Qalander Uween High Camp* (4710m). A small stream provides water.

Day 5: Qalander Uween High Camp to Biatar

7–8 hours, 8.2km, 510m ascent, 1200m descent

Ascend a faint trail up the obvious steep scree slope 1½ to two hours to **Qalander Uween** (5220m). Near the top, pass right of a large rock outcrop. The angle approaches 50 degrees as you near the pass, necessitating use of a trekking pole, taking care to avoid knocking rock onto those below. A small cairn marks the pass. Descend right to rock at the edge of the névé. Travel in roped teams as you descend the centre of the 10- to 15-degree névé field, working left towards the rock wall on the glacier's left margin probing for hidden crevasses. Exit the glacier's left margin into the rocky ablation zone, 1½ to two hours from the pass. Descend steeply on the left side of the massive icefall from the upper glacial basin into the Biatar Glacier. Looking back, it's hard to imagine a relatively easy route exists above the imposing icefall. Continue down the Biatar Glacier's left margin. The route to the true Chilinji An is clearly visible back up the centre of this glacier. Pass the *Chilinji An Base Camp* and continue another hour down the ablation valley. Then cross the glacier above its terminus, fording its outwash stream to its true right bank. Follow a trail down to *Biatar* (4020m).

Day 6: Biatar to Baba Ghundi Ziarat

5 hours, 12.4km, 360m descent

See Days 1–2 of the Chilinji An & Qalander Uween trek (pp287–8) for a description in reverse.

Kilik & Mintaka Passes

Duration	6 days
Distance	88.4km
Standard	moderate
Season	June–September
Start/Finish	Misgar
Zone & Permit	open, no permit
Public Transport	yes
Summary	For more than 1000 years, Kilik and Mintaka were the Silk Route's primary passes between China and Hunza, and today these broad valleys and extensive alpine meadows, once closed to foreigners, are again accessible.

Kilik and Mintaka, two historic passes on Pakistan's border with China, have been off limits to foreigners since 1947. Now open since 1999, the 1m- to 3m-wide trails to these gentle passes are easy to follow, springs and trees are abundant, and camp sites are grassy, making this one of northern Pakistan's easiest treks.

PLANNING
Maps

The US AMS 1:250,000 topographic map *Baltit (NJ 43-14)* covers the trek except the area between Shireen Maidan and Kilik Pass. The only map to depict this area is the US DMA 1:500,000 topographic map *TPC G-7A*, but the scale renders it useless for trekking. The U502 map doesn't show the road to Kalam Darchi. The trail beyond Boi Hil to Gul Khwaja Uween is shown on the Mintaka River's true left bank, but it's along the true right bank all the way between Murkushi and Gul Khwaja Uween.

Guides & Porters

The system of portering and stages was first introduced to Misgar in 1999. Most village men know Kilik Valley, their primary summer pastures, but few know Mintaka Valley beyond Yatumgoz Harai. They're unaccustomed to carrying loads and don't have metal-frame carriers. Misgar men typically use donkeys to transport their own loads to the pastures, and prefer to do the same with trekkers' loads. One donkey carries up to two loads, but is slow. Start out with don-keys from Misgar because you cannot rely on finding any available donkeys upvalley.

Misgar's nambardar Ataullah and village elders set porters' wages at a flat Rs 250 per stage, including payment for food rations and the clothing and equipment allowance. Misgar also has yaks, but during summer yaks don't go below Murkushi. Additionally, Misgar sets a rate of Rs 300–350 per load for yaks, which carry two loads.

Stages

These stages were set during a July 2000 meeting in Misgar attended by this book's authors and Misgar's Board of Governors, which included the nambardar, religious leaders, representatives of the Pamir Cattle Breeding Farm and village political leaders.

The Last Outpost of the British Empire

Misgar is the farthest village in the upper Hunza Valley. Settled in the 19th century by Burusho from Hunza who were sent by the Mir of Hunza to guard against Qirghiz raiders from the Pamirs, it's today one of Gojal's few Burushaski-speaking villages. The Mir's distant outpost became, after the British conquest of Hunza in 1891, the empire's farthest outpost. From Misgar, British sportsmen travelled across Kilik Pass (4827m) to the Taghdumbash Pamir in China in search of game and to learn of the movements of Russian travellers as part of The Great Game, the 19th-century Anglo-Russian rivalry in Central Asia. Misgar was linked to Gilgit by a telegraph line, and later by a tele-phone line. The British employed men as mail runners to carry weekly British dispatches be-tween Misgar and the British consulate in Kash-gar. The mail runners reached Tashkurgan in six days from Misgar, via the Mintaka Pass (4726m), which was the standard route prior to the 1986 opening of the Karakoram Highway over the Khunjerab Pass. Today's trekkers can also visit Kilik Pass where Lord Curzon, later Viceroy of India (1899–1905), stood in 1894 at the outermost edge of Britain's empire.

The entire village agreed to and accepted these stages: Misgar to Arbab-e-Bul (ie, it's half a stage between Misgar and Kalam Darchi plus half a stage between Kalam Darchi and Arbab-e-Bul); Arbab-e-Bul to Murkushi; Murkushi to Sad Buldi; and Murkushi to Gul Khwaja Uween.

The trek described covers a total of eight stages not including the side trips. When you hire a vehicle between Misgar and Kalam Darchi, subtract half a stage for each direc-tion that porters ride and don't carry a load.

The village prefers Gurgun Pert as the overnight place and stage in Mintaka Valley as opposed to Gul Khwaja Uween, which they feel is too cold and too high for porters to sleep. At the time of research, however, there was no usable porters' hut at Gurgun Pert. It's in the interest of trekkers to camp at the more scenic Gul Khwaja Uween, which is a far superior site for the Mintaka Pass side trip. But, it's in the interests of porters to camp lower at Gurgun Pert so they don't have to walk as far with loads. (It's 8km or 2½ hours between Murkushi and Gurgun Pert, and 3.5km or 1½ hours be-tween Gurgun Pert and Gul Khwaja Uween.) Time will tell how this will work out. Meanwhile, it's important to discuss this and reach an agreement before starting.

When you visit either pass on a day trek and your porter accompanies you with no load, you pay one stage for each day trek. Therefore, you pay one stage round trip when you go from Sad Buldi to Kilik Pass and back, or from Gul Khwaja Uween to Mintaka Pass and back. When you do both side trips to Kilik and Mintaka passes as day treks, the trek becomes a total of 10 stages.

The side trip to Hapuchan Valley is also done as a single-stage day trek. When porters carry a load to the head of Hapuchan Valley, it's one stage. A final wrinkle is that if you have porters move your camp above Sad Buldi or Haaq to Luto Harai, it's one stage.

NEAREST VILLAGE
Misgar

Sitting high above the Kilik River's true left bank, the sunny village has its own electricity supply, telephone and post office. Misgar

(3075m) was once populated by Wakhi speakers who abandoned the valley due to intense raiding by Qirghiz nomads from Wakhan. The village was resettled in the 19th century by Burushaski speakers from Hunza, who gave their own pronunciation to the area's many Wakhi place names. In Wakhi, *mis* means 'nose' and *gar* means 'rock', a description of the shape of the rock inside the flag-festooned roadside shrine (*astan*) in the village's centre. Legend has it that butter used to drip from the stone until a greedy villager attempted to gather too much, and the blessed butter ceased to flow.

Places to Stay The 90-year-old British customs house on the village's east side has been revamped into the small *Kilik Guest House* by its owner, Shifaullah. A small grassy area surrounded by a pretty flower garden has space for two tents. The old officer's bedroom inside costs Rs 200 per bed and the camping fee is Rs 50. The welcoming family serves good food on the attractive covered porch. Other villagers offer rooms in their homes at comparable rates and, at the time of research, plans were afoot to build commercial hotels in the village and a camping area on its outskirts.

Getting There & Away Misgar is beyond the Afiyatabad check post, so immigration

---

Warning

Trekkers can go to Kilik and Mintaka passes as far as the large concrete border markers, erected by the Survey of Pakistan in 1964, but should not enter Chinese territory. Chinese guards patrol the border area and will arrest anyone attempting to illegally enter China. Any such incident would likely result in the immediate closing of Misgar to foreigners. Misgar villagers have no interest in seeing their earnings from tourism brought to a premature end. Therefore, they justifiably insist that no foreigner should visit the pass areas unless accompanied by a villager. Respect their legitimate concerns and cooperate in keeping this fascinating and historic area open.

---

officials ask to see your passport. The 16km well-maintained Misgar Link Rd leaves the KKH 15 minutes north of Afiyatabad. Wagons to Misgar (Rs 135) depart Gilgit's Jamat Khana bazaar directly for Misgar at 7am, stopping in Afiyatabad at 1pm, and arriving in Misgar shortly after.

From Afiyatabad, the 30-minute ride to Misgar costs Rs 15, and special hires cost Rs 250. Daily wagons depart Misgar for Gilgit between 6 and 6.30am.

GETTING TO/FROM THE TREK
The road continues north to Kalam Darchi. Misgar–Kalam Darchi special hires cost Rs 200 (7km, 20 minutes).

THE TREK
Day 1: Misgar to Murkushi
6–7 hours, 21km, 584m ascent
It takes 1½ hours to walk 7km along the road between Misgar and Kalam Darchi. Follow the Kilik River's true left bank past several springs. Fifteen minutes before Kalam Darchi, the road crosses a bridge to the river's true right bank. At the base of Kalam Darchi Fort it crosses another bridge over the Dilisang River back to the Kilik River's true right bank. Here a sign posted by the Pamir Cattle Breeding Farm shows a 'Y' with the left fork pointing north-west to 'Dilleson' (Dilisang) and the right fork pointing north to 'Kilik/Mintaka'. The road ends and the trail begins near the abandoned riverside army barracks. Kalam Darchi, locally called KD, was built as a Gilgit Scouts post in the late 1930s on the site of an old Hunza watchtower, and was manned by the Pakistan Army until 1994. Now only caretakers occupy the post.

The trail follows the Kilik River's true right bank a few minutes and crosses a well-built footbridge to its true left bank. In five minutes is the grassy area of **Khan Wali** (3205m), above which are the remnants of a British check post. Soon the trail goes along talus at the base of a scree slope as it parallels and then crosses a clear tamarisk-lined side stream called **Bahadur Khan-e-Bul** (Bahadur Khan's spring). Fifteen minutes farther is a faint trail junction. Veer left on the trail that drops and crosses the river on a footbridge. Called Phari Bridge, it was built to replace a footbridge farther upstream that washed away in a flood.

Once on the river's true right bank, climb a short rough bit to the level sandy area where the footbridge used to be. Here the Kilik River is broad and shallow in contrast to the swift-moving river downvalley. Thirty minutes farther is Arbab-e-Bul (the arbab's spring). Mature birch trees and willows line a clear stream through this grassy area. Across the river is a black terminal moraine from a side glacier. The trail stays along the Kilik River's true right bank all the way to Murkushi, passing through a series of inviting level grassy birch groves about every 30 minutes, named Rung Hil, Put Hil and Lup Jangal. Between each grassy area is a stony section, but the well-made broad trail is easy to follow and allows you to enjoy the towering cliffs on either side of this broad, well-watered valley.

Murkushi (3659m), the last and largest of these grassy birch-dotted plains, is 14km from Kalam Darchi at the confluence of the Kilik and Mintaka rivers. A herders' hut and livestock pen lies at Murkushi's south end, but the best camp sites are among birch trees towards the north end beneath huge granite cliffs. Clear water flows in a small tamarisk-lined stream near the Kilik River.

Day 2: Murkushi to Sad Buldi
4½ hours, 11.7km, 585m ascent

Between Murkushi and Sad Buldi the landscape changes radically from the steep spires and rocky summits of the Karakoram to the rounded, rolling grasslands of the *pamir*. Cross a sloping footbridge to the Kilik River's true left bank and make a short but steep climb to join the main trail heading north-west upvalley. The broad trail rises steadily beneath huge, sheer, water-polished granite cliffs and spires, and one hour from Murkushi reaches the first

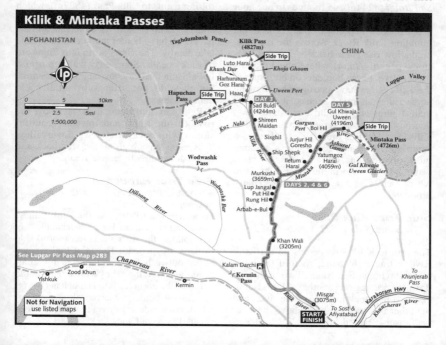

Kilik & Mintaka Passes

GOJAL

grassy area (3870m), which has a spring and a few birch trees. The area between here and the livestock gate upvalley is called **Ship Shepk**.

Thirty minutes farther, a huge trailside spring emerges from rock and in five more minutes the trail passes through the livestock gate. Ahead the trail crosses a former lake bed and continues another hour to ford a large clear side stream through a grassy area called **Sisghil**. Gumbish, a Qirghiz tomb bedecked with Marco Polo sheep horns, marks the south end of *Shireen Maidan*, a level plain with a polo field marked out in stones and some crumbling stone walls and a spring at its north end. The Kilik Pass is visible from here.

Beyond Shireen Maidan and Kuz Nala, the side valley directly opposite, the landscape changes to that of the pamir. The gentle trail continues along closer to the river, and crosses a clear stream at **Shapt Pud** (wolf's foot). The broad windswept plain of *Sad Buldi* (4244m), 45 minutes to one hour from Shireen Maidan, has a herders' hut and livestock pen amid boulders near the tumbling Kilik River. Across the river behind a low rise is the herders' hut and livestock pen of *Haaq*, where the village's herders live. Large boulders on both side of the Kilik River have petroglyphs showing horse riders, hunting scenes, ibex, naked male figures and Buddhist swastikas, evidence of a long and varied human usage of Kilik. Sad Buldi is preferable to Haaq as a camp site, with more grass, less grazing, more privacy and easier access to clear water. Misgar men prefer staying at Haaq where there's more activity and fresh dairy products.

Side Trip: Kilik Pass
4–4½ hours, 11km, 583m ascent, 583m descent
The trail to Kilik Pass begins on the Kilik River's true right bank, so ford the river when staying at Sad Buldi. Two trails lead upvalley, joining one another at Luto Harai. One is a livestock trail along the river, and the other is a traverse high above the river on flower-carpeted hillsides. It's easier to follow the river route upvalley and return along the high route.

From the Haaq side of the river, follow the livestock trail along the grassy flower-strewn stream bank. Pass the confluence of the stream descending from the rounded Uween Pert, to the right, then cross the Khush Dur stream flowing in from the left 30 minutes from Sad Buldi. Continue along the Kilik River's true right bank, occasionally hopping rocks from side to side as needed. Pass through the extensive grassy area of **Harhurutum Goz Harai** (the grassy plain where yaks come to sit and stay). At **Luto Harai** (Luto's pasture), two hours from Sad Buldi, are several tumbledown stone walls once used as a herders' camp. A side stream opposite (east of) Luto Harai, fed by a gigantic snowfield, is Khoja Ghoom (where the Khoja got lost).

Leaving the Kilik River, head left up a rocky hillside trail to the level grassy area above. Continue north across the broad rolling pamir to **Kilik Pass** (4827m), which is half an hour from Luto Harai. The pass area is a 2km- to 3km-wide plateau, and the pass itself has a border marker and a sizable lake nearby. The views north into China are of rocky peaks. Some easy walk-up peaks, in Pakistan territory, are near the pass area, but they do not offer substantially enhanced views.

Return to Luto Harai, then stay above the river (to the right) and traverse beautiful slopes with excellent views downvalley. This route stays high all the way back and drops down directly above Haaq.

Side Trip: Hapuchan
4½ hours, 14km, 200m ascent, 200m descent
Hapuchan is a tributary of the Kilik Valley, branching west from Haaq. A leisurely day trek follows the river's true left (north) side to the valley's head. The faint trail crosses rocky outwash fans interspersed by small grassy areas. At the valley's upper end, a side valley to the north leads to Hapuchan Pass on the Chinese border, a Marco Polo sheep habitat. Another side valley leads south to Wodwashk Pass (see Other Treks, p300).

Day 3: Sad Buldi to Murkushi
3–3½ hours, 11.7km, 585m descent
Retrace your steps downvalley to *Murkushi* (3659m). If you're fit, feeling strong, and can convince any porters, this day combines easily with Day 4.

Day 4: Murkushi to Gul Khwaja Uween
4 hours, 11.5km, 537m ascent
The broad Mintaka Valley retains a typical Karakoram feel, and its reddish-brown granite terraces and cliffs, level grassy areas, numerous side streams and waterfalls give it a dramatic but pleasant quality. The easy walk is on a 2m- to 3m-wide, well-built trail that ascends four short rocky sections, remnants of ancient landslides that once dammed the river, and crosses four broad level grassy areas, former lake beds, now home to many marmots. The trail stays along the Mintaka River's true right bank the entire way.

From Murkushi, cross the sloping footbridge to the Kilik River's true left bank and continue east, passing above a small hut. The trail climbs and stays above the milky Mintaka River as the valley bends north-east. In one hour reach **Iletum Harai**, the first long level grassy area where island-like mounds carpeted by wildflowers dot the broad river. A braided cascade tumbles over granite across the river. At the upper end of this area, more than 1km long, is Jurjur Hil Goresho, with another impressive cascade across the river. Clear water from more falls along the river's true right bank make this a possible camp site.

Beyond the waterfalls, climb a rocky area 15 minutes to another level area. Fifteen minutes farther, **Yatumgoz Harai** (4059m, 'upper grass'), a herders' hut and livestock pen, sits along the river's true left bank, two hours from Murkushi. This stretch has no clear water. The glacier on the valley's east (right) side is Ashural Gamu, and on the valley's west (left) side, hidden from view high above the trail, is a grassy area and lake called Gurgun Pert.

Fifteen minutes beyond Yatumgoz Harai, pass a footbridge, the route back to the hut. Shortly beyond it, cross a side stream, the outwash from Gurgun Pert. The trail heads north-east through a mixed rock and grass area, soon passing a herders' hut and livestock pen with collapsed walls (also called Gurgun Pert). The whole area is known as **Boi Hil**.

The trail continues through a flatter grassy area with a clear stream coming from the base of a big black terminal moraine that emerges from the north-west. This moraine dammed the river in the not-distant past, and the trail traverses the talus-covered moraine, then drops into the valley's last level upper section after 45 minutes. This recently dammed area has significantly less vegetation than those below and the river lies in braided channels across the grey expanse.

Skirting the river's edge, the trail soon reaches **Gul Khwaja Uween** (Gul Khwaja's Pass) with a dramatic granite cliff behind it, over which two free-leaping cascades tumble. Attractive grassy terraces on the cliffs above and the clear white central ice of the Gul Khwaja Uween Glacier to the south-east give this camp site a dramatic appeal. Two huts provide porters' shelter, near which are several grassy camp sites (4196m). The Pakistan Army, which used this area until the early 1990s, built many roofless stone shelters, now weed-filled and tumbling down. Those that face the route to Mintaka Pass have small apertures in their walls for gun placements.

Side Trip: Mintaka Pass
4–4½ hours, 7.5km, 530m ascent, 530m descent
The route to Mintaka Pass is visible from Gul Khwaja Uween. The pass lies just beyond the low saddle in the cliff walls above the glacier's north-east margin. The military-made 1m-wide trail is still serviceable and easy to follow, although rock fall and some moraine collapse means scrambling over short sections. Flowers decorate the moist hillside, which supports good marmot and ram chukor populations. The area around Mintaka Pass abounds in brown bear and wolf signs, and even those of the elusive snow leopard. All in all, Mintaka is the more dramatic of the two passes.

From Gul Khwaja Uween, head southeast and cross the braided clear side stream. Follow its true left bank upstream, then past the base of a cliff onto the Gul Khwaja Uween Glacier's lateral moraine. The trail leads to gently graded switchbacks that wind up a grassy slope to the obvious saddle, two hours from Gul Khwaja Uween. Turn east and walk through a marshy flower-filled area. The trail keeps left (west) across black talus to Mintaka Pass (4726m), half an hour from the saddle. The pretty 500m-wide pass lies between two large rocky peaks. At the border marker, look into the broad, lush Lupgoz (big grass) Valley, but be aware that a Chinese border post sits about 500m beyond the border marker. Return via the same route.

Day 5: Gul Khwaja Uween to Murkushi
3½ hours, 11.5km, 537m descent
Retrace your steps downvalley to Murkushi. You can do this following your visit to Mintaka Pass if you're fit and your porters are willing.

Day 6: Murkushi to Misgar
5 hours, 21km, 584m descent
The valley stays shaded well into mid-morning, which is a good incentive to start early on hot days. Stroll easily downvalley on the broad trail to Kalam Darchi, then follow the even easier road back to Misgar.

Other Treks

The following treks are all in an open zone, except where noted.

SHATUBAR GLACIER
From Gulmit, follow the road behind the village one hour to Kamaris village (2800m). A side trip goes 30 minutes north-east to the ruins of Andra Fort, built about 200 years ago to protect against Nagyr raiders. Heading west from Kamaris, follow the trail towards the Gulmit Glacier's terminus in one hour and continue along its south margin 1km, or half an hour, then turn south and ascend 800m to the summer pastures of Rajabhil. From the ridge-top saddle above Rajabhil, the trail descends south to the pastures of Bulkishkuk

and Shatubar, below the Shatubar Glacier, before turning east and south returning to Gulmit. Allow two or three days for this moderate loop trek.

AROUND PASSU
Borit Sar
Borit Sar (4105m) is the rocky ridge top between the Ghulkin and Passu glaciers (see map, p247). It can be done as a day trek from Passu (2400m) or Borit Lake, as an overnight trip from Passu, camping at Passu Ghar, or as a side trip to the Patundas trek from Passu Ghar. The in-your-face views of peaks and glaciers from Borit Sar make it the best day trek along the KKH for mountain scenery. The moderate trek is possible mid-May to October, and takes seven to eight hours round trip when going quickly or eight to 10 hours when going more leisurely. This stiff trek gains 1705m and descends 1705m in elevation.

The trail to Borit Sar leaves the trail to Patundas at the slate platform (see Day 1 of the Patundas trek, p246). From the slate platform (2865m) to Borit Sar and back takes from six to seven hours, covering 5.5km. Follow an old faint trail along the ridge line up through broken rocky sections, marked by small cairns. Continue up over open artemisia-dotted slopes, past scattled juniper trees to the level top of Borit Sar, five hours from Passu. From this high point overlooking the Passu and Ghulkin glaciers and Borit Lake, 10 7000m peaks, including distant Rakaposhi, Diran and Malubiting, are visible in a 360-degree panorama. Immediately in front of you are killer views of Shīshpar, Bojohagur-Duanasir and Ultar's north face.

Two Bridges
An easy and popular five- to six-hour day trek from Passu, locally known as the 'two bridges' trek, crosses the Hunza River twice over hair-raising suspension bridges (see the Avdegar map, p243). The trek offers good views of the Ghulkin, Passu and Batura glaciers and peaks above Ghulkin and Passu, and is much easier than the trek to Avdegar. Follow the Day 1 description of the Avdegar trek (p243) from Passu via Yashbandan over the first footbridge to Zarabad. Follow the trail that skirts the cliffs above the Hunza River's left bank to an equally interesting footbridge crossing back over the Hunza River to Hussaini. Return to Passu along the KKH, or spend the night at Borit Lake.

Yunz
The glacially formed north-south Yunz Valley lies parallel to and west of the Hunza Valley, between the Passu and Batura glaciers (see the Patundas map, p247). The easy 15.8km loop through Yunz

Valley is a popular six- to eight-hour day trek with excellent glacier views, but lacks any big mountain views. The trail ascends 480m and descends 480m, and is feasible April to October. A guide isn't necessary, yet every year trekkers get lost along this trail. If you're uncertain about finding your way through unfamiliar terrain, hire someone or look for a companion. It's two stages total: Passu to Yunzben; and Yunzben to Passu. Yunz Valley is dry and water at Passu Lake and Yunzben is silty, so carry water from Passu.

From Passu (2400m), walk 10 minutes south on the KKH to the first building (2580m) on the KKH's west side before the bridge. Follow a trail past a usually empty concrete water tank and follow the canal through thorny scrub. The clear trail, marked by small cairns, skirts the base of a rock buttress. Cross a flat, stony area 15 minutes from the KKH and ascend the old terminal moraine to see **Passu Lake** (not marked on any map), formed about 1989 when the Passu Glacier retreated. (The old trail to Yunz Valley was destroyed by a landslide, so the only trail now is via Passu Lake.)

Continue around the lake's north shore to its far west end. Follow cairns and ascend the gravelly gullies amid dark, glacially polished rock. At times, the trail and the cairns are hard to find. As you ascend, Passu Glacier's dark ice is to the south (left). Don't stray too far left, and don't go onto the crevassed glacier. The trail soon becomes more obvious. As the angle begins to lessen, the white-toothed seracs of the Passu Glacier to the west and the Yunz Valley to the north appear.

Continue up the now scree-covered trail to the top of the rock formation, 30 minutes from the lake. A clear trail angles up and to the east (right), across the face of the grey lateral moraine on the valley's north side. Reach the base of this moraine in 15 minutes and go up the trail. At the top, turn west and enter an ablation valley with a few junipers, sage and wild rose bushes. Follow a trail through the ablation valley 10 minutes. Then turn north up a gully and in five to 10 minutes reach a slate slab bench at the top and the actual start of **Yunz Valley** (2775m). After one hour, at the upper (north) end of the valley, there are two huts (3000m) west of the trail where the worthwhile side trip to **Zart Sar** (yellow top), a scenic overlook of Passu village, Tupodan and the Hunza Valley, starts and finishes. The side trip to Zart Sar (labelled as Sart on the Swiss map) takes 1½ to two hours round trip, following the trail that heads east and around the north end of the rocky bluffs that rise above the Yunz Valley's east side to a rocky plateau.

The main Yunz Valley trail continues north from the huts. Stay right and descend briefly to a

small terrace (3060m) overlooking the Batura Glacier with some tumbledown huts, a scenic lunch spot. Descend steeply over scree and loose soil 15 minutes to **Yunzben** in the ablation valley along the Batura Glacier's south margin. See Day 1 of the Batura Glacier trek (p250) for a description back to Passu.

SHIMSHAL
Momhil Sar Base Camp

Momhil is an enormous 26km-long glacier that flows north from Momhil Sar (7343m), east of and parallel to Shimshal's Lupgar Valley (see the Shimshal River map, p262). Momhil Sar, Trivor, Destaghil Sar and Mulungutti Sar (7025m) are the prominent peaks attracting mountaineers to this valley. It's a moderate four-day trek to the base camps for these four peaks of the Hispar Muztagh.

The trail heads south from the road, east of the bridge over the Momhil River a few minutes' jeep ride beyond Dūt. On Day 1 reach Yazmis in three to four hours. On Day 2 reach Chikareen in eight hours, passing Khumreg and then Shilmin halfway. On Day 3, reach Momhil Base Camp (4300m) in seven to eight hours, passing Ambareen just beyond halfway. The return trip from base camp to the bridge can be done in one long day on Day 4. It's 10 stages total round trip from Dūt: (1) Yazmis; (2) Shilmin; (3) Chikareen; (4) Ambareen; (5) Momhil Base Camp; and (6–10) five stages to return via the same route.

A three-day climb of Ambareen Sar (6175m), east of Momhil Glacier, is possible from Ambareen. Set a high camp (5000m) on Day 1, summit and descend to 5800m on Day 2, returning to Ambareen on Day 3.

Yazghil Sar Base Camp

Yazghil (sheep pen by the glacier) are the summer pastures nearest Shimshal village. From Shimshal village, you can reach Yazghil in one long day, explore the area for another day, and return to Shimshal the third day. Perched high above the 31km-long Yazghil Glacier's southeast margin, the huts (4500m) and pastures above have excellent views of the peaks at the glacier's head: Yukshin Gardan, Kunyang Chhīsh, and the Yazghil Domes.

The trail heads east from Shimshal village, staying along the Shimshal River's true left bank, three hours to the huts at Yazben (at the glacier's base). Head up the lateral moraine along the glacier's west margin and cross to the south-east margin reaching Yazyand (after the glacier), the first hut along the Yazghil Glacier's south margin, three to four hours from Yazben. From the ablation valley, ascend the grassy hillside steadily another three to four hours to herders' huts and Yazghil Sar Base Camp (3600m).

A local guide is necessary to show the way across the glacier. This moderate trek totals six stages round trip from Shimshal village: (1) Yazben; (2) Yazyand; (3) Yazghil; and (4–6) three stages to return via the same route.

From base camp, it's a three-day snow and ice climb to reach the summit of **Yazghil Sar** (5964m). Set a high camp (4670m) on Day 1, then ascend the south summit and bivouac (5180m) on Day 2, returning to base camp on Day 3.

Kanjut Sar Base Camp

Kanjut Sar (7760m), one of the hard-to-see summits of the Hispar Muztagh, is accessible from Shimshal village on a moderate five- or six-day trek that also offers close-up views of neighbouring Jutmo Sar (7330m) and Yukshin Gardan. Kanjut Sar is known locally as Kunjlaksh (mountain above narrow place, referring to the narrow width of the glacier that resembles a *kunj*, the narrow part of a Wakhi home near its entry). It takes three days one way to reach base camp from Shimshal village, although it's possible to do it in two. It's eight stages total round trip, four up and four back.

The route follows the Shimshal River's true left bank south-east, crosses the Yazghil Glacier's terminus, and continues towards the Khurdopin Glacier. It crosses the Yukshin Gardan Glacier above its confluence with the Khurdopin Glacier to Chagh Chagh (labelled as Cheng Cheng on the Swiss map). Here the route turns south-west and heads up the Yukshin Gardan Glacier, staying near the glacier's north-west (true left) margin most of the way to base camp (4600m). One tricky outwash-stream crossing via a cable adds a little excitement. Flowers carpet the meadow at base camp (marked by a triangle on the Swiss map), which also has junipers nearby, inviting you to spend an extra day.

Qapachpund & Chilinj Passes

Longer and more challenging routes than the standard trek (see the Shimshal Pamir trek, p264) exist to reach Shuwerth in the Shimshal Pamir. Two technical and extreme passes, Qapachpund and Chilinj, link the 38km-long Virzherav Glacier and Shuwerth. Virzherav is Shimshal's most distant pasture and its name probably derives from the Wakhi word *thir*, which means a 'distant' glacial valley (*zherav*).

From Shimshal village, the routes head east towards the Khurdopin Glacier and branch southeast up the Virzherav Glacier. They follow the Virzherav Glacier's north-east (true right) margin to Arjal-e-Dur. Arjal-e-Dur is a narrow side valley,

named for a black and white yak, Arjal, which strayed up this side valley, which meets the Virzherav just at the letter 'b' in 'Virjerab' on the Swiss map.

The route across **Qapachpund Pass** (5270m on the 1:100,000 Russian map *J-43 128*), goes up Arjal-e-Dur and continues north towards the valley's head. From the pass, the route descends to Zhit Badav, the extensive plain just below Shuwerth. It takes six days one way from Shimshal village to Shuwerth via Qapachpund Pass. The pass is not shown on any maps, but is on the ridge east of peak 5930m on the Swiss map.

A longer, higher and harder route crosses **Chilinj Pass** (5600m on the 1:100,000 Russian map *J-43 140*). This route also leaves Virzherav at Arjal-e-Dur, but turns north-east as Arjal-e-Dur bends in a more northerly direction. From the pass, the route descends Bhaktiyar Dur to the Braldu River below its confluence with Wesm-e-Dur. The route stays along the Braldu's true left bank to Chikor, where it turns north-west to Shuwerth. It takes eight days (and 11 stages) one-way Shimshal village to Shuwerth via Chilinj Pass, crossing the pass on the sixth day. It's necessary to place high camps on both sides of the pass, which is marked by an 'X' on the Swiss map.

Ghidims Pass

Ghidims Pass (5486m) crosses the Central Asian watershed between Ghidims Valley, an upper tributary of Ghuzherav, and Sher Ilaq Valley, Shimshal's prized winter pastures. The existence of the pass was unimagined until the first crossing by the book's authors in June 2000. In pioneering the route, the authors were also the first westerners to reach Sher Ilaq. The upper Ghidims and upper Sher Ilaq valleys have many attractive unclimbed alpine peaks, all inviting first ascents.

See Days 1–4 of the Boisum & Chafchingol Passes trek (p271) for a description between Shimshal village and Mandikshlakh where the route leaves Ghuzherav, and discussion of these stages. From Mandikshlakh, allow a minimum of nine days round trip for this 68km very demanding and technical trek to Arab-e-Dur-e-Gush, Sher Ilaq's main herders' hut.

Head north-east up the Ghidims Valley to Laili Camp (4475m) at the confluence of the North and South Ghidims valleys. The route leads up the South Ghidims Valley to the second eastern side valley. Ascend the side valley first along the outwash stream's true left bank and then on scree along the unnamed glacier's true right margin to Sarwar High Camp (5150m). The next day, cross the glacier and ascend scree to an obvious notch left of a yellow-and-brown rock band well before reaching the glacier's upper basin. Three obvious cols at the glacier's head are not the pass. The nonglaciated Ghidims Pass has steep 40-degree scree on both sides, and is snow-free late in the season.

Descend scree to the North Rost-e-Dur Glacier, and cross the crevassed upper glacier to its true left margin. Follow the ablation valley downvalley to grassy Mirza Camp (4642m). The next day, head down Rost-e-Dur, passing the Chap-e-Dur hut, to the confluence of Sher Ilaq and Arab Khan-e-Dur. Blue sheep and brown bears live in Sher Ilaq, and the likelihood of seeing them is high. On the return, set a camp on moraine below the pass on its east side, called Fazal High Camp (5060m).

Mountaineering equipment necessary to travel in roped teams on the glaciers on both sides of the pass is required. It's 11 stages total round trip from Mandikshlakh. It's 1½ stages one way between Mandikshlakh and Laili Camp. It's eight stages round trip from Laili Camp to Sher Ilaq, four stages each way: Sarwar High Camp, Fazal High Camp, Mirza Camp and Arab-e-Dur-e-Gush.

Lukpe La

The northward flowing Braldu Glacier, not to be confused with the Braldu Valley in Baltistan, offers a technical and extreme route across the Lukpe La (5650m), first crossed by HW Tilman in 1937, linking the Shimshal Pamir and Lukpe Lawo. From Shuwerth in the Shimshal Pamir (see Day 3 of the Shimshal Pamir trek, p268), the route descends to the Braldu River, turns south, and begins the difficult ascent along the heavily crevassed 36km-long Braldu Glacier. The Wesm Mountains, named for ibex trails where animals knock rocks down, rise to the east. Crossing Lukpe La, at the valley's head, requires travelling in roped teams and possibly fixing ropes for safety. The 500m descent over 3km from the rounded saddle guarded by gaping crevasses heads south-west on the Sim Glacier to its confluence with the Biafo Glacier, from where you descend the Biafo Glacier to Thungol (see the Hispar La trek, p311). Depending upon who you ask, it ranges from five to seven stages between Shuwerth and Lukpe La. Everyone agrees that it's one stage from Lukpe La to the confluence of the Sim and Biafo glaciers. This extreme technical trek is in a restricted zone where a permit and licensed guide are required (see Trekking Permits, p70). Due to its remoteness, self rescue is the only option in the event of accident or injury.

Khurdopin Pass

The technical Khurdopin Pass (5790m) is an extreme mountaineering route that links Shimshal village with Lukpe Lawo. Although Tilman reached the pass from Lukpe Lawo in 1937, it was first crossed in 1986 by Canadian Cameron Wake with Shimshalis Shambi Khan and Rajab Shah. Accomplished mountaineer Stephen Venables, who crossed the pass in 1987, rates it an alpine Grade III suitable only for experienced mountaineers.

From Shimshal village, follow the Shimshal River south-east, crossing the Yazghil Glacier, and continue along the river towards its source at the Khurdopin Glacier's terminus. Traverse the 37km-long Khurdopin Glacier below its confluence with the Yukshin Gardan Glacier, exiting above its confluence with the Virzherav Glacier. Now along the Khurdopin Glacier's east margin, which flows from Kanjut Sar I (7760m) and II and Lukpe Lawo Brak, the toilsome route heads south along this vast river of ice.

High on the East Khurdopin Glacier, the dangerous route stays to the east, crossing the heavily crevassed base of an icefall before ascending the huge icefall with steep, loose rock in a snowy gully. The route near the pass requires fixing ropes over classic wind slab with avalanche danger. The 600m descent from the pass to Lukpe Lawo is a 50-degree ice wall with acute avalanche danger, requiring fixing ropes. From Lukpe Lawo, you can descend the Biafo Glacier to Thungol (see the Hispar La trek, p311). Allow up to six days between Shimshal village and Lukpe Lawo.

SHIKARZHERAV

East of Sost is a very demanding six-day near-loop trek that accesses the isolated valley formed by the North Qarūn Koh Glacier's outwash stream where more than 300 blue sheep reportedly roam. From Sost, the route heads up the Shikarzherav for the first night's camp, passing beneath the rocky south face of Sost Sar (5200m), and then along the glacier's north margin. At the valley's head, it crosses a ridge (below 6000m) and descends along the river's true left bank. Camp three nights heading upvalley, watching for wildlife. Leaving the valley, the route turns west, ascends a side valley and crosses a 5774m ridge. The descent from this ridge follows a drainage leading to the Khunzherav near Kilik Ilga on the KKH just north of Sost. Hire a local guide who knows the way.

CHAPURSAN
Pamiri

Pamiri is the summer pasture used by Zood Khun herders. The moderate four-day walk to Pamiri starts from Yishkuk and heads south-west along the Yishkuk Glacier's north-west margin. This trek is good for additional acclimatisation before crossing either the Lupgar Pir Pass or Chilinji An. The trailhead (3450m) is on the west side of the bridge spanning the Yishkuk River. As the road bends to the right near old lateral moraine, climb along the river's true left bank. Continue past the glacier's mouth along the ablation valley on its west side to Kuk Chesham, a herders' settlement with a reliable spring. The next day pass Sekr (labelled Lal Mitti on maps), the prominent red rock, just beyond Kuk Chesham. Continue in the ablation valley to Dush Zhui, a small lake with clear water in an open green area. The trail continues up the ablation valley, ascending gradually to Pamiri, a lovely place to rest and enjoy the views. The stream is called Pamiri, locally referred to as Banafshayeen because banafsha grows here. From Pamiri, either retrace your steps back to Yishkuk or cross the Yishkuk Glacier and walk back along the glacier's opposite side, crossing the low ridge to join the trail down from Kit-ke-zherav. It's six stages total round trip from Yishkuk: (1) Kuk Chesham; (2) Dush Zhui; (3) Banafshayeen; and (4–6) three stages to return via the same route.

MISGAR
Chapursan to Misgar
Two passes link Misgar's Dilisang Valley, the westernmost of Misgar's valleys, with Chapursan (see map, p293). **Kermin Pass** links Kermin

village with the lower Dilisang Valley just above Kalam Darchi. It's an easy five-hour day trek across this pass.

Another unnamed demanding pass links Zood Khun with Wergisht Khun in the upper Dilisang Valley; contact Alam Jan in Zood Khun if you're interested in tackling this pass.

Wodwashk Pass
Obscure and little known parts of the Karakoram are still out there. Wodwashk, the glaciated pass linking the Hapuchan Valley, the western tributary of Kilik Valley, and Wodwashk Bar, a northern tributary of the Dilisang Valley, is one (see the Kilik & Mintaka Passes map, p293). The demanding route is reportedly easier when starting from Dilisang. It heads up the well-watered and green Wodwashk Bar, staying on its true left bank. The pass involves 30 to 60 minutes of glacier travel, and the descent is along the true right bank of the stream flowing down into Hapuchan. Bring an ice axe and rope for safety; crampons aren't necessary.

Anyone interested in attempting this pass can contact Misgar's nambardar Ataullah who knows the unmarked route and pass area called Tung-e-Tuk. Correspondence can be sent in advance of arrival to PO Misgar, Village Misgar, District Gilgit, Northern Areas. No stages are set in the Dilisang Valley or across Wodwashk Pass.

Baltistan

Baltistan, called Balti-yul by its inhabitants, is the centre of the Karakoram's glaciers, peaks and towers where villages are oases in a vertical wilderness of rock and ice. The mighty Indus River sweeps through the land, augmented by the glacial Shigar and Shyok rivers. Baltistan's western border with Gilgit is at Shengus village, downstream from the Indus River's Rondu gorge. To the east and south is the line of control with India, and to the north, along the Karakoram's crest, is the border with China. Baltistan, with its Tibetan cultural roots, contrasts sharply with areas to its west. The folklore of the Balti-pa is not that of shamans and fairies, but rather of the Tibetan hero-king Kesar. Nagyr and Hunza are much influenced by Baltistan, with apricots and polo both probably coming from Baltistan.

HISTORY

Baltistan received Buddhism when the Kushan and Gupta empires spread across the Karakoram and Hindukush during the 1st to 5th centuries and Kashmir was the main centre of Mahayana Buddhism. The kingdom of Great Balur, as Baltistan was then known, sent emissaries to China in the early 8th century, but by the mid-8th century, Tibetan power had become pre-eminent. Many Tibetans probably moved into the area during this period. Lhasa's power declined towards the late 9th century and Baltistan became dominated by Buddhist Ladakh. Baltistan remained Buddhist until about 1500 when missionaries from Kashmir brought the Nurbakhshiyya sect of Shi'a Islam to Baltistan.

Baltistan had three main kingdoms, Shigar, Khaplu and Skardu, whose origins are shrouded in legend. Shigar's Amacha dynasty is said to have been founded by a Hunza prince, who crossed the Hispar La to reach Shigar Valley. Tradition tells of Hunza and Nagyr men crossing the Hispar and Biafo glaciers to play polo with Shigar

JOHN MOCK

Imposing Thalle Peak towers over the south side of Thalle La.

- Camping on the Hispar La to watch sunset and sunrise on the glacial wilderness of Lukpe Lawo (Snow Lake)

- Trekking along the Baltoro Glacier in awe of the world's greatest concentration of high peaks and granite spires

- Rejoicing on Gondogoro La, marvelling at four of Pakistan's five 8000m peaks, the best view from any Karakoram pass

men near Askole. Khaplu's Yagbu dynasty may have been founded by Turkic adventurers who crossed the Karakoram from Central Asia and established themselves as rulers over the Tibetan population. Yagbu is a Turkic title, and the Raja of Khaplu's palace stands today. Skardu's Maqpon dynasty, however, became the most powerful kingdom. The greatest of the Maqpons, Ali Sher Anchan, forged ties with the Moghul emperors of Delhi, who ruled Kashmir.

During the Maqpon dynasty's zenith, Skardu conquered Ladakh, but soon became caught up in the intrigues of the Moghul court. By the 18th century, fighting among the Maqpon princes led to a decline in Skardu's importance.

The Sikhs, who inherited much of the Moghul empire, annexed Baltistan in 1840 and the Balti kingdoms' sovereignty ended. Baltistan retained strong trade and cultural links with Ladakh, and a Kashmiri governor, supported by a garrison of Dogra troops, administered Baltistan from Skardu until independence. When the Maharaja of

Kashmir declared his state would join India in 1947, the Gilgit Scouts marched on Skardu and besieged the Kashmiri garrison until it surrendered in 1948, and Baltistan became part of the Northern Areas.

INFORMATION
Maps

The Swiss Foundation for Alpine Research 1:250,000 orographical map *Karakoram (Sheet 1)* and *Karakoram (Sheet 2)* cover most of Baltistan, north of the Shyok and Indus rivers. The US AMS Series U502 India and Pakistan 1:250,000 topographic

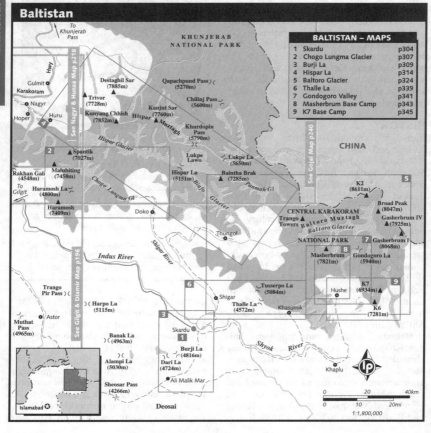

	BALTISTAN – MAPS	
1	Skardu	p304
2	Chogo Lungma Glacier	p307
3	Burji La	p309
4	Hispar La	p314
5	Baltoro Glacier	p324
6	Thalle La	p339
7	Gondogoro Valley	p341
8	Masherbrum Base Camp	p343
9	K7 Base Camp	p345

maps *Mundik (NI 43-3)* and *Gilgit (NI 43-2)* show the Deosai west to Nanga Parbat.

SKARDU

Skardu (2290m) is Baltistan's administrative centre and transport hub. The town lies at the base of a huge 350m rock outcrop along the Indus River's true left (south) bank at the confluence with the Shigar River. Rocky summits rise 3000m above town, dramatically enclosing this scenic 40km-long by 10km-wide valley.

Information

The PTDC Information Centre (☎ 0575-2946) is in the K2 Motel compound.

Supplies & Equipment

The extensive bazaar holds enough food, gear, mountaineering equipment and supplies to outfit a trek. Look in Purana Bazaar for everything including used boots, tarpaulins, expedition barrels and porters' clothing. Mountain Trekking Foods Shop near Yadgar Chowk sells expedition barrels, kerosene drums, plastic containers and stoves. Most mountaineering expeditions stage themselves out of K2 Motel, so ask there if anything is for sale.

Places to Stay & Eat

Budget All hotels serve food and have rooms with attached bathrooms and hot running water, except where noted. Numerous small and dubious eateries line both sides of College Rd west of Yadgar Chowk. Next to Mashabrum Tours east of Yadgar Chowk is *Yadgar Burgers & Juice Center*.

Karakoram Inn (☎ 0575-55438, 2122, *Naya Bazaar)* has reasonable singles/doubles/triples that cost Rs 150/250/350 and deluxe doubles for Rs 500. The management is friendly, and the restaurant, overlooking the bustling bazaar, serves Western and Pakistani food. The *Hotel Sadpara International* (☎ 0575-2951, College Rd) has singles/doubles with cold running water for Rs 100/200, or Rs 150/300 with hot running water; rooms with TV cost Rs 350/500. A small garden is in back and the restaurant cheerfully serves Western and Pakistani food.

Run-down rooms at *Himalaya Motel & Restaurant* (☎ 0575-2576, College Rd) cost Rs 200/300, but some rooms have views out the back of this once-better hotel and restaurant. *Hunza Inn 5 Brothers Hotel & Restaurant* (☎ 0575-2570, College Rd) has dumpy doubles/triples with cold running water for Rs 200/300. The restaurant serves basic Pakistani food.

Mid-Range Run by Ghulam Muhammad, *Indus Motel* (☎ 0575-2608, College Rd) has singles/doubles that cost Rs 300/450 and deluxe carpeted doubles with a view out the back for Rs 600. This place is neat, clean and cooperative. The popular restaurant serves Western and Pakistani food.

Hotel Hillman International (☎ 0575-2175, 2226, e hotelhillmanint@hotmail .com, Naya Bazaar) charges Rs 400/600. Doubles with TV cost Rs 1000. The hotel is relatively new and its restaurant serves Balti, Western and Pakistani food. The *Hunza Tourist Lodge* (☎ 0575-2515), across from K2 Motel, has a pleasant garden. Clean singles/doubles/triples cost Rs 500/800/1000. *North Star Hotel & Restaurant* (☎ 0575-55581/2, Hussaini Chowk), above K-2 Travel Services, has singles/doubles with TV in this newer hotel that cost Rs 600/800. Some rooms overlook the polo ground.

Top End Quiet *PTDC K2 Motel* (☎ 0575-2946, fax 3322) has excellent views and spacious gardens overlooking the Indus River. Managed by Raja Riaz of Hunza, it caters to trekking parties and mountaineering expeditions, offering secure sheds to store gear and plenty of room to pack and sort loads. Singles/doubles in the older (standard) wing cost Rs 1000/1350 and those in the deluxe wing cost Rs 1450/1800. The rather unremarkable Pakistani-style meals are fixed.

Concordia Motel (☎ 0575-55061, 2582, fax 2547), run by Sher Ali of Hunza, is Skardu's only year-round hotel. It's small and clean with a pleasant garden overlooking the river near K2 Motel. Singles/doubles/triples cost Rs 800/1000/1200. *Pioneer Hotel* (☎ 0575-55188), run by Niaz Ali of

BALTISTAN

Chorbat, is in a quiet location near the airport 15km west of town. Singles/doubles are good value at Rs 600/700. The restaurants at both these hotels serve good Pakistani, Chinese and Western food.

Karakoram Yurt 'N Yak Sarai (☎ 0575-2856, Link Rd), in Satellite Town, has single/double *yurts* (large round tents) with electricity, private toilets and hot showers that cost Rs 1080/1260. Catering mostly to groups, it has a large dining room, and offers 40% discount after mid-August. *Masherbrum Hotel (College Rd)* is a luxury hotel under construction at the time of research.

Getting There & Away

Air PIA (☎ 0575-2491, 3325, airport ☎ 0575-2492) schedules a Boeing 737 Islamabad-Skardu flight daily (Rs 2825).

Road A sealed but rough 170km road links Skardu with Gilgit and the rest of Pakistan.

Gilgit The Gilgit-Skardu road leaves the Karakoram Highway (KKH) at Alam Bridge over the Gilgit River north of its confluence with the Indus River, and follows the Indus to Skardu.

NATCO (☎ 0575-3313) has a daily bus (Rs 125, six to seven hours) that departs near Skardu's Chashma Bazaar for Gilgit at 5.30am. Mashabrum Tours (☎ 0575-2616/34, 55195) has a bus (Rs 120) that departs near Skardu's Yadgar Chowk at 5am, a Coaster (Rs 140) at 10am, and wagons (Rs 140) at 8am and noon. K-2 Travel Services (☎ 0575-2855, 55584) has wagons (Rs 140) that depart near Skardu's aqueduct at 9 and 11am and 1pm. Skardu-Gilgit special hires cost Rs 3500.

From Gilgit, Mashabrum Tours departs Cinema Bazaar at 8 and 10am and noon. K-2 Travel Services departs NLI Chowk at 9 and 11am and 1pm. NATCO has a deluxe bus that departs Cinema Bazaar at 6.30am.

Rawalpindi For hard-core fans of long road trips, it's a 760km, 24-hour ride between Rawalpindi and Skardu.

NATCO (☎ 0575-3313) has a deluxe bus (Rs 500) that departs near Skardu's Chashma Bazaar at 3pm. Mashabrum Tours (☎ 0575-2616/34, 55195) has a Coaster (Rs 550) that departs near Skardu's Yadgar Chowk at 1pm (Rs 550) and a deluxe bus (Rs 490) at 4pm. K-2 Travel Services (☎ 0575-2855,

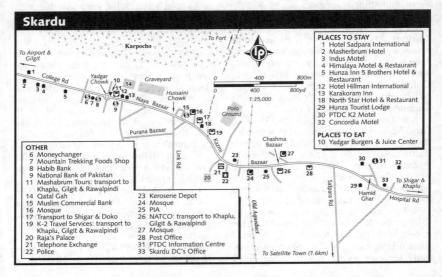

55584) has a coaster (Rs 550) departing near Skardu's aqueduct at 2pm.

Skardu-bound vehicles depart from Pir Wadhai in Rawalpindi. NATCO (☎ 051-4445580) has a deluxe bus (Rs 500) which departs at 3pm. Mashabrum Tours (☎ 051-5477095) has a Coaster (Rs 550) that departs at 2pm and a deluxe bus (Rs 490) at 4pm. K-2 Travel Services (☎ 051-4474112) costs Rs 550.

Getting Around

Suzukis ply the bazaar east from Yadgar Chowk to the hospital for Rs 3, but only until dark. Taxis to and from the airport and the bazaar cost Rs 200. From the K2 Motel to the airport is a special rate of Rs 150. Taxis to and from the K2 Motel and the bazaar cost about Rs 20. The rare Suzuki to or from the airport costs Rs 10.

Special hires anywhere are most easily organised directly with jeep contractors. Some jeeps, operated by Jaffer of Satpara, are often in the K2 Motel compound. Wazir Jaffer Shigri of Alexander Transport Service (☎ 0575-3346, 2946, 2146, fax 3322) in Kazmi Bazaar is helpful, as is Aga Abbas. Most other jeeps depart from an alley off Hussaini Chowk near the aqueduct.

Basha

The Basha Valley offers excellent alternatives to Baltistan's more frequently visited Shigar and Braldu valleys. Trekkers who head north and west into the Basha Valley will encounter traditional Balti villages comparatively unaffected by expeditions and tourism. In Basha, footbridges are made of birch and willow fronds and tight compact settlements are constructed of woven willow plastered with mud. The villages nestle amid fields shaded by poplar, apricot, apple and walnut trees. Women wear broad black *nathing* (hats) with a red rim, and men's nathing are distinctively broad-rimmed also.

NEAREST TOWN

See Skardu (p303).

Chogo Lungma Glacier

Duration	5 days
Distance	72.6km
Standard	demanding
Season	mid-June–September
Start/Finish	Doko
Zone & Permit	open, no permit
Public Transport	yes

Summary Traditional Balti culture, flower-filled meadows and superb alpine scenery reward trekkers who come to this seldom-visited valley and giant glacier.

Godfrey Vigne, who essentially discovered the Karakoram for European science in 1835, called the snout of the 44km-long Chogo Lungma (big valley) Glacier the grandest spectacle that he saw on the whole of his travels. The Basha Valley is especially picturesque above Doko with terraced fields beneath granite Mango Brak, and low-angle granite slabs hundreds of metres high rising above Gon and Arandu. The trail through Basha's villages is relatively easy, and the ablation valleys along the Chogo Lungma Glacier's north margin are lush with trees and flowers, with excellent views of Spantik (7027m) and Malubiting (7458m).

PLANNING
Maps

The Swiss Foundation for Alpine Research 1:250,000 orographical map *Karakoram (Sheet 1)* covers the trek. It labels Churzing as Churtsinks, Chogo Brangsa as Chohob Langsa, Kurumal as Khurumal and Wung as Gongon. It doesn't show Buqon, Manfi Kuru, Gareencho, Bolocho, Skari Byanga or Sharing. It marks Spantik and Laila base camps with triangles. It labels the glacier called Khilburi Gang as Kilwuri Gans. It shows both the Khilburi and Bolocho glaciers as being connected directly to the Chogo Lungma Glacier. They have receded, and now their outwash streams flow into the Chogo Lungma Glacier.

Guides & Porters

Between Doko and Arandu, hire porters from the Basha Valley's lower villages. At

Arandu, select those porters who are most fit and familiar with the route and send back any porters who aren't. Arandu villagers are the best porters because they use the pastures along the glacier.

Porters ask for a flat rate of Rs 220 per stage including payment for food rations. Porters want more trekkers to come, so they don't ask for wāpasi, the clothing and equipment allowance, or rest days.

Stages

It's 10 stages total round trip from Doko: (1) Arandu; (2) Churzing; (3) Chogo Brangsa; (4) Kurumal; (5) Bolocho; and (6–10) five stages to return via the same route. Stage inflation has affected the distance between Arandu and Bolocho, which is now four stages, but was traditionally these three stages: (1) Buqon, (2) Kurumal and (3) Bolocho.

GETTING TO/FROM THE TREK

From Skardu, the small town of Haiderabad, with its two restaurants, lies three hours north up the Shigar Valley. At Haiderabad, jeeps to the Basha Valley turn west, leaving the main Braldu Valley road, and cross the Braldu and Basha rivers. From Haiderabad it's 35km to Doko, which has the last shop with basic supplies. The first village in the Basha Valley is Tissar, from where many men who porter up the Braldu Valley come. Beyond Tissar, landslides occasionally block the road. Skardu-Doko jeeps cost Rs 90 and special hires cost Rs 2000–2500. Skardu-Haiderabad jeeps cost Rs 50. From Haiderabad, jeeps cost Rs 50 and special hires cost Rs 800–1000. Jeeps from Tissar to Skardu (Rs 100) also travel down the Shigar River's true right (west) bank, but this road isn't as good as the road along its true left (east) bank.

THE TREK
Day 1: Doko to Arandu
5–6 hours, 14.5km, 240m ascent
A grassy camp site on Doko's northern outskirts (2530m) is just above the trail under the shade of several large walnut trees near a clear stream. The road between Doko and

Arandu is passable for jeeps only during spring and autumn when the water level in the Basha River is low, but it makes a good, wide walking trail. Ford a large side stream 20 minutes from Doko. Several more clear streams descend from granite cliffs along the valley's west side. As the Basha Valley begins to turn westward, the trail climbs and then descends to the river. It finally rounds the bend in the valley 2½ to three hours from Doko and heads north-north-west over a large plain next to the river.

Across the Basha River near the Berelter River's mouth is Bisil village, which is reached via a wooden basket suspended from a steel cable. Up this side valley is a technical route over the Sokha La, first crossed by HW Tilman in 1937, leading east to the upper Biafo Glacier. The open-zone route offers quick access to Lukpe Lawo, and is still occasionally crossed by mountaineers.

Continue 45 minutes to one hour to Gon. Fractured granite slabs tower above Gon and Arandu, which is 45 minutes to one hour ahead. Just west of **Arandu** (2770m) is a small *camp site*. Villagers can show you where the springs are. Otherwise, the canal offers silty water from the large glacier behind Arandu.

North of Arandu is the Kero Lungma Glacier and the technical route over the Nushik La (called Nashkura La by Arandu villagers), which leads in five days from Doko to Hispar village. The pass, first crossed in 1892 by Major CG Bruce, is heavily corniced with a steep ice slope on the north side. It descends to the Haigutum Glacier, a branch of the Hispar Glacier, which has enormous crevasses that can only be crossed early in the season before snow bridges melt. No Arandu porters have crossed this pass. Reportedly, Burusho men used to cross this pass to raid Shigar.

Day 2: Arandu to Chogo Brangsa
4–5 hours, 11.1km, 552m ascent
The trail heads along the river's true right bank towards the Chogo Lungma Glacier's terminus. This glacier surged in 2000, threatening the village with total disaster.

The glacier's advance may change this section drastically. Ascend the terminal moraine in 30 minutes. A herders' trail crosses the glacier in 45 minutes to one hour to the ablation valley along its north margin. The first clear stream is a few minutes along the trail in the ablation valley. Cross another stream, amid willows and wild roses and, 30 minutes after leaving the glacier, reach Churzing, where some huts cluster against the hillside. A rocky, sloping camp site five minutes farther makes a good lunch spot. Continue through dense willow and rosewood thickets to the ablation valley's end. Contour the hillside, and in 45 minutes to one hour descend into another small, well-wooded valley to huts at **Buqon**. A level camp site is in front of and below the huts, amid willows. Water, however, is often scarce. Continue 45 minutes to one hour to **Manfi Kuru** where herders' huts perch on a small dung-covered knoll overlooking the glacier. The large stream coming from the side valley tends to be silty. The only level ground for camping is next to the stream on sand. From Manfi Kuru are the first views of Spantik. Continue 30 to 45 minutes to **Chogo Brangsa** (3322m, 'big pasture'). Level camp sites are amid willows along the clear stream. Herders' huts cluster against the hillside farther up this pretty side valley, which overlooks the glacier with a good view of Spantik.

Day 3: Chogo Brangsa to Gareencho
4–6 hours, 10.7km, 457m ascent

Continue up the ablation valley with its abundant flowers one hour to **Shing Kuru**, the highest camp site with junipers (*shing* or wood). The side stream here tends to be silty, and is prone to high water in the afternoon. From the lateral moraine are striking views of the Chogo Lungma Glacier's ice and rock, and Malubiting (pronounced locally as Malupiting) first comes into view. Thirty minutes farther is upper Shing Kuru with its smaller, clear stream descending from a waterfall on the cliff. This would also be a nice **camp site**. Fifteen minutes farther, the Kurumal area starts. This wide alluvial area has a big clear stream at its east end, but no good camp sites. A silty brown pool often covers much of the flat area here. At its far west end, 15 minutes' walk, are four porters' shelters and a grassy area for a few tents. Water here is slightly silty. Just beyond these

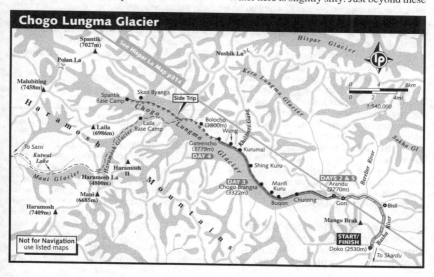

Chogo Lungma Glacier

Not for Navigation use listed maps

porters' shelters is a larger flat area where you can pitch more tents on sand and grass.

From Kurumal, the trail descends 15 minutes and heads out onto the Chogo Lungma Glacier to get around the torrent from the Khilburi Gang. Apparently, there used to be a moraine lake *(khil)* at this spot. It takes 20 minutes to detour this, and another 10 minutes to climb back to the grassy hillside. A trail continues up the ablation valley, over snow pack at times, and after 30 minutes reaches Wung. A single herders' hut lies against the hillside on the alluvial fan's east end. Snow melt provides clear water.

Continue 30 to 45 minutes to the broad, grassy area of **Gareencho** (3779m). The water here has some sediment, which quickly settles. Excellent views of Malubiting, the Polan La and Spantik, and level camp sites on grass beside the stream, make this a nice spot for a rest or acclimatisation day. When continuing to Laila Base Camp or Haramosh La, camp here. Gareencho is more comfortable than the next camp site, Bolocho.

Alternative Camp Site

Bolocho When visiting Spantik Base Camp (see the Side Trip) or heading to Malubiting Base Camp, continue beyond Gareencho and camp at Bolocho, because it's a long walk the next day from Bolocho to Spantik Base Camp. Beyond Gareencho, the trail crosses difficult terrain. Descend over scree to the glacier's edge. Continue along the glacier's margin, through broken areas, where the trail is hard to find. Reach Bolocho after 2.1km and 45 minutes to one hour of toilsome walking from Gareencho. **Bolocho** (3800m) is a sandy area, with water from the glacier, and many porters' shelters. A large mineral spring lies a few minutes to the right of camp. Local people say it's warm and they don't drink it, even though it feels cold to the touch. Alternatively, you can slow down the pace by camping in Arandu, Buqon, and Kurumal, reaching Bolocho on Day 4.

Side Trip: Spantik Base Camp

2 days, 23km, 500m ascent, 500m descent
Spantik (whose name derives from the Balti word *spang,* a grassy place), is at the Chogo

Lungma Glacier's head, and is usually climbed from this glacier via the relatively easy 8km-long south-east ridge. Fanny Bullock-Workman, in her long skirt and laced knee boots, came within a few hundred metres of the summit during their 1902–3 expedition.

From Bolocho, the trail heads onto the glacier. Traversing the glacier between Bolocho and Spantik Base Camp (marked by a triangle 4300m on the Swiss map) requires travelling in roped teams. It takes seven to nine hours from Bolocho to base camp. Villagers say ibex are abundant above the grassy base camp.

You can break up the hike between Bolocho and base camp by camping at **Skari Byanga**, a sandy place along the glacier's north margin. *Byanga* means 'sand', and *skari* refers to a minuscule weight used for weighing gold or silver. Apparently, a villager once found a tiny amount of gold here. The side trip can be done in two days, but allowing more gives time to explore the surrounding area. It's four stages total round trip starting from Bolocho: (1) Skari Byanga (not marked on maps); (2) Spantik Base Camp; and (3–4) two stages to return via the same route.

Days 4–5: Gareencho to Doko

2 days, 36.3km, 1249m descent
Return downvalley to Doko, camping at Arandu on Day 4.

Deosai

Deosai, a vast high-altitude plateau south and west of Skardu, borders on Indian-controlled Kashmir. Nowhere lower than 4000m, this uninhabited alpine grassland has numerous clear streams with unusual snow trout, a significant brown bear population and a multitude of golden marmots. Its remarkable biodiversity has earned it recognition as a national park. Deosai gets its name from *deo,* a powerful spirit. Deosai is snow covered most of the year. Summer brings intense July–August mosquito swarms, which are relieved by strong daytime winds. Early

September frosts restore peace, making late-season trekking pleasurable.

Burji La

Duration	3 days
Distance	39km
Standard	moderate
Season	mid-June–mid-October
Start	Skardu
Finish	Ali Malik Mar
Zone & Permit	open, no permit
Public Transport	start only

Summary Burji La combines tantalising views of the Baltoro Muztagh with the magnificent Deosai Plains in a short trek, which can be combined with other routes for superb longer treks.

Burji La (4816m), the old British route between Srinagar and Skardu, is a snow-covered north-south pass between the Skardu Valley and Deosai Plains. From the pass, only 16km south of, but some 2600m above, Skardu, K2, the Gasherbrums and Masherbrum are distantly visible. The description below is from north to south, so acclimatised trekkers can combine this trek with the Deosai Traverse (see Other Treks, p347). The pass, however, is easier to cross in the reverse direction.

PLANNING
Maps
The US AMS 1:250,000 topographic map *Mundik (NI 43-3)* covers the trek.

GETTING TO/FROM THE TREK
To the Start
Follow the road west from Skardu towards the airport to the bridge over the Satpara stream. You can easily walk or take a Suzuki.

From the Finish
Walk a day or hitch along the road back to Satpara and Skardu or head west to the Astor Valley, since there's no public transport. Special hires cost Rs 1800. (When reversing directions, Burji Lungma is the first clear side stream from the north.)

THE TREK
Day 1: Skardu to Wozal Hadar
6–7 hours, 20km, 1520m ascent

Burji is the first valley west of the large, broad Satpara Valley. From the west side of the bridge over the Satpara stream, reach the obvious narrow opening of the Burji Nala in 1½ hours. Follow a herders' trail along the clear stream, inexorably ascending past stands of birch and willow. Herders' huts and a spring at *Pindobal* offer a camp site three to four hours upvalley for those not yet acclimatised or those crossing the pass from south to north. The treeless camp site of *Wozal Hadar* (3810m) is one to 1½ hours farther.

Day 2: Wozal Hadar to Burji Lungma
5–6 hours, 9km, 1006m ascent, 701m descent

The valley opens into a wide basin. Burji La is the obvious snowy saddle on the east side

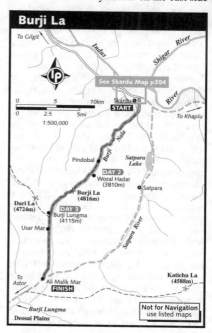

of the ridge above the upper basin two to three hours from Wozal Hadar. A broad snowfield lies below the pass. If crevasses are visible, ascend the rocky spur just west (right) of the snowfield to **Burji La**, marked by a cairn. The giant peaks at the Baltoro Glacier's head rise above the lower ridges in a grand panorama. To the south, several icy blue lakes nestle below a small ridge. Descend south to the valley below, the ***Burji Lungma*** (4115m), and follow it to its confluence with a larger, clear stream, and camp in grass along its banks. Up this stream to the north-west is the Dari La (see p347).

Day 3: Burji Lungma to Ali Malik Mar

3 hours, 10km, 183m descent
Follow the stream south to reach the Deosai Plains and **Ali Malik Mar** at the road.

Biafo, Hispar & Baltoro Glaciers

Out of the centre of the most extensively glaciated high mountain terrain on the planet flows the Braldu River, formed by the confluence of the Biafo and Biaho rivers. The glacial sources of these rivers – the Biafo, Panmah and Baltoro glaciers – form ice highways lined with magnificent peaks and towers that lead to the very heart of the Karakoram. The Sim and Biafo glaciers meet at the vast glacial basin of Lukpe Lawo, beyond which the Hispar La leads to the mighty Hispar Glacier. All along the Baltoro Glacier are monumental rock walls and colossal peaks, culminating in K2. This majestic landscape draws elite climbers from around the world every year, and trekkers who visit the base camps for the towers and peaks share in a once-in-a-lifetime experience. The renowned Balti-pa who live among these Karakoram giants welcome trekkers and climbers alike with a warm cheerfulness that belies their ice-bound surroundings. This is an area of superlatives – the finest, the highest, the most challenging, the most rewarding – that is not to be missed!

PLANNING
Guides & Porters

Typically, the DC in Skardu sets a flat rate per stage each season for Balti porters that supersedes the maximum wage set by the government. You can hire porters in several places: Skardu, the Naib Tehsildar's office in Shigar, Haiderabad and villages around Askole. Hiring porters in Skardu is the best bet. All parties going through the Shigar Valley must hire at least half their porters from Shigar, which includes porters from the Shigar, Basha and Braldu valleys. The remainder can come from elsewhere in Baltistan. In Askole, the headman Ashgar is in charge of porter hire, and Hussain, the late Haji Mahdi's son, sells animals for porters to butcher.

ACCESS FACILITIES
Also see Skardu (p303).

Thungol

In 1995, the staging area, camp site and the valley's final police check post were moved downvalley from Askole to Thungol (2850m). It's nothing more than a dusty area along the river bank, but everyone ends up camping here. Undoubtedly, your guide and porters need to get organised, sort loads and bake bread. During summer, a few 'restaurants' spring up at Thungol selling tea, drinks and local food. The camping fee is Rs 30.

Getting There & Away The road up the Braldu (canyon in Balti) is frequently blocked by high water, rock fall and landslides. In May and June, when water levels are low, the road is usually open. Between mid-July and August, the water levels rise dramatically, along with delays and difficulties. When you encounter a road block, you abandon the jeep and carry your gear across the block to another jeep that takes you as far as the next block, where you repeat the process. It's possible to experience as many as five blocks, necessitating six jeeps. Skardu-Thungol special hires cost Rs 3000 (seven to eight hours, 185km). With multiple blocks, the trip can cost as much as Rs 9000 and can easily turn into a two-day trip since there's usually no rush by local people to clear these lucrative obstacles.

When road blocks force your party to walk, you pay porters for the portions of stages over which they carry loads. It takes two or three days to walk the three traditional stages between Dassu and Askole. The stages from Dassu are: (1) Chakpo; (2) Chongo; (2½) Thungol; and (3) Askole. The road crosses to the true left bank before Chakpo, avoiding the steep climb to that village, and recrosses beyond Hoto before Chongo. When jeeps stop before Thungol, special hires from Skardu cost Rs 1600 to Dassu, Rs 1800 to Apo Ali Ghound and Rs 2500 to Hoto.

Hispar La

Duration	12 days
Distance	130.9km
Standard	extreme, technical
Season	mid-June–September
Start	Thungol
Finish	Huru
Zone & Permit	open, no permit
Public Transport	no

Summary The ultimate classic traverse of the Biafo and Hispar glaciers proceeds through a wilderness of rock and ice up the Biafo, across Lukpe Lawo, over the Hispar La and down the meadow-lined snowy Hispar.

Together the Biafo and Hispar glaciers, the Karakoram's second- (65km) and fifth- (49km) longest glaciers, form the Karakoram's longest continuous stretch of glacier (114km) linked by the Hispar La (5151m).

Warning

Trekkers who attempt the Hispar La trek on their own risk both accident and becoming lost. Almost every year one or two unaccompanied trekkers disappear needlessly, falling into crevasses. In the event of injury or accident, self-rescue is the only option. Hire an experienced individual to show you the way. What would you least like to part with, your money or your life?

Every year, a couple of hundred trekkers traverse these glaciers and cross this difficult pass between Baltistan and Nagyr through what both Francis Younghusband and HW Tilman called the finest mountain scenery in the world, scenery that 'attracts by its grandeur, but repels by its desolation'. It's hard to imagine, but tradition holds that Nagyr men used to travel this route, bringing horses to play polo at Kesar Shaguran near Askole.

Over two thirds of the trekking is actually on glacier, and more than 20km of the route requires travelling in roped teams. Fortunately, only two camp sites, Hispar La Base Camp and Hispar La, are on glacier. Both glaciers have chaotic, debris-covered lower sections and crevasse fields on their upper sections. With the rigours and risks of serious glacier travel, it shouldn't be anyone's first Karakoram trek.

More than a dozen 7000m peaks tower above these glaciers and the Biafo's granite spires – Lukpe Lawo Brak (6593m), Lukpe Brak (6029m), and Baintha Brak (7285m), or The Ogre – form a magnificent cathedral of mountain architecture. Lower pastures along the Biafo Glacier are used by Balti villagers from the Braldu Valley, and lower ones along the Hispar Glacier are used by Burushaski-speaking Nagyrkutz. The upper ablation valleys and meadows along the glaciers, however, are filled with flowers and are unused except by wildlife. Brown bears occasionally appear (raiding camp sites, especially Karpogoro), as do ibex and eagles.

PLANNING
What to Bring
Mountaineering equipment necessary to travel in roped teams is required (see Mountaineering Equipment, p61).

Maps
The Swiss Foundation for Alpine Research 1:250,000 orographical map *Karakoram (Sheet 1)* covers the trek. The Jutmo Glacier is labelled as Yutmaru, and Apiharai as Aplahara. Huru isn't marked. Huru is 150m above the Hispar River's true left bank, west of the two streams shown flowing north from Rush Phari.

The Italian alpine-scientific expedition 'Biafo 77' determined elevations for the Latok group that differ from the Swiss map. Based on its survey, it also propose reversing the designations of Latok I and II, so that the westernmost summit be called Latok I (7151m), and the central peak Latok II (7086m). The easternmost peak Latok III (6850m) is correctly marked.

Guides & Porters
Take an experienced guide who knows the route. If you're experienced with glacier travel, you can reduce costs by hiring savvy porters instead. You cannot, however, expect porters to know how to locate and avoid crevasses, or how to use a rope safely. If you're at all unsure, hire a guide through a trekking company. Even though this is an open-zone trek, police at the Thungol check post have refused to allow unaccompanied trekkers to proceed up the Biafo Glacier and may insist you hire someone for your own safety. Trekkers may want to first request a letter from the DC in Skardu, however, stating that they have permission to go up the Biafo Glacier.

The trek's length and difficulty necessitates hiring porters to carry gear and supplies. The ratio of porters to trekkers typically varies from 3:1 (for smaller scale lower-budget treks) to 6:1 (for trekking parties outfitted by a trekking company). Ensure porters have adequate clothing and equipment. Whether they bring their own gear or you provide it for them, keep in mind that they will be walking, sleeping and cooking on snow and ice for days.

Balti Porters The traverse is usually done from east to west using Balti porters. When you need more than three or four porters, hire them in Skardu. Otherwise, hire them in Haiderabad or Askole. Porters are responsible for paying for their own transport to Thungol. As supplies are consumed and loads eliminated, porters are dismissed. Porters can be released along the Biafo Glacier as far as Hispar La Base Camp. Never dismiss just one porter. It's dangerous for a porter to return down the glacier alone and irresponsible of any trekker to insist upon it. You're committed to take porters that cross the Hispar La all the way to Huru.

Some confusing exceptions to standard porters' wages apply to this trek. Porters bring their own food to Baintha I. For these four stages, porters' wages are a flat Rs 220 per stage. It's customary for porters to butcher an animal at Baintha. For the remaining stages from Baintha I to Huru, you provide all food and fuel for porters and pay a flat rate of Rs 170 per stage. Wāpasi is paid, despite the fact that porters never walk back over the glaciers to Baltistan. Porters instead walk to the KKH and take public transport via Gilgit back to Skardu. You're not responsible to pay for their transport, unless you can get porters to agree not to be paid wāpasi. They also ask for the clothing and equipment allowance. Other trekking parties may negotiate lower wages per stage or fewer stages (the authors have heard as low as 18 stages), but they also pay a lot of baksheesh or face porter strikes.

Nagyr Porters Nagyr porters, eager for work, welcome trekkers doing this route from west to east. A porters' union has effectively eliminated porter disputes that had plagued this area for years. The one hitch is that any trekking party hiring five or more porters must also hire a porter sirdar, who is a village representative and whose responsibility it is to select porters from their village. The porters' wages are a flat Rs 220 per stage, including payment for food rations.

In addition, they ask for Rs 100 for shoes, and a goat from large trekking parties. Nagyr porters don't ask for wāpasi. Instead, they ask for the cost of transport, food and accommodation to get from Skardu back to Nagyr. A representative from the porter union finds you.

Stages

The route totals 22½ stages. It's half a stage between Thungol and Askole, plus these 22 stages from Askole: (1) Namla; (2) Mango I; (3) Shafung; (4) Baintha I; (5) Nakpogoro; (6) Marpogoro; (7) Karpogoro; (8) Hispar La Base Camp (Biafo Glacier side); (9) Hispar La; (10) Hispar La Base Camp (Hispar Glacier side); (11) to first glacier to north; (12) west side of Khani Basa Glacier; (13) Hagure Shangali Cham; (14) west side of Jutmo Glacier; (15) Shiqam Baris; (16) Pumarikish; (17) Bitanmal; (18) Palolimikish; (19) Ghurbūn; (20) Hispar village; (21) Apiharai; and (22) Huru.

NEAREST FACILITIES

See Thungol (p310).

GETTING TO/FROM THE TREK
To the Start

See Thungol (p310).

From the Finish

An unsealed road from Hispar village to the KKH follows the Hispar River, but is subject to blockage by high water, rock fall and landslides. From June to September, you must plan to walk the 16km between Hispar village and Huru, from where the road is usually open. Vehicles from Hispar and Huru are infrequent, so either prearrange a special hire to meet you or walk to the KKH. Some parties send a 'runner' ahead to the KKH to request a jeep in Huru. These are typically VIP jeeps where drivers usually allow a maximum of four passengers. Huru-KKH special hires cost Rs 1700 (1¼ hours, 26km). When the road is open to Hispar village, a Hispar-Nagyr Proper special hire costs Rs 2000.

The walk to the KKH is hot and dry, so carry water from Huru. When porters carry loads from Huru to the KKH, you pay them an additional two stages. This can equal the cost of a jeep, so you may as well hire one and enjoy the ride. Porters with no loads aren't paid for walking between Huru and the KKH.

THE TREK
Day 1: Thungol to Namla

5–7 hours, 14.9km, 690m ascent, 60m descent

Either walk one hour along the road to Askole or stroll two hours through Thungol and Surungo villages to Askole. This upper trail is more shaded and enjoyable, and crosses two streams in steep, but not large ravines.

Walk through Askole (3000m) and follow the canal 30 minutes to its source at a clear stream. Continue past the confluence of the Biafo and Biaho rivers, following the Biafo River's true right bank 1½ hours to **Kesar Shaguran** (Kesar's polo field). A small clear stream is five minutes before this broad, level area (3090m). After crossing the area, the trails to the Biafo and Baltoro glaciers divide. The trail to the Baltoro Glacier continues east below the rock buttress. The trail to the Biafo Glacier turns north-east up a rock gully between a cliff on the left and a rock buttress on the right.

Ascend amid boulders 15 minutes to a large cairn (3360m) and the first view of the Biafo. *Biafo* means 'rooster' and describes the glacier's snout, which resembles the cockscomb. Continue on a trail through the ablation valley, descending to the broken white rock at the glacier's margin in 45 minutes. Move onto the glacier where water lies in moraine pools. Toil gradually up past occasional cairns. After 4.5km, or three hours, on the glacier, head west (left) 15 minutes to its margin. Off the glacier, continue 15 minutes to the grassy area of *Namla* (3690m) with porters' shelters and sandy camp sites. Get water from the glacier or from the silty Namla stream.

Day 2: Namla to Mango I

5–6 hours, 6.7km, 30m descent

Leave Namla on a sandy trail and descend quickly to the glacier. Head straight out through marginal crevasses 1¼ hours to the medial moraine. Cross a medial moraine and a white ice band to a second medial moraine. This eastern medial moraine is more level and easier walking. In 45 minutes, Janping Chekhma (3734m), a large, green, side valley, is visible to the west. This side valley is very hard to reach, blocked by black ice towers and difficult broken glacier. Continue along the medial moraine, passing occasional cairns made by Askole villagers who bring their yaks as far as Mango. Continue two hours from the point on the glacier opposite Janping Chekhma, until directly opposite a side valley to the west, marking the south end of the green Mango area. Cross the white ice, the western medial moraine and then broken rock-covered ice to reach Mango I in 45 minutes. Head for the ablation valley above the side valley. High water in this side stream makes an impassable barrier to approach from below. Two camps exist, Mango I and Mango II. *Mango I*

(3660m), at the south end of this 2km-long ablation valley, is the better camp site with great views, a pond, profuse wildflowers and porters' shelters.

Days 3–4: Mango I to Baintha I
4½–5½ hours, 10.7km, 330m ascent
Walk up the ablation valley 30 minutes to Mango II, a large camp site, but less scenic with silty water. From Mango II, it takes 2½ hours to cross 6.5km of alternating bands of white ice and medial moraine to the Biafo Glacier's opposite (east) margin, with good views of the Latok peaks. Descend onto the glacier and head straight out 30 minutes over broken black rubble-covered ice to a band of white ice. Follow its west (left) edge up 45 minutes, skirting occasional small crevasses. As the white ice levels out, cross it to the east (right) then climb over medial moraine and descend to a larger white ice stream. Work east across that white ice, and ascend another, larger medial moraine.

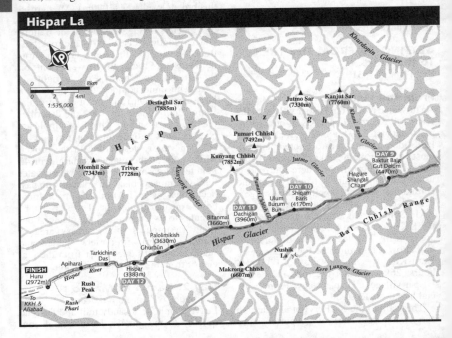

Here, you're directly opposite the Pharosang Glacier, an eastern tributary of the Biafo. Descend the medial moraine east and onto a third white ice stream. Cross it and the medial moraine beyond, to a broad white ice band. Follow this ice highway up 30 minutes, then cross one final medial moraine (4054m), opposite the Gama Sokha Lumbu Glacier and icefall with snowy Gama Sokha Lumbu (6282m) at its head. Cross the broken ice on the Biafo Glacier's east margin at its narrowest point, aiming for a faint trail visible on the grassy hillside ahead.

Enter the dry ablation valley along the Biafo Glacier's north-east margin and climb the short, steep trail along the hillside. Contour through grass and flowers, pass a small rock shelter, and after one hour descend into a large ablation valley with a broad alluvial fan. Below is **Shafung** (3930m), a camp site at the base of a large boulder. Warm, clear water flows by this pretty spot. Follow the stream's true left bank to another side

valley, crossing the stream where it braids into many channels. The water may be high on warm afternoons. Continue north-west, passing a small moraine lake and a possible camp site to reach **Baintha I** (3990m), 1¼ hours from Shafung. Almost all parties take an extra day in Baintha's lush meadow for acclimatisation and so porters can bake bread for the coming days. Tradition also dictates a goat feast for porters. A nontechnical ascent of rocky Baintha Peak (5300m) above camp, which assists with acclimatisation, gives good views of the glacier, Baintha Brak and the Latok peaks. Across the glacier is Ho Brak (5364m), a single-day snow and ice climb.

Day 5: Baintha I to Marpogoro
5½–6½ hours, 14km, 420m ascent
Stroll up the green ablation valley for 45 minutes to **Baintha II** (4050m), a less desirable camp site (marked by a triangle on the Swiss map) at the confluence of the

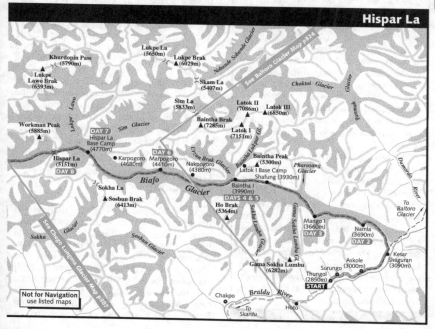

Biafo and Baintha Lukpar glaciers. To the east, up the Baintha Lukpar Glacier, is Latok II Base Camp. The Baintha Lukpar Glacier's northern arm, the Urzun Brak Glacier, leads to Latok I Base Camp, Baintha Brak Base Camp, and a single-day snow and ice climb of a 5669m peak right underneath Baintha Brak.

Move onto the Biafo Glacier, crossing broken ice 20 minutes to the smooth central ice flow. Head up the glacier, working around crevasses and ascending steadily several hours. Early in the season, this section may be snow covered, necessitating use of a rope.

After walking 8km in three to 4½ hours on the ice highway, you're opposite the first of the three 'rock camps' named for the

Snow Lake

Scottish naturalist Hugh Falconer was probably the first European to discover the Biafo Glacier in 1838, and Godwin-Austen did extensive exploration in 1861, but it wasn't until 1892 that Sir W Martin Conway dubbed Lukpe Lawo, the 5000m relatively level, snow-covered glacial expanse at the Biafo's head, as Snow Lake. From the 6000m to 7000m peaks surrounding Lukpe Lawo descend a number of the Karakoram's largest glaciers: the Biafo, Hispar, Khurdopin, Virzherav, Braldu, Nobande Sobande, Choktoi and Sim. Together, the Sim Glacier and Lukpe Lawo form one of the world's largest glacial basins.

This icy playground is best explored on skis, which allows for relatively easy cruising and keeps you out of hidden crevasses. Mountaineers can set a base camp for exploring and straightforward ascents of 5000m peaks. Besides the Hispar La, which is the only pass feasible for most trekkers, four other technical passes lead out of Lukpe Lawo and the Sim Glacier: Khurdopin Pass, Lukpe La, Skam La and Sim La. These high and steep passes are extreme challenges for qualified mountaineers who are experienced at glacier travel through remote areas.

colour of the rock *(goro)* above them: *nakpo* (black); *marpo* (red); and *karpo* (white). **Nakpogoro** (4380m) is a large area in an ablation valley on the Biafo's east margin with clear water, some vegetation and room for many tents. From the Biafo Glacier, a stream from a side glacier tumbling onto a white alluvial fan is visible. A prominent yellow rock spire towers above Nakpogoro. Access to this camp is through broken ice. Start from directly opposite the camp and head straight in. Nakpogoro is used by larger trekking parties, as the higher 'rock' camps are smaller. Camping at Nakpogoro leaves a very long distance the next day if you intend to reach the Hispar La Base Camp.

Continue 3.5km up the ice highway in the glacier's middle. Beyond Nakpogoro 1½ hours, you are just below **Marpogoro**. This small camp site with six or seven tent platforms and stone shelters is just above a side valley with a large icefall. The rock on the north side of the camp site is distinctly red, hence the name. Angle towards the red rock, working cautiously through the large marginal crevasses that guard the approach. A few flowers bloom and a bit of grass grows at Marpogoro (4410m), but the lush vegetation of Baintha is now behind. The tent sites on a lateral moraine are cold and exposed to wind, but dramatic amid the glaciers and snowy peaks. (Marpogoro is marked by a black square on the Swiss map.) Across the glacier, above the confluence with the Ghur Glacier, is a single-day snow and ice climb of Ghur (5796m).

Day 6: Marpogoro to Hispar La Base Camp

5–6 hours, 11.6km, 360m ascent

Leaving Marpogoro isn't as difficult as reaching it. Head out, angling north 15 minutes, detouring occasional crevasses to the broad, white ice highway of the main Biafo. A steady breeze constantly blows down the glacier, making the ascent cold and tiring. It takes two hours to walk 6.5km up the white ice until you're opposite the third rock camp, **Karpogoro** (4680m). The 22km from Baintha I to Karpogoro can be covered in one long day, if you're fit and acclimatised. The camp is at the glacier's east margin, at the confluence of the Sim and Biafo glaciers. It's guarded by marginal crevasses, so approach carefully. To the west is the route to the technical Sokha La.

If you're not going east to camp at Karpogoro, bear west (left) to avoid crevasses. The glacier broadens as the Sim and Biafo glaciers meet, and the ascent is gradual. Measurements here show the ice to be almost 1.5km thick and that the glacier's surface moves 300m per year. With permanent snow cover, travelling in roped teams is mandatory and wearing gaiters is helpful. Continue 5km in three to 3½ hours to *Hispar La Base Camp* (4770m). Avoid placing your camp site in a crevasse field. The usual camp site, marked by litter, is near a large pool of water some 30m below. You may want an extra day here to acclimatise or to explore Lukpe Lawo.

To the west, at the head of a small glacier and on the divide between the Biafo and Solu glaciers, are two climbable granite towers (peaks 5979m and 5957m on the Swiss map).

Day 7: Hispar La Base Camp to Hispar La
3–6 hours, 4.2km, 381m ascent
Start before the sun hits the snow and softens it. The ascent to the obvious Hispar La is a steady climb of a 20- to 30-degree snow slope. Travel in roped teams following a route up the middle, detouring to avoid numerous gaping crevasses and many more hidden ones. The broad and level Hispar La (5151m) makes a magnificent *camp site* in good weather. In inclement weather, get off the pass and camp lower down on the Hispar Glacier.

Conway, the first European to cross the pass, called the view to the east of Lukpe Lawo and Baintha Brak, 'beyond all comparison the finest view of mountains it has been my lot to behold'. Just north of the pass is Workman Peak (5885m), climbed by the indomitable Fanny Bullock-Workman. Far to the west, the Ultar peaks above Hunza are visible.

Day 8: Hispar La to Baktur Baig Gut Delum
6–8 hours, 14km, 681m descent
Start down before the morning sun hits the snow. It takes 45 minutes to one hour to cross the 2.5km-long flat pass, and another hour to descend the middle of the lower angle snow ramp, skirting yawning crevasses with icefalls on either side. The Hispar side of the pass is more heavily crevassed than the Biafo side. Once onto the lower Hispar Glacier (5040m), wend around the fissures and sinkholes 30 minutes. It's possible to *camp* here on the glacier near pools.

Continue for 1½ hours until even with the first large icefall to the north. The crevasses decrease and using a rope becomes optional. Reach red moraine after 45 minutes, and 45 minutes farther, reach the Khani Basa Glacier (4511m), the first of four major glaciers that push into the Hispar Glacier from the north.

Climb 15 minutes over the moraine and cross two white ice sections of the Khani Basa Glacier in 30 minutes, staying right. Kanjut Sar (7760m) is at the Khani Basa Glacier's head. Enter the ablation valley along the north margin of the Hispar Glacier and ascend 30m of talus to the grassy hillside above. Pass two small possible camp sites. Thirty minutes farther, at the end of the ridge descending from point 5198 on the Swiss map, reach a large camp site called *Baktur Baig Gut Delum* (4470m), which means 'Baktur Baig pitched his tent here' in Burushaski. Here are a side stream, wildflowers, porters' shelters and splendid views of the Bal Chhīsh peaks soaring above the Hispar Glacier and Baintha Brak peering over the Hispar La.

Day 9: Baktur Baig Gut Delum to Shiqam Baris
7 hours, 7.9km, 360m ascent, 660m descent
Cross a stream from the small tributary glacier just beyond camp and descend steeply to the ablation valley along the Hispar Glacier's north margin. Move onto boulder-covered medial moraine 30 minutes from

BALTISTAN

camp. On either side of this level moraine are heavily broken sections. Although a trail hugs the grassy hillside above the glacier from Baktur Baig Gut Delum 5km to the Jutmo Glacier, this trail is sporadically obliterated by mud slides and avalanches and may be blocked. A camp site called Hagure Shangali Cham is on the hillside. If this trail is not passable, move out onto the Hispar Glacier, working towards its centre to avoid the Jutmo Glacier's broken east margin where it impacts the Hispar Glacier. After two hours on the Hispar Glacier, cross onto the very convoluted **Jutmo Glacier** (4320m). Work around high ice walls and after two tedious hours, reach the cliff at the north-west corner of the Jutmo-Hispar confluence. A thin, steep trail ascends loose, powdery cliffs 15 minutes to the grassy hillside above (4680m). Traverse the hillside, passing several small *camp sites* along the trail. Each of these camp sites has excellent views and clean water. The largest one, *Shiqam Baris* (4170m), is 1½ hours down the trail at the end of the grassy hill. A large stream descends from a side glacier onto an alluvial plain. Shiqam Baris means 'green canyon' in Burushaski.

Day 10: Shiqam Baris to Dachigan
7 hours, 13.1km, 60m ascent, 270m descent

Continue one hour on a good trail to *Ulum Burum Bun* (white rock ahead), a colder and less desirable camp site with no morning sun and water farther away. Cross the large stream just beyond Ulum Burum Bun in the morning when water is low. Beyond the stream, the trail along the hillside towards the Pumari Chhīsh Glacier is preferable, but occasionally obliterated by rock fall and avalanches. Local people know if it's possible. The alternative is to descend the loose, cliff-like lateral moraine to the Hispar Glacier's north margin and to follow it to the confluence with the **Pumari Chhīsh Glacier** (4080m). This exhausting, awkward route takes three hours. Cross the Pumari Chhīsh Glacier in 1½ to two hours. It's much less broken than the Jutmo Glacier,

and not as wide. Head for the distinctive red lateral moraine of the Pumari Chhīsh Glacier, which bends west beneath cliffs as it merges with the larger Hispar Glacier. Where the red moraine ends and meets the white moraine of the Hispar Glacier (4020m), climb up the powdery cliff above the glacier's north margin on a thin, loose Class 2 trail 15 minutes to the hillside above (4080m). After 30 minutes on a trail, reach a camp site, where water sources may be dry after midsummer. The trail climbs above and around this dry camp site and joins the trail from the west side of the Pumari Chhīsh Glacier. Continue 45 minutes to *Dachigan* (3960m), an ideal camp site. Dachigan refers to a wall *(dachi)* blocking the trail *(gan)* to prevent livestock from straying. A large clear stream waters this beautiful grassy area with grand views of the wall of 6000m peaks south of the Hispar Glacier.

Day 11: Dachigan to Hispar
6½ hours, 17.9km, 340m ascent, 917m descent

Follow a gentle 4km trail 45 minutes to *Bitanmal* (place of the shaman), an expanse of tall, lush grasses used as a pasture by Hispar villagers in late summer. Near the huts and livestock pens is a large rock and shrine. Lofty Makrong Chhīsh (6607m) rises across the Hispar Glacier. Bring water from Bitanmal (3660m) because it's scarce for the next few hours. From Bitanmal, walk 15 minutes across the meadow and descend steep talus to the Kunyang Glacier's edge. A faint trail crosses the stable, rock-covered **Kunyang Glacier** in one hour. The 15-minute climb to the grassy hill (3900m) on the far side (labelled Daltanas on the Swiss map) is the hardest exit from a glacier yet. It requires careful balance and frequent use of small handholds. With no more glaciers to cross, enjoy the stroll through junipers and ephedra down the ablation valley. After an hour, reach Palolimikish (3630m), a field of tall noxious plants named *palolin*. Continue 30 minutes to a large stream, and ford it amid tamarisk shrubs.

continued on page 337

Baltoro Glacier Treks

Baltoro Glacier

JOHN MOCK

Duration	15 days
Distance	143.6km
Standard	demanding
Season	June–September
Start/Finish	Thungol
Zone & Permit	restricted, US$50 permit
Public Transport	no

Summary The world-renowned Baltoro Glacier has some of the planet's most amazing scenery, in a procession of mind-blowing rock towers and shining peaks all the way to K2 Base Camp.

The route up the Baltoro Glacier to Concordia, where the Godwin-Austen, upper Baltoro and Vigne glaciers all converge, is indeed a trek into the throne room of the mountain gods, as photographer Galen Rowell proclaimed. The 62km-long Baltoro Glacier, the Karakoram's third longest, is Pakistan's number one trekking destination. Nearly 70% of the trekking and mountaineering permits issued each year are for the Baltoro. Along the lower Baltoro are amazing granite towers and sheer walls – Uli Biaho, the Trangos, the Cathedrals. These monsters of rock yield above Concordia to the incomparable snow-clad giants. Seven of the world's 25 highest peaks rise above the glacier. Within 25km of one another are the Gasherbrums, Broad Peak and K2 (8611m), so massive yet so ethereal, the ultimate mountain of mountains.

Completion of the road up the Braldu Valley to Thungol in 1992 and to Askole in 1993 and improved trail conditions beyond, both results of the Pakistan Army's year-round deployment along the glacier, have shortened this trek by more than a week from its original length. Today, it takes only eight days to cover the 72km one way to Concordia. Half of the trekking distance and only two camp sites, Goro II and Concordia, are actually on glacier, and all of it's nontechnical. By Karakoram standards, it's gentle glacier travel at its best.

PLANNING
When to Trek
Most expeditions travel up the Baltoro Glacier in June and return in August, making these crowded months on the trail. River crossings along the trail, however, are easier before July when water levels rise dramatically.

Maps & Books
The Swiss Foundation for Alpine Research 1:250,000 orographical map *Karakoram (Sheet 1)* and *Karakoram (Sheet 2)* cover the trek. Thungol, Jula, Skam Tsok and Khoburtse aren't labelled. Gasherbrum IV is mislabelled as Gasherbrum VI (6706m) at the West Gasherbrum Glacier's head.

Other maps feature the Baltoro Glacier and surrounding peaks, but none detail the area south of the Baltoro Glacier. The beautifully coloured 1:100,000 *Ghiacciaio Baltoro* map (US$70) published by the Italian dai tipi

Previous Page: Muztagh Tower above Baltoro Glacier (photographer John Mock).

Above: See main image on p329.

Right: Great Trango Tower from Urdukas camp site at sunrise (John Mock).

dell' Instituto Geografico Militare (IGM) in 1969, and reprinted in 1977, is based on Italian 1929 and 1954 K2 Expeditions. The Xi'an Cartographic Publishing House published the 1:100,000 *(Mount Qogori)* map (US$18) with 40m contour intervals, but it doesn't show international borders. *The Eight-Thousand Metre Peaks of the Karakoram* is a 1:50,000 orographical sketch map (US$14) prepared by Jerzy Wala.

Two classic books on the Baltoro Glacier are *Climbing and Exploration in the Karakoram-Himalayas* (hardcover) by William M Conway, which describes the first expedition to the Baltoro Glacier, and *Karakoram and Western Himalaya* (hardcover), the most sought-after rare book on Himalayan exploration, by Filippo de Filippi who recounts the Duke of the Abruzzi's 1909 Baltoro Glacier expedition with Vittorio Sella's incredible photographs. *In the Throne Room of the Mountain Gods* by Galen Rowell recounts the 1975 American expedition with the best history of Baltoro Glacier exploration and superb photographs (hardcover). *K2: Triumph and Tragedy* by Jim Curran recounts the 1986 season when K2 claimed 13 lives.

Permits & Regulations

This trek is in a restricted zone where a permit and licensed guide are required (see Trekking Permits, p70).

Guides & Porters

Every licensed trekking company has experienced guides and cooks who know the route well. Porters are essential on this route and it's difficult to deviate from the expeditionary-style trekking that has developed. The ratio of porters to trekkers typically varies from 3:1 (for small-scale lower-budget treks) to 6:1 (for trekking parties outfitted by a trekking company). Frustrated budget-conscious trekkers with lightweight gear and freeze-dried food who plan to backpack often wonder why they need so many porters. They're usually unsuccessful in negotiating (with their guide or porters) to significantly reduce the number of porters' loads. Because a guide is required, you usually have to hire a cook since guides don't cook. Then you need a porter to carry the kitchen, a porter for the kerosene, porters for the guide's and cook's food and porters to carry the food for those porters. It all adds up. Try to find a cook who also carries a full porter's load.

Porters are responsible for paying for their own transport to Thungol. Some confusing exceptions to standard porters' wages apply to this trek. Porters bring their own food for the first four stages to Paiju. For these four stages, pay a flat rate of Rs 220 per stage. For the remaining stages from Paiju to Concordia and back, provide all food and fuel for porters and pay a flat rate of Rs 170 per stage. It's customary for porters to butcher animals at Paiju. Small parties can pay each porter a one-time Rs 50 meat ration in lieu of buying an animal. Porters expect to receive either clothing and equipment as per Tourism Division guidelines or to be paid the allowance. It's cheaper to buy all of the required items in Skardu. Although it takes extra effort, you then know your porters have adequate gear. Whether they bring their own gear or you provide it for them, keep in mind that they will be walking and sleeping on snow and ice for many days.

A shop in Paiju sells basic supplies (flour, sugar and kerosene). Unfortunately, beverages in plastic bottles and aluminium cans have made

Left: the colossal form of K2, seen from Concordia (John Mock).

their way here, adding to the rubbish problem. Buying supplies here is more expensive than buying them in Skardu and paying porters to carry them up. However, it provides an option to resupply or to supply porters with food above Paiju, which can reduce the number of porters' loads to Paiju. Porters going down can buy food here to get back to Askole.

Stages

It's 19 stages total round trip. It's one stage round trip (ie, half a stage in each direction) between Thungol and Askole, plus these 18 stages from Askole: (1) Korophon; (2) Jula; (3) Bardumal; (4) Paiju; (5) Liligo; (6) Urdukas; (7) Goro I; (8) Goro II; and (9) Concordia; and (10–18) nine stages to return via the same route.

NEAREST FACILITIES

See Thungol (p310).

GETTING TO/FROM THE TREK

See Thungol (p310).

THE TREK
Day 1: Thungol to Korophon

4–5 hours, 12.6km, 150m ascent

See Day 1 of the Hispar La trek (p313) for a description from Thungol to the trail junction beyond Kesar Shaguran. From the junction, the trail to the Baltoro Glacier continues east below the rock buttress. Thirty minutes past

Below: Masherbrum above a glacial pool on the Baltoro Glacier.

JOHN MOCK

A Fragile Glacier

The Baltoro Glacier is a fragile ecosystem whose carrying capacity is overextended. Fewer than 1000 trekkers and mountaineers make their way up the glacier each year, but the many thousands of porters and staff accompanying them amplify the impact. When you look up, you see beautiful mountain scenery in every direction, but when you look down it's another matter. Rubbish indiscriminately thrown along the way and around camp sites doesn't go away in this frozen landscape. Human faeces are both an eyesore and a health hazard, even though non-government organisations have built pit toilets at many camp sites.

The impact of trekkers, climbers and porters is most concentrated at camp sites. On the glacier, however, the continuing military presence remains the major environmental problem. Rubbish pits announce each army post as you approach. A telegraph wire links all the army camps. Overhead, daily good-weather helicopter flights serve to remind visitors of the long-simmering confrontation between Pakistan and India over the adjacent Siachen Glacier.

the junction reach large rocks and climb 15 minutes onto the Biafo Glacier's terminal moraine. Cross the glacier in 45 minutes on an easy, obvious trail passing above its mouth. *Korophon* (3000m) is a huge plain on the Biafo Glacier's north-east margin with dusty camp sites amid a few willows. The area was more heavily wooded, but is suffering from the many porters chopping wood to cook. Water flows from the glacier and becomes silty in the afternoon. Twenty minutes beyond the camp site is a spring and an enormous boulder called Korophon (bowl-shaped rock).

Day 2: Korophon to Skam Tsok
4½–5½ hours, 13.4km, 300m ascent

Pass the boulder on a good trail and in one hour reach a spring at the river's edge. Walk along the sandy river bed and then climb 15 minutes to a cairn. Here the trail turns east-north-east towards the Dumordo River coming from the Panmah Glacier.

The Dumordo River was once a formidable obstacle, necessitating a tedious cable crossing in low water or, in high water, a half-day detour along an exposed cliffside trail. Now a footbridge, built in 1998, is just 15 minutes upvalley. Villagers charge a Rs 15 bridge toll, but it's worth it for the convenience. Across the footbridge is *Jula* (Urdu for 'swing', referring to the former cable crossing), a broad plain at the confluence of the Dumordo and Biaho Rivers. Jula's exposed location and silty water from the distant river make it an undesirable camp site.

Follow the trail along the Biaho River's true right bank through fragrant tamarisks and ephedra two hours to a side stream with clear water. This is a good lunch spot called Chobrok. Continue 15 minutes to the confluence of the Ching Kang and Biaho rivers, where the Biaho bends east. Beyond the bend is Bardumal, an abandoned camp site with a porter's grave. The preferred camp site, *Skam Tsok* (3300m; *skam* means dry; *tsok*, a thorny bush),

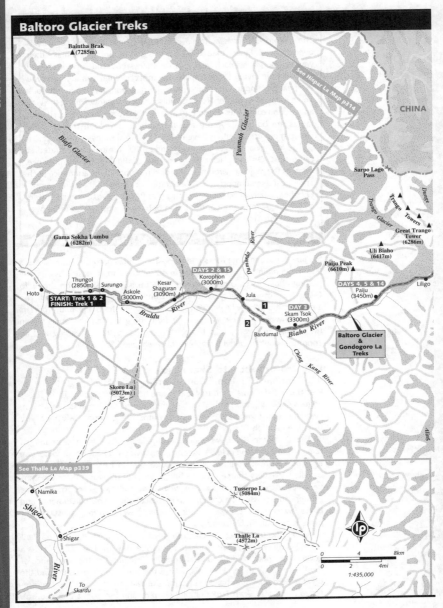

Baltoro Glacier Treks

Baintha Brak
▲ (7285m)

See Hispar La Map p314

CHINA

Biafo Glacier

Sarpo Lago Pass

Dunge

Trango Towers

Great Trango Tower
(6286m)

Gama Sokha Lumbu
▲ (6282m)

Panmah Glacier

Uli Biaho
(6417m)

Braldu River

Dumordo River

Paiju Peak
(6610m) ▲

Thungol
(2850m) Surungo

Kesar
Shaguran
(3090m)

DAYS 2 & 15
Korophon
(3000m)

DAYS 4, 5 & 14
Paiju
(3450m)

Liligo

Hoto

Askole
(3000m)

Jula

**START: Trek 1 & 2
FINISH: Trek 1**

1

Bardumal

2

DAY 3
Skam Tsok
(3300m)

Biaho River

**Baltoro Glacier
& Gondogoro La
Treks**

Chiang Kang River

Skoro La
(5073m)

See Thalle La Map p339

Namika

Tusserpo La
(5084m)

Shigar

Shigar

Thalle La
(4572m)

River

To
Skardu

0   4   8km

0   2   4mi

1:435,000

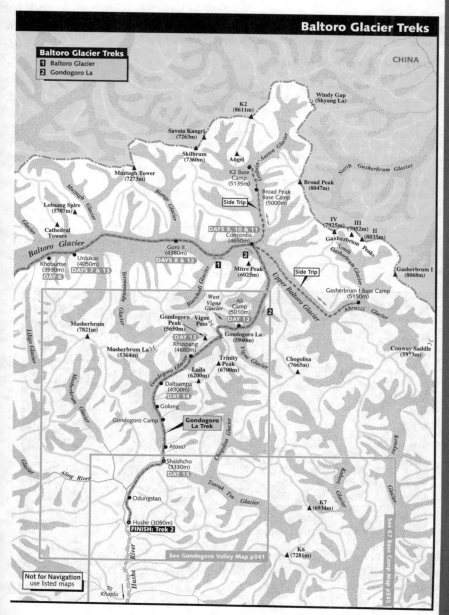

Baltoro Glacier Treks

Baltoro Glacier Treks
1 Baltoro Glacier
2 Gondogoro La

CHINA

Windy Gap
(Skyang La)

K2
(8611m)

Savoia Kangri
(7263m)

Skilbrum
(7360m)

Angel

Muztagh Tower
(7273m)

K2 Base
Camp
(5135m)

North Gasherbrum Glacier

Lobsang Spire
(5707m)

Broad Peak
(8047m)

Broad Peak
Base Camp
(5000m)

Side Trip

Cathedral
Towers

IV
(7925m)

III
(7952m)

II
(8035m)

Gasherbrum
Peaks

Baltoro Glacier

Khoburtse
(3930m)
DAY 6

Urdukas
(4050m)
DAYS 7 & 13

Goro II
(4380m)
DAYS 8 & 12

DAYS 9, 10 & 11
Concordia
(4650m)

South
Gasherbrum Glacier

Gasherbrum I
(8068m)

Mitre Peak
(6025m)

Side Trip

Gasherbrum I Base Camp
(5150m)

Abruzzi Glacier

Masherbrum
(7821m)

West
Vigne
Glacier

Ali
Camp
(5010m)
DAY 12

Conway Saddle
(5973m)

Gondogoro Peak
(5650m)

Vigne
Pass

DAY 13
Xhuspang
(4680m)

Gondogoro La
(5940m)

Masherbrum La
(5364m)

Laila
(6200m)

Trinity
Peak
(6700m)

Chogolisa
(7665m)

Daltsampa
(4300m)
DAY 14

Golong

Gondogoro Camp

**Gondogoro
La Trek**

Atosar

Shaishcho
(3330m)
DAY 15

Tsarak Tsa Glacier

K7
(6934m)

Odungstan

Hushe (3050m)
FINISH: Trek 2

See Gondogoro Valley Map p341

K6
(7281m)

Not for Navigation
use listed maps

To
Khaplu

is 30 to 45 minutes farther amid tamarisks at the first clear side stream. Between Jula and Skam Tsok are several sections with low-water and high-water trails. The low-water trail is quicker and easier with less climbing.

Days 3–4: Skam Tsok to Paiju
3–3½ hours, 8.6km, 150m ascent

The trail alternates between the river bed and terraces above, crossing boulder fields and side streams until coming to the Paiju Glacier's outwash stream. It's easy to ford when the water is low, but when the water is high, you may need a rope for safety. The first glimpses of Paiju Peak (6610m) and Cathedral Towers are from here. Continue around a rocky cliff and drop to the low-water trail along the river; the high-water trail stays high. From the riverside, ascend to the terrace and pass through groves of trees to *Paiju* (3450m), one to 1½ hours from the ford. A small tree-lined stream passes through Paiju, and tent platforms are carved out all over the hillside. Paiju is often crowded and noisy, and always dirty. The tent platforms higher along the stream are quieter with good views. The entire dry area across the stream has become an open toilet.

Some parties reach Paiju in two days, camping at Jula en route. The camp sites, however, are better when taking three days. Regardless, almost all parties take an extra day in Paiju for acclimatisation. Paiju is the last source of wood. Despite kerosene and stoves, and signs urging porters not to cut wood, they do so in order to bake bread for the coming days.

Below: Trango Towers (left) and Cathedral Tower from Baltoro Glacier.

JOHN MOCK

Day 5: Paiju to Khoburtse
4½–5½ hours, 10.8km, 480m ascent

Walk one hour towards the Baltoro Glacier's terminus where an obvious trail leads up the terminal moraine. The trail crosses the glacier angling gently 3.5km to the south-east margin in 2½ hours. Continue up the ablation valley 15 minutes to *Liligo*. The original camp site with a clear stream below a grassy hillside was wiped out long ago by rock fall. Just around the bend is the newer Liligo camp site with stone shelters cramped into a boulder field. Water comes from the moraine lake below. Ibex still wander the grassy slopes above. The incredibly sheer granite towers of the Baltoro's northern wall, separated by steep, broken ice floes, dominate the view. Across the Baltoro along the Dunge Glacier are the base camps (3900–4150m) for Nameless Tower, Great Trango Tower and the Cathedrals.

For the next 1½ hours the trail alternates between the lateral moraine and glacier, finally heading out on the glacier to avoid the Liligo Glacier's outwash stream, which periodically surges to form a lake. *Khoburtse* (3930m), an alternative camp site to Liligo with clear water and a few level tent sites, lies just past the Liligo Glacier. Khoburtse is a bitter but edible fragrant green sage. The tent sites nearest the toilets are subject to rock fall, so pitch tents on the opposite side of the ridge away from the hillside. From the flower-covered hillsides are extraordinary views of Paiju Peak, Uli Biaho (6417m), Great Trango Tower (6286m), Lobsang Spire (5707m) and Cathedral Towers. The scenery is so magnificent, it's worthwhile to walk shorter days and enjoy the views from this and the next camp site.

Day 6: Khoburtse to Urdukas
2–3 hours, 5.1km, 120m ascent

Between Khoburtse and Urdukas, two glaciers from the south-east join the Baltoro. The trail along the lateral moraine moves onto the glacier to skirt these side glaciers. Continue 30 minutes more on moraine to an army camp with a large moraine lake below. On the grassy boulder-strewn hillside 50m above is *Urdukas* (4050m), named for the obvious cracked (*kas*) boulder (urdwa) above camp. Two small streams provide water at Urdukas; the lower (west) one is more frequently used (and polluted), the higher (east) one a few minutes beyond camp is better. The trail between Paiju and Urdukas is now so improved that what was always a two-day walk now can be done by acclimatised trekkers in one day. Heavily used Urdukas is much larger than Paiju. The meadows above Urdukas offer one of the Karakoram's finest panoramas. All the Trango Towers are visible, including Nameless Tower, which has the world's longest granite face.

Day 7: Urdukas to Goro II
6–7 hours, 12.1km, 330m ascent

Head north passing several porters' graves. The trail descends and goes straight out to the glacier's middle. The trail from here to Concordia, although still obvious, is less of a highway, and remains on the glacier. Masherbrum's sheer granite north face and snow-crowned summit (7821m) comes into view as you walk east up the Baltoro Glacier. After 3½ to four hours, stop for lunch near the little-used camp site of **Shakspoon**, the big pile *(spoon)* of little stones *(shak)*. Towering white seracs rise to the right of the trail, which is marked by occasional cairns. This section is more rugged with occasional jumps over small streams. **Goro II** (4380m), 2½ to three hours farther, is just beyond an army camp in the glacier's middle. Tent platforms and porters' circles are fashioned on the ice and rock. Here in mid-glacier, wind blows from the Biange Glacier and Muztagh Tower (7273m). Water comes from the glacier just north of camp. Gasherbrum IV's (7925m) unique squared-off summit beckons towards Concordia and Masherbrum's dramatic summit cap soars behind.

Days 8–10: Goro II to Concordia
5–6 hours, 9.2km, 270m ascent
Follow the black medial moraine up the glacier's centre. The trail marches steadily towards Concordia, working right and close to the Biarchedi Glacier, bounded by a sheer wall of fluted snow. As you approach Concordia, the immense bulk of triple-headed Broad Peak (8047m) emerges. **Concordia** (4650m) where the Godwin-Austen Glacier meets the upper Baltoro and Vigne glaciers, has an army camp. Beyond the army camp 10 minutes is a large level area with many porters' shelters and superb views of the colossal pyramid of K2 (8611m). Mitre Peak (6025m) to the south stands watch over this place of sublime and awesome beauty. Concordia, exposed as it is, receives strong winds and is the Baltoro's coldest camp site. Most trekkers spend three nights to savour its majesty.

Side Trip: Broad Peak & K2 Base Camps
6–8 hours, 20km, 485m ascent, 485m descent
The route to K2 Base Camp and back to Concordia can be covered in one long, tiring day. Most trekkers take a more leisurely pace and move camp from Concordia to K2 Base Camp for one or more nights. As you walk towards K2, and it grows even larger, its incredible size becomes apparent. Leave the Concordia trail 10 minutes beyond (east of) the army camp. Head north, cross a snow bridge, and follow a faint trail through jumbled moraine onto the large light brown medial moraine of the Godwin-Austen Glacier. This moraine runs straight towards K2 with occasional cairns marking the route. It takes 2½ to 3 hours to reach **Broad Peak Base Camp** (5000m), which extends 30 minutes up the moraine. It's easy to tell when you're there by the rubbish. Fifteen minutes after the highest base camp, leave the moraine, as it's easier to walk on the white ice to the west (left). Follow this one hour, then pass through broken glacier and moraine 15 minutes to **K2 Base Camp** (5135m). Here, directly below K2's immense bulk, the mountain appears strongly foreshortened, yet completely fills your view. Camps are on either side of the broken glacier, though most are on its east side. The Gilkey memorial, named for geologist Arthur Gilkey who disappeared on K2 in 1953, lies 100m up the rock slope at the very base of K2. Names of climbers who died on the mountain have been inscribed on steel dinner plates with some more ornate plaques. A few bodies are also interred here. It's four stages total round trip from Concordia: (1) Broad Peak Base Camp; (2) K2 Base Camp; and (3–4) two stages to return via the same route.

Right: Masherbrum (7821m) from Baltoro Glacier.

Side Trip: Gasherbrum I Base Camp
2 days, 500m ascent, 500m descent
The base camp (5150m) for Gasherbrum I, first designated as K5 and later dubbed Hidden Peak by Conway, is at the confluence of the Abruzzi and South Gasherbrum glaciers. From Concordia, follow the upper Baltoro Glacier to the south-east, skirting the base of Gasherbrums IV, V and VI, then head north-east up the Abruzzi Glacier to base camp. This is too far for a day hike, so plan on spending at least one night. It totals two stages round trip – one up, one back. The mountaineering route continues up the South Gasherbrum Glacier to Camp 1 (5943m).

Days 11–15: Concordia to Thungol
5 days, 71.8km, 1800m descent
Most trekkers retrace their route in five days, camping at Goro II, Urdukas, Paiju and Korophon en route to Thungol.

JOHN MOCK

JOHN MOCK

Gondogoro La

Duration	15 days
Distance	114.9km
Standard	extreme, technical
Season	late June–August
Start	Thungol
Finish	Hushe
Zone & Permit	restricted, US$50 permit
Public Transport	finish only

Summary This on-the-edge trek crosses a high glaciated pass with extraordinary views of four 8000m peaks and countless other peaks.

In 1986, a route was established that connects Concordia and the upper Baltoro Glacier to the Hushe Valley over the Gondogoro La (5940m). Since then, this challenging technical pass has attracted trekkers and climbers alike. This route avoids retracing your steps down the Baltoro Glacier and has one of the most overwhelming mountain panoramas anywhere in the world, with all of the Karakoram's 8000m peaks close at hand.

The Gondogoro La, although popular with trekkers, involves Class 4 climbing. The north side is a 50-degree snow slope with avalanche danger requiring fixed ropes. The south side is a continuous 50-degree slope with rock-fall and avalanche danger that requires fixing as much as 300m of rope. Crossing this pass requires good judgment, commitment, top fitness, prior acclimatisation and basic mountaineering skills of all members. Parties must be on top of the Gondogoro La at sunrise to minimise exposure to objective dangers.

Parties cross the pass in both directions. Crossing from north to south from Concordia to Hushe, however, is recommended for four reasons. First, the longer approach up the Baltoro Glacier permits more gradual acclimatisation. Second, the objective dangers of the not-straightforward route up the north side of the pass are more easily visible and take less time on this ascent, which is more than 200m shorter. Third, if conditions prohibit crossing the pass, you don't miss out visiting the Baltoro Glacier and Concordia. Occasionally, especially late in the season, the crevasses on the north side of the Gondogoro La are unbridgeable, and parties have been forced to turn back. Fourth, the road from Hushe to Skardu is usually more free of blocks than the road between Thungol and Skardu.

Large trekking parties, however, may choose to start from Hushe, crossing the pass from south to north, in order to get past the objective rock-fall danger on the south side earlier in the morning when danger is lowest. Such parties then usually slog across the crevassed West Vigne Glacier in soft, treacherous snow. Marathon trekkers also cross in this direction in order to combine this trek with longer traverses of the Baltoro, Biafo and Hispar glaciers. It's advisable to first trek to Masherbrum and/or K7 Base Camps before going up the Gondogoro Valley to facilitate acclimatisation. At the minimum, use Days 1–5 to reach Xhuspang from Hushe, move to Gondogoro High Camp on Day 6, cross the pass to Ali Camp on Day 7, and reach Concordia on Day 8.

Left: Laila Peak above Gondogoro Glacier (photographer John Mock).

Above: see main image (p334).

PLANNING
When to Trek

The pass is easier to cross earlier in the season and can be attempted as early as the last three or four days in June. Any earlier and you are likely to be the first party of the season to break trail. By August, objective dangers from crevasses, avalanches and rock fall increase substantially as the snow cover begins to melt.

What to Bring

Traversing the Vigne and West Vigne glaciers requires travelling in roped teams and crossing the Gondogoro La requires fixing as much as 300m of rope. The Hushe Rescue Team places fixed ropes on both sides of the Gondogoro La each year from late June to late August, and charges a fee to use them: Rs 2500 for one to three trekkers; Rs 3500 for four to six trekkers; Rs 4500 for seven to nine trekkers; and Rs 5000 for nine or more trekkers. Most parties utilise their ropes. Reports are positive because it saves time and reduces weight and the expense of having porters carry rope and anchors. Wearing a climbing helmet is prudent. Crampons are optional, but strongly recommended. See Mountaineering Equipment (p61) for the required equipment.

Maps

Refer to the Maps sections under the Baltoro Glacier trek (p320) and the Gondogoro Valley trek (p341). The Swiss map misrepresents the relationship of the West Vigne Glacier to the Gondogoro Glacier, and the shapes of these glaciers.

Where is Gondogoro La?

Misleading and inaccurate information has been published about three passes between the Baltoro Glacier and Hushe's upper valleys: Gondogoro La, Masherbrum La and Vigne Pass (also called Mazeno La). Of these passes, trekking parties can only cross the Gondogoro La, which links the West Vigne Glacier to the Gondogoro Glacier's large eastern branch. Gondogoro La is misplaced on most maps. Its map coordinates are 35° 39' 18.0" N and 76° 28' 22.0" E. The other two passes present serious technical difficulties. The Masherbrum La (5364m), between the Yermanendu Glacier and a northern branch of the Gondogoro Glacier, has an enormous icefall on its south side. The Vigne Pass connects the Gondogoro Glacier's northernmost section with the West Vigne Glacier's head, north-west of Gondogoro La. The Vigne Pass, although lower in elevation than Gondogoro La, has more rock-fall danger and technical sections impossible for porters to cross. Some maps incorrectly show the Gondogoro La crossing the ridge between the Biarchedi and Gondogoro glaciers. One look, however, at the steep, corniced wall above the Biarchedi Glacier with its multiple avalanche flutes shows that any crossing of this ridge is dangerous and highly technical.

Permits & Regulations

This trek is in a restricted zone where a permit and licensed guide are required (see Trekking Permits, p70).

Guides & Porters

It's essential to hire an experienced guide who knows the pass, and very helpful to have strong porters who have also crossed it. Guides and porters from Hushe may have more experience crossing the Gondogoro La than those from other areas of Baltistan. Having a strong, experienced team helps ensure success and enables all to enjoy it.

Porters cannot ascend or descend this pass without using between 100m and 300m of fixed ropes. Equip each porter with a swami or sling, one locking carabiner, instep crampons and gaiters (you can provide porters with plastic and string to fashion something useful) for one day.

Starting from Thungol See the Baltoro Glacier trek (p321) for rates between Thungol and Concordia. Between Concordia and Hushe, continue paying a flat rate of Rs 170 per stage and providing food for porters.

Starting from Hushe For the four stages between Hushe and Xhuspang, porters ask for Rs 220 per stage, including payment for food rations. Beyond Xhuspang, you provide food for porters and pay Rs 170 per stage. It's customary for porters to butcher an animal at Gondogoro Camp or Daltsampa. Animals can usually be purchased at Shaishcho or Gondogoro Camp. Small parties can pay each porter a one-time Rs 50 meat ration in lieu of buying an animal.

Stages

It's 18½ stages total. It's 9½ stages between Thungol and Concordia (see the Baltoro Glacier trek, p323, for details), plus these nine stages between Concordia and Hushe: (1) corner of Mitre Peak; (2) Ali Camp; (3) Gondogoro La; (4) Gondogoro High Camp; (5) Xhuspang; (6) Daltsampa; (7) Gondogoro Camp; (8) Shaishcho; and (9) Hushe.

Tough bargainers may be able to negotiate eight stages between Concordia and Hushe, eliminating the stage at the corner of Mitre Peak. Reportedly some porters have asked for and received double stages/wages over the pass. Don't follow this precedent, which has no legitimate basis.

NEAREST FACILITIES

See Thungol (p310).

GETTING TO/FROM THE TREK

To reach the trek's start, see Thungol (p310). For transport from its finish, see Hushe (p340).

THE TREK (see map p324)
Days 1–10: Thungol to Concordia

10 days, 71.8km, 1800m ascent

See the Baltoro Glacier trek (pp323–8) for a description. The route over Gondogoro La leaves the Baltoro Glacier trek at Concordia on Day 10.

Day 11: Concordia to Ali Camp

3½–5 hours, 9.5km, 360m ascent

The route to Ali Camp is up the snow-covered Vigne Glacier, so start before the sun softens the snow. From Concordia, head south towards Mitre Peak, crossing the Baltoro Glacier's broken south margin. Follow the lateral moraine around the base of Mitre Peak, paralleling the ridge south from its summit. After 4km, or two hours, reach the Vigne Glacier. Head south-south-west up the Vigne Glacier 5.5km to Ali Camp travelling in roped teams. Firmer snow towards the glacier's middle offers easier walking and avoids crevasses along the west margin. You pass three valleys on the west side of the Vigne Glacier. The first, 15 minutes up the glacier, has a camp site called **Miksus** (eye pain), marked by a cairn along the glacier's margin. 'Snowblindness' camp is infrequently used, yet a reminder to be sure everyone in your party wears sunglasses. In the second small side valley is an alternative Ali Camp. The actual Ali Camp is just beyond the third and largest side valley, three hours up the Vigne Glacier at the base of the spur at the confluence of the Vigne and West Vigne glaciers (ie, the base of point 5943 on the Italian IGM map). Marginal crevasses guard **Ali Camp** (5010m), so carefully approach it straight from the Vigne Glacier's centre. Several tent platforms are wedged against the cliff and on moraine. Painted in red on the cliff is the name of Ali Muhammad Jungugpa, the site's namesake, who crossed the Gondogoro La on 20 June 1986. South-east facing Ali Camp is usually warmer than Concordia. A small shop sells basic supplies such as flour and kerosene.

Below: Trekker ascending steep snow slope towards Gondogoro La (5940m).

Day 12: Ali Camp to Xhuspang
7–10 hours, 8.5km, 930m ascent, 1260m descent

From Ali Camp, it takes four to six hours to reach the pass. Plan to be on top of the pass by 6am. Large parties should start by 1 or 2am; small or very fit parties could start by 3am.

Rope up immediately and move over firm snow along the base of the but-tress to your right. Turn into the snow-covered West Vigne Glacier heading west-south-west. On firm snow it takes one hour to cover the 3.3km to the base of the pass. The angle is gentle heading diagonally towards a black rock band descending from the ridge above the glacier's south side. The pass is south-east (left) of this band, and is not visible until just beneath it. At the West Vigne Glacier's head, an obvious low point is the more difficult Vigne Pass. The steep slope east (left) of the Gondogoro La is prone to avalanche.

From the base of Gondogoro La, the 600m snow ascent takes two hours. Three steep 50-degree sections require fixed ropes; snow anchors are ne-cessary. The first pitch goes 60m to a bench. If no steps exist, kick steps. If steps exist, they may be icy. K2's summit begins to emerge above the ridge to the north as you climb. From the bench, the second pitch is 25m to a sec-ond small bench, with large crevasses on either side. From here, head right up lower-angle snow to the base of a large icy cornice, a part of which avalanched on 24 August 1998, killing two porters. The third pitch turns left and ascends 30m passing left of the cornice. Above, continue up easy low angle snow a short way to the level **Gondogoro La** (5940m).

The spectacular panorama from the pass includes K2, Broad Peak and the four Gasherbrums, I (8068m), II (8035m), III (7952m), and IV (7925m). Trinity Peak (6700m) lies along the ridge south of the pass. The lovely snow and granite cone of Laila (6200m), first climbed unofficially in 1987 by a British expedition and officially in 1996 by an Italian expedition, rises over the Gondogoro Glacier as you turn to descend.

On the south side of the pass, use fixed ropes to angle right and down a ramp 10m to a point in front of an outcrop of exfoliating granite. Here, turn 90 degrees left and descend the 50-degree slope. This slope is snow-covered through early July, but as the snow cover melts, the exposed loose rock presents serious rock-fall danger, giving Gondogoro its name (gondo means 'broken pieces of'; goro, 'rock'). After the first 250m, begin travers-ing right and down for an additional 100m to 150m, at which point the angle begins to ease. Continued use of a rope, although recommended, may unnecessarily slow the descent, particularly when rock-fall danger is present. Reach the glacier, 900m below the pass, in 1½ hours.

Follow along its north (right) margin 45 minutes to a few stone shelters on moraine near a moraine pool. When approaching the pass from Xhuspang, this is **Gondogoro High Camp** (4800m), also known as Doug Scott Camp, named after the well-known British mountaineer. The camp can be snow covered until early July. Continue another hour, 2.7km, along the north (right) side of the lateral moraine in a pretty ablation valley to the confluence of two branches of the upper Gondogoro Valley. This pleasant hillside camp site, called **Xhuspang** (4680m), has several tent platforms and porters' shelters. It's named for the turquoise (xhu) flowers that blanket this grassy place *(spang)* in summer. Just below camp, the ablation valley is often covered by water in summer. Behind camp a flower-blanketed hillside rises to a massive steep-walled granite prow. Water comes from nearby streams, and a latrine has been built a short way upvalley.

Day 13: Xhuspang to Daltsampa
2½–3 hours, 6.8km, 380m descent

Skirt the pool below Xhuspang in 15 minutes and climb onto the moraine where the two branches of the glacier meet. From here, no trail or cairns exist as the route changes regularly. Follow the medial moraine of the east (left) branch 30 minutes. The main Gondogoro Glacier is to the west (right) and its lateral moraine is grey-brown and higher. Continue working left over level ice 30 minutes towards rust-coloured moraine. Cross this and the brown moraine to its left in 45 minutes to a broken and crevassed band of ice. Follow this down until opposite Laila's convex north-east granite face. Cross moraine left to another ice band and head down towards the hillside above the major southern bend of the glacier. The massive granite prow above Xhuspang remains a visible landmark as you descend the glacier. Across the Gondogoro Glacier, to the north-west, is the awesome icefall from the Masherbrum La. After 5km on glacier, exit left off the Gondogoro Glacier through its heavily broken left margin. Once on the hillside, grazed by yaks, follow a trail turning south-west, and after 30 minutes reach *Daltsampa* (4300m). This beautiful camp site is sheltered in a flower-filled ablation valley with a clear stream and two small lakes with superb views of the icefalls from Masherbrum's ridge.

Days 14–15: Daltsampa to Hushe
2 days, 18.3km, 1250m descent

See Days 1–4 of the Gondogoro Valley trek (pp341–2). Camp at Shaishcho on Day 14.

Below: K2 (8611m; left) and Broad Peak (8047m) from Gondogoro La (5940m).

continued from page 318

Another such stream is 30 minutes beyond. A cluster of huts at **Ghurbūn** are 30 minutes farther. The final stream before Hispar village is often difficult to cross in the afternoon. If the water is too high, descend steeply to the Hispar River's true right bank and ford the side stream where it braids out through more level ground. Pass a large spring and cross the footbridge over the Hispar River. Hispar village collects a bridge toll of Rs 30 per person. Climb steeply 100m in 15 minutes to *Hispar* (3383m), two hours from Ghurbūn. Trekking parties stay in the compound of the dilapidated rest house. The camping fee is Rs 50. For Rs 100, your porters can cook and sleep in the single small, intact building. Water here is silty.

Day 12: Hispar to Huru

4½–5 hours, 15.9km, 150m ascent, 548m descent

Follow the road one hour to a bridge to the Hispar River's true right bank. A well-known slide here, called **Tarkiching Das**, causes road blocks. Watch for falling rock. Pass a side stream, with the first water since Hispar, and reach *Apiharai* (grandmother's pasture), a small grassy camp site with a spring and trees in a walled compound. Continue along the true right bank, passing two more slide areas, and reach the second bridge 2½ hours from Apiharai. Cross the bridge to the true left bank, which marks the end of Hispar village's territory. Climb 150m in 45 minutes to reach pleasant *Huru* (narrow canal) with its grass, apricot orchard (2972m), spring and clear willow-shaded pool.

Masochists can follow a seldom-used trail from Huru to Rush Peak for a different perspective of the terrain just covered (see the Rush Phari trek, p231).

Shyok

The Shyok River, a major tributary of the Indus, drains an enormous area of the eastern Karakoram, much of which is Indian territory. In Pakistan, the Shyok is fed by the Thalle, Hushe and Saltoro Rivers. The Shyok River joins the Indus River 40km east of Skardu near Kiris village, which was once the seat of a small kingdom. This easternmost part of Baltistan comprises Ghanche district, headquartered at Khaplu.

NEAREST VILLAGE
Khaplu

Khaplu (2600m), the most prosperous of Baltistan's former kingdoms, is beautifully situated along the Ghanche River above the expansive confluence of the Shyok, Hushe and Saltoro Rivers.

Places to Stay & Eat The bazaar, along an unsealed road uphill from the Khaplu-Skardu road, has a few hotels. *Citizen Hotel* offers singles/doubles with shared bathroom for Rs 50/100 and doubles with attached bathroom with cold-running water for Rs 200. *Konais Hotel* has rooms with shared bathroom for Rs 50/80. *Khaplu Inn* (☎ 62) costs Rs 80/100 for rooms with shared bathrooms. Rooms with attached bathroom cost Rs 120–150.

Karakoram Lodge (☎ 38), uphill 10 minutes' walk from the bazaar, is a pricey Rs 800/1100. *K7 Hotel & Restaurant*, beyond the polo ground and palace, is run jointly by Khaplu Raja Alamdar and a Japanese partner. Singles/doubles cost Rs 300/500, and doubles with a shared bathroom cost Rs 200. Rooms have porches, large windows and outstanding views. The camping fee is Rs 50, but it's free when you make the long hike up from the main road.

PTDC Motel (☎ 79), along the Khaplu-Skardu road east of the bazaar and across the Ghanche River, has spacious singles/doubles with private verandahs for Rs 1250/1500. The camping fee, including a hot shower, is Rs 300.

Getting There & Away NATCO (☎ 0575-3313) buses depart near Skardu's Chashma Bazaar for Khaplu at 7 and 8am, and a Mashabrum Tours (☎ 0575-2616, 2634, 55195) bus departs near Skardu's Yadgar

Chowk at 6.30am. The bus fare costs Rs 55 (three hours, 100km). K-2 Travel Services (☎ 0575-2855, 55584) has a wagon (Rs 60) departing near Skardu's aqueduct at 8am. Jeeps departing from Skardu's Naya Bazaar cost Rs 100. Skardu-Khaplu special hires cost Rs 2000. NATCO buses depart Khaplu for Skardu at 8 and 9am and Mashabrum Tours depart at 9.30am.

Thalle La

Duration	3 days
Distance	48km
Standard	moderate
Season	mid-June–September
Start	Khasumik
Finish	Shigar
Zone & Permit	open, no permit
Public Transport	yes

Summary The best trekking route between Khaplu and Skardu gently ascends the attractive Thalle Lungma and crosses a snow-covered pass, emerging in the dramatic expanse of the Shigar Valley.

The large and green Thalle Lungma leads north-west from the Shyok River, 15km west of Khaplu and 85km east of Skardu. The upper valley divides, and the north branch leads over the infrequently crossed Tusserpo La (5084m), while the south branch leads over the easier Thalle La (4572m). Both passes lead to the Bauma Lungma, which runs south-west to Shigar. The British, who used the route between 1891 and 1947, preferred the Thalle La between Skardu and Khaplu, as it offered grazing for their pack animals.

The Thalle La, one of the few non-glaciated passes and one of Baltistan's easiest, lends itself to backpacking. It can be crossed in either direction, and the Shigar trailhead is easily reached from Skardu. Because many trekkers use the Thalle La as a return trek from Hushe or Khaplu, the description below is from east to west. Early in the season, expect much snow on Thalle La's east side, and even more on Tusserpo La.

PLANNING
Maps
The Swiss Foundation for Alpine Research 1:250,000 orographical map *Karakoram (Sheet 1)* and *Karakoram (Sheet 2)* cover the trek. Doghoni isn't labelled, and Khasumik is labelled as Khusumik.

Guides & Porters
The trail over the Thalle La is not hard to find, so hiring someone is optional. Because the higher and harder Tusserpo La is infrequently crossed, hiring someone is recommended. Porters ask for a flat rate of Rs 220 per stage, including payment for food rations.

Stages
During the British era, the 60km from Shigar to Doghoni over the Thalle La was three stages. Now, porters ask for as many as seven stages. Negotiate carefully; seven is probably too many, but three is not enough.

GETTING TO/FROM THE TREK
To the Start
An unsealed road goes up the Thalle Lungma to the large village of Khasumik and beyond to the open pasture of Thalle Brok (shown as Bukma on maps). Skardu-Khasumik jeeps cost Rs 140 and special hires cost Rs 2000. Khaplu-Khasumik special hires cost Rs 1800.

The least expensive way is to get off any NATCO or Mashabrum Tours bus at Doghoni Bridge west of Khaplu along the Skardu-Khaplu road and walk a day to Khasumik. The Skardu-Doghoni Bridge fare is Rs 40, and Khaplu-Doghoni Bridge costs Rs 10 on NATCO and Rs 15 on Mashabrum Tours. Cross the bridge to the Shyok River's true right bank and Doghoni, the first village on the Thalle Lungma's west side at the valley's mouth. Khaplu-Doghoni jeeps cost Rs 40. From Hushe, you can walk downvalley to Saling, then along the lesser-used unsealed road along the Shyok River's north bank to Doghoni in one day.

From the Finish
A NATCO bus (Rs 19, 32km, 1¼ hours) departs Skardu, from near Hussaini Chowk,

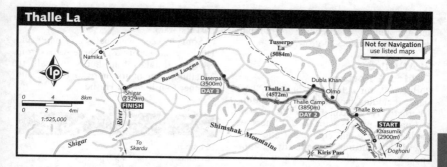

Thalle La

for Shigar at 3pm, returning in the late afternoon. Jeeps (Rs 40) depart from the alley near Skardu's Hussaini Chowk for Shigar in the morning, also returning in the afternoon. Skardu-Shigar special hires cost Rs 700.

THE TREK
Day 1: Khasumik to Thalle Camp
4–5 hours, 16km, 950m ascent

A wide track continues beyond Khasumik (2900m) to Thalle Brok, where another route leads south-west over the Kiris Pass to Kiris village along the Shyok River. Continue north-west up the Thalle Lungma one hour to Olmo, the highest settlement. At the herders' settlement of **Dubla Khan**, two hours above Olmo, the trail splits. The trail to Tusserpo La continues north-west, but follow the trail to Thalle La that branches south-west. One hour beyond Dubla Khan is *Thalle Camp* (3850m), another herder's settlement, along a clear stream.

Day 2: Thalle Camp to Daserpa
6–7 hours, 16km, 722m ascent, 1072m descent

Continue on a good trail through pretty pastures along the stream. Near the pass, the grass ends and the trail becomes rocky. **Thalle La** (4572m), two hours from camp, is marked by a large cairn and has a permanent snowfield on its west side. A steep and snow-covered rocky peak rises dramatically south of the pass. Back to the east is a magnificent view of high snowy peaks on the ridge separating the Thalle and Hushe valleys. To the west are the distant peaks above

Shigar Valley. Descend the snow slope (a fine glissade) and continue through *dzo* pastures to herders' huts at *Daserpa* (3500m), four hours from the pass.

Day 3: Daserpa to Shigar
5–6 hours, 16km, 1171m descent

Continue downstream one hour through stands of cedar to herders' huts at Baumaharel, where the stream from the Thalle La joins the main Bauma Lungma and the track from the Tusserpo La. The good trail down the Bauma Lungma leads in four hours to *Shigar* (2329m).

Hushe

At the head of the Hushe Valley is Masherbrum (7821m) and five large glaciers: Aling, Masherbrum, Gondogoro, Chogolisa and Tsarak Tsa. The popular Hushe Valley offers a variety of short, easy treks, a number of not-too-technical mountaineering peaks, some interesting rock climbs and an exciting route to the Baltoro Glacier.

Hushe (3050m) is the highest village in the once extremely remote and impoverished valley. Hushe men began working as cooks and porters for expeditions in the 1960s. Reinhold Messner's cook, Rozi Ali, is from Hushe. Now, the sons of these men have turned wholeheartedly to tourism and the Hushe-pa have developed an excellent reputation as guides, cooks and high-altitude porters. Hushe villagers are environmentally conscious and work to keep their area nice.

BALTISTAN

Hushe is no longer the poorest of villages, and its popularity as a trekking and climbing destination continues to grow.

PLANNING
Guides & Porters
Porters ask for a flat rate of Rs 220 per stage, including payment for food rations. Alternatively, you can pay Rs 170 per stage and provide porters with food. Porters ask for the clothing and equipment allowance regardless of the trek's length. Hiring someone is recommended on all treks that cross glaciers.

NEAREST VILLAGE
Hushe
Supplies & Equipment The K2 Shop has gear for rent or sale, including tents, sleeping bags, jackets, boots and crampons. Aslam Bakery & General Store, and Mashabrum Shop sell and rent mountaineering equipment and basic supplies.

Places to Stay & Eat Run by Muhammad Hussain, *Mashabrum Inn* has doubles for Rs 100. *Lela Peak Camping*, run by Hamza Ali, the small *K6 & K7 Camping Place*, *Ghandoghoro La Camping Place* and *Ghandughoro Camping Place* serve hot food and charge a Rs 50 camping fee. If you use their kitchens, they charge Rs 100 instead. Large trekking parties usually camp in fields five minutes north of the village where the camping fee is Rs 20. Springs are nearby.

Getting There & Away The road to Hushe, which crosses the Shyok River just east of Khaplu to Saling and follows the Hushe River north, is increasingly reliable, but can be blocked by landslides above Machulu. In 2000, a major flood wiped out a bridge at Kande, seriously damaging Kande village and cutting the road. It may be a year or more until the bridge is rebuilt. Until then, changing transport here is necessary.

Khaplu-Hushe jeeps (Rs 75, 48km, 2½ hours) are infrequent. Khaplu-Kande special hires cost Rs 1500 and Kande-Hushe cost Rs 1200. Skardu-Hushe jeeps cost Rs 150 (six

to seven hours, 148km) and special hires cost Rs 3000.

Some trekkers walk between Khaplu and Hushe village in two or three days. From Khaplu, it takes four hours to walk to Machulu, four hours more to Kande, and another four hours to Hushe.

Gondogoro Valley

Duration	9 days
Distance	50.2km
Standard	demanding
Season	mid-July–September
Start/Finish	Hushe
Zone & Permit	restricted, US$50 permit
Public Transport	yes

Summary This challenging trek up one of Karakoram's most spectacular valleys crosses an impressive glacier and passes astounding icefalls and enchantingly beautiful peaks.

Gondogoro Valley was long used for grazing by Hushe-pa. Now that it's a popular trekking destination, the Hushe-pa no longer use it for grazing, because tourism brings a better economic return. Beautiful camp sites, remarkable mountain views and the major attractions of Gondogoro Peak

Peak Possibilities

Gondogoro Peak
Accessible from Xhuspang (Day 5)
Gondogoro Peak (5650m) lies on the ridge between the two branches of the upper Gondogoro Glacier. The summit has excellent views of Masherbrum and Chogolisa (7665m, also known as Bride Peak), peaks not visible from the Gondogoro La. This single-day, straightforward technical peak involves 970m ascent/descent and requires a pre-dawn start. From Xhuspang, head north (left) and behind the granite prow. Work up the slope, then onto glacier and ascend the snow slope to the summit. Plan to return to camp before noon, otherwise the snow will be too soft.

and the Gondogoro La are the reasons for this popularity. The route up the Gondogoro Valley is steep, but straightforward as far as Daltsampa, beyond which is a tricky traverse of the Gondogoro Glacier.

PLANNING
Maps
The Swiss Foundation for Alpine Research 1:250,000 orographical map *Karakoram (Sheet 2)* covers the trek. Shaishcho is labelled as Chospah. No other camp sites are labelled. The route shown up the middle of the Gondogoro Glacier is incorrect. It inaccurately shows a side glacier from Peak 6294 flowing west into the Gondogoro Glacier. The glacier has evidently receded and now only a stream flows into the glacier at Gondogoro Camp.

Permits & Regulations
This trek is in a restricted zone where a permit and licensed guide are required (see Trekking Permits, p70).

Stages
It's eight stages total round trip from Hushe: (1) Shaishcho; (2) Gondogoro Camp; (3) Daltsampa; (4) Xhuspang; and (5–8) four stages to return via the same route.

GETTING TO/FROM THE TREK
See Hushe (p340).

THE TREK
Day 1: Hushe to Shaishcho
4 hours, 9.3km, 280m ascent
A good trail follows the Hushe River's true left bank north from Hushe village. Two hours from the village, the Aling and Masherbrum rivers join the combined Gondogoro and Tsarak Tsa rivers to form the Hushe River. The trail, with sheer granite cliffs above, fords a side stream and comes soon to the summer settlement of **Odungstan**. Another clear stream is 15 minutes farther, and soon the valley bends east. Continue 30 to 45 minutes, cross a footbridge to the true right (north) bank, and in 15 minutes reach **Shaishcho** (*sha* means 'meat'; *cho*, a 'ruler'). Shaishcho

was the place where the Raja of Khaplu came and ate ibex, brought to this place by his hunters. Shaishcho (3330m) has good water and lots of flat, sandy camp sites amid tamarisks, wild roses and junipers along the river. The camping fee is Rs 20 at either of two sites: *Shaischo Inn*, run by Abdullah Kosar; or *K7 Inn & Camping*, which is run by Mohammad Ali Chana. Both stock food and supplies, prepare meals and rent and sell equipment.

Day 2: Shaishcho to Gondogoro Camp
2–3 hours, 3.9km, 620m ascent
Follow a good trail north one to 1½ hours through the ablation valley on the Gondogoro Glacier's east side to **Atosar** (3750m) with a side stream from the east. This flat grassy expanse has lots of water, willows and junipers. Continue gradually through the ablation valley one to 1½ hours to the next side stream and *Gondogoro Camp* (3950m). A big rock marks the spot and a few huts are across the stream. Camp here to acclimatise. Up this side stream and glacier is the distinctive rock spire of Balti Peak (point 6050 on the Swiss map).

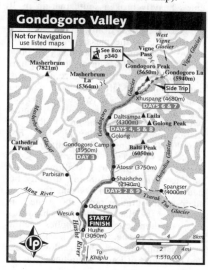

Gondogoro Valley

Days 3–4: Gondogoro Camp to Daltsampa

3–4 hours, 5.1km, 350m ascent

Follow a good trail in the ablation valley one to 1½ hours to **Golong**, a nice lunch spot marked by a large boulder and a stream coming from Golong Peak. Balti Peak is prominent to the south. Landslides have wiped out the trail beyond Golong. At the end of the flat area, drop to the glacier's edge and continue 1.5km over rubble one hour. Watch for rock fall. Climb a hillside to a pasture where unattended male yaks graze. Continue 30 to 45 minutes to lovely *Daltsampa*, sheltered in an ablation valley. A clear stream runs through gorgeous meadows with two small lakes at the south end. Daltsampa (4300m), the valley's most beautiful camp site, deserves an extra day for acclimatisation and to marvel at the incredible icefall from the Masherbrum La and enjoy the meadows, stream and lakes.

Days 5–6: Daltsampa to Xhuspang

3½–4½ hours, 6.8km, 380m ascent

The Gondogoro Glacier bends east beyond Daltsampa, and the trail ends at the glacier's heavily broken south margin in 30 minutes. The point at which you cross onto the glacier changes from year to year. Once on the glacier, the massive granite prow above Xhuspang, 5km away, is your obvious landmark. Work up an ice band until opposite Laila's north-east face, then cross a medial moraine left to a second ice band. Follow this until 1½ to two hours after getting on the glacier. You work left across two medial moraines, one brown, the other rust-coloured, to a more level ice band. Follow this 45 minutes to the medial moraine where the Gondogoro Glacier splits. Cross the moraine, and skirt a shallow moraine lake to *Xhuspang* (4680m), directly beneath flowered meadows and the large, steep-walled granite prow above the confluence of the glacier's two large branches. A small shop sells basic supplies such as flour and kerosene. Spend at least one day at Xhuspang to enjoy the meadows above and the views of Laila. From here, you can also climb Gondogoro Peak (see the boxed text 'Peak Possibilities', p340).

Side Trip: Gondogoro La

1 day, 9.4km, 1260m ascent, 1260m descent

The ascent to the Gondogoro La is higher and more difficult than that of Gondogoro Peak. It requires climbing gear and a pre-dawn start from Gondogoro High Camp. From the pass is an unforgettable view of all the giant peaks at the Baltoro Glacier's head. Be careful of rock fall. See the Gondogoro La trek (p331) for more information.

Days 7–9: Xhuspang to Hushe

3 days, 25.1km, 1630m descent

Retrace your steps downvalley, camping at Daltsampa on Day 7 and Shaishcho on Day 8.

Masherbrum Base Camp

Duration	4 days
Distance	31km
Standard	moderate
Season	mid-June–September
Start/Finish	Hushe
Zone & Permit	restricted, US$50 permit
Public Transport	yes

Summary One of the easiest and quickest treks to the base camp of a Karakoram giant, this trek has superb close-up views of Masherbrum.

A relatively easy trek leads straight towards the foot of mighty Masherbrum (7821m) with excellent views. This short trek into the heart of the Karakoram is recommended by itself or as acclimatisation before tackling higher destinations in the Gondogoro Valley. The only glacier walking is a straightforward 30-minute section before base camp. An alternative route (see Alternative Days 4–6, p344), which is in a restricted zone, is useful when continuing up the Gondogoro Valley or on to K7 Base Camp.

PLANNING
Maps

The Swiss Foundation for Alpine Research 1:250,000 orographical map *Karakoram*

(Sheet 2) covers the trek. No place names are marked except Dumsum, which is misplaced. The trail beyond Dumsum isn't shown. The glacier shown descending from Cathedral Peak, locally called the Drenmo Glacier, doesn't join the Masherbrum Glacier.

Stages

It's six stages total round trip from Hushe: (1) Parbisan; (2) Brumbrama; (3) Masherbrum Base Camp; and (4–6) three stages to return via the same route. Alternatively, it's eight stages total when looping back via Shaishcho. The five return stages starting from Mashabrum Base Camp are: (1) Brumbrama; (2) Darya Chowk; (3) Tir Sir; (4) Shaishcho; and (5) Hushe.

GETTING TO/FROM THE TREK

See Hushe (p340).

THE TREK
Day 1: Hushe to Parbisan

2–2½ hours, 6.9km, 425m ascent
Cross the Hushe River on either of two footbridges. The lower footbridge, directly west of the village, leads to a trail along the Hushe River's true right (west) bank. It crosses the

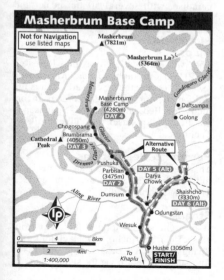

Honbrok stream and ascends through fields past stone huts used to store fodder. A rockier trail stays above the river's east side. In 45 minutes, this trail crosses the higher footbridge and joins the trail along the west bank. Huts at **Wesuk** are 45 minutes farther. Cross the Aling River on a footbridge 30 minutes from Wesuk, with a shaded clear stream 10 minutes beyond near Dumsum summer village. Follow the stony river bed 45 minutes farther to ***Parbisan*** (3475m), a pretty willow grove with a clear spring at the base of a talus slope. Across the river from Parbisan, cliffs tower overhead. Just south of the cliffs is a small, steep side valley called Kyipotama. The name derives from an abandoned hunting practice. Since the steep walls offer no exit, in winter hunters used to send *(tama)* dogs *(kyipo)* to drive ibex into the valley where they proved easy game.

Day 2: Parbisan to Brumbrama

2–2½ hours, 4.1km, 575m ascent
Head along the river's true right bank 30 minutes towards the Masherbrum Glacier's terminus. Cross a side stream from the west and switchback steeply 60m up a faint trail, marked by an occasional cairn in 15 to 30 minutes. At the top, follow a trail parallel to the lateral moraine 30 minutes, passing a *baghath* (a rock wall built to keep animals from crossing to the other side) to Pushuka (little river). Cross to its true left bank via a snow bridge through July, after which you hop rocks. This river is not so little, and parallels the lateral moraine up to the Drenmo Nala. Climb gently, but steadily, 45 minutes to a rise on the lateral moraine, which is covered with flowers and shrubs and offers excellent views of the upper Masherbrum Glacier and Masherbrum itself. Descend gently 15 minutes to the basin called ***Brumbrama*** (4050m), which gets its name from *brama*, a ubiquitous shrub. A stream runs through this flat, grassy, sometimes marshy, ablation valley. Hushe herders use these pastures mid-July to mid-August. Otherwise, unattended male yaks roam the surrounding hillsides. The Drenmo (Bear) Glacier descends the side valley west of the grassy pastures of Brumbrama from Cathedral Peak.

On the glacier's south margin where the river issues from its mouth is a large mound with scattered junipers called Drenmo Saspoon said to have been made by a very large bear.

Day 3: Brumbrama to Masherbrum Base Camp

1½–2 hours, 4.5km, 230m ascent
Follow a trail up the ablation valley. Contour the hillside and cross the outwash stream from an upper ablation valley 15 minutes from Brumbrama. Climb Masherbrum Glacier's lateral moraine on a good trail 10 minutes to huts at **Chogospang** (big meadow). Continue up the ablation valley 15 minutes, contouring along the lateral moraine to another meadow. Climb the moraine of a side glacier, descend to the glacier covered with white rock and cross it in 30 minutes. *Masherbrum Base Camp* (4280m) is just beyond in a meadow with a small pool by the moraine.

Day 4: Masherbrum Base Camp to Hushe

5–6 hours, 15.5km, 1230m descent
Return to Hushe via the same route.

Alternative Route: Masherbrum Base Camp to Hushe

This three-day restricted-zone route is useful when continuing up the Gondogoro Valley or on to K7 Base Camp.

Alternative Day 4: Masherbrum Base Camp to Darya Chowk

4 hours, 10.4km, 1080m descent
Descend along the Masherbrum Glacier's west margin to Pushuka. Cross to the glacier's east margin from just above Pushuka. Descend along the river's true left bank to *Darya Chowk*, opposite the confluence of the Gondogoro and Aling rivers.

Alternative Day 5: Darya Chowk to Shaishcho

6–7 hours, 5km, 130m ascent
Follow the Gondogoro River's true right bank to pastures at **Tir Sir**. Cross the Gondogoro Glacier above its mouth (the river is too big to ford), and descend to **Shaishcho** (3330m).

Alternative Day 6: Shaishcho to Hushe

4 hours, 9.3km, 280m descent
See Day 1 of the Gondogoro Valley trek (p341), following it in reverse.

K7 Base Camp

Duration	5 days
Distance	57.6km
Standard	moderate
Season	mid-June–September
Start/Finish	Hushe
Zone & Permit	restricted, US$50 permit
Public Transport	yes

Summary The Tsarak Tsa Valley, the route to K7 Base Camp, is a tantalising trek for admirers and climbers of big rock walls alike.

K7 (6934m), first climbed in 1984 by a Japanese expedition, and Link Sar (7041m) form a ridge north-east of the upper Tsarak Tsa Glacier. K7's granite face is one of the world's largest. K6 (7281m) is on the ridge south of the upper glacier. The area between Spangser and K7 Base Camp is a climber's paradise, with several 5000m peaks and tons of unclimbed granite.

PLANNING
Maps

The Swiss Foundation for Alpine Research 1:250,000 orographical map *Karakoram (Sheet 2)* covers the trek. Tsarak Tsa is the Balti name for the glacier that is incorrectly labelled as Charakusa. Spangser is labelled as Supanset and Tikchumik as Techimic.

Permits & Regulations

This trek is in a restricted zone where a permit and licensed guide are required (see Trekking Permits, p70).

Stages

It is eight stages total round trip from Hushe: (1) Shaishcho; (2) Tikchumik; (3) Spangser; (4) K7 Base Camp; and (5–8) four stages to return via the same route.

GETTING TO/FROM THE TREK

See Hushe (p340).

THE TREK
Day 1: Hushe to Shaishcho

4 hours, 9.3km, 280m ascent
See Day 1 of the Gondogoro Valley trek (p341) for directions.

Day 2: Shaishcho to Spangser

4 hours, 8.5km, 670m ascent
Head east from Shaishcho into the ablation valley north of the Tsarak Tsa Glacier. The sharp spires of K7 and Link Sar are visible ahead. Tikchumik (small spring), which is in the ablation valley at the base of the ridge west of the Chogolisa Glacier, has good water. Continue along the base of the ridge to the Chogolisa Glacier's west margin. Cross this glacier to the green and flowered **Spangser** above the confluence of the Chogolisa and Tsarak Tsa glaciers. Spangser (4000m) is the highest pasture and is used mid-July to mid-August. Granite slabs rise above Spangser (in Balti *spang* means 'meadow'; *ser*, a 'place to walk about') and Namika (6325m) towers across the Tsarak Tsa Glacier.

Day 3: Spangser to K7 Base Camp

4 hours, 11km, 600m ascent
Continue through the ablation valley north of the Tsarak Tsa Glacier, at times over difficult terrain, to **K7 Base Camp** (4600m).

Days 4–5: K7 Base Camp to Hushe

2 days, 28.8km, 1550m descent
Follow the trail to Hushe, camping at Shaishcho on Day 4.

Other Treks

The following treks are all in an open zone, except where noted below.

NORTH-WEST BALTISTAN

To the west and south of the Basha Valley are the infrequently visited Tormik and Stak valleys. Their rarely crossed passes make for unspoiled and adventurous trekking. Only basic supplies are available in villages, so bring everything you need. Bagicha and Dassu (1½ hours from Skardu), Stak (three hours from Skardu) and Sassi (1½ hours from Gilgit) are trailheads along the Gilgit-Skardu road. It's easy to get on or off any daily transport between Skardu and Gilgit at any of these places.

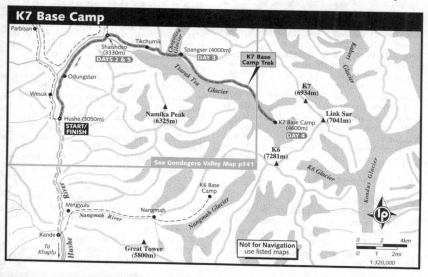

K7 Base Camp

Parbisan · Shaishcho (3330m) **DAYS 2 & 5** · Tikchumik · Chogolisa Glacier · Spangser (4000m) **DAY 3** · K7 Base Camp Trek · Kabari Glacier · Odungstan · Wesuk · Hushe (3050m) **START/FINISH** · Tsarak Tsa Glacier · Namika Peak (6325m) · K7 (6934m) · K7 Base Camp (4600m) **DAY 4** · Link Sar (7041m) · K6 (7281m) · K6 Glacier · Kondus Glacier · See Gondogoro Valley Map p341 · River · Mingyulu · Nangmah River · Nangmah · K6 Base Camp · Nangmah Glacier · Kande · Hushe · To Khaplu · Great Tower (5800m) · Not for Navigation use listed maps · 0 2 4km · 0 1 2mi · 1:320,000

Ganto La

Ganto La (4606m) is a pass, usually open late June to early September, linking the Basha and Tormik valleys. It's an interesting, but steep, exit from the Basha Valley. The moderate trek starts from Hemasil in the Basha Valley, just across a stream north of **Chu Tron**, which means hot springs in Balti. This excellent hot spring, perfect for a pre- or post-trek soak, is around 39°C, has almost no sulphur smell, and gushes forth in a large flow. The villagers have constructed several enclosed bathhouses with doors, open ceilings and cement, walled, knee-deep pools.

It takes two or three days to cross the Ganto La to Harimal in the Tormik Valley from where you can head south to reach Dassu or Bagicha on the Gilgit-Skardu road in one easy day, or head northwest and cross Stak La. From Hemasil, ascend steeply 1000m to the ridge above Chu Tron. Camp in a meadow near huts at **Matunturu**. The next day, continue steeply to the Ganto La, with a permanent steep snowfield below the pass. Descend steeply to a pleasant meadow camp site called **Pakora**. Harimal is a short day's walk farther.

Stak La

Stak La (4500m) links the rugged alpine Stak Nala to the green upper Tormik Valley, both of which have trailheads on the Gilgit-Skardu road. The demanding technical trek makes a four- to five-day loop and can be combined with the Ganto La trek (above). From Dassu, head north up the Tormik Valley. At Harimal (not shown on the Swiss map), the route over the Ganto La branches to the north-east. Continue up the Tormik Valley to Dunsa and camp near the polo field by herders' huts. At the valley's head cross a small glacier and reach the Stak La. The west side of the pass is corniced, so bring a rope and ice axe. Descend the glacier about 500m to a grassy camp site near a large boulder. The view of Haramosh and its large eastern glacier, Khotia Lungma, is stunning. Follow the river's true left bank as it bends south 20km to Stak village. It's possible to get a jeep (Rs 25) between Stak and the Gilgit-Skardu road, 1km east of the bridge over Stak Nala. Transport in a wagon along the Gilgit-Skardu road to either Gilgit or Skardu costs Rs 70, whereas a special hire costs Rs 2000.

HARAMOSH LA

Haramosh La (4800m) is a glaciated pass linking the Chogo Lungma and Haramosh glaciers on its north-east side with the Haramosh Valley to its west (see the Chogo Lungma Glacier map, p307). The pass is enclosed by Laila (6986m), which towers over the confluence of these glaciers,

Mani (6685m) and Haramosh (7409m). This extreme nine-day technical trek, which is possible late July to early September, crosses one of the Karakoram's most formidable and infrequently done passes. Snow and avalanche danger are present on both sides of the pass early in the season with rock fall becoming more of a danger by midsummer. This trek is only suited to experienced trekkers with mountaineering experience. The Haramosh La is usually crossed from east to west.

From Doko in the Basha Valley, the route follows the Chogo Lungma Glacier (see pp306–7) for the first 3½ days as far as Bolocho. From Bolocho, the route crosses the Chogo Lungma Glacier, heads south and west up the heavily crevassed Haramosh Glacier, and reaches a grassy ablation valley along the glacier's north margin and **Laila Base Camp** (4100m) on Day 5.

On Day 6, rope up to reach **Sharing**, the level glacial basin at the base of the pass, five to six hours from Laila Base Camp. On Day 7, travel in roped teams about four hours to the pass, probing carefully for frequent crevasses. Keep to the glacier's west side where it's less steep and fix a rope at the steepest section near the top. Camp on top of the level, open **Haramosh La**. Stronger parties may prefer to combine Days 6 and 7 by leaving Laila Base Camp before dawn to ascend Haramosh La the same day, reaching the top by mid-morning.

Depending on snow conditions, you may need to fix as much as 500m of rope to descend the steep, scary snow slope on the west side of the pass on Day 8. Beware of avalanche and rock-fall danger as you descend steep scree lower down. Mani, at the bottom, is a possible camp site, but a little farther is the inviting **Kutwal Lake** (3260m), seven to eight hours from the pass.

Continue downvalley on a good trail on Day 9 to Dassu with views of high peaks all around. When you prearrange a vehicle, it can meet you at the roadhead in Dassu. Otherwise, walk on the road along the Phuparash River to Sassi on the Gilgit-Skardu road to catch a ride on a passing vehicle.

To attempt to cross the Haramosh La without a qualified companion who knows the route and its dangers is foolhardy. Conflict between Arandu's Balti people and Haramosh's Shina-speakers, however, reportedly prevents Arandu porters from crossing the pass, so be sure to hire a competent Shina speaker. Local porters know the route, but don't know where or how to fix ropes, judge avalanche or rock-fall danger, or make crevasse rescues if necessary. Wearing a climbing helmet is prudent.

It's 14 stages total from Doko: (1) Arandu; (2) Churzing; (3) Chogo Brangsa; (4) Kurumal; (5) Bolocho; (6) Laila Base Camp; (7) Sharing; (8)

Haramosh La; (9) Mani; (10) Kutwal Lake; (11) Kutwal; (12) Iskere; (13) Dassu; and (14) Sassi.

DEOSAI

Numerous little-known routes cross the Deosai Mountains between the Indus River west of Skardu and the Astor Valley. Three valleys along the Indus River's south bank, Shigarthang, Basho and Skoyo, have wildlife conservation programs where the likelihood of seeing wildlife is high. Trekkers can help support these initiatives by visiting them. Dambudas and Bagicha villages, marked by signs along the Gilgit-Skardu road, are where public transport drops you off. Neither village, however, is marked on maps.

Deosai Traverse

Some trekkers simply walk along the 165km-long jeep road between Skardu and Astor across the Deosai Plains in an easy four or five days (see the Burji La map, p309). From Skardu, the road heads south up the Satpara Valley, passing Satpara Lake and village. The road continues west across the Deosai plateau, crossing large clear streams via bridges. As it leaves the Deosai, it skirts the north shore of charming Sheoshar Lake, then crosses Sheoshar Pass (4266m, marked Chhachor Pass on the U502 *Mundik (NI 43-3)* map) into the Chilam Gah, which becomes the Das Khirim Gah as it descends to meet the upper Astor Valley. You can cut the walk shorter by organising a Skardu-Satpara special hire for Rs 300 at the start or by getting on a NATCO bus (Rs 60, five hours) at Chilam for the daily trip to Astor village.

Nanga Parbat is visible in the distance from Deosai hilltops, but a fun two-day side trip offers never-to-be-forgotten views of Nanga Parbat. When heading north-west down the Das Khirim Gah, cross a bridge below Gudai to reach Zail. Follow a trail to the pastures above, and ascend the dry ridge to camp the first night where the entire massif stretches before you. The next day continue down the rugged Bulashbar Gah to meet the Astor Valley at its confluence with the Rupal Gah.

Alampi La & Banak La

A demanding six-day trek across either the Alampi La or Banak La, best crossed mid-June to September, links the Shigarthang and Astor Valleys. Alampi La, also used as a route between Srinagar and Skardu, was probably first crossed by Vigne in 1834–35. Banak La is a more direct and difficult route. The Shigarthang Lungma joins the Indus Valley near Kachura Lake and village (marked Katzarah on the U502 *Mundik (NI 43-3)* map), 30km west of Skardu on the Gilgit-Skardu road. Skardu-Kachura special hires cost as much

as Rs 350 and ones to the road's end at Tsok cost Rs 700. Head south-west up the Shigarthang Lungma to Shigarthang village, whose residents are Brok-pa Shina speakers. Continue west up-valley 10km to huts at **Thlashing Spang** where the valley divides: the west branch leads to Banak La and the south-west branch leads to Alampi La.

To **Alampi La** (5030m), continue up the rocky Shigarthang Lungma and camp below the pass. The ascent to the pass is over snow. The descent, initially more than 35 degrees, is extremely steep and rocky. Continue more gently to a meadow camp (4000m) in the basin below the pass. Continue 5km west down this side valley into Bubind Gah, which joins the Das Khirim Gah and the Deosai road at Gudai, two days from the meadow camp. From Gudai, a side trip offers more Nanga Parbat views (see Deosai Traverse, left).

To **Banak La** (4963m), follow a steep, rocky path along the stream west-north-west and camp above the tree line at Urdukas (3962m), 6km from Thlashing Spang. Continue up across a glacier to the pass, 6km from Urdukas. Crevasses on the glacier are covered by snow bridges until late summer, but use a rope for safety. Descend steeply 8km to Chumik (3657m) and the Urdung Gah. Continue downvalley in two days to Astor.

Dari La

A demanding three-day trek over the Dari La (4724m) links the Shigarthang Lungma with the Deosai Plains. From Shigarthang village, head east then south-east up the Dari Lungma and camp at the lush **Dokhsun** pasture below the pass. On Day 2, cross Dari La, and descend to **Usar Mar** at the confluence of the Burji Lungma. On Day 3, walk south to the road at Ali Malik Mar and ride in a jeep back to Skardu via the Satpara Valley. Alternatively, continue north from Usar Mar and trek over the Burji La (see p309), making it a five-day trek.

Naqpo Namsul La

A demanding five-day near-loop trek crosses the glaciated Naqpo Namsul La (5000m), a pass near the Basho Valley's head. The Basho Valley, whose name means 'grape' for the valley's vineyards, meets the Indus River 36km west of Skardu and 16km south of Bagicha. The Basho River provides hydroelectric power for Basho, Skoyo and Rondu. Basho village (Basha on maps) is linked with the Gilgit-Skardu road via a bridge over the Indus River. Skardu-Basho special hires cost Rs 800. The jeep road goes another 9km up the broad valley to Sultanabad, where the residents are Brok-pa Shina speakers. Skardu-Sultanabad special hires cost Rs 2500.

From Sultanabad (Turmik on the U502 *Mundik* (NI 43-3) map), the trek heads south-west up-valley. It then crosses the pass into the upper Shigarthang Lungma, and descends to Kachura along the Gilgit-Skardu road. Alternatively from the upper Shigarthang Lungma, it's possible to cross Banak La (see Alampi La & Banak La, p347).

Skoyo

Skoyo village, about 60km west of Skardu, is linked to the Gilgit-Skardu road via a bridge over the Indus River (under construction at the time of research). Skoyo is 4km east of Dambudas and 8km west of Bagicha. Skardu-Skoyo special hires cost Rs 1000. Skoyo villagers have implemented the Project Snow Leopard to protect the Skoyo Valley's snow leopard population, which is dependent upon income from trekking for support. An easy three-day loop trek visits pastures beneath the summit of Takht-i-Sulaiman (5632m). Contact the project's Web site (W www.fmntrek king.com) for more information.

Trango Pir Pass & Harpo La

A very demanding four-day trek across either the Trango Pir Pass or Harpo La, two difficult glaciated passes, links the Tukchun Lungma to the Parishing Gah, an eastern tributary of the Astor River, and the Astor Valley. These passes are best done mid-July to September. The trek starts from Shoat village on the Indus River's true left (south) side, 4km west of Dambudas and 2½ hours' drive from Skardu. This area along the Indus River between Bagicha and Shoat, where it flows through a deep gorge called Rondu, was once a separate kingdom. The palace of the former Raja of Rondu is in nearby Mendi. Bridges over the Indus connect both Shoat and Mendi with the Gilgit-Skardu road.

From Shoat, head south up the Tukchun Lungma, past Harpo village to Chutabar, where the valley divides: the south-west (right) branch leads to Trango Pir Pass; and the south-east (left) branch to Harpo La. Both routes have sizable markhor populations.

To **Trango Pir Pass** (conflicting elevations range from 4800m to 5600m), leave the Tukchun Lungma at Chutabar and ascend the rough rocky valley. Camp below the pass near huts at Baltal. The next day, cross the pass, steep near the top, and descend a glacier then a steep rocky spur to Thengi village in the Parishing Gah. Follow a road 10km downvalley to Astor.

To **Harpo La** (5115m), continue from Chutabar up the rough Tukchun Lungma 8km where the route to the pass turns south up a side stream. Continue up the side stream and camp below the pass. The ascent to the snow line is rocky. The pass is glaciated with significant avalanche danger. Descend the steep glacier on the north side below the snow line to camp. The next day continue 4km to the Urdung Gah and 10km to Thengi, and then on to Astor.

Katichu La

Katichu La (4588m) is a pass linking Mehdiabad (formerly called Parkutta) on the Indus River east of Skardu to the Deosai Plains. The pass is usually snow-free July to late September and the moderate trek takes three days. Reportedly, a distant K2 is visible from the pass. When crossing from east to west, this trek is easily combined with the Burji La trek, or return to Skardu via the road down Satpara Valley. Get off the daily NATCO bus (Rs 45) or K-2 Travel Services wagon (Rs 60) between Skardu and Tolti/Kharmang at Mehdiabad, which depart Skardu at 1.30pm and 10am respectively.

SHIGAR & BRALDU

Sosbun

A moderate five-day trek into the rarely visited Sosbun Valley offers wildlife-watching opportunities and, for climbers, ascents of unnamed walls and towers. Ride in a jeep from Skardu up the Braldu Valley to Chakpo (Chokpiong on the Swiss map) and camp. Trek up the Hoh Lungma to camp at Nangmah (Nangmoni Tapsa on the Swiss map). Cross the Sosbun Glacier to Jusma camp at the base of the spur between the Tsilbu and Sosbun glaciers. Trek up the Sosbun Glacier to **Sosbun Base Camp** at the base of the spur between the South and North Sosbun glaciers beneath Sosbun Brak (6413m). Return in two days to Chakpo.

Skoro La

Skoro La (5073m) is a little-used pass, first crossed by Falconer in 1838, linking Askole in the Braldu Valley to Namika and Shigar in the Shigar Valley (see the Baltoro Glacier map, p324). This pass was more frequently used before the road was completed up the Braldu Valley to Askole. It offers an alternative, demanding three-day trek between Askole and Shigar, useful when the road is blocked.

From Askole, cross the Braldu River on a footbridge and ascend steeply to Thal Brok, with fine views. Continue up the Skoro La Lungma's west bank and camp at Darso Brok, a summer pasture at the Skoro La Glacier's edge. The next day continue up the glacier, over snow three to four hours, then turn west and climb to the Skoro La. Descend 450m steeply over snow and rock to the steep grassy slopes below. Camp here or descend another 900m to the Skoro Lungma's head to camp. The next day, follow the stream, crossing it continuously, with several steep sections, to Namika on the road in the Shigar Valley, 6.5km north of Shigar.

Panmah Glacier

The 42km-long Panmah Glacier forms the Dumordo River, which flows into the Biaho Lungma between Korophon and Jula (see the Baltoro Glacier map, p324). Askole villagers use summer pastures along this glacier. The Panmah is fed by two large glaciers, Choktoi to the north-west and Nobande Sobande to the north-east. The Choktoi leads to the base camp for the north face of the Latok spires. At its head is the difficult **Sim La** (5833m), which crosses Baintha Brak's north shoulder. The entire area is in a restricted zone where a permit and licensed guide are required (see Trekking Permits, p70). During the 1990s, experienced Westerners pioneered scenic and extreme technical treks here.

Treks begin from Thungol in the Braldu Valley. The approach follows the Dumordo River's true left (east) bank, crosses to its true right bank below the Panmah Glacier's snout, then continues along its east margin. Technical passes at the head of two eastern side glaciers, First Feriole and South Chiring, lead to the Trango and Baltoro glaciers. The First Feriole is reported to be the easier of the two. Continuing north up the Panmah Glacier, you cross the Chiring Glacier and reach the meadow of Skinmang (many ibex), a fine base for exploring the upper glaciers. The Nobande Sobande is reported to be mostly crevasse free with spectacular scenery. An unnamed pass just east of Biacherahi Tower enables parties to cross to the Choktoi Glacier and return to the Panmah Glacier in a five-day loop.

A longer near-loop trek is possible by crossing the **Skam La** (5407m) at the Nobande Sobande's head, and following the Sim and Biafo glaciers back to Thungol. The east side of Skam La is reported to be straightforward, but the west side requires fixing as much as 300m of rope.

Conditions in this area can change: in 1887 Younghusband found the Nobande Sobande inaccessible with ice blocks the size of houses; in 1929 Ardito Desio found it remarkably smooth and was able to ski to its head; and the 1937 Shipton-Tilman expedition found it almost impassable, 'broken by gaping crevasses and tumbled masses of ice'. Technical trekkers must be prepared for the logistical challenges and changing conditions. Guides and porters don't yet know these routes. If you hire someone make sure they're adequately equipped for the rigours.

KHAPLU

From Khaplu's main bazaar, a 45-minute walk leads past the polo ground to the palace of the Raja of Khaplu, with its impressive four-storey wooden balcony above the entrance. A steep 20 minutes farther is Chakchun village, with an old mosque, and fine views across the Shyok River of Masherbrum at the Hushe Valley's head.

Ghanche Tso

From the powerhouse at the upper end of the road, beyond the K-7 Hotel, it's an easy seven- to eight-hour walk (two stages) up the Ghanche River to Ghanche Tso (lake).

Daholi Tso

From the polo ground, a jeep road climbs southeast to the summer settlements of Khaplutung and Hanjore, easy 1½ and 2½ hours' walks, respectively, from the polo ground. The entire upper settled area, which is called Khaplu Brok, has great Masherbrum views. From Hanjore, a trail climbs behind the ridge in one long day (two stages) to Daholi Tso (lake).

HUSHE
Honbrok

Picturesque Honbrok summer pastures high above the Hushe River west of Hushe village are easily visited on a day hike. It takes four hours to climb steeply to the pastures and 1½ to two hours to return to Hushe. Cross the Hushe River on the lower of the two footbridges to its true right bank. Walk up 15 to 30 minutes to Honbrok Nala. Cross it on a sturdy wooden footbridge. The trail ascends the stream's true left (north) bank all the way to the pastures. Honbrok has reliable spring water. June to October is the best season. Honbrok is labelled Honboro on the Swiss map. Hushe-pa also refer to Honbrok Peak (6459m) as Cigarette Peak.

Aling Glacier

The Aling Glacier, the westernmost of Hushe Valley's glaciers, is very large with multiple upper branches. Two summits above the upper glacier, Mitre (5944m) and Sceptre (5800m), attract climbers. From Hushe, cross the river to its west bank and reach the footbridge over the Aling River in two hours. Across the footbridge, the trail turns west into the Aling Valley to Dumsum, a summer village with a two-storey mosque. Continue west along the Aling River's true left (north) bank to Shatonchen pastures, and along the Aling Glacier's north margin to base camp and Drenmogyalba (royal bear), the highest pasture.

Hushe-pa have 14 stages (one-way) up the demanding route, but no one goes beyond the seventh stage. The seven one-way stages starting from Hushe are: (1) Dumsum; (2) Shatonchen; (3) base camp; (4) Drenmogyalba; (5) Sampibrangsa; (6) Khadanlumba; and (7) Tasa.

K6 Base Camp

K6 (7281m), also called Baltistan Peak, is usually approached from Kande village, midway up the Hushe Valley (see the K7 Base Camp map, p345). The steep granite walls that line the Nangmah Valley, including the Great Tower (5800m) south of the summer pastures, make this a popular rock-climbing destination.

From Kande, cross a footbridge over the Hushe River, then cross to the Nangmah River's true right (north) bank and Mingyulu village (labelled Minjlu on the Swiss map). Continue up the river's north bank to Nangmah summer pastures and on to K6 Base Camp along the Nangmah Glacier's north-west margin. Kande's K6 Hotel & Restaurant, above the road's west side, is the place to hire porters. The moderate trek totals six stages: three stages from Kande to K6 Base Camp; and three stages to return via the same route.

KONDUS & SALTORO

The beautiful Kondus and Saltoro valleys have been in a closed zone since the dispute between Pakistan and India over the Siachen Glacier began in 1984. These valleys were always the preferred approach route to the peaks along the giant Siachen. The southern approach to the Siachen, up the Nubra Valley, was impossible in summer due to high water and quicksand. Now, Kondus and Saltoro villagers no longer see expeditions and so lose the opportunity to earn much-needed income. These eastern Baltistan valleys have some of the finest clean granite towers in Baltistan, rivalling the Trango Towers for size and sheer verticality. Despite the closed status of the valleys, climbers have their eye on first ascents of big walls in these valleys, and the Pakistan government has shown signs of relaxing the restrictions. In the summer of 2000, a group of US rock climbers received a trekking permit for the Kondus Valley and made a first ascent of a 5000m

tower just above Karmading village. Contact the Tourism Division (see Trekking Permits, p70) through a trekking company to request permission – it may say no, but it might say yes!

From Halde village in the lower Hushe Valley, across the river from Machulu, a jeep road follows the Saltoro River's true right (north) bank through Tsino (Chino on the Swiss map) with its magnificent granite towers to Brakhor where the valleys divide: Kondus is to the north, and Saltoro to the east.

Kondus

The road up the Kondus Valley goes to Karmading, the highest village. A few hours' moderate walk above Karmading to the north-east is the Khorkondus Valley and Khorkondus village. A waterfall tumbles over granite cliffs behind the village, and a small hot spring is 15 minutes north. The towers above Karmading can be approached without traversing a glacier. Above, the Sherpi Gang descends from Sherpi Kangri (7380m) and Saltoro Kangri (7742m). Above the pastures called Lisar (hunting ground) are clean granite walls, a climber's delight. From Karmading, a trail leads up the main valley under the Karmading Wall several hours to the Kondus Glacier's snout. It's two stages to the highest pasture, Rahout Chen, passing through Byangeparo near the confluence of the Kaberi and Kondus glaciers en route. The Kondus Glacier is perhaps the Karakoram's most difficult and chaotic glacier, but beautiful clean granite pinnacles rise above its upper reaches. From the Kaberi Glacier, some technical passes lead to Hushe's Tsarak Tsa Valley.

Saltoro

From Brakhor in the Saltoro Valley, a bridge crosses to the river's south bank. The road up the Saltoro Valley follows the south bank to Goma, the highest village. Women in the Saltoro Valley wear unique red-dyed raw wool hats with brown beaver-like tails. At Goma, the Bilafond, Gyang and Chulung streams meet, descending from the glaciers above. The Bilafond Glacier is also renowned for its granite towers. Beyond the passes above these glaciers are Indian troops.

Mountaineering

Mountaineers often follow a trekking route on what Tourism Division calls the 'approach march' to base camp, and climbers can use this book as a planning tool to reach base camp with minimum hassle. Thirty percent of the treks in this book describe routes or side trips to a major base camp, including 18 different 7000m peak base camps, and five 8000m peak base camps. Most treks also offer access to 5000m and 6000m peaks.

The densest concentration of Hindukush peaks clusters around Tirich Mir in Turikho. In the Karakoram, the densest concentrations are in the Rakaposhi-Haramosh Range in Gilgit and Nagyr, the Batura and Hispar Muztagh in Nagyr and Gojal, and the Baltoro Muztagh in Baltistan. The mountaineering season starts late May and finishes by September.

Major peaks usually draw large expeditions. Other peaks and the many granite walls and towers draw smaller parties that tend to favour alpine-style climbs. No matter what the height, all mountaineers approach their climb with seriousness and commitment. Understanding the basic government regulations is the first step to a successful expedition.

PERMITS & FEES

The Tourism Division of the Ministry of Tourism regulates mountaineering, which it defines as any activity higher than 6000m. It publishes the brochure *Mountaineering Rules and Regulations*, which is available from the following offices:

Deputy Chief of Operations, Tourism Division (☎ 051-9203509, fax 9202347) Ministry of Tourism, Sports Complex, Kashmir Highway, near Aabpara, behind Liaqat Gymnasium, Islamabad.
PTDC Tourist Information Centres in Islamabad and Rawalpindi (see Tourist Offices, p78).

Mountaineering Rules and Regulations contains the necessary application forms, and details the permit process and fees, the duties of the liaison officer and high-altitude porters, insurance requirements and equipment and rations you're required to provide to porters. It also gives rules about payment of porters' wages and transport, the import and export of equipment, foreign exchange and photography. The stipulated load limits per high-altitude porter are: 17kg between 6001m and 7000m; 14kg between 7001m and 8000m; and 12kg higher than 8001m. It offers guidelines for providing medical treatment and what to do if an accident occurs. Tourism Division requires all expeditions to attend briefing and debriefing meetings at its office.

To apply for a permit, complete and submit one original copy and one photocopy of Annexure A – Application Form for Mountaineering Expeditions to the nearest Pakistan embassy or consulate (see Embassies & Consulates, p80) in the calendar year preceding the year of the planned expedition. Submit a copy of the royalty receipt and original application directly to Tourism Division in Islamabad. Applications are processed and permits issued on a first-come, first-served basis. Tourism Division usually sends a permit within 60 days of receipt of completed applications.

The royalty for each peak depends on its elevation (see the boxed text 'Royalties'). Tourism Division requires a liaison officer

Royalties

Peak/Elevation	Royalty per expedition	Additional Royalty per person*
K2	US$12,000	US$2000
8001–8500m	US$9500	US$1500
7501–8000m	US$4000	US$500
7001–7500m	US$2500	US$300
6000–7000m	US$1500	US$200

* starting with eighth team member

to accompany every expedition, the cost of which averages US$5000 per expedition, or about US$3000 for his kit and US$2000 for transport and hotels. Typically, budget US$30 per day in cities and US$15 per day in the mountains for the liaison officer. Expeditions also pay a US$200 nonrefundable environmental protection fee and an additional US$1000 refundable deposit in case the expedition pollutes the environment.

All peaks are also classified into zones (see the discussion of zones in Trekking Permits, p70). Some companies are pressing to eliminate the liaison officer requirement for peaks in open zones.

GUIDED CLIMBS
Almost every expedition works with a Pakistani trekking company (see Organised Treks, p44, for a list of companies that handle expeditions). Some reliable companies abroad that market out-there mountaineering expeditions and guided climbs follow.

The UK
High Adventure (☎ 02476-395422, fax 394465, Ⓔe high.adventure@btinternet.com; Ⓦw www.highadventure.org.uk) David Hamilton, 67 Castle Rd, Hartshill, Nuneaton, Warwickshire, CV10 0SG

Jagged Globe (☎ 0114-276 3322, fax 276 3344, Ⓔe expeditions@jagged-globe.co.uk, Ⓦw www.jagged-globe.co.uk) 45 Mowbray St, Sheffield S3 8EN

OTT Expeditions (☎ 0114-258 8508, fax 255 1603, Ⓔe info@ottexpeditions.co.uk, Ⓦw www.ottexpeditions.co.uk) Unit 56, Southwest Centre, Troutbeck Rd, Sheffield, S7 2Q8

Continental Europe
ITMC – Germany (☎ 6201-3 37 15, fax 3 37 16, Ⓔe infos@itmc-germany.com) Heddesheimer Strasse 9, 69469 Weinheim–Ofling, Germany

Terres D'Aventure (☎ 08 25 84 78 00, fax 01 43 25 69 37, Ⓔe terdav@terdav.com, Ⓦw www.terdav.com) 6 rue Saint Victor, 75005 Paris, France

Trekking Y Aventura (☎ 91-522 86 81, fax 523 1664, Ⓔe mad@trekkingviajes.com, Ⓦw www.trekkingviajes.com) Calle Pez 12, 28004 Madrid, Spain and (☎ 93-454 3702, fax 323 5288) Calle Gran Vía 523, 08011 Barcelona, Spain

Australia & New Zealand
Adventure Consultants (☎ 03-443 8711, fax 443 8733, Ⓔe info@adventure.co.nz, Ⓦw www.adventure.co.nz) PO Box 97, Wanaka 9192, New Zealand

Language

Urdu

Pronunciation

Vowel length in Urdu can affect meaning. Long vowels are differentiated by the use of a macron (a line above the vowel).

a	as in 'above'
i	as in 'bit'
u	as in 'put'
ā	as in 'father'
ī	as the 'ea' in 'seat'
ū	as the 'oo' in 'pool'
e	as in 'they'
o	as in 'go'
ai	as in 'bait'
au	as in 'haul'

Urdu vowels are sometimes nasalised (ie, spoken with the nose open). The symbol ~ above a vowel (eg, ĩ) indicates nasalisation. Urdu also distinguishes between aspirated and unaspirated consonants, and aspiration has a direct effect on meaning, eg, *pir* means 'Monday', while *phir* means 'again'. Aspirated consonants are pronounced with a clearly audible breathiness, while unaspirated consonants get hardly any breath. Aspirated consonants are indicated by the letter h after the consonant.

Greetings & Civilities

Hello.	*asalām aleikum* (peace be with you)
response	*wa aleikum salām* (and with you too)
God willing.	*inshallah*
How are you?	*kyā hāl hai?*
Fine/OK.	*thīk hai*
Goodbye.	*khudā hāfiz* (God be with you)
See you again.	*phir milēge*
Good night.	*shab bakhair*
Thank you.	*shukriā*
Special thanks.	*mehrbānī*
Excuse me.	*māf kījiye*

Essentials

Yes.	*hã*
No.	*nahĩ*
Maybe.	*shayad*
Do you speak English?	*āpko English ātī hai?*
Does anyone here speak English?	*kisīko English ātī hai?*
I don't speak Urdu.	*mujhe Urdū nahĩ ātī*
I understand.	*samajh gayā*
I don't understand.	*nahĩ samjhā*
How do you say ... in Urdu?	*Urdu mē ... kaise kahate haī?*
Please write it down.	*likh dījiye*
Please show me.	*dikhā dījiye*
I have a visa/permit.	*visā/ijāzat hai*
Sir/Madam	*jenāb/begum*
surname	*khāndānī nām*
male/female	*mard/aurat*

Pronouns

I/we	*maĩ/ham*
you (sg & informal)	*tum*
you (pl & polite)	*āp*
he, she, they	*ye* (nearby)
he, she, they	*we* (not nearby)

Small Talk

What's your name?	*āpkā nām kyā hai?*
My name is ...	*merā nām ... hai.*
Where are you from?	*ap kahã ke haī?*
Your country?	*āpkā mulk?*
I'm from ...	*maĩ ... kā hū̃*
I'm a tourist/student.	*maĩ tourist/student hū̃.*
Are you married?	*shādī hai?*
I'm ... years old.	*merī ūmar ... sāl hai*
Do you like ...?	*... pasand hai?*
I like ... very much.	*mujhe ... bahut pasand hai*
I don't like ...	*mujhe ... pasand nahĩ*
Just a minute.	*ek minut*
May I?	*maĩ karū̃?*

It's all right/ No problem.	*thīk hai/koī bāt nahī̃*

father/mother	*vālid/validē*
husband/wife	*shohar/bīvī*
friend	*dost*
person in charge	*wālā* (eg, rickshaw *wālā*, hotel *wālā*)
He's my husband.	*Wo merā shohar hai.*
She's my wife.	*Wo merī bīvī hai.*

Questions

You can make a phrase into a question by raising the tone at the end of the sentence, just as in English, or by preceding the phrase with the question marker *kya*.

What?	*kyā?*
Who?	*kaun?*
Where?	*kahā̃?*
When?	*kab?*
Why?	*kyõ?*
How?	*kaisā?*
How much/many?	*kitnā?*

Getting Around

What's the name of this place?
is jagekā nām kyā hai?
Where are you going?
āp kahā̃ jāte haĩ?
I want to go to ...
maĩ ... jānā chāhatā hū̃.
I want to book a seat to ...
mujhe ... keliye sīt chāhīye
What time does the bus leave/arrive?
bus kitne baje ravāna/pahũchtī hai?
Where does the bus leave from?
bus kahā̃se ravana hai?
How long does the trip take?
kitne ghante lagte haĩ?
Please stop (here).
rūkiye

bicycle/motorcycle	*saikul/motar saikul*
car	*gārī*
plane	*jehāz*

Directions

Where is...?	*... kahā̃ hai?*
Is it near/far?	*nazdīk/dūr hai?*

(Go) straight ahead.	*sidhā*
(Turn) left.	*bayã*
(Turn) right.	*dayã*
street/road	*sarak/rāstā*
village	*gāõ*
at the (next/ second) corner	*(āge se/dusri) mor par*
up	*upar*
down	*nīche*
behind	*pīche*
opposite	*sāmne*
here	*yahā̃*
there	*wahā̃*
ahead	*āge*
north	*shumāl*
south	*janūb*
east	*mashriq*
west	*maghrib*

Around Town

Where is the/a ...?	*... kahā̃ hai?*
city centre	*markaz*
embassy	*sifārat khāna*
hospital	*hospitāl*
market	*bāzār*
mosque	*masjid*
police	*thāna*
post office	*dāk khāna*
telephone centre	*pī sī o* (PCO)

I want to make a telephone call.
maĩ telephone karnā chāhatā hū̃.
I'd like to change some ...
maĩ ... change karnā chāhatā hū̃

Accommodation

Where is a ...?	*... kahā̃ hai?*
hotel	*hotel*
guesthouse	*guest house*

Is a ... available?	*... milēgā?*
room	*kamrā*
cheap room	*sastā kamrā*
rope bed	*chārpoī*

the manager/owner	*mālik*
caretaker	*chowkidār*
travellers' inn	*sarai/musāfir khāna*
one night	*ek rāt*
two nights	*do rāt*

How much is it per night/person?	*fī rāt/ādmī kitnā?*	chillies	*lāl mirch*
May I see the room?	*maĩ kamreko dekhū̃?*	coffee	*kāfī*
		egg	*andā*
Where is the toilet?	*paikhānā kidhar?*	egg (boiled)	*ublāhūā andā*
It's very dirty/ noisy/expensive.	*bahut gandā/shor/ mahẽgā hai.*	egg (fried)	*andā frai*
		fish	*machlī*
We're leaving now.	*chelte haĩ*	flour (whole-wheat)	*ātā*
		food	*khāna*
Do you have ...?	*āpke pās ... hai?*	fruit	*phal*
a clean sheet	*sāf chādar*	lentils, pulses	*dāl*
hot water	*garam pānī*	mango	*ām*
a key	*chābī*	meat	*gosht*
bedding	*bistrā*	milk	*dūdh*
blanket	*kambal*	mutton	*chhotā gosht*
quilt	*razai*	oil (cooking)	*tel*
water heater	*gīzar*	okra	*bhindī*
		onion	*pyāz*
		orange	*santarā*

Food & Drink

		peas	*mattar*
I'm hungry/thirsty.	*mujhe bhūkh/pyās lagtī hai*	peanut	*mumphalī*
Do you have (food)?	*āpke pās (khānā) hai?*	pepper (black)	*kālā mirch*
		potato	*ālū*
Is there hot water?	*garam pānī hai?*	rice	*chāwal*
I don't want tea.	*mujhe chai nahī̃ chāhiye*	rice (fried)	*pulāū*
		rice (plain)	*sādhā chāwal*
I'd like some ...	*mujhe ... chāhiye*	salt	*namak*
Another ..., please.	*ek aur ..., mehrbānī*	spice	*masālā*
I don't eat ...	*maĩ ... nahī̃ khātā*	spinach	*pālak*
I'm a vegetarian.	*maĩ sabzī khor hū̃*	sugar	*chīnī*
hot/cold	*garam/thandā*	tea	*chāī*
without spice	*bagair masālā*	tea (green)	*sabz chāī*
		tea (with milk)	*dūdh-chāī*
		vegetable	*sabzī*
apple	*seb*	water	*pānī*
apricot	*khubānī*	water (boiled)	*ublā hūā pānī*
banana	*kelā*	yogurt	*dahī*
beef	*barā gosht*		
bread	*rotī*		

Shopping

bread (flat/ unleavened)	*chapātī*	How much is it?	*kitnā paisā?*
		I'll take this.	*maĩ ye letā hū̃*
bread (fried)	*parāthā*	It's very expensive.	*bahut mahẽgā*
bread (white/ leavened)	*dābel (double) rotī*	May I look at it?	*maĩ dekhū̃?*
		I'm just looking.	*sirf dekhtahū̃*
butter	*makkhan*	I'm looking for ...	*mujhe ... chāhiye*
cabbage	*band ghobī*	Do you have another colour?	*dusrā rang hai?*
carrot	*gājar*		
cauliflower	*phūl gobhī*		
cheese	*panīr*	clothing	*kaprā*
chicken	*mūrgī*	big/bigger	*barā/isse barā*
chickpea	*chanā*	small/smaller	*chotā/isse chotā*
		cheap/cheaper	*sastā/isse sastā*

Useful Words & Phrases

The following 'postpositions' are like prepositions except they go after the word. For example, 'in the hotel' is *hotel-mē*; 'John's wife' is *Jān kī bīvī*. 'From here to there' is *yahāse wahā̃ tak*.

to	-ko
from	-se
in	-mē
belonging to, of	kā, kī
on	par
for	ke liye
with (a person)	ke sath
up to/until	tak

To say you want 'to do something', add the verb to the phrase *maī ... chāhatā hū̃*, (*chāhatī hū̃* for a female speaker), meaning 'I want ...'.

bring	lānā
buy	kharīdnā
climb	chārhnā
cook	pakānā
drink	pīnā
eat	khānā
go	jānā
sleep	sonā
take	lenā
walk	paidal jānā
wash (clothes)	dhonā

The word *achhā* (good) is an all-purpose expression that litters every conversation. Depending on the tone of voice it can also mean 'as you wish', 'I understand', 'I agree', 'right', 'really?' and more.

a little/a lot	thorā/bahut
beautiful	khubsūrat
big/small	barā/chhotā
cheap/expensive	sastā/mahēgā
closed/open	band/khūlā
cold/hot	thandā/garam
delicious	lazīz
difficult/easy	mushkil/āsān
empty	khāli
enough	kāfī
first-rate	pakkā (lit: 'ripe')/
second-rate	kacchā (lit: 'unripe')

forbidden	manā
good/bad	achhā/kharāb
happy	khush
heavy/light	vazandār/halkā
hungry	bhūkhā
ill	bimār
important	khās
necessary	zarūrī
one more, another	ek aur
right/wrong	thīk/galat
too much	zyādā

The word *bas* (enough) is another handy word; use it when you've had enough tea, silly questions, crowds, etc. Saying it twice – *bas, bas!* – gives it an edge.

next, after this	dūsrā, dūsrī
here/there	yahā̃/wahā̃
inside/outside	andar/bāhar
right now	abhī
on foot	paidal
slowly	ahiste

Time & Dates

When?	kab?
How long?	kitna vaqt?
today	āj
tonight	āj rātko
tomorrow/yesterday	kal
every day	har roz
now	ab
hour	ghantā
day	din
month	mahinā

Monday	pir
Tuesday	mangal
Wednesday	budh
Thursday	jūmarāt
Friday	jūmā
Saturday	haftā
Sunday	itwār

| What time is it? | kitne baje? |

It's ... o'clock.	... baje.
5.15	sawā panch
5.30	sarhe panch
5.45	paune chhe

in the morning	*sūbah*
in the afternoon	*dopaherko*
in the evening	*shāmko*

Numbers

Words for numbers are quite regular. Don't confuse 25 and 50, or seven and 60. To add ½ to a number (except one or two, which have special forms) precede it with *sarhe* (eg, 3½ is *sarhe tīn*). This is a common form with prices and clock times.

1	*ek*
1½	*derh*
2	*do*
2½	*dhāi*
3	*tīn*
4	*chār*
5	*pāch*
6	*chhe*
7	*sāt*
8	*āth*
9	*nau*
10	*das*
11	*gyāra*
12	*bāra*
13	*tera*
14	*chauda*
15	*pandra*
16	*sola*
17	*satara*
18	*athāra*
19	*unnīs*
20	*bīs*
25	*pachīs*
30	*tīs*
35	*pantīs*
40	*chalīs*
45	*pantalīs*
50	*pachās*
60	*sāth*
70	*sattar*
80	*assī*
90	*nabbe*
100	*sau*
1000	*hazar*
100,000	*lākh* (written 1,00,000)
10,000,000	*kror* (written 1,00,00,000)

Emergencies – Urdu

Help!	*madad karo*
Call a doctor!	*dāktar bulāo!*
Call the police!	*polīs bulāo!*
I'm allergic to penicillin/antibiotics.	*penicillin band hai*
I'm diabetic.	*shakar kī bimārī hai*
Go away!	*chele jāo!*
diarrhoea	*jelāp, pecchas*
medicine	*dawāī*
danger	*khatarā*
dangerous	*khatarnāk*

On the Trail

How many days?	*kitne din?*
How many stages?	*kitne parāo?*
stage	*parāo*
return wage	*wāpasi*

Check the weight.	*vazan dekho*
Pick up the load/ baggage.	*lod/sāmān ūthāo*
Let's go.	*chelo*
Stop here.	*yahā̃ roko*
Take a rest.	*dam karo*
baggage	*sāmān*
a lot of baggage	*bahut sāmān*
weight	*vazan*
heavy/light	*vazandār/halkā*
scales	*kīl*
How is the trail?	*rāstā kaisā hai?*
trail	*rāstā*
ascent	*charāī*
descent	*utarāī*
Is there a bridge?	*pūl hai?*
bridge	*pūl*
camp	*kemp*
dirty water	*gadlā pānī*
garbage	*kacherā*
map	*nakshā*

Weather

cloud	*bādal*
cold	*thandā*
rain	*bārish*
snow	*baraf*
sun	*sūraj*
wind	*hawā*

Clothing & Equipment

candle	*mombattī*
cloth/clothes	*kaprā*
cookpot	*bartan* or *degchī*
cup	*pyālā*
fire	*āg*
firewood	*lakrī*
foam sleeping mat	*shīt*
fork	*kāntā*
gloves	*dastānā*
hat	*topī*
kerosene	*mittīkātel*
kerosene container	*jerkan*
kettle	*ketlī*
knife	*chhūrī*
matches	*machiz*
needle/thread	*sūī/dāgā*
rope	*rassī*
scales	*tarāzu/kāntā/kīl*
shoes	*jute* or *boot*
soap	*sābun*
socks	*jerāb* or *moze*
spoon	*chamach*
store	*dukān*
stove	*istov*
sunglasses	*kālā ainak*

Trail Features, Flora & Fauna

avalanche danger	*baraf girne kā khatrā*
bridge	*pūl*
canyon/valley/ gorge/stream	*nālā*
cliff	*chatān*
crevasse	*crevas*
flower	*phul*
forest	*jangal*
gorge	*nala/gol*
hut	*jhomprī*
lake	*jhīl*
mosque	*masjid*
mountain	*pahār*
pass	*tap*
pasture	*charāgāh*
path/trail	*rāstā*
river	*daryā*
rock	*patthar*
spring	*chashmā*
spring (hot)	*garam chashmā*
summit	*choti/sār*
tree	*darakht*

Body Language

A common way Pakistanis say 'yes' is by a sideways tilt or waggle of the head; foreigners often mistake this for 'I don't care'. Pakistanis may say 'no' with a single 'tsk' or 'tut', often with raised eyebrows or a slight backwards flick of the head. It is neither rude nor does it necessarily imply disapproval or surprise. A mere raising of the eyebrows has the same meaning: you may see taxi drivers and rick-shaw-wallahs give it when refusing a fare.

A twist of the wrist with fingers outspread can be a generalised question, such as 'what's going on here?' or 'where are you going?'. Thumbs-up and thumbs-down gestures are either rude or likely to be misunderstood.

cow	*gāī*
goat	*bakrā*
livestock	*māl maveshī*
sheep	*bherā*
yak	*khushgāo*

Balti

Balti, the language of the Balti-pa, is spoken throughout Baltistan. It is an archaic Tibetan language closely related to Ladakhi, which is spoken in adjacent Indian territory. Balti ascribes gender only to animate beings. The suffix *po* indicates male, *mo* female. Like other Tibetan languages, Balti uses subject-object-verb word order.

Pronunciation

Balti still pronounces the consonant clusters that modern spoken Tibetan has lost. The combination **ng** is nasal, pronounced as a single sound like the 'ng' in 'singing'. Consonant clusters are also pronounced as one sound.

a	as in 'above'
i	as in 'bit'
u	as in 'put'
ā	as in 'father'
ī	as the 'ea' in 'seat'

ū	as the 'oo' in 'pool'
e	as in 'they'
o	as in 'go'
ai	as the 'ei' in 'height'
au	as the 'aw' in 'law'

Greetings & Civilities

Welcome to you.	*yāng shok*
What's up?	*chī khabar?*
How are you?	*yāng chī hālyo?*
I'm well.	*lyākhmo*
Where are you from?	*kyāng gār paīn?*
I'm from ...	*... paīn*
What's your name?	*yari ming tākpo chīin.*
My name is ...	*nge ming tākpo ... yin.*
His name is ...	*khwe ming tākpo ... yin*

Useful Words

How is the road?	*lāmpo chīnā yod?*
It's good.	*lyākhmo dū.*
It's not good.	*lyākhmo med.*
Where does this trail go?	*di lampo gār wīn?*
This trail goes to ...	*di lampo...wīn.*
How far is ...?	*... tsātse tāring yod?*
What is this?	*dyū chī īn?*
It is ...	*... yod.*
Bring ...	*... khyon*
Yes.	*yāyā/kasal*
No.	*men*
father/mother	*āta/ango*
husband/wife	*ashīpa/zanzus*
head man	*trangpā*
I/we	*ngā/ngātang*
you	*yāng*
he/she	*kho/mo*
they	*khong/don* (m/f)
What	*chī*
Which?	*go*
Who?	*sū?*
When?	*nām?*
Where?	*gār?*
How many?	*tsam*
this	*dyū*
that	*do*
these	*dyung*
those	*dong*
here	*dyūwā*
there	*owā*
big/small	*chhogo/tsūntse*

good/bad	*lyakhmo/changmen*
hot/cold	*tsho/drakhmo*
near/far	*nyīmor/thagrīng*
right/left	*trang/khyun*
beautiful	*rgāshe*
tasty	*zhumbo*

Trail Words

boulder	*urdwā*
fire	*me*
flower	*mendoq*
grass	*spāng*
hat	*nāting*
ibex	*skin*
ice	*gāng*
mountain	*brok*
path	*lam*
rain	*charphā*
river	*gyāmtso*
rope	*thaqpa*
snow	*khā*
spring	*chhūmik*
valley	*lungbā*
water	*chhū*
wind	*hlung*
yak	*yak*
yak-cow (cross breed)	*dzo/dzomo*

Food

apple	*kūshū*
apricot	*chūli*
apricot (dried)	*fading*
bread (thick)	*khurbā*
butter	*mār*
buttermilk	*darbā*
chicken	*byango*
egg	*byapjun*
flour (barley)	*nas fe*
flour (whole wheat)	*baq fe*
food	*zāchas*
goat	*rabuk*
meat	*shā*
milk	*ongā*
peas	*pokshan*
rice	*blas*
salt	*payū*
sheep	*lūq*
tea	*chā*
tea (salted)	*payū chā*
walnut	*stargāh*

Time & Dates

Monday	*tsandār*
Tuesday	*angāru*
Wednesday	*batu*
Thursday	*brespot*
Friday	*shukuru*
Saturday	*shingsher*
Sunday	*adid*
morning	*gyukhpa*
night	*tshan*
today	*dirīng*
tomorrow	*haske*
yesterday	*gunde*

Numbers

1	*chīk*
2	*ngīs*
3	*khsūm*
4	*bjī*
5	*gā*
6	*trūk*
7	*bdūn*
8	*bgyet*
9	*rgū*
10	*phchū*
11	*chūschīk*
12	*chongas*
13	*chuksūm*
14	*chūbjī*
15	*chogā*
20	*ngī shū*
30	*khsūm chū*
40	*ngī shū ngīs*
50	*ngī shū ngīs na phchū*
60	*ngīshū khsūm*
70	*ngīshū khsūm na phchū*
80	*ngiū bjī*
90	*ngīshū bjī na phchū*
100	*bgya*

Burushaski

Burushaski, the language of the Burusho, is unrelated to any other spoken language in the world. Neighbouring Khowar and Wakhi speakers call it Werchikwor. Burushaski is spoken in parts of the Yasin Valley in Ghizar district, in Upper Nagyr and Hunza, and in Chapursan's Raminj village and Misgar in Gojal.

Pronunciation

a	as in 'above'
i	as in 'bit'
u	as in 'put'
ā	as in 'father'
ī	as the 'ea' in 'seat'
ū	as the 'oo' in 'pool'
e	as the 'a' in 'take'
o	as in 'go'
ai	as in 'bait'
au	as in 'haul'

Greetings & Civilities

How are you?	*besan hāl bilā?*
How do you do?	*be mei bān?* (polite)
I'm well.	*shūā bā*
What's your name?	*meik besan bilā?* (polite)
	gwik besan bilā? (informal)
Where are you going?	*ām nichen?*
I'm going to ...	*je ... nichā bā*

Useful Words & Phrases

Where is the post office?	*dak khana amulo bila?*
Is this the road to Sost?	*gute gan Sostar niche la?*
Yes.	*awā*
No.	*beyā*
Let's go.	*nichen na*
Bring me (a thing).	*... ditso*
Bring me (a drink).	*... dutsua*
eat bread	*shapīk shīn*
drink tea	*chaī mīnin*
father/mother	*yū/īmī*
husband/wife	*mūyār/yūs*
I/we	*je/mi*
you	*un*
he or she	*īn*
they	*ū*
this/these	*gūse/gūtse*
that/those	*īse/ītse*
day/night	*gunts/thap*
morning/evening	*tshordīne/shām*
in the morning	*tshordīmo*

now	*mū*
tomorrow	*jhī māle*
yesterday	*sabūr*
What?/Which?	*besan?*
When?	*beshal?*
Where?	*āmūlo?*
Which?	*amīs?*
Who?	*menan?*
Why?	*bes?*
How much?	*bearūm?*
big/small	*ūyūm/jot*
cold/hot	*chhāgūrūm/gārūrūm*
good/bad	*shūā/gūneqīsh*
left-side/right-side	*gaypā/doypā*
many/very	*būt*
near/far	*āsīr/māthan*
here/there	*khole/ele*
ahead	*yar*
beautiful	*daltās*

Trail Words

animal	*haiwān*
bird	*balas*
bridge	*brosh*
cloud	*quronch*
cow	*būā*
fire	*pfū*
firewood	*gashil*
flower	*āsqūr*
glacier	*haguts*
goat	*tshīir*
hat	*pfartsin*
hawk	*bāz*
horse	*hagur*
house	*hā*
herders' huts	*harai*
ice	*gamū*
lake	*phari*
marmot	*tushūn*
mountain	*chhish*
trail/path	*gan*
rain	*hāralt*
river	*daryā*
rope	*gashk*
shaman	*bitān*
snow	*geh*
stone	*dan*
tree	*tom*
tent	*gut*
valley	*bar*
wind	*tish*

Food

apple	*bālt*
apricot	*jū*
apricot (dried)	*batering*
apricot·nut	*hāni*
bread	*shapīk*
bread (thick wheat)	*phitī*
butter	*maltāsh*
buttermilk	*diltār*
cheese (white)	*burūs*
cream	*iran*
egg	*tīngān*
flour (whole-wheat)	*diram*
meat	*chap*
milk	*māmū*
mulberry	*biranch*
onion	*gāshū*
pear	*phesho*
peas	*gark*
rice	*bras*
salt	*bāyū*
soup	*daudho*
walnut	*balring*
water	*tshil*
wine	*mel*
yogurt	*dūmānū māmū*

Numbers

1	*han*
2	*ālta*
3	*ūsko*
4	*wālto*
5	*tshūndo*
6	*mishīndo*
7	*thalo*
8	*altāmbo*
9	*hūncho*
10	*tūrūmo*
11	*tūrmāhan*
12	*tūrmāālta*
20	*āltar*
100	*thā*

Kalashamun

Kalashamun is an Indic language, somewhat related to Khowar with which it has been in long contact. Kalashamun is only spoken in the three Kalasha valleys and in Jinjeret Kuh, all of which are in Chitral.

Greetings & Civilities

Hello	*ishpadeh*
Are you well?	*tabiyet prūsht?*
Good/OK.	*prūsht*
Very good.	*bo prūsht*
Thank you.	*shukriā*
Yes.	*prūsht*
No.	*ne*
No problem.	*ne mishkil*
husband/wife	*berū/ja*
father/mother	*dādā/āyā*

Useful Words & Phrases

Where is ...?	*kawa ...?*
Where are you going?	*kawa pariz?*
I'm going to ...	*... ah parim.*
I want ...	*ah ... khushan.*
I/we	*ā/ābī*
you	*tū*
he	*asa*
they	*elī*
What?	*ki?*
Where?	*kawā?*
Who?	*kūrā?*
When?	*kāya?*
this/these	*īa/emī*
that/those	*se/elī*
big/small	*gonā/chūtyak*
good/bad	*prūsht/shūm*
hot/cold	*tāpālā/osh*
near/far	*taā/desha*
right/left	*drach/kewī*
day/night	*bās/rāt*
today	*onjā*
tomorrow	*chopa*
yesterday	*dosh*
cow	*gakh*
flower	*gambūrī*
goat	*pāi*
hail	*badwash*
lightning	*indochik*
path/trail	*pon*
rain	*pīlīwe*
tree	*mūt*
water	*uk*
wind	*sīra*

Food

bread	*aū*
cheese	*chaska*
clotted cream	*oshāla*
food	*aū*
grapes	*drāch*
meat	*mos*
milk	*chīr*
onion	*kachindūk*
salt	*lõ*
tea (milky)	*chīr chai*
walnuts	*birmo*
water	*ūkh*
wine	*dā*
yogurt	*trunachīr*

Numbers

1	*ek*
2	*dū*
3	*tre*
4	*chāo*
5	*poin*
6	*sho*
7	*sat*
8	*asht*
9	*no*
10	*dash*
11	*dashyega*
12	*dashyedūa*
20	*bīshī*
30	*bishi-das*
100	*shor*

Khowar

Khowar, the language of the Kho, is an archaic Indic language with significant Iranian influence. Khowar is spoken in most of Chitral and in about half of Ghizar including parts of the Ishkoman Valley. The Khowar spoken in Chitral's Turikho area is regarded as the purest form of the language.

Pronunciation

a	as in 'above'
i	as in 'bit'
u	as in 'put'
ā	as in 'father'
ī	as the 'ea' in 'seat'
ū	as the 'oo' in 'pool'
e	as in 'they'
o	as in 'go'
ai	as in 'bait'
au	as the 'aw' in 'law'

Greetings & Civilities

How are you?	*tū kichā āsūs?*
Fine, thanks.	*bo jām, mehrbānī.*
Are you well?	*jām āsūsā?*
Are you fresh?	*tāzāgīyā?*
What's your name?	*ta kīāgh nām?*
My name is ...	*ma nām ...*
husband/wife	*mosh/bok*
father/mother	*tat/nan*

Useful Words & Phrases

Where are you going?	*tū kurī besān?*
I'm going to ...	*āwā ... oten biān.*
We're going to ...	*ispā ... oten bīsīān.*
Where are you coming from?	*kurār gosān?*
I'm coming from ...	*āwā ... ar gomān.*
Where does this trail go?	*heyā pon kuī birān?*
This trail goes to ...	*heyā pon ... ote birān.*
Please bring ...	*... ange.*
Is ... available?	*... lā boyā?*
Yes.	*di*
No.	*no*
I don't understand.	*hosh no koman*
Let's go.	*bisī*
I/we	*āwā/ispā*
you/you (plural)	*tū/pīsa*
it/he/she	*hes*
they	*het*
What?	*kīāgh?*
When?	*kia wat?*
Where?	*kura?*
Which?	*kīwālū?*
Who?	*kā?*
Why?	*ko?*
How?	*kicha?*
ahead	*prushtī*
now	*hanisen*
that/those	*hes/het*
this/these	*hāyā/hamit*
beautiful	*chust*
big/small	*lut/tsak*
good/bad	*jām/shūm*
hot/cold	*pech/ūshak*
left side/right side	*kholī/hoski*
many/very	*bo*
near/far	*shoī/dūderi*
morning/afternoon	*chhūchī/shām*
day/night	*ānūs/chuī*
today	*hanūn*
tomorrow	*chuchi*
yesterday	*dosh*

Trail Words

Khowar nouns have no gender. Plural is formed by adding *an* to the singular.

bed	*zhen*
black bear	*oths*
blanket	*zhūl*
cloud	*kot*
cow	*leshū*
fire	*angār*
flower	*gambūrī*
glacier/ice	*yoz*
goat	*paī*
hat	*khaoī*
Chitrali-style hat	*pakol*
hawk	*yurj*
hemp	*bong*
horse	*istor*
house	*dūr*
ibex (male)	*tonīshū*
markhor (male)	*shārā*
mountain	*zom*
pass	*ān*
plain	*lāsht*
rain	*boshīk*
river	*sīn*
snow leopard	*purdūm*
spring	*uts*
stone	*bort*
trail	*pon*
tree (cedar)	*rogh*
valley	*gol*
water	*ūgh*
wind	*gān*

Food

apple	*palogh*
apricot	*zhūlī*
apricot (dried)	*chambor*
bread	*shāpīk*
butter	*māskā*
buttermilk	*shātū*
cheese	*shapināk*
egg	*ayūkūn*
flour (whole-wheat)	*peshīrū*
grape	*dratch*
meat	*phūshūr*
milk	*chīr*
mulberry	*marāch*

mushroom (morel)	*qutsi*
onion	*treshtū*
pear	*tang*
rice/cooked rice	*grinj/pakhtī*
rhubarb	*ishpar*
salt	*trūp*
tomato	*patīnggel*
walnut	*birmogh*
yogurt	*machīr*

Numbers

1	*ī*
2	*jū*
3	*troī*
4	*chor*
5	*ponch*
6	*chhoī*
7	*sot*
8	*usht*
9	*nīu*
10	*jush*
11	*jush ī*
12	*johjū*
20	*bishir*
30	*bishir jush*
40	*jū bishir*
50	*jū bishir jush*
60	*troī bishir*
100	*ī shor*

Shina

Shina is an Indic language, whose original speakers probably migrated from the south. Several dialects exist, notably Gilgiti, Kohistani and Astori, with Gilgiti the main one. Shina gives its name to Shinaki, the areas in Lower Nagyr and Lower Hunza where Shina speakers live. The Brok-pa, who are the Shina-speakers living on the western edge of Baltistan, call their language Brokskat. Shina speakers also live in the Punial area of Ghizar, parts of the Ishkoman Valley, in Gilgit and in the valleys of Diamir near Nanga Parbat.

Pronunciation

Shina shares its sound system and a fair amount of vocabulary with Burushaski, suggesting they've been neighbours for a long time.

a	as in 'above'
i	as in 'bit'
u	as in 'put'
ā	as in 'father'
ī	as the 'ea' in 'seat'
ū	as the 'oo' in 'pool'
e	as the 'a' in 'safe'
o	as in 'go'
ai	as in 'bait'
au	as the 'aw' in 'law'

Greetings & Civilities

Hello.	*alā*
Goodbye.	*hudā hafīz*
How are you?	*jhek hāl haī?*
Fine.	*mishto hān/mehrbāni*
Yes.	*awā*
No.	*neh*
What's your name?	*tei jek nom hān?*
My name is ...	*mei nom ... hān*
father/mother	*bābo/ājhī*
husband/wife	*barao/jamāt*

Useful Words & Phrases

I'm going.	*māh bojhimer*
Eat bread.	*shapīk khāh*
Drink tea.	*chai pīh*
I/we	*māh/beh*
you	*tū*
he/she	*o/e*
they	*eī*
Who?	*ko?*
What?	*jhek?*
Where?	*kon?*
When?	*kāre?*
How many?	*kachāk?*
Which?	*kok?*
this/these	*ānū/ānī*
big/small	*baro/chūno*
good/bad	*mishto/khacho*
hot/cold	*tāto/shīdalo*
near/far	*kachīl/dūr*
right/left	*dashīno/khabū*
morning	*chalbūjī*
evening	*shām*
today	*āsh*
tomorrow	*lūshtākī*
yesterday	*bālāh*

Food & Trail Words

buttermilk	*mel*
cave	*kor*

cheese	*brus*
chicken	*kārkāmosh*
cow	*go*
day/night	*dez/rātī*
egg	*hanai*
fire	*āgār*
firewood	*jhūk*
flower	*phūnar*
glacier	*gomukh*
goat	*āī*
house	*got*
meat	*mos*
milk	*dūth*
onion	*kāshū*
rain	*āzho*
rice	*brīū*
rope	*bālī*
salt	*pājhū*
stone	*bath*
trail	*pon*
tree	*tom*
water	*weī*
wind	*ōshī*
yogurt	*munto dut*

Numbers

1	*ek*
2	*dū*
3	*che*
4	*chār*
5	*posh*
6	*shā*
7	*sat*
8	*ānsh*
9	*nāū*
10	*dāī*
11	*akāī*
12	*bāī*
20	*bī*
100	*shal*

Wakhi

Wakhi (called Xikwor by the Wakhi people who speak it) belongs to the Pamir group of Iranian languages, all of which belong to the greater Indo-European language family. Wakhi is spoken throughout Gojal, in Broghil in the upper Yarkhun Valley, in Imit, Bilhanz and Bort villages in the Ishkoman Valley, and in Rich Gol in Chitral.

Pronunciation

a	as in 'above'
i	as in 'bit'
u	as in 'put'
ā	as in 'father'
ī	as the 'ea' in 'seat'
ū	as the 'oo' in 'pool'
e	as the 'a' in 'safe'
o	as in 'go'
ai	as in 'bait'
au	as in 'haul'
x	as 'kh', pronounced further back
zh	as the 's' in 'treasure'

Greetings & Civilities

How are you?	*chiz hol he?/tut sīyeta?*
I'm fine.	*bidurt em.*
I'm well.	*wuzem siyet.*
What's your name?	*ī nunge chīst?*
My name is ...	*zhu nunge ...*
husband/wife	*shohar/jamāt*
father/mother	*tat/nān*
friend	*dost*

Useful Words & Phrases

Where are you going?	*kūmeret takh?*
Where is ... available?	*... esh kūmer goten?*
I need ...	*mārey ... dirkor.*
Bring me ...	*mazher ... rand.*
I'm hungry.	*merz vitk*
I'm thirsty.	*wesk vitk*
I'm tired.	*washk vitk*
Sit down.	*nezdita*
Drink tea.	*choī pev.*
Eat food.	*shapīk yāo.*
Yes.	*yau*
No.	*ne*
Go!	*chow*
I/we	*woz/sak*
you	*tū*
he, she	*yao*
they	*yasht*
How?	*tse sokht?*
How much/many?	*tsūmar?*
What?	*chīz?*
When?	*tsogdar?*
Where?	*kūmar?*
Which one?	*kūmdī?*
Who?	*kui?*

Why?	*chizer?*
this/these	*yim*
that/those	*yao*
a little	*safkek*
good/bad	*baf/shak*
beautiful	*khushrūī*
below	*dest*
big/small	*lup/zaqlāī*
cold/hot	*sūr/thin*
easy/difficult	*ausān/zur*
enough	*chok*
ill	*bimaur, galeez*
important	*nayaft*
light/heavy	*ranjhkh/gorung*
long/short	*daroz/kūth*
open	*heth*
right/left	*rost/chap*
small	*zaqlāī*
too much	*gafch*
ahead	*terperit*
behind	*tertsabas*
in front	*perit*
here/there	*drem/drar*
near	*qarīb*
day/night	*ror/naghd*
morning/evening	*sahār/purz*
today	*wothg*
tomorrow	*pīgā*
yesterday	*yezī*

Food

apple	*mūr*
bread	*xich*
butter	*rūghan*
cheese (dried)	*qurūt*
cream	*mirik*
egg	*tukhmūrg*
flour (whole-wheat)	*yumj*
food	*shāpik*
fruit	*mewā*
goat	*thug*
meat	*gusht*
milk	*zharzh*
peas	*shakh*
potato	*ālū*
rhubarb	*shpod*
rice	*grinj*
salt	*namik*
vegetable	*savzi/gazg*
yogurt	*pāī*

Trail Words

birch	*furz*
blue sheep	*rāmapo*
bridge	*skord*
butter churn	*sogo*
cloud	*wītīsh*
clothes	*luqpar*
fire	*rakhnīgh*
firewood	*ghoz*
flower	*spregh*
glacier/ice	*yāz*
hat	*skith*
hearth	*dildung*
house	*xun*
ibex	*yuksh*
juniper	*yārz*
knife	*khezh*
Marco Polo sheep	*rūsh*
mountain	*koh*
needle	*sits*
rain	*mor*
rope	*shīven*
spoon	*kapch*
stone	*gar*
stream (clear)	*zherav*
stream (glacial)	*dur*
sun	*yīr*
tamarisk	*targ*
thread	*wusāī*
trail/path	*videkh*
water	*yupk*
wind	*damā*

Numbers

1	*yīū*
2	*būī*
3	*troī*
4	*tsabur*
5	*pānz*
6	*shāth*
7	*hub*
8	*hāth*
9	*nao*
10	*thas*
11	*thas yīū*
12	*thas boī*
20	*wīst*
100	*yīsad*

Glossary

The language of origin of many glossary terms appears in parentheses after the entry. Terms in italics within definitions have their own entries.

ablation valley – a small valley that runs parallel to a *glacier* at its margins

abseil – a means of descent over a steep incline or overhang whereby a climber makes a controlled slide down a rope from a solid anchor; also *rappel*

AIG – Assistant Inspector General (of police)

an – a mountain pass (Khowar)

arête – a sharp mountain ridge, produced by glaciation; a *crag*

asalam aleikum – universal Muslim greeting for 'peace be with you' (Arabic)

baksheesh – a tip or donation (Urdu)

bar – river, valley or stream (Burushaski)

bashali – a women's birthing and menstrual house (Kalashamun)

bazaar – market area; a market town is called a bazaar

bergschrund – the large *crevasse* found at the upper limit of a glacier's movement, formed where the moving *glacier* breaks away from the icecap

bowl – a basin, sometimes glacial (see also *cirque*)

brak – a mountain or mountain pasture (Balti)

burqa – a long tent-like garment that completely hides the body shape and face, worn in public by conservative Muslim women

cairn – a heap of stones that marks a route or pass

canal – a waterway for irrigation

channel – the bed or deeper part of a river

chapatti – flat, unleavened wheat bread baked on a griddle

charpoy – a simple bed made of ropes knotted together on a wooden frame

chhīsh – a mountain (Burushaski)

chit – slip of paper (eg, a letter of recommendation or confirmation for a hotel reservation)

chowk – intersection

chowkidar – watchman/guard

cirque – a bowl-shaped steep-walled mountain basin carved by glaciation, often containing a small, round lake

col – a pass or physical depression in a mountain ridge

cornice – deposits of wind-drifted snow or ice projecting over the lee edge of mountain ridges

couloir – a steep gorge or *gully* on the side of a mountain

crag – an *arête*

crevasse – a fissure or deep cleft or crack in glacial ice

DC – Deputy Commissioner of a district in NWFP and in the Northern Areas

DFO – District Forestry Officer

dhobi – a washerman

dupatta – long scarf often worn by Muslim women to cover their hair in public

dur – a valley (Wakhi)

dzo – a cross between a yak and a cow (Balti)

erratic – a boulder carried by glacial ice and deposited some distance from its place of origin

ford – to cross a river by wading because there is no bridge or cable

fork – the place where a trail or river divides into branches

gah – river, valley or stream (Shina); place (Persian)

gali – a mountain pass (Shina)

gang – a *glacier* (Balti)

glacier – an extended mass of ice, formed by snow falling and accumulating over the years, that flows/moves slowly down a mountain or valley

gol – river, valley or stream (Khowar)

gomukh – a *glacier* (Shina)

gree – a *col* (Khowar)

gully – a small ravine on a mountain worn by erosion that serves as a 'rubbish' chute for rock and snow

haghost – a mountain pass (Burushaski)
hammam – public bathhouse and barber shop (Urdu)

icefall – a jumbled mass of ice in a *glacier*
IG – Inspector General (of police)
imam – leader; title of one of 12 descendants of the Prophet Mohammad *(PBUH)* who, according to orthodox Shi'a belief, succeeded him as temporal and spiritual leader of Muslims
imamate – the region governed by an imam
inshallah – 'God willing' (Arabic)
Isma'ili – a branch of Shi'a Islam asserting Ismail to be the seventh Imam in the succession from Ali, son-in-law of the Prophet Mohammad *(PBUH)*

jataka – stories of the past lives of Buddha (Sanskrit)

kafir – Muslim term for non-Muslim
khayaban – boulevard or avenue
Khoja – rulers of Kashgar during the 17th and 18th centuries and their descendants, some of whom live in Wakhan
KKH – Karakoram Highway
kot – a fort (Urdu)
kūch – semi-nomadic migratory practice of livestock management (Persian)
kūchi – people who do the work of the *kūch* (Persian)

la – a mountain pass (Balti)
lungma – river, valley or stream (Balti)

maidan – a level plain often used to describe gently sloping alpine grasslands (Urdu)
mehtar – title of the former rulers of Chitral (Khowar)
memsahib – respectful title for a woman, used alone (like 'Madam'; Urdu)
mir – title of the former rulers of Hunza and Nagyr
moraine – ridge, mound or irregular mass of boulders, rocks, gravel, sand or clay, left by a *glacier*; along a glacier's margins (lateral moraine), in its centre (medial moraine), and at its mouth, marking the glacier's farthest point (terminal moraine)
Muharram – the first month of the Muslim calendar
muztagh – ice mountain (Turkic)

nala – river, valley or stream (Urdu)
nambardar – the head man of a village (also called lambardar)
névé – boundary on *glacier* between accumulation zone (where snowfall exceeds melt) and ablation zone (where melting is predominant), characterised by granular snow subsequently compacted into ice

paisa – a unit of currency, 100 in a rupee
pamir – glacially formed high-elevation valleys renowned as summer grazing grounds (Wakhi)
parāo – traditional stage/length of a day's walk, used to calculate porters' wages (Urdu)
pari – magical female spirit beings (Persian)
pax Buddhica – the long period of peace most of Central and South Asia experienced during the heyday of Buddhism
PBUH – Peace Be Upon Him; translation of the obligatory Arabic phrase used after the Prophet Mohammad's name
punji – *cairn* (Burushaski)
purdah – the segregation and veiling of post-pubescent women from all men outside the immediate family in orthodox Muslim communities

qutsi – morel mushrooms (Khowar)

raja – title for ruler (Urdu)
rappel – *abseil*
route – a course for travelling where no visible trail exists
rui – magical, usually malevolent, female spirit beings (Shina)
rupee – the currency in Pakistan

saddle – a low place in a ridge
sahib – respectful title for a man, used alone (like 'Sir') or after a surname or title (like 'Mr'; Urdu)
sar – summit, the head of (Persian)

sarai – a caravan stopping place, now used for a motor transport staging place (Urdu)

scree – small rock accumulated on a slope, usually collected in a *gully* which spreads into a fan-shaped cone

serac – a large pinnacle of glacial ice

shalwar kameez – traditional men's and women's clothing, consisting of a knee-length long-sleeved shirt worn over very loose trousers gathered at the waist

shenakti card – Pakistani national identity card (NIC)

Shi'a (Shi'ite) – a Muslim who regards Ali, the son-in-law of the Prophet Mohammad *(PBUH)*, as the legitimate successor of Mohammad

shikar gah – hunting grounds (Urdu)

shpūn – small group of men who tend livestock during winter (Wakhi)

sirdar – a porter who is selected as headman of porters on a trek or mountaineering expedition (Urdu)

snout – *terminus* of a *glacier*

SP – Superintendent of Police

SSP – Senior Superintendent of Police

Sunni – a Muslim who regards the first four caliphs as legitimate successors of the Prophet Mohammad *(PBUH)*

switchback – a trail or route that follows a zigzagging course up a steep grade

talus – large boulders accumulated on a slope, fanning out at its base

tandoor – clay-lined kiln for baking bread (Urdu)

tang – a gorge (Persian)

tarn – a small mountain lake in a *cirque*

tawa – an iron griddle for cooking *chappatis* (Urdu)

technical – referring to climbing or mountaineering skills and techniques required to complete a route

tehsil – administrative zone within a district in a province (Urdu)

terminus – the lowest part of a *glacier* where melting produces an outwash stream

Tham – title of the former rulers of Hunza and Nagyr (Burushaski)

trail – a visible path for walking

true left – the left bank of a river or *glacier* when facing downstream or downvalley

true right – the right bank of a river or *glacier* when facing downstream or downvalley

uween – a mountain pass (Wakhi)

wāpasi – portion of a porter's wage equal to one half of a stage wage, paid when a porter is released at a place different from where he was hired and hence must walk back to the place where he was hired

wazir – royal adviser or minister (Urdu)

yak – long-haired member of the ox family kept for dairy and as a beast of burden at high altitude

yaz – a *glacier* (Wakhi)

zherav – a river or stream with a glacial source (Wakhi)

ziarat – a shrine to a saint (Urdu)

zom – a mountain or summit (Khowar)

LONELY PLANET

ON THE ROAD

Travel Guides explore cities, regions and countries, and supply information on transport, restaurants and accommodation, covering all budgets. They come with reliable, easy-to-use maps, practical advice, cultural and historical facts and a rundown on attractions both on and off the beaten track. There are over 200 titles in this classic series, covering nearly every country in the world.

 Lonely Planet Upgrades extend the shelf life of existing travel guides by detailing any changes that may affect travel in a region since a book has been published. Upgrades can be downloaded for free from **www.lonelyplanet.com/upgrades**

For travellers with more time than money, **Shoestring** guides offer dependable, first-hand information with hundreds of detailed maps, plus insider tips for stretching money as far as possible. Covering entire continents in most cases, the six-volume shoestring guides are known around the world as 'backpackers bibles'.

For the discerning short-term visitor, **Condensed** guides highlight the best a destination has to offer in a full-colour, pocket-sized format designed for quick access. They include everything from top sights and walking tours to opinionated reviews of where to eat, stay, shop and have fun.

CitySync lets travellers use their Palm™ or Visor™ hand-held computers to guide them through a city with handy tips on transport, history, cultural life, major sights, and shopping and entertainment options. It can also quickly search and sort hundreds of reviews of hotels, restaurants and attractions, and pinpoint their location on scrollable street maps. CitySync can be downloaded from **www.citysync.com**

MAPS & ATLASES

Lonely Planet's **City Maps** feature downtown and metropolitan maps, as well as transit routes and walking tours. The maps come complete with an index of streets, a listing of sights and a plastic coat for extra durability.

Road Atlases are an essential navigation tool for serious travellers. Cross-referenced with the guidebooks, they also feature distance and climate charts and a complete site index.

LONELY PLANET

ESSENTIALS

Read This First books help new travellers to hit the road with confidence. These invaluable predeparture guides give step-by-step advice on preparing for a trip, budgeting, arranging a visa, planning an itinerary and staying safe while still getting off the beaten track.

Healthy Travel pocket guides offer a regional rundown on disease hot spots and practical advice on predeparture health measures, staying well on the road and what to do in emergencies. The guides come with a user-friendly design and helpful diagrams and tables.

Lonely Planet's **Phrasebooks** cover the essential words and phrases travellers need when they're strangers in a strange land. They come in a pocket-sized format with colour tabs for quick reference, extensive vocabulary lists, easy-to-follow pronunciation keys and two-way dictionaries.

Miffed by blurry photos of the Taj Mahal? Tired of the classic 'top of the head cut off' shot? **Travel Photography: A Guide to Taking Better Pictures** will help you turn ordinary holiday snaps into striking images and give you the know-how to capture every scene, from frenetic festivals to peaceful beach sunrises.

Lonely Planet's **Travel Journal** is a lightweight but sturdy travel diary for jotting down all those on-the-road observations and significant travel moments. It comes with a handy time-zone wheel, a world map and useful travel information.

Lonely Planet's eKno is an all-in-one communication service developed especially for travellers. It offers low-cost international calls and free email and voicemail so that you can keep in touch while on the road. Check it out on **www.ekno.lonelyplanet.com**

FOOD & RESTAURANT GUIDES

Lonely Planet's **Out to Eat** guides recommend the brightest and best places to eat and drink in top international cities. These gourmet companions are arranged by neighbourhood, packed with dependable maps, garnished with scene-setting photos and served with quirky features.

For people who live to eat, drink and travel, **World Food** guides explore the culinary culture of each country. Entertaining and adventurous, each guide is packed with detail on staples and specialities, regional cuisine and local markets, as well as sumptuous recipes, comprehensive culinary dictionaries and lavish photos good enough to eat.

LONELY PLANET

OUTDOOR GUIDES

For those who believe the best way to see the world is on foot, Lonely Planet's **Walking Guides** detail everything from family strolls to difficult treks, with 'when to go and how to do it' advice supplemented by reliable maps and essential travel information.

Cycling Guides map a destination's best bike tours, long and short, in day-by-day detail. They contain all the information a cyclist needs, including advice on bike maintenance, places to eat and stay, innovative maps with detailed cues to the rides, and elevation charts.

The **Watching Wildlife** series is perfect for travellers who want authoritative information but don't want to tote a heavy field guide. Packed with advice on where, when and how to view a region's wildlife, each title features photos of over 300 species and contains engaging comments on the local flora and fauna.

With underwater colour photos throughout, **Pisces Books** explore the world's best diving and snorkelling areas. Each book contains listings of diving services and dive resorts, detailed information on depth, visibility and difficulty of dives, and a roundup of the marine life you're likely to see through your mask.

LONELY PLANET

OFF THE ROAD

Journeys, the travel literature series written by renowned travel authors, capture the spirit of a place or illuminate a culture with a journalist's attention to detail and a novelist's flair for words. These are tales to soak up while you're actually on the road or dip into as an at-home armchair indulgence.

The range of lavishly illustrated **Pictorial** books is just the ticket for both travellers and dreamers. Off-beat tales and vivid photographs bring the adventure of travel to your doorstep long before the journey begins and long after it is over.

Lonely Planet **Videos** encourage the same independent, tough-minded approach as the guidebooks. Currently airing throughout the world, this award-winning series features innovative footage and an original soundtrack.

Yes, we know, work is tough, so do a little bit of deskside dreaming with the spiral-bound Lonely Planet **Diary** or a Lonely Planet **Wall Calendar**, filled with great photos from around the world.

TRAVELLERS NETWORK

Lonely Planet Online. Lonely Planet's award-winning Web site has insider information on hundreds of destinations, from Amsterdam to Zimbabwe, complete with interactive maps and relevant links. The site also offers the latest travel news, recent reports from travellers on the road, guidebook upgrades, a travel links site, an online book-buying option and a lively travellers bulletin board. It can be viewed at **www.lonelyplanet.com** or AOL keyword: lp.

Planet Talk is a quarterly print newsletter, full of gossip, advice, anecdotes and author articles. It provides an antidote to the being-at-home blues and lets you plan and dream for the next trip. Contact the nearest Lonely Planet office for your free copy.

Comet, the free Lonely Planet newsletter, comes via email once a month. It's loaded with travel news, advice, dispatches from authors, travel competitions and letters from readers. To subscribe, click on the Comet subscription link on the front page of the Web site.

Lonely Planet Guides by Region

Lonely Planet is known worldwide for publishing practical, reliable and no-nonsense travel information in our guides and on our Web site. The Lonely Planet list covers just about every accessible part of the world. Currently there are 16 series: Travel guides, Shoestring guides, Condensed guides, Phrasebooks, Read This First, Healthy Travel, Walking guides, Cycling guides, Watching Wildlife guides, Pisces Diving & Snorkeling guides, City Maps, Road Atlases, Out to Eat, World Food, Journeys travel literature and Pictorials.

AFRICA Africa on a shoestring • Botswana • Cairo • Cairo City Map • Cape Town • Cape Town City Map • East Africa • Egypt • Egyptian Arabic phrasebook • Ethiopia, Eritrea & Djibouti • Ethiopian Amharic phrasebook • The Gambia & Senegal • Healthy Travel Africa • Kenya • Malawi • Morocco • Moroccan Arabic phrasebook • Mozambique • Namibia • Read This First: Africa • South Africa, Lesotho & Swaziland • Southern Africa • Southern Africa Road Atlas • Swahili phrasebook • Tanzania, Zanzibar & Pemba • Trekking in East Africa • Tunisia • Watching Wildlife East Africa • Watching Wildlife Southern Africa • West Africa • World Food Morocco • Zambia • Zimbabwe, Botswana & Namibia
Travel Literature: Mali Blues: Traveling to an African Beat • The Rainbird: A Central African Journey • Songs to an African Sunset: A Zimbabwean Story

AUSTRALIA & THE PACIFIC Aboriginal Australia & the Torres Strait Islands •Auckland • Australia • Australian phrasebook • Australia Road Atlas • Cycling Australia • Cycling New Zealand • Fiji • Fijian phrasebook • Healthy Travel Australia, NZ & the Pacific • Islands of Australia's Great Barrier Reef • Melbourne • Melbourne City Map • Micronesia • New Caledonia • New South Wales • New Zealand • Northern Territory • Outback Australia • Out to Eat – Melbourne • Out to Eat – Sydney • Papua New Guinea • Pidgin phrasebook • Queensland • Rarotonga & the Cook Islands • Samoa • Solomon Islands • South Australia • South Pacific • South Pacific phrasebook • Sydney • Sydney City Map • Sydney Condensed • Tahiti & French Polynesia • Tasmania • Tonga • Tramping in New Zealand • Vanuatu • Victoria • Walking in Australia • Watching Wildlife Australia • Western Australia
Travel Literature: Islands in the Clouds: Travels in the Highlands of New Guinea • Kiwi Tracks: A New Zealand Journey • Sean & David's Long Drive

CENTRAL AMERICA & THE CARIBBEAN Bahamas, Turks & Caicos • Baja California • Belize, Guatemala & Yucatán • Bermuda • Central America on a shoestring • Costa Rica • Costa Rica Spanish phrasebook • Cuba • Cycling Cuba • Dominican Republic & Haiti • Eastern Caribbean • Guatemala • Havana • Healthy Travel Central & South America • Jamaica • Mexico • Mexico City • Panama • Puerto Rico • Read This First: Central & South America • Virgin Islands • World Food Caribbean • World Food Mexico • Yucatán
Travel Literature: Green Dreams: Travels in Central America

EUROPE Amsterdam • Amsterdam City Map • Amsterdam Condensed • Andalucía • Athens • Austria • Baltic States phrasebook • Barcelona • Barcelona City Map • Belgium & Luxembourg • Berlin • Berlin City Map • Britain • British phrasebook • Brussels, Bruges & Antwerp • Brussels City Map • Budapest • Budapest City Map • Canary Islands • Catalunya & the Costa Brava • Central Europe • Central Europe phrasebook • Copenhagen • Corfu & the Ionians • Corsica • Crete • Crete Condensed • Croatia • Cycling Britain • Cycling France • Cyprus • Czech & Slovak Republics • Czech phrasebook • Denmark • Dublin • Dublin City Map • Dublin Condensed • Eastern Europe • Eastern Europe phrasebook • Edinburgh • Edinburgh City Map • England • Estonia, Latvia & Lithuania • Europe on a shoestring • Europe phrasebook • Finland • Florence • Florence City Map • France • Frankfurt City Map • Frankfurt Condensed • French phrasebook • Georgia, Armenia & Azerbaijan • Germany • German phrasebook • Greece • Greek Islands • Greek phrasebook • Hungary • Iceland, Greenland & the Faroe Islands • Ireland • Italian phrasebook • Italy • Kraków • Lisbon • The Loire • London • London City Map • London Condensed • Madrid • Madrid City Map • Malta • Mediterranean Europe • Milan, Turin & Genoa • Moscow • Munich • Netherlands • Normandy • Norway • Out to Eat – London • Out to Eat – Paris • Paris • Paris City Map • Paris Condensed • Poland • Polish phrasebook • Portugal • Portuguese phrasebook • Prague • Prague City Map • Provence & the Côte d'Azur • Read This First: Europe • Rhodes & the Dodecanese • Romania & Moldova • Rome • Rome City Map • Rome Condensed • Russia, Ukraine & Belarus • Russian phrasebook • Scandinavian & Baltic Europe • Scandinavian phrasebook • Scotland • Sicily • Slovenia • South-West France • Spain • Spanish phrasebook • Stockholm • St Petersburg • St Petersburg City Map • Sweden • Switzerland • Tuscany • Ukrainian phrasebook • Venice • Vienna • Wales • Walking in Britain • Walking in France • Walking in Ireland • Walking in Italy • Walking in Scotland • Walking in Spain • Walking in Switzerland • Western Europe • World Food France • World Food Greece • World Food Ireland • World Food Italy • World Food Spain **Travel Literature:** After Yugoslavia • Love and War in the Apennines • The Olive Grove: Travels in Greece • On the Shores of the Mediterranean • Round Ireland in Low Gear • A Small Place in Italy

Lonely Planet Mail Order

Lonely Planet products are distributed worldwide. They are also available by mail order from Lonely Planet, so if you have difficulty finding a title please write to us. North and South American residents should write to 150 Linden St, Oakland, CA 94607, USA; European and African residents should write to 10a Spring Place, London NW5 3BH, UK; and residents of other countries to Locked Bag 1, Footscray, Victoria 3011, Australia.

INDIAN SUBCONTINENT & THE INDIAN OCEAN Bangladesh • Bengali phrasebook • Bhutan • Delhi • Goa • Healthy Travel Asia & India • Hindi & Urdu phrasebook • India • India & Bangladesh City Map • Indian Himalaya • Karakoram Highway • Kathmandu City Map • Kerala • Madagascar • Maldives • Mauritius, Réunion & Seychelles • Mumbai (Bombay) • Nepal • Nepali phrasebook • North India • Pakistan • Rajasthan • Read This First: Asia & India • South India • Sri Lanka • Sri Lanka phrasebook • Tibet • Tibetan phrasebook • Trekking in the Indian Himalaya • Trekking in the Karakoram & Hindukush • Trekking in the Nepal Himalaya • World Food India **Travel Literature:** The Age of Kali: Indian Travels and Encounters • Hello Goodnight: A Life of Goa • In Rajasthan • Maverick in Madagascar • A Season in Heaven: True Tales from the Road to Kathmandu • Shopping for Buddhas • A Short Walk in the Hindu Kush • Slowly Down the Ganges

MIDDLE EAST & CENTRAL ASIA Bahrain, Kuwait & Qatar • Central Asia • Central Asia phrasebook • Dubai • Farsi (Persian) phrasebook • Hebrew phrasebook • Iran • Israel & the Palestinian Territories • Istanbul • Istanbul City Map • Istanbul to Cairo • Istanbul to Kathmandu • Jerusalem • Jerusalem City Map • Jordan • Lebanon • Middle East • Oman & the United Arab Emirates • Syria • Turkey • Turkish phrasebook • World Food Turkey • Yemen **Travel Literature:** Black on Black: Iran Revisited • Breaking Ranks: Turbulent Travels in the Promised Land • The Gates of Damascus • Kingdom of the Film Stars: Journey into Jordan

NORTH AMERICA Alaska • Boston • Boston City Map • Boston Condensed • British Columbia • California & Nevada • California Condensed • Canada • Chicago • Chicago City Map • Chicago Condensed • Florida • Georgia & the Carolinas • Great Lakes • Hawaii • Hiking in Alaska • Hiking in the USA • Honolulu & Oahu City Map • Las Vegas • Los Angeles • Los Angeles City Map • Louisiana & the Deep South • Miami • Miami City Map • Montreal • New England • New Orleans • New Orleans City Map • New York City • New York City City Map • New York City Condensed • New York, New Jersey & Pennsylvania • Oahu • Out to Eat – San Francisco • Pacific Northwest • Rocky Mountains • San Diego & Tijuana • San Francisco • San Francisco City Map • Seattle • Seattle City Map • Southwest • Texas • Toronto • USA • USA phrasebook • Vancouver • Vancouver City Map • Virginia & the Capital Region • Washington, DC • Washington, DC City Map • World Food New Orleans **Travel Literature**: Caught Inside: A Surfer's Year on the California Coast • Drive Thru America

NORTH-EAST ASIA Beijing • Beijing City Map • Cantonese phrasebook • China • Hiking in Japan • Hong Kong & Macau • Hong Kong City Map • Hong Kong Condensed • Japan • Japanese phrasebook • Korea • Korean phrasebook • Kyoto • Mandarin phrasebook • Mongolia • Mongolian phrasebook • Seoul • Shanghai • South-West China • Taiwan • Tokyo • Tokyo Condensed • World Food Hong Kong • World Food Japan **Travel Literature:** In Xanadu: A Quest • Lost Japan

SOUTH AMERICA Argentina, Uruguay & Paraguay • Bolivia • Brazil • Brazilian phrasebook • Buenos Aires • Buenos Aires City Map • Chile & Easter Island • Colombia • Ecuador & the Galapagos Islands • Healthy Travel Central & South America • Latin American Spanish phrasebook • Peru • Quechua phrasebook • Read This First: Central & South America • Rio de Janeiro • Rio de Janeiro City Map • Santiago de Chile • South America on a shoestring • Trekking in the Patagonian Andes • Venezuela **Travel Literature**: Full Circle: A South American Journey

SOUTH-EAST ASIA Bali & Lombok • Bangkok • Bangkok City Map • Burmese phrasebook • Cambodia • Cycling Vietnam, Laos & Cambodia • East Timor phrasebook • Hanoi • Healthy Travel Asia & India • Hill Tribes phrasebook • Ho Chi Minh City (Saigon) • Indonesia • Indonesian phrasebook • Indonesia's Eastern Islands • Java • Lao phrasebook • Laos • Malay phrasebook • Malaysia, Singapore & Brunei • Myanmar (Burma) • Philippines • Pilipino (Tagalog) phrasebook • Read This First: Asia & India • Singapore • Singapore City Map • South-East Asia on a shoestring • South-East Asia phrasebook • Thailand • Thailand's Islands & Beaches • Thailand, Vietnam, Laos & Cambodia Road Atlas • Thai phrasebook • Vietnam • Vietnamese phrasebook • World Food Indonesia • World Food Thailand • World Food Vietnam

ALSO AVAILABLE: Antarctica • The Arctic • The Blue Man: Tales of Travel, Love and Coffee • Brief Encounters: Stories of Love, Sex & Travel • Buddhist Stupas in Asia: The Shape of Perfection • Chasing Rickshaws • The Last Grain Race • Lonely Planet ... On the Edge: Adventurous Escapades from Around the World • Lonely Planet Unpacked • Lonely Planet Unpacked Again • Not the Only Planet: Science Fiction Travel Stories • Ports of Call: A Journey by Sea • Sacred India • Travel Photography: A Guide to Taking Better Pictures • Travel with Children • Tuvalu: Portrait of an Island Nation

LONELY PLANET

You already know that Lonely Planet produces more than this one guidebook, but you might not be aware of the other products we have on this region. Here is a selection of titles that you may want to check out as well:

North India
ISBN 1 86450 330 0
US$21.99 • UK£13.99

Indian Himalaya
ISBN 0 86442 688 7
US$19.95 • UK£12.99

Healthy Travel Asia & India
ISBN 1 86450 051 4
US$5.95 • UK£3.99

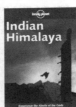

Nepal
ISBN 1 86450 247 9
US$19.99 • UK£12.99

Pakistan
ISBN 0 86442 535 X
US$17.95 • UK£11.99

Hindi & Urdu phrasebook
ISBN 0 86442 425 6
US$6.95 • UK£4.50

Karakoram Highway
ISBN 0 86442 531 7
US$17.95 • UK£11.99

Central Asia
ISBN 0 86442 673 9
US$24.95 • UK£14.99

South-West China
ISBN 1 86450 370 X
US$21.99 • UK£13.99

Read This First: Asia & India
ISBN 1 86450 049 2
US$14.95 • UK£8.99

Trekking in the Indian Himalaya
ISBN 0 86442 357 8
US$17.95 • UK£11.99

Trekking in the Nepal Himalaya
ISBN 1 86450 231 2
US$19.99 • UK£12.99

Available wherever books are sold

Index

Bold indicates maps.
For a list of treks, see the
Table of Treks, pp 4-8.

Bold indicates maps.
For a list of treks, see the Table of Treks, pp 4-8.

Bold indicates maps.
For a list of treks, see the
  Table of Treks, pp 4-8.

Boxed Text

MAP LEGEND

BORDERS

---·---·---·--- International
---··---··--- Provincial
---- · ---- · ---- District
--- --- --- --- Disputed
· · · · · · · · · · · · Line of Control

ROUTES & TRANSPORT

================ Major Road
================ Minor Road
= = = = = : Unsealed Major Road
--- --- --- --- Unsealed Minor Road

████████ Described Trek
■ ■ ■ ■ ■ ■ Alternative Route
● ● ● ● ● ● ● ● ● Side Trip
- - - - - - - Walking Trail

POPULATION CENTRES

◎ **CAPITAL** .... National Capital
● **Town** .... Town
◦ Village .... Village
● Place Name .... Place Name

HYDROGRAPHY

.... Glacier
.... Creek, River
.... Underground flow
.... Lake
.... Canal
⊙ .... Spring

AREA FEATURES

██████ .... Building
████ .... Park (Regional Maps)
▭ .... Park (Trek Maps)
.... Ridge Line
.... Rock/Scree Slope
.... Sand

MAP SYMBOLS

✈	.... Airport	▲	.... Mountain/Peak	+m	.... Spot Height
⊖	..Bank/Moneychanger	⬛	.... National Park	DAY 2	.... Start Day 2
⌂	.... Cave	⬛	.... Oasis	☎	.... Telephone
⬛	.... Embassy	℗	.... Parking Area	⊙	.... Toilet
⋈	.... Footbridge	)(	.... Pass	ⓘ	... Tourist Information
⬛	.... Fort	⊙	...Petrol/Fuel Station	◨	.... Transport
⊕	.... Garden	▼	.... Place to Eat	⋀	.... Trig Point
✛	.... Hospital	▲	.... Place to Stay	◪	.... View Point
⩕	.... Islamic Shrine	●	.... Point of Interest	▬▬	.... Wall
⚲	.... Monument	⬛	.... Police Station	🚶	Peak Climb (described in boxed text)
⬛	.... Mosque	⬛	.... Post Office		

Note: not all symbols displayed above appear in this book

LONELY PLANET OFFICES

Australia
Locked Bag 1, Footscray, Victoria 3011
☎ 03 8379 8000 fax 03 8379 8111
ⓔ talk2us@lonelyplanet.com.au

USA
150 Linden St, Oakland, CA 94607
☎ 510 893 8555 or ☎ 800 275 8555 (toll free)
fax 510 893 8572
ⓔ info@lonelyplanet.com

UK
10a Spring Place, London NW5 3BH
☎ 020 7428 4800 fax 020 7428 4828
ⓔ go@lonelyplanet.co.uk

France
1 rue du Dahomey, 75011 Paris
☎ 01 55 25 33 00 fax 01 55 25 33 01
ⓔ bip@lonelyplanet.fr
ⓦ www.lonelyplanet.fr

World Wide Web: ⓦ www.lonelyplanet.com *or* AOL keyword: lp
Lonely Planet Images: ⓔ lpi@lonelyplanet.com.au